Fundamentals of Health Psychology

Fundamentals of Health Psychology

Edited by

Thomas Hadjistavropoulos
& Heather D. Hadjistavropoulos

OXFORD
UNIVERSITY PRESS

Oxford University Press is a department of the University of Oxford.
It furthers the University's objective of excellence in research, scholarship,
and education by publishing worldwide. Oxford is a registered trade mark of
Oxford University Press in the UK and in certain other countries.

Published in Canada by
Oxford University Press
8 Sampson Mews, Suite 204,
Don Mills, Ontario M3C 0H5 Canada

www.oupcanada.com

Copyright © Oxford University Press Canada 2019

The moral rights of the authors have been asserted
Database right Oxford University Press (maker)

First Edition published in 2015

Library and Archives Canada Cataloguing in Publication

Fundamentals of health psychology/Thomas Hadjistavropoulos and Heather D.
Hadjistavropoulos.–Second edition.

Includes bibliographical references and index.
Issued in print and electronic formats.
ISBN 978-0-19-902864-1 (hardcover).—ISBN 978-0-19-902868-9 (PDF).

1. Clinical health psychology–Textbooks. 2. Textbooks. I. Hadjistavropoulos,
Thomas, 1963-, editor II. Hadjistavropoulos, Heather D., 1967-, editor

R726.7.F86 2018   616.001'9   C2018-903700-8
                                            C2018-903701-6

Cover image: Jordan Siemens/Getty Images
Cover design: Sherill Chapman
Interior design:Laurie McGregor

Oxford University Press is committed to our environment.
Wherever possible, our books are printed on paper which comes from
responsible sources.

Printed and bound in the United States of America

1 2 3 4 — 21 20 19 18

To our sons, Nicholas and Dimitri.

Thomas Hadjistavropoulos

Heather D. Hadjistavropoulos

Brief Contents

Contents

7   Health Anxiety and Other Psychological Responses to Bodily Symptoms   142

Heather D. Hadjistavropoulos

PART II Health Conditions   161

8   Chronic Health Problems: Risk Factors, Prevention, Adjustment, and Management   162

Michelle M. Gagnon
Thomas Hadjistavropoulos

9   The Psychology of Pain   188

Thomas Hadjistavropoulos

10 Cardiovascular Disease   207

Amanda C. Kentner
Eric J. Connors
Adrienne H. Kovacs
Sherry L. Grace

11 HIV and Sexually Transmitted Infections   229

Tyler G. Tulloch
Natalie L. Stratton
Stanley Ing
Bojana Petrovic
Trevor A. Hart

15 Cross-Cultural Issues in Health Psychology   327

Jaime Williams
Chantelle Richmond

Preface

It was a pleasure for us to work with the authors and with Oxford University Press on the preparation of a second edition of this important volume. This edition incorporates updated references and information in all of its chapters and features two brand-new chapters. The first of these new chapters focuses on appetitive behaviours (i.e., eating, drinking, smoking, and recreational drug use). The second new chapter incorporates broad information on psychological influences on health as well as general principles of psychological chronic disease management (e.g., coping techniques and psychological interventions to address depression and anxiety that may result from having a chronic illness). This chapter replaces six short chapters that, in the previous edition, covered a variety of very specific health conditions.

This text, most suitable for health psychology courses offered in the United States, Canada, and elsewhere, is unique in many ways. Unlike many university textbooks in the Canadian market, this volume is not a Canadian edition (i.e., an edition with added Canadian content) of a pre-existing US text. We felt that such an approach would not be optimal. Instead, this book was developed from the ground up with the intent of providing both US and Canadian content (e.g., prevalence information for each country, descriptions of the health systems of both countries, emphasis on cultural diversity) in order to be optimally suited for both countries. Given its breadth, the book would also be appropriate for adoption by universities outside North America.

A second strength of this volume is its collection of contributors. Most university texts are written by one to four authors who are not experts in each and every major topic covered. Unlike such texts, chapters in this volume are authored by individuals who are leading experts on the topics covered.

A third strength of the book is that it contains chapters dedicated to special populations and issues (i.e., children, older adults, cross-cultural issues). Most health psychology university textbooks do not include specialized chapters covering these most important areas.

This book was written with advanced (i.e., third- and fourth-year) undergraduate students in mind but would also be appropriate as an introductory health psychology text for more advanced students. It is organized conceptually so that Chapters 1 to 7 cover very general, broad issues as well as common problems that affect both healthy individuals and those with a wide variety of chronic illnesses (e.g., introduction to health psychology, body systems, psychological determinants of health and immunity, stress and health, appetitive behaviors such as eating and drinking, the health-care system and the role of psychologists within that system, and disease prevention and health promotion). In Chapters 8 to 12 the focus shifts to serious chronic health conditions (e.g., cancer, cardiovascular disease, chronic pain, and HIV) as well as to psychological influences on such conditions. Representing one of the most significant strengths of this book, Chapters 13 to 15 are among the most important in the volume. They cover special populations (e.g., children and older adults) as well as cross-cultural issues. Study of the issues affecting these populations are of critical importance within our pluralistic society.

We hope that you will enjoy this book and that it will kindle your interest to learn more about health psychology.

Thomas Hadjistavropoulos, Ph.D., ABPP, FCAHS
Heather D. Hadjistavropoulos, Ph.D.
Editors

From the Publisher

Oxford University Press is pleased to present the second edition of *Fundamentals of Health Psychology*. Bringing together an internationally respected team of experts, the second edition continues to offer a comprehensive introduction to the key topics and approaches in the fast-growing field of health psychology. Building on the basics, this contributed volume introduces students to general areas of health psychology—such as body systems, health-care systems, stress, and illness prevention—before moving on to examine health conditions, issues affecting special populations, and cross-cultural concerns. Compelling and thought-provoking, *Fundamentals of Health Psychology*, second edition offers students the foundation they need to engage critically with the most pressing issues in health psychology and to pursue future study in this fascinating field.

Important Features of This Book

Fundamentals of Health Psychology, second edition incorporates a number of high-interest features that enhance its value as a reliable, useful, and up-to-date teaching and learning tool:

- **Two new chapters**—one on eating, smoking, and recreational substance use; and the other on chronic health problems—provide coverage of health behaviours and conditions.
- **Distinguished contributors**—hailing from throughout North America offer authoritative and up-to-date insight into the current state of research and collaboration in health psychology.
- **Balanced coverage** of general issues as well as specific conditions and illnesses provides students with a well-rounded understanding of the field.
- **In-depth discussion of special populations** in Part III explores pediatric psychology, geropsychology, and cross-cultural concerns, allowing students to learn about issues and challenges that extend beyond their personal frames of reference.
- **Coverage of the latest research in the field**, including new material on sleep, end-of-life care, and the influence of technology and social media on health, ensures students receive an up-to-date look at this dynamic field.
- **Two types of themed boxes** highlight significant issues, theories, and practice-based solutions.
    - prevention, research, and treatment.
    - **"In Practice" boxes** present students with case studies and show how health psychologists apply theories to explain and solve health issues.
- **Visually engaging photos, figures, and tables** help students envision and interpret complex concepts and data, bringing the discussion to life.
- **"Future Directions" discussions** explore where current research and treatments may lead, providing highly relevant insight to students considering a career in the field.
- **End-of-chapter summaries, questions for critical thought, and reading lists** improve student comprehension and encourage active engagement with key concepts.

Online Supplements

Fundamentals of Health Psychology, second edition is supported by an outstanding array of ancillary materials, including a **test bank**, **PowerPoint slides**, and a **brand-new video guide** for instructors as well as a **study guide** and **practice quizzes** for students. These resources are available online at **www.oupcanada.com/HealthPsychology2e**.

Acknowledgements

We express our sincere gratitude to all of our distinguished chapter contributors for their work and to Rhonda Stopyn for her assistance with the formatting and organisation of the manuscript. We also grateful to Rhiannon Wong and Dave Ward of Oxford University Press, Canada for encouraging and facilitating this work.

The editors, along with Oxford University Press, would like to acknowledge the reviewers whose thoughtful comments and suggestions have helped to shape this text:

Theresa Bianco, Concordia University
Christopher Ashley Cooper, University of Saskatchewan
Ken Fowler, Memorial University of Newfoundland
Sylvette La Touche-Howard, University of Maryland, College Park
Shelley Delano Parker, University of New Brunswick
Gabrielle Rigney, Dalhousie University
Elizabeth Russell, Trent University
Hannah Peach Windell, University of North Carolina at Charlotte

Thomas Hadjistavropoulos
Heather Hadjistavropoulos
Editors

About the Editors

Thomas Hadjistavropoulos, Ph.D., ABPP, FCAHS is Professor of Clinical Psychology, Research Chair in Aging and Health, and Director of the Centre on Aging and Health, University of Regina. He has served as the 2007–8 President of the Canadian Psychological Association (CPA). His research, which has been funded by the Canadian Institutes of Health Research (CIHR), the Saskatchewan Health Research Foundation, the Canada Foundation for Innovation, the AGE WELL Network of National Centres of Excellence, and the Social Sciences and Humanities Research Council of Canada, focuses on psychological issues in pain. An area of recent focus has been pain assessment and management among seniors with a special emphasis

on seniors who have severe limitations in ability to communicate because of dementia. He has been honoured with numerous prestigious awards including a CIHR Investigator Award, the Year 2000 Canadian Pain Society Early Career Award for Excellence in Pain Research, the Canadian Association on Gerontology Distinguished Member Award, the Saskatchewan Health Research Foundation Career Achievement Award, a Saskatchewan Health Care Excellence Award, and many others. He has also been elected Fellow of the Canadian Psychological Association as well as of the American Psychological Association in recognition of his distinguished contributions to the science and profession of psychology. More recently, he was inducted as Fellow in the Canadian Academy of Health Sciences, which represents one of the highest honours available to Canadian health scientists. Thomas is Editor-in-Chief of Ethics & Behavior and in the past has served as Editor of *Canadian Psychology/Psychologie canadienne,* Psychology Section Editor of the *Canadian Journal on Aging,* as well as on other editorial boards. He has published over 160 peer-reviewed papers and book chapters as well as five books.

Heather Hadjistavropoulos (Ph.D. University of British Columbia 1995) is a Professor of Psychology at the University of Regina (U of R), Canada. She founded the Psychology Training Clinic at the U of R in 2002, and trains graduate students in the assessment and treatment of anxiety and mood disorders, commonly among individuals with co-morbid medical conditions. Heather's research is focused on (a) assessing and treating psychological problems that impact health and (b) understanding and improving the quality of health care in an attempt to reduce the burden of illness. Heather received a Canada Innovation Foundation grant to develop a state-of-the-art Clinical Health Psychology research area. She has published and presented her research widely and received funding through the Canadian Institutes of Health Research, Canadian Health Services Research Foundation, and the Saskatchewan Health Research Foundation. She has been the recipient of many awards for her research as well as her contributions to training and the profession of psychology. In 2010, Dr Hadjistavropoulos founded the Online Therapy Unit (onlinetherapyuser.ca). This unit has (1) overseen the development of a website and policies and procedures for the delivery of

therapist-assisted Internet-delivered cognitive behavioural therapy (I-CBT) in Saskatchewan; (2) trained community providers and graduate students on how to use I-CBT; and (3) co-ordinated, monitored, and evaluated the delivery of I-CBT for multiple conditions. The Online Therapy Unit is having a substantive impact on delivery of psychological care in Saskatchewan and inspiring the development of similar services in other provinces.

Contributors

Rebecca S. Allen, Ph.D., ABPP
University of Alabama

Casey B. Azuero, Ph.D., M.P.H
University of Alabama at Birmingham

Christine T. Chambers, Ph.D.
Dalhousie University

Nicholas J.S. Christenfeld, Ph.D.
University of California, San Diego

Eric J. Connors, M.A.
Alliant International University

Blaine Ditto, Ph.D.
McGill University

Michelle M. Gagnon, Ph.D.
University of Saskatchewan

Sherry L. Grace, Ph.D.
York University & University Health Network, Toronto

Heather D. Hadjistavropoulos, Ph.D.
University of Regina

Thomas Hadjistavropoulos, Ph.D., ABPP, FCAHS
University of Regina

Trevor A. Hart, Ph.D.
Ryerson University & University of Toronto

Stanley Ing, M.P.H.
Chatham-Kent Public Health Unit

Amanda C. Kentner, Ph.D.
Massachusetts College of Pharmacy & Health Sciences

Gerald P. Koocher, Ph.D., ABPP
Quincy College

Adrienne H. Kovacs, Ph.D.
Knight Cardiovascular Institute & Oregon Health & Science University

Britta A. Larsen, Ph.D.
University of California, San Diego

Gregory P. Marchildon, Ph.D, FCAHS
University of Toronto

Swati Mehta, Ph.D.
University of Regina

Anne Moyer, Ph.D.
Stony Brook University

Bojana Petrovic, M.P.H.
University of Toronto

James O. Prochaska, Ph.D.
University of Rhode Island

Janice M. Prochaska, Ph.D.
Pro-Change Behavior Systems, Inc.

Chantelle Richmond, Ph.D.
University of Western Ontario

Arseny A. Ryazanov, M.A.
University of California, San Diego

Elizabeth A. Sarma, Ph.D., M.P.H.
National Cancer Institute

Natalie Stratton, M.A.
Ryerson University

Tyler G. Tulloch, M.A.
Ryerson University

Perri R. Tutelman, B.H.Sc.
Dalhousie University

Jaime Williams, Ph.D.
University of Regina

PART I
Fundamentals of Health Psychology

1 Introduction to Health Psychology

Thomas Hadjistavropoulos
Heather D. Hadjistavropoulos

Learning Objectives

In this chapter you will:

- Learn what health psychology and behavioural medicine are.
- Read a brief history of health psychology from its roots in ancient Greece to the tremendous growth the field has experienced in recent years.
- Find out about careers in health psychology (e.g., research vs clinical positions).
- Be introduced to key theories and models in health psychology (e.g., the bi-opsychosocial model, social cognitive theory, theory of planned behaviour, health belief model).

What Is Health Psychology?

When most people think of a practising psychologist, they most often think of a psychologist who works with individuals suffering from mental health problems, such as depression and anxiety. Although this is frequently the case, the number of psychologists who work with people who are trying to adjust to and overcome medical conditions has shown explosive growth over the last 40 years. It is now commonplace for psychologists to work with people who are trying to manage conditions such as chronic pain, cancer, or obesity. Psychologists who specialize in working with people who have physical health problems are known as health psychologists. A survey of practising psychologists conducted by the American Psychological Association (2016) showed that clinical health psychology was the fourth most common of 15 specialties of practising psychology, with 19 per cent of psychologists indicating that they considered health psychology to be either their primary or secondary practice specialty.

Health psychology can be thought of as a subspecialty of psychology, but also as a discipline-specific descriptor within the broad interdisciplinary field of **behavioural medicine**. The 1977 Yale Conference on Behavioural Medicine was organized to support the early stages of behavioural medicine, which at that time was a young, growing interdisciplinary field (Belar, Mendonca McIntyre, & Matarazzo, 2003). The conference led to the following definition of "behavioural medicine":

> "Behavioral medicine" is the field concerned with the development of behavioral-science knowledge and techniques relevant to the understanding of physical health and illness and the application of this knowledge and these techniques to diagnosis, prevention, treatment and rehabilitation. Psychosis, neurosis and substance abuse are included only insofar as they contribute to physical disorders as an end point (Schwartz &Weiss, 1977).

Three years after the Yale conference, a formal definition of health psychology was developed by American psychologist J.D. Matarazzo (1980, 1982; Gatchel, Baum, & Krantz, 1989), who was the first president of the Health Psychology Division (Division 38) of the American Psychological Association (APA). This definition remains widely accepted to this day:

> Health psychology is the aggregate of the specific educational, professional and scientific contributions to the discipline of psychology to the promotion and maintenance of health, the prevention and treatment of illness, and the identification of etiologic and diagnostic correlates of health, illness and related dysfunction.

Over the years, several applied subspecialties of health psychology have developed. **Clinical health psychology** is one of the most influential (American Psychological Association, 2011). Clinical health psychologists help people diagnosed with health conditions manage the symptoms of their health condition and address the psychological consequences of these symptoms. **Occupational health psychology** is another subspecialty that focuses on the prevention and management of occupational stress, the prevention of injury, and the maintenance of health of workers (Centers for Disease Control and Prevention, 2012). Another subspecialty, **community health psychology**, concerns itself with community-wide health needs and health-care systems. More specifically, community health psychologists aim to effect change and to promote access and cultural competence within health-care systems so that these systems can more effectively serve diversity within communities (De La Cancela, Lau Chin, & Jenkins, 1998).

By permission of Joe Matarazzo

Joseph D. Matarazzo developed the formal definition of health psychology.

Psychologists have made tremendous contributions to the prevention of illness, the maintenance of good health, and the management of a variety of conditions including but not limited to asthma (e.g., Grover, Kumaraiah, Prasadrao, & D'souza, 2002), diabetes (e.g., Fisher, Thorpe, Devellis, & Devellis, 2007), cardiovascular disease (e.g., Smith & Ruiz, 2002), and chronic pain (e.g., Ehde, Dillworth, & Turner, 2014). They have also helped thousands of people cope with the psychological consequences of serious illnesses such as cancer (e.g., McGregor et al., 2002) and AIDS (Smith Fawzi et al., 2012). Moreover, psychological interventions for patients with chronic illnesses can result in substantial medical cost savings (e.g., Hunsley, 2003). For example, Arving, Brandberg, Feldman, Johansson, and Gimelius (2014) conducted a randomized controlled study in order to evaluate the cost utility of psychosocial support interventions' effectiveness (in addition to standard medical care) for breast cancer patients. Total healthcare costs (estimated in euros) were at least €5000 less for people who received a psychosocial support intervention as compared to people who received standard medical care. Moreover, quality-of-life scores were significantly higher in the psychosocial intervention group compared to the standard care group. The researchers argued that unmet psychosocial needs result in increased utilization of health-care resources. Analogous results were obtained in a Canadian study involving cancer patients (Simpson, Carlson, & Trew, 2001). Specifically, women who completed medical treatment for breast cancer were randomly assigned to receive either standard psychosocial care available to patients or a structured group therapy intervention. The results showed that patients in the structured group intervention fared better with respect to adjustment and quality of life and that there were significant per patient cost savings even after accounting for the cost of the psychological intervention.

A Brief History of Health Psychology

The roots of health psychology can be traced back to early thinkers such as Hippocrates (460–377 BCE), who is considered by many to be the father of modern medicine, and Galen (129–99 CE). These early Greek physicians held a holistic view of health and considered the mind and the body to be part of the same system (Belar et al., 2003). They also believed that a balance between physical and emotional states was necessary to sustain overall health (Belar et al., 2003). Over the years, the popularity of these ideas varied. During the Renaissance, Descartes (1596–1650) argued in favour of what is now referred to as **Cartesian dualism** or the idea that mind and body are separate entities and that explanations for illness can be found in the body alone. This idea formed the basis for much of physical medicine in Western societies (Belar et al., 2003). Following Descartes, the role of psychological factors in illness was revived again in the nineteenth century. This eventually gave rise to the development of psychosomatic medicine, with the word "psychosomatic" having been coined by Johann Christian August Heinroth (1773–1843), a German psychiatrist (Belar et al., 2003; Lipsitt, 1999). Psychosomatic medicine initially focused on illness behaviour that could be attributed to psychological causes. Consistent with this, Benjamin Rush (1746–1813) argued that "actions of the mind could cause many illnesses." Rush is considered to be the father of modern psychiatry for publishing the book *Medical Inquiries and Observations upon the Diseases of the Mind* (1812) and is credited with founding the American Medico-Psychological Association, which later became the American Psychiatric Association (Belar et al., 2003).

Development of the ideas that led to the emergence of health psychology are also linked to more recent thinkers, including Freud and other psychoanalysts who believed that certain symptoms such as paralysis and blindness represented manifestations of unconscious conflicts. In the 1940s, Franz Alexander helped establish psychosomatic medicine, which focused on the idea that physical disease can be the result of "fundamental, nuclear, or psychological conflict." Although these views did not adequately capture the multifactorial causation of disease (Straub, 2007), they led to explorations that contributed to today's accumulated knowledge of health. These explorations concerning the multifactorial causation of disease have been more directly stimulated by the behavioural sciences (Schwartz & Weiss, 1977).

In contrast to behavioural medicine, which has been more directly concerned with behavioural approaches (e.g., biofeedback, health-promoting behaviours) to the treatment and prevention of physical disease (Schwartz & Weiss, 1977), psychosomatic medicine has traditionally emphasized etiology and pathogenesis of physical disease. Gradually, psychosomatic medicine developed as a field through the work of clinicians such as Helen Flanders Dunbar, who became the founding editor of the *Journal of Psychosomatic Medicine*, which published its first issue in 1939 (Belar et al., 2003). The American Psychosomatic Society was founded in 1942 by an interdisciplinary group that included psychiatrists, psychoanalysts, psychologists, physiologists, and internists, with neurologist Tracy Putnam as its first president (Belar et al., 2003). Over time, psychodynamic theory and psychoanalysis gradually became less popular in North America because of criticisms about insufficient scientific rigour. Nonetheless, a variety of scholars and clinicians continued to explore the interdependence of psychological factors, such as stress and disease. Guze, Matarazzo, and Saslow (1953) published an account of the **biopsychosocial model** as a foundation of comprehensive medicine, although later work by George Engel (1977) on the biopsychosocial model became more widely cited (Belar et al., 2003).

In terms of the organized discipline of psychology, in 1973 the American Psychological Association appointed a task force to explore psychology's role within behavioural medicine and in 1978 created a health psychology division (Division 38) (Straub, 2007). The Health Psychology Division of APA is one of the five largest divisions within the organization (France, 2011). The Health Psychology Section (which has since been renamed as the Health Psychology and Behavioural Medicine Section) of the Canadian Psychological Association (CPA) was founded in the early 1980s (John Conway, personal communication, 10 November 2011). According to a 2017 count, the Health Psychology

Benjamin Rush (1746–1813).

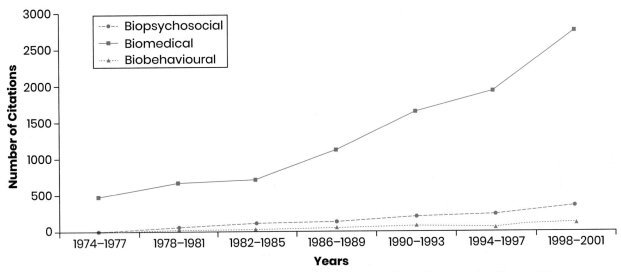

FIGURE 1.1 Frequency of citations of "biopsychosocial," "biobehavioral," and "biomedical" in Medline.

Source: Suls, J., & Rothman, A. (2004). Evolution of the biopsychosocial model: Prospects and challenges for health psychology. *Health Psychology*, 23(2), 119–125..

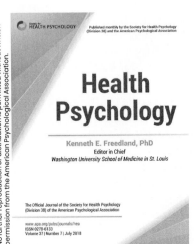

The journal *Health Psychology* is published by the American Psychological Association and its mission is "to advance the science and practice of evidence-based health psychology and behavioral medicine."

and Behavioural Medicine Section of the CPA was the eighth-largest section (out of a total of 32 sections). Developments similar to those pertaining to the formation of formal health psychology groups in North America also took place in Europe and Asia, with a variety of special-interest groups and organizations developing over the 1980s and 1990s (Belar et al., 2003). Health psychology is also recognized as a specialty by the American Board of Professional Psychology, the oldest credentialling group in psychology (Belar, 1997).

The growth of the field is demonstrated not only by an explosion in the number of articles in the field of health psychology but also by dramatic growth in government research support for health-related behavioural and psychological research, especially in the United States (Suls & Rothman, 2004). As an example of the growth, during the years 1974–7 the term "biopsychosocial" was mentioned in six articles, but in the 1999–2001 period it appeared in 350 articles (Suls & Rothman, 2004). Another way of illustrating the rapid growth of the field is to point out that the word "biomedical" increased in frequency by a factor of 5 during the same period whereas the word "biopsychosocial" increased by a factor of 60 (Suls & Rothman, 2004) (see Figure 1.1).

Careers in Health Psychology

Health psychologists are often trained to conduct both applied (e.g., clinical) work and research. However, health psychologists interested in academic or related research careers are sometimes trained exclusively as researchers. Generally speaking, health psychologists in North America tend to seek doctoral or post-doctoral training, although some acquire terminal master's degrees. A program leading to a doctoral degree typically requires five to seven years of graduate study. Clinical health psychologists are often trained within clinical psychology doctoral programs with faculty members qualified and interested in health psychology. This allows these graduate students to conduct health psychological research, take courses relevant to health psychology, and complete internships and practica with a focus on health psychology. Post-doctoral training opportunities are also available. The following In Focus box lists the core competencies, according to the Health Psychology Division of the APA, that health psychologists should have.

Many CPA-accredited graduate programs in clinical psychology have faculty members with strong interests and expertise in health psychology.* For example, within the

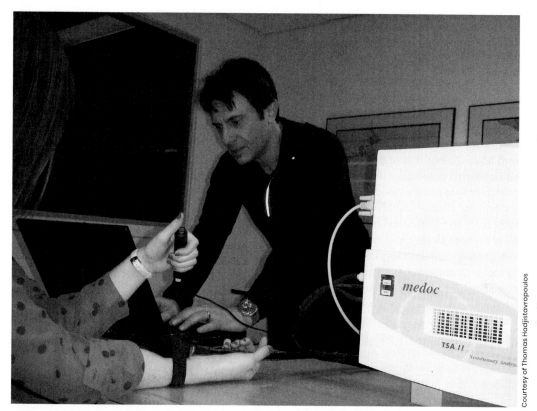

Courtesy of Thomas Hadjistavropoulos

Using safe and sophisticated equipment, the health psychology laboratory at the University of Regina has studied social and psychological influences on pain as well the effects of anxiety on balance. The lab is equipped with sophisticated equipment including a computerized sensor mat (the GaitRite® System) that has been used in the evaluation of gait and balance in older adults while psychophysiological indicators of anxiety (heart rate and skin conductance) are being recorded using wireless psychophysiological monitoring equipment. Pictured here is the TSA-II neurosensory analyzer (made by Medoc Medical Systems), which is controlled by a computer and is used to document responses to stimuli that vary in intensity (e.g., heat, cold, etc). The TSA-II can be used in laboratory studies of pain reactions (e.g., in response to pain induced by exposure to heat). A release button, controlled by the volunteer participant, can instantly terminate the stimulation if the participant finds it to be too discomforting.

---

* The material and examples concerning training and research opportunities in health psychology are based on information gathered at the time of writing of this chapter. Some of the information concerning program offerings and research interests in various universities may have changed since then. Interested students are encouraged to examine university websites and contact departments of psychology directly for more up-to-date information.

In Focus

Competencies in Research for Health Psychologists

The following lists describe the suggested competencies that are taught in many programs in health psychology without reference to clinical training. Of course, not all health psychology programs require all of the same competencies from all of their graduates. It is the unique feature of research-oriented Ph.D. programs to provide sufficient flexibility to allow the developing scientist to acquire a unique set of skills. Similarly, different health psychology programs have different research emphases ranging from epidemiological studies, to exploring mechanisms of disease, to developing individual or population-based interventions. Nevertheless, it is appropriate at this time for our academic colleagues to ask about the competencies that help to define health psychology researchers and for health psychology programs to emphasize such competencies in their curriculum. The list of competencies described is intended to cover in a general way the broad field of health psychology research as it exists today. Central to the work described below is the concept of health behaviour, which refers to all actions or behaviours related to health and well-being. Health behaviours can range from adaptive (e.g., exercising, taking medications as prescribed, and getting regular checkups) to maladaptive (e.g., overeating, under-eating, drinking, smoking, and engaging in high levels of sedentary behaviour).

A. Knowledge base: The entry-level health psychologist researcher should have knowledge of:

   1. The historical relationship of health psychology to the basic sciences, public health, and clinical investigation.

   2. Scientific foundations and methods of psychology and exposure to allied health disciplines (e.g., epidemiology, physiology, genomics, bioinformatics).

   3. Biobehavioural, social-environmental, and psychological factors associated with health behaviours, illness, and disease.

   4. Mechanistic and mediational pathways between contextual, psychosocial, and biological phenomena as they relate to disease progression, health promotion, and illness prevention.

   5. Biological, psychological, behavioural, and sociocultural tools (e.g., psychophysiological assessment, interview techniques, assessment development, observational coding, focus groups, web-based informatics tools) relevant to individuals and systems.

   6. Dynamic interactions between populations and contextual variations (age, gender, ethnicity, culture, religion, etc.) on health behaviour and health outcomes.

   7. Pathophysiology of disease and the implications for development of biopsychosocial treatments.

   8. Appropriate methods and procedures to develop a program of research.

   9. Strengths and potential pitfalls of role relationships that characterize interdisciplinary collaborative research.

   10. Regulatory and ethics competence in relation to interdisciplinary research.

University of Regina Clinical Psychology graduate program, there are strong interests in the areas of pain and health anxiety. A wide range of health psychology interests are represented in Canadian psychology departments (e.g., McGill University, Université de Montréal, Ryerson University, and many others). Research interests in health psychology can be found in numerous departments in the United States (e.g., University of Florida, George Washington University). Training in experimental health psychology with a primarily research focus is

B. Applications: The entry-level health psychologist should be able to:

1. Evaluate biopsychosocial findings related to physical health or physical illness, injury, or disability.
2. Assess biopsychosocial and behavioural risk factors for the development of physical illness, injury, or disability.
3. Assist in assessment of new and emerging health technologies.
4. Develop health psychology research protocols and evaluate their effectiveness and quality.
5. Evaluate biopsychosocial and cognitive assessment tools appropriate to understanding physical illness, injury, or disability.
6. Design and evaluate empirically supported health promotion, prevention, and other interventions appropriate to target populations in the context of an interdisciplinary team.
7. Apply diverse methodologies to address contextual, psychosocial, and biological processes as they relate to disease progression, health promotion, and illness prevention.
8. Select, apply, and interpret data-analytic strategies that are best suited to the diverse research questions and levels of analysis characteristic of health psychology.
9. Work towards translation of research findings to applied settings.
10. Translate issues presented by professionals from other disciplines into research questions and appropriate methods for investigation.
11. Integrate the talents and skills of professionals from different disciplines and different levels of training (e.g., master's, doctoral) to optimize research.
12. Integrate within and lead in the formulation of interdisciplinary research teams.
13. Accurately and efficiently communicate research findings in a manner that is consistent with the highest standards within the profession in ways that can be understood by fellow psychologists, professionals from other disciplines, and lay audiences alike.
14. Write a research proposal of a quality sufficient to be submitted to a granting agency.
15. Publish in peer-reviewed journals in the area of health psychology.
16. Understand the bounds/limits of one's research competence.
17. Obtain proficiency in a traditional area of psychology such as psychophysiology, psychometrics, statistics, affect and cognition, or social psychology.
18. Obtain knowledge, exposure, and competency outside of an area of traditional psychology (e.g., epidemiology, genetics, neural imaging, body imaging, assaying biomarkers, nutrition, exercise, sleep).
19. Demonstrate adequate training and evidence of skill as a teacher, and have the requisite knowledge to develop and implement an undergraduate health psychology course.
20. Understand the role and responsibilities of an effective mentor, and have the ability to promote the development of research and teaching competencies in graduate and undergraduate students.

Source: American Psychological Association Division 38 (2014).

also offered at some universities (e.g., the University of British Columbia and the University of Pittsburgh).

At the time of this writing, specialized occupational health psychology training was offered by several universities, including but not limited to the University of Nottingham (UK), Leiden University (The Netherlands), and several US schools such as the University of Connecticut, Central Michigan University, Portland State University.

Health psychologists are employed by general and specialized (e.g., cancer, physical rehabilitation) hospitals and private clinics treating patients with complex problems (e.g., chronic pain), as well as in private practice. As private practitioners, health psychologists often serve as consultants to the legal and insurance systems and provide expert opinion about a variety of case scenarios (e.g., psychological consequences of accidents, extent of disability). They also provide psychological treatment services to patients diagnosed with various health conditions. Many practising health psychologists often combine their professional work with some university teaching (e.g., teaching an evening course or supervising practica and internships of graduate students in psychology). Health psychologists often are employed as instructors and researchers in psychology, psychiatry, and a wide variety of other university (e.g., health studies, gerontology, anaesthesiology, general medicine) and teaching hospital departments. Funding sources for health psychology research include such agencies and organizations as the National Institutes of Health (US), the Canadian Institutes of Health Research, and the Heart and Stroke Foundation.

TABLE 1.1 | Activities of Clinical Health Psychologists

Types of Conditions: Chronic Pain, Cancer, Cardiovascular Disease, Diabetes, HIV, Multiple Sclerosis, Obstetrics and Gynecology, Asthma, Chronic Obstructive Pulmonary Disease, Gastrointestinal Conditions, Renal and Urological Conditions

Example Assessment Questions:

1. How is the individual emotionally adjusting to the health condition?
2. What impact is the health condition having on the client's quality of life and functioning?
3. Are pre-existing mental health conditions or psychological variables impacting the individual's ability to cope with the health condition?
4. To what extent is the individual adhering to medical treatment and does the he or she require assistance with this treatment?
5. How is the medical condition impacting the social environment and how is the social environment impacting the individual's health condition?
6. To what extent is the person engaged in maladaptive lifestyle behaviours (e.g., substance use, smoking, over-eating, under-eating) that are impacting his or her health condition and does he or she require support in changing maladaptive lifestyle behaviours?

Example Goals of Therapy:

1. To assist the client in identifying, understanding, and managing emotional responses to health (e.g., depression, anxiety, health anxiety, pain-related anxiety), including pre-existing mental health conditions that may be impacting health.
2. To assist the client in identifying and challenging negative thoughts that could be interfering with managing health conditions (e.g., beliefs about inability to cope, lack of support, lack of control).
3. To help the client identify, understand, and explore various strategies for coping with health conditions (e.g., relaxation, problem solving, mindfulness, pacing).
4. To identify and problem solve on strategies for improving adherence to medical recommendations.
5. To identify and effectively engage with persons who provide social support to clients with health conditions.
6. To identify, discuss, and cope with concerns about relationships with health-care providers.
7. To identify and manage maladaptive lifestyle behaviours impacting health (e.g., weight, smoking, substance use).

At the time of this writing, valuable information about careers and training in health psychology was available on the website of the health psychology division of APA (www.health-psych.org). Additional information about health psychology was available on the website of the health psychology and behavioural medicine section of CPA (www.cpa.ca/aboutcpa/cpasections/healthpsychology).

Major Theories and Models in Health Psychology

Throughout this text we present a variety of theories and models that have been used and validated within the context of health psychology and behavioural medicine. These theories and models include, but are not limited to, the biopsychosocial model of health (Chapters 9 and 15), the gate control theory of pain (Chapter 9), cognitive behavioural theory (Chapters 7, 9, and elsewhere), and the stages of change model (i.e., transtheoretical model, Chapter 5). The broad strokes of some of these perspectives are presented in this chapter. The biopsychosocial model is discussed because of its breadth and impact on the entire discipline, while other formulations (e.g., the health belief model, social cognitive theory) are presented as specific introductory examples of the wide range of theoretical foundations that influence the work of health psychologists.

The Biopsychosocial Model

Health psychology operates within the biopsychosocial model of health that considers the interplay and integration of biological, psychological, and social factors on health (see Figure 1.2).

The biopsychosocial model forms the conceptual basis of health psychology (Suls & Rothman, 2004). This approach contrasts with the traditional medical model of disease that separates the physical and psychosocial. An assumption of the medical model of disease is that illness is entirely physical and questions about illness are answerable objectively and deterministically (Child, 2000). However, such conceptualizations fail to fit the data because the role of psychological, social, and behavioural factors in the causation and maintenance of disease are well established (Rozanski, Blumenthal, & Kaplan, 1999; Schneiderman, Antoni, Saab, & Ironson, 2001). For example, social support has been shown to have a positive effect on health-related self-care behaviours of cardiac patients (Salyer, Schubert, & Chiaranai, 2012), and inadequate social support and reduced use of problem-solving coping strategies by patients are associated with increased pain and lower functional outcomes in post-surgical samples (Lopez-Olivo et al., 2011). It is also well documented that psychological stress can have negative consequences for human immune responses (Segerstrom & Miller, 2004).

Many health problems can be conceptualized through the biopsychosocial model (e.g., obesity, drug addiction).

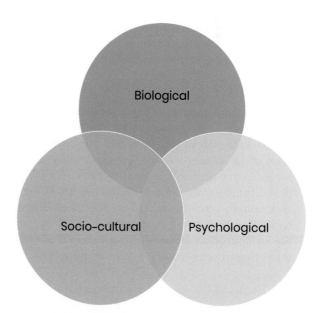

FIGURE 1.2 The biopsychosocial model of health recognizes the importance of biological, psychological, and socio-cultural influences.

Source: Figure I Biopsychocultural Framework July 10, 2010 © A.E. Núñez available at http://culturegenderhealth.blogspot.com/2010/07/which-is-correct-term-sex-gender-both.html

In Practice
A Day in the Life of a Health Psychologist: Dr Christine Chambers

Dr Christine Chambers is a pediatric health psychologist at the IWK Health Centre and a professor of pediatrics and psychology at Dalhousie University. Clinically, she has expertise in providing behavioural and cognitive behavioural interventions for children with acute and chronic medical illnesses and their families, with a focus on management of chronic pain and preparation for painful medical procedures. Her research examines the role of a variety of developmental, psychological, and social factors that influence children's pain, with a focus on family factors in pediatric pain and pain measurement in children.

8:30 a.m. to 10:00 a.m.: Undergraduate health psychology class

Dr Chambers delivers a lecture at the university on the topic of managing chronic illnesses to a classroom of undergraduate students, most of whom are interested in various careers as health professionals, such as medicine, nursing, physiotherapy, and psychology. The students have a few last-minute questions, before the paper is due next week, about their personal health projects, for which they have chosen a health-related behaviour to modify and measure, and then assess the effectiveness of their intervention.

10:00 a.m. to 11:00 a.m.: In the office

Dr Chambers heads over to the IWK Health Centre to her office and research lab in the Centre for Pediatric Pain Research, where she catches up on the latest issue of the *Journal of Pediatric Psychology* and gives feedback to a graduate student on the results section of the student's dissertation on the role of children's memories for pain. She also speaks briefly with a reporter from *Today's Parent* magazine who has contacted her for input on an article about how parents can help their children better cope with immunization pain.

11:00 a.m. to 12:00 p.m.: Teleconference

Just before lunch, Dr Chambers has a teleconference with colleagues on the development of a multi-site Internet-based intervention to address children's sleep problems. This work is a team grant funded by the Canadian Institutes of Health Research and is led

Christine Chambers

Dalhousie University health psychologist Christine Chambers.

by a colleague of Dr Chambers at the university, but includes team members at various other universities and children's hospitals across Canada.

12:00 p.m. to 1:00 p.m.: Lunch and clinical rounds

Dr Chambers enjoys her lunch during an interesting clinical rounds presentation by a colleague on the Pediatric Health Psychology Service. The colleague describes a challenging case of an adolescent with celiac disease who has had difficulties adhering to a gluten-free diet—if the youth cannot maintain the diet, this could have a significant negative impact on long-term health. The psychologists on the service, including Dr Chambers, offer various ideas and suggestions.

1:00 p.m. to 2:30 p.m.: Lab meeting

After lunch Dr Chambers attends her weekly lab meeting with her research team. An undergraduate honours student working with Dr Chambers presents preliminary results from a study examining the relationship between general parenting style and how parents report responding to the pain children experience during daily minor injuries.

2:30 p.m. to 3:30 p.m.: In the clinic

Dr Chambers follows up with one of her patients, a 10-year-old boy, who was referred for treatment of a severe needle phobia. It is their second session together and today they are gradually working their way through various exposure exercises related to the fear hierarchy they generated in the first session. For example, today Dr Chambers has brought pictures of children getting needles and a toy needle for the child to view and manipulate.

3:30 p.m. to 5:00 p.m.: Treatment group for children with recurrent abdominal pain

Dr Chambers provides supervision for a group of practicum students who are leading a six-week cognitive behavioural therapy group for children with recurrent abdominal pain and their parents. The group focuses on teaching children coping strategies to deal with their pain by targeting the thoughts, feelings, and behaviours associated with their pain and symptoms by employing evidence-based strategies, like deep belly breathing, guided imagery, and positive self-talk. In this session, the children practise progressive muscle relaxation while the parents learn about the importance of their own responses to their child's pain.

5:00 p.m. to 10:00 p.m.: Evening at home

Dr Chambers heads home and enjoys some play time with her young children before preparing dinner and helping her husband put the children to bed. She replies to a few e-mails from her students and colleagues and does some last-minute editing on the final draft of the chapter she has been writing on families and pain before heading to bed to get a good night's sleep.

In the case of obesity, for instance, biological factors (e.g., some people may inherit a tendency to gain more weight or a slower metabolic rate), psychological factors (e.g., depression and low self-esteem may lead a person to eat more calorie-dense foods such as in desserts and/or to become physically inactive), and social factors (e.g., socio-economic factors such as in ability to afford healthier foods that may be more expensive than "junk food"; absence of social support) can contribute to the problem as well as play an important role in one's ability to lose weight and maintain the weight loss.

The biopsychosocial model is detailed elsewhere in this volume. Chapter 9, for example, presents a detailed illustration of the model in relation to pain; Chapter 15 discusses the important role of culture in biopsychosocial conceptualizations of health and illness. The breadth of the biopsychosocial perspective has encouraged the development of other theories and models that provide more detailed descriptions and hypotheses related to specific components of the biopsychosocial model (e.g., the specific role of beliefs and cognitions and the role of reinforcement in health and illness). Some of these key models and theories (e.g., the health belief model, social cognitive theory, and the theory of planned behaviour) are introduced below because of their breadth and applicability to a variety of health-related issues.

Health Belief Model

The **health belief model** (Janz & Becker, 1984; Rosenstock, 1974) has been very influential in health psychology (Glanz & Bishop, 2010). The model postulates that readiness to take action in relation to health problems is a function of people's beliefs (e.g., perceived severity of one's health condition, perceived risk of getting the condition, perceived barriers to adopting a health-promoting behaviour) and of their perception of the benefits of taking action to prevent health problems (Champion & Skinner, 2008; Rosenstock, 1974). The model, therefore, facilitates an understanding of possible reasons for non-compliance with health-care recommendations (Turner, Hunt,

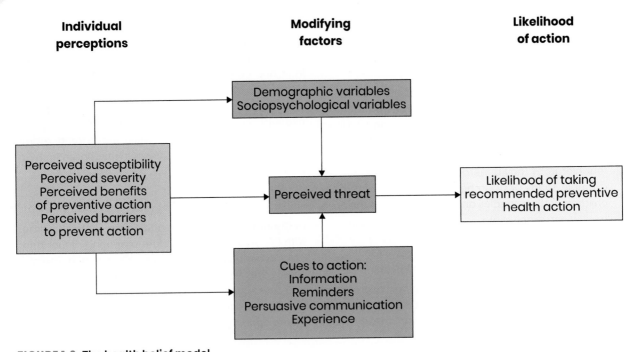

FIGURE 1.3 The health belief model.

Source: Simons-Morton, *Introduction to Health Education and Health Promotion*, 2e, Waveland Press

Dibrezzo, & Jones, 2009). Factors that may affect these types of beliefs (e.g., demographic variables) are also considered in the model (see Figure 1.3). Empirical support for the model is available in that attitudes and beliefs have been shown repeatedly to affect health-related behaviour (Janz & Becker, 1984). For example, beliefs regarding susceptibility to disease (i.e., the flu) and beliefs regarding disease severity and potential benefits of influenza vaccines predict whether individuals will obtain an influenza vaccine (Larson, Olsen, Cole, & Shortell, 1979). On the other hand, the model does not fully explain the full range of reasons (e.g., economic factors) that affect decisions to engage in health behaviours (Janz & Becker, 1984) (see also Chapter 15).

Social Cognitive Theory

Social cognitive theory is based on the work of Albert Bandura (1986, 1991a, 1991b) and considers human behaviour as being reflected in a three-way model in which personal factors, environmental influences, and behaviour commonly interact (McAlister, Perry, & Parcel, 2008). Reinforcement, observational learning, self-control, and self-efficacy (i.e., people's beliefs about their ability to effectively address a situation and to yield desirable results) are central constructs in this theory. According to Bandura, self-efficacy develops through social experiences, observing others, and personal experiences, including any internal experiences that provide the person with information about his or her personal strengths and weaknesses. For example, self-efficacy to manage pain may be influenced by our observations of how family members have coped with pain as well as by our personal experiences of coping with pain. Social cognitive theory helps explain the socio-cultural and personal determinants of health (Bandura, 1998) and is largely consistent with the biopsychosocial model of health, with the greatest emphasis, however, placed on describing social variables involved in health.

Many aspects of the theory have been well supported. For example, self-efficacy beliefs concerning one's ability to control one's health play an important role in our understanding of health-related functioning, including recovery from coronary artery surgery (Allen, Becker, & Swank, 1990; Bastone & Kerns, 1995), coping with cancer (Beckham, Burker, Lytle, Feldman, & Costakis, 1997), renal disease (Devins et al., 1982), adherence to medication (Brus, van de Laar, Taal, Rasker, & Wiegman, 1999; De Geest et al., 1995), decreasing risk of osteoporosis through calcium intake and physical activity (Haran, Kim, Gendler, Froman, & Patel, 1998), and other conditions. This influence occurs largely as a result of the behaviours (e.g., health-promoting behaviours) that self-efficacy beliefs influence and regulate. Specifically, beliefs about self-efficacy influence our health behaviours, which then affect health outcomes. Similarly, social support helps alleviate depression and physical dysfunction, and leads to health-promoting behaviours largely because it raises perceived coping self-efficacy (Bandura, 1998; Cutrona & Troutman, 1986; Duncan & McAuley, 1993; Major, Mueller, & Hildebrandt, 1985). Moreover, effective coping with stressors has been shown to improve immune function (Antoni et al., 1990; Gruber, Hall, Hersh, & Dubois, 1988; Kiecolt-Glaser et al., 1986).

Originally from Alberta, Canada, Stanford University psychologist Albert Bandura has served as honorary president of the Canadian Psychological Association.

Theory of Planned Behaviour

The **theory of planned behaviour** (e.g., Ajzen, 1991) is an expansion of a pre-existing formulation known as the theory of reasoned action (e.g., Ajzen & Fishbein, 1980). According to Ajzen (1991; n.d.), our behaviour is determined by three types of beliefs: (1) *behavioural beliefs* (i.e., beliefs about the likely consequences of behaviour), (2) *normative beliefs* (i.e., beliefs about others' expectations), and (3) *control beliefs* (i.e., beliefs about factors that facilitate or prevent performance of behaviour). As an example, whether we exercise or not may be influenced by our beliefs about whether exercise is beneficial (behavioural belief), beliefs about whether others expect us to be physically active (e.g., normative beliefs), or beliefs about how much control we have over our actions, such as whether we can afford to purchase exercise gear (e.g., control beliefs). As Figure 1.4 illustrates, behavioural beliefs lead to favourable or unfavourable *attitudes* about the behaviour; normative beliefs lead to perceived social pressure related to the *subjective norm*; and control beliefs lead to a *perception of behavioural control*. In turn, the attitudes, subjective norms, and perceived behavioural control affect the strength of the *intention* to perform the behaviour and, ultimately, the actual performance (or lack thereof) of the behaviour. The theory also gives consideration to the extent to which the individual has *actual* (as opposed to just *perceived*) *control* over the behaviour, as shown in the figure.

A considerable body of research has supported the use of the theory of planned behaviour in the prediction of intention and behaviour, although the prediction of self-reported behaviour appears to be stronger than the prediction of actual behaviour (Armitage & Conner, 2001). Similarly, evidence has shown a distinction between desire and intention, as well as between self-efficacy and

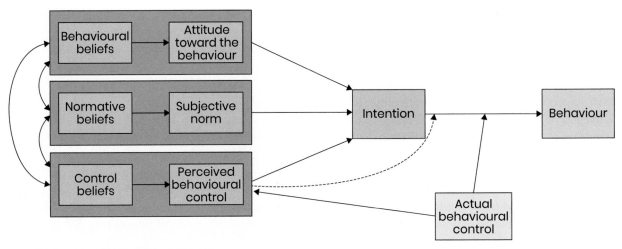

FIGURE 1.4 **Theory of planned behaviour.**

Source: Icek Ajzen, Professor Emeritus, University of Massachusetts.

perceived control over behaviour (Armitage & Conner, 2001). Nonetheless, the theory has been criticized for neglecting the important role of emotion, as well as cultural factors, in the determination of behaviour (e.g., Munro, Lewin, Swart, & Volmink, 2007). Within health psychology, the theory of planned behaviour has been used to study a wide range of health-related behaviours, such as adherence to diet and physical activity, in diverse clinical populations (e.g., Vallance, Lavalee, Culos-Reed, & Trudeau, 2012; Welsh et al., 2013). This theory is discussed further in Chapter 11.

The Common-Sense Model of Self-Regulation/Illness Representation

The **common-sense model (CSM) of self-regulation** (Leventhal, Phillips, & Burns, 2016; also referred to as the **CSM of illness representations**; Leventhal, Meyer, & Nerenz, 1980) is a theoretical framework within health psychology that describes the way people process and cope with health threats. The model specifically suggests that individuals form a lay view of their health based on various sources of information and this lay view guides their coping responses (e.g., whether they seek help or follow advice on how to manage illness). For example, people form beliefs about the identity, cause, consequences, timeline (acute/chronic and cyclical), controllability (personal and treatment control), and emotional impact of physical sensations that they experience. These beliefs, related to the physical sensations, are influenced by past experiences with their health, cognitive heuristics (i.e., rules that people use to make decisions and judgements), social factors, culture, personality, and mood. The model suggests that there is continuous feedback between the efficacy of how people cope with health threats and their perceptions of the health threat. The model has been used to develop interventions to assist people in coping with illness. For example, targeting perceptions of cure/control of illness assists with improving medical adherence (Jones et al., 2016). This model is discussed in more detail in Chapter 7.

Cognitive Behavioural Perspective

The cognitive behavioural perspective is often employed within the field of health psychology. Most commonly this perspective is used to assist clinicians in understanding how individuals respond to physical symptoms or medical conditions (White, 2001). The perspective was originally developed to understand depression, but has been extended to other mental health conditions as well as in explanations of the way in which people respond to health problems (Beck & Dozois, 2011).

In the case of medical conditions, our cognitive appraisals of internal sensations (e.g., physical symptoms) and external events (e.g., receiving a medical diagnosis) play an important role in how we act or respond (e.g., our reactions to our medical condition) as well as how we feel (e.g., depression, anxiety). The cognitive behavioural perspective also emphasizes that thoughts, behaviour, and emotions are interconnected and thus our behaviours and emotions also influence our thoughts. In other words, different people with the same health condition may show different emotional responses to their health depending on their thoughts (e.g., "this symptom is catastrophic" vs "I will be able to cope with this symptom") and behaviours (e.g., engaging in adaptive health-promoting vs self-destructive behaviours). A substantial body of research has provided empirical support for the cognitive behavioural perspective in general and specifically for the relationship between negative beliefs and adjustment (Beck & Haigh, 2014).

Cognitive behavioural therapy (CBT), based on the cognitive behavioural perspective, is often the treatment of choice for psychologists working with patients who are having difficulties managing health conditions (Jensen et al., 2013; Kerns et al., 2014; Stagl et al., 2015) The treatment is typically short-term, goal-oriented, and present-day focused, with the therapist helping the patient identify and challenge unhelpful thoughts and learn individual skills that will assist with or improve her or his health condition (White, 2001). In the chapters that follow, we illustrate applications of CBT with specific conditions.

The Transtheoretical Model of Behaviour Change

The transtheoretical model (detailed in Chapter 5) specifically focuses on five stages of change people may experience when modifying health behaviours (e.g., smoking, alcohol use) (Prochaska, Wright, & Velicer, 2008). The stages include precontemplation, contemplation, preparation, action, maintenance, and termination. For example, consider a person who would like to quit smoking. This person can be viewed as going through varying stages of quitting, ranging from fleeting thoughts of quitting without a specific plan (precontemplation), to intending to quit within the next six months (contemplation), to preparing to quit by picking a quit date in the immediate future and by taking other preparatory steps such as buying a self-help book (preparation), to taking action by using a nicotine patch and making other lifestyle changes (action), to working to prevent relapse by planning to have coping strategies for use in situations where the risk of smoking might be high (maintenance), and, finally, to having 100 per cent confidence that he or she will not smoke again (termination). Different thoughts and behaviours are associated with each stage. Along with stages of change, this model also discusses various processes of change (i.e., behavioural and experiential actions that people use to make changes) and the way in which decisions about change are made. There is some evidence to suggest that interventions that are matched to the individual's stage of change tend to be more effective (e.g., Noar, Benac, & Harris, 2007).

Future Directions

In a review of the state of the discipline of health psychology, Miller, Chen, and Cole (2009) concluded that although health psychology has shown considerable growth in documenting the relationship between psychological factors and disease, the most significant challenge that remains for future research involves the need for a better understanding of the biological processes mediating this relationship. Miller and colleagues also identified a series of advanced methodologies that are becoming increasingly influential and have the potential to help resolve the puzzle of how psychological variables impact health. These methodologies include, but are not limited to, sophisticated statistical approaches for testing complex relationships among variables, use of non-invasive imaging systems (e.g., magnetic resonance imaging [MRI]), use of biomarkers such as C-reactive protein (CRP; an inflammatory biomarker that appears to increase in response to stress), and use of laboratory analyses that permit the capture of a wide range of basic scientific information, including patterns of gene activity. With respect to applied areas, future research is expected to emphasize questions about the cost-effectiveness of health psychology, how to translate knowledge in health psychology into practice, and how to improve delivery of health psychology services through the use of technology, such as the Internet and mobile apps. While there is a proliferation of health-related mobile apps (e.g., targeting behaviours related to weight loss, for example), more systematic research is needed to evaluate their efficacy and establish standards for best practices (Payne, Lister, West & Bernhardt, 2015). Health psychologists must also not lose sight of changing demographics, and ensure that interventions are appropriate for a population that is becoming increasingly ethnically diverse and older (Smith, Orleans, & Jenkins, 2004). Health psychology must also pay greater attention to non-industrialized parts of the world, where it is estimated that 90 per cent of the global burden of disease exists, but where only 10 per cent of the world's health-care resources are found (Lyons & Chamberlain, 2006).

Summary

Health psychology is a subspecialty within the field of psychology, but also a discipline-specific descriptor within the interdisciplinary field of behavioural medicine. The field is concerned with education, research, and practice related to the promotion and maintenance of health and the prevention and treatment of illness. The discipline has grown tremendously since it was defined by Matarazzo (1980), and now has several subspecialties, including clinical health psychology, occupational health psychology, and community health psychology.

The roots of health psychology can be traced back to early Greek physicians who believed that the mind and body are part of the same system and intricately related. These holistic ideas of health re-emerged in the nineteenth century, after a predominant conceptualization in Western society of the mind and body as separate entities (Cartesian dualism) over the previous two centuries. This re-emergence began with the field of psychosomatic medicine, which acknowledged that psychological factors could explain physical symptoms. Gradually, scholars and clinicians began to explore the interdependence of psychological factors and physical health, and the field of behavioural medicine emerged, with an emphasis on behavioural approaches to treating physical disease.

The field has attracted many psychologists, and today health psychologists are often trained to conduct both applied (e.g., clinical) work and research. Health psychologists in North America tend to seek doctoral or post-doctoral training. In terms of employment settings, health psychologists are often employed in academic institutions or in clinical settings, such as general and specialized (e.g., cancer, physical rehabilitation) hospitals, private clinics treating patients with complex problems (e.g., chronic pain clinics), or private practice.

Health psychologists typically conceptualize health and illness using a biopsychosocial model of health that regards both health and illness as stemming from interactions among biological (e.g., genetic), psychological (beliefs, emotions, behaviours), and social (relational) variables. Other models/theories/perspectives that health psychologists commonly draw on in both research and clinical work are the health belief model, social cognitive theory, the theory of planned behaviour, the common-sense model of self-regulation, the transtheoretical model of behaviour change, and the cognitive behavioural perspective. These models are consistent with the assumptions of the broader biopsychosocial conceptualization, but focus on identifying variables that predict health behaviour.

Critical Thought Questions

1. Have you considered a career in health psychology? If you were to consider such a career, would you be most interested in the applied or research aspects of the discipline? Which areas of focus within health psychology (represented in the various chapters of this book) would interest you the most and why?

2. To what extent do you believe that in 25 years professional psychologists will be engaged in clinical work with people who present primarily with physical conditions (e.g., chronic pain, cancer, cardiovascular disease) as opposed to working largely with people whose primary problems are related to mental health issues? Justify your response.

Recommended Reading

Janicke, D., & Hommel, K. (Eds.) (2016). Special Section: Cost effectiveness and economic impact of pediatric psychology interventions. *Journal of Pediatric Psychology, 41,* 831–902.

Miller, G., Chen, E., & Cole, S.W. (2009). Health psychology: Developing biologically plausible models linking the social world and physical health. *Annual Review of Psychology, 60,* 501–24.

Suls, J., & Rothman, A. (2004). Evolution of the biopsychosocial model: Prospects and challenges for health psychology. *Health Psychology, 23,* 119–25.

2 An Introduction to Body Systems and Psychological Influences on Health

Blaine Ditto

Learning Objectives

In this chapter you will:

- Learn the basic functions of key body systems.
- Discover how these body systems work together to support behaviour and health.
- Explore some of the ways these systems malfunction and produce disease.
- Be introduced to how the brain, behaviour, and psychological processes influence risk for disease.

Body Systems

Introduction

Imagine you're a single-celled organism floating in a primeval sea. Life is good! The warm sun stimulates cellular activity and food is plentiful. On the other hand, things aren't perfect. Without a means of locomotion, you rely on currents and waves to make contact with food. Your ability to avoid becoming someone else's food is also limited.

There are problems with this fanciful scenario, including the fact that without a central nervous system you have no organ with which to consider these issues. However, the example raises several issues, including the origin of the field of health psychology. Biological structures and processes evolved because they allowed animals to *do* things that increased their chances of survival and reproduction, such as obtain food and avoid predators. This went beyond the development of simple structures such as legs to complex nervous systems that could support perception, evaluation of the environment, decision making, and emotion. In a sense, Charles Darwin (1872) became the first health psychologist when he suggested that emotional reactions such as fear and anger are the product of evolution and have widespread effects on behaviour and the body. Unfortunately, close integration of thought, emotion, and physiology cuts both ways. In the context of early evolution (or participation in the "Hunger Games"), emotions such as fear and anger increased one's chances of survival by motivating behaviour (e.g., to flee or fight), preparing the body for an emergency, and communicating one's situation to others by facial and bodily expression. On the other hand, in the modern world where vigorous physical reactions are usually unnecessary and most people die of chronic, degenerative illness, the wear and tear of these ancient responses has become a major source of illness (Sapolsky, 2004).

This chapter is an introduction to body systems and psychological influences on health. We begin with a brief overview of some of the body's major systems before introducing mechanisms of psychological influences on body function, such as the autonomic nervous system. The concept of stress is introduced (though discussed in more detail in Chapter 3), followed by some examples of stress-related illness. Throughout the chapter, the integration of psychological processes, physiological activity, and risk for illness is emphasized.

The Cardiovascular System

Complex multicellular organisms require some means of distributing nutrients internally since not all cells can be in contact with the environment. This was a crucial step in evolution, though different species developed different circulatory systems. For example, a number of species have more than one heart, for example, octopi have three and hagfish have five (Choy & Ellis, 1998).

In comparison, the human circulatory system (Figure 2.1) seems relatively simple and similar to closed-loop arrangements, such as a heating system, that circulate water. A strong central pump—the heart—maintains blood flow through a system of outgoing and incoming "pipes" (arteries, capillaries, and veins). Pressure in the system is higher after the heart beats and ejects blood (the systolic phase of the heart) compared

Charles Darwin (1809–82).

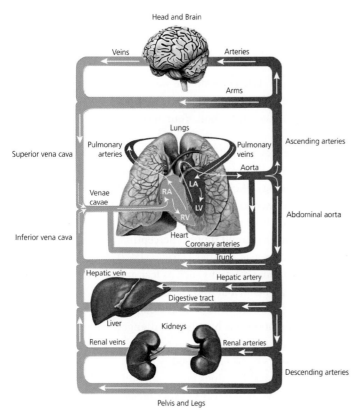

FIGURE 2.1 Schematic view of the cardiovascular system.

Source: Medical Artist Joanna Culley BA (Hons) MAA MIMI.

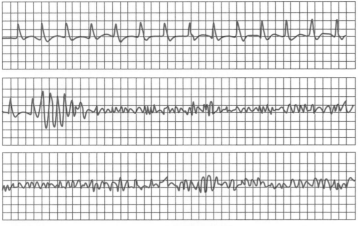

FIGURE 2.2 A normal electrocardiogram (heart rhythm), top, and two cases of ventricular fibrillation.

Source: Figure 3, pg 9 of Ventricular fibrillation is not provoked by chest compression during post-shock organized rhythms in out-of-hospital cardiac arrest, by Erik P. Hessa, Roger D. White, *Resuscitation*, Volume 66, No. 1.

to the resting phase (the diastolic phase), but in general flow is uninterrupted. The obvious importance of continual flow is indicated by what happens when the heart becomes an inefficient pump during a heart attack. Although there are some interesting exceptions (e.g., when someone falls in ice-cold water, slowing metabolism dramatically), death usually occurs within a few minutes in the absence of treatment. See Chapter 10 for a more detailed discussion of cardiovascular disease.

While the basic features are simple, the details of the cardiovascular system are complex and interesting. The human heart is actually two pumps side by side. Blood from the venous circulation collects in the right atrium and is ejected into the right ventricle. At the same time, blood that has just passed through the lungs collects in the left atrium and is ejected into the left ventricle. Afterward, simultaneous contraction of the right and left ventricles sends the blood out to the lungs and rest of the body via the aorta. These actions are co-ordinated by a repeated, reliable pattern of electrical activity that spreads from the atria to the ventricles. The activity associated with the contraction of the two atria is reflected as the P-wave in the electrical signature of the heart, the electrocardiogram (a normal rhythm is displayed in the top panel of Figure 2.2). Contraction of the more powerful ventricles is reflected by the R-wave (the large spikes in the top panel of Figure 2.2). Death of heart muscle cells as the result of a myocardial infarction can produce, depending on the area of cell death, various forms of fibrillation—an interruption of the smooth flow of electrical activity across the heart. This may cause the remaining cells to contract in an unco-ordinated fashion, decreasing the efficiency of the pump (bottom panels of Figure 2.2). Typically, defibrillation involves the use of a large shock in the hope of resetting the electrical profile of the heart.

In general, myocardial infarctions are the result of the process of atherosclerosis. That is, a number of stimuli such as cigarette smoke and high blood pressure can damage the interior lining of the arteries, the endothelium. This may lead to an excessive repair process involving **inflammation**,

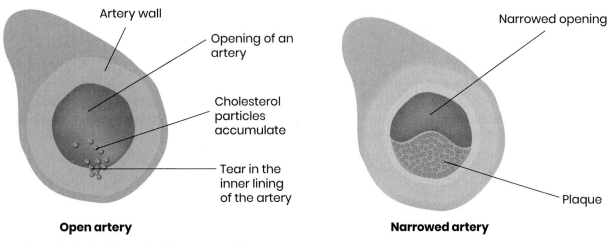

FIGURE 2.3 **The build-up of atherosclerosis in an artery.**

Source: Adapted from an image courtesy of http://www.virtualmedicalcentre.com/health-investigation/cholesterol-testing/65

clotting, cholesterol buildup, and eventually plaques that extend into the artery and reduce blood flow (Figure 2.3). Atherosclerosis can occur in any artery, but those that supply the heart muscle are especially important, given the body's dependence on the heart to distribute oxygen and nutrients.

As can be seen by the effects of wrapping a rubber band around your finger, pain is often experienced in areas of the body that have a reduction in blood flow. In the case of reduced blood flow to the heart, pain is often experienced in the form of angina, a pain or tightness in the chest or shoulder. Angina is an important though not universal warning sign of risk for myocardial infarction and fibrillation.

The Gastrointestinal System

The human body is often described humorously as a doughnut—its exterior surface includes an interior passage (Figure 2.4). That said, the movement of food through the gastrointestinal system is not a leisurely journey. Digestion transforms food using both mechanical and chemical processes to a form where nutrients can be easily absorbed. The breakdown begins in the mouth where it is chewed and mixed with

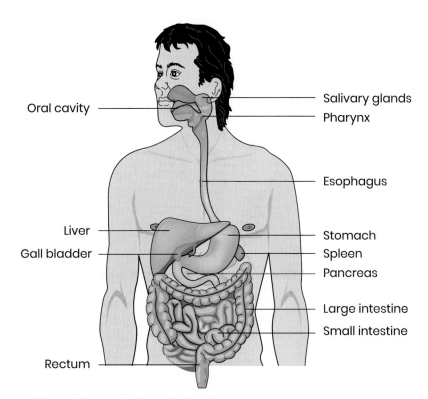

FIGURE 2.4 **The gastrointestinal system.**

Source: Adapted from an image courtesy of http://www.virtualmedicalcentre.com/anatomy/gastrointestinal-system/7

saliva. Patterned muscle contractions move the mixture through the esophagus to the stomach. Smooth muscle in the stomach contracts, further mixing food with corrosive substances such as hydrochloric acid. Additional materials from the liver and pancreas are added in the small intestine. Eventually, the component parts such as sugars and amino acids are small enough for absorption into capillary blood. Waste materials proceed through the large intestine.

This active process is monitored locally (e.g., more fat in the mixture will trigger release of the digestive fluid bile, originally produced by the liver, from the gallbladder into the small intestine) as well as by the brain. While most people acknowledge the influence of the brain on cardiovascular activity, the idea of central control of digestive activity is less appreciated. However, the involvement of muscle activity throughout the process suggests possible means of disruption and a mechanism for functional gastrointestinal disorders that some experience during stress. A more positive example is the increase in saliva often experienced in anticipation of a tasty meal. Some of the mechanisms of such control and their adaptive and maladaptive effects will be discussed below.

The Respiratory System

The respiratory system is also involved in bringing materials from the environment to cells deep within the body (Figure 2.5). Most animals require oxygen to utilize nutrients absorbed from the gastrointestinal system. Oxygen is required to convert glucose to the important molecule adenosine triphosphate, which, in turn, powers the body's chemical reactions. Carbon dioxide is a waste product of this process. Since both oxygen and carbon dioxide are gases, a different system for their intake and excretion was necessary. The primary organs in the respiratory system are the lungs. Other organs include the nose, mouth, trachea, and diaphragm. Similar to the cardiovascular system, air passes through progressively narrower passages in the lungs to allow efficient extraction of oxygen and uptake of carbon dioxide. At the end of the trachea, the pathway divides into two bronchi (the primary bronchi), one for each lung. After entering the lungs, the bronchi subdivide into secondary bronchi, bronchioles, and alveoli. Alveoli are small cavities surrounded by a mesh of capillaries. Carbon dioxide–rich blood from the venous circulation is pumped through the lungs by the heart's right ventricle. Carbon dioxide diffuses out into the alveoli, and oxygen from inspired air is absorbed and proceeds to the left atrium for circulation to the rest of the body. Air is moved in and out of the lungs primarily by contraction of the diaphragm located below the lungs.

Although they require the activity of nearby muscles to move air in and out, the lungs are not simply passive bags of air. As in the gastrointestinal

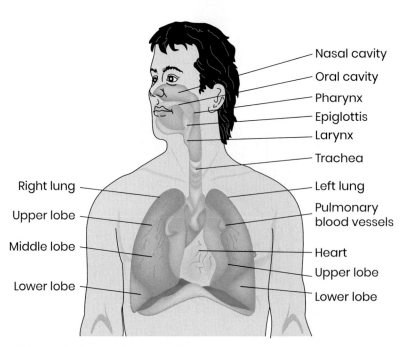

FIGURE 2.5 The respiratory system.

Source: Adapted from an image courtesy of http://www.virtualmedicalcentre.com/anatomy/respiratory-system/18

system, the brain monitors the chemical composition of the blood and can speed or slow respiration via stimulation of the diaphragm. Smooth muscle cells surrounding bronchioles also control airflow. Degree of bronchodilation or constriction can be influenced by both the central nervous system and local processes if inspired air seems problematic, or in response to other environmental challenges.

The Renal System/Urinary System

The gastrointestinal and respiratory systems are involved in both the intake of substances into the body and the removal of waste products, for example, carbon dioxide. The renal system also participates in waste removal as well as other processes such as blood pressure regulation. At any point in time, a considerable amount of the body's blood is being filtered in the two kidneys, the main component of the system. They remove waste products from the blood, concentrate urine that is subsequently passed through the urinary system, control the retention and excretion of electrolytes such as sodium and potassium, and are important in blood-pressure control. As a result, kidney disease can have widespread effects on the body.

The Immune System

As suggested by the previous discussion, a great deal of human physiology is involved in the intake and distribution of nutrients to cells in the interior of the body (this is not to imply that other systems, such as the reproductive system, are unimportant, but these will not be discussed here due to space limitations). Yet not everything that is eaten, inhaled, or otherwise enters the body is useful. Some substances, e.g., certain microorganisms, can be especially harmful. The **immune system** protects the body from infection.

The immune system is more diverse and much less compartmentalized than previously discussed systems. A widespread system is necessary given the diversity of ways that substances can enter the body. As a result, the primary components of the immune system are individual cells that circulate in the bloodstream, though there are also fixed components such as lymph vessels and nodes, the thymus, and the spleen.

Circulating leukocytes (i.e., white blood cells) develop from stem cells located in bone marrow. They have the potential to develop into many different kinds of blood cells and are initially distinguished into myeloid and lymphoid types. A number of different cells develop from the myeloid line, including some that are not part of the immune system such as oxygen-carrying erythrocytes (red blood cells) but also immune system components neutrophils, eosinophils, and macrophages (Figure 2.6). Most of these attack and digest suspect substances. Some also release substances to aid destruction and organize the immune response. For example, macrophages release molecules called cytokines, which activate other immune cells and promote inflammation.

Inflammation is a classic sign of infection. Cytokines and other inflammatory mediators such as histamine dilate and increase the permeability of blood vessels in the area, facilitating the influx of other immune cells attracted to the mediators. An increase in fluid in the area also causes

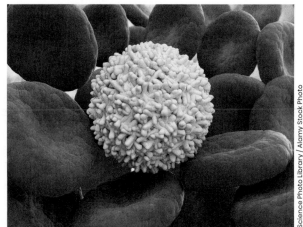

A white blood cell, or leukocyte.

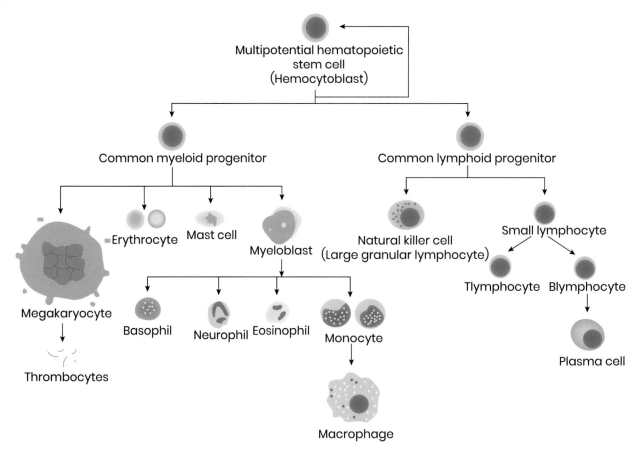

FIGURE 2.6 Circulating immune system cells.

Source: Mikael Häggström from original by A. Rad/Wikipedia.

it to balloon out, tightening connections between cells to create a physical barrier to isolate the infection. Red, puffy areas are a sign that the immune system is working.

Cells derived from the myeloid line as well as some from the lymphoid line (natural killer cells) provide what is described variously as natural, innate, or "non-specific" immunity. They are pre-programmed to attack many types of invaders by the presence of receptors that lock on to common proteins used by these bacteria, etc. However, this leaves open the possibility of attack by novel threats that may have developed recently, such as a new strain of the flu virus. "Specific" immune cells derived from the lymphoid line are more flexible in that they can be programmed to respond to protein patterns on new threats. Although this two-pronged system usually works well, it also means that specific immunity is ineffective during one's first encounter with the threat. For example, most people become quite sick when infected by the chickenpox virus the first time, though non-specific immune activity usually prevents death. However, lymphocytes are programmed to attack and remember the virus, thus providing more-or-less lifelong immunity after the initial infection.

Different types of lymphocytes have complementary functions and are classified as T or B cells (depending on where the cells mature) and subdivided into groups with the prefix CD (cluster of differentiation refers to molecules on cell surface). Cytotoxic T cells (CD8⁺ cells) are similar to neutrophils and macrophages in the sense that they directly attack dangerous cells, especially those infected with a virus. Other T cells support the immune response in various ways. For example, helper T cells ($CD4^+$ cells) stimulate cytotoxic T cells and macrophages by releasing cytokines. Although they do not attack cells directly, their importance is indicated by the devastating effects of the human immunodeficiency virus (HIV), which targets $CD4^+$ cells. B-lymphocytes play a key "humoral" support role, releasing antibodies that bind to invaders and attract immune cells.

The immune system developed to respond to a variety of threats. However, the process of detection is not perfect. At times, the system reacts to innocuous external and internal stimuli. Allergies are caused by unnecessary responses to innocuous external stimuli. Reactions are usually mild but can be life-threatening, as in the case of peanut allergy. The immune system can also attack healthy internal cells. Autoimmune disorders such as rheumatoid arthritis, type 1 diabetes, and lupus are caused by inappropriate targeting of healthy cells in the joints, pancreas, etc. To some degree, immune system cells are like a gang of hired gunslingers who generally follow orders but occasionally shoot the wrong person. Thus, there are mechanisms to dampen as well as stimulate immune activity, some of which involve central nervous system control mediated by actions of the **peripheral nervous system** and hormones. Central nervous system control of immune function will be discussed in the section on psychoneuroimmunology.

Psychological Influences on Body Systems

Complex organisms that could adapt to their surroundings were more likely to survive and produce offspring. The development of systems for the internal delivery of nutrients was a key step as this allowed other systems to execute behaviour. Nervous systems process information about the environment and internal condition of the body, adjusting physiology and behaviour accordingly. The human central nervous system can exert incredible control over physiology and behaviour via the peripheral nervous system and the **endocrine system**. Imagine the rapid-fire adjustments of muscle activity necessary to play a Mozart concerto (or at least to play it well)! At the same time, the brain has to adjust blood flow, respiratory activity, perspiration, etc. to support the behaviour.

Physiological activity is also adjusted according to internal as well as external sensory information. In addition to "efferent" fibres that transmit orders from the brain to muscles, the peripheral nervous system includes "afferent" fibres that transmit information from receptors sensitive to pressure, temperature, chemicals, and pain to the brain. A simple example is the baroreflex. To maintain adequate blood flow to the brain and reduce the chances of fainting as we move through daily activities, receptors sensitive to stretch are attached to the carotid arteries in the neck and elsewhere. If blood flow in this area goes down (e.g., if you stand up quickly), information is transmitted to the brain by afferent fibres in the glossopharyngeal nerve. This is combined with other information about the state of the cardiovascular system and organism, usually leading to compensatory cardiovascular responses organized by efferent fibres of the autonomic nervous system (discussed below), such as an increase in heart rate. The reverse—a decrease in heart rate—occurs when the arteries are stretched by an increase in blood pressure. Interestingly, external pressure to this area, such as wearing a tight collar or tie, can also produce a decrease in heart rate and, at times, fainting (for *Star Trek* fans, this is the origin of the Vulcan death grip). The baroreflex is a simple example of the continuous back-and-forth of information about the external and internal environment to the brain and adjustment of body function.

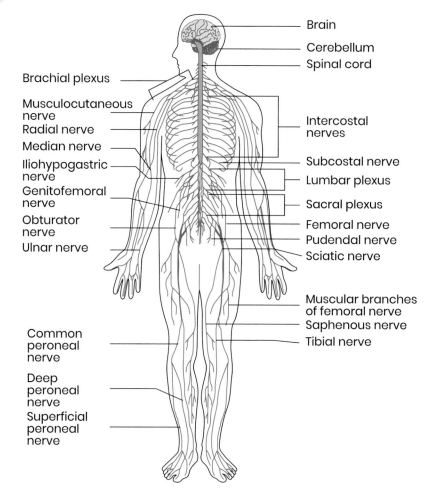

Brain
Cerebellum
Spinal cord

Brachial plexus

Musculocutaneous nerve
Radial nerve
Median nerve
Iliohypogastric nerve
Genitofemoral nerve
Obturator nerve
Ulnar nerve

Intercostal nerves

Subcostal nerve
Lumbar plexus
Sacral plexus
Femoral nerve
Pudendal nerve
Sciatic nerve

Muscular branches of femoral nerve
Saphenous nerve
Tibial nerve

Common peroneal nerve

Deep peroneal nerve
Superficial peroneal nerve

FIGURE 2.7 The peripheral nervous system.

The Peripheral Nervous System

The peripheral nervous system (Figure 2.7) allows the brain to make quick adjustments of body function. The central nervous system (CNS) is comprised of the brain and spinal cord. Neurons (i.e., nerve cells) of the peripheral nervous system are located outside the CNS. Fibres of the peripheral nervous system exit in bundles (nerves) from the brain stem or from the spinal cord between spinal vertebrae. Some fibres proceed directly to their "target organ" whereas others synapse with other neurons along the way in clusters called ganglia.

The peripheral nervous system has two subsystems—the **somatic nervous system** and the **autonomic nervous system**. The somatic nervous system consists of neurons that exit the spinal cord and proceed without synapse to striated muscle cells that control body movement, often referred to as voluntary muscle cells. As exemplified by the impact of severe spinal-cord injury, proper function of the somatic nervous system is important. If the spinal cord is severed due to an event such as car accident, the brain is unable to control somatic nervous system neurons that exit the spinal cord below the injury, resulting in paralysis of muscles innervated by those fibres. That said, since somatic nervous system neurons do not innervate organs such as the heart and the lungs, they are less important in terms of the major causes of illness. As a result, the autonomic nervous system will be described in greater detail.

The Autonomic Nervous System

The autonomic nervous system (ANS) consists of neurons that exit the brain stem or spinal cord, synapse with other ANS neurons, and proceed to cardiac muscle or smooth muscle cells that influence activity in different organs. Muscle activity influenced by the ANS is often referred to as "involuntary" since it occurs continuously without conscious thought, for example, you do not have to remember to tell your heart to contract. On the other hand, the word "involuntary" is somewhat inaccurate since the results of biofeedback experiments indicate that it is possible to develop some control over processes such as heart rate (Levenson & Ditto, 1981). Regardless, the ongoing nature of muscle tension means that ANS effects are revealed by increases and decreases in activity, such as increased or decreased heart rate, rather than the presence or absence of activity. It also means that ANS activity affects muscle tension somewhat more slowly than somatic nervous system activity but has longer-lasting effects (imagine pushing a moving automobile as opposed to a stationary one).

Another similarity to automobiles is the fact that the ANS is subdivided into two relatively independent parts, similar to acceleration and braking systems (Figure 2.8). In general, the **sympathetic nervous system** (SNS) stimulates smooth muscle activity whereas the **parasympathetic nervous system** (PNS) usually inhibits activity.

The PNS is sometimes called the craniosacral system since these ANS fibres exit the central nervous system in the upper (cranial) and lower (sacral) regions. Typically, "pre-ganglionic" neurons proceed most of the way to their target organs before they synapse with "post-ganglionic" neurons. The post-ganglionic neurons are relatively short. Acetylcholine is used as the neurotransmitter at the junctions of the pre- and post-ganglionic PNS neurons and at the junctions between post-ganglionic PNS neurons and the target organ.

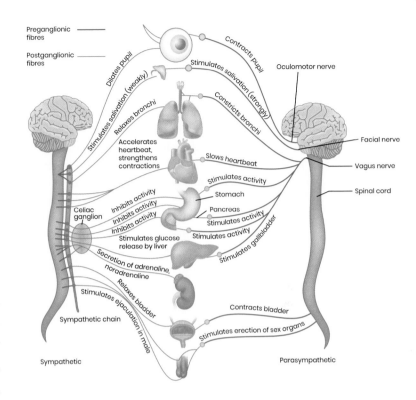

FIGURE 2.8 **The autonomic nervous system.**

The SNS is sometimes called the thoracolumbar system since these fibres exit the spinal cord in the central thoracic and lumbar regions. In contrast to the PNS, these pre-ganglionic neurons do not travel far before synapsing in large clumps called sympathetic ganglia, which are located close to the spinal cord. As a result, the post-ganglionic neurons of the SNS are much longer. As in the PNS, acetylcholine is used as the neurotransmitter at the junctions of the pre- and post-ganglionic SNS neurons, whereas norepinephrine is used as the neurotransmitter at the junctions between post-ganglionic SNS neurons and the target organ.

These differences in anatomy influence function. Though slower and less precisely targeted than somatic nervous system activity, PNS activity is generally quicker and more specific than SNS activity. There is much greater opportunity for sympathetic activity to spread and linger compared to parasympathetic activity. Imagine walking down a deserted street late at night. Unexpectedly, a cat knocks over a trashcan. Sympathetic activity will probably lead to a number of different responses—increased sweating, heart rate, constriction of blood vessels, etc.—that may leave you feeling "wired" for some time. Another interesting example has to do with nicotine. Nicotine from cigarette smoke stimulates a subtype of receptor for acetylcholine that is found in the brain and peripheral nervous system. This might suggest that nicotine produces physiological relaxation, consistent with the subjective experience of many smokers. However, since acetylcholine is also used as a transmitter in sympathetic ganglia, nicotine is mostly a stimulant in terms of its effects on peripheral physiology. Exceptions to this "all-or-nothing" description of SNS activity will be discussed later.

The Endocrine System

In addition to the peripheral nervous system, the brain can influence body function by stimulating the release of hormones. Hormones are similar and in some cases identical to neurotransmitters released by neurons of the peripheral nervous system and influence different aspects of target organ function. However, since they are released into the bloodstream they can influence physiological activity longer. The effects of hormones complement and extend peripheral nervous system activity. This is especially the case for hormones released from the central portion of the **adrenal glands**, the adrenal medulla (Figure 2.8). The adrenal medulla is somewhat unusual in that release of its hormones, primarily epinephrine and norepinephrine, is controlled by sympathetic nervous system fibres. SNS activity stimulates the adrenal medulla to release epinephrine and norepinephrine into the bloodstream, reinforcing and maintaining SNS activity.

Most other hormones are controlled by the hypothalamus and the pituitary gland, often referred to as the "master gland" (Figure 2.9). Descending activity from the brain stimulates different patterns of hypothalamic output to the pituitary. Neurons connecting the hypothalamus to the posterior portion of the pituitary gland control release of hormones such as antidiuretic hormone, which influences water retention by the kidneys and blood pressure, and oxytocin. Traditionally, oxytocin was viewed primarily in terms of its effects on reproductive activities, though more recently it has also been found to have stress-buffering properties. In fact, Taylor et al. (2006) have suggested that oxytocin is a key component of a motivational system ("tend and befriend") promoting social engagement to address collective needs, including safety and protection.

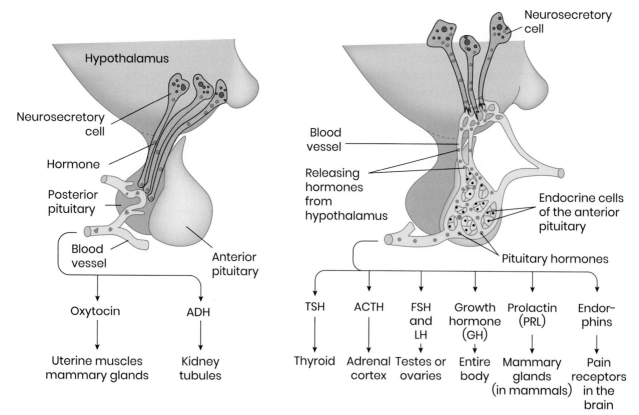

FIGURE 2.9 Pituitary hormones.

The anterior pituitary releases a wider array of hormones than the posterior pituitary and functions somewhat differently. The primary function of hormones released from the anterior pituitary is to stimulate the release of hormones from more distant glands. For example, thyrotropic hormone is released to control the thyroid gland. As well, the hypothalamus controls anterior pituitary function by secreting its own set of "releasing factors," that is, hormones that travel the short distance to the anterior pituitary to influence function. For example, hypothalamic gonadotropin-releasing factor controls the release of pituitary hormones regulating the gonads (testes and ovaries). Similarly, corticotrophin-releasing factor (CRF) controls the release of adrenocorticotrophic hormone (ACTH) from the anterior pituitary, which in turn regulates the adrenal cortex.

The hypothalamic-pituitary-adrenal (HPA) axis is especially important vis-à-vis psychological influences on body systems and the development of illness. The adrenal cortex releases a number of hormones, including glucocorticoids, mineralocorticoids, androgens, and estrogens. As the name suggests, mineralocorticoids (e.g., aldosterone) affect mineral balance (e.g., sodium) and often reinforce the effects of stress on variables such as blood pressure. Glucocorticoids (e.g., cortisol) free up glucose and other energy resources during times of stress. While this may be useful in some circumstances it can pose problems in others. Glucocorticoids also influence inflammation and other aspects of immune system activity that may have beneficial effects in some circumstances and adverse effects in others. This will be discussed in the section on psychoneuroimmunology.

The Development of the Stress Concept

The brain strives to maximize the efficiency of body function and adjust to the environment. Typically, adjustments are small and involve specific aspects of ANS or hormonal activity. For example, standing up may produce a brief decrease in baroreceptor stimulation that triggers an increase in cardiac-related SNS activity and a decrease in cardiac-related PNS activity (causing an increase in heart rate), but not much else occurs in terms of ANS or hormonal activity.

However, the brain also responds to stimuli that challenge the entire human organism. Stimuli such as extreme cold or heat, exercise, and blood loss elicit complex, widespread patterns of ANS and hormonal activity to prepare the body for different challenges. In the early 1900s, the physiologist Walter Cannon noted many common features of responses to strong, challenging stimuli, including stimuli primarily psychological in nature. In his classic book, *Bodily Changes in Pain, Hunger, Fear, and Rage* (1929), he argued that we possess a broad pattern of response to threat that he called the "fight-or-flight response pattern." Cannon believed that the extensive connections of the sympathetic nervous system allow the brain to prepare the body for a potentially life-threatening situation. SNS activity during a fight-or-flight response increases heart rate to facilitate delivery of nutrients to the muscles. It also constricts blood vessels in the skin and gastrointestinal system, though SNS activity *dilates* vessels supplying large muscles in the arms

"It was the classic fight or flight response. Next time, try flight."

In Focus

Cannon and "Voodoo Death"

Walter Cannon was a well-travelled man with diverse interests. Although not an epidemiologist (someone who studies disease trends in human societies) or an anthropologist, Cannon became fascinated by examples of death that seemed to be linked to extreme stress in several non-Western societies. In particular, he was interested in a phenomenon he called "voodoo death," where someone died after being "cursed" by a religious leader. He collected records from adventurers, anthropologists, missionaries, and physicians in South America, Africa, Australia, the Caribbean, and elsewhere. Given the unusual nature of the events, these were case reports rather than controlled experiments, but they were often quite detailed and allowed him to discount alternative explanations such as murder by poison or intentional suicide. Occasionally, Cannon was able

and legs. The fact that SNS activity stimulates smooth muscle in some blood vessels and relaxes it in others shows that the view of the SNS as producing uniform "arousal" is oversimplified. The SNS produces a pattern of peripheral physiological activity that prepares the body for vigorous physical action. Some processes are stimulated; others are inhibited. SNS activity also inhibits smooth muscle contraction in the gastrointestinal system (though this may disrupt digestion) and the bronchioles of the lungs (to allow greater intake of oxygen). The impact of the fight-or-flight response—more commonly described today as the stress response—on a wide variety of body functions has become increasingly recognized and now extends to aspects of physiology once believed unaffected, such as immune function.

Cannon was not an epidemiologist and thus did not extensively study associations between the fight-or-flight response and illness (an interesting exception was his study of the extreme example of voodoo death; see In Focus box, above). World events in the 1930s and 1940s also slowed appreciation of his work (Cannon had an interesting life that included rescuing scientists in the turmoil of the Spanish Civil War and World War II). However, interest in the topic of stress skyrocketed after World War II. To a large degree, this was due to the physician and researcher Hans Selye. Similar to Cannon, Selye believed that a wide range of stimuli can elicit a pattern of physiological activity—the stress response—that is problematic in modern life. His focus on the effects of stress on hormonal activity, particularly the adrenal hormone **cortisol**, complemented Cannon's interest in the ANS. As a physician, he was also more focused on how stress contributed to disease and was noted for his work linking stress, cortisol, and ulcer formation in rats. Selye's greatest contribution, though, may have been to popularize the idea of stress in the scientific community and the general public. His classic book, *The Stress of Life* (1956), was read widely largely because it argued that stress is a daily occurrence. This idea struck a chord in the years of the Cold War and, more generally, during an era of growing concern about the effects of industrialization, the growth of suburbs, and the "rat race" of modern, Western human life. Selye's message fit the times and provided a boost to stress research and the development of health psychology.

to correspond with the observer to extend his detective work.

Cannon viewed voodoo death as essentially the flip side of the placebo effect—a powerful effect of expectation on health. However, in this case, the expectation was death, leading to intense fear and a self-fulfilling prophecy of "death from fear" (Cannon, 1942). In addition to cultural beliefs, this was usually accentuated by withdrawal of all social support and acceptance of the victim's fate by others. Although he could not examine the victims directly, Cannon suggested that strong sympathetically mediated blood vessel constriction was the key feature of the process. Reports of looking extremely pale and "white as a sheet" were common. He believed that this led eventually to a state of physiological shock not unlike a wartime injury. It is likely that other processes were involved, such as cardiac arrhythmias (Sternberg, 2002), but this was an early, creative attempt to link life stress, emotion, physiological activity, and health.

Theories of stress and coping will be discussed in Chapter 3. For the moment, the only issue to note before turning to a few examples of stress-related illness is the association between stress and emotion.

Emotion

Although Cannon and Selye emphasized the idea of a broad, generic stress response, subsequent research revealed interesting differences as well as similarities in reactions to many strong stimuli, including emotional stimuli. These findings complement rather than undercut the notion of a stress response since the differences usually seem to match the nature of adaptive behaviour most likely to occur in the situation. However, the precise pattern of the stress response is more tailored to the situation than once believed. One of the most important differences concerns reactions to situations that elicit anger as opposed to fear. Both being in an angry confrontation and walking on a deserted street late at night, for example, can elicit large increases in heart rate mediated by an increase in SNS activity and decrease in PNS activity directed at the heart. However, anger-inducing situations are more likely to elicit sympathetically mediated blood vessel constriction than are fear-inducing situations, which may even elicit vasodilation (Ax, 1953; Sinha, Lovallo, & Parsons, 1992). This may be due to the fact that the odds of an angry confrontation leading to physical aggression, injury, and blood loss are much greater (at least in an evolutionary context) than a fearful situation that encourages you to run. Blood vessel constriction might reduce blood loss due to injury.

Differences in stress responses may set the stage for different stress-related disorders and be part of the reason that not everyone suffers from a stress-related illness. For example, the development of stress-related hypertension appears to be associated with a certain type of stressful life environment and emotional predisposition that, along with genetic susceptibility, increases risk for high blood pressure. This idea of environmental and emotional patterning will be elaborated in the discussion of specific illnesses.

The fact that emotions are the immediate stimulus for many stress reactions raises one other important issue. Stress responses do not require actual exposure to challenging life situations.

Strong reactions can be produced by the anticipation of an event that may never occur or the memory of an event that has already occurred. This may have been a useful conservative error at one time in evolutionary history (better safe than sorry that one hasn't anticipated and prepared for an attack), but it leads to even more unnecessary stress responses involving, for example, irritation of arteries by increased blood pressure.

Psychological Factors in the Development of Medical Illnesses

Without question, environmental challenges or "stressors" can influence body function. However, can the stress response actually make you sick? Since human beings are not assigned randomly to stressful and non-stressful circumstances at birth, this question has always been controversial. A number of different approaches have been employed, often blending human and animal research. These are illustrated in the following discussion of several stress-related disorders.

Gastrointestinal Ulcers: Executive Monkeys and Helpless Rats

Historically, gastrointestinal ulcers were viewed as the prototypic stress-related illness. In the middle of the twentieth century, many believed that the pressures of modern life and business contributed to the development of ulcers, especially among people with executive responsibility. This belief was common in scientific circles (based largely on Selye's research) as well as the popular media (e.g., the high-pressure newspaper editor in the Spider-Man comics, J. Jonah Jameson, had an ulcer).

In addition to stereotypes of the time, the idea was boosted by an influential experiment that seemed to confirm the importance of executive stress. The "executive monkey" experiment (Brady, Porter, Conrad, & Mason, 1958) was one of the most widely cited studies in psychology and a staple of introductory psychology textbooks for decades (see also Chapter 3). In this study, monkeys trained to avoid the delivery of electric shocks by pressing a bar were much more likely to develop ulcers compared to control monkeys who were placed in the same environment and received the same number of shocks but were not given this "responsibility." Unfortunately, the experiment had a crucial flaw that was not appreciated for some time. To save time during initial training, monkeys who learned the desired behaviour quickly were non-randomly assigned to be executives! The other monkeys were assigned to be the controls. As a result, ulcer formation in the executives may have been due to pre-existing differences in activity, fearfulness, or sensitivity to pain.

The executive monkey study is a useful cautionary tale of the dangers of uncritical adoption of stereotypes and over-enthusiasm for the idea that stress causes illness. However, it does not imply that stress cannot cause illness, including gastrointestinal ulcers. In fact, subsequent animal research showed that certain stressful situations reliably increase risk for ulcers. Weiss (Weiss, Pohorecky, Salman, & Gruenthal, 1976) conducted a well-known series of more tightly conducted studies with rats and found that animals placed in the more helpless situation of receiving electric shocks that they were unable to control were more susceptible to ulcers. Unpredictability also increases risk. The similarity between these animal experiments and the learned helplessness paradigm of psychological depression is obvious, and a number of unpleasant, uncontrollable situations have been found to induce ulcers in animals. For example, simply restraining rats for long periods of time significantly increases risk for ulcers. Underscoring the association with depression, recent research indicates that the likelihood of restraint-induced ulcers in rats is reduced by the anti-depressive medication fluoxetine (Prozac) (Abdel-Sater, Abdel-Daiem, & Sayyed Bakheet, 2012). Another interesting finding from Weiss's experiments (Weiss et al., 1976) was that rats exhibiting signs of aggression towards another rat when shocked were significantly *less* likely to develop lesions, even if this did nothing to terminate the shocks. This is an interesting contrast to research that will be discussed below indicating the importance of anger and aggression in the development of cardiovascular disease. In sum, there is good evidence that uncontrollable stress can contribute to gastrointestinal ulcers in animals.

However, the field took another unexpected turn in the 1980s in the context of human research on ulcers. Two Australian researchers, Barry Marshall and Robin Warren, discovered that a bacterium, Helicobacter pylori (H. pylori), was present in many ulcer patients and that antibiotic treatment often produced remarkably beneficent effects. This led some to argue that the problem was essentially "solved" and that even if stress could produce ulcers in animals it was irrelevant for human ulcers. On the other hand, while the importance of H. pylori continues to be acknowledged, views have become more nuanced in recent years. For example, about 30 per cent of people with ulcers do not have H. pylori and ulcers sometimes reoccur in people treated for H. pylori despite elimination of the bacterium. Most important, most people with H. pylori do not develop ulcers (Fink, 2011). Thus, it is more accurate to view it as a strong risk factor for ulcers that can be exacerbated by other factors, including stress. An interesting study found that stomach ulcers increased significantly following the Hanshin-Awaji earthquake of January 1995 in Japan, especially among those most personally affected and less able to rebuild (Aoyama et al., 1998). Another large population-based study found an association between personality disorders and stomach ulcers (Schuster, Limosin, Levenstein, & Le Strat, 2010). Levenstein (2000) developed a model that integrates influences of infection, stress, and lifestyle factors such as smoking and alcohol use on ulcer formation. The idea that stress may contribute to ulcer formation by reducing immune activity is consistent with the growing area of psychoneuroimmunology. It is also consistent with the role of depression, which is known to have a particularly strong effect on cortisol release. Thus, after some interesting twists and turns, there has been a revival of interest in the role of stress in gastrointestinal ulcers that reflects the growing sophistication of stress research. Indeed, study of stress-gastrointestinal connections will likely grow considerably in coming years given developments in understanding of the extent and diversity of microorganisms that reside within the gastrointestinal system, referred to collectively as the microbiome. The effects of the microbiome include both negative and positive influences on physiology and health that extend far beyond the gastrointestinal system to even the brain (Sherwin, Rea, Dinan, & Cryan, 2016).

Vasovagal Reactions: A Brief but Dramatic Response

Most people are familiar with the symptoms of a vasovagal reaction (VVR), often through personal experience, even if they are unfamiliar with the term. Many people experience dizziness, weakness, and even fainting at some point in their lives that is not due to an external insult such as concussion or drug use or internal disease such as epilepsy. Vasovagal reactions are caused by a decrease in blood flow to the brain in the absence of other illness. Historically, this was believed to be due to the combined effects of a large decrease in heart rate (mediated by parasympathetic *vagal* activity) and changes in blood vessel constriction. This description is not incorrect, though more recent research suggests that blood vessel constriction in the brain may be especially important (Folino, 2006). If blood flow to the brain is reduced sufficiently, fainting or "vasovagal syncope" occurs.

Fortunately, the majority of faints are brief and do not require treatment, though injury from falling is not unusual and longer faints can lead to seizures and on rare occasions death. Fainting and milder symptoms are also associated with avoidance of health-care behaviour such as injections and dental exams as well as clinical phobias. As a result, vasovagal reactions are more serious than the comic depictions of a Victorian matron who swoons at the receipt of bad news or a cartoon character who faints when startled. In fact, a vasovagal reaction is probably the clearest, most dramatic example of stress-related illness. In the span of a few moments, an individual with no pre-existing illness can be rendered *unconscious* by a psychological stressor.

Similar to some early views on the development of stress-related ulcers, vasovagal syncope was first thought to be the result of a stress-related parasympathetic rebound—essentially a side effect of "relief." In a classic article, Graham (Graham, Kabler, & Lunsford, 1961) noted that vasovagal symptoms during injections and blood draws generally follow a period of strong sympathetic nervous system activity and often occur towards the end of the procedure, sometimes after removal of the needle. On the other hand, though a full discussion of the psychology and physiology of the vasovagal response is beyond the present scope, the idea of relief is inadequate. For example, students rarely faint at the end of exams! This does not seem to be a general response to the termination of a stressful event. Nor is there a general association with anxiety or fear. For example, among people with strong fears, a number of studies have showed that people with blood, injury, and injection phobias are especially susceptible to vasovagal reactions whereas people who might have extreme fears of animals or social situations are no more likely to faint than people in the general population. Ost (1992) found that 70 per cent of people with blood phobias had fainted at least once during their lives. Vasovagal reactions seem to be related to the anticipation of physical harm.

In some respects, this sounds similar to the situation that sets the stage for stress-related ulcers, though there are differences as well. In particular, people do not faint or get dizzy in the context of every unpleasant, uncontrollable situation. As suggested above, there seems to be a special association with having to endure "puncture" in the context of injections, blood draws, and dental work. Another clue may be the fact that postural stress such as standing contributes significantly to risk for vasovagal symptoms. This has been observed even in people who are otherwise extremely healthy, such as young soldiers required to stand at attention for a long time (Fitch & Rippert, 1992). Finally, the vasovagal reaction is virtually identical to the physiological response to severe actual blood loss. In fact, hemorrhage-related fainting is observed reliably across species when blood loss approaches 30 per cent of total volume.

Diehl (2005) proposed that hemorrhage-related fainting developed as an active, adaptive response to severe injury. Some aspects of sympathetic activity are stimulated to increase perspiration and blood vessel constriction near the surface of the body. However, other aspects of sympathetic activity are decreased and some aspects of parasympathetic activity are increased in an attempt to lower blood pressure and thus blood loss. Lower blood pressure leads to less blood loss from a wound and greater opportunity for clotting. Metabolic activity is also reduced if this leads to loss of consciousness. This may also be a convincing way to "play dead" in the presence of a predator or overwhelming opponent (Bracha, 2004). Regardless, stress-related vasovagal reactions may have developed as a response to the *anticipation* of major blood loss. This would explain why people who are afraid of blood and blood loss are especially at risk of VVR (Ditto, Gilchrist, & Holly, 2012) and why standing, which causes blood to pool in the lower part of body and creates a sensation of blood loss, contributes to this process. While the details remain to be determined, this is an interesting example of how psychological and physical risk factors interact with specific characteristics of a stressful situation to elicit a patterned stress response, including both sympathetic and parasympathetic activity that may lead to a specific illness.

High Blood Pressure

In many respects, hypertension is the flip side of a vasovagal reaction. The most obvious difference is that hypertension is defined by high rather than low blood pressure. It is also sustained across the day rather than acute. The sustained nature of hypertension is exemplified by the fact that pressure does not drop or "dip" to the same extent when hypertensives sleep. In recent years, the degree of nocturnal blood pressure dipping has been used as a predictor of negative outcomes associated with hypertension such as stroke and coronary heart disease. In other words, the less blood pressure goes down at night, the greater the likelihood of stroke or heart disease.

The psychological profile of hypertension is also quite different from vasovagal reactions and ulcers. Vasovagal reactions and ulcers are typically related to uncontrollable stress, though there are some differences between them. Vasovagal reactions are most likely to occur in situations involving short-term uncontrollable stress that may lead to acute physical injury or blood loss, whereas ulcers are more likely to occur in situations involving long-term uncontrollable stress, hopelessness, and depression. In contrast, theories of high blood pressure typically focus on situations and emotions related to struggle and aggression. A simple manipulation found to raise blood pressure in rats is crowding. The number of rats housed in a cage is positively associated with blood pressure, though the effect is stronger among males and those at greater genetic risk for hypertension (Bernatova, Puzserova, & Dubovicky, 2010). This is an interesting contrast to Weiss's (Weiss et al., 1976) finding that rats who engaged in shock-related aggressive behaviour were significantly *less* likely to develop stomach lesions.

Considerable research in humans also suggests that conditions involving irritation, struggle, conflict, and crowding are linked to risk for hypertension and may begin to influence blood pressure early in life. Regecova and Kellerova (1995) found that kindergarten children whose schools were located in neighbourhoods with higher levels of traffic noise had higher blood pressure than children who went to school in quieter neighbourhoods. The young age of participants eliminates alternative explanations involving smoking and alcohol use. As well, they observed an interesting *negative* association between noise and heart rate—children who attended kindergarten in noisier neighbourhoods displayed lower heart rates. The authors attributed this to a normal baroreflex response of healthy children. Over time, the baroreflex becomes desensitized in hypertension, contributing to the upward progression of blood pressure. Associations between environmental noise and blood pressure have also been observed in adults. A recent review showed that chronic exposure to noise is significantly related to blood pressure elevation and risk for hypertension (van Kempen & Babisch, 2012), though the effect is seen mainly in men and those who are more annoyed by noise.

Chronic exposure to noise has been found to be related to blood pressure elevation and hypertension.

Other research has focused more explicitly on the idea of anger, extending from the original psychoanalytic hypothesis that the chronic experience of anger is often important in the development of high blood pressure (Alexander, 1939). An interesting subset of this research concerns the effects of racial discrimination on emotions and blood pressure in African Americans. African Americans are at greater risk for hypertension due to a combination of genetic and environmental factors. For example, Tomfohr, Cooper, Mills, Nelesen, and Dimsdale (2010) found that African Americans who experience more racial discrimination on an everyday basis had smaller decreases in blood pressure at night, possibly as a result of rumination about injustice that maintains anger (Tomfohr et al., 2010). Relatedly, several studies of stress management strategies that may reduce anger (e.g., transcendental meditation) have observed significantly greater effects in African Americans (Schneider et al., 2005).

The mechanisms of stress-induced hypertension are still under study, but one reason for the involvement of anger may be the fact that it often produces strong increases in both cardiac output and blood vessel constriction (Ax, 1953; Sinha et al., 1992), placing extra stress on the endothelium. In principle, increased cardiac output combined with blood vessel constriction and decreased flow to the skin would be useful in situations that might lead to violent conflict. However, repeated exposure may impair the ability of blood vessels to relax and self-regulate (a condition referred to as endothelial dysfunction; it is interesting that one complication of hypertension is erectile dysfunction) as well as thwart other compensatory responses such as the baroreflex. This view is supported by recent findings indicating poorer endothelial function in military veterans suffering from chronic post-traumatic stress disorder (Grenon et al., 2016). Diet, abdominal obesity, and, more generally, the "metabolic syndrome" (a common cluster of symptoms including abdominal obesity, high blood sugar, high cholesterol, and high blood pressure) are also probably involved in this process via the effect of insulin on endothelial function.

Other Diseases

Coronary heart disease will be discussed in Chapter 10. Many similarities have been identified between psychological aspects of hypertension and coronary heart disease, including the focus on anger. Evidence also links stress to many other diseases. Cortisol is often implicated as the culprit. For example, high cortisol reactivity has been associated with poor blood sugar control in diabetes (Dutour et al., 1996). This is perhaps unsurprising given that its primary function is to increase the availability of glucose during emergencies. Relatedly, stress appears to be a risk factor for obesity, over and above the well-known phenomenon of emotional eating. In addition to its effects on glucose, cortisol facilitates the storage of abdominal fat, perhaps preparing the body for the "long haul" of a stressful situation (Epel et al., 2000).

Cortisol also has intriguing effects on central nervous system function, particularly memory. Animal studies indicate that cortisol may even have toxic effects on brain cells in certain areas (Sapolsky, 2000). Some have speculated that this originated as an adaptive means of coping with trauma, preventing excess fear that may inhibit subsequent behaviour. (Some mothers joke that if they remembered all the details of their pregnancy and childbirth, they would never do it again.) Regardless, the belief that stress may contribute to dementia and age-related cognitive decline is a hot though controversial topic (Fink, 2011). Another hot topic with implications for many stress-related disorders is the effect of stress on immune system function.

Psychoneuroimmunology

Development of the Field

The growth of psychoneuroimmunology is probably the most important development in health psychology in the last 20 years. Cannon's description of the autonomic nervous system set the stage for early theories of stress-related problems such as high blood pressure, asthma, and ulcers. Observable connections between the brain and the heart, blood vessels, etc. provided a framework for speculation. Clinicians and theorists wondered for years about associations between psychological variables and a number of other disorders, but they were stymied by the lack of a plausible mechanism. For example, inspired by Cannon's work, Ishigami (1919) studied people with tuberculosis and observed connections between life stress, personality, and progress of the disease. Unfortunately, this work was largely ignored even though the author noted an additional tantalizing clue—the adverse effects of stress were associated with increased blood glucose.

The tide changed with the arrival of Hans Selye. As discussed earlier, he emphasized the role of cortisol release in the stress response (which may have explained Ishigami's blood glucose finding). He was also aware of its anti-inflammatory properties. In fact, he suggested that stress-related ulcers were due to the effect of cortisol on inflammation, reducing the ability of the stomach to protect itself from acid-related damage. In support of this idea, he found that surgical removal of the adrenal glands prevented stress-induced ulcers in rats (Selye, 1956). While connections among stress, cortisol, immune function, and ulcers are more likely to involve control of Helicobacter pylori, the idea that stress and cortisol can impair one aspect of immune function was influential and encouraged further research in the area.

Years later, Ader coined the term "psychoneuroimmunology" and propelled the field by demonstrating that aspects of immune system function can be influenced by classical conditioning (Ader & Cohen, 1975). In general, stress appears to reduce immune system function, perhaps explaining its impact on risk for a number of diseases.

Stress, Immune Function, and Illness

One of the most popular ways to study the impact of stress on immune function has been to look at the effects of examination stress (Glaser, 2005). For example, Kiecolt-Glaser et al. (1984) found lower natural killer cell activity and T-lymphocytes in blood samples obtained from students during exam periods, especially in more lonely students.

However, are such effects strong enough to lead to illness? Cohen conducted a creative set of studies on the clinical implications of stress-related immune suppression (Cohen, 2005). Participants who differed in life stress, social support, etc. were exposed to a virus that produces a common cold. Those with more life stress were more likely to develop symptoms independent of other risk factors such as cigarette smoking and sleep quality. In some studies, participants were hospitalized to further control possible confounds. While the investigators studied a minor health problem, the controlled exposure to a virus in these studies provides strong evidence of the importance of stress in susceptibility to illness. The accompanying In Practice box discusses a possible case example of psychological influences on health.

What about more serious illness? The results are less clear but emerging evidence suggests that stress can influence the progression of more serious diseases such as AIDS and cancer. An effect of stress on the progression and consequences of the human immunodeficiency virus (HIV) that leads to AIDS is especially plausible given that the disease is defined by the influence of HIV on immune function. Life stress has been associated with accelerated progression to AIDS in HIV+ men (Leserman et al., 2002) and possibly faster progression of cervical cancer in HIV+ women (Pereira et al., 2003).

The possible role of stress in the onset and course of cancer in people without HIV is more controversial. In part, this is due to the difficulty of studying the question given the diversity, complexity, and long time frame of most types of cancer. Some of the most persuasive studies in the area concern the effects of stress reduction interventions on the progression of cancer, that is, what happens when stress is *reduced*. Andersen et al. (2008) found that women with breast cancer who participated in stress-reduction groups after surgery were significantly less likely to experience a recurrence and lived longer than women with only medical treatment. While concerns about the reliability and ethics (e.g., raising false hopes) of particular studies have been expressed, examining effects of stress-reduction strategies on cancer provides a more experimental approach where potential confounding variables (e.g., smoking, diet, and exercise) and mediators (e.g., different aspects of immune function) can be measured carefully. The possible benefit of treatments that reduce depression also fits the large body of research showing increased cortisol release in people with clinical depression (Giese-Davis et al., 2011).

Unfortunately, there are some important additional qualifications to this relatively tidy picture. Most important, the impact of stress on immune function is not uniformly inhibitory (Segerstrom & Miller, 2004). In addition to evidence of decreased immune function, investigators have observed *higher* cytokine levels, inflammation, and greater risk for autoimmune disease in some stressed groups. Another puzzle is why stress reduces immune function. At first glance, from an evolutionary perspective, it would make more sense for stress to strengthen rather than weaken immune function. For example, a fight-or-flight situation involving possible injury could lead easily to introduction of bacteria from a cut or bite of a predator.

Recent research on the effects of the sympathetic nervous system on immune function clarifies the picture somewhat (Kin & Sanders, 2006). Historically, SNS activity was viewed as irrelevant to immune function. How could fixed nerves affect the activity of cells moving freely in the bloodstream? However, it has been established that (1) most immune cells have receptors for norepinephrine; (2) SNS fibres innervate organs like the lymph nodes and thymus where many immune cells congregate; and (3) SNS activity can stimulate certain aspects of immune function. A clever study by Benschop et al. (1996) examined SNS, hormonal system, and immune system activity in novice parachutists. Not surprisingly, people who were just about to jump out of an airplane for the first time experienced large increases in sympathetic activity as evidenced

In Practice
Ron vs the Warts

Ron always had problems with warts on his hands. Nothing dramatic—months would pass with nothing, but then one or two would pop up on or between his fingers. Sometimes they went away on their own, though he also became very familiar with his local dermatologist. While they are caused by a virus (the human papillomavirus), his dermatologist joked that the best way to remove them was simply "nuke" the buggers, that is, freeze or cut (after local anaesthesia, of course) them off. This was usually effective in the short term. They seldom returned in exactly the same spot, but they never completely went away, occasionally popping up in a different location. Unfortunately, during a stressful first semester in university, they became much worse. Tired of the nuisance and embarrassment, Ron decided to look into alternative, hopefully more permanent approaches. Being a bright college student, he knew that they definitely did *not* spring from contact with toads (not common in downtown Toronto). He also discounted "distant healing," the idea that illness can be treated by spiritual or mental energy from a healer, after reading about an interesting but unsuccessful test of this popular alternative treatment applied to warts (Harkness, Abbot, & Ernst, 2000). On the other hand, after reading a study that found that hypnotic relaxation and suggestion worked as well as if not better than salicylic acid (Spanos, Williams, & Gwynn, 1990), he decided to give it a try. This approach is based on the idea that viral activity leading to warts is influenced by the immune system, which, in turn, is influenced by emotional state. Following a training session with a psychologist, he practised a tailored 20-minute relaxation and imagery procedure daily for a month. The warts may have gotten a bit smaller (it was hard to tell), but he eventually became impatient and had them frozen. On the other hand, his mood and general physical health were better and he signed up for a yoga class in the winter semester.

by high heart rate and norepinephrine levels. More important, a number of immune changes were observed, such as increases in the number and activity of natural killer cells. The authors demonstrated that these were the result of sympathetic activity by administering the drug propranolol. Propranolol blocks receptors for norepinephrine and eliminated the changes in natural killer cells.

In sum, life stress can both increase and decrease immune function, depending in part on the length of the stressful situation. Brief stressors appear to produce an adaptive, sympathetically mediated increase in immune function that, if repeated, might contribute to problems such as asthma or rheumatoid arthritis. On the other hand, stressors of longer duration can lead to a cortisol-related reduction in immune activity. This may have developed as a way of modulating the immune response to reduce inflammation that may hinder ongoing escape behaviour and perhaps reduce the risk of autoimmune disorders.

That said, even more recent results suggest that the pendulum may swing back to immune enhancement with *very* prolonged stress. Cohen et al. (2012) suggest that long-term release of cortisol may desensitize glucocorticoid receptors, decreasing the body's ability to control immune function. As a result, inflammation and other aspects of immune function may go up. For example, caregivers of children with cancer have been found to have dysregulated cytokine activity (Miller, Cohen, & Ritchey, 2002).

Collectively, these findings fit a reasonable pattern; at the same time, it is clear that further research is required. For example, the duration of stress does not explain all contradictory findings

In Focus

Illness as Metaphor and the Ethics of Stress

Ironically, one problem with the idea that psychological factors can influence health for better or ill is widespread acceptance by the general public. The idea has been around for a long time and is reflected in everyday language—we speak of dying of embarrassment or a broken heart. In 1728, the Scottish physician, John Hunter, is reported to have said, "My life is in the hands of any rascal who chooses to annoy me." Dr Hunter died during an argument at a hospital board meeting.

Illness is portrayed as an invader we need to battle. This is especially the case for cancer, which is often described in terms of the mythological Hydra that springs two more heads after each is cut off. And if you look at newspaper obituaries or media reports generally, invariably you encounter descriptions of cancer victims who succumbed following a brave or courageous "battle" or "fight" with the disease. However, the feminist author Susan Sontag, herself a victim of cancer, warned against the dangers of "illness as metaphor" (Sontag, 1978).

Why? Unfortunately, psychological and behavioural influences on health can convey the notion of blame. There is a long, sad history of illness being viewed as the "wages of sin." In fact, much of modern medicine was built on the idea of removing blame for illness by emphasizing biological causes, leading to more charitable attitudes about the sick.

Even if a person's psychological state may have contributed to an illness, should he or she be blamed for "pushing too hard" or for "not coping with problems"? The goal of reducing depression and maintaining a positive outlook may be useful for many with cancer, but should those whose health deteriorates feel as if this was due to a lack of "fighting spirit"?

© ZU_09/iStockphoto

Hercules battling the Hydra.

(Segerstrom & Miller, 2004). Just as different stressors elicit qualitatively different patterns of autonomic nervous system activity, there seems to be patterning of immune responses to stress (Kin & Sanders, 2006).

Future Directions

Future research will undoubtedly reveal more connections between psychological variables and illness, with implications for treatment. Many of these effects likely will be complex and multi-directional. For example, while long-term depression may contribute to inflammation, recent research suggests that inflammatory cytokines can enter the central nervous system and exacerbate depression. Indeed, developments in the field of epigenetics indicate that bi-directionality extends even to one's genes. Traditionally, a person's genes have been viewed as the blueprint for their physical (including neural) structure that influences how they respond to the environment. However, we now know that environmental experiences can regulate gene expression. Genes promoting inflammation have been found to be particularly active in lonely people (Cole et al., 2007) and those with low socio-economic status (Chen et al., 2009). Certain effects may cross generations, that is, be heritable and/or influence prenatal development. Some recent studies have found that prenatal maternal stress can influence gene expression in children years later (Cao-Lei et al., 2016)! On many levels, you are in a dynamic relationship with the environment.

Summary

The field of health psychology stems from the integration of biological, behavioural, psychological, and social processes in the evolution of complex multicellular organisms. Complex organisms did not evolve to lie quietly on a beach, at least not all the time. Searching for food, defending from predators, and developing collaborative networks to aid in these and other tasks required the development of complex nervous systems and organs to support the intake and distribution of nutrients. This chapter has discussed the key systems involved in the intake and distribution of nutrients and protecting the body from unhelpful substances. To some degree, these systems are capable of self-regulation, though activity is also influenced by the brain in accordance with information about the internal and external environment. Major life challenges can elicit a strong pattern of physiological response called the stress response.

This is not a recent development. Given its importance in the survival of primitive animals, the stress response developed early in evolution. Snakes, frogs, and fish have well-developed stress responses (Bonga, 1997). Stress–immune system interactions even have been observed in insects (Davies et al., 2012). Thus, it appears that humans are "stuck" with these reactions. Unfortunately, modern life challenges do not usually require the kinds of vigorous physical responses that were once necessary. As well, some problems are compounded by transfer to the pervasive 24-hour sphere of electronic culture—an extreme but common example is cyberbullying—providing little chance for respite. Collectively, this seems to set a "perfect storm" for stress-related illness (Sapolsky, 2004). On the other hand, human beings also have the potential for creative problem-solving and stress management so we are not necessarily prisoners of the "stress of life."

Critical Thought Questions

1. What are some similarities and differences between the respiratory and gastrointestinal systems?

2. What are some similarities and differences in control of physiology by the somatic nervous system, the sympathetic nervous system, the parasympathetic nervous system, and the endocrine system?

3. Why did animals develop a stress response and what kind of considerations influence how the stress response is "tailored" to the situation?

4. What are the differences in the effects of stress on immune system function as a function of time?

Recommended Reading

Kiecolt-Glaser, J.K., McGuire, L., Robles, T.F., & Glaser, R. (2002). Emotions, morbidity, and mortality: New perspectives from psychoneuroimmunology. *Annual Review of Psychology, 53,* 83–107.

Krantz, D.S., & McCeney, M.K. (2002). Effects of psychological and social factors on organic disease:

A critical assessment of research on coronary heart disease. *Annual Review of Psychology, 53,* 341–69.

Dockray, S., & Steptoe, A. (2010). Positive affect and psychobiological processes. *Neuroscience & Biobehavioral Reviews, 35,* 69–75.

Stress, Coping, and Health

Nicholas J.S. Christenfeld

Britta A. Larsen

Arseny A. Ryazanov

3

Learning Objectives

In this chapter you will:

- Learn about different sorts of stress—good stress vs bad stress, chronic vs acute stress—and how these distinctions can matter for health.

- Discover what sorts of situations are likely to produce stress, and how it matters how one thinks about, or appraises, the challenges one faces.

- Find out about groups that are most subject to stress and most at risk of long-term health consequences from that stress.

- Explore coping techniques that can mitigate the impact of stress.

- Learn beneficial effects of social support, how this may differ by gender, and how formal support groups can help.

Introduction

We all know the feeling. You're sitting in class waiting for a lecture to begin, and suddenly you realize that people around you have their notes put away and their #2 pencils out: it's exam time. You completely forgot and are totally unprepared. Your heart starts pounding, you start sweating a little, your mouth gets dry, and you feel ready to jump from your seat and sprint out of the class-room. While you may not have experienced this exact scenario, chances are you've experienced something close enough to imagine the feelings involved in stress.

Most people identify stress as a negative experience. However, a life without stress, while conceptually appealing, may be no more medically advisable than extending the life of one's car by never driving it. Nonetheless, stress is linked in various ways to impaired health and reduced well-being, and some understanding of its nature, variety, mechanisms, and impact is worthwhile. As with the car, while stress is unavoidable, where you go and how you navigate your world can impact the wear and tear on the system.

Most generally, stress involves some perturbation of the system, or movement away from homeostasis or resting state, usually in response to some perceived threat or demand. The study of the body's response to stress (also see Chapter 2) was largely launched by Cannon's (1929) work on the fight-or-flight response and by Selye's idea of a **General Adaptation Syndrome** (Selye, 1976). Various situations require rapid preparation for action, and the hypothalamic-adrenal-pituitary axis (HPA) co-ordinates the body's neuroendocrine response. (See Chapter 2 for a detailed discussion of these physiological responses.) While preparation for action is often adaptive, repeated or chronic activation can produce long-term harm. It may also be that the bodily response—a primitive one in evolutionary terms—is well-suited to dealing with immediate physical threats that are acute and worth some long-term risk, but is less functional in dealing with the vaguer psychological threats of modern life, which cannot often be resolved by either fighting or fleeing (Sapolsky, 2004). Because of the breadth of the bodily stress response, involving cardiovascular, immune, digestive, reproductive, and other systems, the health effects of stress are widespread, and are apparent in many health out-comes (see Chapter 2). Heart disease (see Chapter 10) has perhaps received the most attention, with much research based on the "reactivity hypothesis" that repeated blood pressure spikes lead to hypertension and heart disease.

Of course, not all threats or demands are equal; some are frightening, some are exciting. Similarly, some last only a few moments, and others linger for years. When discussing stress and its effect on physical and mental health, important distinctions need to be made in the vast array of deviations from homeostasis we experience.

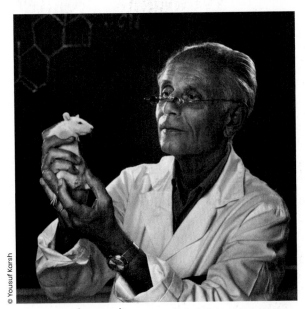

© Yousuf Karsh

Hans Selye (1907–82) of the Université de Montréal.

Good vs Bad Stress

One issue raised by the literature on coping is the distinction between responses likely to be beneficial vs those likely to be harmful. This is an intrinsically difficult issue, as harm and benefit occur along multiple dimensions. Sometimes active coping with a threat, even if it produces some long-term damage to the cardiovascular system, may well be worthwhile if, for example, it prevents one from being fired, or, in more primitive times, eaten by a lion (Sapolsky, 2004). While stress is generally regarded as a negative experience, the stress response, including physiological and cognitive changes, is actually meant to give us the resources to deal with threats, rather than add to the negative experience of the situation.

While Selye (1976) described a General Adaptation Syndrome when demands are placed on the system, he also distinguished between **distress**, which has negative health consequences, and **eustress**, which is positive. This good stress generally comes from confronting challenges that one can adequately deal with, and thus can provide a sense of meaning and well-being (O'Sullivan, 2010). On the other hand, distress comes from feeling that one's resources are insufficient to meet the demands of a situation. There has not been much research on the health benefits of eustress, though it is connected to the notion of optimal arousal, and there is considerable evidence that people can perform better, if not live longer, when they reach an optimal level of arousal (i.e., with some pressure on them) (Le Fevre, Matheny, & Kilt, 2003).

Acute vs Chronic Stress

One factor underlying the difference between positive and negative stress is its duration. While the notions of acute and chronic stress are much used, there is little conceptual clarity about their meaning (Gerin et al., 2012). Most models of how stress leads to disease suggest that the impact will persist even after the stress has passed, with, for example, brief elevations in blood pressure that can gradually cumulate into damage to the arterial wall, and so produce hypertension (Folkow, 1978). As such, the difference between an acute stressor and a chronic one could be simply how many times it recurs and how long it lasts.

Stress researcher Robert Sapolsky (2004) has theorized that the physiological stress response was designed (in evolutionary terms) to address acute threats, such as being chased by a predator. It is when these short-term changes, such as increases in blood pressure, become long-term that stress can lead to disease. There is some evidence that short-term stress can actually be beneficial (Edwards et al., 2006); ample evidence, however, shows that chronic stress is harmful. In one famous example, Cohen, Doyle, Skoner, Rabin, and Gwaltney (1997) exposed willing volunteers to a cold virus, quarantined them, and waited to see who got sick and who remained healthy. While experiencing acute stress over the previous year was not associated with infection rates, people who had experienced chronic stressors, in this case those lasting at least one month, were more likely to become sick than those who had not experienced chronic stressors.

Chronic stress is not always a product of the actual stressor being extended or recurring; rather, dwelling on events that are themselves very brief ("You're fired!" "I'm leaving you!") can turn these acute stressors into chronic ones. This process is known as **rumination**. Research shows that ruminating on a stressor can extend elevated blood pressure response, or later recreate it (Glynn, Christenfeld, & Gerin, 2002). People who tend to ruminate also have a higher incidence of cardiovascular disease (Larsen & Christenfeld, 2009), suggesting that this tendency to extend acute stressors into chronic ones can be damaging to one's health.

Rumination, then, has the potential to turn acute stressors into chronic ones, and also to explain, in part, the difference between positive and negative stressors. It also, as discussed later in this chapter, may be part of the link between stress and various co-morbid disorders.

Whether stress is good, bad, acute, or chronic naturally depends on many factors. Of course, there are the aspects of the events themselves, such as what is at stake (one's grade, one's health, etc.) and how. Also important in determining the nature of a stressful event, however, is the nature of the person experiencing it; the same event (e.g., a failing grade) could happen to two people and evoke very different reactions. In the sections below, we discuss common sources of stress and how some people might find them more stressful than others.

Stressful Situations

Job and Primary Role Stress

Among the most studied sources of situational stress have been various occupations, although attention has also been paid to the stress caused by traumatic life events, and more recently there has been growing interest in stress caused by having chronic caregiver responsibilities. Given the strong indication that stress matters, that people spend a good fraction of their lives at work, and that many people find work stressful, research on this topic is abundant and important.

At the extremes, there is good evidence that occupation matters. Timio et al. (1988) followed for two decades a group with particularly low **job stress**: nuns living in a secluded order in Umbria. They lived isolated from urban life, rarely spoke, spent time praying and meditating, suffered no economic stress, had no family responsibilities, and, to the extent possible, no earthly anxieties. If such things matter, the comparison of these nuns with a control group living in the same area should reveal it. And it does. Over the span of the study, blood pressure rose significantly—roughly 40 mmHg SBP—for people in the control group, while for the nuns it did not rise at all.

Stress is associated with certain occupations and life roles.

This difference emerged despite no difference in body mass index (BMI) increases for the two groups, and withstood control for activities such as bearing children.

There are also health studies of cloistered life roles rather different from life in the convent. D'Atri, Fitzgerald, Kasl, and Ostfeld (1981) studied prisoners, looking longitudinally at changes in resting blood pressure, and found that those assigned to live in solitary cells showed a significant decrease in blood pressure compared to those living in crowded dorms, despite the fact that daily activities, diet, and other lifestyle factors were rigidly controlled and standardized for all prisoners.

While both of these studies show compelling evidence that specific occupations and life circumstances influence blood pressure, neither prisoners nor nuns are representative of the general population. The most simple, intuitive notion of job strain is that some professions intrinsically come with high levels of stress, while others are naturally more relaxing. However, it is not immediately clear what the most stressful jobs would be. Are jobs more stressful if they involve menial tasks, manual tasks, or low wages and endless drudgery? Or instead, are the most stressful jobs ones that involve supervisory positions, with the responsibility not just for oneself but for many or even many thousands of subordinates? Or perhaps stress is not related to status, but instead to the particular details of the job—traders on the floors of the New York or Toronto stock exchanges with relentless time pressure, or Transportation Security Administration screeners who are expected to maintain constant vigilance?

One key question about job stress (and stress in general) is the issue of control; namely, is it more stressful to have control in a demanding situation or to have no control? This has been explored in animal studies with conflicting results. Brady (1958) and Brady and colleagues (Brady, Porter, Conrad, & Mason, 1958) compared rhesus monkeys that could exert control over receiving electric shocks with yoked monkeys that could not. The former died of perforated ulcers, while the latter survived, suggesting that high control in stressful situations may be more damaging. However, there are several reasons not to apply this too literally to human job stress. In addition to methodological objections (see Chapter 2), the finding runs counter to Seligman's animal work (Seligman & Maier, 1967), which suggests that not having control leads to a negative state of learned helplessness and depression. Moreover, the effect does not replicate in another species, namely rats (Weiss, 1968). Thus, it is questionable how useful these studies are in speaking to control and occupational stress in humans; in addition to finding contradictory results, the stressors used in animal studies do not have clear correlates in human jobs.

Studies with humans show that the effect of job stress on health seems to rely on multiple factors, though there is not complete agreement on what those factors are. For example, the model of occupational stress developed by Karasek et al. (1988) suggests that job stress is a function of job demands and "decision latitude," or amount of autonomy. The argument is that jobs with high demands but little autonomy would be highly stressful and, consequently, damaging to health. This clearly moves away from a simple hierarchical view, since upper executives may have high demand, but this can be offset by high control, and those nearer the bottom of the pyramid may have fewer demands, but also less control. People holding high-demand/low-autonomy jobs, such as waiters and firefighters, are roughly four times as likely to suffer heart attacks as those with the greatest balance of autonomy and strain (Karasek et al., 1988). Moreover, it appears that while neither demands (e.g., jobs reported as "hectic") nor control (e.g., jobs affording control over pace) had any predictive value separately with respect to daily blood pressure, the ratio of demands to control predicted both sleeping and waking diastolic blood pressure (Theorell et al., 1991).

Those who put in high effort and receive few rewards are also at risk for high job strain. In other words, the imbalance of effort and reward can predict, in large samples of blue-collar workers, negative health events such as coronary heart disease (CHD, or, colloquially, hardening of the heart's arteries), myocardial infarction (MI, or, colloquially, a heart attack), and death (colloquially, kicking the bucket) (Matschinger, Siegrist, Siegrist, & Dittmann, 1986; Siegrist, 1996). Kivimaki et al. (2002), in tracking workers over 25 years, found that CHD (see Chapter 10) was roughly doubled in those with a high effort–reward imbalance. Another model suggests that damage results from a misfit or incongruence between the person and the environment, or the demands of the job and capabilities of the employee (French, Caplan, & Harrison, 1982). For example, a worker who values creativity would suffer working on an assembly line.

In general, these job strain models rely on some interactive aspect of the effort involved in the job and whether that job includes factors that make its successful completion viable. The models discussed so far deal with such success at the level of structural occupational factors, but this can also be seen as depending on the resources or coping ability of the individual employee. That approach suggests a different sort of model, which is discussed in the section on the interaction of person and situation below.

Life Events

In keeping with the notion that stressful jobs damage health, various views have suggested that life stresses in general, whether at work, at home, in relationships, or elsewhere, should be seen as risk factors for morbidity and mortality. There have been efforts to quantify the general level of stress in a person's life, with one classic tool being the Social Readjustment Rating Scale (SRRS), more commonly known as the Holmes and Rahe Stress Scale (Holmes & Rahe, 1967). This scale includes numerous possible life events, and people obtain a score for each event they have experienced in some given interval, with more points assigned for the more major events (Table 3.1). For example, serious trouble with the law warrants 63 points, and trouble with the in-laws gets 29. One notable feature of this scale is that it does not distinguish between positive and negative events; both contribute to the total stress score. Marriage, thus, gets 50 points, while being fired earns 47. The scores for each event were obtained from subjective magnitude estimates of a group of research participants, and were in fact calibrated off marriage, which was set at 50.

This approach to assessing life stress has received its share of criticism. One argument points out the somewhat arbitrary weighting of the various factors (Rabkin & Struening, 1976). A nuanced response had a panel assign weights to an individual's life stressors based on contextual information, so that the end of a happy marriage, for example, would be rated as more stressful than the end of one that was less idyllic and whose end might even be welcome (Brown & Harris, 1978). Another issue has been the question of whether positive items produce the same sort of stress as negative ones. Few would deny the stress of planning a big wedding but pleasant events such as a vacation also add points in the original formulation.

Another debate about the measurement of life stress is whether stress problems depend on rare major events, or whether they have a greater relationship to frequent and minor ones. The death of a spouse (100 points in the Holmes and Rahe Stress Scale) is unquestionably stressful, but it could be that, given how rare such events are, the damage to the system is more profound from trying to get one's kids to finish their homework every night for a dozen years. To assess such questions, Kanner, Coyne, Schaefer, and Lazarus (1981) developed a scale with questions about more than 100 life hassles. People indicate which events they have experienced in the past month and also rate the severity of the events. The events listed include major changes such as being laid off, but also more minor events like auto maintenance, gossip, and attending too many meetings. Following 100 people for nine months, Kanner and colleagues (1981) found a large and significant

TABLE 3.1 | Events, and Corresponding Points, for Life Stress, from Holmes and Rahe's Social Readjustment Rating Scale

	Life Event	Value		Life Event	Value
1	Death of spouse	100	22	Change in responsibilities at work	29
2	Divorce	73	23	Son or daughter leaving home	29
3	Marital separation	65	24	Trouble with in-laws	29
4	Jail term	63	25	Outstanding personal achievement	28
5	Death of close family member	63	26	Spouse begins or stops work	26
6	Personal injury or illness	53	27	Begin or end school/college	26
7	Marriage	50	28	Change in living conditions	25
8	Fired at work	47	29	Revision of personal habits	24
9	Marital reconciliation	45	30	Trouble with boss	23
10	Retirement	45	31	Change in work hours or conditions	20
11	Change in health of family member	44	32	Change in residence	20
			33	Change in school/college	20
12	Pregnancy	40	34	Change in recreation	19
13	Sex difficulties	39	35	Change in church activities	19
14	Gain of new family member	39	36	Change in social activities	18
15	Business readjustment	39	37	A moderate loan or mortgage	17
16	Change in financial state	38	38	Change in sleeping habits	16
17	Death of close friend	37	39	Change in number of family get-togethers	15
18	Change to a different line of work	36	40	Change in eating habits	15
19	Change in number of arguments with spouse	35	41	Vacation	13
20	A large mortgage or loan	31	42	Christmas	12
21	Foreclosure of mortgage or loan	30	43	Minor violations of the law	11

Source: Holmes, T.H., & Rahe, R.H. (1967). The Social Readjustment Rating Scale. *Journal of Psychosomatic Research*, 11, 213–218.

correlation between reports of these daily hassles and psychological symptoms. In fact, these daily hassles were more associated with scores on a self-reported symptom checklist (including such symptoms as headaches and feeling lonely) than were the more major events.

It does seem clear that people's health and well-being can be impacted by many events of their lives, though questions about the necessary magnitude and valence of those events are not

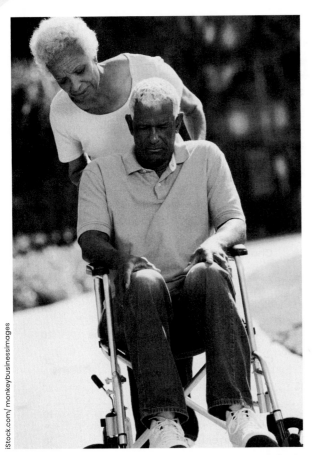

iStock.com / monkeybusinessimages

The role of caregiver is stressful, and increasingly common and long-lasting.

yet fully settled. Questions of causality also complicate the issue, as those with poor coping resources, or those who are simply poor, are likely to encounter more stresses to begin with.

Caregiver Stress

The person tasked with caring for an older or a sick relative experiences significant stress. An aging population, the treatment of infectious diseases, neonatal care, and battlefield first aid have all likely contributed to the number of people needing chronic care, and, accordingly, the number of people providing it. This sort of responsibility perhaps exemplifies the daily hassles approach to stress. The caretaker's role, while interspersed with crises, is mostly known for its relentless responsibility, vigilance, and hassles. This sort of stress has been shown actually to reduce telomere length, which is a marker of cellular aging (Epel et al., 2004). Chronically caring for others, it seems, even makes one's cells feel old.

Some approaches to caregiver stress are conceptually very similar to job stress models. For example, Nolan, Grant, and Ellis (1990) suggested that caregiver stress is produced by the perceived nature of the demand exceeding the perceived capabilities of the person. Other views of caregiver stress are more specific to this stressor and suggest that caregiving is stressful because it interferes with the caregiver taking care of himself or—more

In Focus

Stress and New York City

Cause of death varies by occupation, race, and nationality, but also, more locally, by region. In the southeastern United States—a region known as the "stroke buckle"—there is an excess of stroke mortality (Lanska & Kuller, 1995). Even more locally, New York City is a hot spot for heart-attack mortality (McNutt, Strogatz, Coles, & Fehrs, 1994). While there are numerous possible explanations for this pattern, one is that the level of stress associated with a city is a trigger for MI. If this is the case, then one ought to be able to detect not just an effect of chronic exposure to New York City (NYC) among its residents, but also an acute effect among people who are visiting the city. Similarly, it might be possible to detect

a reduction in heart-attack risk among residents when they are outside the city.

To test such notions, Christenfeld, Glynn, Phillips, and Shrira (1999) used federal death records to examine the fraction of deaths in various groups attributed to ischemic heart disease (IHD). Examining all deaths over the period of a decade, they found a dramatically higher proportion were due to IHD among NYC residents. They also found a significant elevation, about half that observed for residents, among people who did not live in NYC but who died while visiting there. Likewise, NYC residents, out of the city, show a proportion of deaths due to IHD that, while still elevated, is about halfway down commonly—herself. In addition to such objective burdens (Jones, 1996; Maurin & Boyd, 1990), there is also the subjective burden, which includes the feelings experienced when providing care (Nijboer, Triemstra, Tempelaar, Sanderman, & Van den Bos, 1999).

The stress of caregiving does not seem to impact all caregivers equally. With traumatic brain injury, partners seem particularly affected (Verhaeghe, Defloor, & Grypdonck, 2005), perhaps because it represents a more profound or unexpected change to the prior relationship. Women seem to report more caregiver-associated stress and depression than men (Pinquart & Sörensen, 2006). The consequences of caregiver stress include self-reported symptoms (Mioshi, Bristow, Cook, & Hodges, 2009), increased use of medical services despite having less time to seek care (Son et al., 2007), and also an elevation in mortality risk (Schulz & Beach, 1999). Importantly, and it is a point we will return to, subjective assessments of stress are important in understanding the impact of stressors on health (Son et al., 2007). Despite the burden, people value caring for family members (Lawton, Moss, Kleban, Glicksman, & Rovine, 1991).

Sociological Stress: SES, Gender, and Race

Some forms of stress are thought to result not from the particulars of one's employment, family responsibilities, or specific life events, but more generally from one's status in society. The positions thought to be associated with poor health outcomes are those subjected to discrimination, harassment, and limited opportunities. Again consistent with some job-strain models and caregiver stress, people in positions of less power often experience demands that overwhelm their personal resources.

Blood pressure and other health outcomes relate to socio-economic status (SES) (Colhoun, Hemingway, & Poulter, 1998) Some of these relationships seem to be due to the relatively poorer health behaviours of those in lower SES groups as compared to those of higher SES (Nandi, Glymour, & Subramanian, 2014). People of lower SES and those who are marginalized, for example, are likely to have poorer nutrition and are more likely to smoke. Evidence, however, indicates that education interventions improve health (Cutler & Lleras-Muney, 2012). Stress due to societal status

to the population level. All of these effects persist when controls are put in place for age, race, gender, and ethnicity differences and for being in or out of county of residence. The findings taken together suggest that something about being in NYC disposes people to this cause of death, and that about half the effect is from chronic exposure—living there—and about half from acute exposure—being there. The findings do not reveal exactly what it is about the city that matters, but stress, crowding, vigilance, and even excitement could all be involved.

New York City.

iStock.com/tupungato

is different from the other sorts of stress we have discussed in that it is due to relative position, rather than to any absolute level of daily events, task demands, and the like (Eibner & Evans, 2005).

As more women entered the workforce and were unable to correspondingly reduce their burdens at home, researchers addressed the corresponding stress of dual roles. Role conflict for women, for example, has been associated with increased psychosocial symptoms (Coverman, 1989). In contrast to findings showing working women endure greater stress, women have a considerably longer lifespan than men—5.4 more years in Canada, and 4.6 in the United States (CIA World Factbook, 2017)—and, at least through menopause, women have significantly lower blood pressure levels (Oparil, 1995).

Racial minority populations are often studied with respect to health disparities (see Chapter 15). Evidence shows that differences are due not simply to socio-economic factors, but more directly to being the victim of racist interactions. Pascoe and Smart Richman (2009) found that perceived discrimination was associated with poor physical health, as well as psychological distress. Reports of racial discrimination were associated with red blood cell oxidative stress (Szanton et al., 2011). Oxidative stress involves free radicals (which are molecules that, having a single unpaired electron in their outer shell, are highly chemically reactive since they seek to steal an electron from neighbouring molecules) damaging DNA and other cellular components. While African Americans clearly suffer worse health outcomes than Caucasians, the same appears not to be true of persons of Hispanic heritage, an effect at least partly attributable to health behaviour differences such as alcohol consumption and cigarette smoking (Pérez-Stable, Marín, & Marín, 1994).

Contributors to Stress: The Person

Jobs, life events, caregiving, and socio-economic status are all examples of situations or circumstances causing stress. Another approach is to identify the people who, across a wide range of circumstances, are more prone, or vulnerable, to stress. The notion of stressful people has a long history, going back at least to Alexander (1939), who, appropriately in the first issue of *Psychosomatic Medicine*, suggested that people who channel their hostile anger inward activate the autonomic nervous system, and are therefore more likely to develop hypertension. The stress-prone personality reached its apotheosis, in popular fame, if not research support, in Friedman and Rosenman's (1959) notion of a Type A personality (see also Chapter 10). Irvine, Garner, Craig, and Logan (1991) found a significantly higher prevalence of Type A in persons with hypertension than in matched controls, but, going back to Alexander's notion, also found that hostility seemed to be the key factor, rather than the more general Type A pattern, and more recently attention has moved to that dimension (Barefoot, Dodge, Peterson, Dahlstrom, & Williams, 1989; Williams & Barefoot, 1988). There is some debate about just what aspect of the general bundle of anger, hostility, and aggression is critical (Buss & Perry, 1992; Brummett, Maynard, Haney, Siegler, & Barefoot, 2000; Cook & Medley, 1954), with further distinctions such as anger-in vs anger-out used (Spielberger et al., 1985).

Another personality dimension that has received some attention is negative affectivity (NA), a trait that characterizes people prone to negative emotions such as anger, fear, disgust, contempt, and the like. This is related to other constructs such as neuroticism, having to do with anxiety, worry, envy, and such. There seems little doubt that this is associated with reports of poor health, but whether its action is on the reporting or on the health itself is harder to assess. There is some evidence for each, with Eysenck (1991) finding higher death rates (an outcome not so biased by self-report) in those high in NA, and others suggesting that NA can confound reporting (McCrae, 1990).

Contributors to Stress: The Interaction of Person and Situation

In addition to the investigations of the types of situations likely to be stressful and the sorts of people likely to experience stress, there have been studies of the interaction between person and situation to identify the sorts of situations that produce health-damaging stress in particular sorts of people. For example, an effort–distress model (Frankenhauser, 1983) suggests that distress depends not only on effortful situations, but also on the individual seeing events as excessive or feeling out of control. Another model (Dressier, 1990; 1991) has suggested that it is not being poor that is stressful, but rather living beyond one's means—that is, the stressfulness of SES is a combination of available resources and the ways individuals use them.

Another interaction showing that stress depends on the particulars of the person and the situation emerges in work with New York City traffic enforcement agents (TEAs) (Brondolo et al., 2009). In general, most people are in favour of the existence and even enforcement of parking regulations, but nobody is pleased to be ticketed, and the TEA's days are filled with aggressive and hostile encounters. TEAs wore ambulatory blood pressure monitors, and their activities were tracked, so that it was possible to determine whether certain sorts of people in those positions had elevated blood pressure, whether the job in general produced elevations, or whether there was an interaction between person and situation factors. The findings showed that people with the personality trait of high hostility indeed showed high levels of ambulatory blood pressure during the periods of hostile interactions with members of the public. In summary, consistent with the general trend in psychology of moving away from rigid divisions between personality and situational factors, and towards an understanding of the person-by-situation interaction, stress research has embraced the way that people's traits interact with, and create, the situations that can impact health.

Appraisal

The interactionist's view suggests that some stressors are too much for some individuals and overwhelm their resources. Another way of expressing this view is that how people view life's events, rather than just what those events are, is likely to be critical. As Shakespeare suggested in *Hamlet* (Act II, scene ii, 250–1), "there is nothing either good or bad, but thinking makes it so." Going back to the example at the beginning of the chapter, if you don't care about your grade in the class, then you probably won't find a surprise exam very stressful. This process of determining the stressfulness of a situation is known as appraisal.

One of the early, and still most influential, theorists on the role of appraisal is Richard Lazarus. In his early writings on the issue (1966), he illustrated the role of appraisal with the example of his family staying in Japan in a wooden house in a district known for its high risk of fires, and listening at night to the wail, he thought, of nearby fire trucks. The simple discovery, after a few stressful days, that in fact he was near a hospital and was hearing the arriving ambulances transformed the meaning of same stimuli into something no longer considered a threat.

Lazarus's discovery of the nature of the sirens illustrates the concept of **primary appraisal**, which involves a determination of the magnitude and nature of the threat that the situation presents (Lazarus & Folkman, 1984). Primary appraisal is then followed by **secondary appraisal**, a determination of the resources available to deal with that threat. In his case, that appraisal suggested

Richard Lazarus (1922–2002) of the University of California, Berkeley.

there was no threat, and so a secondary appraisal was not necessary. When resources are judged to be adequate, the situation can be seen as a challenge, and when inadequate, as a threat. These judgements have been shown to change physiological responses (Tomaka, Blascovich, Kelsey, & Leitten, 1993). Reappraising electric shocks as interesting new sensations, for example, leads to reductions in physiological response (Holmes & Houston, 1974).

Coping

Problem- vs Emotion-Focused Coping

Just as everyone experiences stress, everyone employs different strategies to cope with that stress. While stress itself tends to spring from primary appraisal, the coping process is focused around secondary appraisal, or an assessment of one's resources available for meeting stressful demands. These resources and the coping strategies that utilize them generally fall into two categories: **problem-focused coping** and **emotion-focused coping**. In problem-focused coping, one copes with stress by directly addressing the demands of the situation, such as borrowing money to pay an unexpected bill. In emotion-focused coping, one copes with stress by addressing the emotions that come with stressful situations, such as turning to friends for encouragement and support (Obrist, 1981).

Some evidence suggests that problem-focused coping for health problems is associated with better health outcomes. There is, of course, a problem with assuming this is causal rather than reflecting a correlation without causality; it could be that people who use problem-focused coping are those who can take specific actions for their health, while those turning to emotion-focused coping may be people who have fewer medical options and can only learn to deal with the emotions that come from being ill. Really, one type of coping is not necessarily better than the other; when facing a serious illness, for example, it is likely that an individual will have to engage in both problem-focused coping, such as seeking treatment options, and emotion-focused coping, such as learning to deal with uncertainty. The most appropriate coping response will depend on the situation, and most situations will call for some combination. In fact, Folkman and Lazarus (1980) have suggested that the most effective coping strategy is a flexible one—that is, being able to switch coping strategies based on the demands of the situation. One type of coping, however, sometimes classified as a type of emotional coping, appears to be less effective than the others: **avoidant coping**. Rather than dealing with the situation or emotions about the stressor, the goal of avoidant coping is to ignore the problem and its resulting emotions. This type of coping is quite robustly shown to lead to worse physical and mental health outcomes (Holahan & Moos, 1986), and is often associated with substance-abuse disorders. This emphasizes that, while there is not necessarily one right way to deal with a stressor, avoidance is often a maladaptive strategy.

Coping strategies can be further differentiated. Coping can be assessed in various ways. Much research on coping has involved the Ways of Coping Scale, a 66-item measure developed by Folkman, Lazarus, Dunkel-Schetter, DeLongis, and Gruen (1986). The scale identifies distinct coping strategies within the categories mentioned above (problem-focused, emotion-focused, and avoidant). Data from couples who completed the Ways of Coping measure to describe their response to a particular recent stressor were used to identify eight distinct coping strategies:

1. Confrontative coping (e.g., "I tried to get the person responsible to change his or her mind").
2. Distancing (e.g., "I went on as if nothing had happened").
3. Self-controlling (e.g., "I tried not to act too hastily or follow my first hunch").
4. Seeking social support (e.g., "I talked to someone about how I was feeling").
5. Accepting responsibility (e.g., "I realized I brought the problem on myself").
6. Escape-avoidance (e.g., "I slept more than usual").
7. Planful problem-solving (e.g., "I made a plan of action and followed it").
8. Positive reappraisal (e.g., "I changed something about myself").

Other measures of coping have included more specific categories, such as turning to religion or substance abuse (Carver, Scheier, & Weintraub, 1989). Measures such as the Ways of Coping Scale can be used to examine how coping changes over time, within or across stressful events (Stone & Neale, 1984). Clearly, coping is a complex, dynamic process. In the pages that follow, we will explore just a few of these specific coping strategies and their interactions with mental and physical health.

Social Support

One of the most common ways of coping with stress—whether everyday hassles like school or work deadlines, or significant stressors like loss of a job or a death of a loved one—is to turn to friends and family for support. **Social support** has many forms, but it can generally be described as a social network in which others care about one's well-being and provide help and assistance. This help is generally divided into four categories (Table 3.2): **emotional support**, such as providing encouragement and empathy; **instrumental support**, which refers to providing tangible goods and services, like loaning someone money or offering them a ride; **informational support**, in which one provides valuable information relevant to addressing the situation; and **appraisal support**, or helping someone identify a stressor and potential coping options (Wills, 1990). It turns out that our inclination to seek social support during stress is a good one, as support is one of the most effective ways of dealing with stress—not just emotionally, but also physiologically. However, determining who will seek social support and the type of benefits they will receive from it is complicated. There are several theories about when and how social support can help us deal with stress. Some of these theories are summarized below.

Main Effects vs Buffering

Is social support only important during severe stress? Certainly not—we enjoy having supportive friends and family whether or not we are facing a stressor. But is social support *more* important during stress? It might be. These two perspectives (i.e., main effects vs buffering) represent two different prevailing theories about social support and health: that social support has a main effect

TABLE 3.2 | Types of Social Support

Type of Support	Description	Examples
Emotional	Providing empathy, sympathy, and reassurance	Assuring a friend that you love and care about him or her; sharing a time you went through something similar
Instrumental	Providing tangible goods and services	Loaning someone money to pay a bill; giving someone a ride to the physician's office
Informational	Providing useful information pertinent to the stressful situation	Telling someone about a newly approved drug for her/his health problem; directing someone to government services she/he qualifies for
Appraisal	Providing feedback about someone's response to a stressor	Reassuring someone that she or he performed well while being evaluated at work; telling a friend that his or her response to an angry co-worker was appropriate

Source: Wills, T.A. (1990). Social support and interpersonal relationships. In M.S. Clark (Ed.), *Prosocial Behavior* (pp. 265–289). Thousand Oaks, Calif.: Sage.

on health, and that social support buffers—or protects us from—the negative effects that stress has on our health (Cohen & Wills, 1985). It is important to remember that these are not duelling or mutually exclusive perspectives. Rather, both can be true, and there is scientific data supporting both models.

The **main effects model** suggests that social support is generally beneficial to health and well-being, whether we are carefree or stress-ridden. This has been shown for myriad measures of health; people with more social support tend to have lower blood pressure, are less likely to suffer from heart disease, have stronger immune systems, and live longer (Uchino, Cacioppo, & Kiecolt-Glaser, 1996). In viral challenge studies, Cohen and colleagues (1997) found that when people were exposed to a rhinovirus (the cause of the common cold), they were less likely to get sick if they had good social support back home. More compelling evidence for the main effects model is shown in studies on marriage and health. Marriage, it turns out, is robustly health-protective: married people live longer and generally get sick less than single people do, one reason being that they have a constant source of social support (Kiecolt-Glaser & Newton, 2001). Of course, it is important to remember that these studies are not randomized trials, so we cannot assume that having better social support actually *causes* better health. It could be that people who are healthy are more easily able to make friends and interact with people, and that people who are chronically ill are kept from participating in social activities. While it may not be possible to randomly assign people to strong or weak social circles, some of these complications can be addressed by conducting prospective studies in which people who are healthy at baseline are followed for many years to see if they develop health problems. Such prospective studies show that among initially healthy people, those with better social support at baseline are less likely to develop health problems (e.g., heart disease) and tend to live longer (Hemingway & Marmot, 1999). While this is not definitive proof of a causal effect, it does suggest that social support may play a protective role.

The buffering model suggests that one of the main ways that social support leads to better health is by reducing stress and, therefore, reducing the negative effects of stress on one's health (Cohen & Wills, 1985). This model has received growing support in recent years. While marriage protects against getting sick in the first place, it also appears to be particularly important when facing a health crisis: married people are more likely to survive a heart attack, more likely to recover from cancer, and less likely to relapse after remission (Chandra, Szklo, Goldberg, & Tonascia, 1983; Goodwin, Hunt, Key, & Samet, 1987). Similar results have been found in prospective studies. In a large prospective study of men in Sweden, Rosengren, Orth-Gomer, Wedel, and Wilhelmsen (1993) found that those who experienced significant stressful events during the seven-year study were more than three times more likely to die (10.9 per cent) than those who had not (3.3 per cent). However, when the authors divided participants into those with low and high emotional support, they found that this increased risk of mortality associated with stress was only found in those with low emotional support. This suggests that those with high social support were somehow protected from the physiological consequences of stress. Again, this study did not involve random assignments so we cannot make causal claims about support being protective.

Some studies on the **buffering hypothesis** have employed an experimental approach because support only needs to be observed during a stressor in order to test the model (rather than throughout daily life, as is the case with tests of the main effects model). Using laboratory studies, researchers evaluated physiological responses to stress, such as changes in blood pressure, when people do and do not have supportive others present. Participants in one study (Glynn, Christenfeld, & Gerin, 1999) were asked to do something many people find particularly stressful: give a speech in front of an evaluative audience. For a random sample of these participants, one of the audience members was a confederate (working for the experimenter) who provided supportive feedback by using body language that might suggest the participant was doing a good job, such as nodding and smiling. The researchers found that those who received this feedback during the speech had lower blood pressure than those who did not receive supportive feedback, suggesting that support during the stressor made the experience not quite as stressful. Short-term increases in blood pressure are not likely to have important effects on health, but over time they can add up and increase risk of heart disease and other health problems (McEwen, 1998). The notion of "allostatic load" captures the idea that not just the magnitude of the elevation but also the duration and frequency of the blood pressure response will contribute to disease outcomes. Having support throughout a chronic stressor, then, could be important for health.

Important health outcomes have been observed with social support during stressors outside the laboratory. Kulik and Mahler (1987) examined the effects of social support in an especially stressful situation: awaiting major surgery. These researchers found that coronary bypass patients whose pre-operative roommate was a patient who had already had surgery had better recovery and returned home from the hospital sooner than those whose roommates had not yet had surgery. In this case, social support was not only a source of encouragement, but also a source of valuable information on what to expect. This study represents a particularly useful real-world example because roommates in hospitals are essentially assigned at random. Thus, while the authors did not plan to conduct a randomized controlled trial, they were able to observe the effects of random assignment in the real world.

Social support, then, appears to be an especially important resource during stressful times. This is one of the most robust findings (across laboratory studies and real-world evidence) in health psychology research.

The Great Gender Divide

People do not use social support equally when they experience stress. Although not all sex and gender stereotypes are true, this one generally is: during stressful times, women are much more likely than men to turn to friends and family for support. In fact, it may be that this is the main difference in the way men and women face stress (Taylor, Klein, Gruenewald, Gurung, & Taylor, 2003). This disparity is seen for different types of support and different types of stress. Given the same physiological symptoms, men are less likely than women to see a physician (Galdas, Cheater, & Marshall, 2005), and men facing personal life stressors are less likely than women to turn to support networks for help (Padesky & Hammen, 1981). This does not mean that men do not benefit from social support—quite the opposite. As mentioned earlier, marriage appears to have great benefits for health, yet these benefits are not distributed equally; men experience more health benefits from marriage than women do (Kiecolt-Glaser & Newton, 2001). This could be for a variety of reasons. The important point is that although men do seem to benefit from support, they do not seek it out the way that women do.

This gender difference is so pronounced that some researchers believe that women's physiological stress response should be classified differently from that of men. Taylor and colleagues (2000) have argued that the typical fight-or-flight response may actually be a more appropriate description of men's response to stress, and that women's much more social response could more accurately be classified as **tend-and-befriend**. This captures the two social responses that women exhibit when experiencing stress: social bonding and caring for children. According to Taylor and colleagues, this social response to stress is not simply socially learned but has an evolutionary basis. In species where females are physically smaller and weaker, relying on a group for protection may be a better survival strategy than fighting or running away. Fight or flight may also be less feasible for females who are pregnant or have young children. Reproductive roles for males and females are such that males can have almost unlimited offspring, whereas reproduction for females is much more finite, making protection of offspring a greater priority for females. Tending and befriending, then, may be the best ways for females to survive and pass on their genes.

The tend-and-befriend hypothesis does not suggest that women do not have a sympathetic fight-or-flight response to stress—of course a woman's heart, like a man's, pounds when she is scared. Central to the tend-and-befriend hypothesis is the idea that women may have a modified stress response due to the hormone oxytocin (Taylor, 2006). Research with oxytocin is still limited, but it appears to encourage affiliation and caregiving. While both men and women secrete oxytocin during stress, oxytocin may affect women more because its effects are modulated by estrogen and suppressed by androgens. Women have especially elevated levels of oxytocin when pregnant and nursing; thus, if oxytocin suppresses the fight-or-flight response, this urge would be especially blunted when women have young offspring.

The tend-and-befriend viewpoint is not universally accepted (Geary & Flinn, 2002). While it is difficult to prove any evolutionary hypothesis, there is some evidence for the tend-and-befriend effect. As part of a study, researchers interviewed children about their parents' behaviours after work and found that the days that children reported the most nurturing from their mothers were the days that women reported the most stress at work. Fathers' stressful days, however, aligned with days children reported their fathers being distant and isolating themselves (Repetti & Wood, 1997). In rodents, group housing acts as a stressor for males but is calming for females (Palanza, Gioiosa, & Parmigiani, 2001). This affiliative response may be stronger for lactating mothers with high oxytocin levels. However, nursing mothers can also become especially aggressive and territorial. There is still a good deal of research to be done on oxytocin and the stress response in women.

A large study of Canadians explored gender differences in the use of social support and the severity and duration of depression (Wareham, Fowler, & Pike, 2007). Positive social interactions were found to be beneficial for both sexes, but men who used more emotional/informational support actually did worse. It may be that men, with less of this sort of support available in reserve, were harmed by using up so much of it.

Some social interactions are stressful for some people and calming for others, which emphasizes an important aspect of social support: the right type of support must be offered in order to be effective in reducing stress. Sometimes, as discussed below, social interactions can actually create more stress than they eliminate.

Social Stress

Are social interactions always good for our health? Certainly everyone can think of some social interactions that have increased their blood pressure rather than decreased it. Being part of social networks is generally good for health, but it can also be stressful when social interactions become negative. Looking at measures of life events, one can see that many major ones are social, such as divorce. Not surprisingly, people who go through major social stressors like divorce report more health problems than people with stable, happy social structures.

Social networks can actually become a liability to health when they do not provide the support that is needed or expected. Kulik and Mahler (1989), in their study of male coronary bypass patients, examined recovery time in relation to how often the patients' wives visited them in the hospital. They found that those who recovered fastest and went home earliest, not surprisingly, were the ones whose wives visited most often. The surprising finding, however, was that the group slowest to recover was not single men, but married men whose wives visited rarely or never. In this case it appeared that having an unsupportive spouse was actually worse for health than having no spouse at all. This effect of spousal support is so strong that one study showed that marital quality predicted the progression of heart disease in heart-failure patients just as accurately as objectively measured physiological risk factors (Coyne et al., 2001).

Just like with social support, not everyone responds to social conflict equally, and in this case the division is again drawn along gender lines. Women generally report more distress over social conflict than men, which is not surprising because women appear to rely more on social networks than men do. However, there is one large exception to this trend: while men receive more health benefits from marriage, they appear to suffer just as many health consequences from divorce as women (Umberson, 1987). One suggested explanation for this disparity is that women tend to have wide, complex social networks, and are often able to list multiple people as close friends and confidants. Men, on the other hand, often list many friends and acquaintances but only one close friend with whom they can discuss their problems: their wives. Thus, when men get married they receive a major boost to their social resources, but when they get divorced they may lose it all at once (Gerstel, Riessman, & Rosenfield, 1985).

People going through significant stressors may also report negative effects of support if they get the *wrong type* of support. People going through treatment for cancer, for example, generally benefit from social support, but report that receiving informational support and treatment suggestions from friends and family can actually be more distressing than helpful, and that they would rather receive such information only from their physicians (Arora, Rutten, Gustafson, Moser, & Hawkins, 2007).

In Focus

Support Groups

Turning to support groups to deal with stressful experiences is an increasingly popular coping option, and it seems these days there is a support group for nearly every type of major stressor: serious physical illness, mental disorders, substance abuse, divorce, single parenting, and so on. By gathering and talking with others who face the same challenges, people can empathize with others who know the stressful experience firsthand and can also glean useful information on overcoming challenges. Whether support groups are actually beneficial for physical and mental health, however, is a matter of some debate. Like with many things, the answer is "it depends." In one study of stage 1 breast cancer, women were assigned to an education group or peer discussion group for eight weeks. The researchers found that those in the education group experienced sustained improvements in physiological and psychological functioning while those in the peer discussion group showed no benefits and experienced more negative affect than those in the control group (Helgeson, Cohen, Schulz, & Yasko, 2000). Conversely, another study showed that women

Other Coping Strategies

Emotional Disclosure

While many benefits are gained from discussing stressful events with others, it appears that there may be some benefits in simply "discussing" a problem with *oneself*. For several decades, James Pennebaker and colleagues have researched the effects of emotional self-disclosure by having participants write about stressful experiences in a journal (Pennebaker, 1997). In a seminal study with college freshmen, Pennebaker, Colder, and Sharp (1990) assigned students to write in a journal three times per week about either stressful experiences and feelings (such as the stress of leaving home and starting college) or trivial topics (such as the weather). Over the course of the study, those who wrote about stressors reported fewer visits to the student health centre than those who wrote about trivial topics, and they showed a slight trend in improvements in their grades from first semester to second semester. Whether this showed actual health improvements due to writing about stress is debatable, as fewer visits to the health centre do not necessarily imply that these people became ill less often. In addition, while the number of visits in the stress writing group differed from the visits taken by those in the trivial topics writing group, it did not actually differ from the number of visits taken by students who were not in the study. An effective intervention ought to be not only better than the placebo, but also better than no treatment at all.

Other studies have since explored further the effects of emotional writing, and have led to mixed results. Pennebaker and colleagues have found that emotional writing may lead to enhanced immune function (Petrie, Booth, Pennebaker, Davison, & Thomas, 1995), fewer absences from work (Francis & Pennebaker, 1992), and enhanced liver functioning (Francis & Pennebaker, 1992), though not all studies have been consistently positive. However, people with chronic diseases benefit more consistently from emotional writing. Smyth, Stone, Hurewitz, and Kaell (1999) showed that patients with asthma and patients with arthritis demonstrated improvements in objective measures of functioning after regularly writing about traumatic experiences.

The question that arises from the writing and stress studies is *why* would emotional writing lead to psychological and physiological benefits? There is no clear answer, but according to with metastatic breast cancer benefited greatly from a support group (Goodwin et al., 2001), and similar results were obtained in a study of HIV+ men with depression (Chesney, Chamber, Taylor, & Folkman, 2003). Overall, research suggests that for those with less serious conditions and/or who already have sufficient support at home, support groups may not be useful and may lead them to focus on the problem rather than coping with it. For others who do not have sufficient support at home and/or who have more serious, potentially terminal conditions, support groups may be a valuable resource.

Many people who suffer from stress attend support groups.

Pennebaker and Seagal (1999), writing about traumatic events can help place these events in a meaningful narrative. Writing about an event could help someone find purpose in relation to the event, or to place it in the context of his or her life in a meaningful way. This is supported by an analysis of the content of these journal entries. Pennebaker and Seagal found that those who benefited most from the writing exercise were those who used the most cause-and-effect words—e.g., "because," "therefore"—which could indicate that these people were recognizing the causes and consequences of the stressors.

Exercise

One common approach to coping with stress is to head to the gym. Given the vast literature on the benefits of exercise and the popularity of this coping strategy, there is surprisingly little research on the effectiveness of exercise as a coping strategy. People who report frequent exercise also tend to report lower levels of stress (Penedo & Dahn, 2005), yet this again is only a correlation, and does not necessarily speak to the effects of exercise on stress.

Limited experimental studies suggest that exercise may be an effective way to cope with and reduce stress. One laboratory study showed that participants who were physically active following an emotional stressor (giving a speech in front of an audience) had greater blood pressure reactivity while exercising than controls who sat quietly (Figure 3.1). When they stopped exercising, however, they returned to baseline blood pressure levels more quickly than controls—that is, the exercise seemed to help them get over the stress faster (Chafin, Christenfeld, & Gerin, 2008). It is not clear whether this is purely a physiological effect, or whether stress actually is lowered by exercise. Randomized controlled trials have also generally shown that those assigned to exercise conditions report less stress by the end of the study than those in control conditions (Penedo & Dahn, 2005).

It is unclear what type of exercise is most beneficial. Norris, Carroll, and Cochrane (1992) found that only high-intensity aerobic exercise was effective in reducing stress in adolescents. Others, however, have found that more mindful forms of exercise, such as yoga and Tai Chi, are effective in reducing depression and anxiety and increasing positive affect (Schell, Allolio, & Schonecke, 1994; Sandlund & Norlander, 2000). Women undergoing radiation therapy for breast

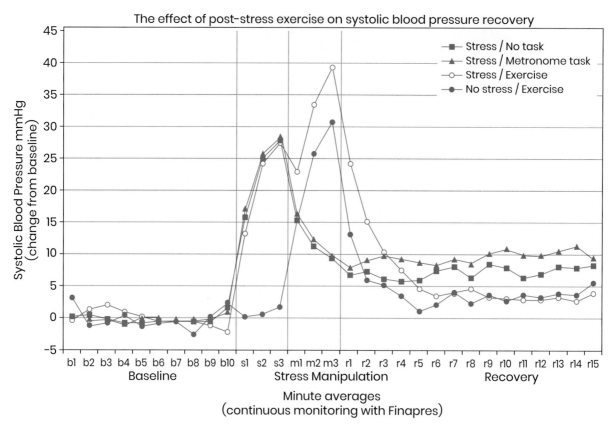

FIGURE 3.1 Average systolic blood pressure (SBP) change from baseline score (per minute) across the experimental session.

Source: Improving cardiovascular recovery from stress with brief poststress exercise, Chafin S. Christenfeld N. Gerin W., *Health Psychology* 2008, Vol. 27, No. 1(Suppl.), S64 –S72

cancer and who were randomly assigned to an integrated yoga therapy not only reported reduced stress, anxiety, and depression, but also showed slightly less damage to their DNA than controls following radiation (Banerjee et al., 2007). Even brief interventions can decrease stress—a 10-day yoga intervention reduced biomarkers of stress and inflammation (Yadav et al., 2012). In summary, evidence supports exercise as an effective coping strategy but it remains unclear how much or what type is needed to prevent or reduce stress, or how and why exercise reduces stress. It could be that planned, purposeful activity in which one accomplishes goals is generally beneficial for mental health. The effects may also be physiological. As stress engages the sympathetic nervous system, using the resulting increased energy could help initiate recovery to baseline. This could also be achieved by actively engaging the parasympathetic nervous system through yoga, Tai Chi, or other mindful, breathing-focused exercises.

Stress and Mental Health

As excessive stress is generally a negative psychological experience, it is not surprising that it is also a significant factor in many psychological disorders. Extreme stress is a major risk factor for depression and, not surprisingly, anxiety disorders (Tennant, 2001; Cutrona et al., 2005).

Post-traumatic stress disorder (PTSD) represents an extreme example of the connection between stress and mental health (American Psychiatric Association, 2013, pp. 271–80). This disorder is characterized by intrusive thoughts, often even when sleeping, of the traumatic event, and this rumination, whether of war, assault, abuse, or other such acute trauma, extends the duration of the stressor and multiplies its impact.

Groups that have been disproportionally exposed to traumatic events exhibit elevated PTSD symptomology and other mental health problems. For example, Indigenous peoples forced to attend residential schools experienced neglect, trauma, and stress after having been torn away from their families, communities, and culture. Such schooling moderates the effects of other negative childhood experiences, such that those who experienced negative childhood events exhibited elevated symptomology if they also attended residential schools (Bombay, Matheson, & Anisman, 2011). The experience can have such an enduring impact that it not only affects the mental health of those forced to attend residential school themselves, but intergenerationally affects the mental health of their children too (Bombay et al., 2011).

Refugees likewise exhibit elevated PTSD symptomology as a result of exposure to traumatic events. In a sample of preschool-age refugees from Iran to Sweden, degree of exposure to war and political persecution even at such a young age correlated with prevalence of PTSD symptomology at follow-up 12 years later (Almqvist & Brandell-Forsberg, 1997). Thus, the effects of extreme stress can endure long after the initial stressor has subsided. Such disadvantaged groups also often experience acculturative stress, or the stress of adapting to a new culture, as well as perceived discrimination, which can exacerbate mental health problems (Ellis, Macdonald, Lincoln, & Cabral, 2008).

Of course, we deal with smaller stressors regularly: feeling anxiety after losing a job or being depressed following the death of a loved one is not unusual and not necessarily a sign of psychopathology or dysfunction. As with stress in general, whether people experience anxiety or depression is only partly influenced by the situations in which they find themselves, and largely by the way they cope with stressful events. In fact, a key component of mood and anxiety disorders is fixating and dwelling on events that might be considered minor—in other words, ruminating. Nolen-Hoeksema (2000) found that trait rumination, or one's usual tendency to ruminate, was predictive of future anxiety and depression, even in people who had not been depressed before. In depressed individuals, ruminating seems to make depression even worse, and learning not to ruminate can actually ameliorate depression (Larsen & Christenfeld, 2009).

This overlap between rumination and anxiety is significant even down to the molecular level: it turns out that neurotransmitters that influence mood, such as serotonin, are also important for shifting and altering thinking patterns (Clarke, Dalley, Crofts, Robbins, & Roberts, 2004). This chronic ruminating and resulting activation of the stress response could partially explain why people with anxiety and mood disorders are at two to three times greater risk for stress-related diseases like cardiovascular disease (Larsen & Christenfeld, 2009). This again emphasizes the interplay of situations and personal characteristics in determining how stress will affect individuals. While stressors are of course significant, the appraisal and coping processes are just as significant, if not more so.

Stress and Sleep

Stress can disturb sleep, and disturbed sleep can in turn increase stress responses. In a broad sample of American workers, job-related stress was shown to be associated with sleep disturbances. Over the course of the month-long study, workers reported 5.3 days of difficulty falling asleep,

iStock.com/OcusFocus

Stress can interfere with ability to sleep.

6.6 days of trouble staying asleep, and 5.0 days of trouble waking up for work, with role conflict, work overload, repetitive tasks, and low levels of job autonomy correlating with at least some of those measures of sleep disturbance (Knudsen, Ducharme, & Roman, 2007). In a study of 5720 Swedes, disturbed sleep was most predicted by an inability to stop thinking about work (Åkerstedt et al., 2002). Rumination appears to mediate the relationship between job-stress and sleep disturbances (Berset, Elfering, Lüthy, Lüthi, & Semmer, 2011), though both stress and sleep disturbances appear to independently contribute to poorer health outcomes (Benham, 2010). Particularly impaired sleep follows particularly stressful days (Åkerstedt, Kecklund, & Axelsson, 2007), and sleep deprivation itself results in lower thresholds for perceiving stress, though not an overall greater stress response (Minkel et al., 2012), suggesting that there is a bidirectional relationship between stress and sleep. Improving sleep habits can decrease stress levels, though stress can also make maintaining healthy sleeping habits more difficult. For example, digital media use before bed is associated with lower sleep quality, (Orzech, Grandner, Roane, & Carskadon, 2016), so avoiding or limiting using your computer or smartphone before bed could, by improving sleep, decrease stress.

Some environmental stressors have a direct effect on sleep and stress, whereas in other instances how one copes with a stressor may be more important than whether a stressor is present. Shift work, a schedule that requires working either earlier or later than the typical 9:00 a.m. to 5:00 p.m. work day, has a direct association with increased social stress and increased sleep complaints in a sample of police officers (Gerber, Hartmann, Brand, Holsboer-Trachsler, & Puhse, 2010). Shift work increases risk of cardiovascular disease, both through psychosocial and biological pathways (Puttonen, Harma, & Hublin, 2010). However, among college students, emotional response to stress, rather then the presence or absence of environmental stressors, predicted aspects sleep quality such as depth of sleep, difficulties in waking up, quality and latency of sleep, negative affect in dreams, and sleep irregularity (Verlander, Benedict, & Hanson, 1999). So, sleep quality, which has a bidirectional relationship with stress, may depend not only on whether one experiences stress, but also on how one handles the stress one does experience.

Stress Management

As stress is a ubiquitous feature of modern life, researchers have explored effective strategies for stress management. Such strategies vary in effectiveness and range from behavioural approaches to medication management. One popular behavioural approach is **cognitive behavioural therapy (CBT)**, a form of therapy focused on changing cognitions and beliefs in order to change behaviour and emotions (Ellis, 1962). As discussed elsewhere in this book (see Chapter 7), CBT is one of the most popular forms of therapy for stress, depression, and other mood and anxiety disorders, and research shows that this intervention, in which people learn to reinterpret stressful situations and inoculate themselves to stress, is generally an effective approach to stress management (Bryant,

In Practice

The Support Group: Stress Welcomes Company

Mary's life, like most, had a mix of challenges and worries. She had just been made regional manager at work, a promotion she had long sought. But with cutbacks by headquarters, the staff she inherited was smaller than what she felt was needed. The vice-president had pointed out that her predecessor had had the same staff, and Mary had thought, but managed not to say out loud, that the reason she now had the job was that her predecessor had predeceased her. There was an early performance evaluation coming up, and Mary had not yet figured out if that would be a chance for her to demonstrate her mastery of the job or instead a moment to let her doubters gloat. She did not feel that her aging father-in-law, to whom she tended almost every day, quite understood the burdens she was operating under, and taking care of him had not been balanced by any reduction in other duties. Mary had talked to her husband about the stress she felt with her new responsibilities, and he had offered a lot of appropriate advice, and even some ideas she had implemented, but she still sometimes felt overwhelmed.

Mary thought she could keep it up, but then she started to get sick. Every virus going around seemed to find a home in her, and it was taking her longer and longer to evict them. One of her friends, listening to Mary talk, suggested that she might try a support group. She did—not with much enthusiasm as first, but she quickly found she treasured the weekly sessions. Other people were going through similar things—taking care of ailing or needy relatives while still working full-time—and just having them listen and understand without even offering advice was very soothing for her. She was as busy as before. In fact, the support group added another commitment each week. But she believed again that she could master the various challenges, and even new tasks at work now were opportunities rather than oppressions. And, she noted to herself in the supermarket checkout line, she had not needed to buy Kleenex.

Harvey, Dang, Sackville, & Basten, 1998; Butler, Chapman, Forman, & Beck, 2006; Saunders, Driskell, Johnston, & Salas, 1996).

Biofeedback, relaxation, and mindfulness are part of a set of strategies, largely inspired by Eastern practices and Buddhism, for dealing with stress. Such strategies involve taking some control over one's own stress responses, both physical and mental. These therapeutic approaches are based on the notion, discussed earlier, that stress responses, while perhaps useful in the face of acute physical threats, may quickly become maladaptive. Biofeedback techniques allow people to monitor, often with the use of devices, their physiological responses, such as heart rate, and so come to have more control over those bodily systems. Relaxation interventions can involve a variety of other techniques to promote calmness, including music, meditation, massage, and the like. While not studied to the degree of CBT, relaxation techniques have been found to be effective in reducing stress (Jacobs, 2001). Mindfulness aims to reduce anxiety about future events and rumination about past ones by having people more focused on their experiences in the moment, and this has also been shown to be effective in reducing anxiety and stress (Kabat-Zinn et al., 1992; Jain et al., 2007; Hofmann, Sawyer, Witt, & Oh, 2010). It may be possible to deliver mindfulness interventions cost-effectively through mobile applications, such as Headspace, though the efficacy of such apps for reducing stress remains unknown (Mani, Kavanagh, Hides, & Stoyanov, 2015). Breathe2Relax, a diaphragmatic breathing exercise app developed by the US Department of Defense, may likewise help stress management (Luxton, Hansen, & Stanfill, 2014). More generally, relaxation may help manage stress—preparing for an oral presentation in the presence of relaxing music prevented both self-reported and physiological stress responses that were experienced by participants not exposed to the music (Knight & Rickard, 2001).

Pharmacological treatments for stress are widely—and some would say sometimes inappropriately—used. A class of drug called benzodiazapines is often prescribed for people experiencing extreme stress and anxiety. Even among people who have never taken these drugs, some of their brand names are quite familiar, the most popular being Xanax and Valium. These drugs are typically taken only on a short-term basis to increase functioning and improve sleep. Common antidepressants, usually selective serotonin reuptake inhibitors (SSRIs) such as Prozac and Paxil, might be prescribed for longer-term stress and anxiety. Much less common in the treatment of short-term stress is the use of beta-blockers, a class of drugs typically used to treat hypertension. Because these drugs reduce heart rate, they have been used experimentally to treat performance anxiety in actors and musicians. The effectiveness of beta-blockers in treating performance anxiety is debatable; they appear effective in addressing physiological manifestations of anxiety, such as shaking, but are less effective in treating cognitive and emotional aspects of stress (Kenny, 2006). While pharmacological treatments are widely prescribed in treating stress and anxiety, people taking these medications are often encouraged to complement them with behavioural approaches.

Social Networking, Stress, and Online Social Support

While it should be by this point clear that in-person social support reduces stress, you may be wondering to what extent online social networks can facilitate these same stress-relieving benefits. Because this is a relatively new area of research, the verdict is still out on whether social networking sites such as Facebook overall decrease or increase chronic stress, but empirical evidence points to the latter being more likely than the former. However, some research suggests that online social networking sites can be used in a way that does confer stress-reducing benefits, notably as platforms for facilitating online social support groups.

Several studies show that online social networks do not confer perceived social support benefits the way in-person social support can. While Nabi, Prestin, and So (2013) found that number of Facebook friends correlated with perceived social support, which in return reduced perceived stress, this relationship was reduced below statistical significance when interpersonal network size was taken into account (neighbours, teachers, relatives, etc. communicated with in real life at least once every two weeks). This suggests that online networks such as Facebook may not offer social support benefits beyond those that interpersonal networks can reflect. Others have found that giving and receiving social support on Facebook is unrelated to perceived social support (Li, Chen, & Popiel, 2015).

Researchers have also uncovered that online social network use, beyond not contributing to perceived social support, can actually have negative effects on stress. More time spent on, and more memberships in, online social networks correlated with higher stress levels and lower quality of life (although in this particular study Facebook use itself did not relate to either on its own; Bevan, Gomez, & Sparks, 2014). Chen and Lee (2013) found that frequent Facebook use correlated with psychological distress as communication overload decreased self-esteem. In experience-sampling studies of Facebook use over time (probing participants via text messaging at regular intervals), the more a person had used Facebook during the previous probe, the worse the person felt during the following probe, whereas in-person social interaction over time showed opposite patterns and made people feel better (Kross et al., 2013). McCloskey, Iwanicki, Lauterbach, Giammittorio and Maxwell (2015) found that only the absence of negative social support, rather than any kind of positive social support, significantly predicted any mental health outcomes such as quality of life and depression, suggesting that online social networks may not improve these outcomes, but can make these outcomes worse. Online social networks have also been shown to affect physical health by inducing stress: Facebook network size (i.e., number of Facebook friends) significantly correlated with increased incidence of upper respiratory infections as a result of Facebook-induced stress (Campisi et al., 2012). The relationship between stress and infection increased in strength as one's online network increased in size (Campisi et al., 2012).

While social media often seem to negatively affect stress and health outcomes, they can also confer benefits when used as a platform for specific online support communities. For example, first-year medical students randomly assigned to a Facebook group addressing stress-related issues were able to anonymously access stress-management coping techniques, leading them to more effectively deal with the stress of their gruelling workload (George, Dellasega, Whitehead, & Bordon, 2013). Thematic analysis of users of an online food allergy bulletin showed that benefits conferred included social support and coping strategies (Coulson & Knibb, 2007). Online support groups may be particularly useful to those not willing or able to seek in-person social support regarding a condition or topic due to it being stigmatizing or when the condition prevents in-person attendance (White & Dorman, 2001). Online social support groups may confer their benefits by facilitating a sense of self-empowerment that helps members cope with distress (Barak, Boniel-Nissim, & Suler, 2008), and by conveying emotional support (Eysenbach, Powell, Englesakis, Rizo, & Stern, 2004). Both active and passive participation appears to confer the same benefits: users randomly assigned to a online smoking cessation community were more likely to quit smoking than nonusers, regardless of whether they were active or passive users, suggesting that "lurking" in such online communities can be as beneficial as actively participating in them (Graham, Papandonatos, Erar, & Stanton, 2015).

It appears there are specific ways of using social networks to decrease stress, though these are distinct from the often stress-inducing way social media are used. We would recommend the reader generally not look to Facebook for the same kind of benefits that in-person social support can give, but to look at online social networks and communities as opportunities for more specific support groups that may be more likely to confer such benefits.

Future Directions

While most are convinced that stress impacts health, and that techniques that reduce stress—its frequency, intensity, and duration—are thereby likely to promote health, central questions about the connection remain unanswered and are the focus of much investigation. One critical question relates to the mechanism by which acute responses are translated into chronic disease. Also, while heart disease has been a main focus of stress researchers, stress has a broad impact, suggesting that the focus on the stress–disease link is broadening. For example, the immune system is involved, with inflammatory responses being connected to a wide range of outcomes. A better understanding of this link would likely shed light on what responses are most likely to be damaging, and whether interventions should focus, for example, on limiting exposure to stressors or on enhancing the speed of recovery from stress.

Various societal trends also make some types of stress research especially important. Among these research areas is work on caretaker stress. Moreover, with relationships becoming increasingly electronically mediated, the role of modern social networking in stress reduction is worth additional investigation. Such research may uncover more effective ways to harness online communication for stress reduction, and ways of avoiding additional stress from social networking.

Summary

Human stress can be broadly understood as resulting from some event that upsets the equilibrium of the system. Moreover, such perturbations are thought to produce long-term damage and adverse health outcomes. This stress can come from aspects of the situation, from aspects of the person, and from the interaction of the two. Job stress has been studied extensively, and most models suggest that it results from the interplay of factors such as a high workload and low autonomy or low reward. Other situational sources of stress include caregiving roles, as well as situations produced by one's position in society (e.g., as a woman, a member of a minority group, having low SES). Looking at aspects of the person, it seems that the sorts of people who are predisposed to stress are those who are prone to hostility and negative affectivity. Such people will find themselves in more stress-provoking situations and respond to them more negatively. The interactionist view is that certain people, those high in hostility, will be prone to stress under certain situations, such as negative interpersonal encounters.

While some efforts to define stress have relied on objective factors, most views recognize that the subjective appraisal of the situation is critical. That is, one must determine whether the situation represents a threat, and then whether one has sufficient resources to cope with that threat. Various external resources can contribute to people's ability to cope, and social support is among the most studied of these. People with more extensive networks enjoy better health, and interventions that provide social support have been shown to reduce blood pressure and promote well-being. Some findings regarding gender differences in the seeking of social support are consistent with women using a different evolutionary strategy when dealing with stress that includes more affiliative responses. Other strategies that may enhance coping include emotional disclosure, with some evidence that expressing one's thoughts on past events can promote health. Similarly, in enhancing recovery after the event has passed, vigorous physical exercise has been shown to be beneficial.

Critical Thought Questions

1. In what way are positive events likely to be as stressful as negative ones, and in what ways might they be expected to cause less damage to long-term health?

2. When should friends help out, and when might it be better to be alone?

3. How readily can stress be dealt with simply by changing the way one thinks about the situation?

Recommended Reading

Sapolsky, R.M. (2004). *Why zebras don't get ulcers: The acclaimed guide to stress, stress-related diseases, and coping* (3rd rev. ed.). New York: W.H. Freeman.

Lazarus, R.S., & Folkman, S. (1984). *Stress, appraisal and coping*. New York: Springer.

Health Psychology within the Health-Care System

Gregory P. Marchildon

Heather D. Hadjistavropoulos

Gerald P. Koocher

4

Learning Objectives

In this chapter you will:

- Discover that health systems in various countries are financed and organized differently and how these differences affect health psychology services.

- Learn how health services are typically classified by time, duration, and complexity of treatment.

- Understand problems with misuse of medical services and how health psychologists can address overuse or delayed medical care.

- Become familiar with the role of health psychologists within health systems.

- Learn how adherence to medical treatment is defined and measured and how health psychologists can improve patients' adherence to treatment.

- Learn about patient satisfaction and dissatisfaction with health systems and services.

- Understand the impacts of interventions by health psychologists, including potential cost savings to health systems.

Introduction

Health problems happen to everyone, but the nature of health care received varies tremendously from individual to individual. Imagine the care received by celebrities such as Angelina Jolie, who had a double mastectomy after learning that she had a gene that increases a woman's risk for breast cancer, or the care received by Charlie Sheen, who shared that he is HIV positive. How do you think their care differs from that of non-celebrities? Would their care differ if they lived in Canada? Do you think they would benefit from access to a health psychologist? Do you imagine they have difficulties adhering to treatment or experience dissatisfaction with the quality or timeliness of the health-care services they receive?

The approach health professionals, including health psychologists, take in caring for patients is largely shaped by the **health system**. The unique public and private funding arrangements, administrative structures, government regulation, and delivery modes all influence the interaction between providers and their patients. This chapter describes the health systems in the United States, Canada, and other areas of the world, and then focuses on the role of health psychologists in North America. In general, all health systems include different levels of care, sources of funding, and administrative and delivery arrangements. Research shows that health-care use varies with patient differences, such as age, gender, and cultural group. The second half of this chapter focuses on several topics of interest to health psychologists in relation to health systems, such as medical service misuse, **adherence** to medical care, patient satisfaction with health care, and **medical cost offset** of psychological interventions.

Pictorial Press Ltd / Alamy Stock Photo

Otto von Bismarck (1815–98).

Health Systems in the United States, Canada, and Elsewhere

The term "health system" has many different definitions. According to the World Health Organization (WHO), a health system consists "of all the people and actions whose primary purpose is to improve health" whether or not these people or actions are "integrated and centrally directed" (WHO, 2000, p. 2). In a published background document prepared for a summit of European ministers of health, the European Observatory on Health Systems and Policies provided a more specific operational definition that identifies the following three functions of a health system: (1) to deliver both personal and population-based health services; (2) to enable the delivery of health services, including finance, resource generation, and *stewardship*; and (3) to influence what other sectors do when it is relevant to health (Figueras, McKee, Lessof, Duran, & Menabde, 2008).

By using the word "stewardship," which means the responsible oversight and protection of something worth caring for and preserving, this definition gives priority to the role of governments in financing, directing, co-ordinating, and regulating health systems. This can occur at the national level or, as is sometimes the case in federations such as the United States and Canada, at both the national and state/provincial levels of government. While the private sector, including relatively autonomous professions (e.g., physicians), can have a significant position in a health system, they can be influenced in performing their roles by government funding and regulation (Saltman & Ferroussier-Davis, 2000). In fact, there has been a long-term trend since 1945 towards greater government involvement in health care in almost all advanced industrial countries, including the United States and Canada (Marchildon & Lockhart, 2012).

Health systems in advanced industrial countries generally follow one of three models based on their financing and organizational mechanisms (Burau & Blank, 2006; Freeman & Frisina, 2010): social health insurance, national health systems, and private health insurance. **Social health insurance systems** originated with employment-based social insurance pools regulated by the state. The version developed in late nineteenth-century Germany was introduced by then German Chancellor Otto von Bismarck (Saltman & Dubois, 2004). National health systems are often called **Beveridge systems**, after William Beveridge, the British public servant who first introduced the idea of a tax-funded health service that later became the National Health Service (NHS) in the United Kingdom. **Private health insurance systems** rely on private insurance carriers setting premiums based on risk and establishing the basic terms of coverage, even if this is done in response to government regulation. Table 4.1 briefly describes these three types of health systems and how various high-income countries can be classified.

Sir William Beveridge (1879–1963).

While the United States represents a mixed health system drawing on all three models, it remains a predominantly private health insurance system. When Medicare and Medicaid were introduced in 1965, they sought to address gaps rather than replace employment-based private health insurance (Hacker, 2002). In order to incentivize physician participation in these plans and address political opposition to "socialized medicine," providers were enticed with a fee-for-service model. Similarly, the reforms introduced through the Affordable Care Act of 2010 (sometimes referred to as Obamacare), although now sharing some features in common with social health insurance, focused on regulating private health insurance and mandating its purchase by individual Americans (Mechanic & Olfson, 2016; Starr, 2011). Unlike European-style universal systems, the United States did not historically provide coverage for everyone. When the Affordable Care Act was passed, the Congressional Budget Office estimated that the law would eventually expand coverage to 94 per cent of the population (Starr, 2011). By 2015, the percentage of Americans without health insurance had dropped to 9.1 per cent compared to 16.0 per cent in 2010 (Centers for Disease Control and Prevention, 2016). Unfortunately, politically and ideologically driven differences in states' implementation policies will result in

TABLE 4.1 | Types of Health Systems

Type of Health System	Definition	Country Examples
Social Health Insurance (Bismarck)	A government-regulated health insurance scheme where the people must buy insurance, but may do so through an employer. In Bismarck's Germany, for example, the government obliged employers to pay and employees to join these social insurance funds. In other countries, trade unions and political parties have played a similar role. The government provides health coverage for those people without jobs and without the means to purchase insurance.	Austria, Belgium, France, Germany
National Health System (Beveridge)	A general tax-funded system directed by government for its entire population. Established in 1948, the National Health Service (NHS) in the United Kingdom provided a reasonably comprehensive set of health services without user fees to all citizens.	Australia, Canada, Italy, Norway, Spain, Sweden, United Kingdom
Private Health Insurance	Funded by private individuals, employees, and employers, private health insurance carriers determine the terms of coverage, payment, and risk assessment, although there may be some government regulation and some targeted programs to address scope of coverage and affordability by the poor or unemployed.	Netherlands, Singapore, Switzerland, United States*

*The United States represents a mixed system drawing from a variety of models, but remains primarily a private health insurance system.

major differences in coverage and affordability based on where people live (Béland, Rocco, & Waddan, 2016). At least some Americans will continue to face financial obstacles in obtaining needed medical care for years to come.

In Canada, the predominant form of financing for the majority of health care is through general government taxation, hence the country's classification as a Beveridge or NHS-style system. Approximately two-thirds of publicly financed health care is provided on a universal basis to 100 per cent of the population, based on a set of five criteria set out in the Canada Health Act. Paid entirely through general taxation at the provincial and federal levels of government and offered free at the medical office or hospital, these universally available services include only medically "necessary" hospital and medical care. As a result, people needing psychological services generally pay through private health insurance or out of pocket unless these services are provided through government-operated clinics/hospitals or school boards by psychologists on salary. The provinces are responsible for administering their own coverage systems while private insurance for medically necessary hospital and medical care services is either prohibited or discouraged (Flood & Archibald, 2001). Figure 4.1 compares the public and compulsory financing of health insurance coverage as a share of the economy for several countries.

With the rapid escalation in health expenditures since the 1980s in the United States and Canada, concerted efforts have been made to contain costs and increase efficiency. This has resulted in changes to permit more effective management of health organizations and health providers. As a consequence, a significant percentage of Americans receive services through health maintenance organizations (HMOs) or preferred provider organizations (PPOs). HMOs provide a range of health services in a single package and typically direct patients to a particular group of medical professionals and facilities. HMOs provide a less expensive alternative to traditional insurance plans that allow consumers to freely choose providers and facilities within limits, based on the nature of the particular plan. In an effort to contain the rapidly growing

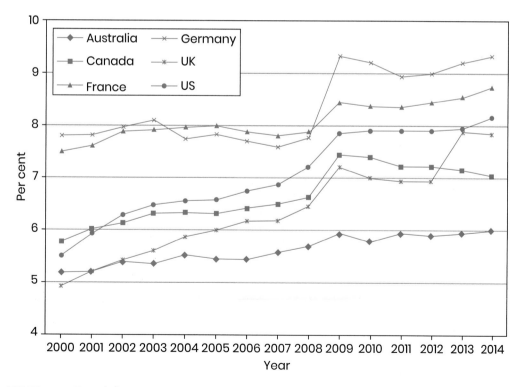

FIGURE 4.1 **Trends in government and compulsory health insurance financing plans as a share of gross domestic product (GDP), selected countries, 2000–14.**

Source: OECD Health Expenditure and Financing, OECD.Stat, http://stats.oecd.org

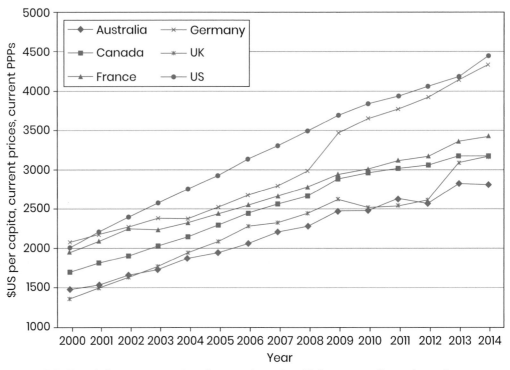

FIGURE 4.2 **Trends in government and compulsory health insurance financing schemes, per capita ($US), selected countries, 2000–14.**

Note: The vertical axis refers to current $US per capita at purchase power parity (PPP).

Source: OECD Health Expenditure and Financing, OECD.Stat, http://stats.oecd.org/

demand for high-tech medical care, HMOs emphasize prevention and more cost-effective treatments (Tovian, 2004). However, HMOs faced a backlash by the mid-1990s led by patients and providers who concluded that quality of care was often sacrificed to achieve cost efficiencies (Gray, 2006). In response to this growing level of dissatisfaction with HMOs, a majority of states began to regulate HMOs in an effort to protect the quality of care (Gray, Lowery, & Godwin, 2007). PPOs allow a wider range of choices by including providers who contract with insurers to offer reduced prices to covered patients. PPOs typically do not co-ordinate patient care as centrally as do HMOs, and patients are free to use "out-of-network" providers at their own incremental expense. Figure 4.2 compares the per capita spending on government and compulsory health insurance in several countries.

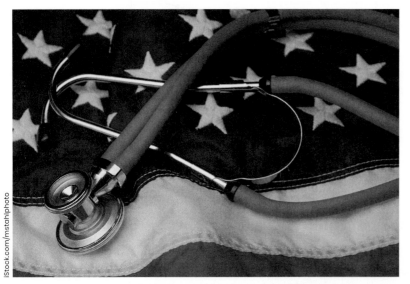

iStock.com/mstahlphoto

The United States has a mixed health system that is highly reliant for its financing on private health insurance.

In the United States, consumers face a diverse patchwork of coverage at the most basic levels, because states have differing coverage mandates under both private insurance and Medicaid. Medicare provides more uniform coverage for those over 65, but many people continue to work or purchase supplemental coverage beyond that age. As a result, making clear generalizations about coverage of psychological services across individuals on a national basis presents a significant challenge. According to the US Census Bureau, the uninsured population declined by more than 4 per cent between 2013 and 2015, while the number of uninsured declined from 10.4 per cent to 9.1 per cent between 2014 and 2015 as the Affordable Care Act intended (United States Census Bureau, 2016).

The bulk of funding for the Canadian health system comes from general taxation.

The Canadian system also emphasizes illness prevention and more cost-effective treatment, but led by provincial governments and their regional health authorities (RHAs) instead of private HMOs. As part of a sweeping effort to contain costs, better integrate and co-ordinate care, and shift resources to illness prevention and health promotion, all provincial governments except Ontario (which has restricted the RHA function to a funding role) have arm's-length RHAs manage most services. The two main exceptions to this delegated administration include prescription drug plans and physician payment, both of which are centrally administered by provincial ministries of health (Marchildon, 2013).

Impact of Health Systems on Health Psychology

The biopsychosocial model (see Chapter 1) posits that biological, psychological, and social processes are "integrally and interactively involved in physical health and illness" (Suls & Rothman, 2004, p. 119). As such, many believe that health psychologists should play an important role in assisting patients with medical concerns. Nevertheless, patient access to health psychologists in the United States and Canada remains limited.

We can summarize the problems addressed by health psychologists in current health systems as follows (Belar, 1997):

- Treating psychological conditions secondary to illness (e.g., post-myocardial infarction depression, and disorders associated with traumatic injuries).
- Addressing physical conditions responsive to behavioural interventions (e.g., anticipatory nausea, improved pain control, reducing medical non-adherence).
- Reducing the physical and psychological discomforts and consequences accompanying stressful medical procedures (e.g., surgery, cardiac catheterization, magnetic resonance imaging, lumbar punctures, bone marrow biopsies, chemotherapy).

- Altering behaviours in terms of risk factors for disease or disability (e.g., promoting smoking cessation, weight reduction, improving exercise levels, and reducing substance abuse).
- Diagnosing and referring people with psychological presentations of organic problems (e.g., steroid-induced psychosis, hypothyroidism presenting as depression).
- Identifying and treating psychological dysfunctions that contribute to physical problems such as tension and migraine headaches, spastic colitis, chest pains as part of panic attacks, and conversion reactions.
- Facilitating the recovery or adaptation of individuals with chronic physical or mental conditions (e.g., cancer, cystic fibrosis, diabetes, muscular sclerosis, depression, schizophrenia).
- Helping health-care providers and patients deal with health system stresses (e.g., improving physician–patient relationships, reducing staff burnout).

Although the United States and Canada have very different health systems, especially when it comes to hospital and physician care, health psychologists have faced strikingly similar obstacles in terms of providing the types of services described above. In particular, both countries lack a comprehensive public payment mechanism to reimburse psychological services, and this has limited their integration into these health systems (Romanow & Marchildon, 2003; Tovian, 2004).

In the United States, under federal Medicare and state Medicaid rules, recent development of "health and behaviour" CPT codes now permit licensed psychologists to access reimbursement for services provided to patients with non-psychiatric conditions without needing to fit their services under existing mental health codes or seeking physician approval. In Canada, publicly funded fee-for-service remuneration is limited to physicians. While RHAs can decide whether to hire health psychologists, doing so remains a relatively rare practice (Romanow & Marchildon, 2003; Tovian, 2004). While citizens of both countries can pay for health psychological services completely out of pocket or use private (largely employment-based) insurance, many people are not aware of these services, cannot afford the services, or do not have access to private practitioners trained to provide services.

Types of Health Services

There are many ways to classify care within health-care systems. A distinction is sometimes made among primary, secondary, and tertiary levels of care. **Primary care** refers to the basic health care aimed at prevention (e.g., immunizations) and a broad spectrum of problems. Typically, we get such care from a family physician, but nurses, physicians' assistants, or other health-care clinic staff may also fall in this category. The primary care provider is usually the first contact, responsible for comprehensive care and, at least initially, co-ordination if referral to specialists is needed. In other words, the primary provider often acts as a de facto gatekeeper to the health system. Psychologists are typically not primary care providers, but may serve on teams in primary health clinics (Frank, McDaniel, Bray, & Heldring, 2004).

Secondary care refers to a broad range of specialized services, such as care provided by medical specialists or health psychologists. While physicians' services can be delivered on an in- or outpatient basis, most health psychology services at the secondary level are delivered on an outpatient basis. These are generally not first-contact services and typically follow a referral from a first-contact health provider. Nonetheless, there are some exceptions. For example, a psychologist on staff at a hospital serving in the emergency department alongside other providers

In Practice
Surviving Myocardial Infarction: A Team Approach

Margaret, a 48-year-old divorcee, did not worry very much about her health. Yes, she did smoke a handful of cigarettes each day. Yes, she was about 15 kg overweight for a woman of her height and age. She'd tell herself that she'd get to work on losing some weight right after the holidays, and could really quit smoking anytime she wanted to—and would someday soon. With that mindset, she did not become concerned when she started to feel some "mild indigestion" at work. One day at work she became a bit more concerned when she started having some trouble catching her breath and felt some pain shooting down her left arm. Margaret mentioned these symptoms to her co-worker, who recognized symptoms of a myocardial infarction (MI, or heart attack). Her colleague had some aspirin in her desk and gave it to Margaret, telling her to chew it up while she called 911.

In some ways, Margaret was very fortunate. Her MI occurred in the presence of someone who recognized what was happening and who assisted her well. Following emergency implantation of two stents to restore cardiac circulation and a few tense days in the cardiac intensive care unit, Margaret was ready for discharge. Her medical condition was stable, but her anxiety shot through the roof. Thoughts of, "How will I manage all the things I have to remember now? What if this happens again?" ran through her mind constantly. On discharge,

a nurse gave Margaret a set of prescriptions, heart-healthy diet instructions, and a warning about her weight and smoking. That night Margaret could barely sleep, feeling intensely aware of her own mortality, and uncertain about how she could possibly manage the lifestyle changes necessary to maintain her health.

Fortunately, she had access to an outpatient cardiac rehabilitation program that used a team approach. The team included a cardiologist, nurse practitioner, dietician, and psychologist. Working together, the team was able to present an integrated plan of care relying on psychological principles to optimize adherence. In addition, the psychologist was able to forewarn Margaret about the hazards of depression during recovery from MI and work with her using cognitive behavioural and medical crisis counselling techniques. She was able to take control of her care, beginning with an improved diet, a moderate exercise program, and a nicotine patch to help end her smoking habit. It wasn't easy, but with the support of the team, Margaret was soon on the road to restored health. She wondered how she'd ever have managed without them. Health statistics show that without such services, Margaret might well have faced a need for expensive and risky re-hospitalizations in the following months.

(e.g., evaluating and providing urgent care to sexual assault victims and suicide attempters) would represent one such exception. Referral to a psychologist for help with a specific health problem, such as coping with a diagnosis of cancer, would be another form of secondary care.

Tertiary care refers to even more specialized care, often delivered in a teaching hospital or academic health centre, that has a supporting infrastructure of specialized equipment and facilities as well as a range of available specialists. Some psychological interventions are delivered within tertiary care settings (e.g., psychological interventions delivered to chronic pain and organ transplant inpatients).

In addition to classifying care in terms of whether it is primary, secondary, or tertiary, health care can be described in terms of duration. Acute care refers to short-term care that is for an injury or illness. Chronic care refers to care for a pre-existing or long-term illness, such as diabetes, asthma, or congestive heart failure. Chronic illnesses form an important part of the work conducted by health psychologists.

Health care is also sometimes classified in terms of the setting in which it is delivered, such as a hospital, the home, the community, a rehabilitation setting, or a long-term care facility. Health psychologists work in all of these settings. For example, in a hospital a health psychologist may assist patients with coping with medical procedures, while in the home, community, or rehabilitation setting health psychologists may assist patients with development of strategies for coping with and adherence to treatment of a chronic condition. In long-term care, health psychologists may assist with development of strategies for working with patients with dementia (e.g., identifying pleasant activities or managing behavioural problems such as agitation, a common precursor to aggression, in the face of changed routines).

Patterns of Health-Care Use

Despite sharp differences in health systems, the health-care cultures of the United States and Canada are remarkably similar. In particular, the health professions, including the medical, nursing, and health psychology professions, are similarly organized. All are self-regulating professions with similar scopes of practices and specializations. Contrary to the European practice of separating social care from health care, long-term care in the United States and Canada, including home and community care, is treated as part of the health-care system—at least from a conceptual perspective.

The people these providers serve are also very similar in terms of their respective demands on the health system. While overall health status is somewhat better in Canada than the United States, both countries have similar rates of acute and chronic disease incidence and suffer from similar high-risk factors for disease (Marchildon, 2013). Table 4.2 compares the two countries to four other mature and high-quality health systems.

Citizens in both Canada and the United States also have high expectations in terms of timely, effective, and high-quality medical interventions. This has led to substantial public and private investments in medical care. At the same time, high expectations may contribute to low patient-satisfaction ratings in both countries relative to other high-income countries in Western Europe and Australasia (Schoen, 2011).

Even with these similarities, some important differences exist between Canada and the United States in their patterns of health-care use. On a per capita basis, Americans spend more on health care than the citizens of any other country. However, in regard to public financing, per capita government health expenditures are almost identical in both countries, in part due to the historical growth and high expense of Medicare and Medicaid in the United States relative to medicare in Canada (Marchildon, 2013).

There are also significant differences in the use of new technologies, particularly advanced diagnostic imaging technologies. The number of CT (computerized tomography), MRI (magnetic resonance imaging), and PET (positron emission tomography) machines per capita in the United States significantly exceeds that in Canada, and evidence suggests that American physicians use health information technology more intensively than their Canadian counterparts (Organisation for Economic Co-operation and Development [OECD], 2011; Schoen et al., 2009).

In both the United States and Canada, health-care use varies with certain demographic variables. For instance, older adults tend to seek and use more care as their health fails and they develop chronic health conditions (Alemayehu & Warner, 2004). Another characteristic involves men making less use of health-care services than women (Alemayehu & Warner, 2004). Pregnancy, female birth control, childbirth, and symptoms associated with menopause account for some of the sex differences in health-care use. Other factors that may contribute to this

TABLE 4.2 | Male and Female Causes of Death (Disease Burden), Selected Countries, Age-Standardized Rates per 100,000 People, 2011

Cause of Death per 100,000 people	Australia	Canada	France	Germany	United Kingdom	United States
Ischemic heart diseases, males	127.8	128	65.3	153.3	143.7	167.4
Ischemic heart diseases, females	73.6	68.8	26.4	86.3	69.2	90.7
Stroke, males	55.4	53.5	30.8	70.0	56.2	53.0
Stroke, females	36.1	28.5	12.9	35.2	27.8	29.3
All cancers, males	251.3	248.7	284.2	261.1	273.3	237.7
All cancers, females	156.2	177.9	145.4	165.6	191.1	164.1
Lung cancer, males	50.8	68.0	70.3	62.5	63.2	68.0
Lung cancer, females	27.3	45.8	19.1	24.7	39.9	42.8
Breast cancer	24.8	25.4	27.6	30.0	30.4	24.5
Prostate cancer	36.6	26.6	29.1	31.3	36.6	23.9
Road accidents, males	10.5	10.4	10.0	7.9	5.1	18.1
Road accidents, females	3.7	3.7	2.7	2.4	1.4	6.9
Suicide, males	16.3	15.9	25.4	17.4	11.1	20.8
Suicide, females	5.1	5.3	7.5	5.0	3.0	5.4

Source: OECD Health Status, OECD.Stat, http://stats.oecd.org (OECD, 2013).

difference involve somatic perception and symptom labelling, as well as socialization that leads men to be less prone to disclose and more prone to ignore symptoms (Barsky, Peekna, & Borus, 2001). Socio-economic status (SES) also plays a role in health-care use. Recent research suggests that in both the United States and Canada, SES is not related to hospital use. In the United States but not Canada, physician use is lower among those with lower income and those without health insurance (Blackwell, Martinez, Gentleman, Sanmartin, & Berthelot, 2009). There is also a significant gap in the extent to which those of lower SES seek preventative health care, such as immunizations against disease (Abramson, Oshea, Ratledge, Lawless, & Givner, 1995). Ethnicity also plays a role, with lower use of health-care services among people from ethnic minority populations (e.g., Quan et al., 2006; Scheppers, van Dongen, Dekker, Geertzen, & Dekker, 2006). This topic is given in-depth consideration in Chapter 15. One implication of these differences is that health psychologists are more likely to provide treatment to patients who are high users of health services. Nevertheless, psychologists must be competent to work with diverse groups and to find ways to ensure that all patients who need their services have access to and are aware of these services.

In Focus

Reducing Medical Services among College Students with Mental Health Disorders

Mental health disorders commonly affect college students. In 2017, a survey by the American College Health Association showed that 30.4 per cent of college students reported being diagnosed or treated by a professional for at least one mental health disorder in the previous 12 months. Depression in the previous 12 months was reported by 17.8 per cent of college students surveyed and anxiety by 21.6 per cent. Mental health disorders cause significant distress and interfere with academic functioning. They also often lead to increased medical care use. Given the comorbidity between mental health disorders and medical conditions, interest in providing integrated medical and mental health services for better co-ordinated care has increased. Integrating care, for instance, could result in better communication and co-ordinated treatment planning between physicians and psychologists who often treat the same patients in parallel care models.

Given the high use of medical services by students with co-occurring mental health disorders, Turner et

Medical Service Misuse

Prevention of medical service misuse is of vital importance to a sustainable health-care system. Such misuse refers not only to the overuse of medical services but also to delays in obtaining medical services. Both situations can harm people and result in increased costs.

Overuse

Overuse of medical services is discussed briefly in Chapter 7 in reference to excessively elevated health anxiety associated with high levels of seeking medical care (Bobevski, Clarke, & Meadows, 2016); Tomenson et al., 2012). People with health anxiety may seek out unnecessary medical services in an attempt to alleviate this anxiety. This results in higher health-care costs, but also in an increased likelihood of patients undergoing unnecessary medical tests or procedures that can cause complications and trigger additional usage.

Other psychological conditions associated with significantly greater use of medical care include depression and general anxiety (Deacon, Lickel, & Abramowitz, 2008; Kimerling, Ouimette, Cronkite, & Moos, 1999). For example, people with panic disorder often become frequent users of medical services, especially if not effectively treated for their psychological condition (Deacon et al., 2008). Panic disorder occurs when people experience recurrent, unexpected panic attacks followed by anxiety about having another attack, worry about the implications of the attack or its consequences, or a change in behaviour (e.g., avoidance) because of the attack (American Psychiatric Association, 2013). Compared to people with other anxiety disorders, those with panic disorder have the greatest number of medical visits overall, as well as the most frequent visits to cardiology, family medicine, and emergency medicine units (Deacon et al., 2008).

Similarly, people with depression also show high levels of medical use (Kimerling et al., 1999). Depression is diagnosed when people have prolonged depressed moods or loss of interest, and al. (2018) explored whether integration of medical services with mental health services in college settings would reduce medical service use by such students. The researchers obtained data from 80,219 post-secondary students with at least one mental health disorder at 21 academic institutions. They compared post-secondary institutions (n = 9) with minimal versus enhanced (n =12) integrated clinical collaboration between medical and mental health services. Enhanced clinical integration in this study involved a high level of collaboration among medical and mental health providers and use of shared electronic health records. The researchers ultimately identified that those patients with mental health disorders in minimally integrated health systems had close to 16 per cent more primary care visits and took 23 per cent more time than patients in the enhanced systems. This has considerable implications for costs. For instance, the study estimated that if students had been treated in an integrated model approximately 19,000 fewer medical visits and ~4500 fewer hours in care during a typical academic year would have occurred. Ultimately, the study concluded that integrated care would prove more cost-effective, and result in more holistic care for students with mental health care needs. In the future, it would be valuable to assess the extent to which integrated care for students also results in differences in health outcomes and perceived suffering.

experience other symptoms, such as a change in weight or appetite, insomnia or hypersomnia, psychomotor agitation or retardation, fatigue, feelings of low self-worth, difficulties concentrating, or recurrent thoughts of death or suicidal ideation (American Psychiatric Association, 2013). Higher levels of depressive symptoms correlate with increased medical usage over a 10-year period, even when controlling for age, sex, marital status, and medical co-morbidity (Kimerling et al., 1999).

It is important for health-care professionals to recognize and treat patients with psychological disorders to prevent the overuse of medical care (Kraft, Puschner, Lambert, & Kordy, 2006). Despite widespread knowledge about these principles, psychological disorders remain consistently undertreated (Andrade et al., 2014). Undertreatment sometimes occurs because the conditions are not identified and instead the focus remains on the unexplained medical symptoms. At other times, undertreatment occurs because of patient interest in self-management of symptoms, inadequate access to appropriately trained mental health providers, or because patients have limited time available to seek care, mobility difficulties, or concerns about stigma (Andrade et al., 2014). This is very unfortunate as there is evidence that psychological treatment reduces physician visits for psychological and social problems and also reduces use of medication (Prins, Verhaak, Smit, & Verheij, 2014).

Delayed Health Care

While overuse of medical services is a significant concern, people who significantly delay seeking health care (including psychological services) when such services could improve their condition also raise concerns. Delayed use of medical services can lead to increased morbidity and mortality and result in increased health-care spending. Some health-system features may encourage or create delays. High user fees, including deductibles and co-payments, are common in private health insurance systems in the United States, as contrasted to the more modest user fees or free services more typical of social health insurance and national health systems. Significant user fees or lack of insurance coverage may encourage people with limited financial means to delay seeking necessary medical care. By the same token, national health systems often have long waiting times for services deemed necessary but not urgent. In addition, they may not cover costs of psychological or other non-medical services.

As an example of the importance of timely care, consider those who delay seeking care after experiencing an acute myocardial infarction or a stroke. Many deaths and significant disability could be prevented if these patients obtained prompt care for such conditions (Kainth et al., 2004). Survival rates after acute myocardial infarction improve by up to 50 per cent if patients receive treatment within one hour of symptom onset. A shorter interval between onset of symptoms and medical treatment is associated with better cardiac function (Moser et al., 2007). Similarly, shorter time of administration of stroke medications is associated with substantially improved outcomes (Hacke et al., 2004).

Aside from the question of costs, why do patients delay seeking or fail to seek health care? As discussed in Chapter 7, often people delay treatment because they fail to recognize early symptoms as requiring intervention, or fail to grasp the benefits of more rapid treatment. If people do not feel vulnerable, or do not believe that care will be helpful, they will likely not seek it (Hagger & Orbell, 2003). At the system level, patients may delay or avoid seeking treatment if they face onerous user charges or potentially long waits for needed treatment.

In the case of acute myocardial infarction, demographic, clinical, social, psychological, and health-care variables are associated with delays in seeking treatment. In the United States, demographic variables associated with delays in seeking care for myocardial infarction include older age, being female, lower education, lower SES, and being Black. In terms of clinical variables, surprisingly, those with more chronic health conditions as well as those who have a history of angina (see Chapter 10) also delay seeking medical care for symptoms of acute MI. It seems these patients may attribute symptoms to other conditions and not to MI and thus delay treatment seeking. Social factors associated with delayed treatment include being at home alone, resting, or sleeping. Psychologically, anxiety is associated with seeking care quickly, while feelings of embarrassment or indecision increase the delay. It also appears that living farther from care is associated with delays in seeking care, and, interestingly, calling a physician for advice is associated with delays in receiving care as compared to calling emergency medical services (Moser et al., 2007).

Although multiple variables are associated with delays in seeking care or underutilization of health care, one variable that seems to be quite consistent across health-care conditions is that individuals from visible minority groups in the United States have lower levels of health-care use than those who identify themselves as White (Burgess, Ding, Hargreaves, van Ryn, & Phelan, 2008). Of note, recent research suggests that perceived discrimination is greater among minority groups and that anticipated discrimination results in decreased utilization of health care among minority groups (Burgess et al., 2008). Chapter 15 discusses cross-cultural considerations in more detail.

Another recent study points to the role of medical mistrust in delaying care, with medical mistrust found to be associated with failing to take medical advice, failing to keep follow-up appointments, postponing receiving care, and failing to fill prescriptions (LaVeist, Isaac, & Williams, 2009). Medical mistrust in the United States and Canada is correlated with individuals of lower education or who belong to an ethnic minority.

What can be done to reduce delays in seeking appropriate medical care? In the case of ischemic stroke and myocardial infarction, it appears that community-based public education has largely been ineffective in reducing patient delays in seeking medical care (Luepker et al., 2000; Moser et al., 2007), even when enormous resources are put into improving education (Hand, Brown, Horan, & Simons-Morton, 1998). More sophisticated approaches are needed to target high-risk populations and address the diverse factors associated with delays in seeking medical care.

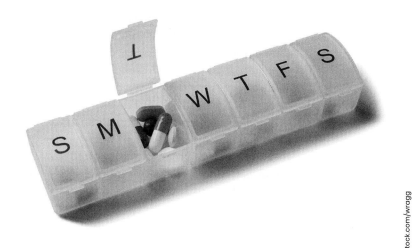

Pill boxes are often used to help ensure that patients remember to take their medication and to improve adherence with medical regimens.

Unfortunately, psychologists do not typically encounter patients who delay seeking medical treatment until the patient's condition has deteriorated to the point where they must seek treatment. When psychologists do work with people who have a history of delaying treatment, in an effort to avoid future delays in seeking care, a component of treatment is likely to involve the review and discussion of factors that may have contributed to this delay. One common strategy that psychologists use with patients who are at risk of treatment delay is to encourage use of a symptom diary so that patients have a better awareness of symptoms. Psychologists encountering new patients routinely screen for symptoms that may signal underlying physical conditions, and make referrals to physicians when a patient has not had the symptoms medically evaluated. For example, hyper and hypothyroidism can present with symptoms of anxiety and depression respectively. Psychologists are also likely to encourage patients to discuss symptoms with significant others so that they have support and assistance in interpreting and responding to symptoms. Psychologists will also review the patient's knowledge and awareness of symptoms that may signal a need to seek care.

Adherence to Medical Care

Adherence to medical care is another issue given considerable attention by health psychologists. Patient adherence to medical recommendations is vital to good health outcomes, including reduced morbidity and mortality. Non-adherence is generally associated with poorer health and increased health-care costs. Patients who follow medical advice are almost three times more likely to have a positive treatment outcome compared to those who are non-adherent (DiMatteo, Giordani, Lepper, & Croghan, 2002).

Definition and Measurement

Adherence refers to patients following treatment recommendations made by their health-care professionals (DiMatteo, et al., 2002). The words "adherence" and "compliance" are sometimes used interchangeably, but "adherence" is a better term as it recognizes that patients are actively involved in sticking to their care. There are many forms of adherence for psychologists to consider, such as whether patients are taking medications as recommended, keeping appointments, or following recommended health behaviours such as exercise or diet plans (DiMatteo et al., 2002). Psychologists can measure adherence in different ways. They can ask patients to keep diaries, count pills, or share results of physical tests related to adherence (e.g., urine or blood assays). Alternatively, they can ask patients to self-report or electronically monitor health behaviours. Self-reporting is often used because it is simple and inexpensive, but this has the disadvantage that memory for the adherence behaviour can be distorted. Many smartphone apps can assist in promoting adherence. Sometimes, collateral information is collected from a family member by a health-care professional, but this assumes the informant has accurate information. Sometimes psychologists think of patients as adhering or not, but, in fact, adherence falls on a continuum ranging from 100 per cent to zero. It can be difficult at times for psychologists to decide whether patients require treatment to improve adherence.

Rates and Predictors of Adherence

Adherence links to a number of different variables. Adherence to medical recommendations, for example, is highest in patients with HIV disease (88.3 per cent), arthritis (81.2 per cent), gastro-intestinal disorders (86.2 per cent), and cancer (79.1 per cent), and lowest in patients with pulmonary disease (68.8 per cent), diabetes (67.5 per cent), and sleep conditions (65.5 per cent) (DiMatteo et al., 2002). What accounts for these differences? It appears that patients are more likely to adhere if the condition is severe, the treatment is believed to be effective, and the treatment recommendations are straightforward and less complex to follow.

Adherence is also related to other variables, such as education, income, and SES, with individuals of higher education, income, and SES more likely to adhere to medical recommendations (DiMatteo, 2004). Adherence decreases with less understanding of what is required, but also decreases as the complexity of the patient's life increases.

Sometimes patients are non-adherent because they do not perceive their condition as severe, because they do not understand the importance of treatment, or because they feel unable to implement the changes required. Emotional problems can also increase non-adherence. Problematic alcohol and drug use and history of mental health problems predict non-adherence (DiMatteo, Haskard-Zolnierek, & Martin, 2012). Social factors are also related to adherence, with adherence found to be greater among those who have good social supports (DiMatteo, 2004). Finally, health-care relationships also factor into adherence, such that the greater trust an individual has in a provider, the greater the adherence (DiMatteo et al., 2002).

Improving Adherence

Health-care professionals, including health psychologists, have worked on improving patient adherence. However, many interventions designed to improve adherence fail. Simplistic interventions that do not target the patients' key motivations are particularly ineffective (McDonald, Garg, & Haynes, 2002). Multi-faceted approaches that combine strategies, regularly review or examine adherence over time, and account for individual patient needs have the greatest chance of success. In a recent review, it was found that interventions that modify attitudes, norms, and self-efficacy are particularly effective at improving health behaviours (Sheeran et al., 2016).

A three-pronged approach, referred to as the information-motivation-strategy model, has been proposed as a method for professionals to assist patients with adherence (DiMatteo et al., 2012). The first step encourages health-care professionals to focus on providing patients with information, and emphasizes the importance of effective patient–provider communication. Adherence cannot take place if patients do not understand the information they are given. For patients to understand, providers must give clear information, check for understanding, allow patients opportunities to clarify misunderstandings, and express empathy towards patients. The second important component of patient adherence, according to this model, is addressing patient motivation. This step recognizes that patient beliefs about disease severity, vulnerability, treatment efficacy, self-efficacy, and barriers to treatment have a significant impact on motivation. As a final step in improving patient adherence, health-care professionals need to clearly and systematically examine the strategies patients use to adhere to treatment recommendations as well as the barriers that may interfere with success. Practical barriers may need to be overcome to help patients with adherence, such as difficulties in coping

ALL YOU HAVE TO DO IS CHANGE EVERYTHING ABOUT THE WAY YOU LIVE.

with the dose frequency and regimen complexity (Ingersoll & Cohen, 2008). Other practical issues that may require consideration include exploring whether patients have the necessary money, skills, resources, or time to adhere to treatment recommendations.

Health-care professionals need to recognize that many treatment recommendations require patients to exert considerable self-control over habits and to give up short-term rewards for long-term outcomes (Hagger, Wood, Stiff, & Chatzisarantis, 2009). Non-adherence results when self-regulation fails or the individual has difficulties overcoming bad habits. Difficulties changing habits, however, does not always reflect a failure of willpower, but instead can be activated by stress and by environmental cues (Wood & Runger, 2016). Difficulties with self-regulation thus need attention from health-care professionals. Some strategies that assist with self-regulation include limiting the number of activities that require self-control and recommending that patients obtain sufficient rest and relaxation to replenish their ability to exercise self-control (Hagger et al., 2009). Health psychologists have an important role to play in helping patients with self-control or similar problems. The accompanying In Practice box discusses how a psychologist worked with an adolescent to improve adherence to diabetes treatment recommendations.

In Practice
Improving Adherence: The Case of Lucas

Lucas, a 16-year-old male, lives with his biological parents. At age 13, Lucas developed Type I diabetes, an autoimmune disease in which the pancreas gradually ceases to produce insulin, making it impossible for the body to process glucose normally. At the time of the assessment, Lucas's prescribed regimen involved injecting two types of insulin (i.e., one long-acting and additional injections of instant-acting insulin with meals) to control his blood-sugar levels. Because of erratic blood-sugar results, Lucas was referred to a psychologist working with adolescents who have diabetes.

The psychologist treating Lucas first evaluated how well he and his parents understood the prescribed regimen and blood-sugar control. The assessment revealed that Lucas thought involving his parents in the psychological management of his diabetes was desirable. Assessment proceeded by having Lucas and his parents keep a detailed record of Lucas's self-management, including food intake, exercise levels, insulin doses, and peripheral blood-glucose levels. The record helped clarify variables affecting good control. Specifically, the psychologist wanted to understand the antecedents of poor self-management (e.g., inadequate diabetes education, dietary issues, lack of exercise, incorrect medication, failure to check blood glucose levels). Lucas had primary responsibility for keeping the journal. The psychologist learned that Lucas's parents both worked full-time and had become less involved in his diabetes care since his initial diagnosis. They expected Lucas to manage his condition by himself. Lucas would often skip meals or snack irregularly. He did not consistently check his blood glucose. The journal revealed that Lucas paid less attention to insulin dosing and monitoring when he was with his friends or busy playing computer games. In fact, he spent considerable time playing sedentary games and got little physical exercise.

Following the assessment period, intervention first began with diabetes management education: the psychologist talked to Lucas and his family about basic diabetes care and effective behavioural strategies for improving adherence. The psychologist also engaged Lucas in developing a list of reasons why he wanted better control of his diabetes. Intervention then focused on developing strategies to assist Lucas in remembering how to balance food intake, exercise, and medication co-ordinated with blood-glucose monitoring. One important strategy involved downloading an app on his smart phone allowing him to better track blood-glucose levels and adherence to medications. This app also sent him reminders to check his blood glucose. Importantly, his parents could also monitor the results. Lucas's parents also agreed to a reward system contingent on improved blood-glucose levels. Rewards were negotiated each week (e.g., use of car, time with friends) and were linked to a progressively higher level of adherence (80 per cent adherence increased to 100 per cent adherence over treatment). Another key to success involved problem-solving and regular meal times (e.g., helping Lucas choose foods when his parents were working), as well as organization of his diabetic supplies (e.g., blood-glucose meter, insulin).

Following treatment, Lucas was able to improve his monitoring of his peripheral blood glucose from one to two times day to at least four times a day (before each meal and at bedtime). He also became more consistent in taking his medications as prescribed. Furthermore, his sleep and meal schedule became much more regular than it had been in the past. His glycosylated hemoglobin (HgA1c) dropped from 11 per cent to a much healthier 7 per cent.

Patient Satisfaction

Patient satisfaction with health care is another topic of interest to health psychologists. When patients feel dissatisfied with care, it is not uncommon to spend time during sessions with a psychologist discussing concerns about individual providers or the health system in general. It is hardly surprising that patients are less likely to follow advice from providers they do not like, understand, or agree with (Taylor, La Greca, Valenzuela, Hsin, & Delamater, 2016).

Since the 1980s there has been a steady increase in research on patient satisfaction (Sitzia & Wood, 1997), with extensive study among different patient groups, different treatments, different settings, and different organizational structures (Xiao & Barber, 2008). The interest in assessing patient satisfaction suggests that health-care providers and organizations value the patient's point of view and collect this information in order to improve services (Worthington, 2005).

When global ratings of care are used, patients report very high levels of satisfaction with care, with as many as 85 per cent reporting they are satisfied with health-care services (Worthington, 2005). When patients are asked about specific aspects of care, however, there is more variability in patient ratings and lower ratings of satisfaction are found (Worthington, 2005).

Given the centrality of physicians within health systems, considerable research has examined patient satisfaction with physicians. This research is highly relevant to health psychologists, as past experience with physicians can become a central topic of discussion when patients seek psychological services. Certain key physician behaviours are related to higher levels of satisfaction with one's physician. Specifically, patients report greater satisfaction with care when their physicians have strong verbal and non-verbal communication skills, question patients effectively, readily share information, express empathy, and collaborate with their patients to make decisions (Zolnierek & DiMatteo, 2009). Thoroughness of care and listening are among the best predictors of patient satisfaction with physicians (Tak, Ruhnke, & Shih, 2015).

Female physicians are generally preferred over male physicians. This may be because female physicians have greater patient-centred communication and more reciprocal interactions with their patients. Female physicians spend, on average, two minutes longer with patients than male physicians, which translates to 10 per cent more time with patients (Roter, Hall, & Aoki, 2002). Female physicians also engage in more positive talk, psychosocial counselling, and emotion-focused talk with patients compared to male physicians.

Perhaps not surprisingly, the better one's health, the more satisfied one feels with one's provider (Xiao & Barber, 2008). It is not entirely clear, however, if greater satisfaction leads to better health outcomes or if better health outcomes result in greater satisfaction with care.

A significant consequence of dissatisfaction with the physician–patient relationship is that patients subsequently seek more health-care services, commonly seeking second opinions (LaVeist et al., 2009), and show lower adherence to medical recommendations and treatment protocols (Zolnierek & DiMatteo, 2009). In other words, if you feel your physician has poor communication skills, you are less likely to follow his or her advice and will be more likely to seek care elsewhere (Zolnierek & DiMatteo, 2009). Clearly, training physicians in communication is extremely important and results in higher adherence among patients than when physicians receive no such training (Zolnierek & DiMatteo, 2009).

Since the 1990s there has been a sustained movement towards more patient-centred care and choice in health systems, in part because of poor patient satisfaction. The Institute of Health-care Improvement (IHI), based in Cambridge, Massachusetts, has been prominent in putting patient-centred care on the agenda of health system decision-makers in the United States and Canada. The first dimension in IHI's influential Triple Aim is improving the patient experience of care, now a key element in the reform agendas of individual health-care organizations, regional health authorities, and governments in both countries.

Medical Cost Offset of Psychological Interventions

As described in other chapters in this book, a growing body of evidence shows that effective psychological treatments can assist individuals with recovery and adaptation to medical conditions, such as diabetes, headaches, arthritis, chronic pain, and medically unexplained physical symptoms (Hunsley, 2003). Suls and Rothman (2004) described three areas in which behavioural interventions by health psychologists have been particularly effective: (1) smoking cessation; (2) reducing stress and mitigating the consequences of medical procedures; and (3) facilitating the recovery or adaptation of persons with chronic illness. One question you may have—and one shared by all governments that fund or subsidize health psychology services—is whether providing psychological services to medical patients ultimately reduces health-care costs. That is, by receiving psychological services, do patients improve their health in a significant way and thus reduce their use of health-care services? From a health-system perspective, government decision makers want to know not only whether costs will be reduced through such interventions, but also their precise impact over successive annual budgets.

In fact, it appears that providing psychological services to patients reduces their subsequent use of other health-care services by approximately 20 to 30 per cent (Chiles, Lambert, & Hatch, 1999). It is very rare for the costs of psychological treatment to exceed cost savings from the psychological intervention. The cost offset is greatest for behavioural interventions delivered to medical inpatients (e.g., surgery, oncology, cardiac rehabilitation) compared to outpatients. The cost offset is also significantly greater when structured psychological interventions (e.g., psycho-education for medical patients) are offered compared to non-specific psychotherapy.

Research on psychological treatment for hostility among coronary disease patients provides a specific example of cost-offset research (Davidson, Gidron, Mostofsky, & Trudeau, 2007). This research involved randomizing male patients with myocardial infarction or unstable angina to either two months of cognitive behavioural group therapy or an information session. Those in the cognitive behavioural treatment condition had a significantly shorter length of hospital stay over six months following therapy and lower hospitalization costs compared to those in the information session. More specifically, for every dollar spent on therapy, there was an approximate savings of two dollars in hospitalization costs over a six-month period. Demonstrating the cost-effectiveness of health psychological interventions is critical for the advancement of health psychology. Nevertheless, as noted above, financial constraints limit the expansion of the profession and delivery of these services to the population, even when cost-effectiveness data are available and favourable.

Future Directions

In addition to helping patients maintain or improve their health, health psychologists have the potential to work with patients on issues that significantly impact the functioning and sustainability of the health system, such as overuse or delayed use of medical services, adherence to medical care, and patient satisfaction. By working with patients on issues that impact health-care use, health psychologists also can help reduce health-care spending and thereby make health systems more fiscally sustainable. Despite the cost-effectiveness of health psychological services, however, the current structure of the health system limits the availability of these services. As we have seen, physicians have a central position in both US and Canadian health systems—though for slightly different reasons—in providing referrals for the services of health psychologists, especially for secondary and tertiary care. As a consequence, there may be an opportunity for health psychologists to play a larger role in the future if more health psychologists are involved in the primary care of patients.

This chapter raises some important directions for future research in the field of health psychology with specific reference to the health system. A question that deserves greater attention is how we can best educate health psychologists to work with diverse health-care disciplines and make their competencies known and valued. Despite being cost-effective and effective in treating individual patients' health and well-being, health psychology interventions are not routinely integrated in clinical practice (Nicassio, Meyerowitz, & Kerns, 2004). We need to ensure that knowledge gained through health psychological research is appropriately disseminated and effectively translated into practice. Health psychologists also need to continue to conduct research that demonstrates the cost-effectiveness of health psychology, and this research should be more effectively disseminated to policy decision-makers. Thus far, research in this area (Chiles et al., 1999) has not had a significant impact on our health system (e.g., increased public access to health psychologists). As a result, considerably more attention should be turned to addressing health-system barriers to incorporating health psychology into routine care (e.g., insurance coverage, both public or private), and this may require greater attention to how best to communicate how health psychology can improve our health systems.

In terms of improving patient access to health psychologists, it is possible that further research on how health psychologists can use technology to improve access to health services would be beneficial. Although this field is growing, we have much to learn about the use of computerized assessment and treatment programs to deliver health psychology services. Internet-delivered cognitive behavioural therapy has been found to be an effective method for assisting patients in coping with a number of health conditions (Glozier et al., 2013; Hedman et al., 2013; Weise, Kleinstauber, & Andersson, 2016). Further research is also needed on how health psychologists can best work with ethnically diverse populations and older adults. Most research in health psychology tends to be on middle-aged, middle-class, and ethnically homogeneous adults in industrialized countries. This is problematic because our population is rapidly becoming more ethnically diverse and older (Smith, Orleans, & Jenkins, 2004), and we need to ensure that health psychologists are competent to meet the needs of all patients who come in contact with our health system.

Summary

Due to different public and private funding arrangements, regulatory structures, and delivery modes, health systems vary from country to country and shape the way health psychologists provide services to their patients. The United States has a predominantly private health insurance system supplemented by public programs, the most notable of which are federal Medicare and state-administered Medicaid. Canada has a predominantly public coverage system in which provincial governments provide medically necessary hospital, diagnostic, and physician services.

Due to restrictive public coverage, patient access to the services of health psychologists is limited in both countries, despite the fact that health psychologists can provide an array of services directly connected to medical care. These include treating psychological conditions secondary to illness; treating physical symptoms that are responsive to behavioural interventions; addressing the physical and psychological consequences of stressful medical procedures; altering behaviours that lower the risk factors for disease and disability; diagnosing and referring individuals with psychological presentations of organic problems; and identifying and treating psychological dysfunctions that first appear as physical problems. Despite these health-system barriers, health psychologists are involved in every stage of care, from primary (first contact) and secondary (specialized outpatient) to tertiary (specialized inpatient) care.

When working with patients, health psychologists often need to consider whether patients are misusing medical services. There are two common types of misuse: overuse and delayed use. Overuse is particularly common among individuals who have health anxiety, depression, and panic disorder. Delayed use is particularly problematic among individuals who delay seeking care for myocardial infarctions, strokes, or cancer and is related to demographic, clinical, social, psychological, and health-care variables.

Health psychologists also often assist patients with adherence to medical care. Adherence refers to patients following treatment recommendations made by their health-care professionals. Psychosocial variables predict adherence, and thus psychologists have an important role to play in assisting patients with adherence to medical recommendations. The information-motivation-strategy model has been proposed as a method to assist professionals in assisting patients with adherence.

Based on a global survey, it is estimated that 85 per cent of patients feel satisfied with the health care they receive. However, when patients are dissatisfied with health care, they may spend considerable time elaborating on their concerns when talking to psychologists. There is growing evidence that there are effective psychological treatments to assist individuals with recovery and adaptation to medical conditions as well to problems they encounter within the health-care system. These psychological services can reduce health-care spending.

Critical Thought Questions

1. What type of health system, if any, do you think is most conducive to ensuring that patients obtain access to health psychology services when they are most needed?
2. What do you perceive to be a greater problem—overuse of medical services, delayed use of medical services, or patient non-adherence to medical recommendations?
3. Could you imagine physicians using the information-motivation-strategy model to improve patient adherence to use of prescribed medications? What would the strengths and challenges of this be?

Recommended Reading

DiMatteo, M.R., Haskard-Zolnierek, K.B., & Martin, L.R. (2012). Improving patient adherence: A three-factor model to guide practice. *Health Psychology Review, 6*, 74–91.

Hunsley, J. (2003). Cost-effectiveness and medical cost-offset considerations in psychological service provision. *Canadian Psychology/Psychologie Canadienne, 44*, 61–73.

Romanow, R.J., & Marchildon, G.P. (2003). Psychological services and the future of health care in Canada. *Canadian Psychology/Psychologie Canadienne, 44*, 283–95.

Tovian, S.M. (2004). Health services and health care economics: The health psychology marketplace. *Health Psychology, 23*, 138–41.

Prevention of Illness and Health-Promotion Intervention

James O. Prochaska*

Janice M. Prochaska*

5

Learning Objectives

In this chapter you will:

- Learn about the importance of a healthy lifestyle.
- Learn the core constructs of the transtheoretical model of behaviour change (TTM).
- Identify which TTM principles and processes to use at each stage of change.
- Learn about multiple behaviour change.
- Read about the challenges to TTM.
- See how TTM interventions have been applied to exercise, nutrition, and smoking.
- Compare patient health to population health.

* Conflict of interest disclosure: The authors of this chapter are affiliated with the Pro-Change Behavior Systems company that is mentioned in this chapter

Importance of a Healthy Lifestyle

Have you, your friends, or your family made important lifestyle changes (e.g., quit smoking, begun to exercise regularly)? Have you met people who have tried to make such changes but did not succeed in the long term? Although change is not always easy, many people succeed; they quit smoking, develop healthier habits, exercise, or otherwise improve themselves and their well-being. Psychologists and other professionals have been trying to understand the processes through which people change and what makes change more likely. This chapter focuses on the process of change, including challenges and successes that people go through to improve their health. Perhaps this chapter will inspire readers to make healthy and beneficial changes to their own lives.

Health-risk behaviours like smoking, inactivity, unhealthy diets, alcohol abuse, and ineffectively managed stress significantly contribute to a population's morbidity, disability, mortality, reduced functioning and productivity, and escalating health-care costs. In contrast, a healthy lifestyle including abstinence from smoking, eating five servings of fruits and vegetables each day, adequate physical activity (e.g., walking **10,000 steps a day** or doing 150 minutes of **moderate exercise** a week), and striving to maintain a body mass index (BMI) of less than 25 is being shown to increase life expectancy up to 14 years (Khaw et al., 2008; van den Brandt, 2011; Pronk et al., 2010). However, having a healthy lifestyle of 0 (smoking), 5 (fruits and vegetables), 10 (10,000 steps), 20 (minutes a day of stress management), and 25 (<25 BMI) has been an elusive goal for 97 per cent of the population (Reeves & Rafferty, 2005).

The World Health Organization (WHO) defines health promotion as "the process enabling people to increase control over, and to improve, their health" (WHO, 1998, p. 1). Health promotion and prevention are needed to reduce health-risk behaviours. Chapter 1 discusses several approaches to guide promotion and prevention including the health belief model (Rosenstock, 1960), theory of planned behaviour (Azjen & Madden, 1986), social cognitive theory (Bandura, 1982), and the transtheoretical model (TTM). To summarize, the health belief model is a framework for motivating people to take positive health action that uses the desire to avoid a negative health consequence as the prime motivation. For example, the perceived threat of a heart attack can be used to motivate a person with high blood pressure into exercising more often. According to this model, in order for behaviour change to succeed, people must feel threatened by their current behavioural pattern and believe that change of a specific kind will result in a valued outcome at acceptable cost. They also feel themselves competent to overcome perceived barriers to take action (Rosenstock, 1960).

The theory of planned behaviour focuses on constructs that are concerned with individual motivation as determinants of the likelihood of performing a specific behaviour. The most important determinant is a person's behavioural intention.

iStock.com/InnaKalyuzhina

A healthy lifestyle consisting of healthy diet and regular exercise has been an elusive goal for much of the population.

This model provides a framework for identifying key behaviour and normative beliefs affecting behaviour. Individuals expend more effort to perform a behaviour when perceptions of behavioural control are high. Perceived control, along with attitude toward behaviour and subjective norm, determine behavioural intention. Interventions can be designed to lead to a change in the intention and behaviour (Azjen & Madden, 1986).

Social cognitive theory addresses psychosocial dynamics that influence health behaviour and methods for promoting behaviour change. Human behaviour is explained in terms of a reciprocal model in which behaviour, personal factors, and environmental influences all interact. In

Physical activity, such as walking, has been shown to lead to increases in life expectancy.

this model, self-efficacy is the most important requisite for behaviour change because it affects how much effort is invested in a given task and what level of performance is attained (Bandura, 1982). This chapter focuses on the transtheoretical model (TTM) because it is the most commonly used model of behaviour change, in part because it does not focus exclusively on those who are motivated to change. The TTM is founded on stages of change and categorizes segments of populations based on where they are in the process of change. Principles and processes are applied to initiate movement through the stages of change. Interventions based on TTM principles can produce interactive and broadly applicable programs for treatment of entire populations. The programs include computer-tailored interventions (CTIs) delivered through various modalities, such as counsellor guidance and coaching face to face or via telephone, the Internet, and texting. CTIs deliver stage-matched interventions for multiple behaviour to individuals via digital technologies, and can have a high impact on disease prevention and management behaviours. CTIs also have the potential to provide the foundation for a well-care system that can complement the existing sick-care system.

Core Constructs of the Transtheoretical Model of Behaviour Change

TTM uses stages to integrate principles and processes of change across major theories of intervention, hence the name "transtheoretical." This model emerged from a comparative analysis of leading theories grounded in psychotherapy and behaviour change. Because more than 300 psychotherapy theories were found, the author determined there was a need for systematic integration (Prochaska, 1979). Ten processes of change emerged, including consciousness-raising from the Freudian tradition, contingency management from the Skinnerian tradition (emphasizing reinforcement for modifying behaviours), and helping relationships from the Rogerian tradition (relating with caring, empathy, and unconditional positive regard to support change).

In an empirical analysis of smokers in self-directed change compared to smokers in professional treatments, researchers assessed how frequently each group used each of the 10 processes (DiClemente & Prochaska, 1982). Research participants indicated that they used different processes at different times in their struggles with smoking. The self-directed individuals exhibited a phenomenon that was not included in any of the multitude of therapy theories. They revealed that behaviour change unfolds through a series of stages (Prochaska & DiClemente, 1983).

From the initial studies of smoking, the stage model rapidly expanded in scope to include applications to a broad range of health and mental health behaviours. Examples include alcohol and substance abuse, stress, bullying, delinquency, depression, eating disorders and **obesity**, high-fat diets, HIV/AIDS prevention, mammography screening, medication compliance, unplanned pregnancy prevention, pregnancy and smoking, radon testing, sedentary lifestyles, and sun exposure. Over time, behaviour studies have expanded, validated, applied, and challenged the core ideas of the transtheoretical model (Hall & Rossi, 2008; Noar, Benac, & Harris, 2007; Prochaska, Wright, & Velicer, 2008).

The transtheoretical model has concentrated on five stages of change, 10 processes of change, **decisional balance** (the pros and cons of changing), **self-efficacy**, and temptation. Stage of change serves as the key integrating construct. Studies of change have shown that people move through a series of stages when modifying behaviour. While the time a person can stay in each stage is variable, the tasks required to move to the next stage are not. Certain principles and processes work best at each stage to reduce resistance, facilitate progress, and prevent relapse. Only a minority (usually about 20 per cent) of a population at risk is prepared to take action. Action-oriented strategies are not helpful for those in the early stages of the change. Strategies based on each of the TTM stages result in increased participation in the change process because they are tailored to each individual rather than to the minority ready to take action.

Stages of Change

None of the leading theories of therapy contained a core construct representing time. Traditionally, behaviour change was often construed as an event, such as quitting smoking, drinking, or overeating, but the TTM recognizes change as a process that unfolds over time and involves progress through a series of stages (see Figure 5.1).

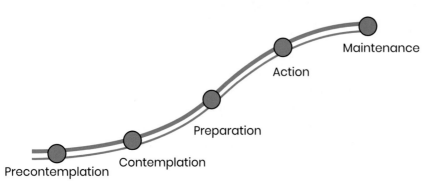

FIGURE 5.1   The stages of change.

Source: Pro-Change Behavior Systems, Inc.

Precontemplation

People in the precontemplation stage do not intend to take action in the foreseeable future, usually measured as the next six months. Being uninformed or under-informed about the consequences of one's behaviour may cause a person to be in precontemplation. Multiple unsuccessful attempts at change can lead to demoralization about ability to change. Both the uninformed and under-informed tend to avoid reading, talking, or thinking about their high-risk behaviours. They are often characterized in other theories as resistant, unmotivated, or not ready for health-promotion programs. In fact, traditional population health-promotion programs were not ready for such individuals and were not designed to meet their needs.

Contemplation

Contemplation is the stage in which people intend to change in the next six months. They are more aware of the pros of changing but are also acutely aware of the cons. In a **meta-analysis** across 48 health-risk behaviours (Hall & Rossi, 2008), the pros and cons of changing were equal. This weighting between the costs and benefits of changing can produce profound ambivalence that can cause people to remain in this stage for long periods of time. This phenomenon is often characterized as chronic contemplation or behavioural procrastination. Individuals in contemplation are not ready for traditional action-oriented programs that expect participants to act immediately.

Preparation

Preparation is the stage in which people are intending to take action in the immediate future, usually measured as the next month. Typically, they have already taken some significant steps towards changing the behaviour in the past year. These individuals have a plan of action, such as joining an exercise class, consulting a counsellor, talking to their physician, buying a self-help book, or relying on a self-change approach. These are the people who should be recruited for action-oriented programs such as traditional smoking cessation or weight-loss clinics.

Action

Action is the stage in which people have made specific overt modifications in their lifestyles within the past six months. Since action is observable, the overall process of behaviour change often has simply been equated with action. But in the TTM, action is only one of five stages. Typically, not all modifications of behaviour count as action in this model. In most applications, people have to attain a criterion that scientists and professionals agree is sufficient to reduce risk of disease. For example, reduction in the number of cigarettes or switching to low-tar and low-nicotine cigarettes were formerly considered acceptable actions towards smoking cessation. Now the consensus is clear—only total abstinence counts, as those other changes do not necessarily lead to quitting and do not lower the risks associated with smoking to zero.

iStock.com/James Brey

Preparation is the stage in which people are intending to take action in the immediate future, usually measured as the next month.

Maintenance

Maintenance is the stage in which people have made specific, overt modifications in their lifestyles and are working to prevent relapse; however, they do not apply change processes as frequently as do people in action. They are less tempted to relapse and grow increasingly confident (have greater self-efficacy) that they can continue their changes. Based on temptation and self-efficacy data, researchers have estimated that maintenance lasts from six months to about five years. While this estimate may seem somewhat pessimistic, longitudinal data in the 1990 Surgeon General's report support this temporal estimate (US Department of Health and Human Services [USDHHS], 1990). After 12 months of continuous abstinence, 43 per cent relapsed to regular smoking. It was not until five years of continuous abstinence that the risk for relapse dropped to 7 per cent (USDHHS, 1990).

Termination

Termination is, in a sense, a sixth stage, when people are not tempted; they have 100 per cent self-efficacy. Whether depressed, anxious, bored, lonely, angry, or stressed, individuals in this stage are sure they will not return to unhealthy habits as a way of coping. It is as if the habit had never been acquired in the first place or as if the new behaviour has become an automatic habit. Examples include people who have developed automatic seatbelt use or who automatically take their medications at the same time and place each day. In a study of former smokers and alcoholics, researchers found that less than 20 per cent of each group had reached the criteria of zero temptation and total self-efficacy (Snow, Prochaska, & Rossi, 1992). The criterion of 100 per cent self-efficacy may be too strict or it may be that this stage is an ideal goal for population health efforts. In other areas, like exercise, consistent condom use, and weight control, the realistic goal may be a lifetime of maintenance. Termination has not been given as much emphasis in TTM research since it may not be a practical reality for populations and it occurs long after interventions have ended.

Processes of Change

Processes of change are the experiential and behavioural activities that people use to progress through the stages. They provide important guides for intervention programs, serving as independent variables that are applied to move from stage to stage. Ten processes have received the most empirical support in our research to date.

In Focus

Mastering Your Own Change

1. Think about what behaviour health risks you may have—smoking, unhealthy diet, sedentary behaviour, being overweight.
2. Choose a risk to focus on.
3. Assess what stage you are in for reducing that health risk, for example, how ready you are to exercise 150 minutes per week: not intending to do so in the next six months (precontemplation); intending to do so in the next six months (contemplation); intending to do so in the next month (preparation).
4. Now go to Table 5.1 and the chapter section on processes of change and work on the processes that match your stage of change.
5. One month later, reassess your stage of change for the risk behaviour you are focusing on and see if there is movement. If so, use the processes of change that match your new stage. If you are still at the same stage, increase your usage of the processes.

TABLE 5.1 | Principles and Processes of Change That Mediate Progression between the Stages of Change

Precontemplation	Contemplation	Preparation	Action	Maintenance
Consciousness Raising				
Dramatic Relief				
Environmental Reevaluation				
	Social Liberation			
	Self–Reevaluation			
		Self-Liberation		
			Counter Conditioning	
			Helping Relationships	
Pros of Changing Increasing			Reinforcement Management	
	Cons of Changing Decreasing		Stimulus Control	
		Self-Efficacy Increasing		

Consciousness Raising (Get the Facts)

Consciousness raising involves increased awareness about the causes, consequences, and cures for a particular problem behaviour. Interventions that can increase awareness include feedback, interpretations, bibliotherapy (i.e., using self-help books or manuals), and media campaigns. Sedentary people, for example, may not be aware that their inactivity can have the same risk as smoking a pack of cigarettes a day.

Dramatic Relief (Pay Attention to Feelings)

Dramatic relief initially produces increased emotional experiences followed by reduced affect or anticipated relief. Role-playing, grieving, personal testimonies, and health-risk feedback are examples of techniques that can move people emotionally.

Self–Reevaluation (Create a New Self-Image)

Self–reevaluation combines both cognitive and affective assessments of one's self-image with and without a particular unhealthy habit, such as one's image as a couch potato vs an active person. Values clarification, identifying healthy role models, and imagery are techniques that can help people apply self–reevaluation. One might ask, "Imagine that you were a regular exerciser. How would you feel about yourself?"

Environmental Reevaluation (Notice Your Effect on Others)

Environmental reevaluation combines both affective and cognitive assessments of how the presence or absence of a personal habit affects one's social environment, such as the effect of smoking on others. It can also include the awareness that one can serve as a positive or negative role model for others. Empathy training, documentaries, and family interventions can lead to such assessments.

In Practice
Motivation for Healthy Change

Sometimes it takes a health scare to motivate us to change—and sometimes witnessing someone else's scare is enough.

Jennifer used the dramatic relief process of change to progress toward action when someone she loved had an unexpected emergency. Her experience may inspire you to get ready to make healthy changes.

"When I first got to school, I had a hard time getting everything done—I felt like I was drowning all the time. So I wasn't sleeping or eating well and there was no way I had time to exercise. But that all changed after my dad had a heart attack."

"He's fine now, but it was really scary. My mom called me to tell me to come home because he had to be rushed to the emergency room. The whole way there I kept thinking, he is so young, how could this have happened? I was terrified that he would die like my grandfather did after his heart attack."

"The doctors put a stent in one of his arteries, so the problem was fixed. But he had to go to a program for three months to start exercising, eating healthier

foods, and learning how to manage stress. The doctors also told me that because so many people in my family have had heart attacks, I need to start living a healthier life too. She said if I changed things now, I could avoid this when I was my dad's age."

"Now I see how important it is to make time to take care of my health. I made a choice to exercise each day. Sometimes I just go for a 30-minute walk between classes, and other times I get **aerobic exercise** by playing tennis with a friend. I'm eating healthier too. Don't get me wrong, I still eat cookies occasionally and don't even try to resist popcorn when we go to the movies, but overall, I'm making better choices. And my dad gave me some good ideas about managing stress—like managing my time better—that he got from his classes. I was surprised at how much of a difference creating a schedule could make."

"I know I am doing a lot to be as healthy as I can. And the best part is that I'm also more relaxed—instead of feeling like I'm just getting by, I feel like I'm doing well. Somewhere along the way, making these changes helped me fit everything in."

Self-Liberation (Make a Commitment)

Self-liberation is the belief that one can change and the commitment, as well as re-commitment, to act on that belief. New Year's resolutions, public testimonies, or a contract are ways of enhancing what is commonly called willpower. One might say, "Telling others about my commitment to take action can strengthen my willpower. Who am I going to tell?"

Social Liberation (Notice Public Support)

Social liberation requires an increase in social opportunities or alternatives, especially for people who are relatively deprived or oppressed. Advocacy, empowerment procedures, and appropriate policies can produce increased health-promotion opportunities for people from diverse cultural groups, LGBTQ persons, and people from impoverished segments of the population. These same approaches can also be used to help populations change; examples include smoke-free zones, salad bars in college dining halls, easy access to condoms and other contraceptives, and workout facilities on campus.

Counter Conditioning (Use Substitutes)

Counter conditioning requires learning healthy behaviours as substitutes for problem behaviours. Examples of counter conditioning include nicotine replacement as a safe substitution for smoking or walking as a healthier alternative than "comfort" foods as a way to cope with stress.

Stimulus Control (Manage Your Environment)

Stimulus control removes cues for unhealthy habits and adds prompts for healthier alternatives. Examples are removing all the ashtrays from the house and car or removing high-fat foods that are tempting cues for unhealthy eating, placing fruit in a bowl on the kitchen counter, and keeping sneakers ready for walks.

Reinforcement Management (Use Rewards)

Reinforcement management provides positive consequences for taking steps in a positive direction. While reinforcement management can include the use of punishment, we found that self-changers rely on reward much more than punishment. Reinforcements are emphasized since a philosophy of the stage model is to work in harmony with how people change naturally. People expect to be reinforced by others more frequently than what actually occurs, so they should be encouraged to reinforce themselves through self-statements like "Nice going—you handled that temptation." They also can treat themselves at milestones as a reinforcement to increase the probability that healthy responses will be repeated.

Helping Relationships (Get Support)

Helping relationships combine caring, trust, openness, and acceptance, as well as support for healthy behaviour change. Rapport-building, a therapeutic alliance, supportive calls, social media, and buddy systems can be sources of social support.

Decisional Balance

The process of reflection and weighing the pros and cons of changing is decisional balance. Originally, TTM relied on Janis and Mann's (1977) model of decision making that included four categories of pros: instrumental gains for self, instrumental gains for others, approval from self, and approval from others. The four categories of cons were instrumental costs to self, instrumental costs to others, disapproval from self, and disapproval from others. In a long series of studies attempting to produce this structure of eight factors, a much simpler structure was almost always found: the pros and cons of changing. Sound decision making requires consideration of the potential gains (pros) and losses (cons) associated with the consequences of a behaviour. For example, there are more than 65 scientific benefits of **regular physical activity**. One could be encouraged to make a list to see how many can be identified. One could also list the cons. The more the list of pros outweighs the cons, the better prepared one will be to take effective action.

iStock.com/mediaphotos

Temptation reflects the intensity of urges to engage in an unhealthy habit while in the midst of difficult situations.

Self-Efficacy

Self-efficacy is the situation-specific confidence that people have while coping with high-risk situations without relapsing to their unhealthy habit. This construct was integrated from Bandura's (1982) social cognitive theory (see Chapter 1).

Temptation

Temptation reflects the intensity of urges to engage in an unhealthy habit while in the midst of difficult situations. Typically, three factors reflect the most common types of tempting situations: negative affect or emotional distress, positive social situations, and craving. People could ask themselves how they will cope with emotional distress (without relying on a cigarette, or lying on a couch) to help them cope more effectively and thereby build their confidence or self-esteem.

Critical Assumptions of TTM

The transtheoretical model is also based on critical assumptions about the nature of behaviour change and population health interventions that can best facilitate such change. The following are a set of assumptions that drive transtheoretical theory, research, and practice:

1. Behaviour change is a process that unfolds over time through a sequence of stages, and health-promotion programs can assist individuals as they progress over time.
2. Stages are both stable and open to change, just as chronic behavioural risk factors are both stable and open to change. Population health initiatives can motivate change by enhancing the understanding of the pros and diminishing the value of the cons.
3. Most at-risk populations are not prepared for action and will not be served by traditional action-oriented prevention programs. Helping individuals set realistic goals, like progressing to the next stage, will facilitate the change process.
4. Specific principles and processes of change need to be emphasized at specific stages for progress through the stages to occur. Table 5.1 outlines which principles and processes to emphasize at each stage.

These critical assumptions need to be taken into consideration when developing health promotion interventions for behaviour change and to facilitate progress through the stages.

Empirical Support

Each of the core TTM constructs (a theoretical dimension represented by two or more variables) has been studied across a broad range of behaviours and populations. Applying TTM to new behaviours involves research and measurement (Redding, Maddock, & Rossi, 2006), followed by intervention development and refinement, eventually leading to studies of intervention success. We have selected a sample of these studies for discussion.

Stage Distribution

If interventions are to match the needs of entire populations, it is important to know the stage distributions of specific high-risk behaviours. A series of studies on smoking in the United States clearly demonstrated that less than 20 per cent of smokers are in the preparation stage in most populations (e.g., Velicer et al., 1995; Wewers, Stillman, Hartman, & Shopland, 2003).

Approximately 40 per cent of smokers are in the contemplation stage and another 40 per cent are in precontemplation. In countries that have not had a long history of tobacco control campaigns, the stage distributions are even more challenging. In Germany, about 70 per cent of smokers are in precontemplation and about 10 per cent of smokers are in the preparation stage (Etter, Perneger, & Ronchi, 1997); in China, more than 70 per cent are in precontemplation and about 5 per cent are in preparation (Yang et al., 2001). With a sample of 20,000 members of a Health Maintenance Organisation (HMO) across 15 health-risk behaviours, only a small portion were ready for the action stage of behavioural change (Rossi, 1992a).

Pros and Cons across 12 Behaviours

In studies of 12 different behaviours (smoking cessation, cocaine cessation, weight control, dietary fat reduction, safer sex, condom use, exercise acquisition, sunscreen use, radon testing, delin-quency reduction, mammography screening, and physicians practising preventive medicine), it was confirmed that helping people to make better decisions involves focus on the pros and cons of changing.

Systematic relationships were found between stages and the pros and cons of changing for these 12 behaviours. In all 12 studies the cons of changing were higher than the pros for people in the precontemplation stage (Prochaska et al., 1994). Likewise, in all 12 studies the pros increased between the precontemplation and contemplation stages, and the cons of changing were lower in the action stage than in the contemplation stage. In 11 of the 12 studies, the pros of changing were higher than the cons for people in action. These relationships suggest that, to progress from precontemplation, the pros of changing need to increase; to progress from contemplation, the cons need to decrease; to progress to action, the pros need to be higher than the cons. These same patterns of relationships have been replicated in a meta-analysis of the pros and cons of changing across the stages of change for 48 different health behaviours (Hall & Rossi, 2008).

Processes of Change across Behaviours

One assumption of the transtheoretical model is that people can apply a common set of change processes across a broad range of behaviours. The higher-order structure of the processes (experiential and behavioural) has received more research support across problem behaviours than have the specific processes (Rossi, 1992b). Typically, support has been found for the stan-dard set of 10 processes across behaviours such as smoking, diet, cocaine use, exercise, condom use, and sun exposure. However, the structure of the processes across studies has not been as consistent as the structure of the stages and the pros and cons of changing. The processes used to initiate change vary by behaviour. An infrequent behaviour such as conforming to an annual screening test (e.g., mammogram) may require fewer processes to progress to long-term maintenance (Rakowski et al., 1998).

Relationship between Stages and Processes of Change

One of the earliest empirical integrations was the discovery of systematic relationships between the stages people were in and the processes they were applying (Prochaska & DiClemente, 1983). This discovery allowed an integration of processes from theories typically seen as incompatible and in conflict. For example, Freudian theory relied almost entirely on consciousness-raising for producing change. This theory was viewed as incompatible with Skinnerian theory, which relied entirely on reinforcement management for modifying behaviour. But self-changers did not know that these processes were theoretically incompatible and their behaviour revealed that processes from very different theories need to be emphasized at different stages of change. This integration suggests that in early stages of health-promotion interventions, efforts should support the application of cognitive, affective, and evaluative processes to progress through the stages. In later stages these programs should rely more on commitments, conditioning, rewards, environmental controls, and support to progress towards maintenance or termination.

Table 5.1 has important practical implications for health-promotion interventions. To help people progress from precontemplation to contemplation, processes such as consciousness-raising and dramatic relief need to be applied. Applying reinforcement management, counter-conditioning, and stimulus control processes in precontemplation would represent a theoretical, empirical, and practical mistake. Conversely, such strategies would be optimally matched for people at the action stage. Integration of the processes and stages has not been as consistent as the integration of the stages with the pros and cons of changing. Part of the problem may be the greater complexity of integrating 10 processes across five stages. The processes of change require more basic research.

Applied Studies

A large, diverse body of evidence on the application of TTM has revealed several trends. The most common application involves TTM computerized tailored interventions (CTIs) that match intervention messages to individuals' particular needs (e.g., Kreuter, Strecher, & Glassman, 1999; Skinner, Campbell, Rimer, Curry, & Prochaska, 1999). Tailored interventions are population based. They combine the best of population health with clinical health to provide individualized help. For example, individuals in precontemplation could receive feedback designed to increase their pros of changing to help them progress to the contemplation stage. These interventions, such as suggested readings, testimonials from others successful in changing, and encouragement to reduce defenses, originally were printed and given to participants at work or mailed to participants at home (Velicer et al., 1993); however, a growing range of applications have been developed, including multimedia, computerized tailored interventions, and texting (Levesque, Johnson, Welch, Prochaska, & Paiva, 2016; Mauriello, Sherman, Driskill, & Prochaska, 2007), that can be delivered in clinic settings, worksites, colleges, online at home, or on tablets and smartphones on the go. To view a demo of a college health Internet intervention, go to https://www.prochange.com/livewell-program.

This health Internet program for college and university students is designed to help students improve their exercise, eating, and stress management habits. Questions and feedback are individualized to each student. Dynamic web activities matched to the individual's readiness to change are also

iStock.com/Mariemlulu

The liveWell health program encourages college and university students to engage in more physical activity, eat healthily, and manage stress effectively.

available. The dynamic portal home page provides specifics on how to apply each principle and process of change. A randomized controlled trial with 1841 first-year students found treated students increasing their well-being, adopting regular exercise, increasing healthy eating, and managing their stress (Broderick, Johnson, Cummins, & Castle, 2015).

The growing range of settings where TTM is being applied also includes primary-care offices (Goldstein et al., 1999; Hoffman et al., 2006; Hollis et al., 2005), churches (Voorhees et al., 1996), campuses (Prochaska, J.M., et al., 2004), and communities (CDC AIDS Community Demonstration Projects Research Group, 1999). Increasingly, employers and health plans are making TTM-tailored programs available to entire employee or subscriber populations. A recent meta-analysis of tailored print communications found that TTM was the most commonly used theoretical model across a broad range of behaviours (Noar et al., 2007). TTM or stage of change model was used in 35 of the 53 studies. In terms of effectiveness, the best results were produced when tailored communications included each of the following TTM constructs: stages of change, pros and cons of changing, self-efficacy, and processes of change (Noar et al., 2007). In contrast, interventions that included the non-TTM construct of perceived susceptibility had significantly worse outcomes. Tailoring non-TTM constructs like social norms and behavioural intentions did not produce significant differences (Noar et al., 2007). These unprecedented impacts require scientific and practice shifts in our approach to health-promotion interventions:

1. From an action paradigm to a stage paradigm.
2. From reactive to proactive recruitment of participants.
3. From expecting participants to match the needs of our programs to having our programs match their needs.
4. From clinic-based to community-based behavioural health programs that apply the field's most powerful individualized and interactive intervention strategies.
5. From assuming some groups do not have the ability to change to making sure that all groups have easy accessibility to evidence-based programs that provide stage-matched tailored interventions. Without such access, behaviour change programs cannot serve entire populations. To reduce health disparities, these programs need to be made available to older people, to people from diverse cultural groups, and to those on social assistance. (See Chapter 15 for more information on health disparities).

Challenging Studies

As with any model, not all of the research is supportive. Here are samples of some of the more challenging studies. Farkas et al. (1996) and then Abrams, Herzog, Emmons, and Linnan (2000) compared addiction variables to TTM variables as predictors of cessation over 12 to 24 months. Addiction variables, like number of cigarettes smoked and duration of prior quits (e.g., more than

Regular physical activity helps people to maintain health and become energized.

100 days) out-predicted TTM variables, suggesting that addiction models were preferable to TTM. Responses to these comparative studies included concerns that Farkas et al. (1996) compared 14 addiction-type variables to just the single-stage variable from TTM (Prochaska & Velicer, 1996; Prochaska, Velicer, Prochaska, Delucchi, and Hall, 2006). The Abrams et al. (2000) study included self-efficacy and the contemplation ladder—an alternative measure of readiness or stage—as part of its addiction model, but these are part of TTM. Also, for those intervening, how much you can predict is less important than how much you can change. Although duration of previous quits (e.g., 100 days) may predict better than stage, little can be done to change history, while stage can be changed.

In one study, Herzog, Abrams, Emmons, Linnan, and Shadel (1999) found that six processes of change did not predict stage progress over 12 months. In a second study, processes predicted stage progress but only when the contemplation ladder measure was used (Herzog, Abrams, Emmons, & Linnan, 2000). In a third report, TTM measures predicted 12-month outcomes, but self-efficacy and the stage measure were not counted as TTM variables (Abrams et al., 2000). Other researchers have found that change processes and other TTM variables predict stage progress (e.g., DiClemente et al., 1991; Dijkstra, Conijm, & De Vries, 2006; Johnson et al., 2000; Prochaska, DiClemente, Velicer, Ginpil, & Norcross, 1985; Prochaska, Velicer, Guadagnoli, Rossi, & DiClemente, 1991; Prochaska, J.O. et al., 2004, 2008; Sun, Prochaska, Velicer, & Laforge, 2007). Johnson et al. (2000) explained some inconsistencies in previous research by demonstrating better predictions over 6 vs 12 months, and better predictions using all 10 processes of change instead of just a few.

One productive response to studies critical of TTM is to conduct further research. In response to the criticism that addiction severity is a better predictor of outcomes than stage of change, a series of studies to determine predictors of outcomes across multiple behaviours was done. To date, four such predictors have been found (Blissmer et al., 2010). The first is the severity effect, in which individuals with less severe behaviour risks at baseline are more likely to progress to action or maintenance at 24-month follow-up for smoking, diet, and sun exposure. This effect includes the level of addiction that Farkas et al. (1996) and Abrams et al. (2000) preferred. The second is stage effect, in which participants in preparation stage at baseline have better 24-month outcomes for smoking, diet, and sun exposure than those in contemplation, who do better than those in precontemplation. This effect is what Farkas et al. (1996) and Abrams et al. (2000) criticized. The third is treatment effect, in which participants in treatment do better at 24 months than those in control groups for smoking, diet, and sun exposure. The fourth is effort effects, in which participants in both treatment and control groups who progressed to action and maintenance at 24 months were making better efforts with TTM variables like pros and cons, self-efficacy, and processes at baseline. Moreover, no single demographic group did better across these multiple behaviours. What these results indicate is that either–or thinking (such as *either* severity *or* stage) is not as helpful as a more inclusive approach that seeks to identify the most important predictors of change, whether they are based on TTM or on an addiction or severity model.

Increasing Impacts with Multiple Behaviour Change Programs

A challenge for any theory is to keep raising the bar, that is, to be able to increase the theory's impact on enhancing health. One challenge for TTM is to treat multiple behaviours, since populations with multiple behaviour risks are at greatest risk for both chronic disease and premature death.

These multiple-problem populations also account for a high percentage of health-care costs. The best estimates are that about 60 per cent of health-care costs are generated by about 15 per cent of populations who have multiple behaviour risks (Edington, 2001).

The studies to date on multiple behaviour changes have been limited by the frequent use of poor research designs, and by not applying the most promising interventions, such as interactive and individualized TTM-tailored communications (Prochaska et al., 2001). From a TTM perspective, applying an action paradigm to multiple behaviours at once risks overwhelming populations, since action is the most demanding stage and taking action on two or more behaviours at once could be overwhelming. Furthermore, in individuals with four health-behaviour risks, like smoking, diet, sun exposure, and sedentary lifestyles, less than 10 per cent were ready to take action on two or more behaviours (Prochaska & Velicer, 1997). The same was true with diabetes patients who needed to change four behaviours (Ruggiero et al., 1997).

Applying best practices of a stage-based multiple behaviour manual and computerized tailored feedback reports over 12 months, researchers reached out to a population of parents of teens who were participating in parallel projects at school (Prochaska, J.O. et al., 2004). Of the eligible parents with cancer risk factors, 83.6 per cent were engaged. The treatment group received up to three computerized, tailored reports at 0, 6, and 12 months. At 24 months, the treatment group was outperforming the controls on three cancer prevention behaviours: smoking cessation, healthier diets, and safer sun exposure practices.

With a population of 5545 patients from primary care practices, we were able to recruit 65 per cent for a second multiple behaviour change project (Prochaska et al., 2005). In this project, mammography screening (i.e., screening aimed at the early detection of breast cancer) was targeted in addition to the three aforementioned cancer-prevention behaviours. Significant treatment effects were found for all four target behaviours at 24 months.

Comparisons across three multiple-risk behaviour studies demonstrated that the efficacy rates for smoking cessation were in the same 22 to 25 per cent abstinence range that we consistently find when targeting only smoking (Prochaska et al., 2006). Further, it was found that smokers with a single risk were no more successful in quitting than smokers who were treated for two or three risk behaviours. The same was found for participants with a single risk of diet or sun exposure compared with those with two or three risk behaviours. Overall, these results indicate that TTM-tailored interventions may be producing unprecedented impacts on multiple behaviours for disease prevention and health promotion.

Applying TTM Interventions to Exercise, Nutrition, and Smoking

With a population of 1277 overweight and obese patients in a workplace who were invited to participate in the study through mailings at work, researchers applied the original strategy for multiple behaviour change. In this modular approach, participants receive a separate TTM computerized tailored intervention (CTI) module for each of their risk behaviours. The treatment groups had significant changes at 24 months on healthy eating, exercise, and emotional eating. This study was the first to report significant coaction in the treatment group and significant changes in fruit and vegetable intake, specific behaviours that were not targeted. **Coaction** is the increased probability that individuals who take effective action on one behaviour (like exercise) are more likely to take action on a secondary behaviour (like diet).

Also, the intervention resulted in a mean of about 0.8 behaviours changed per participant in the TTM group, which was 60 per cent greater than the 0.5 behaviours in the control group (Johnson et al., 2008).

One exciting development in simultaneously changing multiple behaviours is the phenomenon of coaction. Researchers have found that significant coaction typically occurs only in TTM treatment groups (e.g., Johnson et al., 2014; Mauriello et al., 2010; Paiva et al., 2012) and not in control groups, suggesting it is likely to be treatment-induced.

With a population of 1400 employees in a major medical setting, the study by Prochaska et al. (2008) was made available by online modular TTM computerized tailored interventions or by three motivational telephonic or in-person interview sessions (a psychotherapeutic approach designed to enhance motivation for positive change) for each of four behaviours (smoking, inactivity, BMI >25, and stress). Patients chose which behaviours to target and how much time and effort to spend on any behaviour. At six months, both treatments outperformed the health risk intervention (HRI), which included feedback on the person's stage for each risk and guidance on how they could progress to the next stage.

With a population of 1800 students recruited from eight high schools in four states, Mauriello et al. (2010) applied a second-generation strategy with exercise as the primary behaviour. Students received three online sessions of fully tailored CTIs. The secondary behaviours of fruit and vegetable intake and limited television watching alternated between moderate and minimal (stage-only) tailoring. Over the course of the six-month treatment, there were significant treatment effects in each of the three behaviours, but only changes in fruit and vegetable intake were sustained at 12 months. Significant coaction was found for each pair of behaviours in the treatment group but none in the control group. The amount of coaction decreased after treatment, suggesting that longer treatment may be needed for this age population where health-risk behaviours tend to increase.

Prochaska et al. (2012) recruited 3391 adults from 39 states who were at risk for lack of exercise and ineffective **stress management**. This study involved a strategy for multiple tailored behaviour change. One treatment group received a fully tailored TTM online for the primary behaviour of stress management and minimal tailoring for exercise. A second group received three sessions of optimally tailored telephonic coaching for exercise and minimal tailoring for stress. In this study, the TTM telephonic exercise coaching outperformed the TTM online stress management, which outperformed the controls. Also, the exercise coaching produced significant effects on healthy eating and depression management, which were not the focus of treatment. Finally, the same order of effective treatment was found for enhancing five domains of well-being: emotional health, physical health, life evaluation, thriving, and overall well-being. This study represents the greatest impact to date on decreasing health-risk behaviours and increasing health and well-being (Prochaska and Prochaska, 2016). It also underscores the importance of tailoring change interventions.

Limitations of the Model

Although TTM has been applied across at least 48 behaviours and populations from many countries, the model still has limitations. The problem area that has produced the most disappointment has been primary prevention of substance use in children. To date, population studies based on TTM have not produced significant prevention effects (e.g., Aveyard et al., 1999; Hollis et al., 2005).

Unfortunately, little can be concluded from non-significant results. For example, Peterson, Kealey, Mann, Marek, and Sarason (2000) also reported that 16 out of 17 such studies failed, and suggested that the field should move beyond social influence models. Prevention trials have proved challenging across theories.

Part of the challenge from a TTM perspective is that almost all young people who have not yet used substances like tobacco, alcohol, or other drugs are in the precontemplation stage for acquisition of such use. One promising approach was to identify subgroups based on pros, cons, and temptation to try using. Those with a profile of low pros for using, high cons, and low temptations were clearly the most protected. This profile showed the best effort effects at baseline and the least acquisition at 12, 24, and 36 months (Velicer, Redding, Sun, & Prochaska, 2007). The first studies applying such profiles did not produce the expected positive outcomes, but new investigation can involve application of more creative and effective interventions. It remains to be seen whether effective TTM-tailored prevention programs that build on both theoretical and empirical insights can be developed.

A promising new finding (Velicer et al., 2013) is related to the use of an energy balance program (Health in Motion) with middle school students. Specifically, a smoking and alcohol prevention intervention lacked effectiveness to prevent substance use, but the energy balance program in the comparison group did prevent it. A focus on having a healthy lifestyle through exercise, healthy eating, and less than two hours of screen time each day may be a more engaging and helpful intervention than a target of just avoiding substances.

It might be assumed that TTM does not apply very well to children and adolescents. There is a basic question as to the age at which intentional behaviour change begins. Applied studies in bullying prevention in elementary, middle, and high schools, however, have all produced impressive results (Evers, Prochaska, Van Marter, Johnson, & Prochaska, 2007). Similarly, early intervention with adolescent smokers using TTM-tailored treatments produced significant abstinence rates at 24 months that were almost identical to rates found with treated adult smokers (Hollis et al., 2005). This was also true of TTM-tailored interventions targeting sun-protection behaviours in adolescents (Norman et al., 2007). One problem is that there has been much more research applying TTM to reducing risks than to preventing risks.

Given the global application of TTM, it will be important to determine in which cultures TTM can be applied effectively and in which cultures it may require major adaptations. In basic meta-analysis research on the relationships between stages and pros and cons of changing in 10 countries, there was no significant effect by country (Hall & Rossi, 2008).

Future Directions

While research results to date are encouraging, much still needs to be done to advance practical behaviour change through evidence-based efforts such as the transtheoretical model. Basic research needs to be done with other theoretical variables, such as processes of resistance, framing, and problem severity, to determine if such variables relate systematically to the stages and if they predict progress across particular stages. More research is needed on the structure or integration of the processes and stages of change across a broad range of behaviours, including acquisition behaviours such as exercise, and extinction behaviours like smoking cessation (Rosen, 2000). What modifications are needed to better address specific types of behaviours?

Since tailored communications represent the most promising interventions for applying TTM to entire populations, more research is needed comparing the effectiveness, efficiency, and impacts of alternative technologies. Most recently, Pro-Change Behavior Systems, Inc. added tailored texting to its health-risk assessment and computerized tailored programs and improved effectiveness by 11 percentage points for smoking cessation (Jordan, Evers, Spira, King, & Lid, 2013). The Internet is excellent for individualized interactions at low cost but has not produced the high participation rates generated by person-to-person outreach via telephone or visits to primary-care providers. Increasingly, employers are encouraging and offering incentives to employee populations to participate in more integrated Internet, telephone, and provider programs. Interventions once seen as applicable only on an individual basis are being applied as high-impact programs for population health.

How do diverse populations respond to stage-matched interventions and to high-tech systems? How might programs best be tailored to meet the needs of diverse populations? Might menus of alternative intervention modalities (e.g., telephone, Internet, neighbourhood or church leaders, person-to-person, or post-secondary programs) empower diverse populations to best match health-enhancing programs to their particular needs?

Changing multiple behaviours presents special challenges, such as the number of demands placed on participants and providers. Alternative strategies need to be tried beyond the sequential (one at a time) and simultaneous (all treated intensely at the same time). Integrative approaches are promising. For example, with bullying prevention, there are multiple behaviours (e.g., hitting, stealing, ostracizing, mean gossiping and labelling, damaging personal belongings) and multiple roles (bully, victim, and passive bystander) that need to be treated. An integrated approach is needed to address these needs in the given time constraints. If behaviour change is construct-driven (e.g., by stage or self-efficacy), what higher-order construct could integrate all of these more concrete behaviours and roles? In a study where relating with mutual respect was used as a higher-order construct, significant and important improvements across roles and behaviours were found for elementary, middle, and high school students (Evers et al., 2007). The concept of healthy pregnancy was also tested with women receiving Medicaid in the United States as they worked on the multiple behaviours of stress management, smoking cessation, and healthy eating (Mauriello, Van Mater, Umanzor, Castle, & de Aguiar, 2016). As with any theory, effective applications may be limited more by our creativity than by the ability of the theory to drive significant research and effective interventions.

Applying TTM on a population basis to change multiple health risks has required the use of innovative paradigms that complement established paradigms. Table 5.2 illustrates how a population paradigm, using proactive outreach to students, complements the individual patient paradigm that passively reacts when students seek clinical services. The use of the stage paradigm complements the action paradigm, which assumes that because students are seeking services they are prepared to take action. The use of computerized tailored interventions complements the traditional reliance on clinicians, and the treatment of multiple behaviours complements the established clinical wisdom of treating one behaviour at a time. The population theme paradigm based on impacts (reach × efficacy × number of behaviours changed) complements individualized clinical trials with select samples that rely on efficacy. Integrating these new paradigms can produce the foundation for a well-care system to complement the established sick-care system. Combining the two systems would enhance the health and well-being of many more people by healing the sick, while maximizing wellness for all.

TABLE 5.2 | Inclusive Care from Two Clusters of Paradigms for Individual Students, Patients, and Entire Populations

Patient Health	Complemented by	Population Health
1. Individual patients		1. Entire populations
2. Passive reactance		2. Proactive
3. Acute conditions		3. Chronic conditions
4. Efficacy trials		4. Effectiveness trials
5. Action-oriented		5. Stage-based
6. Clinic-based		6. Home-based
7. Clinician-delivered		7. Technology-delivered
8. Standardized		8. Tailored
9. Single target behaviour		9. Multiple target behaviours
10. Fragmented		10. Integrated
11. Specificity		11. Synergy
12. Separate behaviours		12. Behaviour systems
13. Efficacy		13. Impact
14. Reducing risks		14. Reducing risks and enhancing well-being

Summary

In this chapter, we described the core constructs of TTM and how these constructs can be integrated across the stages of change. Empirical support for the basic constructs of TTM and for applied research was presented, along with conceptual and empirical challenges from critics of TTM. Applications of TTM-tailored interventions with entire populations were explored with examples for single behaviours and for multiple health-risk behaviours. A major theme is that programmatically building and applying the core constructs of TTM at the individual level can ultimately lead to high-impact programs for enhancing health at the population level.

The transtheoretical model is a dynamic model of change and must remain open to modifications and enhancements as more students, scientists, and practitioners apply the stage paradigm to a growing number of diverse theoretical issues, public health problems, and at-risk populations.

Critical Thought Questions

1. What are the advantages of a stage paradigm vs an action-oriented paradigm?
2. Historically, it was thought a person could only change one behaviour at a time. Evidence is now showing that multiple behaviours can change. What are some new ideas that make this possible?
3. What stage of change are you in for a health-risk behaviour that you have? What TTM processes of change would you use to get to the next stage of change?

Recommended Reading

Prochaska, J.O. & Prochaska, J.M. (2016). *Changing to thrive: Using the stages of change to overcome the top threats to your health and happiness.* Center City, MN: Hazelden Publishing.

Cancer Prevention Research Center: www.uri.edu/research/cprc

Coaches' Guide for Using ttm with Clients: contact info@prochange.com

Pro-Change Behaviour Systems, Inc.: www.prochange.com

Basic Transtheoretical Model training: contact elearning@prochange.com

MyHealth behaviour change programs: www.prochange.com/myhealth

J & J Prochaska website: www.jprochaska.com

Eating, Smoking, and Recreational Substance Use

6

Swati Mehta

Heather D. Hadjistavropoulos

Thomas Hadjistavropoulos

Learning Objectives

In this chapter you will:

- Understand how eating and substance use can be maladaptive.
- Explore the impact of maladaptive eating and substance-use behaviours on the individual and society.
- Identify risk factors for developing maladaptive eating and substance-use behaviours.
- Examine tools to screen for and assess maladaptive eating and substance-use behaviours.
- Learn about different strategies for managing maladaptive eating and substance-use behaviours.

Introduction

Have you ever felt down and decided to treat yourself to a chocolate bar or a piece of cake? Or had a stressful week with exams and deadlines and just wanted to have a glass of wine or beer to calm down and relax? These are some ways in which people may engage in overeating or consumption of alcohol in their normal lives. In this chapter, we will specifically discuss two types of behaviours that can often be maladaptive, namely eating and substance use. Specifically, we examine the risk factors that may lead to maladaptive eating and substance use, resulting in compromised health. Various assessment and management strategies are also discussed.

Before reading the chapter, take a moment to consider what you think could make behaviours like eating or substance use problematic. What do you think would place an individual at risk of developing problems with eating or substance use? Do you think biological, psychological, or social factors play a key role in the development of problems in these domains? If a person were seeking help for a maladaptive lifestyle behaviour, what kind of treatment would you recommend? Would you see abstinence as the only option or do you think moderation would also work for some substances like alcohol?

People engage in eating and substance use behaviours for various reasons, including social pressure, modelling by peers, and other cultural factors. It is important to remember that eating and substance use have high potential to be maladaptive in response to negative feelings and challenging situations. **Maladaptive behaviours** are defined as behaviours that interfere with the acquisition or use of skills needed for successful adaption and adjustment to situations (McGrew & Bruininks, 1990). We all face stressors in our daily life. However, when we do not have the skills to manage and cope with daily stressors, we often do something (e.g., drink alcohol) to forget about stressors or challenges rather than dealing with or solving the problems that cause the stress. Once a person engages in eating or substance-use behaviours in response to stress, the behaviours have the potential to become habitual responses to negative emotions. The individual may begin to believe that eating or substance-use behaviours are helpful and essential in the management of personal distress.

Although abnormal patterns of eating and substance use can be pleasurable in the short term, they can have long-term negative outcomes. For example, if from previous experience a person has learned that having a couple of drinks has a calming effect, he or she may be likely to engage in the same behaviour in future stressful situations. Though this behaviour (i.e., drinking) may serve to reduce distress in the short term, it is unhelpful in the longer term and does not help the drinker adaptively address the actual stressors (e.g., preparing for exams). Furthermore, drinking may cause more harm to the individual's situation. For example, if someone who is stressed about preparing for exams decides to drink in order to calm down, he or she may end up drinking too much and then not be able to study for the exams. Evidence suggests, for example, that alcohol can impair cognitive performance (Xiao et al., 2013). It is important to examine how maladaptive eating and substance-use behaviours can negatively affect people's lives and how health psychologists may be able to help them engage in healthier and more effective coping strategies.

People often develop problems with maladaptive behaviours (e.g., overeating, smoking, and drug use) at a relatively young age. Nonetheless, problems related to eating and substance use can develop at any age. These behaviours are usually acquired over time and may start as experimentation and/or in response to social pressure and influence. Many maladaptive behaviours can become excessive and impact a person's quality of life and his or her family and friends. As you read this chapter, you will recognize some core risk factors for maladaptive eating and substance use, including genetic predisposition and the influence of psychosocial factors.

Eating Behaviour

Eating not only is essential for survival but also plays an important role in social activities and celebrations. As a child develops, feeding and nurturing play an important role in the bonding process with parents and caretakers. Eating also influences a person's physiological, psychological, and emotional states. Eating behaviour, however, can become a cause for concern when it becomes excessive or abnormal (De Ridder, De Vet, Stok, Adriaanse, & De Wit, 2013). Both overeating and undereating can be a cause for concern and may result in an unhealthy dietary lifestyle and potentially an eating disorder (e.g., **anorexia nervosa**).

Though it is difficult to specify the exact nutrient requirements for a healthy diet, healthy eating can be defined as a food intake pattern that results in health benefits rather than harm (De Ridder, Kroese, Evers, Adriaanse, & Gillebaart, 2017). Some common features of a healthy diet suggested by several dietary guidelines include a diet high in vegetables and fruits and low in saturated fat, sugar, and salt. Healthy diets are also rich in polyunsaturated fatty acids (found in sources such as nuts and fish), whole grains and fibre, low-fat or non-fat dairy, fish, legumes, and nuts and low in refined grains and saturated fatty acids (Wirt & Collins, 2009).

Along with eating healthy foods, it is important to eat the right amount of food. A person's body requires a specific amount of food energy or calories to maintain bodily function while at rest, called the **basal metabolic rate (BMR)**. An individual's BMR is dependent on several factors including age, sex, weight, activity level, body composition, and genetics (De Ridder et al., 2017). A common way of determining if adults are overweight or underweight is through the body mass index (BMI) (De Ridder et al., 2017). People are categorized based on various factors including sex and age. Generally, among adults between the ages of 20 and 65 years, those with a BMI less than 18.5 are categorized as underweight, 18.5 to 24.9 as healthy, 25 to 29.9 as overweight, 30 to 39.9 as obese, and above 40 as extreme or morbidly obese (World Health Organization, 2000) (see Figure 6.1).

$$BMI = \frac{Weight\ (kg)}{[Height\ (m)]^2}$$

Though the BMI is considered a standard tool for assessing body weight, it has several limitations. For example, an individual with a BMI in the overweight range who maintains a healthy diet and exercises may be more fit than someone with a healthy BMI who is sedentary and eats unhealthy foods. Additionally, someone who exercises and lifts weights may have large amounts of muscle resulting in higher BMI but lower body fat compared to someone who does not. Hence, when evaluating body weight, it is important to look beyond BMI. Examination of eating behaviour patterns is important. Normal eating patterns are dependent on the person and can be very flexible. Generally, people eat when they are hungry and stop eating when they are satisfied. But other external signals, for example, smell or exposure to foods (such as attractive displays of food), and psychological factors, such as stress or boredom, can all influence eating behaviour.

Now that you've had a chance to look at how eating behaviours can be adaptive and part of a healthy lifestyle, let's look at what distinguishes this from maladaptive eating. Maladaptive eating behaviour can occur when a person places too much importance on eating and body size and shape (De Ridder et al., 2017). Overeating resulting in obesity can be maladaptive, as can undereating resulting in malnutrition. Both overeating and excessive dieting can be maladaptive and may be related to eating disorders such as bulimia and anorexia nervosa.

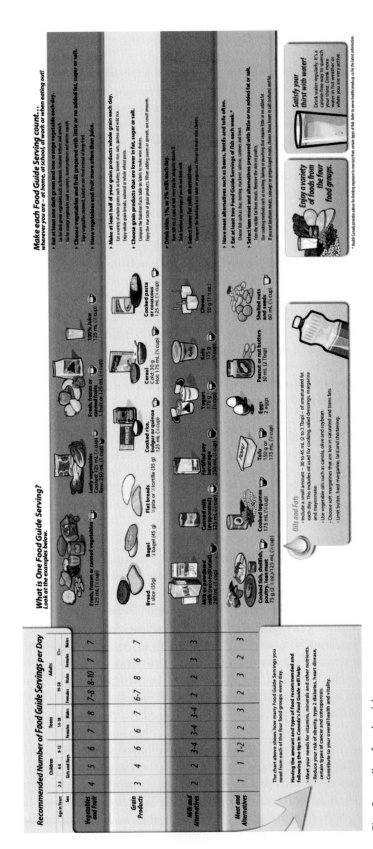

The Canadian food guide.

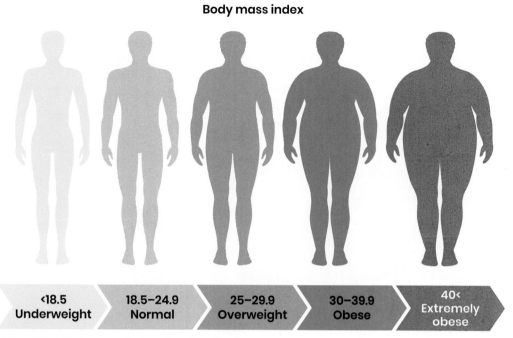

Body mass index

| <18.5 Underweight | 18.5–24.9 Normal | 25–29.9 Overweight | 30–39.9 Obese | 40< Extremely obese |

FIGURE 6.1 Body mass index classification.

Source: MarShot/Shutterstock.com

Obesity

Did you know that obesity has been shown to be a greater contributor to poor health than malnutrition? Global estimates by the World Health Organization (WHO; 2017a) have shown that almost two billion adults are overweight. Of these individuals, over 600 million are obese. In Canada, prevalence of obesity among adults increased from 6.1 per cent to 18.3 per cent from 1985 to 2011 (Twells, Gregory, Reddigan, & Midodzi, 2014). Figure 6.2 shows obesity rates across Canada. The increase in obesity is an especially important concern among the Canadian Indigenous populations where relatively higher rates of obesity have been observed (see Chapter 15 focusing on health disparities) (Kolahdooz, Sadeghirad, Corriveau, & Sharma, 2017). Traditionally, these populations were likely to have a diet of nutrient-dense foods such as caribou, moose, and deer found in the Northern environment (Sharma, 2010). Eating habits have since changed with a decline in eating traditional foods and increased consumption of high-fat and -sugar foods (Kolahdooz et al., 2017). Additionally, limited access to fresh vegetables and fruits has added to the increased prevalence of obesity and related chronic diseases including diabetes (Bruce, Riediger, Zacharias, & Young, 2010). Reduced participation in traditional activities such as hunting among the Indigenous population has decreased levels of physical activity, which has likely contributed to weight increases (Curtis, Kvernmo, Bjerregaard, 2005; Kolahdooz et al., 2017). Increased consumption of high-sugar foods and beverages has resulted in greater daily caloric intake in other populations as well. In the United States, for example, total average daily calorie intake increased from 1803 kcal in the 1970s to 2375 kcal by 2006 (Duffey & Popkin, 2011). Figure 6.3 shows obesity rates across the United States. Counter to the situation in the United States, average caloric consumption does not appear to have increased, over the same time period, in the general Canadian population (Garriguet, 2007). As such, the possibility that a wide variety of other factors (e.g., changes in sleep patterns, increased use of medications with weight gain as a side effect, food pollutants that can affect our hormonal systems) could have contributed to observed population weight increases (Keith et al., 2006).

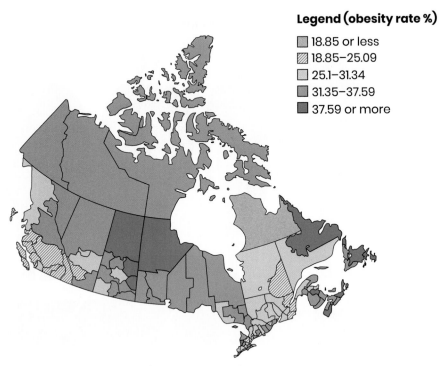

FIGURE 6.2 Rates of obesity across Canada.

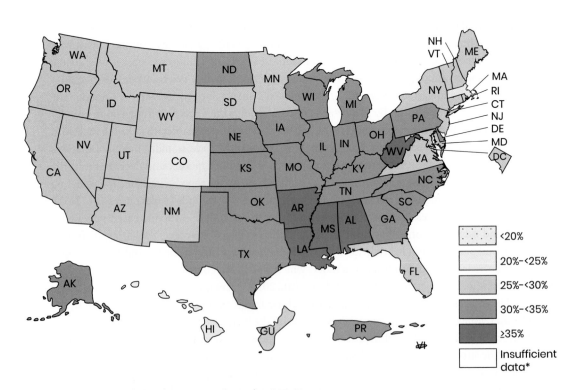

FIGURE 6.3 Rates of obesity across the United States.

Source: Centers for Disease Control and Prevention (2017).

Obesity has a direct impact on every aspect of health, potentially contributing to impairments in physical, psychological, and social functioning. Physical impairments can result through a variety of pathways; excess weight can lead to mechanical stress on the body and imbalances in hormones and metabolism. A meta-analysis showed that among men and women with a BMI greater than 30, there was a 7-fold and 12-fold increase respectively, in developing type 2 **diabetes** compared to those in the normal BMI range (Guh et al., 2009). The meta-analysis also demonstrated direct association between high BMI and specific cancers including breast, colon, rectum, endometrium, kidney, ovary, and pancreas. BMI was also related to cardiovascular risk factors including high blood pressure, low-density lipoprotein cholesterol, blood triglycerides, and inflammation (see Chapter 10).

Along with the physical problems, obesity impacts a person's psychological and social functioning. People who are obese are

Obesity is a risk factor for the development of the following diseases:

Infarction
Stroke
Hypertension
Angina pectoris
Atherosclerosis
Obesity of the heart

Diabetes
Cholecystitis
Pancreatitis
Gastritis
Violation of the endocrine function of the pancreas
Urolithiasis disease
Obesity of the liver
Constipation

Gout
Osteoarthritis
Osteochondrosis
Spondylosis
Flat-footedness

Picture Store/Shutterstock.com

Physical consequences of obesity.

often stigmatized by those with whom they interact, including health-care professionals. This can result in increased stress, social alienation, and low self-esteem (Culbert, Racine, & Klump, 2015). A meta-analysis of 15 studies involved participants who were followed for over 25 years, and showed that people who were obese had a 55 per cent greater risk of developing depression than those who were not obese. Furthermore, those who had heightened levels of depressive symptoms to begin with had a 58 per cent greater risk of becoming obese in the longer term (Luppino et al., 2010). This research demonstrates the impact obesity can have on psychological well-being and also how psychological well-being adversely impacts obesity. Later in the chapter, you will be able to explore how psychologists can work with other professionals such as nutritionists to help improve maladaptive eating behaviours of people who are obese.

Dieting

It is easy to see how excessive eating can result in long-term negative health outcomes. Frequently losing and regaining weight is often referred to as **yo-yo dieting** or weight cycling and can be particularly problematic (Khawandanah & Tewfik, 2016). Diets are often not evidence-based and may not provide people with an adequate amount of calories and nutrients. Some fad diets can result in several negative health consequences. When weight loss is expedited, much of the loss can be water and muscle rather than fat tissue. People may also have lower nutrient and energy intake due to limited food consumption.

Importantly, the weight loss achieved through dieting alone may only last for a short period of time and there may not be long-term maintenance of the weight loss. The percentage of dieters adhering to diet regiments over extended periods of time is generally low (Alhassan, Kim, Bersamin,

King, & Gardner, 2008). This suggests that, for large portions of people, many diet programs may be unsustainable in the long term. One of the main explanations for the lack of long-term weight loss maintenance is unsuccessful lifestyle change and absence of psychological maintenance interventions following successful diets. Presence of external psychosocial cues (e.g., how much others eat in the social environment) can also contribute to failure in maintaining a diet (e.g., Vartanian, Herman, & Wansink, 2008). Successful weight loss maintenance often involves a focus on the development of individualized, appropriate, and realistic goals for healthier lifestyles (e.g., increases in physical activity) and improved eating habits. In addition, development of coping skills (e.g., strategies to help avoid unhealthy foods, changing maladaptive thoughts and beliefs about eating, keeping records of food intake, etc.) is typically necessary for long-term success.

Unhealthy dieting or weight-cycling behaviour can have physical and psychological implications on the functioning of an individual. Some evidence suggests that weight cycling may contribute to risk of cardiometabolic diseases, type 2 diabetes, and hypertension (Montani, Schutz, & Dulloo, 2015). Furthermore, psychological factors such as depression and anxiety may increase the risk of over-eating, which, in turn, could increase anxiety and depression (Puccio et al., 2017).

It is estimated that approximately 44 per cent of men and 65 per cent of women in the United States participate in some form of dieting (Andreyeva, Long, Henderson, & Grode, 2010). Substantial portions of adolescents also go on a diet. In a study of Canadian young people, 29 per cent of Grade 10 girls and 9 per cent of Grade 10 boys reported being on a diet or doing something else in order to lose weight (Boyce, 2004). Among young adults, particularly females, fashion magazines that promote extremely thin models may increase the likelihood of unhealthy dieting in some people (Montani et al., 2015). Role models in the entertainment and sports industries can also affect people's dieting behaviour (Montani et al., 2015). The healthiest approach would be to maintain as healthy a weight as possible through a sensible and healthy diet that is accompanied by positive lifestyle behaviours (e.g., a less sedentary lifestyle).

Eating Disorders

Eating disorders are usually characterized by serious disturbances in eating behaviour and extreme concern about body size or weight. These disorders can sometimes be life threatening if they are not managed effectively. There are three main categories of eating disorders: anorexia nervosa, **bulimia nervosa**, and **binge eating disorder**.

Anorexia nervosa is characterized by extreme weight loss (BMI <17.5) due to extremely low caloric intake stemming from an extreme fear of being overweight (Fairburn & Cooper, 2014). People with anorexia often spend a great deal of time thinking of food but they eat very little. They also tend to have abnormal perceptions of their body image. Many of these individuals see themselves as overweight even when they are dangerously thin (Fairburn & Cooper, 2014). Persons with bulimia nervosa can be distinguished from those with anorexia nervosa based on presence of **binge eating** and purging episodes. Binge eating is characterized by intake of (usually large amounts of food) with a sense of loss of control during the episodes (Fairburn & Cooper, 2014). People with bulimia also engage in purging behaviour such as vomiting or taking laxatives to rid the body of the excess calories (Fairburn & Cooper, 2014). Many individuals diagnosed with bulimia nervosa have a normal BMI.

Another common eating disorder is binge-eating disorder. It is characterized by food binges in which a person eats an excessive amount of food within a discrete period of time with a sense of lack of control during the binging episode. Unlike those with bulimia nervosa, these individuals do not engage in purging behaviour but may feel embarrassed, uncomfortable, or guilty about their food consumption. Individuals with binge-eating disorder often fall in the BMI range greater than 30 (Fairburn & Cooper, 2014).

Over the long term, eating disorders can result in several negative effects on physical health. People with anorexia, for example, may experience bone loss and be at greater risk for fractures (e.g., Legroux-Gerot, Vignau, Collier, & Cortet, 2005). Abnormalities in endocrine, cardiovascular, and gastrointestinal systems may develop (e.g., Mehler & Brown, 2015). Among women with anorexia nervosa, rates of fertility and maternity are greatly reduced (e.g., Ward, 2008). Dental damage as well as cardiac problems among those who engage in frequent vomiting may be typical (Westmoreland, Krantz, & Mehler, 2016). Frequent laxative use can cause serious gastrointestinal complications (Westmoreland et al., 2016). Moreover, comorbid psychological conditions such as depression and anxiety disorders are common among those with eating disorders (Fairburn & Harrison, 2003).

Risk Factors

Engaging in maladaptive eating behaviour is a result of a complex set of biological, psychological, and social risk factors (Figure 6.4) that interplay and influence the person's initial exploratory stages and the long-term maintenance of the behaviour.

Biological

Twin and adoption studies have demonstrated that genetics influence the likelihood of becoming overweight in a number of ways (Ghosh & Bouchard, 2017). Firstly, genes are involved in determining a person's metabolic rate, which affects how fast calories are used up. Secondly, genetic

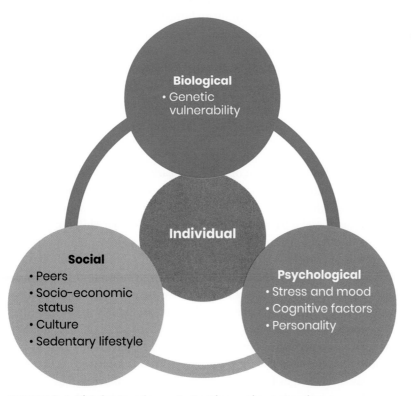

FIGURE 6.4 Risk factors for maladaptive eating behaviours with examples.

factors regulate hormones that are involved in fat storage and metabolism. Lastly, genes regulate energy balance within the organism and are involved in controlling food intake (Ghosh & Bouchard, 2017). A review of the literature reported heritability rates of obesity ranging from 40 to 70 per cent and concordance rates for obesity that were doubled in monozygotic twins (i.e., twin with identical genetic make-up) compared to dizygotic twins (i.e., twins who are as genetically related to each other as non-twin siblings) (Herrera & Lindgren, 2010). Of note, however, genetic factors interact with the environment and psychological factors, which can also increase or decrease the risk of the developing an eating disorder (Suisman et al., 2014; Trace, Baker, Peñas-Lledó, & Bulik, 2013) or obesity. It is important to emphasize that between 30 and 60 per cent of the time, one monozygotic twin is obese while the other is not, underscoring the importance of environmental influences on obesity.

Psychological

Stress is an important risk factor for maladaptive eating behaviours (De Ridder et al., 2017). Sinha and Jastreboff (2013) found that stress combined with anxiety disinhibits the self-control that usually prevents people from overeating. Stress also influences the types of food people eat. Those who are under stress are more likely to eat foods that are poor in nutrients but high in energy such as those with high sugar and fat content (Beydoun, 2014).

Several personality traits also have been associated with engaging in maladaptive eating behaviours. Impulsiveness is an important risk factor for overeating (Nederkoorn, Houben, Hofmann, Roefs, & Jansen, 2010). Other traits such as negative emotionality and neuroticism may also predict development of maladaptive eating behaviours (Cassin & von Ranson, 2005). Individuals with negative emotionality and neuroticism tend to have a disposition towards experiencing unpleasant emotions. Similar to stress eaters, those with negative emotionality are likely to use eating as a way of coping with negative feelings and situations (Cassin & von Ranson, 2005). Moreover, perfectionism has been shown to predict an increased risk of anorexia nervosa and bulimia nervosa symptoms among young females who have low self-esteem and perceive themselves to be overweight (Bardone-Cone et al., 2007). Those individuals with perfectionistic traits and body dissatisfaction are also likely to have an increased drive for thinness (Boone, Claes, & Luyten, 2014). These types of psychological factors underscore the potential utility of psychological interventions in the management of unhealthy eating behaviours.

Social

Peers are important in the development of abnormal eating patterns and practices. Social learning theory states that many behaviours are learned through observation of others' behaviour (Bandura, 1977). Research on peer modelling and food intake has shown that children may regulate their own food intake based on their peers or other older children (Salvy, De La Haye, Bowker, & Hermans, 2012). This relationship may be more significant among young girls than boys (Goldschmidt et al., 2014).

Socio-economic status (SES), including factors such as education level, work status, and income, are also important risk factors for being overweight and obese (see Chapter 15). Those in the lowest income sub-groups have a higher prevalence of obesity than those in the highest income sub-group (15 per cent vs 10 per cent, see Table 6.1) (Pan-Canadian Public Health Network, 2017). Lower SES has been associated with consumption of fewer healthy foods such as fresh vegetables and fruits and lower adherence to dietary guidelines (Pechey & Monsivais, 2016). This association was also true among children ages 4 to 13 years of age (De Jong & Bijleveld, 2015). People with lower SES are more likely to purchase food that is of lower quality and less nutritious since it costs less than food that is nutrient rich (Darmon & Dreqnowski, 2008). Another possibility is that those with lower education may have lower health literacy related to understanding nutritional labels and guidelines (Spronk, Kullen, Burdon, & O'Connor, 2014). Lastly, arguments have been put forward that there may be environmental differences between people with lower SES compared to higher SES. Low-SES neighborhoods in the United States, for instance, were found to be less likely to have stores that carry fruits and vegetables and more likely to include fast-food stores (Darmon & Drewnowski, 2008). In the Canadian setting, health inequalities related to food insecurity (i.e., inability to obtain a sufficient amount of healthy food) are experienced at a greater prevalence rate among those with the lowest income compared to the highest income (27 per cent vs 1 per cent) (Pan-Canadian Public Health Network, 2017). Additionally, food insecurity was more prevalent among Indigenous people living off reserve (27 per cent) compared to the non-Indigenous (9 per cent) population as seen in Table 6.1. Inadequate access to healthy foods can lead to increased consumption of unhealthy foods and obesity.

TABLE 6.1 | Prevalence of Obesity Based on Population Groups

Topic–Indicator	Population Groups[1]	Population Sub-groups	Multi-year Prevalence (%)	Confidence intervals
Health Weights— Obesity prevalence[i]	Income (household)	Lowest income	15.1 (E)[2]	8.0–22.2
		Middle income	14.4	11.4–17.3
		Highest income	9.8	7.8–11.8
	Education (household)	High school graduate or less	15.5	10.3–20.7
		Some post-secondary education or more	11.5	9.8–13.2
	Indigenous populations / visible minority status[4]	First Nations people living off reserve[3] / Inuit/Métis	18.2 (E)	7.1–29.2
		Visible minority	12.1	9.3–15.0
		Not a visible minority	11.7	9.8–13.6

i. *Obesity prevalence*—Body mass index (BMI) score equal to 30.0 or above, based on measured height and weight, population aged 6–17 years, Canadian Health Measures Survey (CHMS; 2009–2013)

1. Results are not directly comparable across population groups.

2. Cells with an (E) notation should be interpreted with caution, as the measure itself or at least one of the components used to calculate the value has a coefficient of variation between 16.6 per cent to 33.3 per cent.

3. To align with OCAP® principles, the Health Inequalities Data Tool does not include data from the First Nations Regional Health Survey (RHS), which is the leading source of health data for First Nations people living on reserve. As a result, data on First Nations people living on reserve are not included in this table. Efforts are being made to work with the First Nations Information Governance Centre to include information on this population sub-group in the 2019 progress report.

4. Obesity prevalence by Indigenous populations/visible minority status: for this indicator, due to the small sample size of the data source (CHMS), children were grouped into three broad sub-group categories large enough to support data disaggregation: Indigenous populations, Visible minority, and Not a visible minority. However, each of these population sub-groups contain high levels of internal heterogeneity. Consequently, while the observed differences in obesity prevalence between these sub-groups may signal real inequalities, the data should be interpreted with caution.

Culture may also be an important trigger for developing maladaptive eating behaviours (see Chapter 15). In the Western world, the ideal body image is often considered to be that of a long, lean, and well-muscled body. Society has developed a culture of thinness through media and advertisements. Media exposure and perceived pressure may be risk factors for maladaptive eating cognitions and behaviours, especially in females (Combs, Smith, Flory, Simmons, & Hill, 2010). However, despite exposure to the sociocultural messages, only some individuals internalize these ideals.

Another important risk factor for obesity is inactivity. Children who engage in sedentary lifestyles such as watching television or playing video games have an increased risk of obesity (Ervin, Kit, Carroll, & Ogden, 2012). Sedentary lifestyle in children is also related to greater intake of unhealthy snacks and drinks and in modelling parental physical inactivity (Ervin et al., 2012; Kozo et al., 2012).

Substance-Use Behaviours

Psychoactive substances are those substances that, when taken, can affect cognitive/mental and affective processes (WHO, 2017b). Did you know that throughout history psychoactive substances have been used in cultural ceremonies and as medical remedies? Psychoactive mushrooms, for example, were used by Indigenous people of pre-Columbian Mexico to induce states of trance in healing rituals and religious ceremonies (Carod-Artal, 2015). Other psychoactive substances, such as opium, were used by various cultures, like the Sumerian and the Greek, for their medicinal properties (Crocq, 2007).

The focus of this section is on substances that are commonly used for recreational purposes: alcohol, tobacco, and recreational drugs (Figure 6.5). Access to large quantities of these substances has increased in modern times and consequently there have been increased morbidity and mortality resulting from these substances (Ouzir & Errami, 2016). Substance abuse is specifically defined as the use of any psychoactive substance that results in "physical, psychological, legal, or social harm to the individual or to others affected by the user's behaviour" (Maisto, Galizio, & Connors, 2011). There is a growing concern about the impact of substance abuse on health impairment around the globe.

There are different ways of defining substance-use issues. **Intoxication** is a state during which the individual has diminished physical or mental control due to the effects of psychoactive substances. **Substance-use disorders** are patterns of symptoms resulting from use of a substance, that the individual continues to take, despite experiencing problems as a result (American Psychiatric Association, 2013). As an example, Table 6.2 provides the 11 symptoms for the diagnosis for alcohol-use disorder. Mild alcohol-use disorder requires two to three symptoms on the list, moderate requires four to five, and severe six or more. **Tolerance** is defined as a need for markedly increased amounts of the substance to achieve intoxication or desired effect. Withdrawal occurs for a time period after an individual who is addicted to a substance stops consuming it, resulting in unpleasant physical and psychological symptoms. These symptoms can include nausea, tremors, headaches, hallucinations, irritability, and anxiety (American Psychiatric Association, 2013).

Substances can be taken orally, through an injection, or by inhalation. Oral administration or swallowing is one of the most common methods and can involve pills, capsules, powders, or liquids. Substances can also be injected into the body through needles and syringes (Maisto et al., 2011). Injection is the riskiest form of administration. It can result in immediate medical complications and long-term conditions such as hepatitis, HIV, and tetanus if non-sterile needles are used. Since an

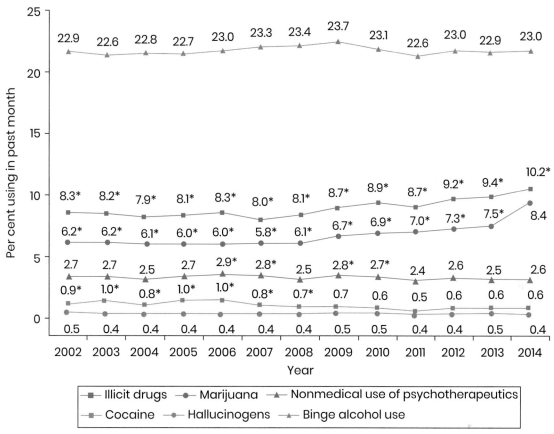

FIGURE 6.5 **Trends of psychoactive substance use in the United States. Reproduced from the Surgeon General's Report.**

Source: U.S. Department of Health & Human Services (2016).

individual is likely to experience immediate effects of the psychoactive substance using injection, this is often the method preferred by people who are dependent and addicted to substances. Inhalation is also a common form of administration that results in fast absorption (Maisto et al., 2011).

Recreational substances are classified into different categories including depressants, stimulants, and hallucinogens. Depressants are substances that slow down the activity of the central nervous system and result in the individual feeling less pain, more relaxed, and sleepy. Stimulants are drugs that heighten mood, increase alertness, and decrease fatigue by speeding up the activity of the central nervous system. Lastly, hallucinogens are a category of substances that result in perceptual and sensory disturbances by distorting messages from the central nervous system (Maisto et al., 2011). Table 6.3 provides examples of the different substances within each category. In the next few sections we will examine the effects of some of the most common substances.

Alcohol

Alcohol is a depressant that slows down the central nervous system. It is usually ingested as a liquid and readily absorbed into the bloodstream. The amount of alcohol in the bloodstream is the **blood alcohol level** (Maisto et al., 2011). Heavy drinking can be defined as a pattern of

TABLE 6.2 | Diagnostic Criteria for Alcohol-Use Disorder

1. Alcohol is often taken in larger amounts or over a longer period than was intended.

2. There is a persistent desire or unsuccessful efforts to cut down or control alcohol use.

3. A great deal of time is spent in activities necessary to obtain alcohol, use alcohol, or recover from its effects.

4. Craving, or a strong desire or urge to use alcohol.

5. Recurrent alcohol use resulting in a failure to fulfill major role obligations at work, school, or home.

6. Continued alcohol use despite having persistent or recurrent social or interpersonal problems caused or exacerbated by the effects of alcohol.

7. Important social, occupational, or recreational activities are given up or reduced because of alcohol use.

8. Recurrent alcohol use in situations in which it is physically hazardous.

9. Alcohol use is continued despite knowledge of having a persistent or recurrent physical or psychological problem that is likely to have been caused or exacerbated by alcohol.

10. Tolerance, as defined by either of the following: a) A need for markedly increased amounts of alcohol to achieve intoxication or desired effect b) a markedly diminished effect with continued use of the same amount of alcohol.

11. Withdrawal, as manifested by either of the following: a) The characteristic withdrawal syndrome for alcohol (refer to criteria A and B of the criteria set for alcohol withdrawal) b) alcohol (or a closely related substance, such as a benzodiazepine) is taken to relieve or avoid withdrawal symptoms.

Reproduced from American Psychiatric Association (2013).

Source: American Psychiatric Association. (2013). *Diagnostic and statistical manual of mental disorders* (5th ed.). Arlington, VA: American Psychiatric Publishing. Reprinted with permission from the Diagnostic and Statistical Manual of Mental Disorders, Fifth Edition, (Copyright ©2013). American Psychiatric Association. All Rights Reserved.

TABLE 6.3 | Categories of Drugs

Depressants	Stimulants	Hallucinogens
Alcohol	Nicotine	Lysergic acid diethylamide (LSD)
Opiates	Cocaine	
Marijuana	Methylphenidate	Phencyclidine (PCP)
	Amphetamines	
	Methamphetamine	

Note: The above list provides examples of common drugs and is not all-inclusive.

drinking that brings blood alcohol level levels to 0.08 g/dL on 5 or more days in the past month (National Institute on Alcohol Abuse and Alcoholism, 2015). Approximately 26.9 per cent of people aged 18 or older have engaged in binge drinking and 7 per cent in heavy alcohol use in the last month in the United States (National Institute on Alcohol Abuse and Alcoholism, 2015). Moreover, approximately 19 per cent of Canadians aged 12 or older were classified as heavy drinkers (Statistics Canada, 2016). Other research has also demonstrated that males are almost three times more likely than females to have alcohol-use problems (Lev-Ran, Le Strat, Imtiaz, Rehm, & Le Foll, 2013).

Alcohol use tends to begin early in an individual's lifetime. A large concern among young adults is binge drinking (Figures 6.6 and 6.7). Young adults encounter numerous social and cultural influences through movies, other media, and their peers that suggest binge drinking is normal activity for young people. Such influences can result in adolescents and young adults engaging in risky behaviour. Substance abuse often occurs in college and university environments as many students move away from home and have access to alcohol and other drugs (Arria et al., 2013). How do you feel your campus fares relative to other campuses in excessive drinking behaviour by students? Are you aware of any support systems on campus to help manage maladaptive drinking behaviours?

Alcohol can have important psychosocial consequences for the individual. Use of alcohol has been associated with problems with attention, anxiety, and depressive symptoms and can increase the risk of developing psychological symptoms (Boden & Fergusson, 2011; Strandheim, Coombes, Bentzen, Holmen, 2009). Alcohol problems have also been associated with increased suicidal ideation as well as suicide attempts and completions (Darvishi, Farhadi, Haghtalab, & Poorolajal, 2015; Norström & Rossow, 2016). Vulnerability to suicide attempts may increase while engaging in heavy alcohol use, especially when other risk factors such as financial distress (Kaplan et al., 2016; Kerr et al., 2017) or depressive symptoms (Grazioli et al., 2018) are present.

Conduct problems have also been strongly associated with alcohol use (Strandheim et al., 2009). Long-term heavy consumption of alcohol has been a major cause of liver cirrhosis resulting in death. Long-term abuse can also result in widespread effects on the brain structure and function

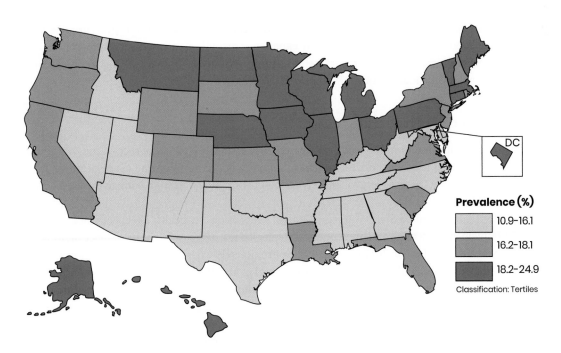

FIGURE 6.6 **Prevalence of binge drinking among adults in the United States, 2015.**

Source: Centers for Disease Control and Prevention (2017).

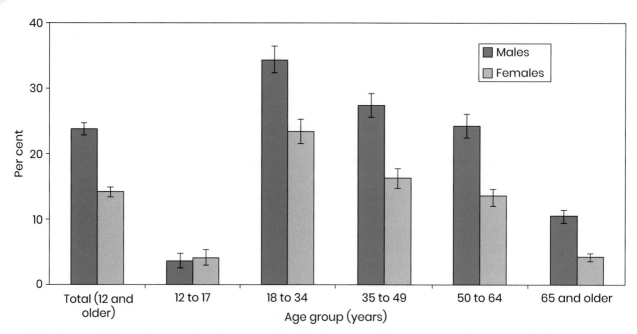

Note: Heavy drinking refers to males who reported having 5 or more drinks, or women who reported having 4 or more drinks, on one occasion, at least once a month in the past year. 95% confidence intervals are denoted by vertical lines overlaid on the bars in this chart. They indicate the degree of variability in the estimates.

FIGURE 6.7 Prevalence of heavy drinking in Canada, 2016.

Source: Statistics Canada (2017).

(Xiao et al., 2013). Heavy drinking during pregnancy can cause **fetal alcohol spectrum disorder (FASD)**, a condition in which the child may experience mental impairment, stunted growth, and facial abnormalities. Guidelines recommend refraining from alcohol use during the pregnancy (Butt, Beirness, Gliksman, Paradis, & Stockwell, 2011).

Tobacco and Nicotine

Nicotine, which is found in tobacco and cigarettes, is addictive and is the second most common psychoactive drug used in the United States. Smoking is the number one cause of preventable deaths (Centers for Disease Control and Prevention [CDC], 2017). At high enough doses, nicotine is lethal (Mayer, 2014).

Based on the United States Surgeon General's report on the health effects of smoking from 1969, implementation of several prevention strategies led to a decrease in the prevalence of smoking by 50 per cent from 1965 to 2011 (CDC, 2017). Approximately 4.6 million Canadians (Government of Canada, 2017) and 36.5 million Americans (Jamal et al., 2016), however, still smoke cigarettes. Like alcohol and other substance use, smoking behaviour starts at a young age. According to the CDC, 9 out of 10 cigarette smokers first tried smoking by the age of 18 (Jamal et al., 2016). Peers play an important role in cigarette use and young females are especially susceptible to use cigarettes based on their peer's attitudes (Mason, Mennis, Linker, Bares, & Zaharakis, 2014).

Although the detrimental effects of smoking are well-established, some smokers report that smoking temporarily enhances their cognitive functioning (Evans & Drobes, 2009). Indeed, nicotine may temporarily facilitate motor and cognitive processes (including fine motor, attention accuracy, and response time) and short-term episodic memory (Evans & Drobes 2009; Heishman, Kleykamp, & Singleton, 2010). On the other hand, given the addictive nature of nicotine, the withdrawal period tends be accompanied by cognitive difficulties such as concentration problems (Ashare, Falcone, & Lerman, 2014; Sweet et al., 2010).

The American Cancer Society classifies tobacco as a **carcinogen** (see https://www.cancer .org/cancer/cancer-causes/general-info/known-and-probable-human-carcinogens.html). A carcinogen is a substance that may initiate alterations in the genetic makeup of the individual resulting in prolific growth of cells at an uncontrollable level. Smoking has been associated with impaired health including lung cancer, respiratory illness, development of nicotine addiction, and a variety of cardiovascular diseases (Milara & Cortijo, 2012). Smoking can lead to bronchial congestion through the production of mucus in the throat and lungs and damage of cilia in the respiratory tract.

Along with its health effects on the individual, smoking has been shown to result in health-care costs of over 97 billion dollars per year in the United States (Jamal et al., 2016). Smoking can also reduce the health of people exposed to second-hand smoke. Second-hand smoke has been shown to reduce blood oxygen capacity and increase levels of carbon monoxide. Exposure to second-hand smoke has been linked to sudden infant death syndrome, which is a main cause of death among babies within the first year of their life (Jamal et al., 2016).

Other Drugs

Marijuana or cannabis is one of the most popular recreational drugs worldwide after alcohol and cigarettes (i.e., nicotine). Over 43 per cent of Canadians aged 15 years or older report having tried marijuana (Statistics Canada, 2012). Similarly, 44 per cent of Americans aged 12 or older reported use of marijuana, with the highest rate (52 per cent) among those aged 18 to 25 (National Institute on Drug Abuse, 2016). Smoking marijuana has been associated with respiratory dysfunction and increased risk of chronic obstructive pulmonary disease (Tan et al., 2009). Due to recent or pending changes in laws related to decriminalization or legalization of marijuana in some jurisdictions, there has been an increase in access to marijuana and as a result a modest increase in risk of motor vehicle collisions and deaths (Hall, 2015). In Canada, marijuana-related costs of collisions were highest amongst young adults (Wettlaufer et al., 2017).

In the last decade, there also has been a sharp increase in nonmedicinal use of prescribed opioid drugs (Atluri, Sudarshan, & Manchikanti, 2014). Opioids are sedative drugs used to help alleviate pain among various chronic pain populations. Approximately 15 per cent of young adults and 6 per cent of adults have been found to misuse non-medically prescribed opioids in Ontario (Fischer et al. 2013). Opioid misuse can adversely affect the respiratory system, with high concentrations of opioids causing the individual to stop breathing and suffocating (Jungquist, Flannery, Perlis, & Grace, 2012). Long-term opioid use can also result in cognitive impairments such as deficits in spatial and working memory performance (Schiltenwolf et al., 2014). Risks are substantially reduced when opioids are taken appropriately as prescribed.

Risk Factors

As with the risk factors related to maladaptive eating behaviour, it is important to examine biological, psychological, and social factors that put individuals at risk for substance-use problems.

In Focus

Legalization of Marijuana

Did you know that the Netherlands decriminalized the personal use of marijuana in 1976? Most other nations, however, continued to prohibit marijuana use. Recently, the Canadian government, under Prime Minister Justin Trudeau, outlined a plan to legalize marijuana in Canada. Jurisdictions in the United States and Australia have also considered or passed relevant legislation. Why the sudden shift in policy? Is it a shift in cultural acceptance? Various factors are linked to the changes in policies. There is emerging evidence of potentially therapeutic effects of medically prescribed cannabis for people with certain pain-related conditions. Another factor that has driven the shift in policy towards use of marijuana is the rise in costs related to policing drug offenders (Pacula & Smart, 2017). Moreover, opening the use of marijuana into the legal trade market may help bring in new sources of funding for the government through increased tax revenue (Caulkins & Bond, 2012; Kilmer, 2014).

Despite these changes in policy and advocacy for its use in medicine, the use of marijuana remains controversial. First it is important to understand the difference between decriminalization vs

Biological

Genetic vulnerabilities may interact with the person's environment and make the individual more susceptible to substance-use problems (Enoch, 2012; Hart & Kranzler, 2015). It is important to remember that for most psychological concerns, including substance use, heredity is not destiny. Although some people may inherit a genetic predisposition that makes them more susceptible to substance-use problems, environmental and psychological influences (e.g., social support and coping skills) are key in determining whether substance-use problems will develop. In the most extreme case, a person will not develop problems with alcohol if he or she never encounters alcohol in his or her life. Moreover, despite genetic predispositions, substance-use problems can be overcome with treatment and even, sometimes, without treatment.

Psychological

Stress can increase the risk of substance-use problems. There is growing evidence that people who have experienced various forms of trauma, including peer victimization or sexual and physical abuse, are at increased risk of developing substance-use problems, perhaps in an effort to manage negative feelings (Whitesell, Bachand, Peel, & Brown, 2013). Among adolescents, peer victimization can play a large role in the development of maladaptive substance-use behaviours (Earnshaw et al., 2017).

People experiencing negative emotional states such as anxiety often engage in problem drinking (e.g., Sabourin & Stewart, 2007). According to the tension-reduction hypothesis, people who believe that alcohol consumption will reduce the stress response are more likely to engage in stress-related drinking (Menary et al., 2015; Rutledge & Sher, 2001). It is important to note, however, that support for the tension-reduction hypothesis has been inconsistent (Menary et al., 2015), suggesting that it can explain drinking behaviour in some but not all situations. Some people may drink because they expect to improve mood and self-esteem (Chassin, Sher, Hussong, & Curran, 2013). For example, they may associate alcohol use with pleasant mood and reduced stress and may begin to drink before social events (Emslie, Hunt, & Lyons, 2015).

legalization. When a substance is decriminalized, it means that having that substance for personal use is not a criminal offence (although, depending on the jurisdiction, it may still be illegal). Legalization of a substance use goes further than decriminalization in that it removes any penalties or criminal offences related to use of the substance.

One of the major concerns regarding legalization of marijuana is related to how to monitor its intake (Schauer, King, Bunnell, Promoff, & McAfee, 2016). Since there are various ways of consuming marijuana (e.g., smoking or eating it), how do we monitor how much is being consumed? We are still not sure how having larger supplies of the substance in the hands of the general population will affect society, including its impact on health and financial markets (Caulkins & Bond, 2012). Another concern regarding marijuana legalization is the regulation of driving after marijuana use. As policies shift, methods for determining impairment while driving must be evaluated. Specially trained police officers may use direct observation along with urine samples to detect use of marijuana. It's important to keep these issues and others in mind when examining how to evaluate the current state of marijuana use in your community. What do you think about the legalization of marijuana? Do you think the potential benefits outweigh the risks?

Although research shows that alcohol is often used in an effort to self-medicate when individuals experience increased levels of negative affect and challenges (Frone, 2016), those who use alcohol or drugs to relieve symptoms of distress are more likely to have persistent anxiety and personality disorders than those who do not (Bolton, Robinson, & Sareen, 2009).

Several personality traits have also been implicated as risk factors for substance-use behaviours. One of the most common is impulsiveness. Impulsiveness has been studied in misuse of alcohol (Dick et al., 2010), as well as in relation to smoking and recreational drugs (Elkins, King, McGue, & Iacono, 2006; Hittner & Swickert, 2006). Impulsiveness strongly correlates with age and an individual's developmental stage. A decline in impulsiveness has been seen from adolescence to adulthood (Harden & Tucker-Drob, 2011). Other traits such as antisocial personality and problems with externalizing behaviours, including bullying or physical assault, also tend to be associated with more substance-misuse behaviours such as heavy episodic drinking (Chassin, Pitts, & Prost, 2002).

Social

Peer relationships are important and can influence behaviours such as smoking and substance use. Conformity to peers is especially important during adolescence as youth seek social acceptance (Onrust, Otten, Lammers, & Smit, 2016). Adolescents become concerned about their role in the social environment. As such, within a social environment, they may disregard the risks associated with using substances (Onrust et al., 2016). During adolescence, reward-seeking behaviours in the presence of peers and risk-taking behaviours begin to increase. Drinking and substance use during social activities may be seen by some adolescents as normal. Individuals with peers who already engage in substance use are more likely to report higher levels of substance use than those without such peers (MacArthur, Sean, Deborah, Matthew, & Rona, 2016).

Familial environments can also influence the development of substance-use issues. A person may learn to use alcohol as a celebratory response from family gatherings and parties. Children may also grow up learning to use substances to cope with stress and negative situations (Whitesell et al., 2013). Family history of substance use has been shown to increase likelihood of children engaging in substance use (Leonardi-Bee, Jere, & Britton, 2011). This could be partly due to the overlap between the genetic contributions and modelling behaviours.

Media also play an important role in the development of substance use, and can do so through direct and indirect messaging. Direct messaging is usually through advertisements of alcohol or tobacco. In the United States between 2001 and 2009, alcohol advertising increased by 71 per cent (Center on Alcohol Marketing and Youth, 2012). Although most of the related research has been conducted in the United States, a Canadian report indicated that almost one-third of the complaints upheld by Advertising Standards Canada in 1998 were for advertisements promoting alcoholic beverages (Advertising Standards Canada, 1998; McKenzie, 2000). It is noted that indirect marketing strategies promote use of substances through images and dialogues. These indirect messages can influence adolescent's perceptions of substance-use desirability and result in increased use (Scull, Kupersmidt, & Erausquin, 2014).

Assessment

When working with people who present with maladaptive eating and substance-use behaviours, health psychologists typically begin by obtaining a detailed clinical history of the individual. This helps identify any history of mental health concerns; medical and comorbidities; biological, psychological and social risk factors; lifestyle characteristics; personal strengths; and prior attempts to manage the problem. Evaluation of an individual's readiness and motivation to change is also important. As described in Chapter 5, a person's stage of change can have important implications for management needs and adherence to treatment. Evaluation of other sociocultural factors, including family and peer support systems, can help to provide a greater understanding of the many factors that may influence maladaptive behaviours. Most often clients are asked to monitor the problem behaviour using diaries designed to identify the antecedents and consequences of the problem behaviour (e.g., what happens before and after overeating). These diaries can later be used to guide treatment. Specific questionnaires focusing on the problem eating and substance-use behaviours are also available to assist with the assessment process.

Eating

Assessment of overeating behaviour may involve the calculation of the client's BMI, which can be estimated during the clinical interview. When assessing overeating, it is important to determine whether or not an eating disorder such as bulimia nervosa is present. Several questionnaires for evaluating eating disorders including the Clinical Impairment Assessment (CIA) (Bohn & Fairburn, 2008) (see Table 6.4) and the Eating Disorder Examination Questionnaire (EDE-Q) (Fairburn & Beglin, 2008) are available.

Two measures have been validated for a primary-care setting in order to screen for potential eating issues. The Eating Disorder Screen for Primary Care (ESP) (Cotton, Ball, Robinson, 2003) (Sample item: Do you ever eat in secret?) and SCOFF Questionnaire (Morgan, Reid, & Lacey, 1999) (Sample item: Do you worry you have lost control over how much you eat?) are short tools that can help primary-care physicians determine if an individual may be experiencing maladaptive eating behaviours.

TABLE 6.4 | Selected Items from the Clinical Impairment Assessment Questionnaire

Over the past 28 days, to what extent have your ... eating habits ... exercising or feelings about your eating, shape, or weight ...	Not at all	A little	Quite a bit	A lot
1. ... made it difficult to concentrate?				
3. ... stopped you going out with others?				
11. ... made you feel guilty?				
14. ... made you feel a failure?				

Reproduced from: Bohn, K., & Fairburn, C. G. (2008). The clinical impairment assessment questionnaire (CIA 3.0). In C.G. Fairburn (Ed.), *Cognitive behavior therapy and eating disorders* [Appendix III]. New York: Guildford Press.

Substance Use

Various measures can help with the initial assessment of substance-use problems. The Alcohol, Smoking, and Substance Involvement Screening Tool (ASSIST) is a comprehensive measure developed by the WHO to help health professionals assess and manage any substance-use issue in the primary-care setting (WHO ASSIST Working Group, 2002). The CAGE Questionnaire Adapted to Include Drugs (CAGE-AID) (Brown & Rounds, 1995) is a short and valid tool to screen for both alcohol and drug use.

Alcohol-specific self-report measures such as the Alcohol Use Disorders Identification Test (AUDIT) (Saunders, Aasland, Babor, De la Fuente, & Grant, 1993), CAGE, which stands for "Cutting down, Annoyance by criticism, Guilty feelings, and Eye openers" (Ewing, 1984), and Michigan Alcoholism Screening Test (MAST) (Selzer, Vanosdall, & Chapman, 1971) are valid tools to screen for alcohol misuse. Among adolescents, the Brief Screener for Tobacco, Alcohol, and Other Drugs (BSTAD) can be used to examine frequency of use in the past year (Kelly et al., 2014). If a client acknowledges using substances in the past year, the questionnaire will also ask which substance was used. Individuals are then placed into three categories of risk: low, moderate, and high.

The Drug Use Disorders Identification Test (DUDIT) (Berman, Bergman, Palmstierna, & Schlyter, 2005) and the Drug Use Questionnaire (DAST) (Skinner, 1982) identify people likely to engage in drug use. The DAST-20 has an adult and adolescent version, while the DAST-10 can be used with either group. DAST total scores are interpreted as none, low, intermediate, substantial, or severe risk in the last 12 months. The interpretation guide also provides suggested actions for each level of risk. Those individuals with total item scores at the intermediate risk are likely to meet diagnostic criteria

TABLE 6.5 | Sample Items from Drug Use Questionnaire 10 (DAST-10)

Questions	Yes	No
Have you used drugs other than those required for medical reasons?		
Are you always able to stop using drugs when you want to?		
Have you ever experienced withdrawal symptoms (felt sick) when you stopped taking drugs?		

Reproduced from: Skinner, H. A. (1982). The drug abuse screening test. *Addictive Behaviors, 7*(4), 363-371.

Management

When developing treatment programs for people with maladaptive lifestyle behaviours, clinicians tend to use strategies that promote patient engagement and education. Furthermore, developing an individual's resilience can improve his or her coping ability and serve as a protective factor for future challenges.

Many people who are referred for the management of substance use (e.g., through the legal system) are not necessarily motivated to overcome the substance-use problem. Motivational interviewing (MI) is a specific therapeutic strategy that involves building a collaborative relationship between the clinician and client in order to achieve behavioural change by enhancing client motivation to change (Elwyn et al. 2014; Miller & Rollnick, 1991). Its primary focus is to help clients identify and resolve any issues related to their motivation to change through examination of perceived barriers to change and of the advantages and disadvantages of change. The approach is patient centred and accepts that behaviour change is difficult and resistance to change is normal (Elwyn et al., 2014).

Most often when working with individuals with maladaptive lifestyle behaviours, health psychologists work collaboratively with other health-care professionals. For example, if working with a client with an eating disorder, the health psychologist may work collaboratively with a nutritionist and a physician. When assisting clients with substance-use problems, psychologists often work together with physicians who are responsible for medication management, if needed.

Cognitive behavioural approaches have shown promise in the treatment of maladaptive behaviour problems (see Chapter 1 for an overview of the theory behind the approach). Activities often include goal setting and behavioural exercises (e.g., relaxation training for stress management). In general, cognitive behavioural therapy focuses on helping clients identify and challenge dysfunctional thoughts and behaviours that are related to their lifestyle problem.

Cognitive behavioural therapy (CBT) is typically provided in individual face-to-face treatment or group format. There is also evidence that Internet-delivered cognitive behavioural therapy is efficacious in improving an individual's ability to develop effective coping skills and manage her or his eating (Fairburn et al., 2015; Melioli et al., 2016; Ruwaard et al., 2013; Wagner et al., 2016) and substance-use issues (Bickel, Christensen, & Marsch, 2011; Boumparis, Karyotaki, Schaub, Cuijpers, & Riper, 2017; Marsch & Dallery, 2012; McTavish, Chih, Shah, & Gustafson, 2012). These online interventions typically provide people with psychoeducational information in the form of online modules. This can be combined with weekly support from a therapist either over secure email or telephone.

A key element shared by cognitive behavioural approaches is relapse prevention (Marlatt & Gordon, 1985). Relapse has been found to remain a significant problem for 50 to 70 per cent of individuals with substance-use issues (McHugh, Hearon, & Otto, 2010). Hence, in addition to the different interventions mentioned below, it is important to incorporate relapse prevention techniques to ensure people do not fall back into the same maladaptive behaviour patterns. Relapse prevention approaches typically help clients identify high-risk situations and plan for how they will manage these situations. Role playing and rehearsing are common strategies used to assist with relapse prevention. In relapse prevention, occasional relapses are conceptualized as "slips" that can be overcome.

Eating

Medical management of maladaptive eating behaviours varies depending on the nature of the client problem. Inpatient treatment is common for people who experience life-threatening weight loss due to anorexia. Pharmacological treatment (e.g., appetite suppressants) and surgical procedures such as bariatric surgery (i.e., surgery that modifies the gastrointestinal tract to reduce capacity to eat large amounts of food) are sometimes used for obesity but involve risks of various complications (Lupoli et al., 2017).

When health psychologists work with individuals who present with maladaptive eating behaviours, they may conduct cognitive behavioural treatment (see Chapter 1). Such treatment often begins with self-monitoring and careful records of food intake that allow clients to become more aware of their eating behaviours and the antecedents of these behaviours. People also learn to control various environmental stimuli that can increase the risk of overeating. Psychoeducation about the health and psychological consequences of maladaptive eating behaviour are key components of management. Thoughts and beliefs about food, body shape, and other issues can be examined and challenged. Coping skills training also takes place. Incorporation of mindfulness exercises, such as meditation training, has also been shown to be helpful (O'Reilly, Cook, Spuijt-Metz, & Black, 2014). Other psychological approaches such as Acceptance and Commitment Therapy (ACT) are used to help people identify and accept emotional experiences (Keesman, Aarts, Hafner, & Papies, 2017) and to identify and participate in valued activities. ACT approaches are still new and further investigation into their efficacy is needed.

CBT programs have been shown to be effective in treating eating disorders (see Fairburn & Cooper, 2014). Moreover, CBT has also been effective in the facilitation of weight loss when combined with diet programs or other weight-loss interventions (e.g. bariatric surgery) (e.g., Doughty, Njike, & Katz, 2015; Gade, Hielmesaeth, Rosenvinge, & Friborg, 2014). CBT may facilitate necessary lifestyle changes for weight loss maintenance.

A variety of public health prevention programs aimed at individuals at high risk for eating-related problems have been developed, including media campaigns. Media messages appear to help reduce rates of maladaptive eating behaviours (De Ridder et al., 2017). In terms of obesity, nutrition and physical-activity education programs have been developed that target families of lower SES and assist parents and children in learning about sensible eating and activity patterns. Lifestyle interventions that involve reinforcing physical activity through sports and encouraging healthy eating practices have also been developed and shown to improve obesity among children (Dietz & Gortmaker, 2001; Wilfley et al., 2007). Moreover, it may be useful to control the availability of unhealthy foods and drinks at schools (Taber, Chriqui, Perna, Powell, & Chaloupka, 2012).

Substance Use

Medical management for substance use may involve inpatient/residential treatment where an individual may detoxify in a monitored environment. Drug consumption rooms (DCR) or supervised injection sites (SIS), such as the first legal facility in Canada called "Insite" located in Vancouver, British Columbia, provide health care and social services for people who might be socially stigmatized and marginalized due to their substance-use issues. This Vancouver facility and others like it combine substance-use management approaches including prevention, treatment, and harm reduction to help individuals use drugs in a non-judgemental environment under the supervision of qualified staff (McCann & Temenos, 2015). SIS aim to significantly reduce fatalities among substance users and provide them with social and health services to help manage their substance use. These sites also allow for sterile injections, which help reduce blood transmissible infections due to viruses such as the human immunodeficiency virus and the hepatitis B and C viruses (Potier, Laprevote, Dubois-Arber, Cottencin, & Rolland, 2014). Though these sites have led to controversy, evidence supports their efficacy in reducing overdose, providing safer injection conditions, and increasing access to health care for those in need. Implementation of these harm-reduction programs for substance use are recommended by best practice guidelines (Strike et al., 2011; Watson

In Practice
Developing Healthy Eating Behaviours through CBT

Jason is a 30-year-old financial advisor who lives on his own. He is 173 cm tall and weighs 118 kg (BMI = 38). In high school, Jason was athletic and did not have problems with his weight. When he moved out of his parents' home to go to university, however, he started gaining weight; in the last year alone, he has gained 50 pounds. At university, Jason used to eat a lot of fast food as he did not have the time to make meals, nor did he know how. Since starting his first full-time job, Jason has become busy with deadlines and has been working overtime. He gets home late at night and primarily eats food from take-out restaurants. He has tried a few different diets over the last year, but finds that he often gives into his temptations.

Jason was referred to a psychologist for help in the management of his weight. He told the psychologist that he feels self-conscious about his weight. He stated that he just wants to lose his excess weight so he can go back to being happy and enjoying his life. The psychologist recommended that Jason meet with a nutritionist to learn about meal planning and substituting nutrient-rich foods for unhealthy ones. The psychologist also explained that she would help Jason learn to manage stress and emotions that may increase the probability of overeating. When she asked Jason about mood and anxiety, Jason shared that he has been feeling sad and does not like himself when he looks in the mirror. Jason shared that, when he meets his friends at restaurants, he feels that they are watching what he eats. Recently, he stopped going out with his friends and instead stays home and watches television while eating junk food. Throughout the session, Jason realized how much he thinks about his weight and eating. The psychologist suggested that they first work primarily on his mood and motivation before starting to focus more on a weight-loss program.

Jason agreed to engage in cognitive behavioural therapy to improve his mood and change his lifestyle. In the first few sessions, Jason learned how to identify and challenge unhelpful thoughts (e.g., "I'm a failure" and "when I'm stressed, I have to eat") and avoidance behaviours (e.g., watching television). He began to think more adaptively (e.g., "I have succeeded in many domains in my life, including at university and work" and "I can learn to manage my stress without using food") and to engage in social activities that he used to find pleasurable. He also learned to be assertive with friends and family about his weight and to be less concerned (and, thus, less stressed) about what others might think of him when he is eating. Instead, he focused on his own goals. He also learned to pace himself with his job and became more efficient in accomplishing work-related tasks.

Once his mood and stress were under control, he began working on lifestyle changes and in enhancing his efforts toward following the diet recommended by his nutritionist. Initially, he practised stimulus control strategies to help change his lifestyle. This started with keeping a food record and identifying situations and emotions that increased the likelihood of over-eating. Early on, he avoided situations (a stimulus-control strategy) that triggered him to give in to his impulses such as fast-food restaurants. He ate at specific times of the day and learned to always eat at a table rather than on the couch while watching television (another stimulus-control strategy). Moreover, he practised assertiveness skills so that he could learn to say "no" to people when they encouraged him to eat unhealthy foods. Over time, Jason began to engage in more physical activities (e.g., skating with friends) that were approved by his family physician. He also learned to cope with high-risk situations (e.g., parties) by not losing control over his eating behaviour. Avoiding such situations was no longer necessary for Jason.

After six months of working with the psychologist, Jason lost 20 pounds through healthy eating and increased physical activity. Moreover, his symptoms of depression and anxiety reduced and his quality of life and social relationships improved.

et al., 2017). It is important to remember that different legal jurisdictions have different regulations concerning SIS and whether or not SIS are permitted to operate.

It is typically recommended that any medical strategies (e.g., use of certain medications designed to manage cravings for a substance) be accompanied by psychosocial approaches, which support changes in behaviour and education that are essential for overcoming problems related to addiction. Clinical guidelines for managing substance-use disorders recommend the use of co-ordinated addiction-focused evidence-based psychosocial interventions that address patient priorities (Management of Substance Use Disorders Work Group, 2015).

CBT has been shown to be helpful in the management of several types of substance-use issues (Chiesa & Serretti, 2014; Cooper, Chatters, Kaltenhaler, & Wong, 2015). This intervention can target use of a specific substance or multiple substances. CBT programs that target comorbid psychological risk factors such as anxiety, depression, stress, and self-esteem may also help to reduce substance use, especially when a person might be using substances as a method of coping with stress. CBT that is combined with motivational interviewing and enhancement approaches has been found to be particularly effective (Hogue, Henderson, Ozechowsky, & Robbins, 2014).

Contingency management methods, in addition to encouraging avoidance of situations that might lead to substance use and offering support and psychological treatment, provide positive reinforcers (e.g., vouchers that can be exchanged for goods when client demonstrate change in maladaptive substance use behaviours) (Davis et al., 2016). If a patient does not engage in behavioural change goals, vouchers can be withheld. The literature on the efficacy of programs that include contingency management for substance-use disorders shows that 86 per cent of studies reported significant positive outcomes (Davis et al., 2016).

Mindfulness-based interventions have become increasingly popular for managing substance use. Unlike other therapies, mindfulness-based interventions help individuals increase their awareness of the present moment and to accept distressing thoughts without judgement (Creswell, 2017). Related to meditation, mindfulness can help reduce psychological distress and ultimately facilitate the management of substance use problems. There is emerging evidence for the use of these interventions among those with substance-use issues (Holzel et al., 2011).

Of interest, during adolescence, effective methods for preventing and managing substance use can be through school-based programs (O'Leary-Barrett et al., 2013; Onrust et al., 2016). The main emphasis of such approaches is to make students aware of the health risks and the various social pressures that are exerted on adolescents to use substances. This helps adolescents to be prepared to resist or manage pressures or influences related to using substances. As mentioned previously, since peers have significant influence during this time of development, incorporation of peer education into substance-use programs can help improve adherence and acceptability (Onrust et al., 2016). Other strategies, such as refusal skills training whereby adolescents practise or role play refusing substances, can also be added as part of preventative interventions (Onrust et al., 2016).

Police officer giving a talk about illegal drugs at a school.

Alcohol

There are several pharmacotherapies for the management of alcohol misuse. Disulfiram (Antabuse) is a drug that causes a person to vomit whenever he or she ingests alcohol. Other drugs are used for their anti-craving properties (Swift & Aston, 2015). Research suggests that combining pharmacotherapy with CBT enhances people's ability to manage their cravings and refrain from substance use, especially among those with comorbid depression (Berglund, 2005; Riper et al., 2014).

Alcoholics Anonymous (AA) is an organization that offers self-help and peer support groups in many countries. The groups provide emotional support and counselling for members with alcohol or substance-use issues. Some evidence suggests that AA can be a beneficial long-term support system for many individuals (Kelly, Magill, & Stout, 2009) although dropout rates may be a problem (Flett, Kocovski, Blankstein, Davison, & Neale, 2017).

In contrast to programs targeting complete abstinence, controlled drinking programs that take a harm-reduction approach (Marlatt & Wietkiewitz, 2010) are also available. Such programs aim to help individuals control problem drinking behaviour rather than engage in total abstinence and have met with at least some success (Sobell & Sobell, 1995), especially in cases where efforts towards complete abstinence goals were previously unsuccessful. Despite some encouraging evidence (Marlatt & Witkiewitz, 2002), the approach has critics who are concerned about its potential for enabling substance use under some circumstances.

In Focus

Allan Marlatt and Relapse Prevention

Dr Gordon Allan Marlatt (1941–2011) is the person whose name is most associated with relapse prevention programs (Rotgers, Fromme, & Larimer, 2012). He completed his Ph.D. in clinical psychology at Indiana University and worked at various universities including the University of British Columbia before settling at the University of Washington as the Director of Addictive Behaviours Research Center (White, Larimer, Sher, & Witkiewitz, 2011).

Dr Marlatt was a strong advocate of the harm-reduction model in managing addictive behaviours. Together with his colleague Dr Judith Gordon, he developed a relapse prevention conceptualization (Marlatt & Gordon, 1985). In contrast to earlier popular views, Dr Marlatt viewed alcoholism as being more of an adjustment issue rather than an illness. Marlatt and Gordon suggest that abstinence is not the only positive outcome in the treatment of alcoholism and that moderation can also be acceptable (e.g., controlled drinking in appropriate circumstances rather than complete abstinence). Marlatt contended that people should learn to distinguish between a lapse and a full-blown relapse. A relapse is considered a warning sign rather than a failure and can be used as a learning experience. In other words, people are not "back at square one" when they experience a relapse. Instead, they can overcome the relapse with the skills that they previously acquired in treatment. The primary focus of the relapse prevention management model is to help individuals develop coping skills, enhance self-efficacy, and make lifestyle changes through CBT interventions. The interventions concentrate on coping with internal cues such as urges and craving along with external cues such as social and environmental triggers (Larimer & Palmer, 1999). Individuals are taught moderation and self-control. Relapse prevention focuses both on the prevention and management of relapse.

Smoking

Smoking-cessation programs often utilize nicotine replacement therapies (NRT) to replace the nicotine from smoking tobacco. These replacement therapies help prevent withdrawal symptoms. Several NRT products are available over the counter or through prescription. Each product differs in the mechanism and rate at which nicotine is delivered. Other medications such as sustained-release bupropion, an antidepressant, and varenicline, a nicotine receptor agonist, are also used in smoking-cessation programs to manage withdrawal and cravings (Hartmann-Boyce, Stead, Cahill, & Lancaster, 2014).

Electronic nicotine delivery systems such as e-cigarettes or vape pens have become increasingly popular among people seeking a lower-risk alternative to smoking. Their use has been advocated as a harm-reduction approach to promote delivery of nicotine in a noncombustible form (Prochaska & Benowitz, 2016). Furthermore, there is some evidence to suggest that they may facilitate smoking reduction (Prochaska & Benowitz, 2016; Rahman, Hann, Wilson, Mnatzaganian, & Worrall-Carter, 2015). These devices deliver nicotine by heating a solution of nicotine, additives, and glycol (Hajek, Etter, Benowitz, Eissenberg, & McRobbie, 2014). Tobacco smoke results from combustion of organic matter leading to toxins such as carcinogens. Since there is no combustion in e-cigarettes, the vapour contains very low levels of detectable toxicants (Hajek et al., 2014). Nonetheless, use of e-cigarettes remains controversial with many debating if its harms

Controlled drinking, as opposed to complete abstinence as a treatment target, has been criticized by some. Specifically, it has been argued that this approach may allow substance users to continue with their maladaptive behaviours (McCambridge & Cunningham, 2014). Nonetheless, there is evidence that a harm-reduction approach can be effective at reducing alcohol abuse (Witkiewitz & Marlatt, 2006). Furthermore, this strategy gives flexibility to therapists when setting treatment goals in collaboration with clients. For clients who have been repeatedly unsuccessful in achieving complete abstinence, controlled drinking in moderation may be a realistic possibility.

Dr Marlatt's model of relapse prevention was initially developed for the management of alcohol abuse; however, it has since been incorporated in the management of a variety of maladaptive behaviours. His work is considered to be the foundation for much of the psychological research in relapse prevention (which is now used to control a variety of habits and problems beyond substance use).

https://depts.washington.edu/abrc/AlanMarlatt.jpg

Psychologist Allan Marlatt was a pioneer in the area of relapse prevention in the management of alcohol-related problems.

outweigh the benefits (Middlekauff, 2015). Opponents of e-cigarettes argue that these may have the potential to become a gateway to smoking or to normalize smoking. Additionally, concerns that nicotine has addictive properties and poses potential long-term health risks are important to consider (Hajek et al., 2014).

Psychological interventions for smoking cessation may include a variety of components (e.g., education, monitoring cravings and smoking through the use of diaries, management of emotions and thoughts that may increase the probability of smoking). Despite initial good results, many of these interventions have high relapse rates (Flett et al., 2017). Combining pharmacotherapy and psychological interventions for smoking cessation can increase the chances of success (Stead, Koilpillai, Fanshawe, & Lancaster, 2016). Moreover, certain Internet-based programs show considerable promise in facilitating smoking cessation, although it is not entirely clear whether these programs are as effective as active treatments (Taylor et al., 2017).

Future Directions

Although research has established the importance of a variety of risk factors related to maladaptive eating and substance use, studies are still needed on the buffering effect of protective factors against developing these behaviours. Models that examine the causal pathways of positive and negative influences may provide guidance on treatment and adherence outcomes research. Furthermore, there still remain gaps in the literature regarding the cultural factors that influence initiation or development of maladaptive eating and substance use behaviours.

Novel approaches to the management of maladaptive lifestyles are being developed through smartphones and other mobile technologies. Mobile health (mhealth) technologies, including calorie trackers such as MyFitnessPal or SparkRecipes, can help people monitor and plan their healthy eating and diet lifestyle. Other apps, such as DrinkControl or Sobriety Clock, may help people to moderate their alcohol intake. Online social media support groups can help people develop a social network of support related to their issue in order to achieve their goal of harm reduction or abstinence. The efficacy of many available apps and online support approaches, however, is not well established through empirical research and more studies are needed.

New technologies such as e-cigarettes, although marketed as safer alternatives to traditional cigarettes and as potential tools for smoking cessation, have opponents who have raised issues regarding their safety (Palazzolo, Crow, Nelson, & Johnson, 2017). In terms of public health prevention strategies, more research is needed in this regard to ensure maximal effectiveness. It is recognized that governments need to develop more engaging marketing strategies to educate people in healthy lifestyles.

Summary

In this chapter, we examined maladaptive eating (e.g., overeating) and substance-use behaviours (e.g., consuming excessive amounts of alcohol) that have been shown to cause health-related disability. Both biological and psychosocial risk factors can place people at increased risk for engaging in such maladaptive behaviours, which often can be managed effectively through appropriate interdisciplinary and other interventions.

Critical Thought Questions

1. Many people have engaged in binge-eating behaviour in the past, either at a party or at an all-you-can eat buffet. What are some external cues that may trigger overeating? What are some protective factors in your life that may help you make healthy choices? What strategies do you use to maintain a healthy diet?

2. What components would you include in a comprehensive program for managing substance use? What factors may affect adherence to treatment?

Recommended Reading

De Ridder, D.T.D., De Vet, E., Stok, F.M., Adriaanse, M.A., & De Wit, J.B.F. (2013). Obesity, overconsumption and self-regulation failure: The unsung role of eating appropriateness standards. *Health Psychology Review, 7*, 148–65.

De Ridder, D., Kroese, F., Evers, C., Adriaanse, M., & Gillebaart, M. (2017). Healthy diet: Health impact, prevalence, correlates, and interventions. *Psychology & Health, 32*, 907–41.

Larimer, M.E., & Palmer, R.S. (1999). Relapse prevention: An overview of Marlatt's cognitive-behavioural model. *Alcohol Research and Health, 23*(2), 151–60.

7 Health Anxiety and Other Psychological Responses to Bodily Symptoms

Heather D. Hadjistavropoulos

Learning Objectives

In this chapter you will:

- Discover how thinking about and appraising physical signs and symptoms influences the way we feel and behave when we experience physical signs and symptoms.

- Learn about the common-sense model of illness representations and how this model can be used to understand how we appraise bodily signs and symptoms as either normal or threatening.

- Examine various influences (e.g., culture, personality, social relationships) on the way we appraise bodily symptoms as being either normal sensations or signs of illness.

- Gain knowledge of the prevalence and nature of health anxiety, which can result when people catastrophically appraise physical signs and symptoms as threatening to their health.

- Develop an understanding of the cognitive behavioural conceptualization of health anxiety and how this conceptualization is used to understand the development and maintenance of health anxiety.

- Learn how health psychologists commonly assess and treat health anxiety.

Introduction

In January 2012, Nick Cannon, actor and comedian, was hospitalized for kidney failure at the age of 31. In a documentary, Cannon shared that one day he was out enjoying time with his family, when he suddenly experienced his body swelling up, shortness of breath, and severe right-sided pain. He was subsequently diagnosed with a disease called lupus nephritis, which is an autoimmune inflammation of the kidney and a serious complication caused by systemic lupus erythematosus (also known as lupus). In patients diagnosed with lupus, the immune system cannot differentiate between harmful and healthy substances and therefore attacks healthy cells and tissues (de Zubiria Salgado & Herrera-Diaz, 2012). Lupus has an unpredictable course, with a wide variety of symptoms such as arthritis, fever, photosensitivity, cold fingers or toes, and mouth sores (Jimenez, Cervera, Font, & Ingelmo, 2003).

Nick Cannon, actor and comedian, was hospitalized for kidney failure at the age of 31.

Cannon documented his extensive medical treatment in a documentary series called *NCredible Health Hustle*. The documentary includes his victories and the obstacles he faced while coping with his condition (Cannon, 2012a). While viewing the documentary, you observe Cannon responding to a life-threatening illness by constantly striving to return to his former state of health. He not only relies on his health-care providers but takes an active role in his own care by exercising and changing his diet, and ultimately reducing some of his work commitments. Cannon's thoughts about his health condition evolve over time. At first, Cannon shared that he was "working on the condition" and feeling very "optimistic" (Cannon, 2012b). Over time, however, he described viewing his condition as "life-threatening" and "unexpected," and noted that he was having increasing thoughts about how "life is important and tomorrow definitely isn't promised." He later described doing all he can to "stay positive" (Cannon, 2012c).

Not all people respond to having a serious medical condition in the same way. Thoughts and behaviours vary widely. Some individuals may rely solely on formal medical care, while others may avoid such care at all costs. Some people are consumed with thoughts about the worst-case scenario, while others attempt to remain positive despite conflicting evidence. This chapter will help you understand diverse responses to bodily sensations, beginning with common reactions and then turning to less common, more anxious responses such as **health anxiety**.

Common-Sense Model of Illness Representation/Self-Regulation

The common-sense model (CSM) of illness representation/self regulation (e.g., Leventhal, Philips, & Burns, 2016) was introduced in Chapter 1 and provides a framework for understanding how we respond to physical signs and symptoms with a cognitive appraisal, evaluating how threatening our physical signs and symptoms are. A *physical sign* refers to observable evidence of a physical change in our bodies. The edema experienced by Cannon is an example of a physical sign. In contrast to a physical sign, a *physical symptom* is something that is only experienced by us and cannot be directly observed by others. Pain is an example of a physical symptom. It cannot be observed directly; others must rely on our non-verbal or verbal reports (see Chapter 9). Surveys that examine the prevalence of physical signs and symptoms suggest that the vast majority of people experience at least one physical sign or symptom a day (e.g., Pennebaker, 1982). Ultimately, this means that there is considerable opportunity for us to appraise and respond to physical signs and symptoms we experience.

According to the CSM (Figure 7.1), after we notice physical sensations (stimuli), we form a "common-sense" or "lay" representation of these sensations in an attempt to determine the meaning of the physical sensations. We are, in essence, processing information and considering whether a health threat is (or is not) present. This mental representation is sometimes called a schema, belief, cognition, or perception. According to the CSM, this mental representation then influences how we cope with the physical sensations we experience. If we ultimately view the physical sensations as threatening, we will employ coping strategies in an attempt to manage the health threat. If we do not regard the physical sensations as threatening, however, no coping behaviours will be required. If implemented, coping behaviour is subsequently followed by a further appraisal process, in which we consider our success in coping with the physical sensations. This appraisal, in turn, influences our representation of the physical sensations. In parallel to processing the meaning of physical sensations, we also simultaneously process our emotional response to the physical sensations. Central to the model is the interaction between our perceptions of physical sensations and our emotional response to the physical sensations. That is, how we view our physical sensations influences our emotions and our emotions influence our views of the physical sensations. According to the CSM model, the way in which we appraise and interpret our physical signs and symptoms affects our reactions to those symptoms. How do you think this model applies to Cannon's experience? Can you see how his appraisals of illness influenced his emotions and behaviours and vice versa?

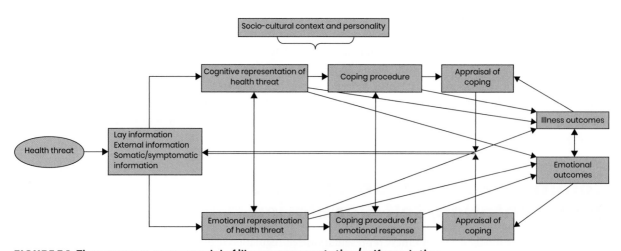

FIGURE 7.1 The common-sense model of illness representation/self regulation.

Source: Jones, C. J., Smith, H. E., & Llewellyn, C. D. (2016). A systematic review of the effectiveness of interventions using the Common Sense Self-Regulatory Model to improve adherence behaviours. *Journal of Health Psychology*, 21(11), 2709–2724.

Dimensions of Illness Representations

Research on the CSM has revealed that we do not develop a single schema or representation of our health/illness, but instead that we conceptualize our health/illness along multiple dimensions. These dimensions include forming a representation of the identity, cause, consequences, timeline, and controllability of the physical signs and symptoms (Hagger & Orbell, 2003). **Identity** refers to how we label the signs and symptoms we experience (e.g., lupus, cancer, heart disease). Identity is often measured by asking individuals about their physical signs and symptoms (e.g., pain, breathlessness, fatigue). **Cause** refers to our beliefs about what brought on the signs and symptoms; we might consider biological, emotional, environmental, or psychological causes. In terms of **consequences**, we also tend to think about the impact of the signs and symptoms on our everyday lives (e.g., self-care, household responsibilities, family, work, emotional well-being). **Timeline** refers to our beliefs about how long the signs and symptoms will last (e.g., acute vs chronic) and whether they will fluctuate or persist over time. Finally, **controllability** refers to our beliefs about whether we have control over our signs and symptoms and whether we believe treatment will be efficacious. These representations of our signs and symptoms are not static but change over time, especially in response to treatment (Fischer et al., 2010).

The Illness Perception Questionnaire was developed to measure these specific illness representations (Weinman, Petrie, Moss-Morris, & Horne, 1996). A revised version of this measure, the Illness Perceptions Questionnaire-Revised (IPQ-R) (Moss-Morris et al., 2002) also assesses these constructs, but includes several other subscales. For instance, control is divided into two subscales, including *personal control* (belief that one can manage signs and symptoms) and *treatment control* (belief that treatment will be efficacious). The timeline construct is also divided into subscales measuring an *acute/chronic timeline* (a short-term or long-term problem) and a *cyclical timeline* (unpredictable and cyclical nature of illness). A further modification is that the questionnaire measures the emotional response to illness with two subscales, *emotional representations of illness* (feelings of depression, anger, worry, and anxiety in response to the illness) and *illness coherence* (how much the individual understands or comprehends the illness). On the IPQ-R, respondents are asked to indicate whether they *strongly disagree, disagree, neither agree nor disagree, agree, or strongly agree* with statements such as "*My illness will last a short time*" and "*There is a lot I can do to control my symptoms.*" At the time of this writing, the full questionnaire, which has been translated into several languages, was available at http://www.uib.no/ipq/index.html.

Relationship between Illness Representations and Coping Behaviour

In terms of coping, the CSM predicts that how we view our signs and symptoms determines how we cope (see Chapter 3 for a broader discussion of coping strategies). The model recognizes wide variability in the types of coping strategies we use, and how we view our signs and symptoms determines how we select a coping strategy. For example, with the advancement of the Internet, many people cope by seeking information about symptoms online (Singh & Brown, 2014). Alternatively, they may attempt to divert their attention and ignore their signs and symptoms. In other cases, people may try to change their beliefs about their signs and symptoms, viewing them as benign and non-threatening (Cameron & Jago, 2008). In contrast to those who attempt to cope with physical symptoms on their own and avoid seeking medical care, some people seek health-care services for very minor medical symptoms (Shapiro, Ware, & Sherbourne, 1986). As many as

40 per cent of individuals seek care for minor medical symptoms that could have been managed without medical intervention (Shapiro et al., 1986).

There are multiple examples of how thoughts about our body influence how we cope with illness. Consider patients with diabetes. Those who hold negative beliefs about their ability to control their illness and negative perceptions about its course and consequences are less likely to attend medical appointments regularly (Lawson, Bundy, Lyne, & Harvey, 2004). Our views regarding illness not only predict whether we seek medical care, but they also predict whether we follow medical advice provided. For example, individuals with asthma who believe that asthma can be cured and/or controlled are more likely to adhere to medical recommendations, while those who believe that asthma has been caused by external factors are less likely to adhere to care recommendations (Jessop & Rutter, 2003). As another example, cardiac patients who perceive their health condition as having few consequences and who believe they have great personal control over their illness and that the treatment is ineffective are more likely to drop out of cardiac rehabilitation programs compared to those who hold the opposite beliefs (Yohannes, Yalfani, Doherty, & Bundy, 2007).

Overall, there is considerable support for the association between how we view our signs and symptoms and our coping behaviour (Hagger & Orbell, 2003). In a meta-analysis of this research, it was found that those who perceive themselves as having many symptoms and view their symptoms as chronic and disabling are more likely to cope with symptoms by using avoidance (e.g., they deny that they have problems and avoid medical care) and emotional expression (Hagger & Orbell, 2003). On the other hand, those who view their signs and symptoms as controllable are more likely to cope by using problem-focused coping strategies (e.g., they use strategies to try and solve their medical problems, such as asking for medical help).

Illness Representations and Health Outcomes

How could our views of illness and how we cope with illness impact our emotional and physical health? Research evidence, in fact, suggests that certain illness representations are associated with improved emotional and physical well-being, while other illness representations are associated with emotional distress and poorer physical health (Norton et al., 2014). In terms of emotional well-being, viewing an illness as within our control is associated with greater psychological well-being and social functioning; in contrast, perceiving one's illness as having multiple symptoms and being chronic is associated with negative psychological well-being (Hagger & Orbell, 2003). These findings are evident across multiple medical conditions such as diabetes, epilepsy, and cardiac disease (Hagger & Orbell, 2003).

In terms of physical well-being, a similar pattern is found. The CSM suggests that our views of an illness determine our behaviours, which in turn impact our physical health. Supporting this idea, McSharry, Moss-Morris, and Kendrick (2011) conducted a meta-analytic study of patients with diabetes. They found that higher scores on identity, negative consequences, cyclical timeline, concern, and emotional representations and lower scores on personal control were positively associated with higher HbA1c in individuals with type 2 diabetes. HbA1c is a measure of blood glucose or glycemic control, with higher scores suggesting that the individual is not following treatment recommendations and is at greater risk of diabetic complications (McSharry et al., 2011). To provide a specific example from a study of young adults with type 1 diabetes, illness representations (e.g., beliefs about ability to control diabetes) predicted blood glucose monitoring; adherence to recommendations for insulin, food, and exercise; and emergency precautions three months later (McGrady, Peugh, & Hood, 2014). Illness representations thus are important targets of change to improve diabetes management.

Also supporting a relationship between illness representations and illness outcomes, there is research showing that interventions that target cure or control perceptions improve patient adherence to medical recommendations and outcomes (C.J. Jones, Smith, & Llewellyn, 2016). As an example, Petrie, Cameron, Ellis, Buick, and Weinman (2002) found that if patients altered their illness perceptions, they experienced improved health outcomes. More specifically, patients who suffered their first myocardial infarction (MI; heart attack) were assigned to usual care or to an intervention (led by nurses) designed to alter their perceptions about their MI (Petrie et al., 2002). The intervention resulted in patients being more likely to believe their heart condition could be controlled and less likely to believe that their heart condition would be chronic and cause serious consequences. In the intervention group, but not the control group, patients reported fewer angina symptoms and more often reported that they were better prepared for discharge. At three-month follow-up, they returned to work at a significantly faster rate than the usual care group. Overall, this is consistent with the view that thoughts influence behaviour, which ultimately influences health.

Determinants of Illness Representations

How do we develop our beliefs or views about our physical sensations? According to the CSM, we actively seek information to understand our physical sensations and base our mental representations on the physical sensations we are experiencing. These illness appraisals, however, are also influenced by other factors, such as our past experiences, cognitive heuristics (e.g., simple mental rules that help us form judgements and make decisions), social factors, and culture, as well as personality and mood.

Physical Stimuli

How we view our signs and symptoms is to some degree influenced by what we feel physically. Take, for example, a study of patients faced with end-stage renal disease. In this study, those who were undergoing dialysis (and thus experiencing many physical symptoms) and those who had a kidney transplant (and thus no longer experiencing significant symptoms) differed in how they perceived illness. Specifically, those who had dialysis had stronger timeline beliefs, lower control beliefs, and stronger beliefs about disruptiveness of illness compared to those who had a kidney transplant (Griva, Jayasena, Davenport, Harrison, & Newman, 2009). In other words, beliefs about illness were shaped by the physical input the individuals experienced. This relationship between physical symptoms and beliefs is also evident in a study of patients with osteoarthritis (Bijsterbosch et al., 2009). In this study, investigators examined if illness perceptions changed over a six-year period in individuals diagnosed with osteoarthritis. Indeed, over time, as osteoarthritis worsened, people with osteoarthritis perceived their condition as more chronic and less controllable.

While physical sensations are important in shaping our beliefs, the CSM recognizes that appraisal of physical sensations is highly individualized and does not always correspond with physical input. As an example, women who have the most invasive breast cancer have been found to have a strong sense of control over their cure (Henselmans et al., 2010). What, then, are the other factors that influence how we interpret and respond to troubling physical sensations?

Personal Experiences

The CSM suggests that our beliefs about our physical signs and symptoms are influenced by our history with illness (Leventhal, Meyer, & Nerenz, 1980). Based on past experience with illness, we develop memories of illness that influence how we interpret and respond to our current physical signs and symptoms. To illustrate, children with a history of previous negative medical experiences demonstrated more distress during a throat culture examination than did children with previous positive or neutral medical experiences (Dahlquist et al., 1986). Knowledge of family history of illness can also be part of our illness history. Our illness history provides a context that colours how we interpret current somatic changes.

Heuristics

Diefenbach and Leventhal (1996) have suggested that, in addition to our personal history, most of us have decision rules or heuristics that influence how we appraise signs and symptoms. One such rule is the *symmetry rule*, which refers to the fact that we tend to believe we are ill if we experience symptoms, and believe we are healthy if we do not experience symptoms. A further rule that influences how we appraise symptoms is the *stress–illness rule*. This holds that symptoms that develop in the context of stressful events are assumed to be part of stress rather than illness. In contrast, the *prevalence rule* refers to the fact that rare conditions are perceived as threatening, whereas common conditions are perceived as less serious. The *age–illness rule* refers to our tendency to believe that mild symptoms that develop gradually are a normal part of aging. In general, these rules are helpful, but they can also lead to errors. Consider, for example, the case of a man in his early sixties who gradually began to experience fatigue. Applying the age–illness rule, he ignored his fatigue and assumed it was associated with the natural aging process, when the fatigue was in fact a sign of coronary artery disease.

Social Influences

How we interpret and view physical sensations is also a function of our social environment. As one would expect, information that medical professionals communicate to us has a powerful influence on how we interpret and respond to physical signs and symptoms (Zolnierek & DiMatteo, 2009). That is, if we are told by a medical professional to be concerned about a sign or symptom, most of us will be concerned. Beyond medical professionals, family, friends, and others we interact with also influence how we interpret and respond to our signs and symptoms and how we cope with illness. A classic study demonstrates how others in our environment impact how we interpret our physical sensations (Craig & Weiss, 1971). In this study, all participants were exposed to experimentally induced pain. Some participants, however, observed a confederate modelling low pain tolerance, while other participants observed a confederate modelling high pain tolerance. Exposure to the confederate displaying low pain tolerance led participants to report greater pain than when they observed confederates displaying high pain tolerance. This experimental study provides a great example of how social factors influence our views of physical sensations and also our behaviour.

Another example of how social variables influence how we respond to symptoms comes from a study conducted by Giannousi, Karademas, and Dimitraki (2016). These researchers found that recently diagnosed cancer patients had more intense psychological symptoms when their views of the consequences of illness were discrepant from their partners. The researchers concluded that adjustment to cancer is a dyadic process impacted not only by the sufferer but also by how others understand his or her illness (Giannousi et al., 2016).

At least three divergent approaches to how family and friends respond to patient illness have been described (Vilchinsky et al., 2011). One such approach is referred to as *active engagement*. This approach involves family and friends discussing illness with the patient, asking how he is or she is feeling, and attempting to assist the patient with constructive problem-solving activities.

Another way in which family and friends influence illness perceptions is through *protective buffering*, which consists of withholding their concerns about the patient and denying being worried about the patient's health condition. A third approach is referred to as *overprotection*, which involves family and friends underestimating the patient's ability to cope and providing unnecessary and excessive assistance. These varying reactions to patients significantly influence how patients view and respond to illness. More specifically, when support involves active engagement compared to the other approaches, patients respond to illness with less distress and greater self-efficacy (Vilchinsky et al., 2011).

Spouses of chronic pain patients respond to their loved one's pain condition in varying ways.

Culture

Related to social influences, one's cultural background also influences how we interpret and respond to illness. The health beliefs of Caucasians, for instance, are quite different from those of other ethnic groups (Landrine & Klonoff, 1992). A study of critically ill patients who were in an intensive care unit for more than three days illustrates this difference (Ford, Zapka, Gebregziabher, Yang, & Sterba, 2010). In this study, African-American patients tended to perceive illness as less enduring than Caucasians did, and reported more confidence in treatment efficacy as well in their own personal control (Ford et al., 2010). They also tended to view illness as being less serious, having less emotional impact, while simultaneously perceiving illness as less coherent. Another example of research showing cultural differences in illness beliefs comes from a study of inpatients with coronary artery disease; in this study, patients who identified themselves as South Asian reported having lower personal control over their illness compared to those who identified themselves as Caucasian (Grewal, Stewart, & Grace, 2010). They were also more likely to attribute their illness to worry and poor medical care in the past, and, compared to Caucasian patients, less likely to attribute illness to aging. Chapter 15 reviews further research on cross-cultural factors in health psychology.

Personality and Mood

Personality, in particular **neuroticism**, influences how we view physical symptoms. Neuroticism, also referred to as negative affectivity, is the tendency to experience negative emotions and emotional instability. Neuroticism is associated with a tendency to report somatic complaints (Charles, Gatz, Kato, & Pedersen, 2008). It appears that negative affectivity influences our attention to and interpretation of symptoms (Charles et al., 2008). For example, women who scored higher on neuroticism were more likely to view their newly diagnosed and surgically treated breast cancer as not being under their control (Henselmans et al., 2010).

Depression, anxiety, and stress, which tend to be correlated with neuroticism, also have a significant impact on how we view and respond to signs and symptoms. For example, when daily mood is negative and stress is high, people tend to report increased pain, miss work more often, and seek out health care more frequently (Gil et al., 2004). Positive mood, on the other hand, has the opposite effect. Those who have a positive mood report lower pain and lower health-care use (Gil et al., 2004). Norman Cousins (1976) is widely known for providing a personal account or anecdotal evidence on how viewing comedy films assisted him in coping with pain and illness. Experimental studies also support the relationship between mood and appraisals of health. In a classic laboratory study, it was found that inducing a positive mood as compared to a negative mood by watching pre-selected movie clips resulted in more favourable perceptions of health (Croyle & Uretsky, 1987). These results serve to highlight that personality and mood influence how we perceive our health. It should also be acknowledged, however, that relationships are bi-directional and our physical health has a direct impact on our mood (Pollard & Schwartz, 2003).

Health Anxiety

Some people, when faced with physical signs and symptoms, become extremely overwhelmed and consequently report experiencing severe levels of health anxiety. Here, our focus on health anxiety emphasizes cognitive behavioural therapy for the treatment of health anxiety. Before proceeding, consider the case of Linda presented in the In Practice box.

Clinical Considerations

The case of Linda, described in the accompanying box, illustrates health anxiety. Health anxiety specifically refers to the experience of excessive anxiety about one's present or future health and is often based on a misinterpretation of signs and symptoms (Rachman, 2012). Health anxiety is recognized as a dimensional construct characterized by a lack of concern about one's health at one end of the continuum and excessive anxiety about health on the other (Ferguson, 2009). Transitory or fleeting health anxiety is a common experience in the general population. In this case, the fleeting health anxiety is suspected to be adaptive by motivating individuals to take necessary action to prevent the development of a medical condition or deterioration of health (Asmundson, Taylor, & Cox, 2001). Health anxiety is regarded as excessive when it is continuous, results in distress, and causes extreme behaviours designed to alleviate anxiety but that ultimately heighten anxiety and interfere with daily functioning.

When health anxiety is extreme, it can be the subject of clinical attention. In the past, extreme health anxiety was referred to as **hypochondriasis**. This label is no longer used in the current edition of the *Diagnostic and Statistical Manual of Mental Disorders*, as it was considered unclear (American Psychiatric Association, 2013). Instead, those with extreme health anxiety are now diagnosed with either somatic symptom disorder or illness anxiety disorder. A diagnosis of somatic symptom disorder is given to those with one or more distressing somatic symptoms who also experience persistently high levels of anxiety about health. A diagnosis of illness anxiety disorder is given to those who are preoccupied with having or acquiring a serious illness and who have a high level of health anxiety but do not have significant somatic symptoms. It is important to note that excessive health anxiety also exists among individuals who have a medical condition (Hadjistavropoulos et al., 2012). That is, even people diagnosed with a medical condition can become overly health anxious. In this case, health anxiety presents as a preoccupation with the medical condition that is substantially greater than typically experienced by other people with the same medical condition and is associated with increased distress and disability (S. L. Jones, Hadjistavropoulos, & Gullickson, 2014).

In Practice
The Fear of Illness

Linda is a self-employed 55-year-old single woman who works as a freelance journalist. She reported being extremely anxious about her health and concerned that she would develop lung cancer. Linda shared that the fear developed in 2005 after she heard that Peter Jennings, a TV reporter and anchorman, died from lung cancer. She noted that as a teenager and young adult she often smoked socially when out with friends. She also described growing up in a home where both her parents smoked. Linda indicated that after hearing about the death of Peter Jennings, she began to notice that she was short of breath when walking up stairs. She also began to notice an unexplained pain in her shoulder. Linda indicated that she subsequently spent several days on the Internet searching the potential meaning of her symptoms. After becoming alarmed by what she was reading, she spoke to her physician. He ordered a chest x-ray, which did not reveal any suspicious areas in her lungs. Linda initially found this reassuring, but later requested that her physician order a CT scan. Her physician complied with her request. Consistent with the x-ray, the CT scan showed no suspicious areas in Linda's lungs. She once again felt reassured, but only for a brief period of time. She later returned to her physician and requested an MRI. Although reluctant, the physician complied with Linda's request and ordered an MRI, which, similar to the other tests, did not reveal any suspicious areas in Linda's lungs.

Despite this reassurance, Linda found that she continued to be preoccupied with the idea that she had lung cancer or would develop lung cancer in the future. Linda reported that she began to keep a daily diary of her symptoms. She also reported spending about a half an hour on the Internet each day reading about lung cancer. Linda described feeling "immobilized" and "fatigued" by her worry, and as a result neglected her regular household chores as well as her work responsibilities. She further reported limiting her recreational activities and isolating herself from her family and friends.

In terms of prevalence among medical patients, approximately 20 per cent have extreme health anxiety (Tyrer et al., 2011), with patients with neurological problems having greater health anxiety than other patient groups. In comparison, extreme health anxiety is found in about 7.7 per cent of the population (Noyes, Happel, & Yagla, 1999). Some argue that as you age and experience an increased number of medical conditions, you will become more health anxious. While this is a common assumption, no solid research evidence supports this (Barsky, Frank, Cleary, Wyshak, & Klerman, 1991). In fact, older adults who are healthy may be at decreased risk of health anxiety compared to older adults with medical problems or younger adults (Bourgault-Fagnou & Hadjistavropoulos, 2009).

Extreme health anxiety is associated with considerable emotional distress and increased disability (Bobevski, Clarke, & Meadows, 2016), including higher rates of unemployment (Barsky, Wyshak, Klerman, & Latham, 1990). Extreme health anxiety

"Our guest speaker called in sick."

© Aaron Bacall/Cartoonstock

also results in a substantial increase in medical care (Bobevski et al., 2016), which then increases the risk of unnecessary, invasive, potentially dangerous, and expensive medical procedures (Abramowitz & Braddock, 2008). Adding to the severity of the condition, elevated health anxiety is associated with lifetime history of diagnoses of anxiety and depressive disorders (Faravelli et al., 1997; Noyes et al., 1999), and it is estimated that 50 to 70 per cent of patients diagnosed with extreme health anxiety do not recover. In a recent study, health anxiety at age 5 to 7 years was associated with health anxiety symptoms at age 11 to 12 years and was associated with the presence of other emotional disorders, unspecific somatic complaints, and health-care costs (Rask et al., 2016).

Genetics

Limited research to date has examined the heritability of health anxiety, and what has been done in this area is largely inconclusive (Torgerson, 1986). On the other hand, a number of predisposing traits are suspected of increasing vulnerability to health anxiety, and these traits seem to have a genetic component. One such trait is anxiety sensitivity or the tendency to be fearful of anxiety-related sensations such as increased heart rate; this trait has been linked to health anxiety and also appears to be inherited to some degree (Stein, Jang, & Livesley, 1999). Similarly, somatization or the occurrence of recurring multiple somatic complaints also appears to have a genetic component and increases risk for health anxiety (Gillespie, Zhu, Heath, Hickie, & Martin, 2000). Finally, neuroticism or a tendency to experience negative affectivity and mood instability is also thought to increase vulnerability to health anxiety (Costa & McCrae, 1985) and again seems to involve genetic predispositions (Birley et al., 2006).

Cognitive Behavioural Model of Health Anxiety

Beyond genetics, it is suspected that health anxiety results through a learning experience whereby people either directly or indirectly (e.g., someone the person knows or hears about) experience a distressing event (e.g., illness) that leads them to believe that their health is in danger (Salkovskis & Warwick, 1986). These experiences are thought to be responsible for the development of core cognitions and behaviours that consequently produce health anxiety. This is referred to as the cognitive behavioural model (see Figure 7.2). This model is commonly used to understand health anxiety. Similar to the common-sense model of illness representation, the cognitive behavioural model recognizes that thoughts significantly impact how people feel about and respond to physical sensations. The approach emphasizes, however, that the individual with health anxiety has developed dysfunctional thoughts based on past experience and that health anxiety arises when these dysfunctional thoughts are triggered. Supporting this hypothesis, death of an ill parent has been found to predict elevated health anxiety in young adults (Alberts & Hadjistavropoulos, 2014). Thoughts about health can be triggered by internal physical sensations but also by external events, such as hearing about another person's illness. These thoughts in essence result in people being preoccupied with their health and misinterpreting innocuous or benign bodily sensations as more threatening than they actually are. Of interest though, while health anxiety is associated with biased tendency to attend to mild and benign bodily sensations, there is no evidence to suggest that people who are health anxious are actually better able to detect body signals than individuals who are not health anxious (Krautwurst, Gerlach, & Witthoft, 2016). That is, it does not seem that abnormalities in interoception (i.e., sensitivity to internal stimuli) account for health anxiety.

Several thoughts are believed to be central in the development of health anxiety, including holding beliefs that (1) the feared disease is serious and catastrophic; (2) one is vulnerable to disease; (3) one is not capable of coping with the feared illness; and (4) inadequate medical resources are available to treat the illness. Indeed, the presence of these thoughts in individuals who are health anxious has been confirmed (Hadjistavropoulos et al., 2012). In addition to these thoughts, people with extreme health anxiety hold other general dysfunctional beliefs, such as the belief that *there must be an explanation for all aches, pains, and unusual sensations and that there is far more illness in the world than people realize* (Fulton, Marcus, & Merkey, 2011). In a recent study, Hedman and colleagues also observed that individuals who are health anxious tend to perceive others as less healthy and to rate the risk of contagion as higher (Fergus, 2014; Hedman et al., 2016). These thoughts specifically are expected to trigger avoidance behaviours.

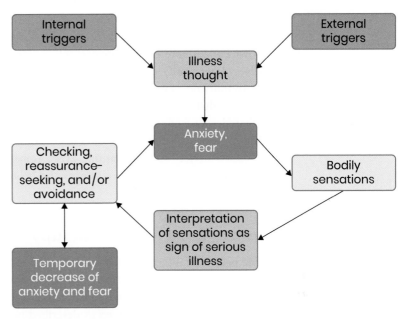

FIGURE 7.2   Cognitive behavioural model of health anxiety.

Source: Adapted from Page 42 of Furer, P., Walker, J. R., & Stein, M. B. (2007). *Treating health anxiety and fear of death: A practitioner's guide.* New York, NY: Springer Science + Business Media; US.

In addition to thoughts or beliefs, people with extreme health anxiety have several cognitive biases that make them vulnerable to anxiety. One such bias is a **confirmatory bias** whereby individuals with health anxiety tend to focus on information that confirms their fears and ignore information that disconfirms their fears (Warwick & Salkovskis, 1990). A second bias of relevance to health anxiety is referred to as *thought–action–fusion bias*, which is the tendency of anxious people to believe that when they think a negative thought the thought will come true (e.g., "If I think about cancer, I will develop cancer") (Shafran & Rachman, 2004). Also identified as relevant to health anxiety is *ex-consequentia reasoning*, which refers to the tendency of anxious individuals to believe that if they feel anxious, there must be danger present (Arntz, Rauner, & Vandenhout, 1995).

The cognitive behavioural approach to health anxiety also identifies behaviour as playing a role in its development and maintenance. Specifically, this approach emphasizes that, when exposed to physical sensations or information about health, people who are health anxious engage in **safety behaviours** that, although designed to reduce threat and anxiety, in the longer term have the opposite effect. Safety behaviours can be quite variable. The classic behaviour associated with extreme health anxiety is repeated *information-seeking* or *reassurance-seeking* from medical professionals or family and friends. *Body monitoring*, which refers to monitoring one's physical sensations and appearance, is another form of safety behaviour. Other behaviours relevant to health anxiety include avoidance behaviours, such as avoiding situations that may provoke health anxiety (e.g., television shows, hospitals, people with illness). It has been suggested that behavioural dimensions of health anxiety (e.g., reassurance seeking) arise as a method of compensation for ineffective cognitive coping strategies (Gorgen, Hiller, & Witthoft, 2014).

The cognitive behavioural model posits that when health anxiety is triggered, the person who is anxious becomes vigilant and engages in these behaviours to reduce threat. A study by Abramowitz and Moore (2007) supports this notion. These researchers had participants expose themselves to personally significant health-related stimuli and found this provoked anxiety and resulted in individuals reporting urges to perform safety behaviours. The problem with safety behaviours is that, contrary to expectations among health-anxious individuals, they increase rather than decrease anxiety (Radomsky, Shafran, Coughtrey, & Rachman, 2010). For example, engaging in hygienic safety behaviours (e.g., using sanitized wipes) increases rather than decreases health-anxiety scores (Olatunji, Etzel, Tomarken, Ciesielski, & Deacon, 2011). It seems that engaging in the behaviour reinforces the belief that there is danger and the individual should be fearful.

Cognitive Behavioural Therapy

Cognitive behavioural therapy (CBT) has emerged in the past 20 years as the treatment of choice for health anxiety. CBT has the greatest empirical support and also has other attractive features, such as being patient-centred and collaborative in nature. CBT for health anxiety focuses on addressing thoughts and behaviours as described previously. A number of books describe this

iStock.com/nullplus

Cognitive behavioural therapy (CBT) has emerged in recent years as the treatment of choice for health anxiety.

approach in considerable detail (Abramowitz & Braddock, 2008; Furer, Walker, & Stein, 2007; Owens & Antony, 2011; Taylor & Asmundson, 2004).

Core Features

Most clients who receive CBT for health anxiety visit their therapist for approximately 12 sessions of 50 to 60 minutes, but the exact number of sessions depends on the client. More sessions are provided to clients who experience greater health anxiety and a greater number of health fears. Also notable about CBT is that clients typically are responsible for the completion of assignments and homework between sessions. The accompanying In Focus box contains some homework sheets completed by Linda as part of her therapy. The assumption is that the more a client works on the homework, the greater the efficacy of treatment and the shorter the treatment duration.

Some factors are known to complicate treatment of health anxiety. Review of the research (Taylor, Asmundons, & Coons, 2005), for instance, suggests that treatment is more difficult if clients:

1. Have had extreme health anxiety for a longer period of time.
2. Suffer from severe symptoms.
3. Have strongly held beliefs.
4. Present with a personality disorder.
5. Experience co-morbid general medical conditions.
6. Report the presence of stressful life events.
7. Appear to benefit in some way (e.g., financially) from having health anxiety.

The relationship between treatment outcome and age is ambiguous, in that some studies show better outcomes with younger clients, while other studies suggest outcomes are not related to age (Taylor et al., 2005).

Typically, CBT begins by providing psycho-education to clients, covering similar details to those described above. The key to this component of therapy is for clients to understand how health anxiety develops, with specific attention to how thoughts lead to health anxiety, which leads to selective attention to bodily sensations or changes and behaviours (e.g., avoidance, seeking reassurance, checking) that serve to further increase health anxiety. Clients are also often encouraged to keep a diary. In the diary, they record the date, the level of health anxiety experienced, triggers for health anxiety, thoughts, behaviours, and physical symptoms they may be experiencing. One challenge during psycho-education is that sometimes clients are focused on proving they have a medical condition, and therefore may not be open to exploring alternative explanations for their physical sensations. Following the initial psycho-education, sessions turn to helping clients identify the specific thoughts they are having about their health that may be triggering health anxiety. It is common at this stage to have clients examine the evidence for and against their thoughts and explore whether they are able to formulate and accept an alternative, more balanced thought. One thought that is likely contributing to Linda's health anxiety is her belief that feelings of discomfort in her chest must be a sign of lung cancer. A further important thought in Linda's case is that she felt she would not be able to cope with a diagnosis of lung cancer and would die if she developed the condition. The following In Focus box presents a sample thought record Linda might complete as part of treatment.

In Focus

Linda's Homework

THOUGHT RECORD: As part of therapy, Linda was required to keep a thought record whereby she identified her anxious thought and then identified evidence for and against the thought. Following this, she was asked to generate a new balanced thought.

Trigger	Anxious Thought	Anxiety (0–100)	Evidence for the Thought	Evidence against the Thought	New Balanced Thought
Noticed that I had a heavy feeling in my chest	This must be a sign that I have lung cancer	85	I used to smoke and so it is highly likely that this is a sign of lung cancer. Peter Jennings had a heavy feeling in his chest and this ended up being lung cancer.	I have been examined extensively and been reassured that I do not have lung cancer. There are many other reasons to cough other than having lung cancer. Focusing on my cough makes it more likely I will cough.	It is not likely that this is a sign that I have lung cancer. I have a habit of thinking the worst. Just because I think the worst does not make it likely.

EXPOSURE HIERARCHY: As part of her therapy, Linda created an exposure hierarchy and then worked on exposing herself to these activities, situations, persons, places, and sensations in order to reduce her anxiety.

Easy (provokes least anxiety: 0–35)	Anxiety rating (0–100)
Watch a movie where the main character has an illness	30
Imagine walking past someone who is smoking	35
Read obituaries	40
Medium (provokes moderate anxiety: 35–70)	
Go for coffee with a friend who had cancer	60
Walk up three flights of stairs	65
Sit near someone who is smoking	70
Hard (provokes the most anxiety: 70–100)	
Imagine I will be diagnosed with lung cancer	90
Visit the oncology ward at the hospital	95
Imagine that I will die of lung cancer	100

SAFETY BEHAVIOUR RECORD: As part of her therapy, Linda identified safety behaviours that she performs to alleviate her health anxiety and was asked to identify both the benefits and drawbacks of the behaviour.

Safety Behaviour	Benefits	Downside
Checking Internet for at least ½ hour a day	Makes me feel that I am keeping up to date on knowledge. Makes me feel like I am doing something to avoid getting lung cancer.	Actually increases my health anxiety because it reinforces the idea that I am in danger. There is always something that is frightening that increases my anxiety rather than decreases it.
Keeping diary of symptoms	Makes me feel like if my symptoms get worse, I will notice this and be able to go to my doctor immediately.	Keeps my attention focused on my symptoms and increases the likelihood that I will identify a symptom that will lead me to go to my doctor.

After this initial attention to thoughts, the cognitive behavioural therapist normally focuses on exposure with response prevention, a therapeutic technique that involves having clients first formulate a hierarchy of the stimuli and thoughts that they tend to avoid. Clients order the hierarchy so that they work on exposing themselves to items that are lower (i.e., less anxiety provoking) on the hierarchy first before graduating to items that are higher on the hierarchy. Key when completing exposure exercises is the concept of response prevention, which involves ensuring that clients do not employ strategies that they typically use to manage their anxiety (e.g., repeatedly checking the body for signs of change, seeking reassurance), but instead fully expose themselves to stimuli or events that produce anxiety. Exposure sometimes begins by presenting images rather than actual stimuli to clients. This can then be followed by direct exposure to a feared object, situation, or stimulus. During exposure exercises, clients rate their fear on the subjective units of discomfort scale (SUDS), which ranges from 0 or no fear to 100 or maximal fear. Ultimately, the therapist helps clients build hierarchies that range from a low level to a high level of fear. The accompanying In Focus box shows a sample exposure hierarchy.

A further component to CBT is helping clients examine their safety behaviours, such as body-checking or reassurance-seeking. It is not realistic to ask clients to never perform a checking behaviour or to never see a physician. Instead, it is important for the therapist to discuss realistic levels of safety behaviours. In terms of medical visits, some authors have suggested that clients be encouraged to take a "wait-for-two-weeks" approach to certain types of symptoms (Furer et al., 2007). This approach assumes that most symptoms resolve on their own in two weeks and do not require further medical attention. If the symptoms persist beyond this period, then it is reasonable to see a physician. In working in this area we have found that, rather than imposing limits on how often clients seek medical services, it is important for clients to decide what is reasonable after discussing it with their physician and/or friends and family members.

Adjunctive Strategies

Additional strategies can be incorporated into treatment, depending on the client. Stress management, for instance, has been advocated by some and involves helping clients identify stressors and applying various strategies to the stressor, such as relaxation, time management, and problem-solving (Taylor & Asmundson, 2004). It is also not uncommon to find clients who are anxious about their health to be fearful of death; when this occurs, this fear must also be addressed in therapy (Furer et al., 2007). Other authors advocate the importance of focusing on improving general life satisfaction and enjoyment since individuals with health anxiety are commonly overly focused and preoccupied with their health at the expense of other activities (Furer et al., 2007). In addition, mindfulness has recently been incorporated into the treatment of health anxiety (Wattar et al., 2005). In this case, therapists assist clients with bringing their complete attention to the present moment to aid clients in learning how to be present-focused rather than focused on future health problems. Beyond working with the individual with health anxiety, it is often necessary in CBT to work with the family during the course of treatment. In this case, the therapist may attend to sick-role behaviours (Barsky & Ahern, 2004). This involves helping clients consider how others respond to their behaviour and how this may be impacting their anxiety (e.g., do others only pay attention to the individual when the individual expresses worry about his or her health?). Furthermore, it can be helpful for therapists to work with health-care providers to ensure they recognize that providing excessive reassurance may exacerbate rather than improve client health anxiety.

Empirical Evidence

Considerable evidence supports the efficacy of CBT (e.g., Barsky & Ahern, 2004; Bourgault-Fagnou & Hadjistavropoulos, 2013; Greeven et al., 2007; Seivewright et al., 2008; Warwick, Clark, Cobb, & Salkovskis, 1996). For instance, when randomly assigned to a CBT or a control condition, clients significantly improve in response to CBT in comparison to the control. Of note, treatment improves not only health anxiety, but also associated problems such as generalized anxiety, depression, social function, and use of medical services (e.g., Seivewright et al., 2008). In a recent randomized controlled trial, investigators explored whether assisting patients with cognitions as compared to behaviours was more important in treating health anxiety. To study this, the researchers compared cognitive therapy (i.e., targeting thoughts and cognitive processes that contribute to health anxiety) to exposure therapy (i.e., exposing patients to stimuli that elicit health anxiety while working with the patients to reduce safety and avoidance behaviours) and found both treatments were effective at post-treatment and one-year follow-up (Weck, Neng, Richtberg, Jakob, & Stangier, 2015). Safety behaviours, however, improved more with exposure therapy than cognitive therapy. Particularly noteworthy, CBT has also been found to be efficacious for treating health anxiety when delivered in a cost-efficient manner. When CBT is provided in a group format, clients improve in comparison to a waiting list control condition (Avia et al., 1996). Furthermore, when CBT is presented online in weekly modules and paired with therapist support, clients improve in comparison to individuals who receive no treatment (Hedman et al., 2011). Internet-delivered CBT (ICBT) also appears to result in better outcomes than Internet-delivered behavioural stress management, although this later approach also results in some improvement in symptoms of health anxiety (Hedman et al., 2014). It also appears that treatment outcomes for ICBT are better among those who view ICBT as credible, who are more adherent to treatment, and who have greater therapeutic alliance with the online therapist (Hedman et al., 2013).

The above review is not meant to suggest that other approaches to health anxiety are ineffective. In fact, studies suggest that medication (e.g., paroxetine) (Greeven et al., 2007), behavioural stress management (Clark et al., 1998), cognitive therapy that incorporates principles related to meditation/mindfulness (McManus, Surawy, Muse, Vazquez-Montes, & Williams, 2012), group psycho-education based on a problem-solving approach (Buwalda, Bouman, & van Duijn, 2007), and short-term psychodynamic psychotherapy (Sorensen, Birket-Smith, Wattar, Buemann, & Salkovskis, 2011) can all be effective in treating health anxiety. The main limitation of the other approaches is that results have generally not been replicated across multiple studies.

Future Directions

Future research is needed to enhance our understanding of the continuum of responses to physical sensations. We still do not fully understand why some individuals become health anxious while others do not. More sophisticated studies that concurrently examine biological and psychosocial determinants of health anxiety are needed. Beyond questionnaires, it is possible that research could be enhanced through a greater use of technology (e.g., evidence-based mobile apps) to capture the dimensions of health anxiety in the context of everyday life. In the area of treatment, evidence clearly shows that CBT is efficacious for health anxiety, and emerging evidence supports other treatment approaches for health anxiety as well. There is a trend in the recent literature to add techniques to CBT; the question remains whether more is better. If all treatments are effective, then it is important that we give further consideration to determining which treatment approaches are the most cost-effective. Preliminary research has been conducted in this area and suggests that when individuals participate in CBT, medical and non-medical costs are substantially lowered (Hedman et al., 2010). Despite the cost-effectiveness of treating health anxiety, the reality is that most patients with health anxiety do not receive psychological treatment. More research is needed on strategies for improving the identification and management of health anxiety. ICBT could be particularly helpful for improving patient access to treatment as it overcomes multiple barriers to receiving care, such as limited time, rural and remote location, and concerns about privacy (Hadjistavropoulos, Alberts, Nugent, & Marchildon, 2014). Other important areas for research include examining the efficacy of CBT with diverse populations. Based on our review of the literature, we do not yet know the extent to which CBT is efficacious among people from ethnic minority populations.

Summary

According to the common-sense model of illness representations, after perceiving physical sensations we form a common-sense representation of these sensations in an attempt to determine their meaning. The representations are multi-dimensional in nature in that we form beliefs about the identity, cause, consequences, timeline (acute/chronic and cyclical), controllability (personal and treatment control), and emotional impact of the physical sensations. The representations we form of our physical sensations are determined not only by our physical sensations, but also by our past experiences with our health, cognitive heuristics, social factors, and culture. Personality and mood are other determining factors.

The mental representations we form are important because they influence how we cope with the physical sensations. In parallel to processing the meaning of physical sensations, we also simultaneously process how we will emotionally respond to these sensations. The way we view our physical sensations influences our emotions and health outcomes, and our emotions and health outcomes influence our representations of the physical sensations.

When physical sensations are perceived to be extremely threatening, people may experience health anxiety. Health anxiety specifically refers to excessive anxiety about one's present or future health and is often based on a misinterpretation of signs and symptoms. Health anxiety is regarded as excessive when it is persistent and results in distress, and extreme

behaviours ultimately heighten anxiety and interfere with functioning.

The cognitive behavioural model of health anxiety was introduced in this chapter. This model suggests that health anxiety results when individuals develop dysfunctional cognitions based on past experience. These cognitions result in the individual being preoccupied with his or her health and misinterpreting innocuous or benign bodily sensations to be more threatening than they actually are. The cognitive behavioural model suggests that individuals who are anxious about their health also engage in safety behaviours, such as seeking information and reassurance, and these behaviours can contribute to the anxiety. While safety behaviours are designed to reduce threat and anxiety, they have the opposite effect and usually exacerbate an individual's health concerns.

CBT has emerged as the treatment of choice for health anxiety. Key strategies include identifying and challenging dysfunctional thoughts and exposing individuals to feared stimuli while simultaneously modifying or eliminating safety behaviours. Randomized controlled trials comparing CBT to usual care suggest CBT reduces not only health anxiety but also associated problems such as generalized anxiety, depression, social function, and use of medical services. CBT is also found to be efficacious for treating health anxiety when delivered online or in groups.

Critical Thought Questions

1. Think of your most recent experience with a health concern. Apply the common-sense model of illness representations to your experience.

2. In the research literature and clinical practice, attention has been given primarily to severe health anxiety. Do you think individuals who significantly underestimate the probability/seriousness of illness and have an unrealistic optimism about their health should also be treated? How could CBT be used with these clients?

Recommended Reading

Jones, C.J., Smith, H.E., & Llewellyn, C.D. (2016). A systematic review of the effectiveness of interventions using the Common Sense Self-Regulatory Model to improve adherence behaviours. *Journal of Health Psychology, 21*(11), 2709–24.

Leventhal, H., Phillips, L.A. & Burns, E. (2016). The common-sense model of self-regulation: a dynamic framework for understanding illness self-management. *Journal of Behavioral Medicine, 39*, 935–46.

Rachman, S. (2012). Health anxiety disorders: A cognitive construal. *Behaviour Research and Therapy, 50*, 502–12.

Weck, F., Neng, J.M., Richtberg, S., Jakob, M., & Stangier, U. (2015). Cognitive therapy versus exposure therapy for hypochondriasis (health anxiety): A randomized controlled trial. *Journal of Consulting and Clinical Psychology, 83*(4), 665–76.

PART II
Health Conditions

8 Chronic Health Problems: Risk Factors, Prevention, Adjustment, and Management

Michelle M. Gagnon

Thomas Hadjistavropoulos

Learning Objectives

In this chapter you will:

- Learn about the prevalence of chronic health problems and their impact on health and well-being.

- Learn about individual and lifestyle factors that increase one's risk of developing a chronic health problem.

- Explore what it means to adjust to chronic health problems and learn about various influences on the adjustment process.

- Be introduced to how health psychologists may contribute to the prevention and management of chronic diseases and conditions.

Chronic Health Problems

Imagine waking up day after day with an illness. For many North Americans, this is a reality. **Chronic disease** represents a significant health concern in both Canada and the United States. The World Health Organization (WHO) describes chronic diseases as being of "long duration and generally slow progression" (WHO, 2017c). Although the classification of chronic diseases varies slightly across various diagnostic systems, the following are some common conditions that are generally subsumed under the umbrella of chronic disease:

- Cardiovascular disease (see Chapter 10).
- Cancer (see Chapter 12).
- **Chronic obstructive pulmonary disease (COPD)** (e.g., asthma).
- Type 1 and type 2 **diabetes.**
- Arthritis.
- Human immunodeficiency virus (HIV)/Acquired immune deficiency syndrome (AIDS; see Chapter 11).
- **Multiple sclerosis (MS).**
- **Inflammatory bowel disease** (Crohn's disease and ulcerative colitis).

In addition to various diseases and illnesses, there are other health problems that are chronic (e.g., chronic pain) and are not necessarily a "disease" in and of themselves. That is, chronic pain can be the result of a wide variety of different health conditions and injuries. In this chapter we consider a number of health problems that create long-term suffering including chronic diseases (e.g., cardiovascular disease) but also other health concerns such as chronic pain. For this reason, we will often refer to chronic health conditions and chronic health problems rather than chronic diseases.

More than half of people over 20 years of age, in both Canada and the United States, report having at least one chronic health condition and approximately 88 to 89 per cent of all deaths are due to chronic diseases such as cancer and cardiovascular disease (Public Health Agency of Canada, 2015; Ward, Schiller, & Goodman, 2014). (Figure 8.1 highlights prevalence rates of major chronic diseases in Canada by age group.) In the various chapters of this book, you will learn about several major chronic conditions and their specific prevalence.

The incidence of chronic health problems generally increases with age (Sanmartin & Healthy Analysis Division, 2015), but there are changing trends and demographic disparities. For example, the risk of developing certain chronic diseases is on the rise in children. Canada, for example, has one of the highest rates of pediatric inflammatory bowel disease (IBD) worldwide, with rates of diagnosis of pediatric IBD increasing at an alarming speed. Between 1999 and 2010, the number of children under five years of age diagnosed with IBD went up by 7.2 per cent per year (Benchimol et al., 2017). Although the cause of these increased rates of IBD in young children largely remains unknown, it is suspected that a combination of factors, including environmental and genetic contributors, are to blame (Bhat et al., 2009; Frolkis et al., 2013). Other trends are also notable in chronic disease prevalence among Canadians. Indigenous populations (see Chapter 15, which discusses cross-cultural issues and health disparities) are disproportionately affected by chronic health problems (Dyck, Osgood, Lin, Gao, & Stang, 2010; Riediger, Bruce, & Young, 2010). In Canada, Indigenous peoples are 1.5 to 2 times more likely to develop heart disease than the general Canadian population (Anand et al., 2001). This population-based difference represents one of many health disparities that occurs in chronic diseases. Disparities in prevalence of

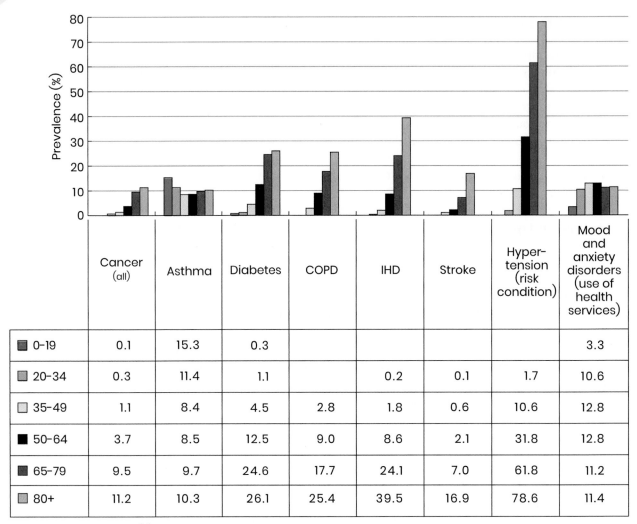

	Cancer (all)	Asthma	Diabetes	COPD	IHD	Stroke	Hyper-tension (risk condition)	Mood and anxiety disorders (use of health services)
0-19	0.1	15.3	0.3					3.3
20-34	0.3	11.4	1.1		0.2	0.1	1.7	10.6
35-49	1.1	8.4	4.5	2.8	1.8	0.6	10.6	12.8
50-64	3.7	8.5	12.5	9.0	8.6	2.1	31.8	12.8
65-79	9.5	9.7	24.6	17.7	24.1	7.0	61.8	11.2
80+	11.2	10.3	26.1	25.4	39.5	16.9	78.6	11.4

FIGURE 8.1 Prevalence (%) of major chronic diseases and risk conditions in Canadians, by age group, Canada (2011–12).

Note: COPD=Chronic Obstructive Pulmonary Disease; IHD=Ischemic Heart Disease.

chronic disease, access to treatment, and treatment outcomes exist among minority groups (Fredriksen-Goldsen, Kim, Barkan, Muraco, & Hoy-Ellis, 2013; Williams, 2002), people of lower educational attainment (Braverman, Cubbin, Gerter, Williams, & Pamuk, 2010), individuals living in rural and remote areas (Pong, DesMeules, & Lagacé, 2009), and those living in poverty (Braverman et al., 2010). Such health disparities are discussed in more detail in Chapter 15.

High rates of chronic health concerns place an enormous strain on health-care systems. In recent years, the economic burden of chronic health problems in Canada approached $200 billion per year (Public Health Agency of Canada, 2014). In addition to lost productivity and income, approximately 67 per cent of all direct health-care costs are attributed to chronic conditions (Pong et al., 2011). Similarly, in the United States, approximately 86 per cent of all 2010 health-care spending went towards individuals with one or more chronic medical concerns (Gerteis et al., 2014).

Impact of Chronic Health Conditions

The pernicious effects of a health problem can trickle into an individual's physical, psychological, social, and financial functioning. Although the nature of symptoms varies across chronic conditions, there are consequences that tend to be experienced by a large number of patients regardless of diagnosis. The most devastating consequence of many chronic diseases is loss of life. The possibility of premature death is a reality faced by many chronic disease patients and their families. Chronic illnesses represent one of the leading causes of mortality in North America (Heron, 2016; Statistics Canada, 2015b). Heart disease and cancers account for the highest number of deaths in both the United States and Canada (Kochanek, Murphy, Xu, & Tejada-Vera, 2016; Statistics Canada, 2015b). Health psychologists develop interventions targeting the psychosocial consequences of the possibility of loss of life, or work with family members after a loved one has passed away as a result of chronic disease. They may also intervene to help people with a variety of other consequences of chronic illness such as fatigue, pain, sleep problems, physical disability, psychological distress, inability to work, and relationship challenges.

Fatigue

Fatigue, which can impede patients' ability to complete daily activities, is reported across a range of chronic conditions, including cancer, HIV, cardiovascular disease, asthma, and arthritis, to name a few. It can be a core symptom of the health condition, as is the case in **fibromyalgia** (Nicassio, Moxham, Schuman, & Gevirtz, 2002), or a side effect of interventions such as the case of chemotherapy in cancer treatment (Butt et al., 2008). Individuals with chronic health problems often report feeling endlessly tired. Even after a full night's sleep, people with various chronic illnesses can wake feeling exhausted.

Pain

Pain (see Chapter 9) is pervasive across many chronic health conditions. In addition to being an obvious consequence in pain-related diagnoses, such as arthritis and fibromyalgia, pain is commonly reported among a wide variety of patients including, but not limited to, those suffering from HIV (Parker, Stein, & Jelsma, 2014), inflammatory bowel disease (Srinath, Walter, Newara, & Szigethy, 2012), diabetes (Abbott, Malik, van Ross, Kulkarni, & Boulton, 2011), cancer (Green, Hart-Johnson, & Loeffler, 2011), and multiple sclerosis (Drulovic et al., 2015). Persistent pain often leads to increased emotional and psychological distress (Gatchel, Peng, Peters, Fuchs, & Turk, 2007). Although patients experiencing chronic pain may be able to achieve some relief through pharmacological and non-pharmacological treatments, chronic pain can be challenging to treat.

Sleep Problems

Individuals with chronic health conditions including heart disease, cancer, high blood pressure, chronic pain, breathing problems, and gastrointestinal problems report more frequent insomnia than people without medical problems (Taylor et al., 2007). Sleep problems are also common among those with mental health concerns, which often accompany chronic disease. Sleep disturbances not only affect general health and immunity, but can also interfere with cognitive functioning and performance on daily tasks (McEwen, 2006b; Van Dongen, Maislin, Mullington, & Dinges, 2003).

Physical Disability

Not surprisingly, many chronic health conditions can lead to functional impairments and physical disabilities (e.g., a person with **osteoarthritis** of the knee may have difficulty with extended walking). Adjusting to loss of ability and physical function can be challenging, particularly as it impinges on one's independence, lifestyle, social roles, and previously enjoyed activities (Ch'Ng, French, & Mclean, 2008). Loss of previously held abilities can also present a threat to emotional and psychological well-being (Katz & Yelin, 2001).

Psychological Distress

Mental health concerns (e.g., anxiety, depression) and chronic health problems commonly co-occur, which makes adjustment more difficult. This relationship is complex; that is, mental health problems may interfere with recovery/rehabilitation from physical illness and physical illness can increase the risk of mental health problems (D.P. Chapman, Perry, & Strine, 2005; Strik, Lousberg, Cheriex, & Honig, 2004).

Across chronic medical conditions, **comorbid** mental health problems are commonly observed at rates higher than seen in the general population (e.g., Graff, Walker, & Bernstein, 2009; Harris, 2003; Musselman, Evans, & Nemeroff, 1998). For example, patients with cancer can become two to three times more likely than people without cancer to have a comorbid mood disorder, substance-related disorder, or anxiety disorder (Honda & Goodwin, 2004). People with MS present higher rates of depression, anxiety disorders, and bipolar disorder than the general population (Marrie et al., 2016). Moreover, comorbid mental health conditions can impede adherence to medical recommendations, which may delay recovery or interfere with the effective management of a chronic disease (DiMatteo, Lepper, & Croghan, 2000).

Loss of Work

Many people with chronic health problems (e.g., cardiovascular disease) are able to manage their condition and continue working. For a portion, however, the illness/condition or associated treatment impairs ability to remain actively employed. Many factors may contribute to an inability to continue working. These factors include pain, physical disability, fatigue, mental health problems, cognitive impairment, and gastrointestinal symptoms (Hewitt, Rowland, & Yancik, 2003; Islam et al., 2014; Schouffoer, Schoones, Terwee, & Vliet Vlieland, 2012). Loss of work can have a significant effect on financial security and is associated with decreased quality of life (Finkelstein, Tangka, Trogdon, Sabatino, & Richardson, 2009). In some cases, family caregivers may also be impacted financially by loss of work that occurs because they need extra time to provide care or support to their ill family member (Longo, Fitch, Deber, & Williams, 2006).

Relationship Challenges

In couples, having a chronically ill partner can place strain on the relationship. It is not unusual for both the healthy and the ill partner to experience psychological distress when one partner has a chronic illness (Hagedoorn, Sanderman, Bolks, Tuinstra, & Coyne, 2008; Honda & Goodwin, 2004). Dyadic adjustment to chronic health problems involves multiple components, such as coping with renegotiating roles within the relationship and dealing with the possibility of a long-term or life-threatening illness (Quittner et al., 1998; Wagner, Bigatti, & Storniolo, 2006). Moreover, people with a chronic health condition may experience decreased sexual desire, disability, or pain that impairs the couple's sexual satisfaction and intimacy (Kwan, Roberts, & Swalm, 2005; Schmidt, Hofmann, Niederwieser, Kapfhammer, & Bonelli, 2005). Similarly, the presence of a chronic condition may increase stress among all members of his or her family.

Cross-Cutting Issues in Chronic Health Conditions: Prevention, Adherence, and Adjustment

There are numerous avenues through which health psychologists can intervene in chronic disease. These include prevention and health-promotion work with at-risk populations prior to the onset of medical conditions, helping patients with adherence to recommended regimens (e.g., eating a healthier diet, taking prescribed medications consistently) as well as with adjustment to one's new life situation. Understanding factors involved in prevention, adherence, and adjustment that span chronic health conditions are central when working with populations who have or who are at risk of developing a chronic health problem.

Prevention

Certain psychological and behavioural factors are known to increase one's risk of developing a chronic health problem. These factors include *stress, lifestyle,* and *personality characteristics.*

Stress

As you recall from Chapters 2 and 3, stress plays an important role in our physical and mental health. Although it is impossible to avoid all stressful life experiences, there are good reasons to be mindful of the implications that stress has on the development and maintenance of chronic disease. Remember that stress can affect the various bodily systems. The wear and tear that chronic stress can have can ultimately increase the risk of chronic disease (McEwen, 2006a).

There are numerous examples linking chronic disease and stress. Populations who experience natural disasters or war, for example, have been found to present with increased incidence of cardiovascular disease (Krantz & McCeney, 2002; Rozanski, Blumenthal, & Kaplan, 1999). Even in the absence of major disasters, persistent life stress increases risk of cardiovascular disease. As discussed in Chapter 3, employees with persistent work stress, for example, are at a much higher

---

Inflammatory Bowel Disease (IBD) and Irritable Bowel Syndrome (IBS): Are they the same?

IBS and IBD share similarities, but they are distinct disorders. Here's how they differ:

IBD	IBS
• IBD is a chronic autoimmune disease.	• IBS is functional disorder.
• Crohn's disease and ulcerative colitis are the two most common types of IBD	• IBS does not typically result in permanent damage to the intestines. People with IBS are not generally at a higher risk of colon cancer or bleeding than the average population.
• Involves chronic inflammation of the intestines.	• Symptoms:
• IBD can result in permanent damage to the intestine. People with IBD are at a higher risk of colon cancer and bleeding.	• Cramps
	• Bloating
	• Gas
• Symptoms include:	• Mucus in stool
• Abdominal pain	• Diarrhea
• Diarrhea	• Constipation
• Rectal bleeding and blood in stool	• Treatment:
• Weight loss or loss of appetite	• People with IBS generally do not require medication. Some patients may take stool softeners, laxatives, or anti-diarrheal medications.
• Anemia	• Diet and lifestyle changes can help control symptoms.
• Fever	
• Ulcers	
• Vomiting	
• Inflammation in the skin, joints, or eyes	
• Treatment:	
• Drug therapy (anti-inflammatory drugs and immunosuppressors).	
• Diet and lifestyle changes may help some patients.	
• Some patients may require surgery.	

FIGURE 8.2 Comparing IBD and IBS.

Illustration source: iStock.com/yuoak

relative risk of developing coronary heart disease than their counterparts who do not report as much work-related stress (Kivimäki et al., 2006).

Even in your own life, have you ever noticed your guts churning during periods of high stress? This is not surprising, as stress increases colonic contractions, can lead to spasm in the colon, and may lead to increased muscle tension in the abdominal area (Collins Jr., Sorocco, Haala, Miller, & Lovallo, 2003). Individuals with persistently high levels of stress are more often seen for conditions such as **irritable bowel syndrome** (IBS), although admittedly, the link between inflammatory bowel disease, such as Crohn's disease, and stress is more tenuous (Targownik et al., 2015). Figure 8.2 highlights some additional differences between IBD and IBS.

Even diseases affecting the nervous system, such as MS, can be impacted by stress. Several researchers have used magnetic resonance imaging (MRI) scans to examine brain changes that contribute to disease progression in MS. Stressful events such as changes in routines and major negative life stressors have been shown to predict new or enlarging lesions in the brains of patients with MS (Burns, Nawacki, Kwasny, Pelletier, & Mohr, 2014; Mohr et al., 2000; Yamout, Itani, Hourany, Sibaii, & Yaghi, 2010). Interestingly, there is some evidence to suggest that positive stressors (i.e., stress that is linked to challenges/goals that provide a sense of meaning and purpose; see Chapter 3 for a more detailed discussion) are associated with reduced risk of developing new or enlarging brain lesions in MS patients (Burns et al., 2014).

Perhaps paradoxically, during stressful periods people may engage in behaviours that further increase the risk of illness. Think back to the last time you were studying for exams. Did you sleep less? Did good eating habits fly out the window? Did you exercise less? It is not uncommon for poor lifestyle practices to crop up in times of stress. Unfortunately, such behavioural changes (see Chapter 3) that occur in response to stressors, (as well as smoking and increased use of alcohol that can result from stress), are known risk factors for disease onset and progression (Cohen, Kessler, & Gordon, 1995).

Lifestyle and Risk Factors

Even when they do not occur in response to stress, certain lifestyle factors such as tobacco smoking, physical inactivity, poor sleeping habits, unhealthy eating, and excessive consumption of alcohol are contributors to the development of chronic disease (see Chapter 6). According to one study, for example, four out of five Canadians (see Figure 8.3) have a least one modifiable risk factor for chronic disease (Public Health Agency of Canada, 2016). These behaviours are seen in youth and adults alike. The WHO has estimated that by improving diet, increasing activity, and eliminating smoking, 80 per cent of heart disease, stroke, and type 2 diabetes cases, as well as 40 per cent of cancer cases, would be prevented.

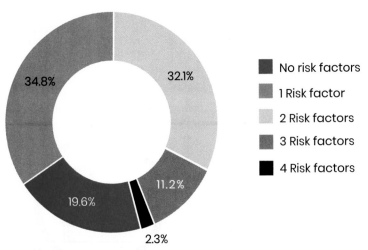

FIGURE 8.3 **Proportion of the Canadian population 20 years and older with 0 to 4 modifiable risk behaviours (heaving drinking, smoking, physical inactivity, consumption of fruits and vegetables less than five times per day) in 2014.**

Physical Inactivity

Physical inactivity is the fourth leading risk factor for global mortality and has been identified by the WHO as a serious health issue. In both adults and children, physical activity can improve cholesterol levels, blood pressure, body composition, bone density, cardiorespiratory and musculoskeletal fitness, and aspects of mental health (Tremblay et al., 2011). In adults, increased exercise can lead to reduced risk of premature death, coronary heart disease, stroke, hypertension, various forms of cancer, type 2 diabetes, and osteoporosis (Tremblay et al., 2011).

Canada and the United States lag behind several other countries when it comes to physical activity in children and youth. Each year, Canada releases a report—the ParticipACTION Report Card on Physical Activity for Children and Youth—which compares Canada to other countries with respect to how well it promotes and facilitates physical activity among children and youth (Barnes et al., 2016). On their recent report cards, both Canada and the United States earned a D in physical activity. In Canada, only 9 per cent of youth aged 5 to 17 years met the physical activity guidelines (60 minutes of physical activity per day) (Barnes et al., 2016). Slovenia came out on top, receiving an A. In Slovenia, 86 per cent of boys and 76 per cent of girls are getting the recommended 60 minutes of activity per day (Physical & Health Education Canada, 2016; Sember et al., 2016). Overall, the message is clear: many North American youth are not getting enough physical activity. Moreover, these trends of inactivity persist into adulthood. Although the recommendation is that adults engage in 150 minutes of moderate-to-vigorous physical activity per week, in increments of 10 minutes or more (Tremblay et al., 2011), 77.8 per cent of Canadians 18 years of age and over are not meeting these physical activity guidelines.

Sleeping Habits

Chronic sleep deprivation—whether caused by one's work schedule, insomnia or sleep disorders, or lifestyle factors, such as staying up late watching movies or surfing the Internet—is a significant problem. Researchers have found that over a quarter of adults do not get enough sleep (Strine & Chapman, 2005). Teenagers, too, are chronically sleep deprived. Despite guidelines from the American Academy of Pediatrics (2016) recommending that teenagers should be getting 8 to 10 hours of sleep, 45 per cent of adolescents sleep fewer than 8 hours per night on school nights (National Sleep Foundation, 2006).

Poor sleep has been associated with a plethora of negative health outcomes. Although having a health condition can impact quality of sleep, not getting enough sleep can also *lead* to chronic health problems. One example of this can be observed among employees who work night shifts or rotating night shifts, such as health-care providers, police officers, and security guards. This type of work schedule inevitably interferes with one's regular sleeping pattern. The impact can be so severe that the World Health Organization has classified night work as a possible contributor to illness (Straif et al., 2007). Studies have linked rotating night shift to diabetes (Pan, Schernhammer, Sun, & Hu, 2011), hypertension (Yeom et al., 2017), and cardiovascular issues (Gu et al., 2015). The relationship between chronic health problems and sleep loss does not only occur for shift workers. Across populations, sleep loss is associated with increased risk of having a heart attack (Ayas et al., 2003; Qureshi, Giles, Croft, & Bliwise, 1997), increased mental distress and alcohol use (Strine & Chapman, 2005), and premature death (Cappuccio, D'Elia, Strazzullo, & Miller, 2010; Fredriksen, Rhodes, Reddy, & Way, 2004).

Eating Habits

The old adage "Eat your fruits and veggies" may cause flashbacks to your childhood, but it holds up when it comes to chronic disease prevention. Increased consumption of fruits and vegetables has been found to lower risk of mortality, especially mortality from cardiovascular disease (Wang et al., 2014). *Canada's Food Guide* recommends that adults (19 to 50 years of age) consume at least 7 to 10 servings of vegetables and fruits per day (Health Canada, 2011a). Of course, it does not all come down to fruits and vegetables. Sugar intake, **trans fats**, and **saturated fats** are associated with cardiovascular diseases and type 2 diabetes, while sodium may be a culprit in many cases of cardiovascular disease (Willett et al., 2006). Additionally, overall caloric consumption can impact overall health. As discussed further in Chapter 6, both underconsumption (e.g., chronic dieting) and overconsumption (e.g., binge eating) can be associated with health problems.

In Canada and the United States, across age groups and sexes, many people are not getting the recommended daily intake of fruits and vegetables, nor the intake of dairy (Garriguet, 2009; Office of Disease Prevention and Health Promotion, 2017). Added sugar (for instance sugars found in soft drinks and juices) often exceeds by far the recommended maximum limits across age groups, and sodium intake tends to also be higher than recommended in many food products (Office of Disease Prevention and Health Promotion, 2017).

Smoking

Smoking tobacco (see Chapter 6) is the leading global cause of preventable death (WHO, 2013) and is associated with a number of chronic diseases, including chronic obstructive pulmonary diseases, cardiovascular disease, and many forms of cancer (Health Canada, 2011b). Smoking can also reduce life expectancy by more than 10 years (Jha et al., 2013)! Although the risks of smoking are numerous (see Chapter 6), quitting can significantly reduce these risks. For instance, within one year of quitting, one's risk of developing heart disease decreases by 50 per cent compared to smokers. Over time, the chances of developing heart disease (for those who have quit smoking) reduce and align more with those observed among non-smokers (WHO, 2017a).

The proportion of smokers in North America has been steadily declining (Janz, 2015), which is good news for the prevention and management of chronic disease. Nevertheless, the number of smokers remains quite high (Centers for Disease Control and Prevention, 2016; Statistics Canada, 2017) (see Chapter 6). Most smokers report starting in their teens. Unfortunately, the younger a person starts smoking, the more difficult it can be to quit later in life (Breslau & Peterson, 1996).

Alcohol

While smoking is on the decline, heavy drinking and binge drinking (see Chapter 6) are on the rise. Alcohol consumption has been linked to a number of physical health conditions, including cancer (Corrao, 2004; Rehm et al., 2003), stroke, and hypertension (Corrao, 2004; Cushman, 2001; Reynolds et al., 2003).

Heavy, excessive, and binge drinking (see Chapter 6) are significant problems in both the United States and Canada. In the United States, 90 per cent of alcohol consumed by youth is consumed while binge drinking (Centers for Disease Control and Prevention, 2015). In Canada, nearly 20 per cent of Canadians over the age of 12 report heavy drinking on a least one occasion per month over the course of the previous year. Rates of heavy drinking are highest among adults aged 20 to 34 years and decrease with age (Public Health Agency of Canada, 2016). Chapter 6 discusses these issues in more detail.

Personality Characteristics

Researchers have suggested that certain personality characteristics contribute to the risk of developing certain diseases. As an example, **Type A personality**—characteristic of people who are driven, hostile, impatient—has a long-standing history of being linked to cardiovascular diseases, such as heart attack and stroke (Friedman & Rosenman, 1959). Over time, it has become clear that, of the various dimensions of Type A personality, hostility has the strongest link to cardiovascular risk (Matthews, 2004) (see also Chapter 10).

High levels of neuroticism and low levels of conscientiousness have also been associated with the development of chronic disease (Sutin, Zonderman, Ferrucci, & Terracciano, 2013). Neuroticism is akin to emotional instability: the tendency to experience strong negative emotions and be emotionally reactive. Conscientiousness refers to self-discipline, self-control, and drive for achievement. Many researchers suspect that the links of neuroticism and conscientiousness with chronic health conditions do not follow a direct path. Rather, personality may influence lifestyle decisions and behaviours, which in turn increase disease risk (Sutin et al., 2013; Terracciano, Löckenhoff, Crum, Bienvenu, & Costa, 2008). Individuals who present with high levels of conscientiousness and low levels of neuroticism, on average, are at reduced risk of chronic disease (Christensen et al., 2002). We know, however, that personality characteristics influence physical activity levels and those individuals who are very conscientious and who present with low levels of neuroticism tend to be the most physically active (Artese, Ehley, Sutin, & Terracciano, 2017; K. E. Wilson & Dishman, 2015). As another example, people with high levels of neuroticism and low levels of conscientiousness present higher levels of chronic inflammation (B. P. Chapman et al., 2011). Inflammation, which can be part of the body's immune response when it attempts to remove harmful stimuli and begin the healing process, can be harmful when it becomes chronic. Chronic inflammation is associated with the development of disease such as cancer, arthritis, and heart disease. While we might jump to the conclusion that individuals with certain personality traits are simply at a higher risk of developing chronic inflammation, other lifestyle factors, such as unhealthy eating and weight patterns (Sutin, Ferrucci, Zonderman, & Terracciano, 2011) or poor sleep (Duggan, Friedman, McDevitt, & Mednick, 2014), which are also more commonly seen among individuals with these personality characteristic, may play a role somewhere on the path between personality and chronic disease. Although it is clear that there is a link between certain personality characteristics and chronic disease, more work is needed in this area to understand fully what aspects of personality, or behaviours that emerge as a result of personality characteristics, are contributing to higher risks of disease in certain individuals.

Adherence

The WHO defines adherence (see also Chapter 4) to long-term therapy as "the extent to which a person's behaviour—taking medication, following a diet, and/or executing lifestyle changes, correspond with agreed recommendations from a health care provider" (WHO, 2003). Across health conditions, non-adherence increases morbidity and mortality. In developing countries, only 50 per cent of patients with chronic disease adhere to recommended treatment regimens (WHO, 2003). This number is staggering, given that lack of adherence to recommended treatments may prolong disability and reduce the likelihood of a speedy recovery. Chapter 4 discusses the role of health psychologists in recommended treatment adherence.

As you learned in Chapter 4, non-adherence is a complex issue influenced by a number of factors. Non-adherence to medication is one of the most familiar forms of non-adherence and can involve not taking prescribed medications, taking them sporadically, or not taking the prescribed dosage. Non-adherence also occurs if patients do not follow recommended changes in lifestyle. This could include, for example, not making the recommended dietary changes, continuing with drug and alcohol use, or not engaging in the recommended amount of physical activity. Consequently, for many conditions, full adherence to a treatment regime may not only require medication on a daily basis, but may also require extensive lifestyle changes. In your own life, you may have experienced the challenges associated with making a significant lifestyle change, such as going to the gym regularly. Imagine the challenges associated with making

In Focus

Non-Adherence in Asthma

Asthma is a chronic inflammatory airway disease that affects 300 million people worldwide (Masoli, Fabian, Holt, & Beasley, 2004). It is the most common chronic health condition in children and one of the most common chronic conditions in adults (Ritz & Janssens, 2014). In Canada, asthma affects 8.1 per cent of Canadians over the age of 12 (Statistics Canada, 2015a). In the United States, 7.6 per cent of adults over the age of 18 reported having asthma in 2015 (Blackwell & Villarroel, 2016). Asthma causes coughing, shortness of breath, chest tightness, and wheezing; affects quality of life; and is related to absence from work, school, and activities (Meng, Babey, & Wolstein, 2012; Statistics Canada, 2015a). Asthma is generally treated with two types of medication. Daily anti-inflammatory medication (typically in the form of inhaled corticosteroid) that reduces swelling and tightening of the airways is used for long-term control. In addition, short-acting beta-adrenergic inhalers are used for quick symptom relief when asthma symptoms flare up (Ritz & Janssens, 2014). The overarching goal in asthma treatment is to achieve asthma control through the right dose and combination of medications. Developing an action plan that outlines how and when to take both forms of medication and when to seek urgent care is the most effective form of asthma management (Gibson et al., 2003).

Although this approach to managing asthma might sound straightforward, treatment non-adherence is a significant issue in asthma patients. In many instances, prescriptions for asthma medications go unfilled. Even when prescriptions are filled, patients report erratic use or discontinuation (Gamble, Stevenson, McClean, & Heaney, 2009). Estimates suggest that non-adherence rates are as high as more than 50 per cent in children (Milgrom et al., 1996), and between 30 and 70 per cent in adults (Reid, Abramson, Raven, & Walters, 2000; WHO, 2003). Non-adherence has consequences. For the individual with asthma, non-adherence often means poorer asthma outcomes, reduced lung functioning, increased hospitalization rates, and decreased quality of life. In addition, there is a significant economic burden. In recent years, the direct and indirect health care costs associated with asthma in Canada were over $1 billion per year (Asthma Society of Canada, 2014). The average direct and indirect cost of asthma in the United States was estimated at $3300 per person with asthma each year from 2002 to 2007 (American Academy of Allergy Asthma & Immunology, 2017; Blackwell & Villarroel, 2016). These high costs are significantly impacted by non-adherence (Masoli et al., 2004).

multiple changes across multiple domains! As you saw in Chapter 4, several factors determine successful adherence, some of which are external. Medication or therapy factors (e.g., medication regime is too complicated), health-care provider/health-care system factors (e.g., insufficient instruction from health-care providers), disease-related factors (e.g., memory deficits), and patient-related factors may all play a role (e.g., attitude toward treatment) (Brown & Bussell, 2011; Gillisen, 2007; WHO, 2003). Unfortunately, across health systems, blaming patients for non-adherence continues to predominate (WHO, 2003).

Adjustment

Receiving a diagnosis of a chronic disease can be life changing. It is not surprising that each person responds to chronic disease in his or her own way. Two people with the same diagnosis will likely not have the same psychological or emotional experience. The process of adjusting to the circumstances of chronic disease is increasingly recognized as integral to disease outcomes. Adjustment can be described in terms of "the presence or absence of diagnosed psychological disorder, psychological symptoms, or negative mood" (Stanton, Revenson, & Tennen, 2007).

Research in the area of adjustment is vast and a number of conceptualizations of the adjustment process have been proposed. Annette Stanton from the University of California, Los Angeles, is a leading health researcher in the area of adjustment and has made significant contributions in this area. In their work examining cross-cutting issues in adjustment to chronic illness, Stanton and her colleagues have come to certain conclusions regarding chronic disease and adjustment processes. First, they note that *chronic disease affects multiple domains of functioning and consequently adjustment must occur across these multiple domains* (e.g., lifestyle, relationships, mental health). Chronic disease and its management could, for example, interfere with ability to work, care for one's family, and function socially, as well as cause strain in couples (Peyrot et al., 2005). This aligns with our understanding of the adjustment process. Positive adjustment is not simply the absence of pathology, but rather involves the integration of interpersonal, cognitive, emotional, physical, and behavioural domains (Stanton et al., 2007).

Second, Stanton and colleagues *do not view adjustment as a static process, but as one that unfolds over time*. Adjustment is necessarily influenced by the nature of the health condition and the environment of the sufferer. Stage theories of adjustment, such as that often seen in grief (e.g., the five stages of grief by Kübler-Ross [1973]: denial, anger, bargaining, depression, acceptance), have been proposed, yet there is relatively little empirical support for many of these theories (Stanton et al., 2007; Wortman & Silver, 2001). Rather, the evidence suggests that adjustment must occur over time as the disease progresses or as symptom flares occur. Take, for instance, an inflammatory bowel disease (IBD), such as Crohn's or ulcerative colitis. Even with strict adherence to treatment and careful monitoring of lifestyle factors, flares can happen. For some patients, flares can be debilitating. They can include diarrhea, rectal bleeding, urgent bowel movements, constipation, abdominal cramps and pain, fever, fatigue, or weight loss, depending on the condition (Crohn's & Colitis Foundation of America, 2009). The unpredictability of these symptoms can make adjustment challenging. Adjustment to IBD is usually influenced by multiple patient factors including disease acceptance, disease characteristics, emotional representation of illness, frequency of gastroenterologist visits, and coping (Kiebles, Doerfler, & Keefer, 2010). As the management of these factors ebb and flow over the course of one's disease, degree of adjustment will also change. Moreover, life circumstances (e.g., pregnancy, varying levels of support from friends and family, work status) will change over the course of the health condition and these changes may require additional adaptations and re-adjustment.

Lastly, Stanton and colleagues point out that *every individual will adjust differently* (Stanton et al., 2007). Given the number of domains in which adjustment must occur, it would be foolish to assume that patients will experience equivalent adjustment within each domain. Patients will be set on distinct adjustment trajectories due to variations in premorbid functioning, social support, and demographic factors (Helgeson, Snyder, & Seltman, 2004; Rodríguez-Artalejo et al., 2006). Differences in symptom presentation will also affect adjustment (Stanton et al., 2007; Stone, Broderick, Porter, & Kaell, 1997). All of the aforementioned factors contribute to diverse adjustment outcomes across populations with chronic health problems.

Psychological Comorbidity and Adjustment

Having a comorbid psychological disorder can play a significant role in chronic illness. Depression is a frequent psychological comorbidity of chronic health conditions; people with chronic health problems are more likely to have a comorbid depressive disorder (D.P. Chapman et al., 2005). Those with diabetes, for example, are twice as likely to have a comorbid depressive disorder as compared to the general population (Anderson, Freedland, Clouse, & Lustman, 2001). Similarly, depression is far more prevalent in individuals with HIV (9.4 per cent) than without

HIV (5.2 per cent) (Ciesla & Roberts, 2001). Among those who experience a myocardial infarction (commonly referred to as a "heart attack"), the incidence of depression increases 15 to 30 per cent compared to the general population (Strik et al., 2004).

Across chronic health problems, there is evidence that having a comorbid mental health problem leads to increased symptom severity, more rapid illness progression, and higher rates of mortality (Ciechanowski, Katon, Russo, & Hirsch, 2003; Cook et al., 2004; Ickovics et al., 2001; Ludman et al., 2004). In a meta-analysis of 31 studies involving over 16,922 patients with a chronic illness (illnesses included diabetes, diabetic neuropathy, asthma, chronic obstructive pulmonary disease coronary disease, heart failure, rheumatoid arthritis, and osteoarthritis) (Katon, Lin, & Kroenke, 2007), patients with a comorbid depression or anxiety diagnosis reported significantly higher numbers of medical symptoms than those without a comorbid anxiety or depressive disorder.

While the diagnosis of a mental health condition in and of itself may be tied to the increase in perceived and actual symptom severity (e.g., anxiety can exacerbate a variety of physical symptoms such as headaches), additional influences are at play. Mental health comorbidity can lead to poorer treatment adherence and reduced likelihood of healthy lifestyle choices (Ciechanowski, Katon, & Russo, 2000; Ziegelstein et al., 2000). Consequently, treating mental health symptoms in individuals with chronic disease can have a positive impact on disease symptoms, functional status, and quality of life (Borson et al., 1992; Lin et al., 2003).

Additional Factors Related to Adjustment

Personal and situational characteristics have been found to be predictive of adjustment to chronic illness. Examples of such characteristics include gender, personality, social support, cultural background, socio-economic status, and personal coping resources.

Gender

Gender can affect adjustment. Gender differences in adjustment have been noted, for example, in patients with diabetes (Iida, Parris Stephens, Rook, Franks, & Salem, 2010), cancer (Hagedoorn et al., 2008), arthritis (Revenson, 2003), and heart disease (Hunt-Shanks, Blanchard, & Reid, 2009; Rohrbaugh et al., 2002), with women experiencing greater difficulties. Gender differences in disease severity can also occur. Women with coronary heart disease have more comorbid health conditions (e.g., diabetes, hypertension, renal dysfunction) and higher rates of complications than do men with the same diagnosis (Bucholz et al., 2014). A number of factors may contribute to these gender gaps in disease adjustment and severity. In heart disease, the discrepancy may be due, in part, to women being older at the onset of the disease (Bucholz et al., 2014). Being at a more advanced age places women at an increased risk of having a comorbid disease, as the prevalence of many diseases can increase with age (e.g., arthritis, hypertension). Social roles in a marital relationship may also contribute to gender differences in adjustment. In heterosexual couples, women provide more support to an ill male partner than male partners provide to their ill wives (Iida et al., 2010; Li, Mak, & Loke, 2013). As a result, men who are ill may receive more support, resulting in improved adjustment (Iida et al., 2010). Moreover, in heterosexual couples where one partner has an illness such as cancer, female partners report more distress, regardless of whether they are the partner with the illness or the caregiving partner (Hagedoorn et al., 2008). This finding of higher distress among women, regardless of who has the illness, is somewhat aligned with rates of distress in the general population where women report more depressive symptoms as well as worse perceived health and more functional limitations than men (Helgeson, 2012). As a result, the discrepancies between men and women observed in chronic disease appear to parallel, to some extent, the trends observed in healthy adults.

Personality

In addition to contributing to disease risk, several personality traits have been linked to disease adjustment. Optimism, in particular, has received notable attention. Higher levels of optimism tend to be associated with better health outcomes (see Rasmussen, Wrosch, Scheier, & Carver, 2006 for review). For instance, among patients recovering from coronary artery bypass surgery, individuals with higher levels of optimism report greater quality of life, more positive mood, and faster rates of recovery (Mahler & Kulik, 2000; Scheier et al., 1989). Similarly, in patients with MS, optimism is associated with more positive appraisals of the illness (S.L. Hart, Vella, & Mohr, 2008). The mechanisms through which optimism improves outcomes appear to be related to coping. Optimism leads to more active and adaptive approaches to coping, such as positive reappraisal, acceptance, and problem-focused coping (Carver, Scheier, & Segerstrom, 2010). Pessimism, in contrast, can increase avoidance, denial, and disengagement from goals (Carver et al., 2010; Rasmussen et al., 2006). Similarly, high levels of neuroticism can impede medication adherence, while high levels of agreeableness and conscientiousness increase the likelihood of adherence to treatment (Axelsson, Brink, Lundgren, & Lötvall, 2011; J.M. Bruce, Hancock, Arnett, & Lynch, 2010; Ediger et al., 2007).

Social Support

Chapter 3 discusses the powerful link between social support and health. Social support is also tied to adjustment and long-term outcomes in chronic disease. This was observed in a study examining readmission to hospital in 371 patients following myocardial infarction. Hospital re-admissions were significantly lower among patients who reported good levels of social support as compared to low or moderate levels of social support (Rodríguez-Artalejo et al., 2006). Similarly, among patients with kidney disease undergoing **dialysis** and **hemodialysis**, greater social support is associated with better patient satisfaction, higher health-related quality of life, and fewer hospitalizations (Plantinga et al., 2010).

Multiple explanations have been proposed for the pathways through which social support enhances adjustment. Evidence suggests that social support could help boost immune functioning, which could help improve health and, consequently, adjustment (Uchino, 2006). Supportive others provide opportunity for ill individuals to participate in conversations and activities that allow them to better understand and cope with their diagnoses and symptoms (Helgeson & Zajdel, 2017). Supportive others may also encourage adherence and positive health behaviours (Miller & DiMatteo, 2013). Social support can also increase self-esteem, which further facilitates psychological adjustment (Symister & Friend, 2003).

iStock.com/katarzynabialasiewicz

Social support is key to adjustment and long-term outcomes in chronic disease.

Culture, Race, and Ethnicity

Racial and ethnic disparities in chronic disease prevalence and mortality are observed in Canada and in the United States (see Chapter 15). In Canada, Indigenous populations are more likely to present with diabetes (Dyck et al., 2010), cardiovascular disease (Riediger et al., 2010), obesity (S.G. Bruce, Riediger, Zacharias, & Young, 2010), and tuberculosis (Smeja & Brassard, 2000) as well as higher rates of mortality from circulatory diseases and cancers (Tjepkema, Wilkins, Senécal, Guimond, & Penney, 2010). Race and ethnicity variables are sometimes compounded with socio-economic status differences (discussed below), which creates a challenge in disentangling the contribution of each variable. Access to care, past experiences with health care, and traditional or cultural healing practices can all influence adjustment to chronic disease (Harper et al., 2013; Jacklin et al., 2017; Lee, Lin, Wrensch, Adler, & Eisenberg, 2000; Peek et al., 2010). A more detailed discussion of the interrelation among cultural, racial, or ethnicity factors and disparities in health outcomes can be found in Chapter 15.

Socio-Economic Status

It is well documented that individuals of lower socio-economic status (SES) experience poorer illness outcomes. For instance, patients with kidney disease, HIV, and chronic obstructive pulmonary disease who are of lower SES, on average, present with greater illness severity (Bello, Peters, Rigby, Rahman, & El Nahas, 2008; Cunningham et al., 2005; Eisner et al., 2011). In patients with diabetes, mortality rate among those of low SES is two times higher than those with the highest SES (Saydah & Lochner, 2010).

The potential contributors to the association between SES and disease are numerous. People of lower SES are more likely to be exposed to chronic stressors (e.g., poorer living conditions, food insecurity, environmental hazards, higher rates of crime) that may directly influence health (Lovasi, Hutson, Guerra, & Neckerman, 2009; Matthews & Gallo, 2011). They may also have reduced access to many health-care services (Bloch, Rozmovits, & Giambrone, 2011; J.T. Hart, 1971; Nicholas, Kalantar-Zadeh, & Norris, 2015; Willems, De Maesschalck, Deveugele, Derese, & De Maeseneer, 2005; Williamson et al., 2006). Additionally, loss of work resulting from chronic disease may be particularly detrimental for individuals of low SES who rely on the income to support their families (Stanton et al., 2007).

Coping Processes

Coping strategies (see Chapter 3 for a more detailed discussion) are thought to mediate the relationship between illness and adjustment (Stanton & Revenson, 2007). In the context of chronic illness, coping efforts can lead to approach or avoidance of aspects of the chronic disease (Stanton & Revenson, 2011; Suls & Fletcher, 1985). Approach-oriented coping involves actively engaging in strategies, such as solving problems, gathering information, seeking support, and actively thinking through one's emotional experience. Avoidance-oriented strategies involve behavioural (e.g., disengagement from treatment) or cognitive (e.g., denial) strategies to distance oneself from the reality of the illness (Stanton et al., 2007). Generally speaking, people who use more approach-oriented coping adjust better to their disease (Hack & Degner, 2004; Karlsen & Bru, 2002), and avoidance-oriented coping is associated with poorer adjustment (Dew et al., 1994; Jim, Richardson, Golden-Kreutz, & Andersen, 2006). That being said, over the course of prolonged chronic illness people are likely to engage in multiple forms of coping at various points.

Prevention and Psychological Interventions for Chronic Health Problems

Given that addressing chronic illness begins with prevention and continues into diagnosis and adjustment, health psychologists may be drawn on at various times throughout a patient's care. Here are some hypothetical examples of how health psychologists are relied on in medical and other community settings to assist with chronic disease prevention and management:

Due to a recent increase in HIV diagnoses in an urban primary-care centre, a community health psychologist was asked to offer educational sessions to community members. Sessions focused on risk factors and lifestyle factors associated with disease prevention, and mental health in people with HIV.

Liam has a fast-paced job as a corporate lawyer. He feels harried and stressed, works long hours, and does not take good care of himself. His physician has noted that his stress levels are taking a toll on his body and are putting him at risk for becoming ill. Liam decides to seek the services of a health psychologist for help with stress reduction.

Julia has kidney disease. Despite many discussions about the importance of regular engagement in treatment, Julia is not taking her medications and has missed several of her dialysis appointments. Her treatment team is growing increasingly concerned. Julia is referred to see the team's health psychologist to explore and address barriers to treatment adherence.

Philip is a 45-year-old cancer survivor. He has been in remission for several years and his physician says that he is doing well. Nevertheless, Philip becomes anxious whenever he experiences certain body sensations because he incorrectly believes that such sensations are a sign of illness. Philip's physician recommended that he see a health psychologist to help him address his health-related anxiety.

Colleen is a 75-year-old woman with **rheumatoid arthritis**. She has been living with this diagnosis for many years, but has recently started feeling frustrated about the degree to which pain is interfering with her life. She has less energy, goes out less often with friends and family, is sleeping poorly, and generally feels sad. At her most recent appointment with her rheumatologist, the physician indicated that Colleen might benefit from seeing the team psychologist to address these changes in her mood and functioning. It is possible for Colleen to improve her mood and quality of life, despite her pain.

Cassandra is a 15-year-old girl with diabetes. She has been taking insulin and managing her diabetes very independently since the age of 12. Recently, however, her parents have noticed that she has become resistant to treatment and self-management, is easily angered, and acts out whenever they try to broach the issue. Cassandra's endocrinologist recommended that the family see a psychologist to support Cassandra with her current concerns regarding treatment and to help Cassandra's parents develop strategies to work with Cassandra on optimizing her self-management and to improve the family's communication around her health condition.

Prevention and Promotion

In many clinical settings, health psychologists play a large role in disease prevention and health promotion. Health promotion is defined by the WHO as the process of enabling people to increase control over, and improve, their health (WHO, 2017b). Health psychologists frequently work with populations that are known to be at higher risk of developing chronic disease. This may include targeted interventions with

Psychologists often work with families in which a child or adolescent has a chronic disease.

individuals who are, for instance, pre-diabetic. When working to prevent chronic disease, psychologists may help patients better manage their stress, quit smoking, become more physically active, or help patients make other lifestyle changes (American Psychological Association, 2017). Health psychologists integrate a number of strategies, such as psychoeducation, problem-solving training (Lilly et al., 2014), and interviewing techniques designed to enhance clients' motivation to make healthier choices and improve the management of their health conditions (Martins & McNeil, 2009). Psychologists may also be involved more broadly with populations to promote health in groups at high risk for disease, such as in communities of lower SES. In addition to working directly with patients and clients, psychologists may be involved in policy making, media campaigns, and program development. Health psychologists are also engaged in research to help identify risk factors for chronic disease and strategies for the promotion of wellness across the lifespan.

Psychologists on Social Media

In recent years, there has been increasing use of Internet and social media by health providers in health care and in research. Social media are used for a number of purposes by health-care professionals, such as to share the latest research, promote best practices in health care, communicate important health-related information to the public, and advocate for patient care. Patients with chronic illness, on the other hand, are taking to social media to discuss their experiences with chronic disease management, diagnosis, and treatment; and as a place to build a community and garner support. Patients are often interested in integrating social media into their care. For instance, in a study of inflammatory bowel disease patients' attitudes towards and use of social media, 84 per cent of patients were interested in having some form of interaction with health-care professionals on social media to manage their health (Timms, Forton, & Poullis, 2014). Of patients using social media, 29.5 per cent reported using it for support for their illness, and 45.5 per cent reported that they belonged to or were following a specific group related to their IBD.

Twitter has been a particularly popular platform for health promotion and disease management. By tweeting about their research or clinical experiences, or retweeting relevant articles, psychologists and health-care providers are speaking out about important issues in the prevention and management of chronic disease. If you are a Twitter user, then you know that hashtags allow people posting about similar topics to connect, and essentially serve as a search function on social media platforms. Hashtags are used by patient and health-care communities for a whole host of conditions. To better promote the use of social media in health care, the *Healthcare Hashtag Project* is a website that was developed as a place where all health care–related hashtags are compiled and their use tracked. The goal of the *Healthcare Hashtag Project* is to promote health-related conversations, advocacy, and community building by uniting tweeters through the use of hashtags (Symplur, 2017). Researchers are also using hashtags to develop campaigns to raise awareness, to combat stigma, or to increase evidence-based practice for specific conditions (Wehner et al., 2014). The #DontHateYourGuts, the #ThisIsDiabetes, and the #itdoesnthavetohurt campaigns are three campaigns directed at inflammatory bowel disease, diabetes awareness, and children's pain, respectively. It is important to note, however, that not all health information that is disseminated through social media and the Internet is accurate (Bailey, LaChapelle, LeFort, Gordon, & Hadjistavropoulos, 2013) and that it is important for patients to be educated on how to distinguish credible from non-credible information.

In addition to social media campaigns, moderated health chats are also used on Twitter, other social media platforms, or through online chat systems. These chats are often scheduled by health centres or health-care providers. Interested individuals such as health-care providers, patients, and caregivers are able to join. During the scheduled chat time, participants can ask questions,

Twitter post by the American Diabetes Association using the #ThisIsDiabetes hashtag to promote diabetes awareness.

discuss concerns, and provide support related to a specific disease. An example of these is the online health chats for adolescents with chronic pain offered by the Boston Children's Hospital (The Comfort Ability, 2016).

Self-Management

Self-management is a process in which a person is actively engaged in understanding and implementing the day-to-day tasks involved in managing his or her chronic health problem (Barlow, Wright, Sheasby, Turner, & Hainsworth, 2002). Self-management programs aim to empower people with chronic disease by increasing their sense of self-efficacy and agency in managing their illness. This may be achieved in conjunction with family members and health-care professionals, and may target lifestyle changes, psychosocial factors, and consequences of the illness (Richard & Shea, 2011). Psychologists are frequently involved in helping patients engage in self-management.

Optimal self-management strategies may, to an extent, be illness dependent as individuals learn to navigate the specific needs and consequences of their health condition. Nevertheless, there are certain commonalities in the self-management process that span diseases and health conditions (Schulman-Green et al., 2012). Generally, the self-management process includes learning about the condition and health needs, taking ownership of the health needs, and performing health-promotion activities. This involves active treatment engagement and modification of lifestyle factors to minimize the impact of the health condition. Good self-management also encompasses activating and/or making use of psychological, social, and community resources.

Formal and informal self-management programs are available to people with chronic health conditions. The Stanford Model provides an example of a formal self-management program. For over 30 years, the research team at the Stanford Patient Education Research Centre has been developing and evaluating self-management approaches (Stanford School of Medicine, 2017b). They offer programs for people with HIV (Gifford, Laurent, Gonzales, Chesney, & Lorig, 1998), type 2 diabetes (K. Lorig, Ritter, Villa, & Armas, 2009), chronic pain (LeFort, Gray-Donald, Rowat, & Jeans, 1998), and cancer, and a general program for individuals with various chronic conditions (K. Lorig et al., 2001). Their programs are offered in a group format, generally through two-hour meetings over six weeks, and are led by peers (i.e., individuals who have health problems of their own). Topics for each program vary, but share similarities. For instance, the HIV program covers the topics of (1) integration of medication regimes in day-to-day life for consistent use; (2) techniques for dealing with frustration, fear, fatigue, pain, and isolation; (3) exercise for maintaining and improving strength, flexibility, and endurance; (4) communicating effectively with family, friends, and health professionals; (5) nutrition; (6) evaluating symptoms; (7) **advance directives**; (8) decision-making; and (9) sex, intimacy, and disclosure (Stanford School of Medicine, 2017a).

Self-management programs are led either by peers or by health professionals, often using manuals or online platforms. Self-management manuals have been developed for a number of conditions such as chronic pain in older adults (Hadjistavropoulos & Hadjistavropoulos, 2019) and HIV (Webel et al., 2016). Internet-based self-management programs have been developed for patients with pain conditions such as arthritis and fibromyalgia (K. Lorig, Ritter, Laurent, & Plant, 2008; Shigaki et al., 2008). Text messaging (Hanauer, Wentzell, Laffel, & Laffel, 2009; Kim, 2007) and email reminders (Hanauer et al., 2009) have been used to reinforce monitoring of glucose and medication adherence in patients with diabetes. Moreover, mobile phone apps for the self-management of chronic disease are also gaining popularity and many may be a useful adjunct to treatment in a number of health conditions (Con & De Cruz, 2016).

Self-management programs are effective for improving certain health outcomes. Although outcomes tend to vary as a function of health condition, patients engaged in self-management programs generally experience more benefits than other patients (Barlow et al., 2002). Self-management programs have been shown to lead to improvements in treatment adherence (Gifford et al., 1998), improvements in ability to cope with the illness (Kennedy, 2004), decreases in symptom severity (Gifford et al., 1998), and changes in lifestyle factors (S.R. Wilson et al., 1993). Importantly, some self-management programs have shown reduced health-care costs and service use (Ahn et al., 2013; Kennedy, 2004; K.R. Lorig, Mazonson, & Holman, 1993). Peer support programs also exist (see Table 8.1). Such programs offer peer and social support, although they vary with respect to which they incorporate self-management approaches.

Psychological Interventions

Psychological interventions for people with chronic disease may be implemented for a variety of reasons. Psychological interventions may target stress or behavioural changes as a means of preventing chronic illness or disease progression. Psychological interventions can also help with adherence, coping and distress, and mental health issues experienced by individuals living with a chronic disease. A number of therapeutic approaches may be used by health psychologists in the context of chronic disease.

Cognitive Behavioural Therapy

As you may recall from Chapter 1, cognitive behavioural therapy (CBT) is an intervention that targets cognitions and behaviours that may be contributing to emotional distress, psychological symptoms, and problematic outcomes. CBT is a widely used, evidence-based approach to treating a number of mental health conditions in children and adults (for review, see Butler, Chapman,

Table 8.1 | Examples of Peer Support Programs (Many of Which Provide Self-Management Information) for Chronic Illnesses in Canada and the United States

Disease	Canada	United States
Arthritis	*Canadian Orthopaedic Foundation* Ortho Connect, a peer support program through which orthopaedic patients are matched with volunteers who have undergone similar surgical treatment for their condition. http://whenithurtstomove.org/my-surgery/talk-to-someone/ (accessed June 14, 2017) *The Arthritis Society:* Online forum (discussion board) for individuals affected by arthritis and their caregivers.	*Arthritis Foundation* Arthritis Support Networks, peer-led, local support networks for adults with all types of arthritis. http://www.arthritis.org/arthritisintrospective/ (accessed June 14, 2017)
Asthma	*Asthma Society of Canada* Asthma Ambassador Program, a peer-to-peer support and education program in which trained ambassadors share their asthma-related knowledge with their friends, family, and communities. Asthma & Allergy Support Line http://www.asthma.ca/ (accessed June 14, 2017)	*Asthma and Allergy Foundation of America* Online support community for parents and caregivers of children with asthma (discussion board). https://community.aafa.org/ (accessed June 14, 2017)
Cancer	*Canadian Cancer Society* Telephone-based peer support for adults 18 years and older diagnosed with cancer or who are a caregiver of an individual with cancer. http://www.cancer.ca/en/support-and-services/support-services/talk-to-someone-who-has-been-there/?region=on (accessed June 14, 2017)	*American Cancer Society* Reach to Recovery, a breast cancer support group in which volunteers provide live or phone support to individuals with breast cancer. Cancer Helpline, a 24-hour service where trained individuals provide information or support by phone or live chat. https://www.cancer.org/treatment/support-programs-and-services.html (accessed June 14, 2017)
Cardiovascular Disease and Heart Disease	*Heart and Stroke Foundation* Living with Stroke™, a community-based support and educational program for stroke survivors and caregivers. http://www.heartandstroke.ca/stroke/recovery-and-support/living-with-stroke (accessed June 14, 2017)	*CardioSmart Initiative, American College of Cardiology* Mended Hearts Program, a peer support organization made up of patients, families and caregivers impacted by cardiovascular disease. http://mendedhearts.org/ https://www.cardiosmart.org/Connect/Community-Peer-Support (accessed June 14, 2017)

Continued

Table 8.1 | Continued

Disease	Canada	United States
		American Heart Association Support Network, online peer-to-peer support for caregivers of individuals with heart disease or stroke. http://www.heart.org/HEARTORG/Support/Support_UCM_001103_SubHomePage.jsp (accessed June 14, 2017)
Diabetes	*Diabetes Canada* Peer-to-peer support groups delivered by trained volunteers in community settings. http://www.diabetes.ca/in-your-community/support-groups (accessed June 14, 2017)	*American Diabetes Association* Online support community (discussion board). https://community.diabetes.org/home (accessed June 14, 2017) 12-month program "Living with Type 2 Diabetes" that offers guidance to help people manage diabetes. Program includes peer support online and by phone. http://www.diabetes.org/living-with-diabetes/recently-diagnosed/living-with-type-2-diabetes/?referrer=https://www.google.ca/ (accessed June 14, 2017)
HIV/AIDS	*Canada's Source for HIV and hepatitis C information (CAITIE)* Provides list of regional hotlines. http://www.catie.ca/en/basics/hiv-and-aids/hotlines (accessed June 14, 2017)	*Health Resources & Services Administration* Provides list of regional hotlines. https://hab.hrsa.gov/get-care/state-hivaids-hotlines (accessed June 14, 2017)
Inflammatory Bowel Disease	*Crohn's and Colitis Canada* "Gutsy Peer Support": an online peer-to-peer support program for Canadians affected by IBD. https://gutsypeersupport.ca/gutsypeersupport (accessed June 14, 2017)	*Crohn's & Colitis Foundation* Online Support Education Group: a four-week program with weekly chat sessions. Chats available for patients and for caregivers. https://www.ccfacommunity.org/chatseries (accessed June 14, 2017)
Kidney Disease	*The Kidney Foundation of Canada* Kidney Connect Program: a peer support program for individuals with kidney disease and caregivers, family members, or friends. Support provided by phone or online. https://www.kidney.ca/document.doc?id=4394 (accessed June 14, 2017)	*National Kidney Foundation* Peers Lending Support: a telephone-based peer support program for patients with kidney disease. https://www.kidney.org/sites/default/files/01-10-599b_cbb_peerspatflyer.pdf (accessed June 14, 2017)
Multiple Sclerosis	*MS Society of Canada* Peer Support Program: a telephone- or Internet-based peer support program connecting patients living with MS with peer volunteers. https://mssociety.ca/support-services/ms-peer-support-program (accessed June 14, 2017)	*National Multiple Sclerosis Society* Peer Connections: a peer support offered via email, telephone, or through an online community to individuals with MS or their family members. http://www.nationalmssociety.org/Resources-Support/Find-Support/Connect-with-Peers-One-on-One (accessed June 14, 2017)

Note: This table does not represent a complete list of programs available in Canada and the United States. This table provides examples of groups associated with national organizations. Local and regional support groups may also be available in certain areas.

Forman, & Beck, 2006). CBT treatment protocols vary in the way they are organized and with respect to their specific emphasis, but generally involve psychoeducation, relaxation training, self-monitoring, identifying and challenging unhelpful thoughts, implementation of behavioural strategies (e.g., pacing, gradual exposure), and relapse prevention. In the context of chronic illness, CBT programs have been used to address both aspects of the disease management (e.g., adherence) and psychological sequelae (e.g., coping, distress) or comorbidity (e.g., anxiety, depression). Although CBT content is adapted and generally made to address disease-related concerns, CBT interventions in the context of medical conditions still share the general framework described above.

CBT interventions in the context of chronic illness can reduce risk of further health issues. For example, in HIV populations where there is an increased prevalence of depressive disorders, which can interfere with treatment and adherence, CBT has been shown to lead to a decrease in symptoms of depression (Kennard et al., 2014). In patients with type 2 diabetes, CBT targeting adherence and depression is effective at increasing adherence, decreasing depression, and improving glycemic control (Gonzalez et al. 2010). Similar programs focused on adherence and depression have been examined on a larger scale in patients with uncontrolled type 2 diabetes (Safren et al., 2014).

In recent years, there has also been a rise in web-based delivery of CBT for chronic health conditions. Such programs can be particularly beneficial among medical populations where disability may impede capacity to attend treatment or where a plethora of medical appointments makes it challenging to add more commitments. Programs have included, for example, a self-guided CBT Internet intervention to cope with cancer-related distress (Beatty, Koczwara, & Wade, 2011), therapist-guided CBT for anxiety and depression following cancer remission (Alberts, Hadjistavropoulos, Dear, & Titov, 2017), CBT pain management program for individuals with fibromyalgia (Friesen et al., 2017), CBT for depression and anxiety in patients with chronic kidney disease (Chan, Dear, Titov, Chow, & Suranyi, 2016), and CBT for symptom management in irritable bowel syndrome (Hunt, Moshier, & Milonova, 2009). Across these various programs, positive changes can be noted in disease-related symptoms, adherence, and mental health symptoms.

Mindfulness and Acceptance-Based Approaches

Mindfulness-based approaches, such as mindfulness-based stress reduction (MBSR), are rapidly gaining popularity as treatment options for people with health problems. Mindfulness can be defined as "paying attention, on purpose, in the present moment, and non-judgmentally" and shares common elements with meditation (Kabat-Zinn, 1990, 1994). Jon Kabat-Zinn originally developed MBSR for patients with chronic pain and associated symptoms in the early 1990s. Since this time, MBSR has been applied across a variety of conditions and concerns. In its original form, MBSR is offered in 2- to 2.5-hour group sessions over 8 to 10 weeks. In these sessions, participants learn to increase their awareness, learn new breathing and mindfulness skills, and change the way in which they respond

Material republished with the express permission of: Regina Leader-Post, a division of Postmedia Network Inc.

Researchers at the University of Regina in Saskatchewan have developed a therapist-led internet cognitive behavioural therapy program to help cancer survivors cope with symptoms of depression and anxiety.

to distressing thoughts, sensations, and emotions. A formal home daily meditation practice is also incorporated in some MBSR programs.

Mindfulness and MBSR interventions have been applied in populations with fibromyalgia (Astin et al., 2003; Grossman, Tiefenthaler-Gilmer, Raysz, & Kesper, 2007), cancer (Smith, Richardson, Hoffman, & Pilkington, 2005; Speca, Carlson, Goodey, & Angen, 2000), chronic low back pain (Cramer, Haller, Lauche, & Dobos, 2012; Morone, Greco, & Weiner, 2008), arthritis (Pradhan et al., 2007), irritable bowel syndrome (Ljótsson et al., 2010), and HIV (Gayner et al., 2012), to name a few. Reviews of effects of MBSR on chronic disease have shown that MBSR can lead to improvements in depression, anxiety, and psychological distress (Bohlmeijer, Prenger, Taal, & Cuijpers, 2010; Merkes, 2010). Preliminary findings even suggest that MBSR may have beneficial effects on cognitive functioning in people with MS (Blankespoor, Schellekens, Vos, Speckens, & de Jong, 2017) and older persons who experience cognitive decline due to dementing illnesses (Quintana-Hernández et al., 2015; Smart, Segalowitz, Mulligan, Koudys, & Gawryluk, 2016) .

Acceptance and commitment therapy (ACT) is based on the notion that our attempts to control distressing and aversive internal experiences are futile and may actually lead to increased distress and interference. Within an ACT framework, patients are encouraged to increase their awareness and engage in non-judgemental acceptance of their experiences. The objective is to improve psychological flexibility and functioning, and to decrease interference of unpleasant experiences by identifying valued life directions and committing to actions that support these values (Hayes, Strosahl, & Wilson, 2012).

ACT has been well-supported for the treatment of depression and anxiety (Forman, Herbert, Moitra, Yeomans, & Geller, 2007). There has been a proliferation of research examining ACT in the treatment of chronic pain, which has shown that ACT leads to decreases in pain interference, depression, and pain-related anxiety (Wetherell et al., 2011), and can be an alternative to CBT (Veehof, Oskam, Schreurs, & Bohlmeijer, 2011). In cardiac patients, initial evidence suggests that an acceptance-based intervention can be helpful for modifying diet and increasing physical activity (Goodwin, Forman, Herbert, Butryn, & Ledley, 2012). Patients with diabetes who participated in an ACT intervention showed better coping and self-care abilities (Gregg, Callaghan, Hayes, & Glenn-Lawson, 2007; Shayeghian, Hassanabadi, Aguilar-Vafaie, Amiri, & Besharat, 2016). There is also evidence that ACT interventions lead to improved quality of life in cancer patients (Feros, Lane, Ciarrochi, & Blackledge, 2011).

Future Directions

Chronic diseases and conditions are prevalent in North America and health psychologists can play an important role in their prevention and management. There have been many advances in recent years leading to increased awareness and better management of chronic health conditions. Current intervention and prevention strategies may need to be adapted to better suit the needs of our aging population (see Chapter 14). Moreover, as certain chronic diseases and conditions continue to affect certain populations disproportionally, such as members of minority groups and individuals of lower SES, there remains an urgent need to address health inequalities.

More basic research is also needed for a better understanding of the relationship between psychological/sociocultural parameters and health functioning. Advances in medical imaging and genetics will become increasingly important in such research. As an example, functional magnetic resonance imaging (fMRI) has been used to document the effect of human relationships in the pain experience; viewing pictures of a romantic partner while experiencing pain led

In Practice
Acceptance and Commitment Therapy in Inflammatory Bowel Disease

Gabbi is 21-year-old second-year university student. At the age of 15, she was diagnosed with IBD. When she was first diagnosed, she had a very tough time getting her IBD flares under control and adjusting to her illness. She missed a great deal of school and, as a result, graduated a year late. Moreover, because she was in and out of school so often, she had difficulty maintaining relationships. When she started university, Gabbi was determined to have a better experience. She wanted to make good friends, be involved in university life, and do well in her studies.

Unfortunately, despite her best intentions, Gabbi found that managing her IBD while at university was harder than expected. In particular, she struggled to engage with other students and be involved in university activities to the degree that she wanted. Although she made a handful of friends, their favourite social outings tended to be going to pubs and bars, and eating out. This was tough for Gabbi. She could not drink when they went out, because she had learned from experience that alcohol caused her IBD to flare. She had to be exceedingly cautious of what she ate, also to prevent flares. Over time, Gabbi started to feel discouraged. Why go out if she would only feel bad about not being able to do what her friends were doing? What is more, Gabbi was worried about having an IBD-related problem in public, which prevented her from doing activities as often as she wanted. These thoughts and worries left Gabbi avoiding social situations and withdrawing from her friends. She noticed that her mood plummeted. To make things worse, the stress of worrying about not having the university experience she had hoped for, paired with her low mood, made it difficult to concentrate. As a result, her school grades took a hit.

To help her cope with her situation, Gabbi decided to start seeing a psychologist, Dr Maladie, through her hospital's IBD program. Dr Maladie is a health psychologist who often uses **acceptance and commitment therapy** with youth and young adults with IBD. Gabbi and Dr Maladie have been working together for several months. Over this time, Gabbi has learned a number of skills and developed new ways of thinking about her experiences. Working with Dr Maladie, it became clear to Gabbi that she was avoiding activities because she worried about embarrassing herself and because she did not want to experience the negative feelings that arose when she felt she could not do what her friends were doing. However, instead of making her feel better, this avoidance was actually making her feel worse! With Dr Maladie, Gabbi was able to identify her life values. One of her main values was to develop meaningful relationships. Her values were not about being able to drink beer and eat onion rings, and they definitely were not about staying home alone! Although it was challenging in the beginning, Gabbi practised making committed actions that aligned with these values, and not letting her fear of negative emotions or experience interfere with her valued actions. She also worked on acknowledging her own limitations and finding ways of making decisions that aligned with her values, while still respecting her health needs. One of the ways in which Gabbi accomplished this was by reaching out to some of her friends and making suggestions of activities like hiking on the nearby trails. Her friends had a blast and really seemed to appreciate Gabbi's initiative. Dr Maladie also helped Gabbi live in the present moment, particularly when with her friends. This meant focusing on her friends and enjoying her interactions with them, rather than getting caught up in her frustration that she could not order what she wanted off the menu. She learned mindfulness exercises to help her with this and integrated them throughout her day. Mindfulness had the added benefit of helping Gabbi feel more focused. As a result, she noticed improvements in her grades. Over time, Gabbi noticed a significant improvement in her mood and her relationships. She went out more and was more engaged when she did go out. Although she still had worries and frustrations about her IBD, her IBD was no longer in control of her.

to increased activity in several reward-processing regions of the brain (Younger, Aron, Parke, Chatterjee, & Mackey, 2010).

Although psychological interventions have been shown to be beneficial in the prevention and management of a variety of chronic health conditions, many patients never get the opportunity to benefit from psychological services. Research and policy change are needed to overcome barriers to accessing such services. It would also be important to pursue more research on the cost effectiveness of psychological interventions in the context of chronic disease, as the findings of such research are likely to drive policy change. Technological advances and the omnipresence of social media have been capitalized upon by health psychologists and can be helpful in improving access to psychological services. Online treatment/self-management programs, social media prevention campaigns, and integration of text message in treatment adherence interventions are examples of technological applications. As technology progresses, psychologists can continue to identify creative ways of integrating these technological advances into their practice and research.

In this chapter, we have acknowledged the similarities that emerge across chronic diseases/conditions. Although each disease/condition brings about unique challenges, there are many parallels, particularly with regard to facets of prevention, adjustment, and adherence. Health psychologists and health providers should be mindful not to work in disease-specific silos, but rather to continue learning from each other's successes.

Summary

The number of people affected by chronic health problems in Canada and the United States is substantial. Chronic illness can have a negative impact on psychological well-being and results in a variety of personal and psychosocial consequences such as relationship strain and loss of work. An individual's level of adjustment to a health problem may wax and wane throughout the progression of a health condition.

There are many ways in which health psychologists may intervene when it comes to chronic diseases and conditions. Prevention is a first avenue. There are many lifestyle factors that increase one's risk of developing chronic disease, such as unhealthy eating habits, sleep deprivation, physical inactivity, and smoking and alcohol use. Stress and personality factors may also increase one's risk of developing a chronic disease.

Health psychologists are involved in health promotion, help individuals at risk of developing a chronic disease engage in healthier behaviours and lifestyles, and conduct research that provides a better understanding of how to prevent and manage chronic health problems. Among people who have a diagnosis of a chronic condition, health psychologists may be involved in helping with adherence to treatment recommendations and adjustment. Adherence to treatment recommendations is often low, which places additional strain on the health-care system as problems may become more severe. Health psychologists help people address barriers to treatment adherence and increase engagement. Self-management programs and psychological interventions may help people with chronic health conditions as they adjust to their illness.

Critical Thought Questions

1. If you had a friend or loved one with a chronic illness, would you be likely to recommend that he or she see a health psychologist? What factors would influence your decision on whether or not to make such a recommendation? Would your friend or loved one be likely to encounter barriers to accessing psychological services? If so, what would those barriers be and what would be needed to overcome them?

2. What are the potential benefits to practitioners of increasing the use of online interventions and social media in the prevention and management of chronic disease? What are the potential benefits to people with chronic health conditions? Are there any risks related to use of Internet and social media for those who are coping with chronic health conditions? How can such risks be minimized?

Recommended Reading

Public Health Agency of Canada. (2016). *How healthy are Canadians? A trend analysis of the health of Canadians from a healthy living and chronic disease perspective.* Ottawa: Author. Retrieved from https://www.canada.ca/en/public-health/services/publications/healthy-living/how-healthy-canadians.html

Stanton, A.L., Revenson, T.A., & Tennen, H. (2007). Health psychology: Psychological adjustment to chronic disease. *Annual Review of Psychology, 58*, 565–92. doi: 10.1146/annurev.psych.58.110405.085615

World Health Organization. (2003). *Adherence to long-term therapies: Evidence for action.* Geneva: Author. Retrieved from http://www.who.int/chp/knowledge/publications/adherence_report/en

9 The Psychology of Pain

Thomas Hadjistavropoulos

Learning Objectives

In this chapter you will:

- Learn the difference between acute and chronic pain.
- Understand how pain is both a psychological and a physical experience.
- Examine important pain theories (e.g., the gate control theory) and models of pain (e.g., the biopsychosocial model).
- Learn about the psychological assessment and management of pain.

Acute and Chronic Pain, Prevalence, and Medical Management

Pain is ubiquitous and does not spare anyone.* According to the Huffington Post (Wenn, 2012), actor George Clooney was injured when filming a scene in the movie *Syriana* in 2005. Clooney has reported that his pain became so intense that he had suicidal thoughts (Bates, 2011). Over time, and with the help of pain management interventions, he was able to manage his chronic pain condition and continued to lead a productive and rewarding life. He was quoted as saying, "I went to a pain-management guy whose idea was, 'You can't mourn for how you used to feel, because you're never going to feel that way again'" (Wenn, 2012). In this chapter you will read about the impact that pain can have on psychological well-being and quality of life as well as about the role of psychological factors on the ways in which pain can be managed and experienced.

Due to its high prevalence, pain represents a serious public health concern. Pain is often classified as acute or chronic. Acute pain is usually associated with recent ongoing tissue damage (e.g., an injury), while chronic pain has persisted beyond the normal expected healing period or is otherwise persistent over time (Merskey & Bogduk, 1994). Often chronic pain is defined as pain that has lasted for at least three to six months (Merskey & Bogduk, 1994). Chronic pain, the primary focus of this chapter, affects people's lives in diverse ways. Its prevalence is estimated to be as high as 30 per cent of the adult population in the Western world (Tsang et al., 2008), but this estimate varies from country to country (e.g., Breivik, Collet, Ventafridda, Cohen, & Gallacher, 2006) and as a result of different research methodologies used. In Canada, close to 20 per cent of adults are estimated to suffer from chronic pain (Schopflocher, Taenzer, & Jovey, 2011). In the United States, approximately 116 million Americans suffer from chronic pain (Skinner, Wilson, & Turk, 2012; Institute of Medicine, 2011). According to the National Center for Health Statistics (2006), up to 10 per cent of adults reported that they had pain that lasted a year or more, and 40 per cent indicated that their pain had a moderate or severe negative impact on their lives (Skinner et al., 2012).

A World Health Organization (WHO) survey of primary-care patients in 15 countries showed that 22 per cent of patients reported pain lasting for six months or longer requiring medical attention or medication, or causing significant interference with activity (Gureje, Von Korff, Simon, & Gater, 1998; Skinner et al., 2012). Persistent pain is also a prevalent problem in children and adolescents, with estimates ranging from 15 to 30 per cent (Stanford, Chambers, Biesanz, & Chen, 2008). According to an Institute of Medicine (2011) report, cumulative costs in the United States, including treatment, disability payments, lost work days and tax revenue, and legal fees, attributed to chronic pain may exceed $600 billion per year. In Canada, where the population is roughly 10 per cent of that of the United States, the costs are also very high. Specifically, the Canadian costs are estimated to be over $37 billion per year, including an estimated $6 billion in direct health-care costs (Phillips & Schopflocher, 2008). Moreover, the typical annual cost of care per pain patient waiting for treatment at Canadian pain clinics is $17,544 (most often this is privately funded by patients) (Canadian Pain Society, 2011; Guerriere et al., 2010).

From a biomedical standpoint, depending on its nature, pain can be managed with medications, surgical interventions, physical therapy, and other related modalities. It is worth mentioning that there has been considerable public awareness of problems related to the abuse of

---

* Extremely rare cases of people who do not experience pain (congenital insensitivity to pain) have been reported (e.g., Cascella & Muzio, 2017). These individuals frequently sustain accidental injuries (e.g., painless burns) due to not realizing that they are being burned or injured. They also face medical difficulties as a result of not noticing early signs of a physical problem or infection.

certain medications that are used in the treatment of chronic pain (e.g., opioids). These medications have found their way into the illegal drug trafficking market and have been used (often with lethal consequences) by individuals who do not necessarily have chronic pain. It is important to remember that, when prescribed and taken appropriately, these medications can be of value in the management of several chronic pain problems (Gallagher & Beattie, 2019). Nonetheless, a review of non-cancer-related chronic pain treatments led to the conclusion that single modality treatments for chronic pain (e.g., medications alone, surgery alone) tend to provide only modest improvements in pain and minimal improvements in physical and emotional functioning (Turk, Wilson, & Cahana, 2011). This finding was not surprising, given the complexity of chronic pain, and points towards the need for interdisciplinary approaches that incorporate psychological modalities.

Understanding the Nature of Pain

Pain is primarily a psychological experience (Hadjistavropoulos & Craig, 2004). The International Association for the Study of Pain (IASP), which is the most highly influential group of pain researchers and clinicians, defines pain as "an unpleasant sensory and emotional experience associated with actual or potential tissue damage, or described in terms of such damage" (Merskey & Bogduk, 1994). This definition stresses the psychological nature of the experience by clarifying that pain is not merely a sensation but a perception that incorporates emotional components.

Although pain is often thought of as a sensation, this is incorrect. A sensation is defined as the process by which stimulation of a sensory receptor gives rise to neural impulses that result from an experience outside the body (Gerrig, Zimbardo, Desmarais, & Ivanco, 2010). A potentially painful sensation, however, will not be perceived as pain until it is interpreted as such by the brain. Related to this, it is important to clarify the distinction between the terms "nociception" and "pain." **Nociception** refers to the processing of stimuli associated with the stimulation of nociceptors (i.e., specific receptors) and has the potential of being experienced as pain (Turk & Melzack, 2011). In other words, nociception frequently (but not always) leads to the experience of pain. In contrast to nociception, pain represents a perceptual process associated with selective abstraction, conscious awareness, ascribed meaning, learning, and appraisal (e.g., Hadjistavropoulos & Craig, 2004; Loeser & Treede, 2008). In fact, motivational and psychological states are of primary importance in the conceptualization of pain (Price, 2000). For example, the experience of pain has been shown to be closely tied to emotions such as anger, sadness, and disgust (Hale & Hadjistavropoulos, 1997). In addition to pain being a psychological experience in and of itself, it also leads to direct behavioural (e.g., facial expressions of pain) and psychological consequences (e.g., mood deflation).

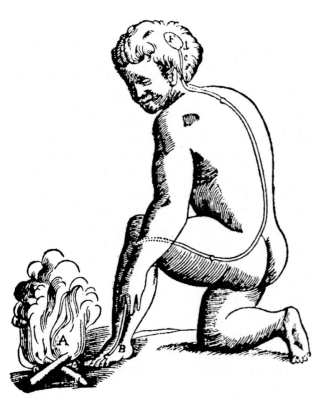

FIGURE 9.1 **Descartes's conception of the pain pathway. From R. Descartes,** *Traite de l'Homme* **(1648).**

For example, a considerable portion of chronic pain sufferers also present with depression. According to a comprehensive literature review, and depending on the study, 5 to 85 per cent of people with chronic pain suffer from depression; the percentage varies as a function of the nature of the patient population studied and the criteria and measures used (Bair, Robinson, Katon, & Kroenke, 2003). Regardless of these discrepancies in the prevalence of depression within chronic pain populations, most investigators seem to agree that patients with chronic pain are at risk of suffering from depression (Miller & Cano, 2009).

Chronic pain can also be associated with other psychological conditions such as anxiety and substance abuse (Morasco, Corson, Turk, & Dobscha, 2011; Cimmino, Ferrone, & Cutolo, 2011), with patients often using alcohol and non-prescribed drugs in an effort to palliate

pain. At the social level, chronic pain can lead to disruption of social relationships, social isolation, and reduced quality of life (e.g., Sessle, 2011; Breivik et al., 2006). Given the strong psychological elements of the pain experience as well as the psychosocial consequences of pain, psychologists have played a central role in research designed to better conceptualize the pain experience (Melzack & Wall, 2004), to better understand the manner in which pain is expressed verbally and non-verbally (T. Hadjistavropoulos et al., 2011), and to treat chronic pain patients whose quality of life suffers as a consequence of pain.

Theories of Pain

Early theories of pain had a biophysical focus. Figure 9.1 depicts the concept of the pain pathway conceptualized by Descartes (1596–1650). This conceptualization has been viewed as being analogous to a string with a bell attached to it. According to this early view, tissue damage results in pain being experienced in the same way as a pull on the string causes the bell to ring. Descartes implied a direct one-on-one correspondence between pain and tissue damage, which is known as **specificity theory**. That is, the greater the tissue damage, the greater the pain. Although specificity theory was influential for many years, it failed to help patients with severe chronic pain (Melzack & Katz, 2004).

Several attempts were made to find a new theory, but these led to accounts of pain mechanisms that were vague and inadequate, and none of these theories considered the brain as anything more than a receiver of pain messages

Ronald Melzack, McGill University psychologist.

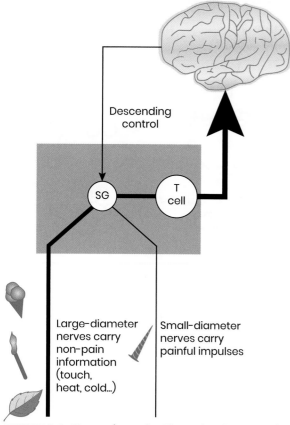

Descending control

SG

T cell

Large-diameter nerves carry non-pain information (touch, heat, cold...)

Small-diameter nerves carry painful impulses

FIGURE 9.2   How pain works: The Melzack–Wall pain gate.

Source: Starkey, C: *Therapeutic Modalities for Athletic Trainers*. FA Davis, Philadelphia, 1993, p. 28.

(Melzack & Katz, 2004). This changed as a result of the pioneering work of Melzack and Wall (1965), who developed the most dominant theory of pain today (i.e., the gate control theory). Subsequent work by these and other pain researchers has moved our focus from pain as a physical experience to pain as a complex psychological phenomenon.

Key elements of the theory are summarized in Figure 9.2. Melzack and Katz (2004) outlined the **gate control theory** as follows: nerve impulses are transmitted from afferent fibres to spinal cord transmission cells modulated by a gating mechanism in the dorsal horn of the spinal cord. This gating mechanism is affected by the amount of activity in small pain pathway fibres and large-diameter sensory neural pathways. Specifically, the large-diameter fibres tend to "close the gate" by inhibiting transmission while small fibres "open the gate" by facilitating transmission. As a concrete example, rubbing a painful area often helps reduce pain because the act of rubbing activates the large-diameter fibres that tend to inhibit nociceptive transmission. These small and large-diameter fibres synapse on projection cells, which go to the brain through the spinothalamic tract (i.e., a sensory pathway originating in the spinal cord and transmitting signals to the thalamus). When the output of spinal transmission cells reaches a critical level, it activates the neural areas that underlie the complex, sequential patterns of experience and behaviour that characterize pain. Cortical descending signals (i.e., messages from the brain) also have the potential to inhibit nociceptive message transmission to the brain and close the "gate." The description of the process whereby descending cortical input (that can represent beliefs, attitudes, attentional processes, and other psychological responses) can close the gating mechanism provides a physiological basis for the role of psychological factors and strengthens justification for use of psychological treatments for pain. Moreover, recognition of the role of cortical function in pain modulation serves to explain a variety of phenomena and establishes the important role of psychological influences in the pain experience (e.g., the ability of many people to endure increased pain under hypnosis) (Facco et al., 2011).

Melzack (2001) has complemented the gate control theory of pain with the **neuromatrix model**, which emphasizes the role of the brain in pain perception. The neuromatrix model is capable of explaining phenomena such as phantom limb pain (i.e., pain felt as if it is coming from an amputated limb that is no longer there). More specifically, Melzack (2001; 2005) argued that the body is perceived as a unit and is identified as the "self" distinct from its surroundings. The perception of unity of the body with all of the qualities felt from the body, including pain, is produced by a central neural process. The anatomical process of the body-self, the neuromatrix, is described as a widespread network of neurons, which form loops between the cortex and the limbic system (comprising complex sets of brain structures) as well as the thalamus and the cortex. The neuronal loops separate to allow for parallel processing in different components of the neuromatrix and come together repeatedly to permit interactions between the processing outputs. Melzack conceptualized the neuromatrix as initially being genetically determined, but subsequently sculpted by sensory inputs. Characteristic inputs from the body undergo cyclical synthesis so that patterns are impressed on them in the neuromatrix. The repeated cyclical processing and synthesis of nerve impulses through the neuromatrix reveal a characteristic pattern, the neurosignature, which is produced by the arrangement of synaptic connections in the entire neuromatrix. The neurosignature can be conceptualized as output from the neuromatrix. In other words, pain perception can be generated by the output of the neuromatrix as a function of sensory inputs as well as of information from regions of the brain involved in affective and cognitive functions. Moreover, pain behaviours can be generated or perpetuated by previously conditioned cues in the environment or by the expectation of pain and suffering (Loeser & Melzack, 1999). Phantom limb pain is therefore believed to be related to activity of the neuromatrix. Various treatments can affect the output of the neuromatrix to the extent that they change the inputs and the influences on the neuromatrix (Loeser & Melzack, 1999).

A variety of **biopsychosocial models of pain** are consistent with and build on the gate control theory of pain by elaborating on social and psychological influences that affect the pain experience. Such models focus on the interplay of biological, psychological, and social parameters in pain. Like the gate control theory, biopsychosocial models contrast with strict biomedical models, which are losing popularity. Specifically, biomedical models do not take into account social and psychological factors on the pain experience and focus only on biological processes. Biomedical models fail to explain a wide variety of phenomena, including but not limited to the effect of hypnosis on the pain experience, the role of coping styles in functioning with pain and rehabilitation outcomes, and the success of psychological interventions in chronic pain management (T. Hadjistavropoulos et al., 2011).

Various influential biopsychosocial models/conceptualizations have been developed to describe and clarify different aspects of the pain experience. These models recognize the importance of biological factors in pain but emphasize the interaction of biology with psychological (including cognition, affect, and behaviour) and social factors (e.g., social support, culture) (e.g., T. Hadjistavropoulos et al., 2011; Waddell, 1987, 1991, 1992; Waddell, Newton, Henderson, Somerville, & Main, 1993). Such models/conceptualizations include, for example, the *operant model*, *fear avoidance model*, *communications model*, and *cognitive behavioural* conceptualizations of chronic pain. We review each of these below.

The Operant Model of Pain

This model stresses the importance of reinforcement in the development and maintenance of pain behaviour. For example, if excessive pain behaviour (e.g., excessive complaining) is reinforced by attention, it tends to persist and be maintained by the attention (e.g., Fordyce, 1976; Fordyce, Shelton, & Dundore, 1982). Moreover, behaviours (e.g., inactivity) that are reinforced because they temporarily reduce pain may also persist and become maladaptive, especially when they are associated with additional rewards such as reduced aversive work-related responsibilities. Empirical support for many aspects of this model exists. Experimental laboratory studies have demonstrated that pain reports in relation to induced pain can increase as a function of verbal reinforcement (Jolliffe & Nicholas, 2004; Flor, Knost, & Birbaumer, 2002). Moreover, therapy based on operant principles has been found to be effective, relative to being on a waiting list, at least in the short term (Henschke et al., 2010). In actual clinical practice, however, therapy components based on the operant model are often incorporated within broader cognitive behavioural therapy approaches (i.e., approaches that incorporate a variety of additional psychological methods). The operant model has been criticized for failing to take into account interpretations and appraisals of pain (Sharp, 2001).

The Fear Avoidance Model of Pain

The fear avoidance model (Vlaeyen & Linton, 2000) is based on the idea that certain movements and behaviours become associated with pain or exacerbations of pain (Meulders, Vansteenwegen, & Vlaeyen, 2011). Such associations, especially when coupled with catastrophic thoughts about pain and concern about the possibility of re-injury, can lead to excessive avoidance. According to the model, excessive avoidance can then lead to stiffness and deconditioning, thus increasing the probability of future pain. Important aspects of the model have been supported with empirical research. For example, fear avoidance beliefs (e.g., "I must avoid most activities because I am afraid of re-injury") are predictors of future disability and chronicity (Fritz, George, & Delitto, 2001). Nonetheless, clinical studies generally find small effects and it has been argued that fear of pain leading to avoidance may be better construed as one of many variables that influence the experience of pain and disability (Moseley, 2011).

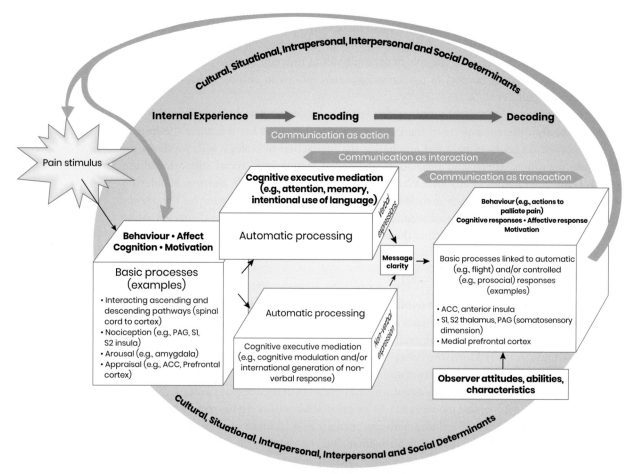

FIGURE 9.3   The communications model of pain.

Source: Hadjistavropoulos et al., (2011). A biopsychosocial formulation of pain communication. *Psychological Bulletin, 137,* 910–939.

The Communications Model of Pain

The communications model of pain (e.g., Prkachin & Craig, 1994; T. Hadjistavropoulos et al., 2011) is summarized in Figure 9.3. Based on an earlier formulation by Rosenthal (1982), the chain of pain communication is seen as a three-step A–B–C process whereby the internal experience of pain (A), which is determined by biological, social/cultural, and psychological factors, is encoded into verbal and non-verbal expressive behaviour (B) that can be potentially decoded (C) by observers. External influences, including cultural, interpersonal, and intrapersonal determinants, can affect this process at any stage. The first step of the model describes a variety of processes that take place during the experience of pain. These include affective (e.g., negative emotion), cognitive (e.g., thoughts about the pain), and brain correlates (reflecting a complex system that conveys nociceptive information from the spinal cord to the cerebral cortex) (Dube et al., 2009; T. Hadjistavropoulos et al., 2011; Price, 2000; Rainville, 2002; Staud, Craggs, Robinson, Perlstein, & Price, 2007).

In terms of the encoding of pain in expressive behaviour (i.e., verbal and non-verbal), the model specifies that expressive behaviours vary with respect to the extent to which they are characterized by automaticity (e.g., reflexive withdrawal) or cognitive executive mediation (e.g., as is the case with self-reported pain) (Hadjistavropoulos & Craig, 2002). Non-verbal pain behaviours are seen as, generally, being more automatic and less under voluntary control than self-report. On the other hand, self-report is considered to be under more voluntary control but easier to decode by an observer. Characteristics of the observer (e.g., sex, gender, health professional or not) (Hadjistavropoulos et al., 1998) and of the person expressing pain have also been shown to affect the decoding process (e.g., LaChapelle, Lavoie, Higgins, & Hadjistavropoulos, 2014; MacLeod, LaChapelle, Hadjistavropoulos, & Pfeifer, 2001). In turn, observer actions (often based on decoding of the pain experience) have the potential to palliate or worsen the pain experience.

Examples of contextual influences on the pain process are derived from studies demonstrating that people are less likely to express pain in the presence of a tolerant model (i.e., an individual who demonstrates that he or she can tolerate well relatively high pain intensities) (Craig & Weiss, 1972; Craig, 1986), that children whose mothers were taught to interact in a pain-promoting manner reported more pain than children in a control group (Chambers, Craig, & Bennett, 2002), and that pain can be expressed with varying levels of intensity as a function of cultural background (Nayak, Shiflett, Eshun, & Levine, 2000). Moreover, social stereotypes such as those based on physical attractiveness seem to affect the decoding of pain, with more physically attractive people being perceived as healthier and as experiencing less pain (e.g., LaChapelle et al., 2014). Although aspects of the model require more testing, particularly in naturalistic contexts (i.e., health-care settings), a strength of the communications model is

Non-verbal pain expressions are believed to be more automatic and less under voluntary control than self-reported pain.

ESB Professional/Shutterstock.com

that it provides a high level of detail with respect to the various variables that influence the pain experience.

Cognitive Behavioural Conceptualization of Pain

Cognitive behavioural conceptualizations focus on the role of cognitive factors and beliefs in the pain experience and recognize the interconnections among thoughts, feelings, and behaviours (Turk, Meichenbaum, & Genest, 1987; Sharp, 2001). The assumption is that a fundamental difference between those who adjust well to pain and those who do not lies in their appraisals and interpretations of the situation (e.g., holding maladaptive beliefs such as "I can never enjoy anything with this pain problem" as opposed to "I can still enjoy many things in my life, despite the pain"). Such beliefs also affect emotions and behaviour (e.g., exaggerated concern about re-injury may lead to reduced activity) and, in turn, negative emotions and associated physiological changes can affect the thinking process (Skinner et al., 2012). As such, this conceptualization also postulates that patients' beliefs have an impact on the manner in which they present themselves to others, such as health-care providers, which in turn would affect how others react to the patient in pain (e.g., by encouraging or discouraging pain complaints) (Skinner et al., 2012). Cognitive behavioural theorists have argued that pain-related beliefs and cognitions develop as a result of the patients' early histories, cultural backgrounds, and other social experiences. Indeed, research has supported many predictions of this model. For example, catastrophic thinking about pain is a risk factor in the development of chronic pain and is an indicator of poor prognosis (Haythornthwaite, Clark, Pappagallo, & Raja, 2003; Linton, 2005; Picavet, Vlaeyen, & Schouten, 2002; Sullivan, Feuerstein, Gatchel, Linton, & Pransky, 2005). Psychological interventions based on this model are reviewed below and incorporate a variety of techniques and procedures designed to influence affective, behavioural, cognitive, and sensory aspects of the pain experience (Skinner et al., 2012).

Psychological Assessment of Pain

Health psychologists are frequently involved in the assessment of patients experiencing pain, especially those who suffer from chronic pain. It is important to recognize that such psychological assessments tend to incorporate complete evaluations of patients' psychological functioning (e.g., psychological co-morbidities, coping efforts) and involve both detailed clinical interviews covering personal and psychological history and psychological tests.

The psychological assessment of pain is typically based on biopsychosocial formulations of the pain experience. It focuses on a variety of domains capturing information about the person, psychological and problem history, co-morbidities, coping styles, dimensions of the pain experience itself, functional analysis of pain behaviour (i.e., examination of antecedents and consequences of pain behaviour), and impact of pain on quality of life.

Full History, Co-morbidities, Coping Styles, and Overall Psychological Functioning

The psychological assessment of the pain patient involves obtaining a full personal and psychological history and assessment of co-morbidities and coping styles. Coping styles are important because some strategies for coping with pain (e.g., strategies that focus on problem-solving) are associated with better outcomes than more passive strategies (e.g., heavy reliance on hope that pain will be alleviated as a result of the actions of others) (e.g., Covic, Adamson, & Hough, 2000). Historical information includes information on past treatments, substance use, and vocational and social history, as well as the client's goals and expectations related to current treatment.

Dimensions of the Pain Experience

Pain is a multi-dimensional experience. In the first instance, a psychologist may assist with the standardized measurement of self-reported pain intensity using scales that vary in complexity. A simple tool would be a 0–10 numeric rating scale anchored by the polar opposites "no pain" and "pain as bad as it can be" or verbal rating scales where the patient selects a word out of a list that depicts different levels of pain intensity (e.g., "no pain," "mild pain," "moderate pain," "severe pain"). However, pain also has affective (i.e., it is accompanied by negative emotions), sensory, and evaluative components (e.g., perceptions of the nature of pain such as throbbing or sharp).

One of the most widely used psychometric tools is the McGill Pain Questionnaire (MPQ) (Melzack, 1975), which consists of groups of words designed to capture various dimensions of the pain experience (see Figure 9.4). The tool consists of pain descriptors that the patient can select from (e.g., throbbing, stabbing, burning, dull). In addition, the questionnaire includes line drawings of the human body so that the patient can mark the spatial distribution of the pain. Moreover, there is an overall rating of pain intensity based on a 1–5 scale (with each number associated with an intensity word ranging from "mild" to "excruciating". Descriptors of the temporal properties of the pain (e.g., brief, momentary, transient, constant) are also included. The MPQ provides assessment of the following pain dimensions: (1) sensory: linked to words describing the sensory quality of the experience in terms of properties such as thermal and pressure; (2) affective: linked to words relating to affective elements such as fear; and (3) evaluative: e.g., whether pain is evaluated as unbearable, annoying, etc.

The MPQ has shown remarkable accuracy in classifying people correctly with a variety of pain syndromes. For example, Melzack, Terrence, Fromm, and Amsel (1986) showed that the tool was 91 per cent accurate in classifying patients who suffered from trigeminal neuralgia, a nerve disorder that causes intense pain in the face, or atypical pain. Moreover, Dubuisson and Melzack (1976) showed that the MPQ was accurate in correctly classifying 77 per cent of patients who presented with eight different types of pain syndromes.

Other aspects of the pain experience commonly evaluated by health psychologists include cognitions. For example, the Pain Catastrophizing Scale (Sullivan, Bishop, & Pivik, 1995) is often used to evaluate the extent to which patients engage in catastrophic thinking. Catastrophic thinking involves a cognitive appraisal in which situations are viewed as being threatening and beyond an individual's ability to cope. Similarly, psychologists often measure whether patients show certain behavioural tendencies, such as the tendency to avoid activity due to fear of pain or fear of re-injury. Dimensions such as pain catastrophizing and fear of pain predict poor rehabilitation outcomes (e.g., Piva, Fitzgerald, Wisniewski, & Delitto, 2009) and are, thus, important to assess.

Pain Behaviour: Its Antecedents, Consequences, and Other Situational/Environmental Determinants of the Pain Experience

Health psychologists assess pain behaviours observed during the interview (e.g., a patient grimacing due to pain) and through discussion of what the patient does when he or she is in pain (e.g.,

McGill Pain Questionnaire

Patient's Name ————————————————————— Date ————————— Time ————— am/pm

PRI: S ——————— A ——————— E ——————— M————————— PRI(T) ————— PPI ———
        (1–10)   (11–15)   (16)   (17–20)   (1–20)

BRIEF ___	RHYTHMIC ___	CONTINUOUS ___
MOMENTARY ___	PERIODIC ___	STEADY ___
TRANSIENT ___	INTERMITTENT ___	CONSTANT ___

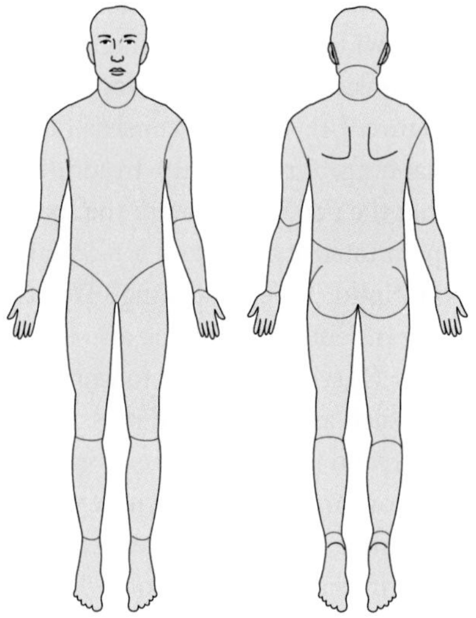

1 FLICKERING ___
QUIVERING ___
PUSING ___
THROBBING ___
BEATING ___
POUNDING ___

2 JUMPING ___
FLASHING ___
SHOOTING ___

3 PRICKING ___
BORING ___
DRILLING ___
STABBING ___
LANCINATING ___

4 SHARP ___
CUTTING ___
LACERATING ___

5 PINCHING ___
PRESSING ___
GNAWING ___
CRAMPING ___
CRUSHING ___

6 TUGGING ___
PULLING ___
WRENCHING ___

7 HOT ___
BURNING ___
SCALDING ___
SEARING ___

8 TINGLING ___
ITCHY ___
SMARTING ___
STINGING ___

9 DULL ___
SORE ___
HURTING ___
ACHING ___
HEAVY ___

10 TENDER ___
TAUT ___
RASPING ___
SPLITTING ___

11 TIRING ___
EXHAUSTING ___

12 SICKENING ___
SUFFOCATING ___

13 FEARFUL ___
FRIGHTFUL ___
TERRIFYING ___

14 PUNISHING ___
GRUELLING ___
CRUEL ___
VICIOUS ___
KILLING ___

15 WRETCHED ___
BLINDING ___

16 ANNOYING ___
TROUBLESOME ___
MISERABLE ___
INTENSE ___
UNBEARABLE ___

17 SPREADING ___
RADIATING ___
PENETRATING ___
PIERCING ___

18 TIGHT ___
NUMB ___
DRAWING ___
SQUEEZING ___
TEARING ___

19 COOL ___
COLD ___
FREEZING ___

20 NAGGING ___
NAUSEATING ___
AGONIZING ___
DREADFUL ___
TORTURING ___

PPI
0 NO PAIN ___
1 MILD ___
2 DISCOMFORTING ___
3 DISTRESSING ___
4 HORRIBLE ___
5 EXCRUCIATING ___

E = EXTERNAL
I = INTERNAL

COMMENTS:

FIGURE 9.4 The McGill Pain Questionnaire.

Source: Copyright R. Melzack 1970, 1975; reprinted with permission. http://www.fcesoftware.com/images/16_McGill_Pain_Questionnaire.pdf

does he or she ask for assistance from significant others?). Standardized observational approaches are also often used with special populations, including persons with limited ability to communicate, such as infants (Ruskin, Amaria, Warnock, & McGrath, 2001) and older adults with severe dementia (Hadjistavropoulos et al., 2014; also see Chapter 14).

Antecedents (i.e., what precedes the pain behaviour) are examined. For example, some patients report that their pain feels worse when they find themselves in stressful situations. Similarly, the consequences of pain behaviour are discussed (e.g., how does a spouse react to pain complaints?). Consistent with the operant model, the environment can sometimes serve to encourage or discourage pain behaviour. For example, an individual may receive more help and attention because he or she is in pain (although the opposite can also occur with potentially detrimental consequences for social relationships). Other environmental/social elements relating to the pain experience are also evaluated. Social support is a good example. An optimal amount of social support has been linked to more positive outcomes and experiences among pain patients (Faucett & Levine, 1991; Hanley et al., 2004; Jensen, Moore, Bockow, Ehde, & Engel, 2010; Kerns, Rosenberg & Otis, 2002). On the other hand, excessive social support (i.e., social support that becomes solicitous) can be counterproductive (Boothby, Thorn, Overduin, & Ward, 2004; Hanley et al., 2004; McCracken, 2005; Schwartz, Jensen, & Romano, 2005). Other examples of environmental/social influences on the pain experience are the work environment the patient is in (or is planning to return to) and whether or not the patient is operating within an adversarial compensation system. Adversarial compensation systems, where the patient's veracity is being questioned, have been linked to poorer rehabilitation outcomes (Hadjistavropoulos, 1999).

Effects of Pain on Quality of Life

Chronic pain often affects a variety of spheres of human functioning. These spheres include the following:

- A person's mood and psychological functioning with pain possibly leading to clinical depression or anxiety.
- Social relationships (pain can result in social isolation due to physical limitations preventing the individual from participating in various social activities).
- Intimate relationships (pain leading to irritability or physical discomfort interfering with sexual activity).
- Vocational functioning, that is, workplace productivity and safety.
- Economic circumstances, resulting, for example, from a person being less able to engage in his or her regular occupation.
- Use of substances, with the individual abusing alcohol and other drugs in order to cope with the pain experience.

As such, using interview techniques and other psychological assessment tools, such as psychological inventories, the psychologist evaluates the extent to which each of these areas is affected and makes treatment recommendations to address these concerns.

Acceptance of the biopsychosocial formulations of pain has supported the development of and increased emphasis on psychological treatments for chronic pain. Cognitive behavioural therapy (CBT) is gaining popularity as a modality designed for the treatment of chronic pain. CBT perspectives recognize the reciprocal relationships among cognition (including beliefs, schemata, automatic thoughts, and appraisals), behaviour, and interpersonal variables.

In Focus

Pain in Persons with Limited Ability to Communicate

The case of Tracy Latimer attracted tremendous Canadian media attention in the 1990s (McGrath, 1998). Tracy was a 12-year-old girl who suffered from cerebral palsy and had serious limitations in her ability to communicate pain due to the severe motor and cognitive impairments associated with her condition. There was little question, though, that she suffered severe pain, which was caused by the neuromuscular pathologies of cerebral palsy and probably by surgery performed to relieve contractures. Nonetheless, systematic assessment of pain represented a real challenge (Hadjistavropoulos, von Baeyer, & Craig, 2001). Tracy's father, Robert, decided to end her life because of what he described as her continuous suffering and pain. His legal representatives argued that he was left with limited choice as he had been told that nothing could be done to relieve his daughter's suffering. Following considerable public debate and legal battles, the Supreme Court of Canada eventually heard the case and ruled that Mr Latimer must spend at least 10 years in jail for killing his severely disabled daughter. Mr Latimer's decision concerning Tracy was supported by many people, who argued that her extreme pain justified euthanasia. Others, however, expressed concern about vulnerable persons who cannot effectively express themselves. Canadian psychologist Patrick McGrath (1998), in an article titled "We all failed the Latimers," argued that although much of the media attention had focused on the right to live or die, the most important issue

Psychological Treatments for Chronic Pain

CBT is used widely. It is not typically considered to be an alternative to medical and physical treatment modalities but complementary to these. Generally, the best approach to address chronic pain is interdisciplinary, and CBT is often offered as a component of such interdisciplinary approaches (Turk et al., 2011). In addition to psychologists, interdisciplinary pain management teams tend to include physicians, physiotherapists, occupational therapists, pharmacists, and/or other health professionals. Rather than simply targeting the pain itself, CBT for chronic pain patients also targets a variety of psychological consequences of pain, such as depression and anxiety.

CBT not only incorporates cognitive techniques, such as challenging dysfunctional automatic thoughts (e.g., "I am useless because I have pain"), but also a wide variety of behavioural procedures, including, but not limited to, pacing of activity, building coping skills, problem-solving, relaxation training, and biofeedback. Skinner et al. (2012) organized the methods that tend to be incorporated into CBT for pain:

1. Cognitive techniques such as cognitive restructuring (e.g., challenging negative thoughts and maladaptive beliefs through Socratic dialogue) and problem-solving (e.g., defining problems and working on solutions).
2. Behavioural techniques such as relaxation training and pacing (e.g., breaking up tasks into smaller components and performing them throughout the day) and behavioural activation (e.g., pleasant activity scheduling, pacing activity).

(i.e., the right of people with severe communication impairments to adequate pain assessment and management) was not discussed sufficiently.

Tracy Latimer's case sparked considerable attention within the pain research community and contributed to considerable efforts to improve pain assessment and management for people with severe cognitive impairments. As an example, the Non-Communicating Children's Pain Checklist (Breau, Finley, McGrath, & Camfield, 2002) was developed and subsequently validated as an effective behavioural observation tool to improve pain assessment in children with severe to profound intellectual disabilities (see Hadjistavropoulos, Breau, & Craig, 2011, for a review of this work). Similar efforts have been undertaken to improve the pain assessment of older adults with severe dementia (see Chapter 14).

Tracy and Robert Latimer.

3. Supportive educational techniques (e.g., offering support and providing information about the nature of pain).

4. Other techniques including biofeedback (a procedure that helps clients become more aware of specific physiological functions using psychophysiological measuring instruments), hypnosis, and relapse prevention strategies (e.g., developing coping skills to deal with possible relapses, identifying triggering events as a means of preventing relapse).

With respect to biofeedback, a variety of different types are used (e.g., thermal biofeedback or electromyography) depending on the type of pain experienced. For example, electromyography biofeedback has been used with tension headache patients who learn to reduce tension in muscles of the head (e.g., the frontalis muscle).

Given that thoughts, emotions, and behaviours can affect one another, targeting maladaptive beliefs can have a positive impact on behaviour. For example, overcoming a belief such as "socialization can never be pleasant when one has a chronic pain condition" could lead the person to participate in social activities more frequently, and rewarding social experiences can lead to improved mood. Cognitive behavioural therapists often aim to modify maladaptive beliefs and behaviours that patients with chronic pain may hold or engage in (e.g., "unless my pain problem can be treated, I cannot experience any joy"). More specifically, such thoughts are challenged through Socratic examination and dialogue. Often, "behavioural experiments" are set up within the context of therapy. Consider, for example, a client who believes that "I can't enjoy going out because I am in pain" and agrees to go to a social event

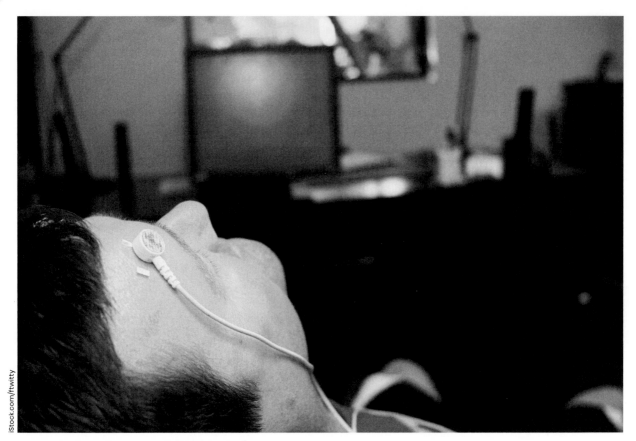

iStock.com/ftwitty

Patient undergoing electromyographic biofeedback therapy for headache pain.

in order to test the belief that "there is no way I can have fun if in pain." Testing such beliefs directly and finding evidence against such beliefs is often a far more powerful tool in changing maladaptive thoughts than trying to convince a client through dialogue that the belief may not be accurate.

Generally, CBT has been found to be effective in the management of chronic pain, leading to reductions in self-reported pain intensity and negative affect, although the effect sizes are only small to medium (Eccleston, Williams, & Morley, 2009; Ehde, Dillworth & Turner, 2014). To put this in perspective, however, it is important to note that many pain problems are highly resistant to treatment, and physical/medical treatment modalities often also lead, at best, to only modest benefits. As is the case with most other treatments for chronic pain, some patients do not benefit from CBT. As such, it has been argued that rather than conducting more studies simply examining the effectiveness of CBT in the treatment of chronic pain, it is important to identify subgroups of patients who are most likely to benefit from this therapy, as well as the circumstances under which CBT is likely to be beneficial (Day, Thorn, & Burns, 2012; Skinner et al., 2012).

More recently, CBT-based programs have begun to be delivered via the Internet and tend to focus on pain education, coping skills acquisition, and other cognitive behavioural procedures. Macea, Gajos, Daglia Calil, and Fregni (2010) conducted a systematic review and meta-analysis of these studies and concluded that such interventions offer a small but statistically significant benefit in terms of pain reduction. More recent investigations have shown even more promising

In Practice
Learning to Adapt to Pain through CBT

Jim is a 49-year-old mechanic who is married with one adult son. He presented with neck and back pain as a result of a work injury, which persisted despite repeated medical and physical treatments. Not only was he unable to work but he was no longer able to play golf, which was his favourite pastime and provided him with social opportunities. Since he went off work and stopped playing golf, Jim began spending more time at home and minimal time with his friends, since most of the socialization took place at the golf club. As a result of boredom and frustration, he became depressed and irritable. In turn, his irritability created considerable strain in his marriage. He believed that he "could not have his life back" as long as he had his pain.

He was referred for psychological therapy by his disability insurance provider. Jim was skeptical when he came for therapy and quickly questioned the purpose of the referral. As he told the therapist, "The problem that I have is with my back and I know that you can't fix that. When my back gets better, I will feel better. So I don't know what you are going to do for me."

The psychologist asked Jim a number of questions about the quality of his life. Jim confided that he was feeling depressed and had many catastrophic and other negative thoughts about pain (e.g., "I can never have a nice time unless my pain goes away"; "there is nothing that I can do to cope with my pain"; and "I can't stop thinking about the pain"). He talked about his marriage and how his irritability had strained his relationship with his wife. Through discussion, Jim also came to recognize that the more he thought about and focused on his pain, the more upset he became. He saw a vicious cycle of how increased distress made him focus even more on the pain, which only increased his distress. The psychologist asked Jim whether he would be willing to see if cognitive behavioural therapy could improve the quality of his life, despite the pain.

Over the weeks that followed, Jim tried a number of "therapy experiments." That is, the psychologist encouraged him to test out some of the beliefs that he held about his pain. For example, Jim created a list of activities that were once pleasurable. These included getting in touch with friends he had not seen for several months as well as high school friends he had not seen for longer. In fact, he was able to attend a high school reunion and had a good time. As he visited with old friends, he realized that he often did not think about his pain. As a result of this, he had tested the beliefs "*I can never have a nice time until my pain problem goes away*" and "*I cannot stop thinking about the pain.*" Through discussions in therapy, he began to adopt more adaptive beliefs, such as "I can distract myself from my pain problem by engaging in activities that interest me" and "When I participate in certain pleasant and interesting activities, I derive a sense of pleasure and a sense of mastery."

Gradually, he started to become more active. He and his wife began to go to the movies together and he even visited the golf club, where he was able to socialize with his friends at the clubhouse. As his mood improved, he explored vocational options and was able to find a job at the service desk of an automobile repair shop. He also learned to use relaxation strategies that reduced muscle tension in his back, which contributed to his pain experience, and he began to pace himself with home projects, breaking each project into small jobs and taking breaks before experiencing pain exacerbation. By doing this, he was able to break the mental association of pain with physical activity. Jim had managed to change his thinking and behaviour and to improve the quality of his life despite the pain.

results, suggesting the possibility that clinician-assisted online CBT may show outcomes that are comparable to those of face-to-face therapy (e.g., Dear et al., 2013).

In recent years, in addition to CBT, acceptance and commitment therapy has also gained in popularity. According to this approach, acceptance of pain rather than changing one's thoughts about pain is the focus of treatment. The approach (Hayes, Strosahl, & Wilson,

2012) emphasizes the manner in which the client relates to distressing thoughts and incorporates mindfulness, which is a mental state of awareness that has commonalities with meditation and involves being intentionally present in the moment, without judgement and while having an orientation that is characterized by openness, curiosity, and acceptance (Bishop et al., 2004). The assumption is that suffering is an unavoidable part of human experience and trying to control distressing thoughts about pain (or other forms of suffering) can ultimately increase distress. Patients are encouraged to be mindful and to notice, observe, and accept private events, rather than fight them. This, in turn, is expected to help them experience life more fully, because they will no longer be consumed and preoccupied with fighting distressing thoughts.

A meta-analysis of the effectiveness of mindfulness-based interventions and of acceptance and commitment therapy showed that, although these approaches were not superior to CBT, they were good alternatives in that the outcomes were comparable (Veehof, Okam, Schreurs, & Bohlmeijer, 2011). Nonetheless, the authors of the meta-analysis acknowledged that the CBT approach remains the standard, given the larger number of quality studies evaluating CBT.

Psychological Management of Acute Pain

Although psychologists are more likely to become involved in chronic pain management, there are many opportunities for clinical health psychologists to engage in the management of acute pain. For example, psychological interventions for post-surgical pain have been associated with reduced post-surgical mental distress although more systematic study is needed before this conclusion can be confirmed (Koranyi, Barth, Trelle, Strauss & Rosendahl, 2014). Psychologists have also been involved in the management of burn pain, dental pain, and pain due to non-surgical medical procedures. The types of psychological interventions typically used for acute pain management include a variety of different relaxation procedures (e.g., progressive muscle relaxation, imagery-based relaxation), hypnosis (i.e., a state of consciousness that involves attention being diverted away from the pain and onto a narrowly focused area or the hypnotist), cognitive procedures (e.g., distraction, use of coping self-statements), and psycho-education (e.g., providing information about the steps involved in the procedure to reduce unrealistic anxiety-provoking expectations that could have a negative impact on pain levels) (Bruehl & Chung, 2004). More recently, technological advances have also been incorporated into these treatments. For example, immersion in virtual-reality environments has been used as a distraction strategy with good results (Li, Montaño, Chen, & Gold, 2011). Psychological interventions for acute pain management have been studied as adjuncts to standard pharmacological approaches

By permission of appliedVR

Immersive virtual reality has been used in the management of acute pain.

and have shown considerable promise, although the extent to which they can be effective in the absence of pharmacological pain management has been studied less (Bruehl & Chung, 2004) and there is a need for more systematic controlled clinical trials.

Future Directions

Plenty of evidence supports the social-contextual elements of the pain experience and expression, but much of this research has been conducted in laboratory settings with healthy research participants (T. Hadjistavropoulos et al., 2011). Thus, more research is needed in real-world settings. Similarly, much of the research on pain assessment (Turk & Melzack, 2011) and management has focused on populations treated in multi-disciplinary settings, yet only a select subsample of patients with chronic pain are treated in such settings. More research with pain patients who receive pain services in more typical community facilities is needed.

An exciting area in which health psychologists are engaged involves the use of imaging such as functional magnetic resonance imaging (fMRI). For example, psychologists have investigated specific brain activity in response to the observation of pain in others (Budell, Kunz, Jackson, & Rainville, 2015; Lamm, Decety, & Singer, 2011). More research, however, is needed to better understand the psychosocial variables affecting brain mechanisms involved in the direct experience of pain but also when observing pain in others (T. Hadjistavropoulos et al., 2011). Increased study of these phenomena with pain patients (as opposed to healthy volunteers) would be especially welcome.

Increasingly we are seeing a greater role for the Internet and social media in pain self-management and patient education. We expect that this trend will continue. Patients rely heavily on pain information obtained through the Internet but the quality of much of the available information is questionable with unsubstantiated claims and promotion of products for commercial purposes being common (Bailey, LaChapelle, LeFort, Gordon, & Hadjistavropoulos, 2013). Nonetheless, the Internet and the social media, when used appropriately, can be great tools in the facilitation of pain education. An example within the area of pain psychology is the "It Doesn't Have to Hurt" initiative led by the Centre for Pediatric Pain Research in Halifax (http://itdoesnthavetohurt.ca), which is discussed in more detail in Chapter 13. In the coming years, we expect and hope to see similar initiatives targeting other groups (e.g., older adults with chronic pain), aimed to bring research results about pain to patients who can use them. Finally, we anticipate increased research and clinical application of well-designed protocols designed to address pain over the Internet (e.g., Dear et al., 2013), with the potential of reaching thousands of patients who now have limited access to psychological services for chronic pain (H. Hadjistavropoulos et al., 2011).

Summary

Pain is both a physical and a psychological experience. The gate control theory of pain describes the mechanisms involved in the perception of pain, while biopsychosocial formulations, consistent with the gate control theory, emphasize the role of social, cultural, psychological, and cognitive influences on pain and its communication. Given the well-documented influence of psychological factors in pain, psychologists have been involved in research and clinical applications with pain patients. Cognitive behavioural and other related procedures are of demonstrated effectiveness in helping people cope with pain problems.

Critical Thought Questions

1. Can you think of psychological strategies (e.g., distraction through engagement in pleasant activities, repeating coping self-statements) that you have used to cope with pain? Did these strategies make it easier for you to manage your pain? Besides what you may have already tried on your own, what are some other psychological strategies that a person could use to manage pain and its consequences?

2. Even today, many health professionals underplay the extent to which psychological intervention can help with serious chronic pain problems. If you were discussing this issue with a health professional who argued that a physical problem can only be managed by physical/medical methods, what position would you take and what arguments and evidence would you use to support your position?

Recommended Reading

Flor, H., & Turk, D.C. (2011). *Chronic pain: An integrated biobehavioural approach*. Seattle: IASP Press.

Hadjistavropoulos, T., Craig, K.D., Duck, S., Cano, A., Goubert, L., Jackson, P., . . . Dever Fitzgerald, T.

(2011). A biopsychosocial formulation of pain communication. *Psychological Bulletin, 137,* 910–39.

Cardiovascular Disease 10

Amanda C. Kentner
Eric J. Connors
Adrienne H. Kovacs
Sherry L. Grace

Learning Objectives

In this chapter you will:

- Learn how psychological distress is linked to the behavioural and biological risk factors that underlie heart disease (the biopsychosocial model).

- Learn to distinguish between types of cardiovascular diseases and their medical management through secondary prevention measures.

- Learn to identify and describe several psychosocial factors that contribute to cardiovascular disease.

- Gain an understanding of how these psychosocial factors are assessed in heart patients.

- Be able to compare and contrast common pharmacological, psychotherapeutic, psycho-educational, and behavioural interventions offered to those living with heart disease.

Cause of Death: Heartbreak

Can one truly die of a broken heart? Perhaps. The belief that one can die of a broken heart has been around for centuries. In Shakespeare's (2008) *Romeo and Juliet* Lady Montague's husband stated, "Alas, my liege, my wife is dead tonight. Grief of my son's exile hath stopped her breath (5.3.225–6)." In more recent times, renowned actress Debbie Reynolds passed away a day after the death of her daughter Carrie Fischer, who is best known for her role as Princess Leia in *Star Wars*. Additionally, there have been countless stories of individuals who may have died from heartbreak, whether it was after the death of a loved one, separating from a significant other, or even moving far away from home.

However, is this scientifically possible? Interestingly, research supports this notion. It is referred to as "broken-heart syndrome" (or *takotsubo* syndrome in Japan), and is a stress-induced cardiomyopathy (disease of the heart muscle; American Heart Association, 2016). When an individual endures a significant amount of emotional distress, the body is flooded with hormones that directly impact the heart. Rapid and immense levels of these hormones can influence the heart to enlarge and pump blood inefficiently (Akashi, Nef, & Lyon, 2015). These effects are typically transient and most individuals fully recover within two months. However, this intense hormonal cascade can lead to heart failure and in rare cases death (Akashi et al., 2015). As such, yes, one can in fact indirectly die from a broken heart and this mind–body phenomenon highlights the cardiovascular impact of severe emotional distress.

Cardiovascular Disease Description, Prevalence, and Medical Management

Diseases of the cardiovascular system include those that occur within the heart and the blood transport or circulatory system (i.e., veins and arteries). Together, these diseases are among the leading causes of death for North American men and women (Table 10.1). Fortunately, due to advances in treatment, mortality rates from cardiovascular disease (CVD) have significantly declined in developed nations such as Canada and the United States (Figure 10.1). Since mortality rates have declined, and onset of disease has not, this means that many people are living with chronic CVD.

Psychological factors are associated with the onset of CVD and its progression, as well as the quality and quantity of life of those with CVD. For example, people suffering from depression are more likely to develop heart disease, and once they do they also have a higher rate of mortality. Further, it is known that optimal management of heart disease requires multiple behavioural changes, such as abstinence from tobacco, regular physical activity, and adhering to a heart-healthy diet. Coping with a heart condition and its treatment can also contribute stress in interpersonal relationships and role functioning (e.g., paid and unpaid work), thus impacting **quality of life**.

iStock.com/Goodluz

Due to advances in treatment, mortality rates due to cardiovascular disease (CVD) have significantly declined in developed nations such as Canada and the United States. This means many more people are living with chronic CVD today than ever before.

Table 10.1 | Male and Female Mortality (%) Due to Cardiovascular Disease, Canada and the United States

Country	All Deaths	Male Deaths	Female Deaths
Canada	27.01%	27.05%	26.97%
United States	23.50%	24.60%	22.40%

Source: Adapted from: Statistics Canada. (2011). Mortality, summary list of causes (2008 numbers: CVD).
Heron, M. (2016). Deaths: Final data for 2013. National Vital Statistics Reports, 65, 1–95.
Mozaffarian, D., Benjamin, E.J., Go, A.S., Arnett, D.K., Blaha, M.J., Cushman, M., . . . Turner, M.B. (2016).
Heart disease and stroke statistics–2016 update: A report from the American Heart Association. Circulation, 133, e38–360.

This chapter explores each of these issues in terms of the psychological risk factors that under-lie CVD development and its prognosis, in addition to the different assessment tools for evaluating the psychological functioning of people with CVD. Finally, the evidence base for common psychological interventions offered to patients living with heart disease is discussed. Information about the physiology of the cardiovascular system is presented in Chapter 2. We recommend that you review it before continuing with this chapter.

The Disease Process

The biopsychosocial model provides a framework describing how behavioural and social factors contribute to the onset of CVD (Ferris, Kline, & Bourdage, 2012). Specifically, injury to the endo-thelium (see Chapter 2) is often caused by hypertension (high blood pressure), diabetes (problems regulating blood sugar), and hyperlipidemia (too much cholesterol). These injuries are associated with modifiable behavioural and social risk factors such as smoking, abdominal obesity, physical inactivity, unhealthy diet, and psychosocial distress (Douglas & Channon, 2014).

The result is atherosclerosis, where endothelial cells become inflamed and lipids start to form plaque in the endothelium, causing calcification (i.e., hardening). This, in turn, means the heart has to work harder to pump blood, and the diameter of the blood vessel often gets smaller. This interrupts blood flow, and hence the distribution of oxygen and nutrients to the body, including the heart. A temporary restriction of blood flow is known as *ischemia* (tissue cells remain alive but their functioning is disrupted), in which the heart tissue by the vessel is deprived of oxygen. Dam-aged arterial walls are also vulnerable to plaque rupture and blood clots, which can completely block the vessel (see Stone & Mancini, 2009). In the instance of complete blockage, there is no distribution of oxygen and other nutrients to the tissues supplied by that artery. When this occurs in the coronary arteries serving the myocardium (heart muscle), this is known as a "heart attack," or **myocardial infarction (MI)**. The continuum from unstable angina (i.e., ischemia causing chest pain that does not remit with rest) to MI is known as acute coronary syndrome.

Over time, while the heart works to pump blood despite death of some of the heart muscle tissue, it can become enlarged, causing more pump inefficiency. **Heart failure** is an end-stage of heart disease, when the heart cannot pump sufficient blood to meet the demands of the body (Figure 10.3). The average lifespan of heart-failure patients is approximately five years following hospital discharge (Alter et al., 2012). There are other heart diseases related to the function of the valves (which ensure proper directional flow of blood through the heart), the contraction of the heart (i.e., electrical disturbances called arrhythmias, some of which can cause sudden cardiac death), the heart muscle (i.e., cardiomyopathies), infections, and structural defects (i.e., congenital heart disease). These are not addressed in this chapter.

In Practice
CVD and Depression

James was a 62-year-old man, happily married, with three adult children and two young grandchildren. He worked long hours in real estate, and was planning to work for five more years in order to retire more comfortably at the age of 67. While showing a house to clients, he experienced the sudden onset of chest pain and collapsed to the ground. His clients called 911 and James was taken by ambulance to the hospital where an angiogram revealed three-vessel blockage. He subsequently underwent emergency coronary artery bypass grafting (CABG). He remained in the hospital for seven days. When he was discharged from the hospital, he was referred to **cardiovascular rehabilitation (CR)** and informed that he could plan to return to work, initially on a part-time basis, in approximately six months.

After James returned home, he spent much of his time sleeping in his bedroom and ignored telephone calls from the CR team to arrange an intake session. James had never behaved like this before, and his wife and children were unsure how to handle the situation. As a result of his wife's encouragement, James discussed his situation with his cardiologist, who easily recognized the symptoms of a major depressive episode. The cardiologist told James about the elevated rate of depression among cardiac patients and co-ordinated a referral to a psychologist. The psychologist provided emotional support as well as cognitive-behavioural therapy. The psychological benefits of physical activity were strongly emphasized. By the end of a 12-session course of psychotherapy, James had initiated CR, re-engaged with his family and professional colleagues, and reported a significantly improved mood.

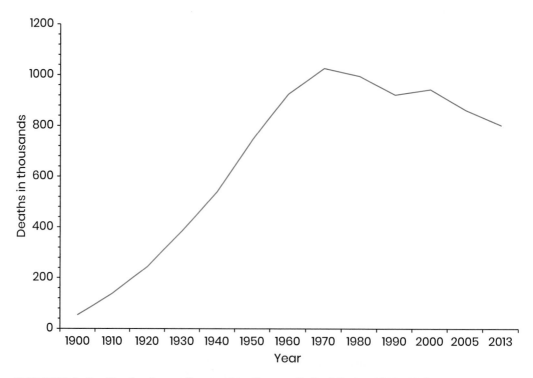

FIGURE 10.1 **Deaths due to cardiovascular disease, United States, 1900–2013.**

Source: Reprinted with permission, Circulation. 2015; CIR.0000000000000350 ©2015 American Heart Association, Inc.

In Focus

Know the Warning Signs of a Heart Attack

- Chest discomfort—most heart attacks involve discomfort in the centre of the chest that lasts more than a few minutes, or that goes away and comes back. It can feel like uncomfortable pressure, squeezing, fullness, or pain.

- Discomfort of other areas of the upper body—symptoms can include pain or discomfort in one or both arms, the back, neck, jaw, or stomach.

- Shortness of breath—with or without chest discomfort.

- Other signs—may include breaking out in a cold sweat, nausea, or light-headedness.

- If these signs are present dial 911!

Source: Reprinted with permission. © 2014 American Heart Association, Inc.

Heart Attack

Did you know that men and women often experience different symptoms?

♂ MEN...

often, but not always, experience the classic warning signs of a heart attack:

Uncomfortable pressure, fullness, squeezing or pain in the centre of the chest that goes away and comes back

Pain that spreads to the shoulders, neck, or arms

Chest discomfort with lightheadedness, fainting, sweating, nausea, or shortness of breath

Trigger: Men most often report **physical exertion** prior to heart attacks.

WOMEN... ♀

may experience the classic symptoms, but they are often milder. Women may also have other symptoms like:

Shortness of breath or difficulty breathing

Nausea, vomiting or dizziness

Back or jaw **pain**

Unexplained **anxiety,** weakness, or fatigue

Palpitations, cold sweats, or paleness

Mild, **flu-like symptoms**

Trigger: Women most often report **emotional stress** prior to heart attacks.

Every Second Counts! If you or someone you know has any of these symptoms, immediately call 911 or get to an Emergency Room as quickly as possible. Our doctors are ready to evaluate any patient complaining of chest pain within 10 minutes of arrival, and to provide the right treatment. We re here for you 24 hours a day, every day.

FIGURE 10.2 Heart attack: Did you know that men and women often experience different symptoms?

Source: http://www.cprsavealife.org/WARNING-SIGNS.html
Illustration credits: iStock.com/Blablo101; iStock.com/Ylivdesign

Prevalence and Cost of CVD

In Canada, over 70,000 individuals experience an MI each year (Public Health Agency of Canada, 2009), and 14,211 of these result in death (Statistics Canada, 2015). In the United States, recent annual estimates suggest that 750,000 adults will have an MI and 3.4 million will experience **angina** each year (Mozaffarian et al., 2016). Heart failure is increasing in prevalence, in part due to our aging population demographic (Hunt et al., 2005). An estimated 5.7 million American adults have heart failure (Mozaffarian et al., 2016). There is an associated financial burden; CVD costs the Canadian and American economies more than $12.1 billion and $316.6 billion, respectively (Figure 10.4), in physician services, hospital costs, lost wages, and decreased productivity (Mozaffarian et al., 2016; Public Health Agency of Canada, 2014).

There are disparities in CVD. With regard to ethnic background for example, CVD tends to occur in men and women of African ancestry at an earlier age than in Caucasians (Feinstein et al., 2012); subsequently, death rates are higher in persons of African ancestry across all age categories (Mensah, Mokdad, Ford, Greenlund, & Croft, 2005). Additionally, ethnic minority groups have been shown to have relatively more limited awareness regarding CVD risk factors and less access to health care (Kim, Hogan, D'Onofrio, Chekijian, & Safdar, 2017). These discrepancies highlight the need for individualized, culturally sensitive methods of CVD prevention, diagnosis, and treatment. Please refer to Chapter 15 for more information on health disparities based on culture. There are also disparities by sex and socio-economic status. For instance, while the prevalence of CVD is comparable in women and men, women often receive less aggressive treatment and are more likely to die in the early months after a heart attack (Anand et al., 2008). Finally, CVD risk factors are most common among people in lower income brackets, such that socio-economic status is a major factor associated with later chronic disease risk and mortality (Johnson-Lawrence, Kaplan, & Galea, 2013).

Medical Management of CVD

Once a patient is diagnosed with acute coronary syndrome, it is important to acutely restore blood flow to the heart. Often, **revascularization** interventions are performed in hospital to restore sufficient blood flow. Revascularization procedures include angioplasty, also known as percutaneous coronary intervention (PCI), and coronary artery bypass graft (CABG) surgery. PCI is a procedure in which a catheter is used to place a mesh tube in the coronary vessels that have narrowed. This mesh tube ("stent") is then expanded so blood can again flow through

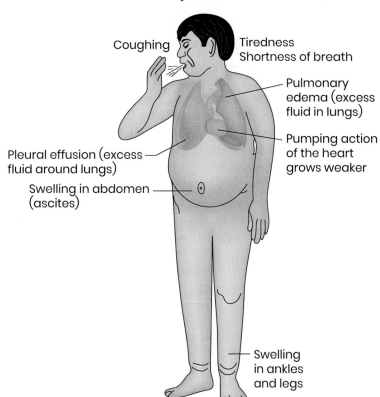

Coughing

Tiredness
Shortness of breath

Pulmonary edema (excess fluid in lungs)

Pumping action of the heart grows weaker

Pleural effusion (excess fluid around lungs)

Swelling in abdomen (ascites)

Swelling in ankles and legs

FIGURE 10.3 **The major signs and symptoms of heart failure.**

Source: National Heart, Lung, and Blood Institute; National Institutes of Health; U.S. Department of Health and Human Services.

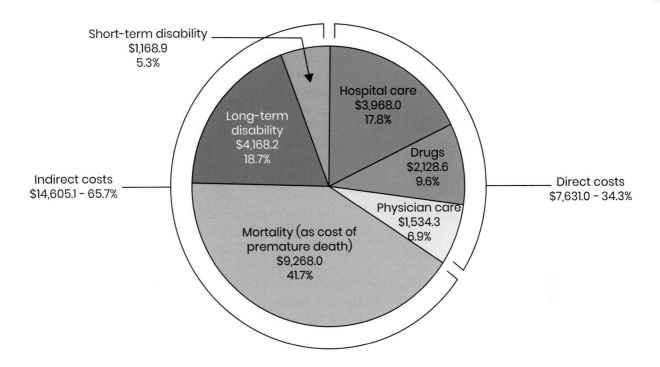

Short-term disability
$1,168.9
5.3%

Long-term disability
$4,168.2
18.7%

Hospital care
$3,968.0
17.8%

Drugs
$2,128.6
9.6%

Indirect costs
$14,605.1 – 65.7%

Direct costs
$7,631.0 – 34.3%

Physician care
$1,534.3
6.9%

Mortality (as cost of premature death)
$9,268.0
41.7%

Economic Burden of Illness in Canada 2000.

FIGURE 10.4 **Percentage of costs due to cardiovascular disease in Canada.**

Note: Costs are in millions.

the vessel to the heart muscle (Figure 10.5). CABG uses arteries or veins from another area of the body to circumvent the blocked flow in the coronary arteries (Figure 10.6), restoring the delivery of the blood supply to heart tissues (Antman et al., 2004). PCI is typically performed as a day procedure, whereas CABG requires an approximately week-long hospitalization and extended recovery period at home.

Patients are also encouraged to work towards improving the long-term health of their vasculature in order to prevent further blockages and preserve the pumping ability of the heart. Secondary prevention refers to the initiation of treatments to stop or slow the progression of diseases and disabilities once they have already occurred. Secondary prevention of **acute coronary syndrome** specifically includes reducing CVD risk

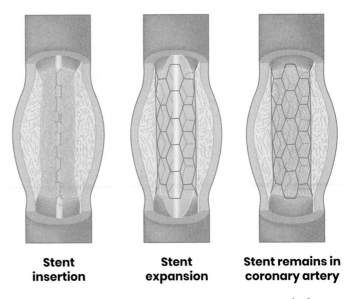

| Stent insertion | Stent expansion | Stent remains in coronary artery |

FIGURE 10.5 Percutaneous coronary interventions (PCI).

Before   **After**

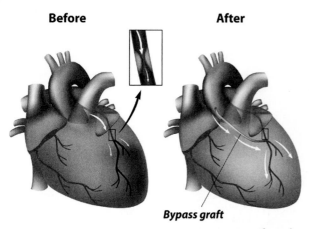

Bypass graft

FIGURE 10.6 Coronary artery bypass grafting (CABG).

Source: © Alila07 | Dreamstime.com

factors through behavioural approaches (e.g., exercise, smoking cessation) and pharmacotherapy (e.g., aspirin, cholesterol-lowering drugs).

When the pumping function of the heart is ultimately permanently damaged, as in **heart failure**, there are unfortunately no cures. Heart transplantation is the most enduring treatment approach. However, there are insufficient organs available to meet need (Lund et al., 2016). Mechanical circulatory support, such as through a ventricular assist device, is becoming a more widely implemented approach. The device supports ventricular contractions to facilitate blood flow throughout the body (Caro, Rosenthal, Kendall, Pozuelo, & Funk, 2016). Advances in the devices have prolonged survival in patients with these implanted devices (Sorabella et al., 2015).

The diagnosis of CVD and the acute experience of having a CVD event may contribute to psychological distress in patients and their loved ones, which can complicate this process of behavioural modification. Some patients will benefit from support to cope with their chronic condition and to successfully modify health behaviours over the long-term. Motivational interviewing can be a helpful strategy employed by health-care professionals by addressing patient ambivalence, and increasing motivation, action, and maintenance of healthy lifestyle behaviours (Miller, 1996). Health professionals can also encourage self-efficacy and self-regulation in the adoption of sustainable health-promoting behaviours and the elimination of health-damaging ones. Interventions have been developed to train physicians in these evidence-based approaches to communication with patients, resulting in greater heart-healthy behaviour changes among their patients compared to usual care (Martins & McNeil, 2009).

Cardiovascular rehabilitation is a comprehensive secondary prevention program providing risk-factor modification through education, behavioural counselling, and individualized exercise training. Participation in CR significantly reduces mortality and repeat hospitalization rates (Anderson & Taylor, 2014).

Following PCI or CABG, patients are ideally referred to CR, which is a comprehensive secondary prevention program that provides risk-factor modification through education, behavioural counselling (e.g., pharmacological therapy adherence, nutrition and weight management, smoking cessation), and structured exercise training. In addition, CR programs provide social support to patients with CVD, and may offer stress-management classes and programs targeting psychological distress (Cahill, Bilanovic, Kelly, Bacon, & Grace, 2015). CR may be provided on an outpatient basis in a hospital setting, in a community gym, or even through telephone support at home. Participation in CR significantly reduces cardiovascular mortality and repeat hospitalization rates, regardless of the setting in which the program is offered (Anderson & Taylor, 2014; Davies et al., 2010).

BSIP SA/Alamy Stock Photo

Unfortunately, these programs are grossly underused (Grace, Turk-Adawi, Santiago Pio, & Alter, 2016). Barriers to CR are multifactorial and thus efforts to improve access to and participation in CR should target patients, providers, and the broader health-care system (Ghisi, Polyzotis, Oh, Pakosh, & Grace, 2013).

Psychological Factors in Cardiovascular Disease

Traditional risk factors (e.g., diabetes, hypertension, smoking, dyslipidemia) only explain about two-thirds of new CVD cases. Psychosocial factors have also been associated with the development of CVD and its prognosis. For example, in the international INTERHEART study, over 24,000 people from 52 countries who had MIs were age- and sex-matched to people who had not. Patients who had MIs were more likely to recall periods of perceived work and home stress, financial stress, and have experienced major life events (i.e., business failure, intra-family conflict), in addition to depression and perceiving lower control over their lives, during the 12 months *prior* to their cardiac events (Rosengren et al., 2004). These factors accounted for a large proportion of their risk for CVD. Moreover, these psychosocial factors were related to MI across all regions of the world, ethnic groups, and in both men and women (Rosengren et al., 2004). These psychosocial risk factors for both the development and prognosis of CVD, namely perceived job and home stress, social isolation, depression, anxiety, and even some personality traits, are discussed further below.

Stress

Stress stems from a discrepancy between a real or perceived appraisal of environmental demands and the biopsychosocial coping mechanisms of an individual. For example, adults with CVD might experience stress when faced with an unexpected hospitalization, attending multiple medical appointments, reduced ability to maintain employment, etc. Stress may be acute or chronic in nature, and each can affect the cardiovascular system. Acute stressors are those of shorter duration but stronger intensity (e.g., losing a job, the death of a loved one, undergoing CABG). Chronic stressors are those of a longer duration, and may be intermittent or continuous (e.g., ongoing financial challenges or relationship conflicts).

Acute Stress

As described in the beginning of the chapter, acute levels of stress can negatively impact the structure and the function of the heart. This rapid onset of impaired cardiac functioning, followed by an identifiable stressor, is known as stress-induced cardiomyopathy or "broken-heart syndrome" (Akashi et al., 2015). The cardiovascular effects of acute stressors have been demonstrated in studies of people experiencing bereavement, environmental disasters, and terrorist attacks. For example, there is heightened risk for cardiovascular events following the death of a spouse for both men and women (Carey et al., 2014; Martikainen & Valkonen, 1996). During the first month following the 1995 Hanshin-Awaji earthquake in Japan, there was a significant increase in MI and stroke among those living near the epicentre. Compared to the two-week period prior to the disaster, one clinic reported prolonged elevations in blood pressure (a risk factor for CVD) two to four weeks after the disaster in well-controlled hypertensive patients (Kario, McEwen, & Pickering, 2003). It appeared that the risk of a fatal outcome following this acute stressor was associated with having underlying CVD prior to the earthquake. In another study, individuals residing in Chicago,

New York, Mississippi, and Washington D.C. had significantly greater systolic blood pressure two months following the 11 September 2001 terrorist attacks (Gerin et al., 2005). Further, data collected from 16 New Jersey emergency departments revealed a 49 per cent increase in patients who experienced an MI 60 days following the September 11th attacks, compared to the 60 days prior (Allegra, Mostashari, Rothman, Milano, & Cochrane, 2005).

It has been suggested that acute mental stress can contribute to cardiac ischemia, particularly "silent" ischemia (i.e., no overt chest pain). For example, Rozanski et al. (1988) assessed cardiac functioning in patients with CVD while they completed either exercise or a series of mental tasks that included arithmetic, reading, and public speaking. In a majority of the patients, mental stress, particularly public speaking, was accompanied by myocardial ischemia similar to what was observed during exercise. This converging literature highlights the negative impact that acute stressors have on cardiovascular functioning.

Chronic Stress

Although chronically stressful situations are those that persist for longer durations, the specific stressors themselves are varied and often arise unexpectedly (such as an argument in an overall situation of marital strife). These types of stressors are often unpredictable in their frequency and duration, but occur numerous times over long periods. The core feature of chronic stress is that the person perceives himself or herself as having limited control over the situation in which the chronic stressor(s) occur. Stressors that have been shown to impact CVD onset and prognosis include job strain, family conflict, and social isolation.

Job Strain

Low decision-making control (i.e., the demand-control model) (Karasek & Theorell, 1990) and an imbalance between employees' efforts at work and the rewards they gain in return (i.e., the effort–reward imbalance model) (Siegrist, 2010) have been shown to be hazardous to heart health (Aboa-Éboulé et al., 2011; Aboa-Éboulé, Brisson, & Maunsell, 2011; Kuper, Singh-Manoux, Siegrist, & Marmot, 2002; Siegrist et al., 2004; Siegrist, 2010). A Canadian study established that chronic job strain, as characterized by "high psychological demands" and "low decision control," is a predictor of *recurrent* CVD events following an initial CVD event (Aboa-Éboulé et al., 2007). In this study, middle-aged male and female participants who returned to work after an MI were followed until (a) their first recurrent CVD event, (b) death, or (c) until six years after their initial heart attack (whichever occurred first). The assessment of psychological work demands included quantity of work, time constraints, and intellectual requirements, in addition to their freedom to use and develop new skills, make independent decisions, and be creative. After adjusting for other work characteristics, sociodemographic characteristics, lifestyle (i.e., alcohol consumption, physical activity), and clinical characteristics, survival rates for patients with greater chronic job strain were lower. These patients had a higher risk for fatal CVD, MI, or angina in the two to six years after their initial MI (Aboa-Éboulé et al., 2007).

As per the effort–reward model, there is an increased risk of CVD and poor physical and mental health functioning in employees who perceive an imbalance between the work they put in for their employer and their rewards (e.g., income, potential for promotion, job security) (Siegrist, 2010; Kuper et al., 2002). The effect of effort–reward imbalances are particularly evident in employees with limited occupational social support networks (Kuper et al., 2002).

Another job strain is shift work that varies from the typical eight-hour workday, disrupts normal biological rhythms, and has been associated with a higher prevalence of atherosclerosis and MI. Shift workers often have more CVD risk factors, such as smoking and reduced physical activity. The negative CVD outcomes associated with shift work occur in people at a younger age than would be expected in the general population (Haupt et al., 2008). For example, in the landmark Nurses' Health Study, female nurses who worked rotating night shifts had a higher rate of MI and death from CVD, even after controlling for other CVD risk factors. Specifically, the risk for CVD among women who worked more than six years on shifts was 1.5 times greater than it was among the women who were not on shifts (Kawachi et al., 1995).

Family Strain

The aforementioned interheart study highlighted the negative effects of chronic family stress on cardiovascular health (Rosengren et al., 2004). Marital strain in particular may be related to the development of CVD. In the Framingham Offspring Study, men and women were assessed on measures of marital status, marital strain, and risk factors for CVD, then followed for 10 years. In

By permission of Amanda Kentner

A discrepancy between the effort that employees put into their work and the payoffs received has been linked to the development of cardiovascular disease (Kuper et al., 2002; Siegrist, 2010). Low decision-making control is also related to cardiovascular risk.

this study, the *development* of a CVD event was primarily related to the reaction to conflict with one's spouse (Eaker, Sullivan, Kelley-Hayes, D'Agostino, & Benjamin, 2007). Importantly, men and women who had marital conflict tended to have higher blood pressure compared to individuals who engaged in collaborative problem-solving (Smith et al., 2009). Moreover, *prognosis* following a CVD event was related to the frequency of marital disagreements, individual marital happiness, and comparison of their marital satisfaction to other couples (Eaker et al., 2007; Orth-Gomer et al., 2000). The impact of marital strain on CVD prognosis appeared to affect both men and women.

Approximately 12 per cent of Americans over the age of 45 have family caregiving responsibilities for someone with a chronic illness or disability (Roth, Perkins, Wadley, Temple, & Haley, 2009). Providing support to a spouse or other family member who requires assistance increases the risk of CVD onset in the caregiver. This is often due to chronic stress and the specific strains associated with physically and psychologically demanding tasks, financial difficulty, filling multiple roles, social isolation, and watching the deterioration and suffering of another person. Caregivers are often older persons and their own health and emotional adjustment to the situation may decline during the process of taking care of another (Haley, Roth, Howard, & Safford, 2010; Low, Thurston, & Matthews, 2010). However, some recent work suggests that the fulfillment that comes with caregiving can prop up the health of the caregiver (Roth, Fredman, & Haley, 2015; see section on positive psychology below).

Social Isolation

Social networks, such as family, friends, co-workers, pets (Friedmann & Thomas, 1995) and even the patient-centred care network (Cossette, Frasure-Smith, & Lespérance, 2001) have been associated with a lower incidence of CVD (Orth-Gomer, Rosengren, & Wilhelmsen, 1993; O'Shea et al., 2002). Higher-quality relationships are particularly protective (Dickens et al., 2004).

By permission of Amanda Kentner

Those who believe they have a poor social network are more likely to suffer from depression and are at an increased risk of a recurrent cardiovascular event (Leifheit-Limson et al., 2010; Schmaltz et al., 2007).

In contrast, social isolation has been related to decreased heart functioning and poor health behaviours. For example, those who know fewer than three people well enough to visit their home are at an increased risk for CVD (Rodriguez et al., 2011). Moreover, social isolation and loneliness are associated with a greater risk of inactivity, smoking, multiple health-risk behaviours, and hypertension (Shankar, McMunn, Banks, & Steptoe, 2011). People who feel that they have limited social support (Burg et al., 2005; Leifheit-Limson et al., 2010) or who live alone are more likely to die, to have a recurrent cardiovascular event (Schmaltz et al., 2007), and to experience decreased quality of life and/or depression (Leifheit-Limson et al., 2010).

Psychological Disorders

Two psychological conditions—depression and anxiety—have been related to CVD onset and prognosis. Depression is characterized by low mood and/or a diminished feeling of pleasure or interest in normal everyday activities. Other prominent features include significant changes in appetite, weight, sleep disturbance, fatigue/decreased energy, psychomotor retardation or agitation, sense of worthlessness or guilt, difficulty concentrating and making decisions, and/or recurrent thoughts of death or suicide. The difference between clinical depression and psychological distress ("the blues") relates to the severity and duration of the symptoms, and the degree of impact on one's life roles.

Adults with CVD have a higher prevalence of depression. The prevalence of depression in the general American population is 7.6 per cent (Kessler, Chiu, Demler, & Walters, 2005; Pratt & Brody, 2014) but 15 to 20 per cent for those with CVD (National Institute of Health, 2004; Thombs et al., 2006) and symptoms of depression persist (Grace et al., 2005). A history of depression is a known psychological risk factor for CVD (Rugulies, 2002; Van der Kooy et al., 2007; Wulsin & Singal, 2003) and MI (Lichtman et al., 2014). Of particular note, this risk level is comparable to that of traditional risk factors such as smoking. The risk for CVD onset remains elevated (albeit lower) for individuals who present with sub-clinical symptoms of depression (Van der Kooy et al., 2007).

Moreover, there is an association between depression and death in patients who have CVD (Freedland et al., 2016; Meijer et al., 2013; Smith & Ruiz, 2002). Depression in the first two years after MI predicts poor prognosis in terms of cardiac symptoms, quality of life, disability, and death (de Jonge et al., 2006; Meijer et al., 2013). These poor outcomes are particularly evident in women (Frasure-Smith, Lespérance, & Talajic, 1995). Specifically, depression in CVD patients is related to two times greater mortality in the two years after CVD diagnosis, when compared to non-depressed CVD patients (Barth, Schumacher, & Herrmann-Lingen, 2004; Meijer et al., 2013). See Figure 10.7 for the theorized relationship between cardiovascular disease and depression.

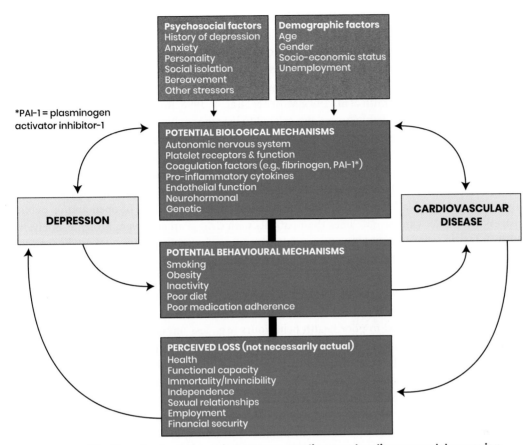

FIGURE 10.7 The theorized relationship between cardiovascular disease and depression.

Source: Hare, D. L., Toukhasati, S. R., Johansson, P., & Jaarsma, T. (2014). Depression and cardiovascular disease: A clinical review. *European Heart Journal*, *35*, 1365–1372.

Anxiety and Trauma/Stressor-Related Disorders

Anxiety refers to a negative emotional state marked by worry, apprehension, and a sense of threat. Other symptoms of generalized anxiety include restlessness, fatigue, irritability, and sleep disturbance. Anxiety disorders include, but are not limited to, generalized anxiety disorder (GAD), phobias, and panic disorder. The overall 12-month prevalence of all anxiety disorder subtypes (including trauma-related disorders) in the general American population is about 18 per cent (Kessler et al., 2005). The documented prevalence of cardiac patients meeting the criteria for at least one anxiety disorder is approximately 36 per cent (Todaro, Shen, Raffia, Tilkemeir, & Niaura, 2007). CVD populations have a higher risk of anxiety disorders irrespective of socio-economic background, geographic location, and culture (Ormel et al., 2007). However, the impact of anxiety on CVD appears to be stronger for men than for women (Fiedorowicz, He, & Merikangas, 2011).

The role of anxiety in the development of CVD is less than that of depression (Fleet, Lavoie, & Beitman, 2000), and may be dependent on the specific anxiety-disorder subtype (Hemingway & Marmot, 1999). For example, the presence of phobic anxiety (which is not a diagnosable subtype per se) increases the risk of sudden cardiac death (i.e., problem of the electrical conduction system of the heart, such that the heart cannot pump effectively and circulation ceases), but not of non-fatal MI (Albert, Chae, Rexrode, Manson, & Kawachi, 2005; Kawachi et al., 1994). It has been proposed that phobic anxiety may elevate this risk of cardiac death through increased ventricular arrhythmia (abnormal rapid heart rhythms) (Albert et al., 2005; Watkins et al., 2006).

As one might expect, anxiety levels tend to be high following a CVD event, and have been shown to persist for longer than six months. Post- MI anxiety has been associated with a range of CVD events, including ischemia, recurrent MI, and sudden death (Allgulander, 2016; Denollet & Brutsaert, 1998; Frasure-Smith et al., 1995; Moser & Dracup, 1996; Roest, Martens, Denollet, & de Jonge, 2010). High levels of anxiety are also related to longer hospital stays (which is costly to the health system, and distressing for patients and their families) and reduced quality of life (Lane, Caroll, Ring, Beevers, & Lip, 2000).

There is more evidence to suggest a differential impact of anxiety dependent on disorder sub-type (Herrmann, Brand-Driehorst, Buss, & Ruger, 2000). For instance, MI patients with a lifetime history of agoraphobia (a specific phobia indicated by an irrational fear of open and/or public spaces) had poorer cardiac outcomes than patients with GAD (Parker, Owen, Brotchie, & Hyett, 2010). It was suggested that the worrying tendencies among individuals with GAD might actually promote help-seeking behaviour and better CVD self-management (Herrmann et al., 2000; Parker et al., 2010).

Post-traumatic stress disorder (PTSD) has also emerged as a potential contributor to CVD onset. PTSD is characterized by intrusive memories of a traumatic event, avoidance, and hyper-arousal. It has been linked to poor health behaviours (e.g., less physical activity, higher rates of medication non-adherence, and smoking) (Zen, Whooley, Zhao, & Cohen, 2012), and may be associated with increased risk of atherosclerosis and mortality (Ahmadi et al., 2011). Furthermore, PTSD may occur in response to a traumatic cardiovascular event, thus further increasing CVD recurrence and death (Sidney, 2013; Vaccarino et al., 2013).

It must be noted that mood and anxiety disorders are highly co-morbid (i.e., they often occur together; Kessler et al., 2005), and thus their unique contribution to CVD development and prognosis can be difficult to determine. In one study, CVD patients with co-morbid depression *and* GAD were not at a greater risk for poorer outcomes (cardiac death, cardiac arrest, or revascularization procedures) than those patients who had either major depression *or* GAD alone (Frasure-Smith & Lespérance, 2008). In another study, anxiety alone (not including depression) was an independent risk factor for hospitalization and outpatient clinic visits (Strik, Denollet, Lousberg, & Honig, 2003). This suggests that although depression and anxiety are highly co-morbid, they may relate to CVD in different ways (Allgulander, 2016).

Personality

In general, "personality" refers to an individual's characteristic way of acting and thinking, although there is little consensus for a specific definition (Griggs, 2017). **Type A personality** was the first aspect of personality hypothesized to have an independent role in the onset of heart disease (Friedman and Rosenman, 1959). Type A individuals are competitive high achievers who display anger and hostility, and tend to be engaged in multiple tasks. Aspects of personality consistently related to both CVD onset and prognosis are anger and hostility (Chida & Steptoe, 2009), which are specific dimensions of the Type A personality. For example, cynical hostility levels in those with and without CVD are associated with a significantly higher risk for mortality and non-fatal CVD outcomes, particularly in healthy men compared to women (Chida & Steptoe, 2009).

The focus of personality subtypes has also centered on the Type D personality, referring to people who display both a high level of negative affect and social inhibition (Denollet, 2005). Negative affectivity is the predisposition for worry and irritability, while social inhibition is the tendency to be insecure and uncomfortable in social situations (Denollet, 2005). While recent studies have demonstrated Type D personality to be associated with severity of CVD (Garcia-Retamero, Petrova, Arrebola-Morena, Catena, & Ramírez-Hernández, 2016), researchers have not consistently shown a connection between this personality type and CVD (Grande et al., 2011; de Voogd, Sanderman, & Coyne, 2012).

Positive Psychology: Resilience and Coping

So far, we have explored the role of negative psychosocial factors (anxiety, depression) on CVD onset and prognosis. Now we shift focus to another arm of cardiac psychology that explores more positive perspectives—specifically, a focus on "resilience" or "psychological thriving" in the face of a cardiac or other health diagnosis, as positive ways of coping that lead to health-protective behaviours (e.g., participating in physical activity, smoking cessation, choosing heart-healthy foods) or engaging one's support networks. Notably, there are significant associations between health-related outcomes and positive psychological constructs such as vitality, optimism, hope, positive affect, and happiness among those with CVD (Boehm & Kubzanksy, 2012; DuBois et al., 2012; DuBois et al., 2015). For example, DuBois and colleagues (2015) explored this relationship among cardiac patients and found a significant correlation between positive psychological states/well-being and a reduced risk of mortality and rehospitalization. To utilize the benefits of positive psychology with this population, interventions are being developed that are focused on increasing a patient's level of positivity to promote better short-term and long-term outcomes (Huffman et al., 2011).

When people who have survived a CVD trauma such as an MI begin to recognize benefits and take steps towards positive changes in their lives, they may undergo "post-traumatic growth," defined as the experience of positive consequences arising from the struggle with a traumatic experience. The resulting transformation is thought to lead not only to a return to previous levels of well-being, but to a higher level of functioning in some aspects of life (Aldwin, 1994; Chan, Lai, & Wong, 2006; Tedeschi, Park, & Calhoun, 1998). In particular, PCI patients who experienced such positive psychology in the weeks after their cardiac event had better health outcomes (i.e., lower cholesterol and better performance on a six-minute walk test) following an exercise rehabilitation program than patients with lower personal growth (Chan et al., 2006).

Psychological Assessment of Patients with Cardiovascular Disease

Psychological risk factors/disorders are commonly assessed via self-administered psychometrically validated questionnaires or surveys. For those whose responses suggest a potential mental health problem, clinical interviews by a trained professional (e.g., psychiatrist or psychologist) are required to "diagnose" a psychological disorder. These professionals are trained on established diagnostic criteria (American Psychiatric Association, 2013). Where positive, results of the assessment, impact on quality of life and medical outcomes, as well as treatment options should then be discussed with the patient.

Notably, most medical care for cardiac patients focuses on their physical health, despite the large burden of psychological distress in those with heart disease. Some experts recommend screening for psychological distress (i.e., brief surveys of depression) within the context of routine cardiac care for patients (Hurley et al., 2017), although this recommendation is not without its critics (see Gilbody, House, & Sheldon, 2005; Gilbody, Sheldon, & House, 2008; Ziegelstein, Thombs, Coyne, & de Jonge, 2009). Unfortunately, however, psychological disorders are under-recognized and undertreated in people with CVD (Czarny et al., 2011).

Depression/Anxiety

Diagnosis of a cardiac patient with a mood or anxiety disorder can be complicated by the fact that many symptoms of depression or anxiety, such as fatigue, sleep disturbance, and appetite-related weight change, are also symptoms associated with CVD (Simon & Von Korff, 2006). For these reasons, structured diagnostic interviews are considered the gold standard (Berkman et al., 2003; Freedland et al., 2002). Self-report assessments of depression/anxiety symptoms are used often because they allow for a quick and cost-effective evaluation of patient populations. Examples include the Patient Health Questionnaire (PHQ) (Kroenke, Spitzer, & Williams, 2003) and the Hospital Anxiety Depression Scale (HADS) (Hunt-Shanks, Blanchard, Reid, Fortier, & Cappelli, 2010; Zigmond & Snaith, 1983).

Social Support

Many scales are available to assess social support, but these are typically administered within the research setting. One recommended measure in the CVD literature is the ENRICHD (Enhancing Recovery in Coronary Heart Disease) Social Support Inventory (ESSI) (Vaglio et al., 2004). The ESSI was developed for use in a major randomized controlled trial (i.e., a gold standard method of study in which patients are randomly allocated to receive an intervention or a comparison treatment, ensuring that any unmeasured alternative explanations for the findings would be balanced in both groups) called ENRICHD (Berkman et al., 2003) to identify patients who had low social support following an MI. The ESSI can be administered as either a five- or a seven-item test that allows for validated quick and reliable scoring in CVD populations (Berkman et al., 2003; Mitchell et al., 2003; Vaglio et al., 2004). The items on the ESSI evaluate factors such as love and affection, help with daily chores, and whether someone is available to help sort through problems and/or offer advice (Vaglio et al., 2004).

Personality Factors

In the laboratory setting, hostility, arguably the most hazardous trait of the Type A personality, can be measured via the Cook-Medley Hostility (Ho) Scale (Barefoot, Peterson, & Harrell, 1989). The Ho Scale assesses hostility according to six subscales: cynicism, hostile attributions, hostile affect, aggressive responding, social avoidance, and "other." High scores on cynicism, hostile affect, and aggressive responding are most predictive of mortality (Barefoot et al., 1989).

Interventions for Patients with Cardiovascular Disease

Given the burden of psychological distress in patients with CVD and the negative effects on health, therapies demonstrated to reduce distress in non-medically ill populations have been applied and tested in CVD patients. Treatments for psychological disorders include pharmacological, psycho-therapeutic, and behavioural approaches. Ideally, patients are engaged in the decision of which therapy to initiate first, and these approaches are not mutually exclusive (Davidson et al., 2013). This is because the magnitude of benefit for pharmacological and psychotherapeutic approaches is comparable (although psychotherapy is associated with more sustained remission of distress, and has no associated side effects as medications do). The goals are to reduce psychological distress such as depression, and also to reduce the increased rates of morbidity and mortality in distressed cardiac patients.

Pharmacotherapy (Medications)

Anti-depressant and anxiolytic medications are used to treat depression and/or anxiety. Guidelines recommend that patients begin at an initial fairly low dose (i.e., potentially non-therapeutic) that minimizes potential side effects. These medications often take 4 to 6 weeks to have an effect. Treatment response should be monitored through regular follow-up appointments with the prescribing physician, and the dose increased until symptoms are reduced. It has been recommended that if symptoms are not reduced, patients should be prescribed a different medication or offered therapy if not already receiving it (i.e., so-called "stepped" care), and again followed up (Hare, Toukhsati, Johansson, & Jaarsma, 2014; Mavrides & Nemeroff, 2013).

There have been a series of randomized trials undertaken to test different antidepressant medications in cardiac populations in particular, and many of these are summarized below. Overall, the class of anti-depressants called selective serotonergic reuptake inhibitors (SSRIs) is recommended as the first-line approach for heart patients, given their efficacy and safety in this population (Bradley & Rumsfeld, 2015). Indeed, some antidepressants such as monoamine oxidase inhibitors and tricyclic antidepressants have cardiotoxic effects and are rarely prescribed to patients with cardiac disease (Carney & Freedland, 2017)

An initial study to evaluate antidepressant medication in CVD patients was the Sertraline Antidepressant and Heart Attack Randomized Trial (SADHART) (Glassman et al., 2002), which was conducted across seven countries, including the United States and Canada. Eligible male and female patients had had an MI or had been hospitalized for unstable angina and also had been diagnosed with a current episode of depression. Half of the patients were given the SSRI drug sertraline. In this study, sertraline was not associated with negative changes in any cardiovascular indicators, suggesting that it is safe for use in CVD populations (Glassman et al., 2002). In addition, sertraline was more effective than a placebo in reducing depressive symptoms. More recently, Glassman, Bigger, and Gaffney (2009) conducted a seven-year follow-up study of the SADHART participants. They found that baseline depression severity and a lack of improvement of depressive symptoms, regardless of being in the sertraline or placebo group, were the two strongest predictors of mortality. These results highlight the importance of long-term follow-up of depressed cardiac patients to ensure treatment is sufficient to achieve remission and that patients do not relapse.

In the MI and Depression Intervention Trial (MIND-IT) (Honig et al., 2007), MI patients with depression were randomized to receive either mirtazapine or a placebo for a 24-week period. Mirtazapine is part of a newer class of antidepressants, activating serotonin and other receptors in the brain involved in mood. In MIND-IT, MI patients who received mirtazapine had lower depressive symptoms at follow-up. Similar to SADHART, those who responded best to the antidepressant treatment tended to be those with a history of depressive episodes. Overall, a review of the studies in this field concluded that SSRIs offer a small, but clinically meaningful, effect in reducing depression symptoms in CVD patients, and that hospitalization rates may also be reduced (Hare et al., 2014; Mavrides & Nemeroff, 2013; Rutledge, Redwine, Linke, & Mills, 2013; Thombs et al., 2013).

Psychotherapy

Psychological therapies are effective in treating psychological distress in both mental health-care settings and medically ill populations. Well-established therapies include cognitive behavioural therapy (CBT) (see Prior, Francis, Reitav, & Stone, 2009) and interpersonal psychotherapy (IPT) (see Prior et al., 2009). These structured interventions of short duration involve the interaction between a client and a trained therapist for the purpose of addressing the underlying factors that contribute to anxiety or mood disorders. As indicated in previous chapters, the goal of CBT is to identify cognitive patterns and behaviours that generate these psychological manifestations, while IPT is focused more on the patient's relationships and social environment.

Given the evidence suggesting depression and low social support are related to poor CVD prognosis following MI, the ENRICHD trial (Berkman et al., 2003) was designed to address whether treating depression and increasing social support would reduce recurrent CVD events and death. In this American study, MI patients who were depressed and/or had low social support were assigned at random to either a usual care or a CBT intervention. Part of the CBT intervention was for patients to complete homework assignments that addressed maladaptive cognitive patterns and behaviours that contributed to their psychosocial distress, including low social support. Usual care consisted of the standard care provided by physicians, in addition to written materials about CVD risk factors.

Results were disappointing; Treatment allocation had no effect on recurrent MI or death during the four-year follow-up period. Depression symptoms were reduced and social support was significantly increased in the intervention group vs patients in usual care; however, benefits were not sustained over the long term (Berkman et al., 2003). A closer look at the findings showed that improvements in mood and social support were found to be related to the adherence of the patient to the CBT-related homework assignments (Cowan et al., 2008), as well as exercise (Vasamreddy, Ahmed, Gluckman, & Blumenthal, 2004). Moreover, depressed patients who did not benefit from the CBT were at higher risk for mortality (Carney et al., 2004).

Cognitive behavioural therapy is used to identify maladaptive thoughts and behaviours that contribute to anxiety and mood disorders. Evidence suggests that this form of therapy assists to elevate mood but may not significantly improve cardiovascular outcomes (Thombs et al., 2008).

Another trial tested combination therapy: an SSRI antidepressant, citalopram, alongside IPT. The Canadian Cardiac Randomized Evaluation of Antidepressant and Psychotherapy Efficacy (CREATE) study (Lespérance et al., 2007) was a 12-week trial that included patients with both clinical depression and CVD (i.e., MI, PCI). Patients were randomized to one of four groups: (1) IPT + clinical management + citalopram, (2) IPT + clinical management + placebo, (3) clinical management + citalopram, or (4) clinical management + placebo. Clinical management was a standardized protocol of patient depression treatment offered by a clinician. Results showed that citalopram was significantly better than the placebo in the reduction of depression scores 12 weeks after initiation of the antidepressant treatment. There was no effect of IPT. Therefore, the investigators recommended that citalopram be considered as a first-line treatment for co-morbid depression in CVD patients (Lespérance et al., 2007).

Another psychotherapy intervention is stress management. This typically involves relaxation training, cognitive restructuring (see Chapter 9), and communication and problem-solving skill development to provide patients with the skills to manage acute episodes of stress and chronically reduce depression, anxiety, and hostility (Blumenthal et al., 2005; Blumenthal et al., 2010). In one randomized trial, patients who received either comprehensive CR, or comprehensive CR plus stress management training (SMT), had significant improvements in cardiac biomarkers, physical activity, and perceived level of stress. When compared to those receiving comprehensive CR without SMT, the individuals in the comprehensive CR plus SMT group had significantly greater reductions in self-reported stress, which correlated with a reduction in adverse cardiac events (Blumenthal et al., 2016).

In the Secondary Prevention in Uppsala Primary Health Care Project (SUPRIM) trial (Gulliksson et al., 2011), patients who had been discharged from hospital with CVD in the last year were randomized to CBT with a focus on stress management, or traditional care. CVD patients who were randomized into the CBT/stress management intervention demonstrated a significant decrease in recurrent cardiovascular events compared to controls. Moreover, higher attendance rates across the 20 CBT stress management sessions was associated with the lowest recurrent CVD risk (Gulliksson et al., 2011).

Overall, despite the lack of efficacy evidence for IPT in the management of depression in CVD patients, CBT and pharmacotherapy are recognized as having a modest role in the improvement of mood (Thombs et al., 2008). The importance of treatments in reducing distress and hence improving quality of life should not be overlooked. Some more recent trials suggest that depression treatment may also improve CVD outcomes (Carney & Freedland, 2017; Kronish et al., 2012; Davidson et al., 2013; Gulliksson et al., 2011). More randomized clinical trials are necessary to properly evaluate how the elements of these interventions (i.e., timing of treatments and effectiveness) impact on both physical and psychosocial health outcomes. Finally, there are currently no clinically effective treatment programs to specifically address low social support, job stress, or hazardous personality traits in CVD patients.

Psycho-Educational and Behavioural Interventions

Behavioural interventions aim to address the physical and psychosocial aspects underlying the CVD process, such as smoking cessation, increasing physical activity, medication adherence, improvements in diet, and stress management (as outlined above). Education is also necessary for patients to understand their disease, its causes, and treatments, and hence initiate and sustain these behaviour changes (Ghisi, Abdallah, Grace, Thomas, & Oh, 2014). CR is a comprehensive model of care offering each of these components.

Physical activity, a core component of CR, is effective in the primary and secondary prevention of CVD (Grace et al., 2016). The effectiveness of CR is arguably in large part due to its ability to increase physical activity. Physical activity is associated with significantly reduced psychological distress in the form of depression, anxiety, and hostility. In one CR intervention study, patients were followed for one year and their anxiety and depression were measured by the HADS. Participation in CR significantly lowered both depression and anxiety severity across the follow-up period. Interestingly, a reduction in depression severity independently accounted for improvements in quality of life (Yohannes, Doherty, Bundy, & Yalfani, 2010). Combined, the ability of physical activity to positively impact both physiology and psychological well-being makes it an important intervention for the improvement in long-term prognosis of CVD patients. Indeed, those who participate in CR have a reduced risk for death during the first two years or more following participation (Milani & Lavie, 2009).

Given these findings, adherence to CR is crucial. However, patients typically attend only two-thirds of the recommended sessions, with women being significantly less adherent than men (Oosenbrug et al., 2016). Patients also often stop exercising after CR. In order to mitigate this, Reid and colleagues (2016) are currently testing an exercise facilitator-based intervention rooted in the socio-ecological model. The intervention consists of repeated contacts with patients via telephone over a one-year period to promote their transition from the structured CR program to self-managed or community-based exercise.

Given atherosclerosis develops over time, it is important individuals engage in heart-health behaviours and optimize their psychosocial well-being across the lifespan. Accordingly, behavioural interventions and psychoeducation geared toward young adults may have protective effects against CVD. For instance, research shows that students have an increased risk of gaining weight during their first two years of college (Deforche, Van Dyck, Deliens, & De Bourdeaudhuij, 2015). Additional CVD risk behaviours that emerge during this period include unhealthy eating, harmful use of alcohol, a reduction in sport participation, and an increase in sedentary activities (Deforche et al., 2015). Students should be encouraged to exercise regularly, eat a well-balanced diet, socialize with peers, as well as cease tobacco use and reduce alcohol consumption.

Future Directions

In recent years, numerous phone applications (apps) and Internet resources have been developed to facilitate changes in behaviour that are consistent with the guidelines established by the American Heart Association (AHA) to combat CVD (Burke et al., 2015). One systematic review reported that mobile phone–based interventions, via text-messages, were effective in promoting smoking cessation, one of the major risk factors of CVD (Whittaker, McRobbie, Bullen, Rodgers, & Gu, 2016). In addition, results from a randomized clinical trial supported the use of mobile phone text message interventions to promote physical activity among those diagnosed with coronary heart disease (Thakkar, Redfern, Thiagalingam, & Chow, 2016).

There have been some trials testing CR delivered via telehealth, the Internet, and smartphones. Indeed, two recent **meta-analyses** have demonstrated that CR delivered via these means is beneficial (Huang et al., 2015; Rawstorn, Gant, Direito, Beckmann, & Maddison, 2016), although more work needs to be done to understand the optimal degree of interaction, duration, etc. to maximize effectiveness (Turk-Adawi & Grace, 2014). However, the results from both meta-analyses supported the comparable benefit of telehealth interventions, when compared to standard CR, in modifying cardiac risk factors.

Further, social media (i.e., Facebook, Twitter) may be effective as a form of social support for individuals who would like to communicate with others with CVD. Given the advances in mobile technology and the widespread use of smartphones, future research should consider the benefits of Internet-based interventions or support groups to reach more patients with CVD. There are now studies where CBT is successfully delivered via information and communication technologies (Andersson et al., 2013; Andrews, Cuijpers, Craske, McEvoy, & Titov, 2010; Cuijpers, Donker, van Straten, Li, & Andersson, 2010; Donker et al., 2013; Glozier et al., 2013; Hedman, Ljótsson, & Lindefors, 2012; Spek et al., 2007; Wagner, Horn, & Maercker, 2014), although these need to be tested in CVD populations.

Moreover, numerous phone apps have been designed to track health-related activities and self-monitoring is essential in behaviour modification (Helsel, Jakicic, & Otta, 2007). For instance, there are phone apps that are designed to track physical activity such as Map My Run by Under Armour, FitBit, RunKeeper, and Couch to 5K. In addition, phone apps have been created to facilitate smoking cessation and popular apps for this target behaviour include The LIVESTRONG MyQuit Coach and Quit Smoking. There are also apps that are considered to be high-quality programs that allow individuals to track their medication intake and these apps include Medisafe Pill Reminder, MyMeds, and CareZone (Santo et al., 2016). Caution is warranted with regard to phone apps however, as many have not been developed based on behaviour change theory nor tested through research (Azar et al., 2013). This is particularly true for apps geared toward diet modification and weight loss, although certain apps have been found to include components of behaviour change theories such as Lose It! by FitNow Inc. and Calorie Counter by MyFitnessPal (Azar et al., 2013). Future studies are needed to investigate the effectiveness of these programs at facilitating the modification of intended target behaviours.

Summary

CVDs are among the leading killers of North American men and women. Advances in treatments have reduced the risk of mortality, such that an increasing number of individuals live with CVD. The chronicity of CVD requires long-term medical follow-up and multiple behaviour changes on behalf of patients, yet these patients remain at heightened risk of a recurrent CVD event and death.

Psychosocial factors are associated with CVD onset and progression, in addition to quality and quantity of life. Major psychosocial factors implicated in the development and prognosis of CVD include depression and anxiety, job and marital/family stress, social isolation, and personality factors such as hostility. These factors may directly influence the disease process through pathophysiological changes, such as inflammation and endothelial damage, resulting in atherosclerosis. Psychosocial distress also indirectly affects disease progression through its association with poor health behaviours (i.e., smoking, low physical activity, poor treatment adherence) that can lead to the development of traditional risk factors such as diabetes, hypertension, and high cholesterol. Altogether, there is substantial evidence that anxiety, and predominantly depression, are associated with CVD development and worse prognoses.

In summary, the role of psychology in the management of heart patients is substantial. This chapter has established that psychological distress: (a) is linked to behavioural and cardiovascular risk factors, and may itself be a risk factor for CVD; (b) may trigger acute cardiac events; (c) can masquerade as cardiac symptoms, and hence be unrecognized and untreated; (d) is highly prevalent in cardiac patients; (e) can form a barrier to use of evidence-based therapies; and (f) is associated with poorer quality of life, and greater morbidity and mortality (Rozanski, Blumenthal, & Davidson, 2005).

Critical Thought Questions

1. How might mood or anxiety disorders impact CVD patients throughout their medical management process and in their interactions with health-care providers?

2. How can researchers assess the effectiveness of a psychosocial intervention for heart patients?

3. How might a psychologist approach a patient whose social support circle includes people thought to negatively influence health behaviours?

4. What psychological factors might be at play for a CVD patient undergoing a PCI?

Recommended Reading

Bradley, S.M., & Rumsfeld, J.S. (2015). Depression and cardiovascular disease. *Trends in Cardiovascular Medicine, 25*, 614–22.

Carney, M., & Freedland, K.E. (2017). Depression and cardiovascular disease. *Nature Reviews Cardiology, 14*, 145–55.

Garcia, M., Mulvagh, S.L., Merz, N.B., Buring, J.E., & Manson, J.E. (2016). Cardiovascular disease in women: Clinical perspectives. *Circulation Research, 118*, 1273–93.

Jordan, J., Bardé, B, & Zeiher, A.M. (Eds.). (2007). *Contributions towards evidence-based psychocardiology: A systematic review of the literature.* Washington, DC: American Psychological Association.

HIV and Sexually Transmitted Infections

11

Tyler G. Tulloch

Natalie L. Stratton

Stanley Ing

Bojana Petrovic

Trevor A. Hart

Learning Objectives

In this chapter you will:

- Identify common sexually transmitted infections (STIs) and learn how their transmission is facilitated by behaviour.

- Learn about the human immunodeficiency virus (HIV) and how its transmission is facilitated by behaviour.

- Learn how thoughts and behaviours are associated with the transmission of HIV and STIs.

- Learn about the psychological effects of living with HIV and STIs.

- Identify different types of psychological interventions to prevent HIV and STIs.

- Identify different types of psychological and community-level health-promotion interventions for people living with HIV.

Sexually Transmitted Infections in the National and Global Contexts

Charlie Sheen is among the most famous actors in Hollywood, having starred in films and television shows such as *Anger Management* and *Two and a Half Men*. Charlie publicly disclosed he was HIV-positive in November 2015, adding that some people had attempted to extort money from him in order to keep his secret. HIV stigma, discussed in this chapter, is a problem for many people living with HIV as it can lead to unfair treatment, poorer mental health, and may even contribute to the spread of HIV if people are afraid to get tested. HIV stigma is just one of many things that have contributed to the global spread of HIV and other **sexually transmitted infections** (STIs).

According to the World Health Organization (WHO), 357 million new cases of four curable STIs occur annually among people aged 15 to 49 years throughout the world (WHO, 2016a). The four STIs deemed curable are chlamydia, gonorrhea, syphilis, and trichomoniasis. The WHO estimated that, at any point in 2012, 131 million people were infected with *Chlamydia trachomatis* (chlamydia), 78 million people with *Neisseria gonorrhoeae* (gonorrhea), 6 million people with *Treponema pallidum* (syphilis), and 142 million people with *Trichomonis vaginalis* (trichomoniasis). In addition to these four curable STIs, **human immunodeficiency virus** (HIV)/**acquired immunodeficiency syndrome** (AIDS) and other non-curable STIs continue to adversely affect the lives of individuals worldwide. At the end of 2015, approximately 33.3 to 36.7 million people were living with HIV/AIDS, and the areas most affected were eastern and southern Africa (19 million) and western and central Africa (6.5 million); when combined, 69.4 per cent of all people living with HIV/AIDS reside in these areas (The Joint United Nations Programme on HIV and AIDS; UNAIDS, 2016; WHO, 2016b). Furthermore, an estimated 2.1 million people were newly infected with HIV, a decline from 3.2 million in 2000 (UNAIDS, 2016). Across the world, social, economic, political, and environmental factors, such as poverty, discrimination, and gender inequalities, influence the susceptibility of HIV/AIDS and STI transmission among a variety of communities and populations (WHO, 2016a; WHO, 2016b). A comprehensive and sustained response to these social and structural factors may adequately address HIV/AIDS globally (Seeley et al., 2012; WHO, 2016b). The investment in resources for the HIV response in the past 15 years has led the decline of new HIV infections. The WHO and UNAIDS established new global HIV targets (also known as 90–90–90 HIV targets) for 2020 with respect to HIV testing and treatment: (1) 90 per cent of all people living with HIV will know their HIV status; (2) 90 per cent of all people with diagnosed HIV infection will receive sustained antiretroviral therapy; and (3) 90 per cent of all people receiving antiretroviral therapy will have viral suppression (UNAIDS, 2014). When these targets are collectively achieved, at least 73 per cent of all people living with HIV worldwide will be virally suppressed (very low levels of HIV in one's blood).

STIs are mainly transmitted through unprotected sexual contact, but can also be transmitted through non-sexual means, such as blood transfusions, contaminated needles (used by infected individuals),

Actor Charlie Sheen.

Tinseltown/Shutterstock.com

and from mother to child during birth or while breastfeeding. If left untreated, HIV and STIs can pose serious health risks, so it is important for individuals who are sexually active to be tested for HIV and STIs to prevent further spread of infection and to seek appropriate treatment.

Overview of STIs in the United States and Canada

STIs, especially incurable viral infections such as herpes and HIV, are a public health concern in the United States and Canada. Many people with STIs do not experience symptoms and, therefore, may not get tested. As a result, asymptomatic individuals may unknowingly transmit STIs. The pathogenic agents that cause STIs can be **viruses**, **bacteria**, or parasites.

Unless otherwise specified, all STI and HIV/AIDS descriptions and epidemiological data in this overview are provided by the Centers for Disease Control and Prevention (CDC) in the United States, the Public Health Agency of Canada (PHAC), and the BC

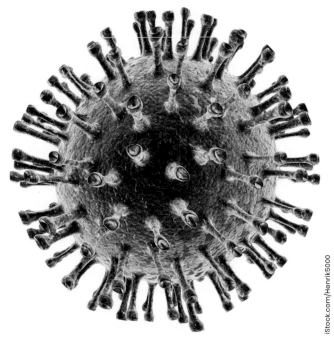

An isolated HIV virus.

Centre for Disease Control (BCCDC) (BCCDC, 2016a; CDC, 2016a; PHAC, 2015a). Table 11.1 outlines common types of STIs, their pathogens, and how they are transmitted and treated medically.

Adolescents and young adults (15 to 24 years old) in the United States and Canada comprise the group with the highest STI rates (PHAC, 2013; CDC, 2016b). National survey studies report low rates of condom use during sexual intercourse as well as low rates of STI testing among adolescents and young adults (Rotermann, 2012; Kann et al., 2016). In light of this situation, there have been many sexual-health support and education programs developed for adolescents. In addition to the high prevalence of STIs in adolescents and young adults, other factors such as socio-economic status, gender, and ethnicity/race can influence whether people are at greater risk of getting an STI (CDC, 2011; CDC, 2016b; Harling, Subramanian, Barnighausen, & Kawachi, 2013). Females are more likely to suffer long-term consequences of STIs due to differences in anatomy—bacteria and viruses more easily penetrate the lining of the vagina than they penetrate a penis—and symptoms of STIs may not be seen as quickly and easily for females when compared to males (CDC, 2011). In the United States, African Americans bear a disproportionate burden of STIs due to factors that relate to (1) higher prevalence of HIV/STIs within the African-American community; (2) stigma from fear of disclosing various risk behaviours or sexual orientation, which impacts health-seeking behaviours; and (3) socio-economic factors, which include poverty, racial discrimination, lack of access to health care, and higher rates of incarceration (CDC, 2016b; CDC, 2016c). The CDC highlights the distribution and trends of STIs among four population groups (women and infants; adolescents and young adults; racial and ethnic minority groups; and gay, bisexual, and other men who have sex with men) that are most vulnerable to help state and local health departments guide and prioritize STI prevention efforts (CDC, 2016b).

HIV is a viral infection that weakens the immune system and causes AIDS. AIDS is diagnosed when an individual has HIV and/or an opportunistic illness (such as AIDS-related cancer(s), including Kaposi's sarcoma, non-Hodgkin lymphoma, and cervical cancer), or an **opportunistic**

iStock.com/Henrik5000

infection(s) (infections associated with severe immunodeficiency) (WHO, 2016c). In the United States, an AIDS diagnosis (also known as stage 3) is based on the CD4+ T-lymphocyte count and the presence of opportunistic illnesses (Selik et al., 2014). A person infected with HIV who is six years of age or older will receive an AIDS diagnosis if his or her CD4+ T-lymphocyte count is less than 200 cells per µL or opportunistic illnesses indicate stage 3. Comparatively, an AIDS diagnosis in Canada is based on a positive test for HIV infection and the presence of one or more AIDS indicative diseases (i.e., opportunistic illnesses) (PHAC, 2009). CD4+ T-cells are responsible for orchestrating the immune response, so a low number of these cells lead to the poor immune system found in people with HIV/AIDS. In Canada, a total number of 2096 new cases of HIV were reported in 2015 (PHAC, 2016a).

Since 2000, the rate of HIV infection among adults has been relatively stable. In Canada, the most vulnerable populations are men who have sex with men (MSM), people who inject drugs, street youth, and Indigenous populations (PHAC, 2016a). In 2014, an estimated 65,040 individuals were living with HIV in Canada, of whom 52,220 were diagnosed and 12,820 were not aware of their HIV positive status, 39,790 were on antiretroviral therapy, and 35,350 had suppressed viral load (PHAC, 2016b). That is, an estimated 80 per cent of people living with HIV were diagnosed, 76 per cent of those diagnosed were in treatment, and 89 per cent of those in treatment had a suppressed viral load (PHAC, 2016b). In the United States, an estimated 39,513 new HIV infections were reported in 2015, a number that has declined since 2005. In 2013, an estimated 1,242,000 persons were living with HIV in the United States. A disproportionate number of new US HIV infections are men who have sex with men, African Americans, and Hispanics/Latinos (CDC, 2016d). In 2011, it was previously estimated that 1.2 million people were living with HIV in the United States, of whom 1,032,000 (86 per cent) were diagnosed, 478,433 (40 per cent) were engaged in care, 441,611 (37 per cent) were on antiretroviral therapy, and 361,764 (30 per cent) had suppressed viral load (Bradley et al., 2014).

As HIV is a virus, it needs a host to replicate itself. The routes by which HIV enters the body are unprotected sexual contact, sharing of contaminated needles, transmission from mother to child, and, less commonly, through tattooing, body piercing, or transfusion of HIV-infected blood (see Figures 11.1 and 11.2). Also less commonly, HIV can enter the body via accidental needle stick injuries that occur when a needle pierces the skin, which can be a workplace hazard for medical health providers and for medical laboratory workers. Once the virus enters the body, it invades the CD4+ T-cells (National Institutes of Health, 2016a; AVERT, 2016). The virus enters the CD4+ T-cell by first fusing with the outside surface of the cell (National Institutes of Health, 2016a). CD4+ T-cells therefore become host cells for HIV and help the virus to self-replicate. Once new copies of the virus are produced by the host cell, they leave to enter other CD4+ T-cells. Antiretroviral medications, which are used to treat viruses such as HIV, do not cure HIV but instead reduce the ability of HIV to enter cells or replicate itself. Highly active antiretroviral therapy is the use of a combination of antiretroviral medications to treat HIV, which is now often called **combination antiretroviral therapy (cART)**. HIV/AIDS symptoms occur in three primary stages (National Institutes of Health, 2016b), illustrated in Table 11.2.

Genital human papillomavirus (HPV) (BCCDC, 2016b; CDC, 2016e) is the most common STI transmitted in the United States and is mainly transmitted through genital contact and oral sex; it can be transmitted even when an infected person is asymptomatic. A number of serious health problems can arise from HPV, including genital warts and various types of cancers (i.e., cancers of the head, neck, vagina, cervix, anus, and penis). However, HPV usually goes away (in 90 per cent of cases) before it causes any serious complications. To prevent HPV infection, vaccines are recommended for males and females between 11 and 12 years of age, which could potentially protect

TABLE 11.1 | Summary of Sexually Transmitted Infections

Disease and Pathogen	Transmission	Medical Treatment
Viral Infections		
HIV/AIDS Human immunodeficiency virus	Unprotected sexual intercourse; injection drug use; mother to child	*Not Curable* Treatment available: combination antiretroviral therapy reduces the rate at which the virus will replicate.
HPV Genital human papillomavirus	Unprotected sexual contact	*Not Curable* No specific treatment available. Treatment for the health problems that HPV can cause is available. Vaccine is also available.
Genital herpes Herpes simplex virus 2	Unprotected sexual contact	*Not Curable* Treatment available for symptom management. Antiviral medications can shorten and prevent outbreaks during period of time person takes medication.
Hepatitis A Hepatitis A virus	Fecal–oral route	*Curable* No specific treatment available. Recommend bed rest and adequate intake of fluids.
Hepatitis B Hepatitis B virus	Direct blood-to-blood contact; contaminated needles; unprotected sexual intercourse; mother to child	*Not Curable* No specific treatment available. Recommend bed rest, adequate nutrition, and intake of fluids. Some people may need to be hospitalized. Vaccine available.
Hepatitis C Hepatitis C virus	Direct blood-to-blood contact; contaminated needles; unprotected sexual intercourse	*Potentially Curable* Treatment available. Antiviral medications are taken for as little as eight weeks.
Bacterial Infections		
Chlamydia *Chlamydia trachomatis*	Unprotected sexual contact	*Curable* Preferred treatment (antibiotics): single dose of azithromycin or a week of doxycycline twice a day
Gonorrhea *Neisseria gonorrhoeae*	Unprotected sexual contact	*Curable* Preferred treatment (antibiotics): single dose of ceftriaxone plus azithromycin or cefixime plus azithromycin
Syphilis *Treponemapallidum*	Direct sexual contact with sore from infected individual	*Curable* Treatment: a single intramuscular injection of penicillin, an antibiotic, will cure a person who has had syphilis for less than a year. Additional doses are needed to treat someone who has had syphilis for longer than a year.
Parasitic Infections		
Trichomoniasis *Trichomonasvaginalis*	Direct sexual contact	*Curable* Recommended regime: a single dose of the antibiotics metronidazole or tinidazole

Continued

TABLE 11.1 | Continued

Disease and Pathogen	Transmission	Medical Treatment
Parasitic Infections		
Pediculosis (pubic lice) *Phthirus pubis*	Sexual contact May also spread by close personal contact or contact with articles used by an infected person	*Curable* Treatment: a lice-killing lotion can be used to treat pubic ("crab") lice.
Scabies *Sarcoptesscabiei*	Direct, prolonged, skin-to-skin contact with person infected with scabies; indirectly by sharing articles such as clothing, towels, or bedding used by an infected person	*Curable* Treatment: products used to treat scabies are called *scabicides* because they kill scabies mites; some also kill eggs

Source: Based on BC Centre for Disease Control (2016a); CDC (2016c); PHAC (2015a).

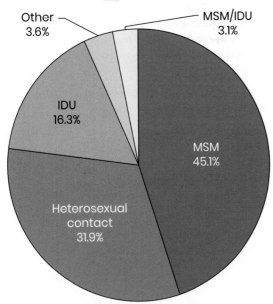

FIGURE 11.1 Proportion of new HIV infections by exposure category (15+ years old), Canada, 2015. *N* = 2084. MSM = Men who have sex with men. IDU = Injection drug use. MSM/IDU = Men who have sex with men and use injection drugs.

Note: 703 cases had no identified risk or exposure category was not reported. One case had an exposure category of blood/blood products.

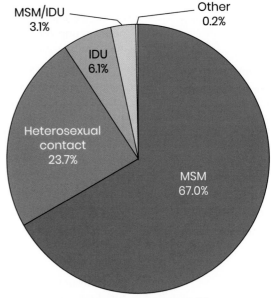

FIGURE 11.2 Proportion of new HIV infections by transmission category (13+ years old), United States, 2015. *N* = 39,513. MSM = Men who have sex with men. IDU = Injection drug use. MSM/IDU = Men who have sex with men and use injection drugs.

Source: Centers for Disease Control and Prevention (CDC). (2016d). *Diagnoses of HIV infection in the United States and dependent areas*, 2015.

people from the most common types of HPV. Although there are no treatment options for HPV infection, there are treatments to alleviate the symptoms of HPV.

Genital herpes (BCCDC, 2016c; CDC, 2016f) is transmitted through sexual contact with infected individuals. Most individuals with herpes will never have sores or will experience only very mild symptoms. Symptoms usually occur two weeks after transmission and resolve within two to four weeks. Symptoms during the initial episode may include secondary sores and flu-like symptoms (i.e., fever, swollen glands). Although genital herpes cannot be cured, treatment such as antiviral medication is available for symptom management. Treatment can shorten and/or prevent future outbreaks.

Hepatitis A (BCCDC, 2016d; CDC, 2015a) is caused by the hepatitis A virus and is transmitted through anal–oral contact or contaminated food and water from infected food handlers with poor hygiene. Individuals generally experience fever, fatigue, loss of appetite, nausea, vomiting, abdominal pain, dark urine, clay-coloured bowel movements, joint pain, and jaundice. Symptoms usually last less than two months, although 10 to 15 per cent of individuals have prolonged or relapsing disease for up to six months. There is no specific treatment for hepatitis A, but adequate bed rest and fluid intake aid in the healing process. The hepatitis A vaccine prevents acquiring hepatitis A.

Hepatitis B (BCCDC, 2016e; CDC, 2015b) is an infection caused by the hepatitis B virus (HBV). Differing from hepatitis A transmission, hepatitis B is transmitted mainly through sexual contact, contaminated needles, and from mother to child during childbirth. Some people are asymptomatic yet can still spread the virus. Symptoms during the acute phase of HBV are similar to those of hepatitis A. Symptoms may last from a few weeks to as long as six months. Chronic HBV occurs when the disease is left untreated and people may either experience ongoing symptoms or remain symptom-free for as long as 20 to 30 years. Approximately 15 to 25 per cent of persons with chronic HBV develop serious liver conditions such as cirrhosis (scarring of the liver) or liver cancer, and some individuals may require hospitalization. Like hepatitis A, no specific treatment is available for HBV, but adequate bed rest and fluid intake aid in the healing process. The hepatitis B vaccine prevents acquiring HBV.

TABLE 11.2 | Stages of HIV Infection

Acute HIV Infection	Earliest stage of HIV infection where HIV multiplies in the body; many (but not all) people develop flu-like symptoms (e.g., fever, headache, rash, muscle and joint aches and pains, swollen glands, sore throat) within 2–4 weeks. Because of the high levels of HIV in the bloodstream, people are at high risk of transmitting HIV during this stage.
Chronic HIV Infection	Second stage of HIV infection (also known as clinical latency or asymptomatic HIV) where HIV continues to multiply in the body at very low levels but without producing symptoms. People can still spread HIV to others. This stage can last up to 10 years for people who are not on antiretroviral therapy but for some people, this stage can progress faster. For people who are on antiretroviral therapy, this stage can last for several decades because the treatment helps to control the virus from multiplying.
AIDS	Final stage of HIV infection where the immune system is severely damaged. Since the body's immune system has weakened, people become vulnerable to opportunistic illnesses. At this stage, CD4$^+$ T-cell count is less than 200 cells per μL or one or more opportunistic illnesses are present. Without adequate treatment, people with AIDS typically survive about three years.

Hepatitis C (BCCDC, 2016f; CDC, 2015c) is a bloodborne infection caused by the hepatitis C virus. Also unlike hepatitis A, hepatitis C is transmitted mainly through contaminated needles, other forms of contact with blood such as an open sore or wound, through penetrative sexual contact, and, more rarely, from mother to child during childbirth. Some people are asymptomatic yet can spread the virus. Symptoms during the acute phase of hepatitis C are similar to those of hepatitis A and B. Symptoms can last indefinitely. Unlike hepatitis B, treatments may cure the infection. New developments in hepatitis C treatments have improved cure rates, are easier to take, involve a shorter course of treatment, and have fewer side effects when compared to pre-existing drugs.

Chlamydia (BCCDC, 2016g; CDC, 2016g) is transmitted through vaginal, oral, or anal intercourse with an infected person. Although most infected individuals are asymptomatic, some may experience symptoms such as painful or difficult urination, inflammation of the rectum, genital discharge, or rectal pain and bleeding. For men, testicular pain and swelling are other common symptoms. For women, additional symptoms include abnormal vaginal bleeding and lower abdominal pain. In rare cases, infected women may experience pelvic inflammatory disease, in which infection of the uterus, fallopian tubes, and other reproductive organs causes lower abdominal pain. Chlamydia is curable with antibiotics. Chlamydia is prevalent among youth and young adults and is the most commonly reported notifiable disease in the United States and Canada (CDC, 2016b; PHAC, 2013). In 2015, the rate of reported cases of chlamydia was higher among African Americans (5.9 times), American Indians/Alaska Natives (3.8 times), Native Hawaiians/Other Pacific Islanders (3.3 times), and Hispanics (2.0 times) when compared to Caucasian Americans (CDC, 2016b). Since 2003, the incidence rates of chlamydia have increased in both countries. The increase in chlamydia cases in the last 20 years may be due to increases in actual incidence, but also may reflect improved screening, testing, and diagnostic and reporting practices for the disease in medical and public health settings. This increase in chlamydia is illustrated in Figures 11.3 and 11.4.

Gonorrhea (BCCDC, 2016h; CDC, 2016i) can lead to severe complications and spread to other parts of the body, such as the eyes, if left untreated. It is transmitted mainly via sexual contact and common symptoms include anal itching, soreness, bleeding, or painful bowel movements.

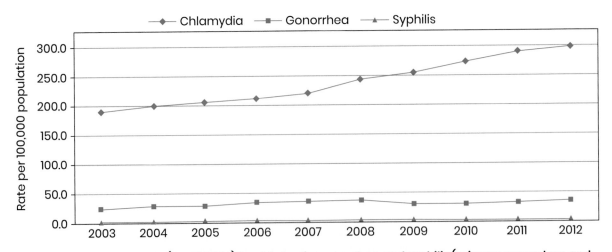

FIGURE 11.3 **Reported rates (per 100,000) for chlamydia, gonorrhea, and syphilis (primary, secondary, and early latent stages), Canada, 2003–12.**

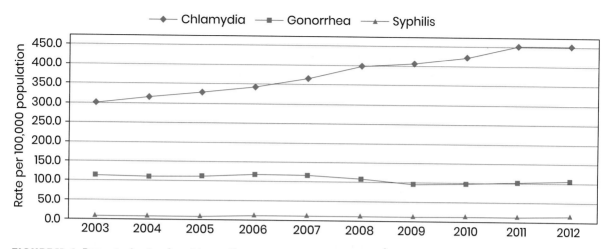

FIGURE 11.4 **Reported rates for chlamydia, gonorrhea, and syphilis (primary, secondary, early latent, and late latent stages), United States, 2003–12.**

Source: Centers for Disease Control and Prevention (CDC). (2016a). *Sexually Transmitted Disease Surveillance* 2015.

Some men and most women never experience any symptoms. Some symptomatic men experience a burning sensation when urinating; a yellow, white, or green discharge from the penis; and painful or swollen testicles. For women, symptoms may include increased vaginal discharge, burning sensation while urinating, and vaginal bleeding between periods. Furthermore, women with gonorrhea are at risk of developing serious complications, even if symptoms are mild or absent. Gonorrhea is curable with antibiotics. The bacterium, *Neisseria gonorrhoeae*, has progressively developed resistance to antibiotics used for treatment of gonorrhea. In 2015, the rate of reported cases of gonorrhea was higher among African Americans (9.6 times), American Indians/Alaska Natives (4.4 times), Native Hawaiians/Other Pacific Islanders (2.8 times), and Hispanics (1.8 times) when compared to Caucasian Americans (CDC, 2016b).

Syphilis (BCCDC, 2016i; CDC, 2016j) is contracted through sexual contact. Most people who contract syphilis are asymptomatic for years, but remain at risk for later complications if it is left untreated. Syphilis occurs in three stages: primary, secondary, and late, with a latent stage between the secondary and late stages when the virus remains hidden. In the primary stage, sores appear approximately 21 days after infection and usually last from three to six weeks, healing without treatment. If treatment is not administered, infection can progress to the secondary stage. During the secondary stage, a non-itchy rash appears, as well as other symptoms like fever, swollen lymph glands, headaches, weight loss, muscle aches, and fatigue. Secondary-stage symptoms heal without treatment; however, infection will progress to the latent and late stages of disease. The final latent and late stage begins when symptoms of the primary and secondary stages of syphilis disappear. Without treatment, individuals remain infected yet symptom-free for years. In the late stage of syphilis, internal organs and tissues such as the brain, nerves, eyes, heart, and liver may be damaged. Symptoms of late-stage syphilis include paralysis, numbness, gradual blindness, and dementia. Fortunately, syphilis is often curable in the primary and secondary stages with injections of penicillin. In Canada and the United States there has been an increase in the rate of syphilis among men who have sex with men and in African-American communities (CDC, 2016b; PHAC, 2013).

Trichomoniasis (BCCDC, 2016j; CDC, 2015d) is a parasitic infection. Most individuals have no symptoms, but when symptoms occur they range from mild irritation to severe inflammation of the genital area. Without treatment, infection can last for years. Itching or irritation may occur during urination, and for men, during ejaculation. A thin discharge with an unusual smell may accompany symptoms. Trichomoniasis is curable with antibiotics.

Pediculosis, or *pubic lice* (BCCDC, 2016k; CDC, 2013a), is caused by a tiny insect called *Phthirus pubis* and is usually transmitted through sexual contact with someone infected with pubic lice but can occasionally be spread via close personal contact or contact with articles of clothing used by an infected individual. The most common symptom of pediculosis is itching in the genital area. Pediculosis is curable with a lice-killing lotion.

Scabies (BCCDC, 2016l; CDC, 2010) is caused by *Sarcoptesscabiei*, a type of mite, and is usually transmitted by direct, prolonged, skin-to-skin contact with an infected individual. Just like pediculosis, scabies can sometimes be spread indirectly by sharing articles of clothing, towels, or bedding used by an infected person. The spread of scabies may be increased if the person has crusted scabies. The illness is characterized by intense itching and a rash that may include tiny blisters and scales. Sometimes sores become infected with bacteria due to scratching the rash. Topical treatments, also called scabicides, kill scabies mites and some also kill scabies eggs.

Psychosocial Risk and Protective Factors in HIV/STI Acquisition

Knowledge, Motivation, and Skills

Knowing how STIs are transmitted and the level of risk of contracting an STI from a given behaviour allows people to make informed choices about which sexual activities they feel comfortable performing. The level of risk associated with certain sexual behaviours varies depending on the STI's mode of transmission. Table 11.3 illustrates the level of risk of STI transmission for given behaviours.

Condom Use

Engaging in condomless vaginal or anal sex is considered a high-risk activity for transmission of HIV and STIs (see Table 11.3). Despite having accurate knowledge about STIs and the risks associated with certain sexual behaviours, many people continue to engage in unprotected sex. Although condoms remain the most effective method of protection against the transmission of STIs and unintended pregnancies (e.g., CDC, 2013b; Kulig, 2003), rates of consistent condom use among adolescents and young adults are low (e.g., Shiely, Horgan, & Hayes, 2009). One explanation for these low rates may be that adolescents and young adults tend to engage in unplanned sexual activity, especially when using alcohol or illicit substances (e.g., Poulin & Graham, 2001). Another explanation is that adolescents may be uncomfortable obtaining condoms or discussing condom use with sex partners. In a US national survey, more than one-third of adolescents reported that purchasing condoms was embarrassing and found discussing condom use challenging (Kulig, 2003). Cost may be another barrier to consistent condom use (Sarkar, 2008).

In order to protect against the transmission of STIs and unintended pregnancies, condoms must be used consistently and correctly. Common improper techniques include using a condom after first putting it on inside out, not holding the base of the condom during withdrawal, and not leaving enough air at the tip of the condom, thus increasing its chance of breaking (Grimley, Annang, Houser, & Chen, 2005). People who feel confident that they are capable of and likely

TABLE 11.3 | Level of Risk of STI Transmission Associated with Sexual Behaviours

	Skin on Skin; Rubbing of Genitals	Mutual Masturbation	Oral Sex without a Condom	Vaginal/Anal Intercourse without a Condom
Viral Infections				
Genital herpes	High risk if sores are present or just before an outbreak	Low risk if hands are clean before touching genitals	Receiving: High risk if sores are present on the mouth Giving: High risk if sores are present on the genitals	High risk
Hepatitis A	Low risk if fecal matter is not present	Low risk if hands are clean and fecal matter is not present on hands	Receiving: No real risk Giving: Low risk	High risk
Hepatitis B	No real risk	No real risk	Receiving: No real risk Giving: Low risk	High risk
Hepatitis C	No real risk	No real risk	Receiving: No real risk Giving: Low risk	High risk
HIV/ AIDS	No real risk	No real risk	Receiving: No real risk Giving: Low risk	High risk
HPV (genital warts)	High risk if sores are present or just before an outbreak	Low risk if hands are clean before touching genitals	Receiving: No real risk Giving: High risk	High risk
Bacterial Infections				
Gonorrhea (the clap)	No real risk	No real risk	Receiving: No real risk Giving: High risk	High risk
Chlamydia	No real risk	No real risk	Receiving: No real risk Giving: High risk	High risk
Syphilis	High risk if chancre or rash is present	Low risk	Receiving: High risk Giving: High risk	High risk
Parasitic Infections				
Trichomoniasis	High risk	Low risk if hands are clean before touching genitals	Receiving: No real risk Giving: Low risk	High risk
Pubic lice (crabs)	High risk	Low risk if hands are clean before touching genitals	Receiving: No real risk Giving: High risk	High risk
Scabies	High risk	Low risk: If hands are clean before touching genitals	Receiving: No real risk Giving: High risk	High risk

Note: Activities listed as no real risk either never lead to infection or never pose a potential risk of transmission, or the possibility is extremely unlikely. Low-risk activities include behaviours where a few reports of transmission have been documented. A significant number of scientific studies link high-risk activities with transmission.

Source: CDC (2012); Rathus, Nevid, Fichner-Rathus, Herold, & McKenzie (2007).

Safe sex practices can help prevent the spread of sexually transmitted diseases.

to use condoms correctly during sexual activity are more likely to use condoms consistently and to refuse to have sex when condoms are not available (DiIorio et al., 2001; Farmer & Meston, 2006). Individuals who intend to use condoms during their next sexual encounter are also less likely ever to have contracted an STI, which suggests that they may use condoms consistently (Small, Weinman, Buzi, & Smith, 2009). These individuals report more positive attitudes toward taking responsibility for their health and are less concerned with whether their partner endorses condom use (Small et al., 2009). Although knowing how to properly use condoms is important in protecting against transmission of HIV and STIs, this may only be helpful if individuals first have the skills and confidence to negotiate condom use with sex partners (French & Holland, 2013). Some condom negotiation skills that have been identified include asking directly, introducing condoms nonverbally in the context of sexual behaviour, withholding sex unless condoms are used, introducing condoms out of concern for one's partner or relationship, presenting HIV/STI risk information to introduce condom use, and using false pretences to deceive a partner into condom use, such as expressing fear of pregnancy rather than fear of contracting an STI (Noar, Morokoff, & Harlow, 2002). While all of these are commonly used strategies, deceiving one's partner may be ethically problematic. Learning and practising assertive communication skills is a more ethical way to negotiate condom use with partners.

Number of Sexual Partners

People who have a higher number of sexual partners are at greater risk for acquiring STIs (e.g., Shiely et al., 2009; Tapert, Aarons, Sedlar, & Brown, 2001). Participating in sexual activity with numerous casual partners (e.g., "one-night stands") increases an individual's chance of acquiring an STI, as the sexual history of each partner then becomes linked to the individual. Each partner who has previously engaged in unprotected sex with others exponentially increases the number of partners an individual has indirectly come into contact with. Furthermore, condom use declines throughout the duration of a relationship with a primary partner (Kulig, 2003). To minimize the chance of acquiring STIs, it is important for individuals (1) to discuss whether the relationship is monogamous and (2) to be tested for STIs before making the decision to stop using condoms.

Communication

Similar to gaining accurate information about the transmission of STIs, it is important to find out about a potential partner's sexual and drug history. That knowledge allows people to make informed decisions about which activities they are comfortable performing. In fact, partners who discuss each other's sexual history and condom use are more likely to use condoms than those who discuss safe sex in general (e.g., Noar, Carlyle, & Cole, 2006). However, partners who do not communicate with one another about condom use or STI- and pregnancy-prevention strategies are less likely to use condoms (Crosby et al., 2002; Sarkar, 2008).

Substance Use

Illicit drug and alcohol use before or during sexual situations may facilitate sexual activity by lowering inhibitions, calming anxiety, and improving confidence (Drumright, Patterson, & Strathdee, 2006). At the same time, individuals who consume alcohol before or during a sexual encounter are less likely to use a condom (e.g., Logan, Cole, & Leukefeld, 2002; Sarkar, 2008), specifically with a casual sexual partner (Brown & Vanable, 2007). In fact, alcohol and substance abusers are more likely to have a higher number of casual sexual partners and a history of STIs (Tapert et al., 2001).

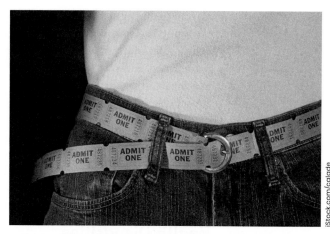

Individuals with a high number of sex partners are at greater risk for acquiring sexually transmitted infections.

Personality Factors

Sensation-seeking and impulsivity are examples of personality factors related to unsafe sexual behaviour (e.g., McCoul & Haslam, 2001; Teva, Bermudez, & Buela-Casal, 2010). Sensation-seeking describes people who search for new, exciting, and intense experiences and are willing to take various risks (e.g., physical, financial, etc.) to attain those experiences (Zuckerman, 2009). Extreme sensation-seekers are more likely to not use condoms (Kalichman & Cain, 2004), to have

Partners who discuss each other's sexual history are able to make informed choices and are more likely to practise safe sex.

a greater number of sexual partners (e.g., McCoul & Haslam, 2001), and to use substances before or during their sexual encounters (e.g., McCoul & Haslam, 2001; Teva et al., 2010). Impulsive people react in the moment whether or not they recognize the risks associated with their behaviours (Kahn, Kaplowitz, Goodman, & Emans, 2002). Highly impulsive persons are more likely to participate in sexual activity without a condom, to use drugs and alcohol before or during sexual encounters, and to have a history of STIs (e.g., Kahn et al., 2002; Winters, Botzet, Fahnhorst, Baumel, & Lee, 2009).

Personality factors associated with distress may also be risk factors for contracting HIV or STIs. For example, social anxiety or anxiety about being evaluated in social situations is associated with sexual risk behaviour among gay and bisexual men (Hart & Heimberg, 2005; Hart, James, Purcell, & Farber, 2008).

Health Disparities

Socio-cultural and demographic factors also play an important role in risky sexual behaviour, with some groups experiencing higher rates of HIV and STIs than others. Some minority groups, specifically African-American and Latina women, represent a disproportionate number of new US cases of STIs and HIV (CDC, 2016b). However, racial and ethnic differences may not be the reason for the increased incidence rate among these groups. In fact, persons with lower income experience more stress and are more likely to participate in unsafe sexual practices (e.g., Capaldi, Stoolmiller, Clark, & Owen, 2002; Ickovics et al., 2002). Moreover, poverty is more common among African-American and Latino men and women than Caucasian Americans (Aral, Adimora, & Fenton, 2008; Ickovics et al., 2002). Furthermore, religious affiliation, rather than ethnicity, is associated with a higher likelihood of participating in vaginal sex without a condom (e.g., Sarkar, 2008). Catholic, non-Catholic Christian, and non-religious or agnostic students are more likely to have vaginal intercourse without a condom compared to students who are Muslim or who practise East Asian religions (e.g., Buddhism, Hinduism) (James et al., 2011). Other possible factors that may explain the higher incidence rate of STIs among minority groups include unequal power between partners (e.g., Teitelman, Tennille, Bohinski, Jemmott, & Jemmott, 2011) and age differences of six or more years between sexual partners (e.g., Hurt et al., 2010). See Chapter 15 for more information on health disparities based on culture.

Stress in People from Ethnic Minority Populations

A **syndemic** is defined as "two or more afflictions, interacting synergistically contributing to excess burden of disease in a population (Wilson et al., 2014). According to syndemic theory, certain populations may experience worse health outcomes due to the additive effects of two or more diseases or psychosocial problems (Singer, 2009). For instance, gay, lesbian, and bisexual persons experience unique stressors such as stigma and discrimination due to their sexual minority status, which may account for worse health outcomes in this population (e.g., Meyer, 1995, 2003; Wolitski & Fenton, 2011). Sexual minority individuals may internalize society's negative beliefs and assumptions regarding same-sex attraction, which is known as internalized homophobia (e.g., Newcomb & Mustanski, 2011). Gay and bisexual men with high internalized homophobia may feel more shame (Kashubeck-West & Szymanski, 2008), which may explain why gay and bisexual men with high internalized homophobia are more likely to engage in unprotected anal intercourse (Dew & Chaney, 2005). Gay and bisexual men who experience high internalized homophobia and loneliness also report a greater number of sexual partners (DeLonga et al., 2011). In addition, gay and bisexual men who endorse a higher number of psychosocial problems are more likely to engage in high-risk sexual behaviour (Tulloch et al., 2015).

Internet and Social Media

With the ever-increasing accessibility of the Internet, finding sexual partners online has become more commonplace (e.g., Al-Tayyib, McFarlane, Kachur, & Rietmeijer, 2009; Rietmeijer, Bull, McFarlane, Patnaik, & Douglas, 2003). Although meeting a sexual partner online does not increase the likelihood of, or lead to, STI acquisition (e.g., Al-Tayyib et al., 2009), using the Internet to find sexual partners is associated with a number of higher-risk sexual behaviours. Specifically, individuals who seek sexual partners online are more likely to engage in condomless vaginal and anal intercourse (e.g., Bolding, Davis, Hart, Sherr, & Elford, 2005; McFarlane, Kachur, Bull, & Rietmeijer, 2004; Mustanski, 2007; Rosser et al., 2009a, 2009b), are less likely to discuss their own and their partners' sexual histories (Mustanski, 2007), and report a greater number of sexual partners (e.g., Horvath, Rosser, & Remafedi, 2008; McFarlane et al., 2004; Mustanski, 2007; Ogilvie et al., 2008) than those who meet sexual partners offline. At the same time, the Internet may also play an important role in STI education and prevention, as an increasing number of people use the Internet to access STI information (e.g., Rietmeijer et al., 2003).

Psychology of Living with HIV/STIs

Stressors

HIV Stigma

Stigmatizing is the devaluing or discrediting of an individual (or group) who has an undesirable attribute, such as a physical characteristic or behaviour (Brown, Macintyre, & Trujillo, 2003). One of the main attributes shared by diseases with the highest level of stigma (Goffman, 1963) is that persons with the disease are viewed as being responsible for having it. Therefore, people living with HIV and incurable STIs, such as herpes and hepatitis B, may experience high levels of stigmatization. Some members of society hold the belief that the ill person is to blame for contracting the disease due to morally reprehensible or irresponsible decisions or actions (Herek, 1999). Discrimination as a result of the stigma attached to HIV may be perceived as coming from society in general or from specific sources such as family members, friends, employers, colleagues, or even health-care professionals. Almost half of people living with HIV report being treated negatively due to their HIV status, and about half are concerned about HIV stigma (Whetten et al., 2008). This concern about stigma among people living with HIV appears to be justified, because almost one-third of Americans report that, if possible, they would avoid interacting with someone with HIV (Herek, Capitanio, & Widaman,

Earvin "Magic" Johnson, retired NBA player, announced in November 1991 that he was HIV positive. To prevent his HIV infection from progressing to AIDS, Johnson takes daily antiretroviral medications. He has been active in campaigns to educate others about HIV and has raised money to provide free testing and treatment for HIV.

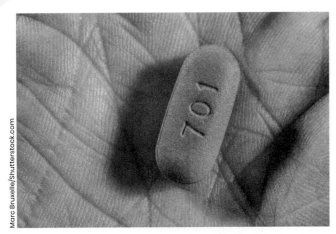

Marc Bruxelle/Shutterstock.com

People living with HIV/AIDS must closely adhere to a daily antiretroviral medication schedule in order to benefit from treatment. While most recent regimens now consist of a single daily pill, adherence must be carefully maintained.

2002). Furthermore, HIV stigma may impact employers' hiring decisions, leading to higher unemployment rates and greater poverty among people living with HIV (Liu, Canada, Shi, & Corrigan, 2012).

HIV stigma has been associated with poorer mental health among people living with HIV. Adults who experience greater stigma have higher levels of anxiety (Ivanova, Hart, Wagner, Aljassem, & Loutfy, 2012; Wagner et al., 2010), more severe depressive symptoms, and are more likely to seek psychiatric care (Vanable, Carey, Blair, & Littlewood, 2006). These findings were replicated in a student-aged sample of adolescents and young adults, among whom experiencing greater HIV stigma was associated with depression, anxiety, and post-traumatic stress disorder (PTSD) symptoms (Bennett, Hersh, Herres, & Foster, 2016). Similarly, people who experience or internalize HIV stigma show greater levels of depression, anxiety, and hopelessness than those who do not (Ivanova et al., 2012; Lee, Kochman, & Sikkema, 2002).

HIV stigma may also contribute indirectly to the severity of the HIV epidemic. Perceiving HIV as a stigma is associated with lower quality of life in general (Holzemer et al., 2009), and people living with HIV who perceive greater stigmatization from health-care providers are less likely to visit their physician (Kinsler, Wong, Sayles, Davis, & Cunningham, 2007). HIV stigma is also associated with poorer medication adherence (see review by Whetten et al., 2008), and some individuals may fear taking medication in public for fear their HIV status will be discovered by others (Golin, Isasi, Bontempi, & Eng, 2002). The stigmatizing of HIV may inhibit people from getting tested for HIV (Ma et al., 2007; Mahajan et al., 2008; Obermeyer & Osborn, 2007; Pitpitan et al., 2012), either by delaying HIV testing (Chesney & Smith, 1999) or by avoiding testing altogether (Fortenberry et al., 2002). Furthermore, individuals who endorse HIV stigma are more likely to engage in higher-risk HIV transmission behaviour than those who do not endorse HIV stigma (Pitpitan et al., 2012). Fear of stigmatization is also associated with a lower likelihood of being tested for other STIs, such as gonorrhea and chlamydia (Fortenberry et al., 2002; Balfe et al., 2010). People who experience discrimination as a result of HIV may be less likely to disclose their HIV status to sex partners (Calin, Green, Hetherton, & Brook, 2007; Simbayi et al., 2007). HIV stigma indirectly perpetuates the HIV epidemic through its impact on increasing sexual risk behaviour, reducing testing for HIV and other STIs, inhibiting disclosure of HIV status to sexual partners, and reducing treatment adherence.

HIV Disclosure and the Law

In the United States, there is no overarching federal law mandating that people living with HIV must disclose their HIV status prior to engaging in behaviour likely to result in HIV transmission (i.e., unprotected sex, sharing needles). In some states, there is no legislation surrounding HIV disclosure; in others non-disclosure has been deemed a criminal offence (American Civil Liberties Union, 2008) and punishment ranges from monetary fines to imprisonment. As of 2011, 24 states had enacted laws requiring disclosure of HIV-positive status to sexual partners, and 14 states had enacted laws requiring disclosure of HIV-positive status to needle-sharing partners.

Among these, 25 states have laws criminalizing behaviours associated with low or negligible risk of HIV transmission (Lehman et al., 2014). In some states, the same laws apply equally to the disclosure of HIV and of other STIs and infectious diseases. In Canada, federal law states that an HIV-positive status must be disclosed prior to engaging in any sexual activity that poses a "realistic possibility of HIV transmission"; however, the Supreme Court of Canada has characterized even low-risk sexual activities as involving a "realistic possibility." Some examples of sexual activities that would require HIV disclosure include vaginal or anal sex without a condom (regardless of viral load), and vaginal or anal sex with a condom (if viral load is higher than "low"). It is unclear whether the Supreme Court of Canada rulings would require HIV disclosure prior to engaging in oral sex without a condom, despite oral sex being considered very low risk for HIV transmission (Canadian HIV/AIDS Legal Network, 2014). The punishment for non-disclosure in Canada can result in a charge of aggravated sexual assault that carries a maximum sentence of life imprisonment. Between 1989 and January 2014, approximately 155 people had been criminally charged for HIV non-disclosure in Canada, including 17 women (Canadian HIV/AIDS Legal Network, 2014). Many individuals charged under this law engaged in behaviour not generally considered to pose a significant risk for HIV transmission, such as having oral sex (Canadian HIV/AIDS Legal Network, 2011). However, UNAIDS recommends that criminal law should only apply to non-disclosure if there is malicious intent and transmission actually occurs (UNAIDS, 2008). When a health professional discovers that an HIV-positive patient is having unprotected sex, he or she may feel conflicted as to whether the patient's right to confidentiality supersedes the professional's legal duty to warn the individual(s) at risk. Currently, no universal standard practice exists regarding one's duty to warn someone in the case of risk of HIV transmission. Depending on the jurisdiction, local laws may conflict with professional codes of ethics so that the professional is placed in a potential lose-lose situation (Alghazo, Upton, & Cioe, 2011). Health professionals must navigate this complex ethical issue on a case-by-case basis with great care, weighing legal obligation, patient confidentiality, and duty to warn.

Psychiatric Diagnoses

The prevalence of some types of mental disorders (e.g., depression, anxiety, post-traumatic stress disorder, insomnia, schizophrenia, and substance-use disorders) is higher among people living with HIV than among the general population (Brandt et al., 2016; Owe-Larsson, Säll, Salamon, & Allgulander, 2009; Rubinstein & Selwyn, 1998). It is not clear whether this is because certain types of mental disorders put people at greater risk of contracting HIV or whether having HIV puts people at greater risk of suffering from mental disorders.

Depression

The prevalence of major depression among people living with HIV is higher than among the general adult population of the United States (Ciesla & Roberts, 2001; Treisman & Angelino, 2007), with estimates ranging from 10 to 20 per cent, as compared to 5 to 10 per cent in the general population (Klinkenberg & Sacks, 2004). Estimates for the prevalence of lifetime depressive disorder among people living with HIV range from 30 to 50 per cent, as compared to 6 to 17 per cent in the general population (Klinkenberg & Sacks, 2004). It is quite common for people living with HIV who are depressed to also be diagnosed with an additional mental disorder. In one study, 62 per cent of depressed people living with HIV had a comorbid anxiety disorder, and 28 per cent had a comorbid substance-use disorder (Gaynes et al., 2015). Among people living with HIV, there is a higher prevalence of depression among women than among men (Evans et al., 2002; Ickovics et al., 2001).

Depression is sometimes difficult to accurately diagnose in this population because some of the physiological symptoms of depression are also associated with HIV: fatigue, weight loss, and decreased appetite and sex drive (Rabkin, 1996).

The higher prevalence of depression among people living with HIV does not necessarily mean that HIV causes depression. Depression and HIV interact in complex ways and may be interrelated. For example, people with depression may be more likely to have unprotected sexual intercourse, putting them at greater risk for contracting HIV or other STIs. Alternatively, HIV may damage subcortical brain structures (i.e., parts of the brain beneath the cerebral cortex), thus leading to a sense of hopelessness that is often seen among people who are depressed (Treisman & Angelino, 2007), and depression may result from HIV-related events such as HIV infection, side effects of antiretroviral medications, and opportunistic infections (Goforth, Cohen, & Murrough, 2008).

Depression negatively impacts the immune system functioning of people living with HIV and is associated with disease progression (Evans et al., 2002) and with higher mortality rates (Mayne, Vittinghoff, Chesney, Barrett, & Coates, 1996). Depression is also associated with poor HIV medication adherence (Treisman & Angelino, 2007; Wagner et al., 2011); however, this effect is more common among individuals with low vs high treatment self-efficacy (Houston et al., 2016).

Anxiety

There is a higher lifetime prevalence of anxiety disorders such as generalized anxiety disorder and panic disorder, as well as a higher rate of anxiety symptoms among people living with HIV relative to the general population (Brandt et al., 2016). Some of the physical symptoms of anxiety are similar to the physical symptoms of HIV/AIDs and medication side effects, so particular attention must be given to determine whether people living with HIV are experiencing effects of the disease and its management, or whether they are experiencing anxiety, for which treatment is available (Hofman & Nelson, 2006). People with high anxiety may tend to avoid stressors associated with HIV such as taking medication, accessing health care, and thinking about the diagnosis. This avoidance negatively impacts disease management and may lead to a worsening of symptoms and a more rapid decline in health (Antoni, 2003). Anxiety among people living with HIV is associated with poorer medication adherence (Ammassari et al., 2002; Campos, Guimarães, & Remien, 2010; van Servellen, Chang, Garcia, & Lombardi, 2002) and an increased rate of mood or substance-use disorders (Gaynes, Pence, Eron, & Miller, 2008). Furthermore, anxiety, in combination with HIV-associated neurocognitive disorders (see below), is associated with poorer everyday functioning (Brandt et al., 2016).

PTSD

Estimates of the prevalence of PTSD among people living with HIV vary widely, ranging from 13 per cent among adolescents and young adults (Radcliffe et al., 2007) to 30 per cent among gay men (Theuninck, Lake, & Gibson, 2010) and 64 per cent among individuals who have problems with medication adherence (Safren, Gershuny, & Hendriksen, 2003). Among people recently diagnosed with HIV, the prevalence of lifetime PTSD and HIV-related PTSD in one study was approximately 54 per cent and 40 per cent, respectively (Martin & Kagee, 2011). By contrast, the prevalence of PTSD among US adults is about 6.8 per cent (Kessler, Berglund, Demler, Jin, & Walters, 2005). Theuninck and colleagues (2010) reported that half of HIV-infected gay men mentioned receiving an HIV diagnosis as a traumatic event. PTSD is also associated with poorer HIV medication adherence (Boarts, Sledjeski, Bogart, & Delahanty, 2006).

Insomnia

Although estimates of insomnia prevalence among people living with HIV vary widely, from 33 to 100 per cent (Smith, Huang, & Manber, 2005), a prevalence estimate of 73 per cent is commonly used (Rubinstein & Selwyn, 1998). This is much higher than the prevalence of insomnia in the general population, which ranges from 6 to 10 per cent (Chung et al., 2015). This range of estimates is also higher than the prevalence of insomnia among individuals living with other medical conditions, which is estimated at 22 per cent among people with one medical disorder, 28 per cent among those with two medical disorders, 34 per cent among those with three medical disorders, and 39 per cent among those with four or more medical disorders (Budhiraja, Roth, Hudgel, Budhiraja, & Drake, 2011). It is unknown why the prevalence of insomnia is so high among people living with HIV, but some possible explanations include HIV medication side effects, increased stress as a result of living with a stigmatizing and chronic medical condition, the presence of co-existing mental disorders (e.g., depression, anxiety, PTSD), physiological changes resulting from HIV infection, or any combination of these factors (Taibi, 2013).

Substance Use

A higher prevalence of current substance-use problems occurs among people living with HIV (44 per cent) than among the general population (11 per cent) (Klinkenberg & Sacks, 2004). Klinkenberg and Sacks also reported a higher prevalence of lifetime alcohol and drug-use disorders among people living with HIV as compared to the general population: 26 to 60 per cent vs 14 to 24 per cent for alcohol use disorders and 23 to 56 per cent vs 6 to 12 per cent for drug-use disorders. For people living with HIV, having a substance-use disorder diagnosis is associated with a greater likelihood of having a comorbid mood or anxiety disorder (Gaynes et al., 2008).

HIV-Associated Neurocognitive Disorder

Advanced HIV infection has been shown to impact the central nervous system, and is associated with neuropsychological deficits such as declines in cognitive and behavioural functioning (e.g., Owe-Larsson et al., 2009; Sperber & Shao, 2003). Approximately half of all people living with HIV experience some type of cognitive impairment due to HIV; however, severe neurocognitive impairment is now rare due to advances in antiretroviral medication treatment (Clifford & Ances, 2013). HIV-associated neurocognitive disorder includes three categories: asymptomatic neurocognitive impairment, mild neurocognitive disease, and HIV-associated dementia (HAD) (Antinori et al., 2007). Asymptomatic neurocognitive impairment and mild neurocognitive disease are both associated with lower performance on neurocognitive tests; however, they are differentiated from one another by the degree of impairment in daily activities, with asymptomatic neurocognitive impairment being associated with no functional impairment, and mild neurocognitive disease being associated with some functional impairment. In contrast, HAD is associated with worse performance on neurocognitive tests and notable functional impairment in daily activities (Antinori et al., 2007). HAD typically occurs during late stages of HIV infection once CD4$^+$ T-lymphocyte counts drop to low levels (Sperber & Shao, 2003). Symptom severity increases over time as disease progression moves from asymptomatic to symptomatic HIV infection, then on to late symptomatic HIV disease (Owe-Larsson et al., 2009). In developed countries where combination antiretroviral therapy (cART) is available, the prevalence of HAD decreased from 20 per cent to about 10 per cent among people with advanced AIDS (Brew & Gonzalez-Scarano, 2007; Geraci & Simpson, 2001). Some common symptoms of HAD are memory problems, difficulty concentrating, impaired fine motor movements, apathy, social withdrawal, and decreased interest in sex, and in some cases, mania, psychosis, and tremors (Sperber & Shao, 2003; Geraci & Simpson, 2001). Older adults with HIV may be especially susceptible to cognitive impairment compared to older adults without HIV, although it is not clear if this is due to HIV or other factors, such as previous substance use (Hardy & Vance, 2009).

Coping with HIV

People living with HIV routinely face a number of serious problems simultaneously, such as stigmatization, mental illness, physical health problems, and the stress of living with a chronic and potentially fatal disease. Lazarus and Folkman (1984), pioneers in the field of coping research, identified two main types of coping: problem-focused and emotion-focused (see also Chapter 3). Problem-focused coping involves dealing with the stressor itself by removing, working around, or confronting it, whereas emotion-focused coping is an attempt to reduce or eliminate the emotional distress associated with the stressor (e.g., Siegel & Schrimshaw, 2000). People who use a problem-focused coping style tend to be better adjusted to living with HIV. The emotion-focused coping style involves both active (i.e., having a fighting spirit) and passive (i.e., avoiding thinking about problems) strategies. People who use active strategies are better adjusted to living with HIV, whereas those who use more passive strategies have greater distress than those who use other approaches and coping styles (Pakenham & Rinaldis, 2001). Another form of coping is through the social support of friends, family, and others. People living with HIV who are more satisfied with social support report less increase in HIV-related physical health problems over time such as CD4+ T-cell count, diarrhea, fever, night sweats, or persistent fatigue (Ashton et al., 2005).

The attitudes people adopt towards their illness may impact their adjustment to living with HIV and STIs. Evidence that an optimistic attitude is associated with improved adjustment to living with HIV is conflicting (e.g., Anderson, 1995; Peterson, Folkman, & Bakeman, 1996; Taylor et al., 1992). In light of these conflicting results, it has been proposed that situational optimism (a person's optimism in a specific situation) is associated with improved adjustment whereas dispositional optimism (a person's long-term level of optimism across many situations) is unrelated to adjustment (Pakenham & Rinaldis, 2001).

Medications and Adherence

HIV is treated using antiretroviral medication, which must be taken daily. Different types of antiretroviral medications target HIV disease progression by suppressing the replication of the virus in different ways, such as preventing the virus from entering cells and from replicating itself. Classes of antiretroviral medications include nucleoside-analog reverse transcriptase inhibitors, non-nucleoside reverse transcriptase inhibitors, integrase inhibitors, protease inhibitors, and fusion inhibitors (Arts & Hazuda, 2012). Combination antiretroviral therapy (cART) is the use of two or more types of antiretroviral medications simultaneously, often combined into in a single pill, whereas monotherapy is the use of a single antiretroviral medication alone. Monotherapy is associated with medication resistance, and is no longer recommended as a treatment for HIV. The use of cART is more effective than monotherapy at suppressing HIV replication and preventing viral resistance to medications. Using cART daily as prescribed reduces the risk of dying from AIDS-related conditions (Ray et al., 2010). Guidelines indicate that cART should include at least three classes of antiretroviral medications, and should be initiated as soon as someone is diagnosed with HIV, regardless of CD4+ T-cell count (Becker, Cox, Evans, Haider, & Shafran, 2017).

People living with HIV who have low adherence to HIV medications have a five-fold increase in risk of HIV disease progression compared to those with moderate or high adherence (Kitahata et al., 2004), and adherence levels must often be as high as 80 to 85 per cent in order to fully benefit from these medications (Kobin & Sheth, 2011). It is therefore extremely important to adhere to medication schedules (see Chapter 4 for additional discussion of medication adherence). Many factors are associated with poor medication adherence among people living with HIV, such as medication side effects (Al-Dakkak et al., 2013), mental disorders (e.g., anxiety, depression) (Ammassari et al., 2002; Boarts et al., 2006; Campos et al., 2010; Wagner et al., 2011), substance use (Begley, McLaws, Ross, & Gold, 2008), HIV stigma (Rintamaki, Davis, Skripkauskas, Bennett, & Wolf, 2006; Vanable et al., 2006; Whetten et al., 2008), and sexual dysfunction in males (Miguez-Burbano, Espinoza, & Lewis, 2008). Commonly reported reasons for missing medication include feeling sick or ill, having too many pills to take, feeling like the drug is toxic or harmful, wanting to avoid side effects, feeling depressed or overwhelmed, and having problems taking pills at specified times (Saberi et al., 2015). Medication side effects associated with poor adherence include fatigue, insomnia, confusion, taste disturbance, nausea, loss of appetite, and diarrhea (Al-Dakkak et al., 2013). The widespread use of smartphones has led to the development of medication-adherence applications (apps). Features of these apps include medication information, electronic reminders for taking doses and refilling prescriptions, dose logging, and the ability to prepare and electronically submit activity summaries to health-care providers (Dayer, Heldenbrand, Anderson, Gubbins, & Martin, 2013). The efficacy of smartphone medication-adherence apps remains to be determined; however, the use of these apps represents a potentially useful solution to improving medication adherence in societies that are increasingly reliant on technology. Given that hundreds of medication-adherence apps exist across several operating systems, it can be difficult for users and health-care providers to choose an appropriate app. The website www.medappfinder.com contains a searchable database to assist users and health-care providers in making an informed decision (Heldenbrand et al., 2016).

Assessment of HIV/STI Risk Behaviour and Medication Adherence

Although health psychologists working in clinical settings with people who are at risk for or who are living with HIV and STIs tend to use similar measures to assess personality, psychopathology, and other clinically relevant variables, two additional types of measures have been created when working with these populations. The first type of measures assesses risk behaviour that predisposes a person to contract HIV and STIs. Sexual behaviour is typically assessed via self-report, such as number of instances of unprotected vaginal or anal intercourse in the past three months (e.g., Koblin et al., 2003). There are also standardized sexual risk-behaviour assessments, such as the Risk Assessment Battery (Navaline et al., 1994). The Risk Assessment Battery contains 45 questions that assess risk related to both drug use and sexual behaviour, and includes questions such as *"In the past month, how often have you injected amphetamines, meth, speed, crank, or crystal?"* and *"In the past six months, how often did you use condoms when you had sex?"* Respondents indicate how frequently they engaged in risk behaviours by checking off the most appropriate response. Injection risk behaviour is also assessed, especially for people at risk for HIV and hepatitis B and C. Injection risk behaviour is also assessed via self-report. Self-report measures, while potentially subject to social desirability, are necessary because of the ethical problems involved with directly observing an individual's sexual or drug-use risk behaviour, or doing frequent biomedical

Mauricio Jordan De Souza Coelho/© 123RF.com

HIV-prevention interventions may be provided individually or in small groups, and may be delivered in a variety of settings, including schools, community-based organizations, health centres, and sexual health clinics.

assessment of evidence of risk behaviour of clients or patients (e.g., conducting vaginal or rectal swabs to assess for presence of semen; drug screening via blood draws).

Medication adherence is also frequently assessed for people living with HIV or STIs. Medication adherence can be assessed via self-report using standardized measures such as the Adherence to Anti-Retroviral Medications Questionnaire (Chesney et al., 2000) or the single item Self-Rating Scale Item (SRSI) (Feldman et al., 2013), or via patient interviews (e.g., Catz, Kelly, Bogart, Benotsch, & McAuliffe, 2000). The SRSI asks respondents to rate their ability to take their HIV medications over the previous four weeks by circling one of six options ranging from *very poor* to *excellent*. There is evidence that individuals are less likely to over-report their medication adherence when asked about their adherence ability more generally rather than specifically in terms of a frequency or percentage (Lu et al., 2008). Other more objective measures may also be used, such as pharmacy reports of medication refills, evidence of biological outcomes such as amount of medication in the blood, amount of bacteria or virus in the blood, or, in the case of HIV, number of CD4+ T-cells in the blood, which would be expected to increase with proper medication adherence. Another innovative method is the use of electronic pill caps, or Medication Event Monitoring System (MEMS). These pill caps contain a chip that records the date and time of each instance a pill bottle is opened.

Evidence-Based Treatments and Other Interventions

Many psychological interventions have been developed for HIV and STI prevention as well as to support or treat people living with HIV and STIs. The term "intervention" is used as opposed to "treatment" because many clinicians working in the field of HIV and STIs, such as in public health clinics, may also be working to prevent new cases among people at higher risk. With the advancement of research on behavioural interventions, public health agencies such as the CDC developed standards to assess interventions that reduce risk behaviours. The CDC's HIV/AIDS Prevention Research Synthesis (PRS) Team outlined efficacy criteria for behavioural interventions focusing on study design, implementation, analysis, and strength of evidence. In order for an intervention to be classified as being based on best evidence, all criteria must be met. Evidence-based interventions include those aimed at reducing HIV risk behaviours across a variety of populations, such as MSM, drug users, adolescents, heterosexual adults, and people living with HIV (Lyles, Crepaz, Herbst, & Kay, 2006; Lyles et al, 2007).

Although most of these interventions are rooted in psychological models, they typically view any psychological changes (e.g., decreases in sexual risk behaviour, increases in medication adherence) through the lens of the biopsychosocial model. For example, sexual risk-reduction interventions for people living with HIV are biopsychosocial because they may discuss the societal effects of HIV stigma or focus on specific demographic or social groups (socio-cultural) and help them to change their attitudes and behaviours (psychological). These interventions consider biomedical factors because the purpose of the interventions is to reduce HIV and STI incidence and HIV transmission. Most interventions focus on the individual psychological and behavioural problems that contribute to HIV transmission risk; however, greater attention is being drawn to the broader systemic problems that contribute to HIV transmission, such as poverty and discrimination (Newman & Poindexter, 2010).

Theoretical Frameworks Used in Evidence-Based Interventions

Several theoretical frameworks, such as social cognitive theory (Bandura, 1998), the health belief model (Rosenstock, 1974), and the transtheoretical model (Prochaska & Velicer, 1997; see Chapter 5), provide a foundation for evidence-based interventions. Other theoretical models commonly used for planning sexual health-promotion interventions include the theory of reasoned action (Ajzen & Fishbein, 1980), the theory of planned behaviour (Ajzen, 1991), and the information, motivation, and behavioural skills model (Fisher & Fisher, 1992).

Theory of Reasoned Action and Theory of Planned Behaviour (TPB)

These theories assert that behavioural intention is the best predictor of a behaviour, which is influenced by the attitude towards performing the behaviour and the subjective norms associated with the behaviour (see Chapter 1). Attitudes are determined by individual beliefs regarding outcomes or characteristics of performing the behaviour. Likewise, subjective norms are based on normative beliefs (e.g., approval/disapproval of performing the behaviour) and the individual's motivation to comply with norms. The theory of planned behaviour also includes perceived control with regard to performing a behaviour as an additional variable that may predict behavioural intentions. Both theories have been used to successfully predict behaviours with which individuals demonstrate substantial control, including behaviours and intentions of substance use, sexual behaviour, exercise, cancer screening, and health-service utilization (Montaño & Kasprzyk, 2015). Regarding HIV and STI risk behaviours, the theory of reasoned action and theory of planned behaviour have been applied to addressing HIV risk behaviours through culturally sensitive programs. In a South African study (Jemmott, 2012), Xhosa-speaking male and female facilitators delivered a six-session HIV risk reduction intervention to grade six students using comic workbooks, homework assignments to engage parents, and other activities. This intervention resulted in improved condom use self-efficacy and knowledge, increased belief that using condoms would not interfere with sexual pleasure, and decreased belief in cultural myths regarding HIV (Jemmott, 2012).

Information, Motivation, and Behavioural Skills Model

Developed by Fisher and Fisher (1992), this model is recommended by the Canadian Guidelines for Sexual Health Education (PHAC, 2008). The core principles of the model include information (e.g., knowledge regarding STI transmission), motivation (e.g., to change risky behaviour), and behavioural skills (e.g., performing preventative behaviours, such as negotiating condom use). The information, motivation, and behavioural skills model specifies that HIV-prevention information and motivation directly affect preventive behaviour, and also affect preventive behaviour through their impact on behavioural skills. In addition, the model requires that elicitation research (i.e., exploring the most appropriate information, motivation, and behavioural skills for the target populations) should be conducted prior to developing the intervention. This model has been used effectively to reduce sexual risk behaviours for a variety of populations, including minority youth, young adults, and low-income women (PHAC, 2008). The model has also been used outside of HIV, such as to improve glycemic control among people with diabetes (Mayberry & Osborn, 2014), and adherence to medical recommendations for coronary artery bypass grafting patients (Zarani, Besharat, Sadeghian, & Sarami, 2010).

Methods of Delivering Interventions

Interventions for preventing HIV/STIs and supporting individuals living with HIV/STIs may be approached through one or several levels. The social-ecological approach for health promotion acknowledges that health is influenced through the interplay of factors related to people, their immediate surroundings (e.g., family and friends), and broader social structures (e.g., organizations and communities) (Bartholomew, Parcel, Kok, Gottlieb, & Fernández, 2011). Individual-level interventions are delivered in one-on-one counselling sessions, and interpersonal interventions may use a small-group format. Community-level interventions adopt a systems approach to changing the behaviour of a population and may be delivered through multiple venues and outreach activities. Interventions that take into account an ecological perspective are more likely to result in health-behaviour change (Glanz & Bishop, 2010). However, incorporating multi-level interventions poses numerous challenges, and it is inconsistent with current HIV-related policy that tends to focus on brief interventions that can be easily replicated and disseminated (Kaufman, Cornish, Zimmerman, & Johnson, 2015).

With the expansion of digital media in recent years, there is an opportunity to harness the Internet and other communication technologies for sexual health promotion through text messaging, social networks, blogs, and gaming. New media approaches allow for targeted messaging and applicability to a variety of behaviours (e.g., sexual initiation, HIV/STI testing, adherence to medication) (Guse et al., 2012). Intervention research in this area has generally focused on MSM and youth, and few studies have involved women, HIV-positive populations, injection drug users, or sex workers (Garett, Smith, & Young, 2016). Research evidence suggests that digital media interventions can improve sexual health outcomes, such as increasing the likelihood of HIV testing, improving condom use self-efficacy, and increasing HIV/STI knowledge, but sometimes the research findings are inconsistent from study to study (Guse et al., 2012). Implementing social media interventions can pose challenges due to ethical concerns. It is important that researchers are mindful of privacy policies and settings. For example, participants have reported concerns that information shared through an HIV/STI intervention Facebook group may appear on their friends' newsfeeds (Chiu, Menacho, Fisher, & Young, 2015). Future research is needed to further explore the long-term effectiveness and ethical implications of using digital media for HIV prevention and creating supportive online communities for people living with HIV.

Interventions to Prevent HIV and STI Transmission

Interventions that focus on preventing HIV and STIs are delivered in a variety of settings, including educational institutions, community-based organizations, health centres, and sexual health clinics. Such sexual health-promotion programs focus largely on providing information regarding risk factors for contracting HIV and STIs and on providing resources to health services in local communities that provide testing and contraceptives.

Behavioural interventions addressing condom-use skills and motivational training can be effective in reducing the risk of contracting HIV and STIs among youth. A meta-analysis on interventions for adolescents concluded that programs focused on sexual behaviour beyond an abstinence-only approach (one that encourages adolescents to abstain from sex), such as encouraging condom use, were more successful in reducing risky sex in the long term than were abstinence-only approaches (Johnson, Scott-Sheldon, Huedo-Medina, & Carey, 2011). Abstinence-only education may not have a significant effect on reducing engagement in unprotected sex or on postponing sexual activity (Kohler, Manhart, & Lafferty, 2008), and in some jurisdictions, it has been associated with increased rates of teenage pregnancy (Stanger-Hall & Hall, 2011). In addition, abstinence-only approaches to sexual health education do not prepare youth to use condoms when they decide to become sexually active (Johnson et al., 2011), and these approaches may violate individuals' rights to access complete sexual health information (Santelli et al., 2006).

Examples of Interventions

The Study to Reduce Intravenous Exposures is a group-level intervention designed for injection drug users who are HIV-negative and are living with hepatitis C. This intervention is delivered over six sessions in groups of five to nine participants with two facilitators. It uses a harm reduction approach, which seeks to minimize the harmful consequences associated with illegal or stigmatized behaviours, to promote safer injection behaviours, and to reduce hepatitis C transmission. The sessions focus on knowledge improvement, skills building, hepatitis C management, and peer mentoring to engage other injection drug users in safer injection behaviours (Latka et al., 2008). The Mpowerment Project is a community-level HIV-prevention program aimed at young men who have sex with men. The intervention included peer outreach activities in venues frequented by young men who have sex with men, peer-led groups offered in community settings, and a social marketing campaign (Kegeles et al., 2012).

Treatments and Interventions Involving People Living with HIV/STIs

Prevention Interventions

Most of the focus in HIV prevention has been on working with HIV-negative populations to reduce sexual and drug-use risk behaviours. However, the benefits of working with people living with HIV to reduce HIV transmission have increasingly been recognized (CDC, 2003). In a review of research related to prevention with people living with HIV, interventions delivered to individuals and/or groups were found to decrease HIV risk behaviours (Gilliam & Straub, 2009). Although many of the interventions were delivered by health-care providers, peers who themselves are living with HIV have also been involved in facilitating interventions. Peer-delivered interventions have been used with various populations and have been successful in improving HIV knowledge and condom use, reducing the sharing of drug-use equipment among injection drug users, and improving medication adherence for people living with HIV (Chang et al., 2013; Medley, Kennedy, O'Reilly, & Sweat, 2009; Simoni, Nelson, Franks, Yard, & Lehavot, 2011). In addition to providing support to clients, peer interventions have been beneficial to the educators themselves through reciprocal support, learning, and empowerment (Marino, Simoni, & Bordeaux Silverstein, 2007).

One intervention with a focus on people living with HIV is called Healthy Relationships. Based on social cognitive theory, Healthy Relationships is a group-level intervention delivered through five two-hour sessions over two-and-a-half weeks, and is offered for groups of six to ten

In Focus

The Role of Evidence in Policy Development: Spotlight on Insite

Injection drug use is associated with high risk for the transmission of HIV, hepatitis C, and other blood-borne illnesses (Hagan & Des Jarlais, 2000). Many of these negative health outcomes result from limited access to sterile injection equipment and fear of legal prosecution. Harm-reduction programs address the needs of injection drug users by providing access to syringes, needles, and other safer drug-use equipment (e.g., tourniquets, sterile water, alcohol swabs, cookers, etc.). Between 1986 and 2009, 61 cities across the globe opened safe injection facilities to provide injection drug users with a safe environment where they can inject drugs under the supervision of health-care providers (Hedrich, Kerr, & Dubois-Arber, 2010).

In 2003, the first North American safe injection facility, Insite, was opened in Vancouver, Canada. Insite began operations after receiving a special exemption from the Canadian federal government (Dooling & Rachlis, 2010). The exemption was provided for a three-year period and required an external scientific program evaluation (Wood, Tyndall, Montaner, & Kerr, 2006a). Since its first two months of service, Insite has consistently had an average of about 500 visits per day. Nursing staff and addiction counsellors provide injection drug users with access to safer drug-use equipment and first aid, offer counselling and referrals to treatment programs, and assist in cases of overdose (Wood et al., 2006a).

Within the initial three-year phase, 22 peer-reviewed studies were published demonstrating the effectiveness of Insite, such as reductions of HIV risk behaviour, decreased injections in public places (Kerr, Tyndall, Li, Montaner, & Wood, 2005), and increased engagement in drug treatment programs

(Wood, Tyndall, Zhang, Montaner, & Kerr, 2007). Using mathematical modelling, researchers calculated that Insite prevents between 2 and 12 deaths due to overdose per year (Milloy, Kerr, Tyndall, Montaner, & Wood, 2008). Insite's services were not associated with increased relapse among former drug users and did not have a negative effect on those attempting to discontinue drug use (Kerr et al., 2006). Further, there was a significant decrease in crime, public injecting, and litter related to drug use (Wood et al., 2006b). Insite was also found to be a cost-effective program (Bayoumi & Zaric, 2008; Pinkerton, 2011).

Although Insite was granted an additional three-year extension, the continuation of the safe injection facility was questioned once the Canadian federal government was led by a different political party. Despite the various health benefits to drug users as well as to the community, the federal government believed Insite encouraged injection drug use and continued to oppose it. Following several short-term extensions for exemptions and three years of legal proceedings in the British Columbia Supreme Court and the Supreme Court of Canada, the Supreme Court announced on 30 September 2011 that Insite should be allowed to continue its operations (Canadian Broadcasting Corporation; CBC, 2011). Amidst the surge in fatalities from opioid overdoses, the federal health minister recently proposed changes to the Controlled Drug and Substances Act, which would make it easier to establish supervised injection sites in Canada (*Toronto Star*, 2016). Cost-effectiveness studies suggest that implementing similar programs in other jurisdictions could reduce taxpayers' expenses while averting HIV and hepatitis C infections (Enns et al., 2016; Jozaghi & Jackson, 2015; Jozaghi, Reid, &

participants. The goals of Healthy Relationships is to develop coping skills related to HIV and situations of sexual risk, improve self-efficacy for decisions to disclose HIV status, and develop and maintain safer sex behaviours. The intervention uses role-playing activities, videos, skills-building exercises, and personalized feedback reports based on the risky behaviours participants reported prior to the intervention (Kalichman et al., 2001). In a randomized controlled trial with

THE CANADIAN PRESS/Jonathan Hayward

The innovative but controversial Insite program offers free needles and a safe and sanitary area to use injection drugs. The purpose of this evidence-supported program is to reduce the risk of transmitting HIV and other diseases for people who are dependent on injection drugs.

Andersen, 2013; Jozaghi, Reid, Andersen, & Juneau, 2014). Additional cities that are exploring whether to offer supervised injection facilities include Toronto, Ottawa, Montreal, Edmonton, Surrey, and Victoria (CBC, 2016).

The case of Insite demonstrates the challenges of implementing evidence-based policy for addressing the HIV and hepatitis C epidemics via reducing the harms associated with illicit drug use. This case also demonstrates the relevance of the biopsychosocial model for injection drug users: there are legal challenges rooted in societal attitudes that prevent access to harm-reduction services that need to be addressed for the Insite program to run (socio-cultural factors); the program allows changes in behaviour such as use of clean needles (psychological factors); and the purpose of the program is to reduce HIV transmission among drug users and the larger community (biomedical factors).

HIV-positive women participating in a videoconferencing group, this intervention resulted in reduced engagement in unprotected sex six months later (Marhefka et al, 2014).

Recently there has been increased interest in "treatment as prevention," which is the use of CART to decrease the chances of transmitting HIV by reducing the amount of virus in the body of an individual living with HIV (Williams et al., 2011). Thus, in addition to helping people living with HIV maintain their health, this approach could help to reduce HIV transmission on a large scale. cART can be used as a preventative measure by reducing the rate of transmission between partners who are serodiscordant (opposite HIV status) and from mother to child (Granich et al., 2010). Given that some may continue to engage in unprotected sex even when on cART, HIV prevention should include evidence-based behavioural interventions to reduce HIV risk behaviours in addition to the use of cART (WHO, 2008). Research into the implementation of this method for HIV prevention is ongoing.

Antiretroviral therapy may also be used as part of pre-exposure prophylaxis (also known as "PrEP"), which is intended for individuals who are at high risk for HIV infection. For example, this approach may be helpful for serodiscordant couples during conception and pregnancy to avoid infecting the HIV-negative partner. The regimen involves taking HIV medication (a combination of tenofovir disoproxil fumarate and emtricitabine, under the brand name Truvada) on an ongoing basis to reduce the chances of becoming infected. If taken as prescribed, PrEP has the potential to reduce the risk of infection by over 90 per cent (US Public Health Service, 2014). One concern is the potential for generating drug-resistant viruses, although mathematical models have shown that PrEP may have a limited impact on future levels of drug resistance (van de Vijver et al., 2013). Recent research examining alternative drug regimens, such as taking antiretroviral medications before and after sexual intercourse, suggests the approach can be effective in reducing the risk of HIV infection (Molina et al., 2015). Similarly, antiretroviral medications can be taken after possible exposure to HIV (referred to as post exposure prophylaxis, or "PEP") in emergency situations, such as following a sexual assault or if a health-care worker is potentially exposed. This approach requires that daily medication be taken for 28 days, starting within 72 hours from possible exposure to HIV (CDC, 2016j). Findings from a recent systematic review support the use of tenofovir combined with lamivudine or emtricitabine as preferred drugs for PEP (Ford et al., 2015). However, PEP is not 100 per cent effective as there have been reports of failed PEP treatments (Beekmann & Henderson, 2014).

Psychotherapeutic Treatments

Most psychotherapy is offered one-on-one or in small-group format. The treatments offered to people living with HIV or incurable STIs like herpes are typically the same as those offered to people in the general population.

Research-supported psychological treatments specifically useful for people living with HIV are available. For example, the Life-Steps intervention (Safren, Otto, & Worth, 1999) is a single-session treatment that incorporates cognitive behavioural, motivational interviewing, and problem-solving techniques designed to improve medication adherence (see In Practice box). For clients with comorbid problems such as substance use and homelessness or severe mental health problems, more than one session may be needed. A brief follow-up phone call is scheduled one week after the intervention to review strategies and cues that were identified during the session.

More intensive treatments may also combine health psychology techniques with techniques from clinical psychology, such as cognitive behavioural therapy for medication adherence and depression among HIV-infected individuals (Safren et al., 2009). Another example is a brief risk-reduction intervention developed by Sikkema and colleagues (2011) designed for men who have sex with men recently diagnosed with HIV. This intervention comprises three 60-minute sessions within one month of diagnosis and involves developing a personalized risk-reduction plan, increasing motivation for transmission risk reduction, and developing behavioural skills to protect the individual's health. This brief intervention is more effective than standard care procedures at reducing risk behaviour, alcohol use, STI symptoms, and traumatic stress as well as increasing use of clinical services (Sikkema et al., 2011).

In Practice
HIV and Depression

Mark is a 30-year-old heterosexual man who presented to the HIV clinic at the local hospital to get more of the combination antiretroviral therapy (CART) medications to control the amount of HIV virus in his body. Mark's CART regimen helped change his diagnosis from a possible death sentence to a chronic but manageable disease. He has been living with HIV for five years now, and after a period of two years during which Mark was too sick to work, he is back at work as a server at a restaurant. Mark was referred to the psychologist at the HIV clinic, Dr Jimenez, because he has been experiencing depressed mood, irritability, and sleep problems over the last two months.

Dr Jimenez has extensive expertise working at the HIV clinic, and knows that people living with HIV are more likely to suffer from depression than people in the general population. Dr Jimenez also knows that depression is associated with increased risk of death from HIV and difficulties taking medications as prescribed. Mark has informed his psychologist that he has skipped a few doses of his medications because he has been feeling too tired and apathetic. Dr Jimenez therefore views Mark's depression as being dangerous not only for mental health reasons, but also because it may affect Mark's physical health.

Dr Jimenez, who is aware of the latest treatments available for people living with HIV, provided a psychological treatment called Life-Steps (Safren et al., 1999) to help Mark reduce his depression and become more adherent to his HIV medications. Life-Steps is a single-session treatment in which the therapist and client proceed through 11 informational, problem-solving, and cognitive behavioural steps in order to help the client identify and develop strategies to overcome problems with medication adherence. Some examples of steps addressed in treatment are obtaining medication, coping with side effects, cues for pill-taking, and responses to slips in adherence (Safren et al., 1999). Dr Jimenez informs Mark about the availability of smartphone applications for improving medication adherence and assists him in selecting an appropriate application based on his needs. Dr Jimenez then follows up this initial session with eight sessions of cognitive behavioural treatment for medication adherence and depression, which aim to reduce Mark's depressive symptoms while continuing to increase his medication adherence (Safren et al., 2009).

Future Directions

Although much research has already been conducted examining risk factors for HIV and STIs, less research has examined factors that protect uninfected people against these infections (e.g., Hart et al., 2017; Kurtz, Buttram, Surratt, & Stall, 2012). Similarly, there is a paucity of research that examines which factors are associated with positive mental health and well-being among people living with HIV and other incurable STIs. Regarding interventions to prevent HIV and STIs and to promote better HIV and STI health outcomes, most of these interventions may need to be administered face to face, which may limit the ability of health psychology programs to reach people from rural populations or others who are unable to attend weekly

iStock.com/oatawa

Social media and smartphone applications may be useful tools for increasing HIV and STI testing, knowledge, and prevention; however, more research is needed in this rapidly growing area.

counselling sessions. It has been recommended, therefore, that health psychologists increase the use of the Internet to improve access for marginalized populations (Hart & Hart, 2010), including social media-based interventions to increase HIV/STI testing or to increase safer sex and drug harm-reduction knowledge and risk-reduction behaviours. The use of Internet apps is another area where more research is needed, as apps can be used to monitor medication adherence but may also facilitate a role in increasing risk for STIs via apps where people can easily meet each other for sexual encounters.

Summary

HIV and STIs are of psychological interest because they are transmitted largely through sexual behaviour. In the case of HIV, another common route is through injection drug use. These infections are also psychological because psychological factors like personality traits and beliefs predict someone's susceptibility to engaging in risky behaviour. Living with HIV and STIs can also have psychological consequences, such as poor mental health outcomes due to societal stigmatization. Fortunately, health psychologists and other researchers and health providers operating within the biopsychosocial model have created psychological interventions that promote improved sexual health outcomes, reduce sexual risk behaviours, and help people living with STIs and especially people living with HIV to live longer and fuller lives.

Critical Thought Questions

1. Which psychological factors may explain why younger adults may be more at risk for STIs than older adults?
2. How would you respond to a friend who does not understand why psychologists would study STIs and HIV?
3. What role do you think you would have if you were a health psychologist working in a clinic for clients with HIV?

Recommended Reading

Cohen, M.A., & Gorman, J.M. (2008). *Comprehensive textbook of AIDS psychiatry*. Toronto: Oxford University Press.

Wolitski, R.J., Stall, R., & Validserri, R.O. (2008). *Unequal opportunity: Health disparities affecting gay and bisexual men in the United States*. Toronto: Oxford University Press.

Acknowledgements

T.G. Tulloch and N.L. Stratton are supported through Ontario Graduate Scholarships. T.G. Tulloch is also supported through Engage, a Team Grant funded by the Canadian Institutes of Health Research in HIV-prevention research for gay, bisexual, and other men who have sex with men. T.A. Hart is supported through an Applied HIV Research Chair from the Ontario HIV Treatment Network. The authors would like to thank the staff at the HIV Prevention Lab at Ryerson University for their help with this chapter.

Cancer

Anne Moyer
Elizabeth A. Sarma

12

Learning Objectives

In this chapter you will:

- Learn to explain the basic biological processes underlying cancer.
- Familiarize yourself with the most common types of cancer.
- Learn to describe cancer risk factors and cancer prevention strategies.
- Learn to explain how psychosocial factors may contribute to cancer initiation and progression.
- Compare and contrast the features and purpose of different psychological treatments for cancer patients.

Understanding Cancer

In 2013 and 2015, Angelina Jolie Pitt wrote opinion articles in *The New York Times* describing her decisions to undergo removal of her breasts and, subsequently, her fallopian tubes and ovaries as preventive measures against cancer. Her decisions were made in response to testing positive for a genetic mutation conferring a high susceptibility for breast and ovarian cancer, an intense desire to remain alive for her children, and the loss of her own mother to cancer. She went public about her medical choice so that others could benefit from her experience, but maintained "the most important thing is to learn about the options and choose what is right for you personally" (Jolie Pitt, 2015, p. A23).

Cancer is not a single disease, but rather a term to refer to a group of more than 100 illnesses (Benson & Liau, 2010; National Cancer Institute [NCI], 2015a). The basic process underlying different types of cancer, however, is the same. Cell proliferation normally is stringently regulated so that new cells are created to replace damaged or dying cells. Mechanisms are in place during cell division to repair damaged deoxyribonucleic acid (DNA, the basic genetic material that controls cell growth, division, and death) or to activate programmed cell death if the DNA damage is too extensive to repair. DNA damage can occur due to genetic processes or damage from *carcinogens* or viruses. Importantly, cancer is typically a result of multiple gene mutations, and these mutations are usually acquired during the lifespan. When genes that regulate cell division have mutations (i.e., DNA damage), the result is a breakdown in the regulation of cell division, leading to uncontrolled cell proliferation (see photo of hepatic cancer cells). The new tissue that develops from unregulated cell growth is called a tumour or neoplasm.

The resulting tumour may or may not be harmful. Malignant tumours are cancerous. Cells in malignant tumours can invade surrounding tissue and spread to a distant site in the body through the blood or lymph systems in a process called **metastasis**. Benign tumours are not cancerous and typically are not life-threatening. Often, they can be removed and do not invade nearby tissue or metastasize (Benson & Liau, 2010). The main categories of cancer are broadly classified according to the tissue in which the cancer originates. These categories include the following (NCI, 2015a):

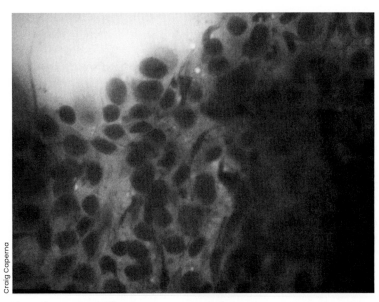

Craig Caperna

Hepatic cancer cells.

1. Carcinoma: Malignant neoplasms (i.e., new, abnormal tissue growth) that develop in the cells of the skin or tissues that line or cover organs (e.g., respiratory tract, reproductive tract). Most human cancers are carcinomas.
2. Sarcoma: Malignant neoplasms that develop in connective tissue, muscle, or bone.
3. Leukemia: Cancer that develops in blood-forming tissue (e.g., bone marrow), causing a rapid proliferation of white blood cells.
4. Lymphoma: Cancers of the lymphatic system.
5. Central nervous system cancer: Cancers that develop in brain tissue or the spinal cord.

Cancer type is typically named for the organ or type of cell in which the cancer initially develops (e.g., breast cancer for cancer that begins in breast tissue).

Types and Prevalence of Cancer

Cancer is a leading cause of death worldwide: approximately 8.2 million (13 per cent) of all deaths are cancer related (Ferlay et al., 2015). In Canada, cancer is the leading cause of death, accounting for 30 per cent of all deaths each year (Statistics Canada, 2015). Every day, over 500 people are diagnosed with cancer, and 200 die of cancer-related causes (Canadian Cancer Society [CCS], 2016). In 2016, it was estimated that approximately 202,400 Canadians would be newly diagnosed with cancer and 78,800 Canadians would die of cancer.

Over the past 30 years the number of new cases diagnosed and cancer-related deaths have increased, mainly due to the growth of the aging population (CCS, 2016). However, incidence rates are becoming stable or increasing only modestly, and mortality rates are decreasing, suggesting that survival rates are improving for some cancers (see Figure 12.1). The five-year survival rate for all cancer types is between 60 per cent and 70 per cent in North America (American Cancer Society [ACS], 2016; CCS, 2016). In the next section, we examine incidence and mortality trends for the most common cancers in North America: lung, prostate, and breast. Table 12.1 shows the annual incidence and mortality rates for these select cancers, adjusted for age of the patient, in Canada and the United States.

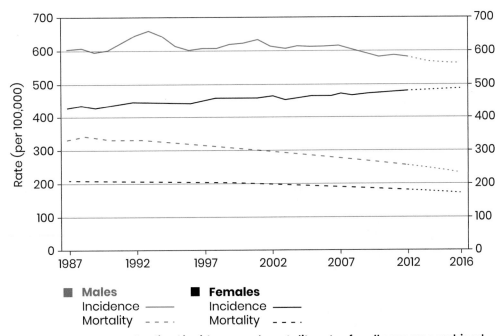

FIGURE 12.1 Age-standardized incidence and mortality rates for all cancers combined, by sex, Canada, 1987–2016.

Source: Canadian Cancer Society's Advisory Committee on Cancer Statistics. *Canadian Cancer Statistics 2016.* Toronto, ON: Canadian Cancer Society; 2016.

TABLE 12.1 | Annual Age-Standardized Incidence and Mortality Rates of Select Cancer Types per 100,000 Males and Females, Canada and the United States

	Overall		Lung		Prostate	Breast
	M	F	M	F	(M only)	(F only)
Canada						
Incidence	562.4	488.2	78.9	66.2	114.7	130.1
Death rate	235.9	171.2	60.5	45.8	24.2	23.4
United States						
Incidence	504.5	409.9	67.9	49.4	129.4	125.0
Death rate	204.0	143.4	57.8	37.0	20.7	21.5

Sources: Canada data: Canadian Cancer Society's (CCS) Advisory Committee on Cancer Statistics. (2016). Canadian cancer statistics 2016. Toronto, ON: Canadian Cancer Society. US data: Howlader, N., Noone, A.M., Krapcho, M., Miller, D., Bishop, K., Altekruse, S.F., ... Cronin K.A. (Eds). (April 2016). SEER Cancer Statistics Review, 1975–2013. Bethesda, MD: National Cancer Institute. Retrieved from http://seer.cancer.gov/csr/1975_2013/.

Lung Cancer

Lung cancer is the most common cancer worldwide, accounting for 13 per cent of all cancer cases (Ferlay et al., 2015). In North America, lung cancer is the second most commonly diagnosed cancer, accounting for approximately 14 per cent of new cancer diagnoses (ACS, 2016; CCS, 2016). Over 28,400 people in Canada and 224,390 people in the United States were expected to be diagnosed with lung cancer in 2016. In addition, lung cancer is the most common cause of cancer death in the world (Ferlay et al., 2015). Indeed, approximately 26 per cent of all cancer deaths in Canada are attributed to lung cancer. In both Canada and the United States, the five-year survival rate for lung cancer for all stages is just 17 per cent. The survival rate is 55 per cent when the cancer is localized, but unfortunately only 16 per cent of lung cancer diagnoses are made at this early stage (ACS, 2016).

Lung cancer incidence and mortality rates began to decrease in the mid-1980s for men but did not do so until the mid-2000s for women (ACS, 2016; CCS, 2016). This lag is attributed to gender differences in smoking behaviour. Specifically, tobacco consumption decreased among men in the mid-1960s but did not decrease among women until the mid-1980s. It should be noted, however, that men still have higher incidence and mortality rates of lung cancer than women (see Figures 12.2 and 12.3).

Prostate Cancer

Prostate cancer is the most commonly diagnosed cancer among North American men (CCS, 2016; National Center for Health Statistics [NCHS], 2016). Prostate cancer accounts for approximately 20 per cent of new cancer diagnoses in men, and an estimated 21,600 men in Canada and 180,890 men in the United States were expected to be diagnosed with prostate cancer in 2016 (ACS, 2016; CCS, 2016). In Canada, prostate cancer is the third leading cause of cancer death, while in the United States it is the second leading cause. The five-year survival rate for all stages of prostate cancer combined is between 95 per cent in Canada and 99 per cent in the United States (ACS, 2016; CCS, 2016). This rate becomes 100 per cent when the cancer is localized, an encouraging fact given that 92 per cent of prostate cancers are discovered in the local or regional stages. Incidence rates have fluctuated due to increased rates of cancer screening but have generally decreased since the early 2000s in both Canada and the United States. Mortality rates have also decreased since the mid-1990s because of the improved effectiveness of treatment.

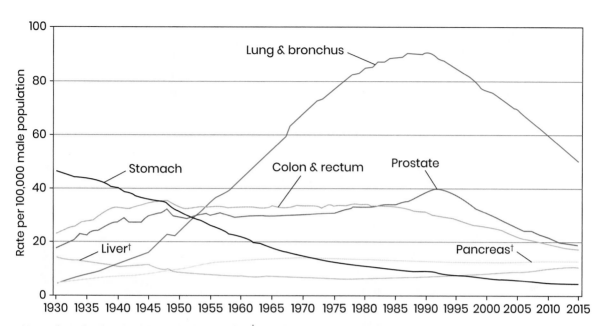

*Age adjusted to the 2000 US standard population. †Mortality rates for pancreatic and liver cancers are increasing.

Note: Due to changes in ICD coding, numerator information has changed over time. Rates for cancers of the liver, lung and bronchus, colon and rectum, and uterus are affected by these coding changes.

FIGURE 12.2   Age-adjusted cancer death rates,* males by site, United States, 1930–2015.

Source: American Cancer Society. *Cancer Facts and Figures 2018.* Atlanta: American Cancer Society, Inc.

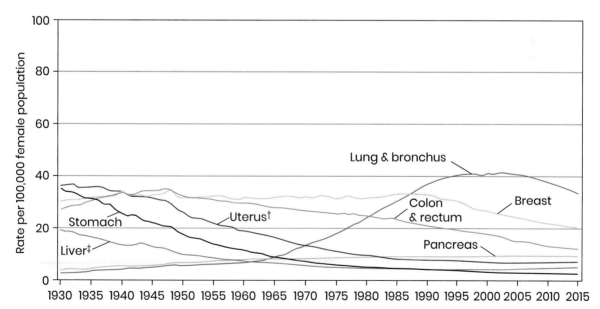

*Age adjusted to the 2000 US standard population. †Uterus refers to uterine cervix and uterine corpus combined.

‡The mortality rate for liver cancer is increasing.

Note: Due to changes in ICD coding, numerator information has changed over time. Rates for cancers of the liver, lung and bronchus, colon and rectum, and uterus are affected by these coding changes.

FIGURE 12.3   Age-adjusted cancer death rates,* females by site, United States, 1930–2015.

Source: American Cancer Society. *Cancer Facts and Figures 2018.* Atlanta: American Cancer Society, Inc.

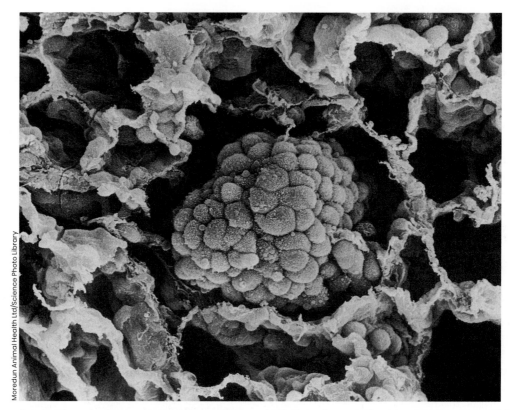

Moredun Animal Health Ltd/Science Photo Library

A scanning electron micrograph provides a depiction of a small cancerous tumour within a human lung. The tumour is covered in microscopic hair-like structures called microvilli, which enable absorption and secretion. Smoking and other tobacco use are responsible for nearly all cases of lung cancer.

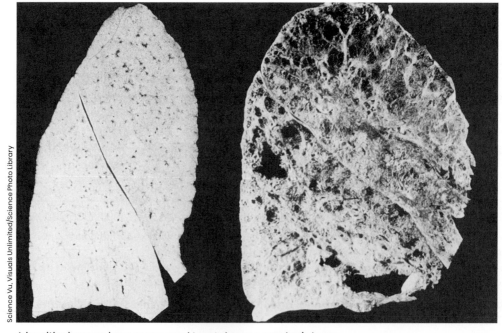

Science Vu, Visuals Unlimited/Science Photo Library

A healthy human lung compared to a tobacco smoker's lung.

Breast Cancer

Around the world, breast cancer is the most diagnosed cancer among women, with an estimated 1.67 million cases diagnosed in 2012 (Ferlay et al., 2015). Breast cancer is also the most commonly diagnosed cancer among North American women, with an estimated 25,700 and 246,660 new cases in Canada and the United States, respectively, in 2016 (ACS, 2016; CCS, 2016). Breast cancer accounts for approximately 26 to 29 per cent of all cancer diagnoses and is the second-most common cause of cancer death among women in North America (CCS, 2016; NCHS, 2016). Across all stages of the disease, 87 per cent of Canadian women and 89 per cent of American women survive at least five years after diagnosis (ACS, 2016; CCS, 2016). This rate is as high as 99 per cent when the cancer is localized and is 85 per cent when the cancer has spread to surrounding regions (ACS, 2015a). Fortunately, approximately 61 per cent of breast cancer diagnoses are at the local stage (NCI, 2016). Incidence rates have generally remained stable since the early 2000s (ACS, 2015a; CCS, 2016), and mortality from breast cancer has generally decreased since the mid-1980s thanks to early detection and more effective adjuvant therapy after surgery.

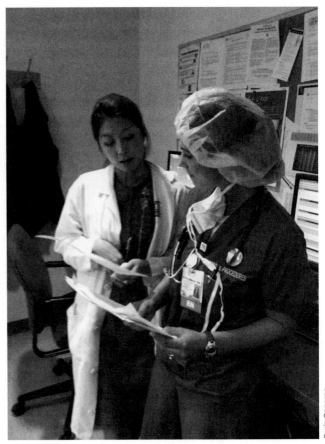

Screening is designed to detect cancer at an early stage, before symptoms have developed.

Medical Management Approaches

Treatment for cancer involves procedures that address cancerous cells locally, such as surgery and radiation, and treatments, such as chemotherapy, that eradicate cancerous cells that may have metastasized to other areas of the body where they may develop into secondary tumours. Surgical removal of tumours allows them to be examined further by a pathologist to determine how aggressive they may be and whether they are likely to respond to particular types of adjuvant treatment. Radiation therapy may be given daily over an extended period of time, often necessitating time off from work or even temporary relocation to be near a treatment centre. Radiation may be delivered by external beams or by the insertion of radioactive seeds or needles to a target area of the body (Rosenbaum et al., 2005). While a person receiving external beam radiation is not radioactive, radioactive seeds are, and necessitate caution, for example, by avoiding close proximity to other people. There are more than 250 kinds of cancer drugs (NCI, 2017). Chemotherapy may be given as intravenous infusions or taken orally as pills. For example, Cisplatin is used to treat ovarian, bladder, and testicular cancer (NCI, 2018). Hormonal therapy is given to combat tumours whose growth is promoted by hormones, such as breast, ovarian, and uterine cancer in women and prostate cancer in men. For example, tamoxifen is used for estrogen-sensitive breast cancers and anti-androgens for men with prostate cancer include bicalutamide (CCS, 2018). Bone

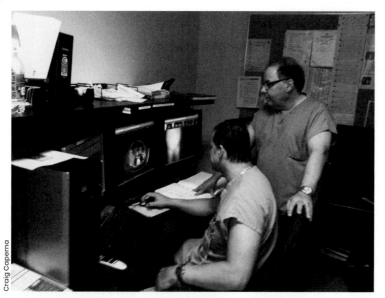

Craig Caperna

Surgical removal of tumours allows them to be examined further by a pathologist to determine how aggressive they may be and whether they are likely to respond to particular types of adjuvant treatment.

marrow transplant is performed following very high-dose chemotherapy treatment that is so radical that it depletes one's bone marrow (Rosenbaum et al., 2005). Sometimes chemotherapy is administered to shrink a tumour before surgery, or even palliatively, to alleviate symptoms associated with a tumour's growth.

Cancer Risk Factors

The long delay between exposure to risk factors, such as carcinogens, and the onset of cancer makes the determination of the cause of cancer a challenge (NCI, 2016; Swerdlow, Peto, & Doll, 2010). Although different cancers share similar clinical characteristics, the causes and risk factors associated with cancers at different sites varies. In addition, cancer is often the result of the interaction of various risk factors, which can include genetic factors, environmental factors, infectious agents, and behavioural and sociodemographic factors. Epidemiological research provides much of the information regarding risk factors for cancer.

People who carry cancer gene mutations are at a heightened risk of developing cancer. For example, mutations in the BRCA1 and BRCA2 genes confer an increased risk of breast and ovarian cancers (NCI, 2015b; Swerdlow et al., 2010). Approximately 5 to 10 per cent of all breast cancers are due to inherited genetic mutations, although most cancers are due to sporadic mutations that are acquired during the lifespan (ACS, 2015a). In addition, a family history of cancer, specifically in first-degree relatives, can confer increased risk; however, families share not only genetics, but may also share lifestyle behaviours that increase risk, such as diet, or exposure to the same

In Focus

Patenting and Commercializing Breast Cancer Susceptibility Genes

Since the discovery in the early 1990s that mutations in the BRCA1 and BRCA2 genes confer increased susceptibility to breast, ovarian, and other cancers in both men and women, battles have raged about whether it should be allowable to obtain US patents on genetic material and on methods to use that genetic material for diagnostic tests. Proponents suggest that patenting is necessary to protect the significant investments of companies that have conducted essential scientific research. Such protection, it is argued, allows companies to develop further products and services, advancing environmental risk factors. Genetic testing for gene mutations that suggest increased risk for cancer has become increasingly popular, as tests have become more accessible (see In Focus box). Those who test positive for carrying a mutation can opt for increased surveillance, prophylactic surgical removal of potentially affected organs (e.g., breasts or ovaries), or preventive medications (NCI, 2015b). They may also share this information with family members, particularly first-degree relatives, who have a 50 per cent chance of carrying the mutation themselves, and who may also opt for testing. Those who test negative for a mutation should continue to engage in screening at recommended rates.

In addition to and in interaction with genetic risk factors, environmental factors and infectious agents may also increase one's risk for cancer. Exposure to certain environmental factors called carcinogens, such as asbestos, radon, and formaldehyde, can increase the risk of some cancers (Ljungman, 2014; Swerdlow et al., 2010). Exposure to ionizing radiation, such as ultraviolet radiation (the principal cause of skin cancer), can increase cancer risk through damaging DNA. Infections with particular viruses, bacteria, and parasites can also increase the risk of specific cancers. Approximately 9.2 per cent of cancers in developed countries are attributable to infectious agents, including *Helicobacter pylori*, human papillomavirus (HPV), and hepatitis B (Plummer et al., 2016). As an example, HPV16 and HPV18, which can be sexually transmitted, cause about 70 per cent of cervical cancers worldwide (Buck & Ratner, 2014).

It is estimated that 35 per cent of cancer deaths are related to lifestyle choices (WHO, 2009). Tobacco is a major cause of cancer, especially lung and bronchial cancers, in developed countries (Centers for Disease Control and Prevention [CDC], 2016; Swerdlow et al., 2010) (see Figure 12.4). It is estimated that tobacco use is linked to 20 to 30 per cent of cancer deaths worldwide. Tobacco smoke contains over 70 carcinogens and greatly increases the risk of lung cancer. In fact, smokers are 15 to 30 times more likely to develop or die from lung cancer than non-smokers (CDC, 2016), and the risk increases with the amount smoked (US Department of Health and Human Services [USDHHS], 2014). Other behavioural factors linked to increased risk of some cancers include high alcohol consumption, a diet low in fruits and vegetables, lack of exercise, and obesity (ACS, 2015b; NCI, 2016).

Finally, several sociodemographic factors are associated with risk for cancer. For example, the incidence of cancer generally increases with age. Indeed, 89 per cent of new cancer cases and 96 per cent of cancer deaths in Canada are among adults age 50 and over (CCS, 2016).

innovations in the field of personalized medicine. Detractors, including some scientists and professional medical organizations, counter that patenting stifles the open sharing of information and data essential to scientific discovery. For companies that seek to hold the patents on tests for hereditary cancer, such testing represents significant revenues. However, in 2013 the US Supreme Court ruled against the current patent holder, allowing several academic and commercial laboratories to offer this testing (Lynch, Venne, & Berse, 2015). The commercialization of such testing has been criticized, based on concerns about conflicts of interest and the lack of appropriate counselling and delivery of such information outside of clinical settings (Matloff & Caplan, 2008).

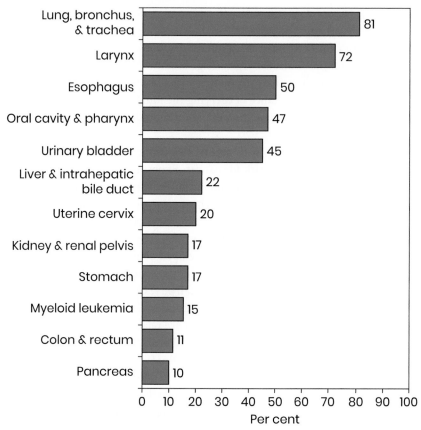

FIGURE 12.4 **Proportion of cancer deaths attributable to cigarette smoking in adults 30 years and older, US, 2014.**

Source: American Cancer Society. *Cancer Facts and Figures 2018*. Atlanta: American Cancer Society, Inc.

The increased risk with age may be due to a combination of risk factors, including an accumulation of genetic mutations, a weaker immune system, and more carcinogen exposure (Parkin & Bray, 2006). When age is taken into account, men generally have higher cancer incidence and mortality rates than women (CCS, 2016; Swerdlow et al., 2010). For instance, the lifetime probability of developing cancer is approximately 45 per cent in men and 42 per cent in women living in Canada (CCS, 2016).

Socio-economic status (SES) is linked to increased risk for certain types of cancer. Low SES is associated with increased risk of developing cancer, including lung and gastrointestinal cancers (Hastert, Beresford, Sheppard, & White, 2015; Kawachi & Kroenke, 2006). In addition, low SES is a risk factor for cancer mortality in general (Booth, Li, Zhang-Salomons, & Mackillop, 2010; Hastert et al., 2015). The reasons for the association between SES and cancer risk and survival are unclear. It has been suggested that later stage of diagnosis, a more aggressive biology of cancer, lower quality of care, and differences in behavioural risk factors (e.g., higher smoking rates, higher rates of obesity) may help to explain the SES difference in cancer risk and mortality (Clegg et al., 2009; Kawachi & Kroenke, 2006; Woods, Rachet, & Coleman, 2006).

Differences in cancer incidence and mortality have also been observed based on geography and ethnic ancestry. For example, breast cancer is most common in Western nations, such as the United States and Europe, whereas breast cancer incidence is relatively low in Africa and Asia (Ferlay et al., 2015; Parkin & Bray, 2006; Swerdlow et al., 2010). Asian-American women born in the United States have been found to have a breast cancer risk 60 per cent higher than Asian-American women who were born in the East (Ziegler et al., 1993). Furthermore, those who had lived in the United States longer had an increased risk of breast cancer, with incidence rates closer to those of White women than rates of women in their home country. Geographic differences in cancer incidence and mortality are believed to be due to environmental and behavioural differences, though genetic differences may also contribute (Parkin & Bray, 2006). For instance, the differences observed in breast cancer incidence are likely related to lifestyle factors in the host country that are adopted after immigration, such as an increase in caloric intake that may increase body mass index, and the influence of reproductive hormones (Keegan, Gomez, Clarke, Chan, & Glaser, 2007; Kolonel & Wilkens, 2006; Parkin & Bray, 2006).

There are also racial and ethnic differences in the incidence and mortality of various cancers. For example, non-Hispanic White women in the United States are more

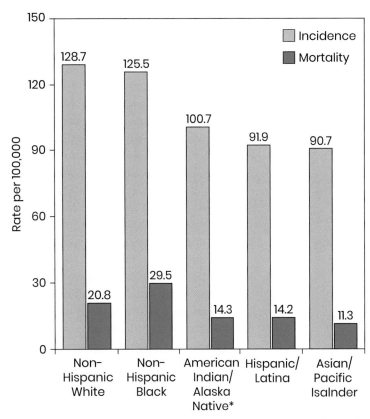

*Statistics based on data from Contract Health Service Delivery Area (CHSDA) counties. Note: Rates are age adjusted to the 2000 US standard population.

FIGURE 12.5   Female breast cancer incidence (2010–14) and mortality (2011–15) rates by race and ethnicity, US.

Source: American Cancer Society. *Breast Cancer Facts and Figures 2017-2018*. Atlanta: American Cancer Society, Inc

likely to develop breast cancer than any other race/ethnicity group, but African-American women are more likely to die from the disease (ACS, 2015a) (see Figure 12.5). This discrepancy is attributed to later stages at detection and poorer stage-specific survival among African-American women (Curtis, Quale, Haggstrom, & Smith-Bindman, 2008; Iqbal, Ginsburg, Rochon, Sun, & Narod, 2015) (see also Chapter 15 for health disparities related to culture).

Biopsychosocial Factors in Cancer Incidence and Progression

We have thus far considered the biological, environmental, behavioural, and sociodemographic risk factors for cancer. The biopsychosocial model posits that, besides biological factors, social and psychological factors must be taken into account in explaining and treating patients' dysfunction (Engel, 1977). In this section, we consider the role of psychosocial factors, particularly stress, in concert with biological mechanisms that may play a role in the initiation and progression of cancer.

In general, the evidence linking psychosocial factors to cancer initiation has been equivocal (Antoni et al., 2006; Lutgendorf & Andersen, 2015; Lutgendorf & Sood, 2011). The most consistent evidence has linked cancer incidence with severe life events (e.g., bereavement), extreme distress, and chronic depression (Chida, Hamer, Wardle, & Steptoe, 2008; Lutgendorf & Andersen, 2015; Lutgendorf & Sood, 2011). For example, major life events, such as the death of a loved one, have been linked to an increased risk of developing cancer (Levav et al., 2000). Lillberg and colleagues (2003) examined whether major life events were related to increased cancer incidence in a prospective study with approximately 11,000 Finnish women. At baseline, women in the study were asked to report stressful life events that had occurred in the past five years. Cancer registry information was checked 14 years later to determine which women developed breast cancer. Women who had experienced a major life event, including divorce or separation, death of a spouse, or death of a friend or relative, were at an elevated risk for breast cancer. Depression has also been linked to an increased risk of developing cancer (Chida et al., 2008; Penninx, Guralnik, & Havlik, 1998).

It is difficult to establish a causal link between psychosocial factors and cancer onset for several reasons. The use of retrospective designs can greatly limit our ability to make causal conclusions (Chida et al., 2008; Reiche, Nunes, & Morimoto, 2004; Sklar & Anisman, 1981). Cancer patients who are asked to recall past life events may remember these events differently based on having knowledge of their diagnosis. In addition, it is possible that the disease was present before and during the stressful life events. Importantly, there is typically a long delay between the development of and the detection of cancer, further obscuring causal links between psychosocial factors and cancer onset (Bleiker, Hendriks, Otten, Verbeek, & van der Ploeg, 2008; Reiche et al., 2004).

In general, the evidence linking psychosocial factors to cancer progression and mortality has been stronger than the evidence for cancer onset (Antoni et al., 2006; Lutgendorf & Andersen, 2015). In particular, depression, stressful life events, and social isolation have been associated with more rapid cancer progression and poorer survival in individuals with cancer (Lutgendorf & Sood, 2011). Depression in cancer has been associated with mortality rates up to 39 per cent higher (Chida et al., 2008; Satin, Linden, & Phillips, 2009). Stressful life events, such as loss of a spouse, have also been associated with higher mortality rates in cancer patients (Chida et al., 2008). In a study investigating the experience of traumatic and stressful life events in women with metastatic or recurrent breast cancer, women who had experienced at least one traumatic or stressful life event had a significantly shorter disease-free interval, relative to women who had not had such an experience (Palesh et al., 2007).

Cancer progression and mortality are associated with social isolation and a lack of social support (Pinquart & Duberstein, 2010; Reynolds & Kaplan, 1990), although not all studies support this relationship (e.g., Chida et al., 2008). For example, in a study of women with breast cancer, women who reported they were socially isolated before their diagnosis were twice as likely to die of breast cancer. Furthermore, women without close relatives, friends, or living children had a higher risk of breast cancer mortality than women with more social ties (Kroenke, Kubzansky, Schernhammer, Holmes, & Kawachi, 2006). However, a decrease in cancer mortality is associated with high levels of perceived social support, a larger network size, and being married (Pinquart & Duberstein, 2010). Among those not currently married, cancer mortality appears to be differentially associated with marital history. In a study of marital status and cancer survival, patients who were separated from their spouse at the time of their diagnosis had the lowest five- and ten-year survival rates, followed by those patients who were widowed, divorced, and never married (Sprehn, Chambers, Saykin, Konski, & Johnstone, 2009).

How might psychosocial factors influence the initiation and progression of cancer? Both indirect behavioural and direct physiological pathways have been proposed. First, behavioural changes that accompany psychosocial factors may play a role in cancer onset and development. For instance, psychosocial factors can lead to behavioural changes that increase one's risk of cancer, including increased smoking, less exercise, and poor diet (Reiche et al., 2004; Sprehn et al., 2009). Furthermore, psychosocial factors, such as stress and depression, can lead to a decrease in compliance with medical regimens, which may increase the progression of cancer (Spiegel & Giese-Davis, 2003; Sprehn et al., 2009). Social support may be linked to lower mortality because one's social network encourages healthy behaviours and allows for greater access to the health-care system (e.g., getting to medical appointments).

Psychosocial factors have also been postulated to influence cancer initiation and progression through physiological pathways. Psychoneuroimmunology research (see Chapter 2 for a general discussion of psychoneuroimmunology) has helped to clarify possible biological mechanisms. Stress and the immune system are linked through the sympathetic nervous system (SNS), which releases catecholamines (e.g., norepinephrine and epinephrine), and the hypothalamic-pituitary-adrenal (HPA) axis (a pathway that connects the brain with the endocrine system), which releases cortisol (Antoni et al., 2006; Lutgendorf & Andersen, 2015; Segerstrom & Miller, 2004). Chronic stressors (e.g., bereavement, depression, isolation) and the resulting constant exposure to stress hormones generally impair immune function (Antoni et al., 2006; Glaser & Kiecolt-Glaser, 2005). When the immune system detects transformed cells, it attempts to destroy these cancerous cells, a process referred to as **immunosurveillance** (Dunn, Koebel, & Schreiber, 2006). If the immune system is inhibited and all tumour cells are not destroyed, the tumour will grow, leading to cancer.

How do stress hormones and immunosuppression influence cancer? Stress hormones can cause DNA damage, impair mechanisms involved in DNA repair, and inhibit programmed cell death in cancer cells, all of which may promote the onset and progression of cancer (Antoni et al., 2006; Cole, Nagaraja, Lutgendorf, Green, & Sood, 2015; Reiche et al., 2004). Stress, through the release of catecholamines, may also promote tumour growth by facilitating angiogenesis (the development of a blood supply for the tumour, allowing growth, invasion, and metastasis) (Cole et al., 2015; Lutgendorf & Sood, 2011). High levels of social support have been associated with lower levels of these growth factors in women with ovarian cancer, suggesting a potential physiological pathway through which a lack of social support influences cancer progression (Costanzo et al., 2005; Lutgendorf et al., 2002). Cortisol, which is a significant steroid hormone (a glucocorticoid, produced by the adrenal cortex), has also been shown to stimulate growth and proliferation of cancer cells (Lutgendorf & Sood, 2011). Negative psychosocial states, through their effects on stress hormones, have been associated with inhibition of the cellular immune response, thus decreasing immunosurveillance (Lutgendorf & Andersen, 2015). For example, women who were diagnosed and treated surgically for breast cancer and who reported high levels of psychological distress (intrusive and avoidant thoughts and behaviours about cancer) had reduced natural killer (NK)-cell response relative to women who reported low levels of psychological distress (Andersen et al., 1998). Breast cancer patients with higher levels of perceived social support, especially high-quality emotional support from a spouse or intimate other, had greater NK-cell activity and increased NK-cell cytotoxicity (Levy et al., 1990).

Cancer Prevention

Behavioural changes can be made to help reduce one's risk of developing cancer. For example, wearing sunscreen to protect against harmful ultraviolet radiation can help reduce risk of skin cancer. Avoiding smoking can help reduce risk of lung cancer. Exercising regularly can help reduce the risk of colon and breast cancer. Receiving the HPV vaccine can reduce the risk of cervical cancer. Apps are available for several areas of cancer prevention such as exercise, nutrition, smoking, sun safety, and risk-assessment tools; information can be found at https://www.mdanderson.org/publications/focused-on-health/february-2014/cancer-prevention-apps.html. However, as we have seen in previous sections, cancer is typically caused by multiple factors, so primary prevention measures can reduce but not entirely eliminate the risk of developing cancer.

Cancer screening is a secondary prevention measure. Screening is designed to detect cancer at an early stage, before symptoms have developed. Screening reduces cancer morbidity and mortality through early detection because early-stage cancer is typically easier to treat, and treatment interventions tend to be less aggressive and invasive (PDQ˚ Screening and Prevention Editorial Board, 2016). Examples of efficacious cancer-screening tests are mammography for breast cancer, Pap tests for cervical cancer, and fecal occult blood tests and colonoscopy for colorectal cancer.

Although screening tests have benefits for morbidity and mortality, there are also associated harms. Some screening tests can be directly harmful to the patient, for example, perforation of the colon from a colonoscopy (Levin & Prorok, 2006). Also, screening tests may incorrectly detect absent cancer or may miss present cancer. False positives (i.e., a positive screening result when cancer is not present) cause stress and anxiety. In addition, unnecessary follow-up diagnostic tests, such as biopsies, can be painful and invasive. False negatives (i.e., a negative screening result when cancer is present) usually result in a delay in diagnosis and treatment. The issue of **overdiagnosis** has also been identified as a problem of cancer screening in that it can lead to unnecessary treatment (Levin & Prorok, 2006; Løberg, Lousdal, Bretthauer, & Kalager, 2015). When making their screening recommendations, task forces weigh these harms against the reduction in cancer-specific mortality due to the test. In recent years, the use of the prostate-specific antigen (PSA) test to detect prostate cancer has been discouraged in both Canada (Canadian Task Force on Preventive Health Care, 2014) and the United States (Moyer & USPSTF, 2012) due to its high false-positive rate, risk of overdiagnosis, and lack of a reduction in prostate cancer-specific mortality.

Screening mammography is a low-dose x-ray procedure used to look at breast tissue and detect early-stage breast cancer. Mammography screening decreases breast cancer mortality by 19 to 31 per cent (Nelson et al., 2016a; Siu & USPSTF, 2016). Although mammography involves radiation, the radiation risk from mammography is small, and the mortality benefit of screening outweighs the risks of radiation exposure (Yaffe & Mainprize, 2011). In general, mammography correctly identifies those with breast cancer approximately 77 to 95 per cent of the time and those without breast cancer approximately 94 to 97 per cent of the time (Siu & USPSTF, 2016). In Canada, it is recommended that women between the ages of 50 and 69 years of age be screened every two to three years (Canadian Task Force on Preventive Health Care, 2011). Similarly, women in the United States are advised to receive screening every two years between the ages of 50 and 74 (Siu & USPSTF, 2016). Approximately 69 per cent of women aged 50 and older in the United States and 62 per cent of women in Canada have had a screening mammogram in the past two years (Canadian Partnership Against Cancer, 2015; NCHS, 2016).

Although screening mammography can help to reduce breast cancer morbidity and mortality, some women do not receive mammograms. Barriers to engaging in mammography screening exist at the health-care system level, the social level, and the individual level (Sarma, 2015). Reasons for non-adherence include a fear of radiation (Champion & Skinner, 2003), fear of pain (Rawl, Champion, Menon, & Foster, 2000), anxiety about a positive screening result (Miller, O'Hea, Block Lerner, Moon, & Foran-Tuller, 2011), and lack of accessibility to a screening centre (Ogedegbe et al., 2005). Despite this, health psychology researchers have used mainly individual-level theories such as the health belief model (Rosenstock, Strecher, & Becker, 1988) to examine such barriers to obtaining mammograms. For instance, the health belief model (see Chapter 1), in predicting the likelihood of getting a mammogram, considers one's beliefs about barriers to engaging in a behaviour (e.g., mammography is painful) in combination with one's beliefs about one's susceptibility to a condition (e.g., breast cancer), the severity of the consequences of that condition (e.g., surgery, death), the perceived benefits of the behaviour (e.g., a clear mammogram would provide peace of mind), and one's perceived sense of self-efficacy in performing the behaviour.

Like other screening tests, mammography can sometimes be inaccurate. Indeed, the chance of receiving at least one false-positive mammography result after 10 years is 42 per cent with biennial screening (Nelson et al., 2016b). What are the psychological consequences of false positive results? In the short term, women may be anxious when they receive the results (Brett, Bankhead, Henderson, Watson, & Austoker, 2005; Salz, Richman, & Brewer, 2010). In the long term, women with false positives may experience an increase in thoughts, anxiety, and worry about breast cancer (Brewer, Salz, & Lillie, 2007), although it is not known how long this anxiety lasts.

Psychosocial Adjustment to Cancer

As treatments have improved and cancer mortality has decreased in some cancer types, cancer is increasingly becoming a chronic illness. For cancer patients and their families, cancer diagnosis and treatment mean multiple adjustment challenges due to the disease, including changes in interpersonal relationships and social roles, the physical effects of treatment, and coping with the uncertainty and stress of the diagnosis and treatment (Franks & Roesche, 2006; Helgeson & Cohen, 1996). In this section, we consider how patients adapt to and cope with living with cancer.

A diagnosis of cancer can create a period of crisis. Major concerns for many patients include death, disability, dependence on others, and disfigurement. Common initial reactions to a cancer diagnosis include disbelief and denial of the veracity of the diagnosis. This initial phase typically lasts less than a week. Patients then move to the dysphoria phase, during which the diagnosis is acknowledged. This dysphoria phase is characterized by anxiety, depression, insomnia, poor concentration, lack of appetite, and trouble maintaining daily activities, and usually lasts one to two weeks, although this varies. Finally, patients typically adjust to the diagnosis and treatment for cancer and attempt to resume regular routines. The quality of this long-term adaptation phase depends on many factors and varies greatly among individuals (Holland & Weiss, 2010).

Psychosocial adaptation to cancer is an ongoing process that changes with the disease stage, symptoms, prognosis, and treatment (Holland & Weiss, 2010). Patients need to attend treatment sessions, manage emotional distress, and adjust to changing social roles. In addition, patients are faced with the consequences of cancer and its treatment, including pain, fatigue, lack of appetite, and sexual dysfunction, all of which can cause impairment and influence the patient's daily life (Nicholas & Veach, 2000).

Coping with cancer involves the use of different coping strategies according to the nature of the stressor. For instance, patients receiving palliative care for cancer reported using problem-focused coping less frequently for existential issues and emotion-focused coping less frequently for physical stressors (De Faye, Wilson, Chater, Viola, & Hall, 2006). The appraisal of cancer-related stressors is also an important factor that determines which coping strategies a patient will use. For example, if cancer is appraised as a threat or a challenge, problem-focused coping is more likely to be used to deal with the stressor (e.g., medical compliance, problem-solving). On the other hand, if cancer is appraised as a harm or loss, then avoidance coping is more likely to be used (e.g., denial, minimizing the threat of cancer, wishful thinking, substance use). Again, cancer patients use multiple types of coping to deal with the stress of cancer (Franks & Roesch, 2006). Helplessness and hopelessness are associated with poor adjustment (van't Spijker, Trijsburg, & Duivenvoorden, 1997). Although the evidence linking helplessness and hopelessness to cancer survival has not been consistent (Petticrew, Bell, & Hunter, 2002), some studies have shown an increased risk of cancer relapse or death (e.g., Price et al., 2016; Watson, Haviland, Greer, Davidson, & Bliss, 1999). Optimism has been linked to greater psychological well-being in cancer patients (Costa, Mercieca-Bebber, Rutherford, Gabb, & King, 2016; van't Spijker et al., 1997). In a study of newly diagnosed cancer patients, psychological well-being was associated with higher optimism and lower pessimism before the start of chemotherapy, and pessimism predicted a negative change in psychological well-being nine months after chemotherapy (Pinquart, Fröhlich, & Silbereisen, 2007).

Social support is thought to have positive effects on psychological and physical health both directly, by enhancing health behaviours, and indirectly, by acting as a buffer against cancer-related stressors (Costanzo, Sood, & Lutgendorf, 2011; Nicholas & Veach, 2000). Emotional support and, more specifically, emotional expression (i.e., having someone to talk with about cancer-related concerns) may be especially important for successful adjustment to cancer (Helgeson & Cohen, 1996). For instance, in a sample of breast cancer patients, women who reported high emotional expression about cancer had fewer medical morbidities, better physical health, and less distress eight months after medical treatment than women who reported low emotional expression (Stanton et al., 2000). Emotional expression is also associated with better survival (Reynolds et al., 2000). Cancer is a strain on interpersonal relationships and is also stressful for the patient's friends and family (Helgeson & Cohen, 1996). The patient may have to limit social activities due to treatment schedules and side effects. Friends and family may act in unintentionally harmful ways towards the patient, such as avoiding physical contact or open communication about cancer, because they are unsure of how to behave (Wortman & Dunkel-Schetter, 1979).

Cancer is a major source of stress, and more severe psychological problems, such as depression, can develop in patients. The likelihood that a patient will develop psychological problems depends on medical (e.g., site, stage, hospitalization) and personal factors (e.g., quality of social support) (Manne et al., 2008). Depression affects between 7 and 24 per cent of patients (Krebber et al., 2014), and is more common among cancer patients than in the general population (Massie, 2004). However, depression can be difficult to diagnose in cancer patients because the symptoms of depression (e.g., weight loss, insomnia, fatigue) may be mistaken for symptoms of the disease (Spiegel & Giese-Davis, 2003). Patients who are socially isolated and have greater physical impairment due to cancer are more at risk for poor adjustment (Holland & Weiss, 2010; Manne et al., 2008). Knowledge of risk factors that predict poor adjustment can help health-care providers to identify patients who may be at risk.

Psychological Assessment of the Cancer Patient

Treatment for cancer has changed from being focused solely on medically managing the disease to also preserving quality of life. This has become especially important as medical advances have allowed cancer patients to live long after their treatment is complete. Thus, more attention has been paid to the psychological needs of patients. Psychosocial health needs can be identified when patients bring this up themselves, when providers ask about them directly, or when clinicians administer screening assessments (Adler & Page, 2008). Screening is useful in that it may identify patients who do not perceive themselves to be in need of psychosocial services. Specific instruments include the Distress Thermometer, a single-item scale that depicts a thermometer and asks respondents to indicate the level of distress that they have experienced over the past week from 0 (no distress) to 10 (extreme distress). The Patient Care Monitor 2.0 uses 86 items to identify difficulties commonly encountered by cancer patients, including psychological distress, problems with performing their roles in life, physical problems, and lowered overall quality of life. Individual items assess things such as "fatigue, tiredness, or weakness" or "trouble focusing or concentrating" (Fortner, Baldwin, Schwartzberg, & Houts, 2006). The instrument is administered via computer, taking about 11 minutes, and the results can be forwarded automatically to clinicians in advance of meeting with a patient (Adler & Page, 2008).

Current practice guidelines recommend that psychological assessment be part of an ideal plan to identify cancer patients whose psychosocial needs are likely to affect their health. None theless such screening is not yet routine in cancer care (Adler & Page, 2008). Moreover, such is useful only in environments where resources are available to link patients to assistance.

A predominant belief underpinning the development of psychosocial interventions for cancer patients was that the challenges that cancer presents are so disruptive that most patients could benefit from some type of psychological intervention. Recent research, however, has shown that those who are more distressed appear to benefit the most from such interventions (Hart et al., 2012; Schneider et al., 2010), suggesting that screening and then targeting treatment to those who are actually experiencing difficulties may be a more appropriate approach. Nonetheless, it has also been suggested that psychological interventions may be instrumental in preventing distress, even in patients who are not currently troubled, as they go through the stages of cancer treatment and beyond.

Psychological Interventions for Cancer Patients

As has been outlined above, the challenges that cancer patients face are many. As Karen's example (see In Practice box) demonstrates, upon diagnosis, in addition to the shock of a potentially life-threatening diagnosis, there is often much new information to take in and understand, and decisions regarding the course of treatment often need to be made. Like Karen,

In Practice
Adjusting to a Cancer Diagnosis

Karen, a 61-year-old mother of two grown daughters, was looking forward to spending more time in her garden and travelling during her upcoming retirement. She was relatively active, took vitamins and calcium supplements, and, at the recommendation of her physician, received a mammogram semi-annually. One morning in the shower she felt a pea-sized bump under her left arm. Although somewhat alarmed, she wondered whether it really could be an indicator of something serious. Her most recent mammogram had been clear, so she decided to just keep an eye on it for a while and not let herself get too worked up thinking about the "C word." She felt healthy and the lump wasn't painful. About a month later, when the lump hadn't changed, she scheduled an appointment with her physician who, upon physical examination, ordered a mammogram. When the diagnostic mammogram indicated suspicious findings in the form of visible calcifications, Karen was scheduled to have a needle biopsy. This would allow the cells themselves to be examined, to definitively determine if the tumour was cancerous. She was anxious about the procedure, which would occur under a local anaesthetic, but, although it was somewhat uncomfortable, it was over quickly.

Although Karen had been fairly composed when she had identified the lump, waiting for the results of the biopsy sent her into a bit of a tailspin. She began to worry about worst-case scenarios, wondering if she would lose her breast, her femininity, the admiration of her husband, her robust lifestyle and social life, and, most importantly, she wondered if she would live to see grandchildren. She sat up late into the night searching the Internet for information, and at times it was overwhelming to process so many new terms and concepts: tumour staging, lumpectomy, mastectomy, breast prostheses, reconstructive surgery, the dangers of silicone breast implants. When the news came that she indeed had breast cancer, Karen felt shocked and numb, despite having prepared herself as best she could. It was difficult to concentrate on all that was said during her consultation and she was relieved when she learned that a **patient navigator** would help her negotiate the process of understanding her options and getting information from the various specialists that formed her medical team.

Fortunately, like a large proportion of women diagnosed with breast cancer, Karen's cancer was detected at an early stage and she could be effectively treated by either mastectomy, having her entire breast removed, or lumpectomy, having just the tumour removed. The breast-conserving treatment, however, would involve several weeks of daily radiation therapy to eradicate any remaining malignant cells. Removing the entire breast might make her feel as if she'd had a more "complete" procedure, but what would it be like to be without a breast? Although she did not consider herself vain and felt confident in her husband's love and support, she was somewhat invested in her image of herself as healthy, "whole," and attractive. She found testimonies on the Internet from women satisfied with each of the procedures, and even from women who had had breast reconstruction following a mastectomy and a breast augmentation on the other side that resulted in an overall enlarged bust. She didn't think that an enhanced body image was worth that amount of follow-up surgery, so she opted for lumpectomy plus radiation. The surgery went smoothly, and during the procedure the surgeon also biopsied one of the lymph nodes under her arm. The pathology report revealed that, because cancer had not appeared to have metastasized beyond the breast, chemotherapy would not be necessary.

Karen's radiation therapy was five days a week over six weeks. Each session was brief and wasn't painful, but the sight of unfamiliar medical equipment was somewhat alarming at first. Although she kept working through her treatment, she experienced some additional fatigue, and the skin of the treated breast often felt sunburned and dry.

Karen's family and friends were as supportive and caring as she could have wished and her husband took on additional household tasks to allow her extra time to rest. However, intimacy between them dropped off for a while, arousing insecurities for Karen that she was no longer a vibrant, sexually attractive woman. After some frank and tearful discussion, Karen realized that her husband's withdrawal was based in a concern for her comfort and well-being. With that, the pressure to resume sexual activity felt lessened and they settled into more affectionate forms of intimacy, a time that intensified their bond and led to the eventual resumption of their regular patterns of lovemaking. As the completion of her treatment approached, Karen was looking forward to having these trips to the hospital behind her, but, somewhat unexpectedly, without the schedule of appointments and the care, attention, and concern of the medical staff, she felt somewhat unmoored. Although she would have regular follow-up visits to monitor her condition, she felt strange when no longer taking an active role in fighting her cancer.

Karen was an avid reader and noticed how many self-help books related to cancer there were in the bookstores and her local library. Some were authoritative, written by doctors, and some were written by women who had cancer themselves. Some of the books were irreverent and upbeat in tone, and focused on how to maintain a positive body image and family and sexual relationships; some were more clinical in tone and packed with medical terminology and information. She read one focused on life beyond cancer and found it useful and encouraging. However, Karen craved some kind of personal connection with others who had been through what she had experienced. But she was busy, and admittedly somewhat hesitant to discuss her concerns in a group of people. She noted that several mainstream cancer support organizations such as The Wellness Community, Cancer Care, and American Cancer Society had online support communities where one could post one's own concerns and read the posts of others. This worked well for her, as she often found herself brooding later at night after the concerns of the day had faded. When she had trouble sleeping, spending some time online gave her some peace of mind. Soon she found that not only was it uplifting to connect with others in her situation but that sharing her own insights and encouraging others was empowering. This forum was a place where more personal issues, such as how to communicate with her husband about intimacy post-cancer and worries about her own daughters' health, could be explored with people who knew what she was going through.

Part of what had spurred her concern about her daughters' risk for also developing breast cancer was seeing an advertisement about genetic tests to determine if one carried a breast cancer mutation that could be passed on. Karen began thinking about other cases of cancer in her family—an aunt on her mother's side who also had breast cancer, a sister who had had skin cancer, and a great-aunt on her father's side who she seemed to remember may have had some kind of ovarian or gynecological cancer—and she worried there might be something genetic going on.

When she asked her physician about this at her next follow-up visit, she was referred to a **genetic counsellor** specializing in cancer. Karen found the genetic counsellor supportive and especially good at communicating the complexities of genes, mutations, and what types of information genetic testing could and could not provide. The counsellor took a detailed family history and created a diagram, called a pedigree. It depicted all of the relatives on both sides of her family and documented whether they were alive, and, if dead, what they had died of, and at what age. There were some details of distant relatives' health histories that were hard for her to remember, but telephone calls to her older sister and a still-living aunt filled in some of the details. The counsellor explained that, despite the multiple cases of cancer in Karen's family, cancer is a common disease and her family history did not appear to be indicative of a hereditary pattern. Because genetic testing is uninformative in cases like this, it was not recommended for her. This assessment was reassuring for Karen to hear, along with the fact that hereditary cancers represent a very small proportion of all cases of breast cancer. The counsellor explained further, however, that Karen's daughters, because they had a family history of breast cancer in a first-degree relative, had a risk twice that of women without a family history of cancer (Rosenbaum & Rosenbaum, 2005). Thus, they should continue to obtain screening mammography at recommended intervals and to have regular clinical breast exams by their physicians.

many women with breast cancer will be in the position of deciding between being treated with **mastectomy** vs **breast-conserving surgery** plus radiation. Being offered this type of choice is helpful in allowing patients to maximize the aspects of quality of life that are particularly important to them, such as body image concerns vs worry about being exposed to radiation. However, this latitude also brings with it the burden of making a decision during an already stressful time.

Patients often vary in the extent to which they desire to share their treatment-related decision making with their physicians. Some make their decisions on their own while others rely on their physician's best clinical recommendation, so this process must be negotiated skilfully by clinicians (Adler & Page, 2008). Several American states mandate that women diagnosed with breast cancer who are medically eligible for them be informed of breast-conserving options in addition to mastectomy. These mandates arose in reaction to a history of surgical treatment for breast cancer that was extensive in its degree of breast tissue removal. This radical surgical approach was in keeping with a now-outdated notion of cancer's spread and a treatment focus that was primarily on survival per se rather than on the quality of that survival. Breast cancer activists and individuals within the medical community equally were important in bringing about these changes, both in the revised standards of medical care and in legal actions (Lerner, 2001).

Men diagnosed with prostate cancer may be offered a similar type of decision between having their tumour surgically removed or treated with radiation and "active surveillance" or watchful waiting to detect signs that a cancer is aggressive or has started to progress. This is because most prostate cancers are not life-threatening and evidence suggests that survival time is similar for men who are treated with either radical prostatectomy or active surveillance (Wilt et al., 2012). Deciding between treatment or watchful waiting is made more arduous by the fact that the side effects of prostate cancer treatment, including impotence and urinary incontinence, are threatening to quality of life, and some men may consider these quite problematic. However, taking no action against a tumour may also be anxiety-promoting and risky.

As described earlier, the array of treatments for cancer, including surgery, radiation therapy, chemotherapy, hormone therapy, and bone-marrow transplant, bring side effects that often are debilitating. These include loss of function, disfiguration, **lymphedema**, fatigue, nausea, vomiting, hair loss, skin burns or irritation, mouth sores, neuropathy, and even "chemo brain," the awareness that one's thinking is no longer sharp. These side effects result in diminished body image and self-esteem; depression and anxiety; disruptions in family, marital, and social relationships; and occupational and financial consequences. The side effects or ramifications of cancer treatment may last months or even years so that ongoing support is essential. Even the end of treatment may present a difficult adjustment for patients, as it brings about a change in routines, the withdrawal of frequent contact with medical personnel, and a halt to a sense of actively engaging with the disease.

eireann/© 123RF.com

Hair loss can be a consequence of chemotherapy.

Fortunately, now more than ever, a wealth of psychosocial resources are available for cancer patients through various social service and charitable organizations. These resources assist in meeting the informational, emotional, social, and practical needs that arise during the various stages of cancer diagnosis, treatment, and recovery. They include information on cancer-related treatments, peer support, counselling/psychotherapy, pharmacological management of mental symptoms, medical supplies, transportation, family and caregiver support, assistance with activities of daily living, legal services, cognitive and educational services, financial and insurance advice, benefits counselling, and financial assistance (Adler & Page, 2008).

Among the types of treatments that have been subjected to empirical evaluation, a major theoretical orientation has been the cognitive behavioural approach (Moyer, Sohl, Knapp-Oliver, & Schneider, 2009), which focuses on recognizing and altering problematic thoughts and behaviours and on reducing negative emotions related to cancer. An example of this type of treatment involved developing effective problem-solving skills and identifying and challenging maladaptive thoughts; learning relaxation techniques; and using resources such as family and friends and pleasurable activities to cope (Edelman & Kidman, 1999). Supportive-expressive group therapy focuses on expressing emotions, generating social support among group members, and exploring existential concerns like the fear of dying (Classen et al., 2008). Another type of well-researched treatment is education, which focuses on increasing knowledge and reducing uncertainty by providing information on topics such as treatment options, side effects, and psychosocial challenges.

One popular type of coping assistance is provided in the form of support groups. These may be offered through organizations such as Cancer Care, The Wellness Community, or through the hospitals where medical treatment occurs. These may be offered in person or online, and may be led by professionals such as nurses, social workers, or clinical psychologists, or by cancer survivors or "peers." These groups may be comprised of members with various types or stages of cancers, or may be restricted to those with a particular cancer, gender, age, or stage of disease or treatment. Opinion varies regarding the extent to which insisting on commonalities among support group members is important or not. One reason why this may be important is that group members often engage in social comparison, a process whereby they contrast their own condition, abilities, qualities, etc. to those of similar others. Often, cancer patients selectively use downward social comparison (comparing oneself to those who are doing less well) and upward social comparison (comparing oneself to those who are doing better). Women being treated for breast cancer were observed to use downward social comparison spontaneously and frequently (Wood, Taylor, & Lichtman, 1985). This strategy is presumed to be a means of coping and self-enhancement when under threat. This suggestion was borne out by the fact that downward social comparison was used more frequently by women who were closer in time to their surgery and presumably experiencing more threat. However, in some instances, downward social comparisons to similar others who were physically much worse proved to be frightening and sobering. In a review of the ways in which individuals in threatening situations satisfy their need to be with others and gain information, cancer patients were found to seek contact with individuals they perceive as more fortunate (Taylor & Lobel, 1989). Thus, peer discussion groups may be problematic when they expose cancer patients to others doing poorly psychologically or physically.

Another type of intervention useful for many cancer patients is physical activity, including aerobic exercise and resistance training. Such training can actually reduce fatigue and improve mood (Brown et al., 2011; Puetz & Herring, 2012). In previous years, cancer patients experiencing fatigue were encouraged to rest, take things easy, and refrain from exerting themselves. However, this strategy is thought to lead to a vicious cycle that promotes deconditioning and further fatigue. Research indicates that even patients currently undergoing chemotherapy can benefit physically and psychologically from exercise training. Similarly, breast cancer patients were once discouraged from using the arm on their treated side to lift heavy objects like groceries or grandchildren. This advice was intended to prevent lymphedema, irreversible damage to the lymphatic system that may have already been weakened by surgery and radiation. However, research now indicates that weight training is safe for women with breast cancer who have or are at risk for lymphedema and decreases the symptoms or incidence of lymphedema (Ahmed, Thomas, Yee, & Schmitz, 2006). Interventions for terminally ill cancer patients aim not only to manage psychological distress, but also to promote coping with the **end of life** and fostering a good death by focusing on spiritual well-being and finding meaning in one's life. One such activity used to do this is a short-term life review (Ando, Morita, Akechi, & Okamoto, 2010). This involves bringing to mind and sharing the important events and memories from one's life during an interview with a therapist. Patients respond to questions such as "What was the proudest moment in your life?" and then review their recorded statements with a therapist who has compiled them, along with relevant images, into an album, to develop a sense of continuity and coherence in these memories. Meaning-centred psychotherapy (van der Spek et al., 2014) is a new therapy based on psychiatrist Viktor Frankl's ideas forged from his experience as a concentration camp inmate and outlined in his book, *Man's Search for Meaning*. Such programs may be particularly valuable for advanced-stage cancer patients, for whom more spiritually oriented concerns may be focal, and feelings of hopelessness, despair, and even a desire for hastened death can prevail.

For students interested in specializing in working psychotherapeutically with cancer patients it is important, in addition to appropriate psychotherapy training, to become knowledgeable about the medical aspects of cancer (Watson & Kissane, 2011). Such professionals must often communicate with medical personnel to be aware of the disease, prognostic, and treatment context affecting their patients. Most importantly, such professionals must manage their own emotional responses to this potentially demanding work. The supportive care of cancer patients involves dealing with highly charged psychological, physical, relationship, and existential issues.

Future Directions

Both medical and psychosocial treatment for cancer is likely to become more individualized with the emergence of personalized medicine and more emphasis on screening and targeting of appropriate psychological services. Future research investigating psychosocial interventions for cancer patients will likely focus on understanding the role of particular patient characteristics (e.g., personality traits, mental and physical quality of life, social environment, and self-efficacy) that moderate their effects (Tamagawa, Garland, Vaska, & Carlson, 2012) and the mechanisms of action as well as the active ingredients of treatment that are most effective in improving quality of life (Moyer et al., 2012; Stanton, Luecken, Mackinnon, & Thompson,

2012). Enthusiasm regarding e-Health interventions (which include those delivered via the Internet, email, mobile phone text or applications, interactive voice response, automated and electronic programs, CD-ROMs, and computer-tailored print) for cancer prevention and control will need to be matched by research on their feasibility and effective translation to real-life settings (Sanchez et al., 2013).

Summary

"Cancer" is the term used for a number of diseases. Cancerous tumours result when genes that regulate cell division have damaged DNA, leading to uncontrolled cell proliferation. Mortality rates for some cancers are decreasing. Treatment for cancer includes surgery, radiation therapy, chemotherapy, hormonal therapy, and bone marrow transplant.

Risk for cancer involves the interaction of biological, environmental, behavioural, and demographic factors. Specific factors include genetic susceptibility, age, sex, exposure to carcinogens, infections, tobacco use, high alcohol consumption, a diet low in fruits and vegetables, lack of exercise, and obesity. The evidence linking psychosocial factors to cancer initiation has been ambiguous. The evidence linking psychosocial factors such as depression, stressful life events, and social isolation to cancer progression and mortality is somewhat stronger. Potential mechanisms include behavioural factors, such as adherence to treatment, and physiological factors, such as elevated stress hormones and immunosuppression. Primary prevention measures, like avoiding smoking, can reduce but not entirely eliminate the risk of developing cancer. Cancer screening, including mammography, is a secondary prevention measure designed to detect cancer at an early stage, before symptoms have developed. Screening has both benefits and harms.

Cancer diagnosis and treatment bring changes in interpersonal relationships and social roles, physical effects, and uncertainty and stress. Targeting coping strategies appropriately, appraising threats as challenges, maintaining optimism, and benefiting from interpersonal support are related to psychological adjustment and well-being. Screening for distress is not yet routine in oncology care and needs to be linked to follow-up psychosocial care services. Treatment decision making, side effects, and survivorship pose burdens that often require assistance. Resources such as information, peer support, counselling/psychotherapy, pharmacological agents, medical supplies, transportation, family and caregiver support, and practical, legal, educational, and financial assistance are readily available to cancer patients through social service and charitable organizations.

Critical Thought Questions

1. As screening has both benefits and harms, how do we decide whether the general population should use a screening test, such as mammography?
2. For an individual with a family history indicating a high likelihood of a hereditary cancer, what are the potential advantages and disadvantages of pursuing a genetic test to determine if he or she carries a cancer-related mutation?
3. Is it appropriate to patent a gene?

Recommended Reading

Love, S. (2010). *Dr. Susan Love's breast book* (5th ed.). South Boston, MA.: Da Capo Press.

Miller, S.M., Bowen, D.J., Croyle, R.T., & Rowland, J.H. (2009). *Handbook of cancer control and behavioral science: A resource for researchers, practitioners, and policymakers.* Washington, DC: American Psychological Association.

Mukherjee, S. (2011). *The emperor of all maladies: A biography of cancer.* New York, NY: Scribner.

Rosenbaum, E.H., & Rosenbaum, I. (2005). *Everyone's guide to cancer supportive care: A comprehensive handbook for patients and their families.* Kansas City: Andrews McMeel.

Watson, M., & Kissane, D. (Eds.). (2011). *Handbook of psychotherapy in cancer care.* Hoboken, NJ: John Wiley & Sons.

PART III
Special Populations

13 Pediatric Psychology

Christine T. Chambers
Perri R. Tutelman

Learning Objectives

In this chapter, you will:

- Learn how children and their families cope with a diagnosis of a chronic medical condition.

- Discover the role of pediatric psychologists in helping children and their families adhere to pediatric treatment regimens and cope with painful medical procedures.

- Understand common parenting challenges with young children, including sleeping, feeding, and toileting issues, and the role of pediatric psychology in addressing these issues.

- Become familiar with the role of technology in pediatric psychology, including the use of e-Health tools and social media.

- Consider future directions in the field of pediatric psychology, including the unique needs of children with medical conditions transitioning to adult care, and the implementation of research evidence into practice and policy.

What Is Pediatric Psychology?

Joshua was only six years old when he was diagnosed with acute lymphoblastic leukemia, a form of blood cancer. Joshua was immediately admitted to the hospital and, as part of his treatment, was required to undergo several painful procedures per day ranging from surgery, to lumbar punctures, to needle pokes. Over time, Joshua became so fearful of needles that he would scream and flail his arms and legs in protest, making procedures long and distressing. Joshua's parents struggled with balancing life with their other children at home and supporting Joshua in the hospital, and worried what Joshua's uncertain future would mean for him and for their family. Unfortunately, these challenges are not specific to Joshua's family, but reflect the unique needs of children with chronic medical conditions and their families: a focus of the field of pediatric psychology.

Up to 25 per cent of children and adolescents in North America have a diagnosed chronic illness or potentially life-limiting medical condition, such as asthma, diabetes, or cancer (Bethell et al., 2011; Butler-Jones, 2009). Figure 13.1 shows the percentages of children reported to have various common health conditions. With advances in modern medicine, a range of available medical treatments now can reduce condition-related symptoms and improve quality of life. These medical treatments, however, are often complex and multi-faceted in nature, including medications, dietary restrictions, and physical therapy. Further, as a result of improvements in medical treatments, children now live longer or survive what would previously have been life-threatening illnesses associated with high mortality. For example, in the case of pediatric acute lymphoblastic leukemia, the most common cancer diagnosed in children, survival rates have improved dramatically, from 70 per cent in the 1980s to 90 per cent in recent years (Siegel, Miller, & Jemal, 2016). Children with medical conditions and their families often experience psychological effects associated with their conditions and multiple interactions with the health-care system, and they can also experience cognitive and psychological effects as a direct result of their treatments (e.g., radiation, chemotherapy) (Cheung & Krull, 2015; Padovani, André, Constine & Muracciole, 2012). This means that millions of children and adolescents in North America now live with chronic illnesses and medical conditions that can contribute to significant emotional and behavioural difficulties and negatively impact treatment adherence and child and family adjustment. Furthermore, it has been shown that chronic medical conditions in childhood can be associated with psychological issues in adulthood (Pless, Power, & Peckham, 1993). Importantly, disparities in a range of health outcomes (both physical and psychological) have been documented in children belonging to minority groups, including disproportionate rates of disease incidence, treatment adherence and response, and differences in risk factors (Lescano, Koinis-Mitchell, & McQuaid, 2016). Chapter 15 provides an in-depth discussion of health disparities based on culture.

The field of **pediatric psychology** was developed to address the needs of patients in pediatric settings and brings together several areas within psychology, including health, clinical, and developmental psychology. The term "pediatric psychology" was first coined in 1967 by Logan Wright in the article "The pediatric psychologist: A role model," and was defined as "dealing primarily with children in a medical setting which is non-psychiatric in nature" (Wright, 1967). Today, the field of pediatric psychology is acknowledged as a specialized field within health psychology that integrates both scientific research and clinical practice to address the psychological aspects of children's medical conditions and the promotion of health behaviours in children and their families.

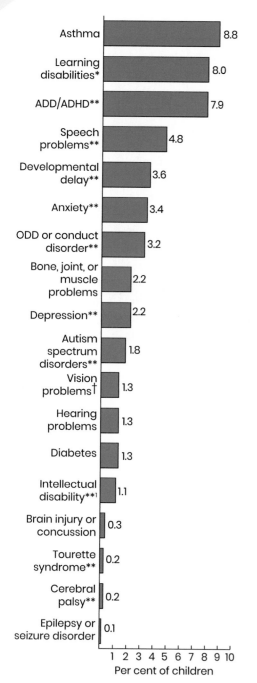

FIGURE 13.1   Percentage of children with reported chronic conditions by health condition.

*Children aged 3–17 years only
**Children aged 2–17 years only
†Includes only problems that cannot be corrected with glasses or contact lenses.
[1]Previously labelled as intellectual disability/mental retardation when the prevalence data was captured.

Source: U.S. Department of Health and Human Services. (2014). *The health and well-being of children: A portrait of states and the nation, 2011–2012.* Rockville, MD: Author.

For example, pediatric psychologists might be called upon to help children with diabetes manage their treatment regimen, help children with cancer and their families cope with their diagnosis, or teach children psychological strategies to deal with painful medical procedures.

The professional face for the field of pediatric psychology is the Society of Pediatric Psychology (SPP), which is Division 54 of the American Psychological Association (APA) (see www.apadivisions.org/division-54/index.aspx). The Society aims to promote the health and psychological well-being of children, youth, and their families through science and an evidence-based approach to practice, education, training, advocacy, and consultation. SPP publishes two journals: the *Journal of Pediatric Psychology (JPP)* and *Clinical Practice in Pediatric Psychology (CPPP).* Founded in 1967, *JPP* primarily publishes empirical research articles that examine theory and intervention in pediatric psychology. *CPPP* was established in 2013 as a peer-reviewed forum to publish research articles, reviews, and commentaries focused on professional and clinically applied issues in the field. However, research studies in pediatric psychology are published in a broad range of journals, including general psychological and medical journals. The role of psychological factors in children's health is generally recognized as important by all medical specialty and subspecialty groups.

Despite the varied nature of health conditions in children, pediatric psychologists deal with a number of cross-cutting themes that are described throughout this chapter. These include **coping** with chronic medical conditions, adherence to pediatric treatment regimens, coping with medical procedures, pediatric **chronic pain**, and pediatric **palliative care**. Furthermore, pediatric psychologists have expertise in dealing with health issues unique to childhood that often present as significant parenting challenges, including sleeping, feeding, and toileting problems. The impact of pediatric chronic medical conditions on parents and siblings is also addressed by pediatric psychologists. Further, there are many exciting future directions in pediatric psychology, including innovative models of delivery of health services, such as use of electronic and mobile health interventions, and addressing the needs of youth with medical conditions transitioning from pediatric to adult care. Each of these topics is described in this chapter.

Coping with Chronic Medical Conditions

How a child copes with a chronic medical condition is related to patient outcomes and can play an important role in health behaviour and health-care utilization in children (Feeney, 2000). The study of coping with chronic medical conditions is challenging in pediatrics as a result of the unique developmental and familial contexts in which children with medical conditions live and are dependent (Compas, Jaser, Dunn, & Rodriguez, 2012). Diagnosis of a chronic medical condition can cause significant stress for the whole family and affect children's functioning across multiple domains and points in time. Typically, a chronic medical condition begins with a sudden onset of medical symptoms (e.g., fatigue, pain, fever), which prompts the family to seek initial medical consultation and care. In most cases, this initial phase concludes with diagnosis of a specific medical condition and identification and implementation of an appropriate medical management plan. However, for some children and their families, a clear medical diagnosis and accompanying management plan may not always be immediate or evident, as in the case of children experiencing some forms of chronic pain, which is discussed further below. This uncertainty can create considerable additional stress for the child and family. Provided an appropriate diagnosis and management plan are identified, the child and family enter a longer-term phase where they gradually adjust to the impact of the medical condition and management on their day-to-day lives. Further, many children with chronic medical conditions and their families

Journal of Pediatric Psychology.

must learn to deal with an uncertain course associated with their condition. For example, many medical conditions experienced by children, such as inflammatory bowel disease and arthritis, are associated with flares or crises that may be unpredictable.

Children with chronic medical conditions face a range of stressors associated with their conditions and management. These stressors are in addition to the typical stressors associated with normal development (e.g., challenges with peer relationships, school transitions) experienced by all children (Olson, Johansen, Powers, Pope, & Klein, 1993). As an example, Rodriguez et al. (2012) surveyed children with cancer and their parents regarding perceptions of stressors associated with childhood cancer. The three most common areas of stressors identified by children included (1) interruptions in daily role functioning (e.g., missing school days, falling behind in school work, not being able to do the things they used to do); (2) physical effects associated with treatment (e.g., feeling sick or nauseous from treatments, pain from medical procedures); and (3) uncertainty about the cancer (e.g., concerns about their future health or about length of life). The study revealed that children reported interruptions in their daily role functioning (i.e., interruptions in their school and social activities) as the most frequently experienced stressor, and as more stressful than uncertainty about disease/chance for survival, indicating that it is the disruption of typical activities and tasks associated with childhood, rather than the specific limitations imposed by a medical condition itself, that is most problematic for children. Parents, on the other hand, reported cancer caregiving (e.g., effects of treatment, not knowing if child's cancer will get better) as most stressful (Rodriguez et al., 2012). They also reported high levels of stress associated with interruptions in daily role functioning (e.g., paying bills, having less time for other children) and cancer communication (e.g., talking with their child or others about cancer). Parents who expressed high levels of stress in the areas of cancer caregiving and cancer communication were more likely to report post-traumatic stress symptoms as a result of their child's condition.

The extent to which a stressor is perceived as stressful depends on a number of internal and external factors associated with the child, parent, and the specific medical condition. Not all coping responses are equally effective. Considerable attention has been given in the theoretical and empirical literature to conceptualizations of children's coping with medical conditions and medical stressors (for reviews, see Compas et al., 2012; Rudolph, Dennig, & Weisz, 1995; Schmidt, Peterson, & Bullinger, 2003; Thompson & Gustafson, 1996). The majority of this work has generally examined the fit between appraisal of medically related stressful events and corresponding coping responses. A variety of developmental and familial factors that can affect how a child copes, and how a child generally approaches a stressful event, are typically addressed in these models. Coping with medical conditions in children is intertwined with development. As children get older, coping approaches change and become more sophisticated. For example, use of behavioural strategies (e.g., **distraction**) is more common in early childhood, and evolves into more complex cognitive strategies (e.g., cognitive restructuring) in later childhood. It is important to note that medical conditions differ considerably in their level of associated symptoms and challenges across conditions (e.g., treatment regimens, life expectancy) and these variables are typically considered in theoretical conceptualizations of children's coping with medical conditions (Thompson & Gustafson, 1996).

Several specific theoretical models to guide the understanding and study of how children can and do cope in the context of medical conditions have been put forward in the literature, including Wallander and Varni's disability-stress-coping model of adjustment (Wallander & Varni, 1992) and Thompson's stress and coping model of adjustment (Thompson, Gustafson, Hamlett, & Spock, 1992). A recent review of coping with chronic illness in childhood and adolescence was published by Compas and colleagues (2012). They present a control-based model of coping that includes primary control or active coping (i.e., efforts to act on the source of stress or one's emotions), secondary control or accommodative coping (i.e., efforts to adapt to the source of stress), and disengagement or passive coping (i.e., efforts to avoid or deny the stressor). Research has shown that children with a variety of medical conditions, including diabetes, chronic pain, and cancer, who engage in secondary control coping, generally adjust and cope better than children who use disengagement coping (Compas et al., 2012). While there are many common elements

In Focus

Relaxation Script for Children

You are lying down on your back.... Start to take slow, deep breaths into your belly. Make your belly bigger as you breathe in, and let it flatten down as you breathe out. [Perhaps the child wants to place a small stuffed animal on his or her belly.] Don't worry about your breathing. Just let it happen. You can feel your whole body begin to relax with each breath...breathing out stress and worry...breathing in relaxation and calm. Centring yourself...inwardly smile. Deep breathing, relaxing...now imagine a warm ball of light in your belly. Every time you take a breath in, the warm ball of light climbs up the front of your body, becoming bigger, expanding. It is now in your chest, making it feel warm and light...with another inhalation, it travels up into your throat and neck...each time you breathe in, the warm ball of light grows bigger...it is filling you....

across the various theoretical models of children's coping with medical conditions that have been proposed, the lack of a universal conceptual model for guiding research has been a challenge for those conducting work in this area.

An additional challenge in the study of children's coping with medical conditions is the difficulty associated with appropriate assessment (Blount et al., 2008). Measures of stress and coping in children typically require them to rate the extent to which they find various aspects of their medical condition stressful (as done in the study by Rodriguez et al. [2012]) and the degree to which they engage in a variety of coping strategies, such as problem-solving, distraction, social support, and catastrophizing. Most of what we know about the assessment of children's medical stress and coping is in the area of children's pain (e.g., the Pain Coping Questionnaire) (Reid, Gilbert, & McGrath, 1998). The best-known coping questionnaire that has been used across various childhood medical conditions and in children ranging in age from 7 to 16 years is the Kidcope (Spirito, Stark, & Williams, 1988). Similar to other coping measures, children rate commonly used coping strategies (e.g., problem-solving, distracting), but also the degree of anxiety, unhappiness, and anger experienced in dealing with stressful situations related to their condition. Children's questionnaire responses can be analyzed separately by specific sub-scale or in two categories of coping: positive/approach or negative/avoidance. The review by Blount et al. (2008) was helpful in identifying coping and stress measures that can be used both in research and in clinical practice with children with medical conditions. This paper has also made important contributions to the field by highlighting the importance of improving assessment of children's coping in order to advance the field and to test the efficacy of interventions aimed to improve children's coping.

The development and evaluation of interventions to improve children's abilities to cope with the range of stressors they may experience as a result of their medical condition have been a focus in pediatric psychology for a long time. Progress in the area has been hindered in part by the challenging measurement issues and lack of a universal theoretical model. Regardless, psychological interventions to improve coping have taken many forms, ranging from simple provision of written materials to more intensive individual or group interventions (for example, see an outline of a group-based intervention in Table 13.1).

Your face is now filled with this warm light and your jaw loosens...let your mouth open slightly....The ball of light reaches the top of your head...relaxing your scalp...it travels with each inward breath down the back of your head to your spine...warming and relaxing your entire back...softening each bone in your back. The ball of light rolls slowly down both arms...then to your hands...making them heavy and warm....This warm flow slowly moves into each of your legs...travelling to your knees...ankles...softly on to your feet...warming you...each toe and bone in your foot is relaxed...softened. This is everywhere. Keep breathing and let all your tension and worry be gone...quiet...melted away. Go back to any area that has any tightness and bring the warm ball of healing light back to it. Take your time. You are warm, relaxed, happy, and safe. Your body is heavy and comfortable...filled with relaxation.

TABLE 13.1 | Overview of a Six-Week Cognitive Behavioural Treatment Program for Children with Recurrent Abdominal Pain and their Parents.

	Sessions for Parents	Sessions for Children
Week 1	How Does Pain Work?	How Does Pain Work?
Week 2	Behaviour and Pain	Relaxation
Week 3	Relaxation	Imagery, Distraction, and Pain
Week 4	Thoughts, Feelings, and Pain	Thoughts, Feelings, and Pain
Week 5	Daily Living	Thoughts, Feelings, and Pain (continued)
Week 6	Review and Relapse Prevention	Review and Relapse Prevention

Source: Author-created based on Noel, M., Petter, M., Parker, J.A., & Chambers, C.T. (2012). Cognitive Behavioural Therapy for pediatric chronic pain: The problem, research, and practice. *Journal of Cognitive Psychotherapy, 26,* 143–156.

These psychological interventions are often referred to as psycho-educational in nature because they typically include basic information about disease management in addition to providing instruction in specific cognitive behavioural coping skills (e.g., relaxation, problem-solving, communication skills) to address psychosocial aspects of living with a chronic medical condition. (The accompanying In Focus box provides a sample relaxation script.) The strongest research support is for the efficacy of psycho-educational interventions that incorporate cognitive behavioural techniques in improving a range of outcomes, including self-efficacy, self-management of disease, family functioning, general psychosocial well-being, reduced isolation, social competence, knowledge, and hope (Barlow & Ellard, 2004). Furthermore, these interventions can produce improvements in a number of disease-specific outcomes for various medical conditions, including reduced pain (for headache), improved pulmonary function (for asthma), and improved metabolic control (for diabetes) in the short and long terms (Beale, 2006).

Adherence to Pediatric Treatment Regimens

Chapter 4 provides a broad discussion of adherence with medical treatments. In this section, the focus is on issues particular to children.

Most parents struggle to get their children to complete simple tasks of daily living like brushing teeth or making their beds. Getting children to adhere to treatment regimens can seem overwhelming, yet there are potentially life-threatening outcomes associated with failure to comply (Modi et al., 2012). High rates of non-adherence to treatment have been reported across numerous pediatric conditions (Kahana, Drotar, & Frazier, 2008) with an estimated overall non-adherence rate of 50 per cent for pediatric patients across various medical conditions (Modi et al., 2012). Similar to adult outcomes, non-adherence is known to be associated with increased morbidity, use of the health system, and mortality (Modi et al., 2012).

Numerous variables have been associated with adherence to treatment in children (Modi et al., 2012). These include child age, child emotional development, family factors, and disease- and treatment-specific considerations. Adolescents are at particularly high risk for non-adherence to prescribed medical regimens, potentially due to less parental involvement and other developmental aspects of adolescence. Family relationships and parental beliefs about medical conditions and treatments demonstrate consistent relationships with treatment adherence (Drotar & Bonner, 2009). Across medical conditions, greater levels of both child and parental involvement in condition management have been associated with improved adherence and better outcomes. More complex treatment regimens generally are associated with lower levels of adherence then simpler regimens (Modi et al., 2012). Identification of factors associated with treatment adherence is important in enhancing treatments to improve adherence.

A variety of creative interventions have been developed to improve adherence. Reinforcement-based interventions, such as the use of simple sticker charts or other forms of positive reinforcement, can be very powerful for children (Luersen et al., 2012). Figure 13.2 shows a sample rewards chart used with children. A range of additional behaviour-management techniques have also been applied with children, including monitoring, goal setting, contingency contracting, problem solving, and linking medication with established routines (La Greca & Race Mackey, 2009). More complex regimens typically require more intensive education and intervention, such as instruction in social support and family-based problem solving (La Greca & Race Mackey, 2009). Education efforts alone generally are insufficient to promote adherence; adding a behavioural-management component enhances adherence-related outcomes (Dean, Walters, & Hall, 2010; Kahana et al., 2008). Multi-component interventions, which typically incorporate some variety of social skills training or family therapy, are also effective (Kahana et al., 2008). Successful interventions usually target adherence to a narrow age range, include the family, and improve access to care (Modi et al., 2012). More customized interventions are needed to target adherence in children who have established poor adherence and children who are at different developmental stages.

Addressing barriers to adherence to treatment regimens is important. For example, many parents of children struggle with basic issues related to condition management. A simple problem such as an inability to swallow pills may cause considerable stress for families. Up to 20 per cent of children have difficulty swallowing pills (Meltzer, Welch, & Ostrom, 2006), and it is reasonable to assume that these difficulties could lead to some degree of avoidance and/or inappropriate medication use and health-care use. Many parents receive extensive coaching from health professionals and pharmacists in how to "hide" medication (e.g., in foods) rather than in the best methods for teaching their children how to swallow pills. Pill-swallowing is an excellent example of application of a children's health intervention based on basic behavioural principles (e.g., modelling, shaping, and reinforcement) (see In Practice box). Although there have been no large-scale randomized trials, numerous published case studies

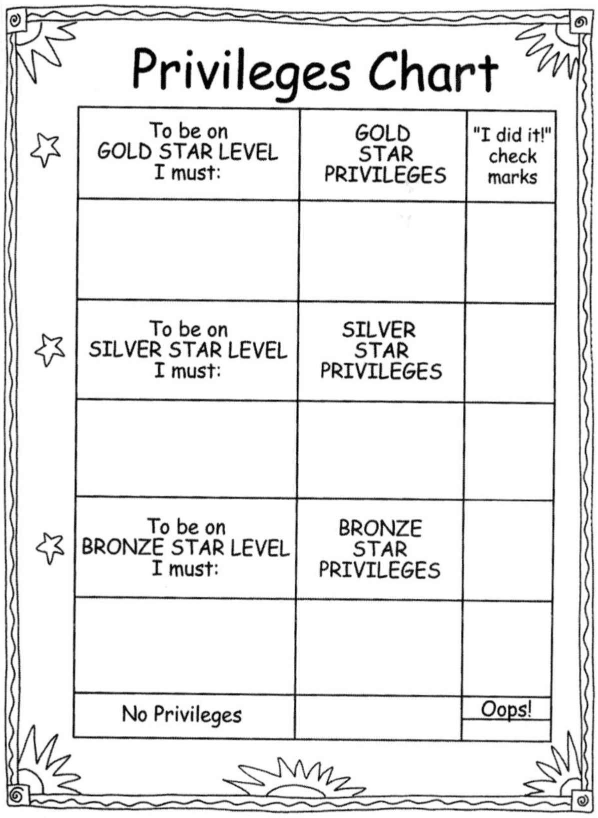
Privileges Chart

To be on GOLD STAR LEVEL I must:	GOLD STAR PRIVILEGES	"I did it!" check marks
To be on SILVER STAR LEVEL I must:	SILVER STAR PRIVILEGES	
To be on BRONZE STAR LEVEL I must:	BRONZE STAR PRIVILEGES	
No Privileges		Oops!

FIGURE 13.2 Sample reward chart commonly used with children as positive reinforcement.

Source: *Rewards for Kids: Ready to Use Charts and Activities for Positing Parenting*, Virginia Shiller PhD. APA Press 2003, p. 127.

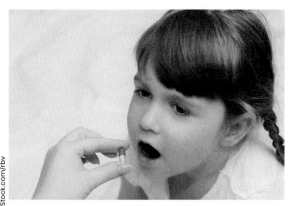

One area of children's health that is effectively managed with behavioural intervention by a pediatric psychologist is pill-swallowing.

and single case designs have revealed success rates in the range of 75 to 90 per cent with excellent maintenance at three months and longer in children with a variety of health issues (e.g., cancer, autism, attention deficit hyperactivity disorder) (Beck, Cataldo, Slifer, Pulbrook, & Ghuman, 2005; Blount, Dahlquist, Baer, & Wuori, 1984; Cruz-Arrieta, 2008; Funk, Mullins, & Olson, 1984; Ghuman, Cataldo, Beck, & Slifer, 2004; Reitman & Passeri, 2008; Walco, 1986). Research has shown that pill-swallowing training improved adherence to antiretroviral medication treatment in pediatric patients with HIV/AIDS (Garvie, Lensing, & Rai, 2007). Pill-swallowing is just one example of the unique contributions that pediatric psychologists can make in applying psychological principles and interventions to address health issues in children.

Coping with Medical Procedures

Needle procedures, such as immunizations and **venepuncture**, and the pain associated with such procedures are frequently cited as among the most feared experiences of children, including healthy children and children with chronic medical conditions (Broome, Bates, Lillis, & McGahee, 1990). These fears tend to persist over time and can cause considerable distress not only for the child, but also for his or her parents, siblings, and any health professionals working with the child. Children with significant fears towards medical procedures are likely to avoid seeking appropriate health care in the future (Taddio et al., 2009). It is estimated that one in 10 adults avoids medical procedures, such as immunization, due to severe needle-related fears or phobias (Taddio et al., 2009).

Painful medical procedures unfortunately are commonplace even for healthy children, who now undergo up to as many as 20 routine immunizations by age five. Preterm infants who spend time in the neonatal intensive care unit (NICU) are at particular risk of experiencing repeated painful medical procedures (Craig, Whitfield, Grunau, Linton, & Hadjistavropoulos, 1993; Stevens, Johnston, Petryshen, & Taddio, 1996). Unfortunately, the majority of children undergoing painful medical procedures receive no pain-relieving interventions. For example, a recent survey of **procedural pain** management practices at eight children's hospitals across Canada showed that 80 per cent of hospitalized children experienced at least one painful procedure over the previous 24 hours (the average was six procedures per child) and more than two-thirds of these procedures had *no* documented pain management intervention (either pharmacological, psychological, or physical) (Stevens et al., 2011). In the past it was believed by many health professionals that young infants did not feel pain and as a result they were often denied appropriate pain management. This situation is troubling because poorly managed painful procedures early in childhood have been shown to be related to later increased pain sensitivity (Grunau, Whitfield, Petrie, & Fryer, 1994; Porter, Grunau, & Anand, 1999; Taddio, Goldbach, Ipp, Stevens, & Koren, 1995; Taddio, Katz, Ilersich, & Koren, 1997). A recent study showed that, after controlling for a range of clinical factors, the frequency of painful medical procedures was related to impaired brain development in a sample of preterm infants hospitalized in the NICU (Brummelte et al., 2012).

In Practice

Practice in Pill-Swallowing

Case Description

Mark is a seven-year-old boy recently diagnosed with ulcerative colitis by the gastroenterology clinic at the local pediatric health centre. The medical team recommends an oral medication, and these can sometimes be very large tablets that need to be taken two to four times per day. The family panics. As the parents try to process the impact of this significant diagnosis on their child's health and future, they become anxious as they realize that Mark has never had to swallow a pill before. The clinic sends the family home with some oral medication and a pill-swallowing cup, which is purported to be able to help individuals learn how to swallow pills without stress. The family spends a nerve-wracking evening trying to help Mark learn to swallow pills. They try using the cup but with no luck. They try to encourage him to swallow the pills, but by this time Mark and his parents are agitated and stressed. "Did you swallow it?" "No, it's still on his tongue." "Try again." "Try!" "Yes you can. It's important." "It's going to help your belly." The pill is dissolving in his mouth. Mark cries and storms off, indicating that he will never be able to swallow pills. The parents wonder how they can ever make this happen. How will the babysitter or grandparents manage? They place an exasperated call to the gastronterology clinic, and a referral to the pediatric psychology service for assistance with pill-swallowing is made.

Treatment Description

The psychological intervention used for pill-swallowing is based on principles of behaviour therapy, primarily "shaping," in which successive approximations to the desired behaviour are rewarded. Children are initially taught to swallow very small cake decorations (e.g., chocolate sprinkles) and once this task is mastered, the child is offered larger and larger candies, and then placebo tablets and capsules of varying sizes. The hospital pharmacy and the local candy store are helpful resources for psychologists who need to create a pill-swallowing placebo kit. It is important that the psychologist always check with parents first regarding any potential allergies or concerns they might have about the use of different types of placebo pills/candies. Children are provided with praise and reinforcement (e.g., a sticker) for effort and eventual mastery of each step. Treatment can also include behavioural modelling, with the therapist demonstrating and the child trying in a game-like manner, and relaxation strategies (e.g., deep breathing). For children with disruptive or inattentive behaviours, basic behaviour management principles (e.g., ignoring, time-out) may need to be integrated into the session.

Source: Modified from Chambers (2012).

An impressive body of literature highlights the importance of family factors in children's responses to painful medical procedures (Birnie, Uman, & Chambers, 2013; Chambers, 2003). Numerous studies in the field have documented a strong relationship between certain parent behaviours (e.g., use of reassurance) and increased child pain and distress, while other behaviours (e.g., use of distraction, humour) have been associated with child coping when used by mothers, fathers, and health professionals (Blount et al., 1989; Blount et al., 1997; Chambers, Craig, & Bennett, 2002; Moon, Chambers, & McGrath, 2011). The counterintuitive relationship between adult reassurance and child pain and distress is one that has begun to receive considerable support in the literature. It has been suggested that parental reassurance likely serves as a signal to children that the parent is nervous or worried (McMurtry, Chambers, McGrath, & Asp, 2010; McMurtry, McGrath, Asp, & Chambers, 2007; McMurtry, McGrath, & Chambers, 2006). A study by McMurtry et al. (2010) involved a pairing of clinical and lab-based methodologies in children undergoing blood work to provide a detailed examination of the complexities of adult

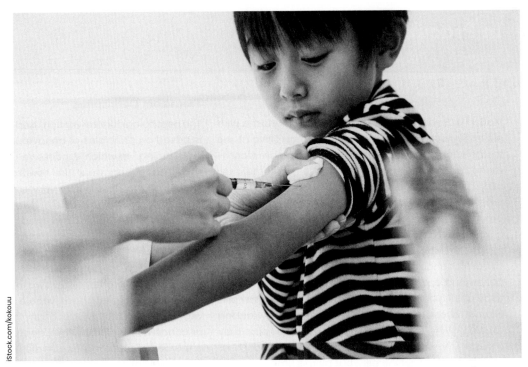

Medical interventions involving needles are often reported as children's most feared experiences.

reassurance during painful medical procedures. They solicited children's impressions of their parents' reassurance via asking children to rate the emotional context associated with clips of their own parents reassuring them during a blood draw. Children also rated parental reassurance in a series of videotaped vignette clips where parental facial expression, vocal tone, and verbal content were manipulated during children's painful procedures. Results supported that children do indeed perceive their parents as more fearful and less happy when they reassure, and that this was particularly the case for reassurance spoken in a rising vocal tone (indicative of uncertainty) (McMurtry et al., 2010).

Pain as a subjective experience can be challenging to assess in children due to communication problems or children too upset or distressed to report on their pain. Children above the age of five years are generally able to provide self-reports of their pain using validated self-report tools such as the Faces Pain Scale–Revised (FPS–R) (Figure 13.3) (Hicks, von Baeyer, Spafford, van Korlaar, & Goodenough, 2001). Children use these scales to point to the face that best shows how much hurt or pain they have. It is important that scales for pain assessment begin with a relatively neutral face, as is the case in the FPS–R. Research has shown that faces that begin with a smiling face instead of a neutral face can confound more general distress with pain and make pain self-report more challenging for children (Chambers & Craig, 1998; Chambers, Giesbrecht, Craig, Bennett, & Huntsman, 1999; Chambers, Hardial, Craig, Court, & Montgomery, 2005). When children are unable to provide self-reports of pain, pain can be assessed using a variety of validated behavioural measures that assess either broadband behaviours (e.g., flailing) or fine-grained facial movements (e.g., eye squeeze, nasolabial

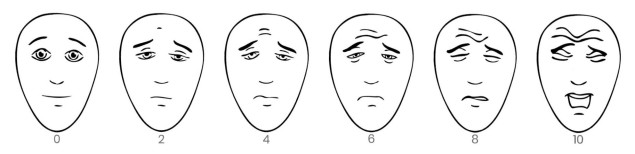

FIGURE 13.3 **Faces Pain Scale–Revised.**

Source: Faces Pain Scale – Revised, ©2001, International Association for the Study of Pain. http://www.iasp-pain.org/Education/Content.aspx?ItemNumber=1519

furrow) that quantify pain. Parents and health professionals can also be asked to provide an observer report of children's pain, although research has shown that these observer reports generally tend to underestimate children's pain (Chambers, Reid, Craig, McGrath, & Finley, 1998; Zhou, Roberts, & Horgan, 2008).

A variety of pharmacological, psychological, physical, and combined pain management strategies can significantly reduce procedure-related pain in children. This research evidence has been gathered in the form of randomized clinical trials and summarized in comprehensive meta-analyses and systematic reviews (e.g., for immunizations: Birnie et al., 2015; Shah et al., 2015; Pillai Riddell et al., 2015a, 2015b; Taddio et al., 2015b), and for painful procedures in general (Birnie et al., 2014; Uman et al., 2013; Uman, Chambers, McGrath, & Kisely, 2008). In the case of psychological interventions specifically, strong evidence supports the use of cognitive behavioural strategies for decreasing pain and distress associated with medical procedures (Powers & Rubenstein, 1999; Uman et al., 2013; Uman et al., 2008). These reviews conclude that the psychological interventions with the most support include distraction, **hypnosis**, and some combination of cognitive behavioural interventions (e.g., deep breathing combined with positive self-statements).

Despite the compelling evidence showing the efficacy of a variety of pain-relieving interventions in children, a significant gap looms between what is known in the research literature about pain management for procedures and what is happening for children and their families in the real world (Taddio et al., 2009). Barriers to proper pain management are present at many levels, including the level of the patient, primary caregiver, health-care provider, and the health-care system (Cohen & MacLaren, 2007; Craig, Lilley, & Gilbert, 1996). Incorporating information about evidence-based pain management in children in the case of immunization, for example, has been distilled into clinical practice guidelines directed towards health professionals (Taddio et al., 2015a). These guidelines have identified simple, cost-effective, evidence-based pain-relieving interventions for immunization pain management, which include breast-feeding (for infants), sweet-tasting solutions (i.e., sucrose, for infants), sitting position (vs lying down), use of topical anaesthetic creams (e.g., eutectic mixture of local anaesthetics; EMLA), use of parent-led distraction, coaching, and deep breathing by the child. The publication and dissemination of the clinical practice guideline has already supported changes at a global level; in 2015, the World Health Organization (WHO) issued a policy on the mitigation of pain, distress, and fear during vaccinations, which was developed on the basis of the clinical practice guideline recommendations (World Health Organization, 2015).

TABLE 13.2 | Behavioural Management Tips for Parents for Procedural Pain Management.

- Prepare yourself and stay calm.
- Prepare your child by using age-appropriate words and be honest; children five years old and up should be told about the procedure at least one day in advance.
- Distract your child using age-appropriate strategies, such as toys, books, or music or videos.
- Encourage your child to take slow, deep breaths, for example, with bubbles or pinwheels.
- Avoid words that focus on the pain or the procedures, such as "It'll be over soon" and "You'll be okay"; it's better to talk about things not related to the procedure.
- Use other age-appropriate pain-relieving interventions, such as breast-feeding or sucrose for infants, or topicalanaesthetic creams.
- After the procedure, praise your child for a job well done.

Source: Birnie, Boerner, & Chambers (2013), p. 113. By permission of Oxford University Press.

All national immunization programs are expected to implement the WHO's policy to reduce vaccination pain.

It is also important that parents have the opportunity to access important information about pain-relieving interventions directly, so they are in a position to advocate for and implement these strategies on behalf of their child (see Table 13.2). Parents have been the target of recent **knowledge translation** efforts aimed at communicating evidence-based strategies to reduce vaccination pain in their children. For example, a group of researchers partnered with *ParentsCanada* magazine to distill the major points of the 2015 vaccination pain practice guidelines into a brief, plain-language summary for parents. The resource was published in the August 2016 issue of *ParentsCanada* (see photo, p. 297).

Guidance from health professionals regarding how parents can best prepare and provide information to children about forthcoming medical procedures is also critical. It is generally recommended that children above the age of five years receive at least a five-day notice for procedures, although this will vary depending on the age and temperament of the child and the severity of the procedure (Jaaniste, Hayes, & von Baeyer, 2007). Jaaniste et al. (2007) provide a useful review and summary of how to best provide children with information about forthcoming medical procedures. They note the importance of including both sensory and procedural information, of giving advice on coping skills, and of informing the child of whether the procedure is going to be painful, in neutral language.

While many to most children experience some distress around medical procedures and can benefit from instructions in basic coping skills (e.g., deep breathing) that can be directed by parents, children with more severe needle phobias often require more in-depth therapeutic support from a pediatric psychologist. For these children, coping skills interventions to decrease procedural pain and distress are often folded into a more general psychological treatment protocol for specific phobia, which typically includes desensitization via exposure, contingency management, modelling, and self-control procedures.

NEEDLES **DON'T HAVE TO HURT**

Keep this timeline handy to make your child's vaccinations easy peasy

A FEW DAYS BEFORE THE NEEDLE	30-60 MINUTES BEFORE THE NEEDLE	RIGHT BEFORE, DURING AND AFTER THE NEEDLE

ALL AGES

> Stay calm and interact normally with your child.

> **Be honest.** Talk with your children about strategies to manage their pain and distress.

> Ask children over 10 if they want **you to be there for the needle.**

> Apply **numbing creams or patches** (topical anesthetics such as EMLA™, AMETOP™, and Maxilene™), available for purchase from pharmacies without a prescription. Follow instructions – product must be applied 30 to 60 minutes before the needle to the area where the needle will go.

> Apply cream to multiple areas if your child is having more than one needle.

> Ask if you are not sure exactly where on the body the needle will be given.

BABIES UP TO AGE TWO

> **Sit upright.** Newborns (younger than one month) can be held skin to skin against your chest. Young children can sit on your lap. Hug but don't hold too firmly.

Needle location:
- Babies under 1 year: upper outer thigh.
- Babies 12 months and older: upper arm.

> **Breastfeed** (if possible). If your child unlatches, gently reposition when your child is ready.

- Or **give sugar water** 1-2 minutes before the needle (1 tsp white sugar dissolved into 2 tsp boiled or distilled water).
- Or have your child **suck a finger or a pacifier.**

CHILDREN TWO TO 17

> **Use neutral language** rather than drawing attention to pain.

- Let children/teens know when things are going to start by saying "Ready?" or "Here we go!"
- Avoid reassuring (e.g., "It'll be over soon" and "You're OK") as it can increase distress and pain.

> **Distract** by taking their attention away from the pain.

- Watch a video together and ask questions about it.
- Encourage listening to music through headphones.
- Talk about something fun (e.g., birthday party).
- Play with toys that encourage deep breathing, such as blowing a pinwheel or bubbles.

> **Get support** from a registered psychologist if your child has severe needle fear or phobia.

CHILDREN SEVEN TO 17 WHO FEEL FAINT WHEN GETTING NEEDLES

> A simple technique called **muscle tension** can raise blood pressure and stop these feelings.

- Ask your child to recline or lie down if possible and tighten his/her leg and stomach muscles (not the arm where the needle is going to be given).
- Tensing should continue for about 20 seconds until your child is feeling flush in the face. Stop tensing for five seconds (without fully relaxing) before tensing again.

TIP:

IF MORE THAN ONE NEEDLE IS TO BE GIVEN AT AN APPOINTMENT, ASK THE HEALTHCARE PROVIDER TO GIVE THE MOST PAINFUL VACCINATION LAST.

BROUGHT TO YOU BY:

HELP Eliminate Pain in Kids & Adults

It Doesn't Have to Hurt
Prevent Pain Control for Children

SUPPORTER:
Immunize Immunisation Canada
immunize.ca

INSTITUTIONS:
IWK Health Centre
SickKids

FUNDERS:

NOVA SCOTIA Health Research FOUNDATION
CIHR IRSC
Canadian Institutes of Health Research / Instituts de recherche en santé du Canada

Evidence summarized by Dr. Christine Chambers, Dr. Meghan McMurtry, Dr. Noni MacDonald, Dr. Melanie Barwick, Dr. Anna Taddio, Kathryn Birnie and Katelynn Boerner
Adapted from Taddio A., McMurtry CM., Shah V., et al. Reducing pain during vaccine injections: clinical practice guideline. CMAJ 2015;187:975-982.

ParentsCanada

ParentsCanada vaccination pain resource.

Pediatric Chronic Pain

Chronic pain is a serious health concern that affects a surprisingly large number of children and adolescents (see Chapter 9 for a broader discussion of pain). A population-based survey of Canadian adolescents aged 13–17 years found that approximately 20 per cent of adolescents report experiencing weekly or more frequent chronic pains such as headaches, stomach aches, or backaches (Stanford, Chambers, Biesanz, & Chen, 2007). Many other studies from around the world yield similar prevalence rates and provide further support for the commonplace nature of chronic pain in children and adolescents (King et al., 2011). Chronic pain can occur as a result of associated medical conditions or in the absence of any identifiable organic pathology. It is important to note that not all children who experience chronic pain are significantly disabled by this pain. It is a subgroup of children (estimated at around 5 per cent) who experience significant pain-related interference (Huguet & Miro, 2008). However, for these children the negative consequences of their pain are far-reaching, affecting emotional functioning, school performance, peer relationships, sleep, and family functioning (Palermo, 2000). Pain was once viewed by scientists and clinicians as a purely biological phenomenon, but it is now understood that pain is a complex experience where psychological factors play an important role (Simons & Basch, 2016). There is evidence that as many as two-thirds of children with chronic pain continue to experience chronic pain as adults, and psychological factors have been shown to play an important role in predicting this trajectory (Walker, Sherman, Bruehl, Garber, & Smith, 2012).

iStock.com/pzRomashka

Some children experiencing chronic pain require more intensive interventions and are treated by a multidisciplinary team through inpatient and outpatient clinics specializing in chronic pain.

A variety of measures have been developed to assess chronic pain and pain-related outcomes in children. Core outcome domains for assessment of pediatric chronic pain include not only pain intensity, but also physical functioning, emotional functioning, role functioning, and sleep (McGrath et al., 2008). Two recent reviews summarize the efficacy of psychological interventions for improving pain, disability, and mood in children with chronic pain delivered either face to face (Eccleston et al., 2014) or remotely (i.e., via the Internet, CD-ROMs, audiotapes, or the telephone) (Fisher, Law, Palerma, & Eccleston, 2015). The psychological interventions tested included relaxation, hypnosis, coping skills training, biofeedback, and cognitive behavioural therapy. These interventions were applied to a variety of chronic pain conditions, which for the purposes of the reviews were grouped as either headache or non-headache (i.e., recurrent abdominal pain, musculoskeletal pain, and arthritis). The reviews found that psychological treatments delivered face to face and remotely were effective in reducing pain intensity associated with both headache and non-headache pain. However, long-term therapeutic gains were limited to children and adolescents with headache who received face-to-face treatment. Overall, there was limited evidence for the effects of psychological interventions on mood and disability (Eccleston et al., 2014; Fisher et al., 2015).

While psychological interventions delivered on their own can certainly be helpful for some children, many children with chronic pain require more intensive, multidisciplinary interventions and are seen in clinics specializing in chronic pain (for a review, see Hechler et al., 2015). Treatments offered in these clinics usually include a combination of medication, nursing support, and physical therapy, in addition to psychological interventions and support with school-based modifications. For example, in 2015, the pediatric chronic pain clinic at the Stollery Children's Hospital in Alberta, Canada launched Chronic Pain 35, an innovative education program, in collaboration with the provincial government (Reid, Simmonds, Verrier & Dick, 2016). Chronic Pain 35 allows teens in the chronic pain clinic enrolled in Grades 10 to 12 to earn high school credits for attendance at a group-based cognitive behavioural therapy program. The benefits of this program are multifaceted. By participating, teens are able to socialize with same-age peers and maintain their academic progress all while engaging in an evidence-based chronic pain intervention (Reid et al., 2016).

Pediatric Palliative Care

Over the last 20 years there has been tremendous growth in the field of pediatric palliative care, which originated within oncology but is now beneficially applied to children with other medical conditions, including conditions where curative treatments have failed or that require intensive long-term treatment aimed at maintaining quality of life (Moody, Siegel, Scharbach, Cunningham, & Cantor, 2011). That said, pediatric palliative care has significantly lagged behind care provided to adults with life-threatening illnesses. It is estimated that only 10 per cent of dying children each year receive hospice or palliative services (Moody et al., 2011). The goals of pediatric palliative care are multi-faceted and include establishing goals of care, symptom (e.g., pain, fatigue) management, and advanced-care planning, as well as ethical and legal considerations. Pediatric palliative care is different from adult care in that the types of medical conditions experienced by children, their needs for education and support, their family environment, and their understanding of death and dying all differ significantly from those of adults (McCulloch, Comac, & Craig, 2008). The potential or impending death of a child can have a huge impact on a family; parents of children with life-threatening illnesses require unique support (Bergstraesser, 2013).

Pediatric psychologists involved in caring for dying children typically work as part of an interdisciplinary palliative care team that provides comprehensive physical, psychological, and spiritual support. There is evidence that involvement of pediatric palliative care can significantly improve the quality of children's remaining lifetime and address other palliative care goals, such as pain (Moody et al., 2011).

Common Parenting Challenges: Sleeping, Feeding, Toileting

In addition to their expertise in dealing with children with chronic medical conditions, pediatric psychologists also have considerable knowledge in dealing with several common parenting challenges that are often problematic in healthy children as well as in children with medical conditions. These common challenges include difficulties in the areas of sleeping, feeding, and toileting.

Sleep problems are very common among young children and are associated with a range of emotional and behavioural issues (Honaker & Meltzer, 2016; Meltzer & Montgomery-Downs, 2011;

Vriend, Davidson, Rusak, & Corkum, 2015). Sleep problems are a very strong correlate of emotional and behavioural issues, and children's sleep problems are known to exacerbate their emotional and behavioural problems (Coulombe, Reid, Boyle, & Racine, 2010; Reid, Hong, & Wade, 2009). Sleep problems are a greater issue for children with medical conditions (Lewandowski, Ward, & Palermo, 2011). The most common sleep difficulties in childhood include bedtime resistance and night wakings. Most often related to a parental lack of education about appropriate sleep habits for children and inappropriate reliance on parental intervention (e.g., rocking, feeding, staying in the room or bed with the child), these negative sleep habits have their roots in early infancy (Meltzer & Montgomery-Downs, 2011). They are likely to persist throughout childhood without intervention, although the specific nature or presentation of the sleep problem can change over the course of development (Meltzer & Montgomery-Downs, 2011). There is very strong support for the efficacy of behavioural interventions for pediatric sleep (Allen, Howlett, Coulombe, & Corkum, 2016), most often involving gradual reduction of parental involvement and attention using principles of graduated or full extinction in order to promote independent sleep and self-soothing. Many pediatric sleep problems can be managed effectively using basic principles of sleep hygiene, such as deciding on appropriate bed and wake times and eliminating television and other screen use while in bed (see Table 13.3) (Allen et al., 2016).

Feeding issues are a common concern of parents of young children. Common challenges reported by parents include trying to get children to eat food at assigned, structured mealtimes (vs snacking or on the go) and encouraging children to try new foods (those who will not are referred to as "picky eaters") (Crist & Napier-Phillips, 2001). Mealtime lengths greater than 30 minutes are often associated with feeding problems (Crist & Napier-Phillips, 2001). Children's eating behaviours are influenced by a host of factors. Some factors are related to overeating, such as food responsiveness, enjoyment of food, and emotional overeating, while other dimensions relate to under-eating, such as slowness in eating, fussiness, or refusal of new foods (Birch & Fisher, 1995; Birch & Fisher, 1998). Parent attitudes show significant relationships with children's

TABLE 13.3 | Sleep Tips for Parents.

	Core concept	Details and Recommendations
A	Age appropriate	It is important that children go to bed and wake up at times that ensure that they receive an age-appropriate amount of sleep. For children who have outgrown naps (which usually occurs during the preschool age period), napping during the day could be an indication that children are not getting sufficient quality and/or quantity of sleep at night.
B	Bedtimes	Set bedtimes and wake times, as well as routines in the evening and morning, are key to good sleep. It is recommended that bedtimes be no later than 9 p.m. across childhood.
C	Consistency	It is very important that these bedtimes and wake times are consistent, even on weekends (i.e., no more than a 30–60-minute difference between weekday and weekend bedtimes and wake times).
S	Schedule	The child's schedule in general is important—in addition to having routines at bedtime and wake time, it is also important that they have consistency throughout their day, including the timing of homework, extracurricular activities, etc.

TABLE 13.3 | Continued

L	Location	It is important that the child's location for sleep includes a comfortable bed; the room is quiet, dark, and cool; and the location remains consistent and familiar. Also, the child's bedroom should only be used for sleeping—children should not be sent to their bedroom for a time out. Their bedroom also should not be too exciting or distracting, and should be conducive to relaxation.
E	No Electronics in the bedroom or before bed	The use of electronics, including both the timing of use and the location, should also be considered—children should not be using stimulating electronic devices (i.e., iPods, cell phones, laptops, etc.) too close to bedtime (most commonly defined as one hour prior to going to bed), and it is recommended that these items not be placed in the bedroom.
E	Exercise and diet	Exercise and diet are both important factors that should be considered when evaluating sleep hygiene—physical activity during the day is important to healthy sleep, but should not be undertaken too close to bedtime (defined in the literature as anywhere from 1 hour to 4 hours prior to bedtime). The child's day should be organized so that there is time for a "cool down" period before bedtime, where he or she slowly comes down from the regular level of activity into a quiet, more restful state. Diet includes things like caffeine consumption—children should limit or totally eliminate caffeine consumption (i.e., caffeinated soft drinks)—as well as the timing of meals. Children should not be going to bed hungry, but they also should not be consuming a large meal right before bedtime. A healthy balanced diet is also important to the child's sleep as well as to his/her overall health.
P	Positivity	Positivity surrounding sleep is also an important aspect of sleep hygiene. Parents should have a positive attitude towards sleep and the bedtime/wake time routine, and the atmosphere in the house should be positive, in order to be conducive to creating a positive mood in the child. It is important that this positive mood is relaxing and calming, rather than fun and exciting—we want the child to be winding down before bedtime. Also, doing frustrating activities right before bed (i.e., math problems for a child who struggles with math) is not recommended, as this may interfere with the child's ability to fall asleep.
I	Independence when falling asleep	Independence is also important. Once the child reaches an age where he or she is capable of settling into sleep without the presence of a parent, independence when falling asleep should be encouraged, in order to discourage dependence on someone else in order to fall asleep. For children, independence means no calling out and no getting out of bed, and for parents, no responding to their child calling out and returning the child to the bedroom if he/she does get out of bed.
N	Needs met during the day	Finally, the needs of the child should be met throughout the day. This refers to both the child's emotional needs (i.e., love, support, hugs, etc.), as well as basic physiological needs (i.e., thirst, hunger, etc.).
G	All of the above equals a Great sleep!	

Adapted from: Bessey, J., Coulombe, A., & Corkum, P. Sleep hygiene in children with ADHD: Research findings and clinical recommendations. *The ADHD Report*, 21(3). (Acronym created by M. Gendron, Project Co-ordinator, Corkum LABS).

nutritional behaviours, including their food intake and eating motivations (Birch & Fisher, 1995; Birch & Fisher, 1998). Parents create environments for children that may foster the development of healthy eating behaviours and weight, or that may promote overweight and aspects of disordered eating. These dietary habits acquired in early childhood are likely to persist through to adulthood (Birch & Fisher, 1995; Birch & Fisher, 1998). Behavioural interventions for pediatric feeding issues, which include setting reasonable expectations, removing attention from undesired behaviours, and providing reinforcement for desired behaviours, are well supported in the literature (Silverman, 2015).

Enuresis and **encopresis** are two common yet often poorly understood toileting-related issues that occur in childhood and are often treated by pediatric psychologists (Christopherson, 2010). Encopresis is defined as the passage of feces in inappropriate places, such as clothing. For the vast majority of these children (>90 per cent), this soiling occurs as the direct result of overflow incontinence, which is involuntary and results from constipation. A variety of predisposing biopsychosocial factors may make a child likely to get constipation, which is typically then followed by painful defecation and withholding. The colon walls stretch and this leads to an accumulation of stool, creating a vicious cycle that can result in frequent soiling incidents. In some cases, this stretching of the colon can reduce a child's sensitivity to the urge to defecate, further increasing the frequency of accidents. Encopresis is an extremely frustrating problem for children and their families and is a frequent source of conflict (Christopherson, 2010). Evidence-based behavioural interventions for encopresis include biofeedback and enhanced toilet training (ETT). With **biofeedback**, electrodes are placed in and/ or around the anus with the goal of teaching children to contract and relax their anorectal muscles to achieve effective bowel movements (Shepard, Poler & Grabman, 2017). ETT is a behavioural management program. ETT typically includes education about the nature of constipation and soiling, defecation modelling, breathing exercises, and behavioural reinforcements to encourage toilet use (Shepard et al., 2016). ETT has yielded outcomes superior to medical management (Borowitz, Cox, Sutphen, & Kovatchev, 2002).

Nocturnal enuresis (bedwetting) is also a common disorder and affects as many as 5 to 10 per cent of five-year-olds, decreasing in frequency with age, although 1 per cent of older adolescents are estimated to continue to struggle with enuresis (Christopherson, 2010). It is more common in boys than girls. While the specific mechanisms that produce bedwetting are not well understood, there is strong empirical evidence in support of the urine alarm as the most effective intervention.

Anzacare Limited

A modern version of a urine alarm, a small, ultra-light weight alarm that can be comfortably attached to a child's pyjamas.

These alarms, worn in undergarments or pajamas, alert the child when he/she starts to urinate, and after consistent usage most children begin to be able to rouse themselves prior to urination. Use of the urine alarm results in complete resolution of bedwetting in up to 80 per cent of patients (Brown, Pope, & Brown, 2010; Christopherson, 2010; Shepard et al., 2016). Despite this compelling evidence, this treatment approach is relatively unknown to parents and is used less commonly by physicians than medications, even though medications for enuresis are generally less effective and any improvements cease following discontinuation of the medication (von Gontard, 2003; von Gontard, Baeyens, Van Hoecke, Warzak, & Bachmann, 2011). Pediatric psychologists assist with providing education about the urine alarm, assessing for factors that may influence the success of this treatment (e.g., child motivation, ability of child to awake independently) and providing support to increase the effectiveness once it is implemented (e.g., charting, reinforcement of effort, over-learning to prevent relapse).

Impact on Family

In addition to the impact on the child, parenting a child with a chronic or life-limiting illness can have a major negative impact on the child's parents and family. For example, taking care of a child with chronic illness can impact a parent's ability to go to work, have a social life, care for other children, and accomplish necessary chores around the house. A healthy family environment is critical in supporting children's physical and mental health and development (Repetti, Taylor, & Seeman, 2002). Recently, research has focused on developing psychological interventions specifically directed at parents of children with medical conditions. A systematic review identified 47 studies for six common childhood chronic illnesses (pain, cancer, diabetes, asthma, traumatic brain injury, and eczema) (Eccleston, Fisher, Law, Bartlett, & Palermo, 2015). Four types of psychological interventions directed towards parents were examined: cognitive behavioural therapy, family therapy, problem-solving therapy, and multi-systemic therapy. Cognitive behavioural therapy was found to be associated with improvements in the child's medical symptoms, while problem-solving therapy improved parents' distress and their ability to solve problems.

The needs of siblings of children with medical conditions have also been acknowledged. Frequently, having a child with a medical condition in the family can pull attention and resources away from other children, placing them at risk for a range of negative outcomes. In a recent review, Vermaes, van Susante, and van Bakel (2012) examined the psychological functioning of siblings of children with a range of chronic physical and medical conditions such as cancer, diabetes, cystic fibrosis, and spina bifida. They found that having a sibling with a chronic health condition had a small but significant effect on siblings resulting in more internalizing and externalizing problems and less positive self-attributes (e.g., self-esteem, self-concept). Older siblings, and siblings of children with life-threatening (e.g., cancer) or highly intrusive disorders that impact daily life (e.g., diabetes), were at greater risk for negative outcomes (Vermaes et al., 2012). Intervention programs have been developed to address the psychosocial needs of siblings (Incledon et al., 2015). These interventions, usually group-based, typically include developmentally appropriate information regarding the sibling's condition, coping skills training, and the opportunity to meet others with similarly ill siblings. Incledon and colleagues (2015) found that these types of treatments, in addition to emotional support from parents, and consistency in family routines, can effectively reduce psychological maladjustment in siblings of children with chronic conditions.

Technology Applications in Pediatric Psychology: e-Health and Social Media

The application of technology in pediatric psychology over the past decade has allowed for significant advancements in assessment, intervention, and research. A major development in the field has been the implementation of **e-Health** (electronic health) tools that deliver health services and information through the Internet and other related technologies. Telemedicine delivery of pediatric psychology services, with families participating in assessment and treatment from their own communities through an interactive phone or video interface, can address important barriers to psychological treatment for children and families, such as cost, transportation, and missed time from school or work. Additionally, Internet-based self-management interventions for youth with health conditions have been developed and reviews have found that these interventions are effective in improving symptoms across a range of common pediatric health conditions (e.g., asthma, recurrent pain, encopresis, traumatic brain injury, and obesity) (Stinson, Wilson, Gill, Yamada, & Holt, 2009). In recent years, the use of technologically enhanced distraction devices, such as humanoid robots, have emerged as novel tools to reduce procedural pain and distress in pediatric patients. One example is MEDi, otherwise known as Medicine and Engineering Designing Intelligence. MEDi is an interactive humanoid robot (see photo of MEDi the humanoid robot) that can serve as an engaging, multisensory distraction tool for children undergoing medical procedures by dancing, playing games, and telling stories. MEDi can also be programmed to deliver cognitive behavioural interventions (e.g., deep breathing) and positive reinforcements (e.g., high fives). In one study, children undergoing routine vaccinations were randomized to receive usual care or to interact with MEDi during the procedure. Children in the MEDi condition reported significantly lower pain and distress than those who received usual care, with effect sizes in the moderate to large range (Beran, Ramirez-Serrano, Vanderkooi & Kuhn, 2013). **m-Health** (mobile health) is a subset of e-Health that involves the use of mobile phones and other wireless technology (i.e., tablets). For example, in the case of pain, electronic pain diaries using smartphones are being used to capture real-time data (Lalloo, Jibb, Rivera, Agarwal & Stinson, 2015). Smartphone applications have also been developed to promote medication adherence in pediatric populations and include features such as reminders, behavioural reinforcements, and education (Nguyen et al., 2016).

Social media have become an increasingly important research tool in pediatric psychology. Surveys estimate that as many as 83 per cent of parents with children under the age of 18 (Duggan, Lenhart, Lampe, & Ellison, 2015) and 91 per cent of youth between the ages 13 and 17 (Lenhart, 2015) use social media. Thus, one of social media's strongest applications in pediatric psychology is as a method to facilitate direct communication and engagement between clinicians, researchers, youth, and their families. In pediatric psychology research, social media have been used to deliver health-promotion

Christine Chambers.

MEDi the humanoid robot can help children manage procedural pain and distress.

programs for children with medical conditions and their parents, run virtual focus groups, and recruit hard-to-reach clinical populations (Akard, Wray, & Gilmer, 2015; Gorman et al., 2014; Hamm et al., 2014). Recently, social media have also been used as a knowledge translation tool to deliver research evidence on pediatric health to parents in a way that is functional, accessible, and that can be implemented in everyday life. One such example is the #ItDoesntHavetoHurt (#IDHTH) social media initiative. #IDHTH is a science-media partnership between the Centre for Pediatric Pain Research (Halifax, NS) and the YummyMummyClub.ca, (Canada's leading online magazine for mothers) that places evidence-based information on pediatric pain management directly into the hands of parents through blogs, posts, videos, social media images, Twitter chats, and Facebook polls (Canadian Institutes of Health Research, 2016). The photo shown from the

A social media image on procedure pain management from the #ItDoesntHavetoHurt campaign.

#ItDoesntHavetoHurt campaign shows a social media image that was developed to educate parents on procedure pain management. Similar initiatives include the #KidsCancerPain campaign in collaboration with the Cancer Knowledge Network (Gerrard, 2016), and the #ShitHappens campaign for parents of children with Hirschsprung's Disease (Wittmeier et al., 2014). As part of these initiatives, parents can also engage with the research team over social media to ask questions, share their experiences, and identify priority areas for future research.

Applications for technology in pediatric psychology are growing exponentially, as are the ethical issues (e.g., informed consent, privacy, and participant safety) associated with these types of interventions and research (Bull et al., 2011; Henderson, Rosser, Keogh, & Eccleston, 2012; Moreno, Goniu, Moreno, & Diekema, 2013). Ethical issues related to the use of technology in pediatric psychology must be carefully considered, and with the rapid development of new technology, it is likely that unique ethical issues will continue to emerge.

Future Directions

Several exciting new themes are emerging in the field of pediatric psychology. Opportunities for social media and other e-Health and m-Health tools will continue to evolve with the arrival of new technological features. For instance, the emergence of social media live video streaming (e.g., Facebook Live, Periscope) and real-time communication (e.g., Twitter chats) have the potential to facilitate dynamic, two-way contact between patients, families, and pediatric psychologists. To optimize patient uptake, engagement, and adherence with these tools, future work with social media in pediatric psychology may consider the utility of multi-platform integrated interventions. Unfortunately, despite the rapid development of evidence-based e-Health and m-Health interventions in pediatric psychology, few are available for use outside of a research setting. Changes in the way scientists conduct and disseminate their research in this area will be required to ensure that interventions shown to be effective are readily accessible to the public.

A rapidly evolving area in pediatric psychology is the need to properly anticipate and meet the needs of children with medical conditions as they progress into adolescence and young adulthood and require transition to adult-oriented care for continued management. Adolescence is a unique developmental period that has not been extensively studied in pediatric psychology; yet, challenges specific to this population require attention. Canadian population-level research suggests that adolescence is a time when mental health problems first emerge, and in fact, adolescents and young adults between the ages of 15 and 24 years are more likely to be diagnosed with a mental health or substance-use disorder than Canadians of any other age (Pearson, Janz, & Ali, 2013). Further, adolescents are also likely to experiment with risky behaviours (e.g., sexual risk-taking, experimenting with drugs and alcohol) that can pose significant health threats, particularly to those with pre-existing medical conditions. The serious consequences that substance use can have on metabolic control in youth with type 1 diabetes (Hogendorf et al., 2017) is one common example. These unique challenges highlight the need to ensure that developmentally appropriate care is provided to adolescents, particularly during their transition to adult health care. Coordinated transition to adult care is associated with improved health, better disease management, and more appropriate use of health-care services (Schwartz, Tuchman, Hobbie, & Ginsberg, 2011). Attention to the transition process of these young adults, their unique psychological and social needs, their evolving family relationships, their transition readiness, planning, and transfer of care are all important variables in facilitating this important process (Schwartz et al., 2011).

Another emerging area is related to the opportunities and challenges associated with implementing research evidence into pediatric psychology policy and practice. Pediatric psychology is a robust field with a strong scientific knowledge base to inform evidence-based assessment and intervention. But unfortunately, many children do not benefit from the best available research evidence in real-world practice (Boerner, Gillespie, McLaughlin, Kuttner, & Chambers, 2014; Woody, Weisz, & McLean, 2005). Barriers to the adoption of evidence-based approaches include limited resources (e.g., staff, time, funds), organizational culture, and gaps in clinician knowledge and skill (Boerner et al., 2014; Yamada et al., 2017). The principles of implementation science (Peters, Adam, Alonge, Agyepong, & Tran, 2013) must be carefully applied to the field of pediatric psychology to promote the widespread uptake of the best available research evidence into policy and practice.

Finally, there will be a continued need for pediatric psychologists with expertise in dealing with the unique psychosocial issues faced by children with health conditions and their families. A Society of Pediatric Psychology task force has made recommendations for the continued training of pediatric psychologists (Palermo et al., 2014). The underlying principles of these recommendations include that clinical child psychology is the foundation for developing skills and expertise in pediatric psychology. The task force recommended that pediatric psychologists demonstrate competence in the following *knowledge* areas: the scientific foundations of pediatric psychology; clinical child psychology; contextual influences on child health; disease process and management; familial, socio-economic, and cultural influences on child health; influence of systems and contexts; the role of different disciplines in service delivery systems; functions of health information technology; and the process of transition from pediatric to adult health care (Palermo et al., 2014). In addition, six core *skill areas* were identified that reflect competence: scientific methods; professional conduct; interpersonal skills; evidence-based assessment and intervention; education, teaching, and supervision; and practising within an interdisciplinary system of disciplines and settings (Palermo et al., 2014).

Summary

Pediatric psychology is a specialized field in health psychology that integrates both scientific research and clinical practice to address the psychological aspects of medical conditions and the promotion of health behaviours in children and their families. The field addresses the unique needs of patients and their families in pediatric settings. Areas of major focus in pediatric psychology include coping with medical conditions; adherence to pediatric treatment regimens; coping with medical procedures; pediatric chronic pain; pediatric palliative care; common parenting challenges in the areas of sleeping, feeding, and toileting; and the impact of pediatric health conditions on the family. Pediatric psychologists make important contributions to supporting children with health conditions and their families.

Critical Thought Questions

1. What can explain the continued failure to appropriately manage children's pain from procedures despite the availability of numerous evidence-based interventions to reduce this pain?

2. How can we adapt psychological interventions to make them most effective for children with medical conditions based on various individual differences (e.g., age, cognitive ability)?

Recommended Reading

Drotar, D. (2006). *Psychological interventions in childhood chronic illness.* Washington, DC: American Psychological Association.

Roberts, M.C., & Steele, R.G. (2017). *Handbook of pediatric psychology.* New York, NY: Guilford Press.

Spirito, A., & Kazak, A.E. (2006). *Effective and emerging treatments in pediatric psychology.* New York, NY: Oxford University Press.

14

Health Geropsychology

Casey B. Azuero

Rebecca S. Allen

Thomas Hadjistavropoulos

Learning Objectives

In this chapter you will:

- Learn about the demographics of aging in relation to health in North America and to theories that reflect individuals' response to chronic illness, stress, and coping.

- Familiarize yourself with common health issues (e.g., pain, falls) affecting older adults and the role of health psychologists in the management of these health issues.

- Come to know behavioural interventions used to enhance long-term care residents' response to chronic illness and enhance their health and quality of life.

- Learn about interventions designed to improve the quality of life of older adults who live independently in the community.

- Learn about the psychologist's role in working with individuals at the **end of life.**

Introduction

"But no matter how they make you feel, you should always watch your elders carefully. They were you and you will be them. You carry the seeds of your old age in you at this very moment and they hear the echoes of their youth each time they see you." This quote comes from Kent Nerburn's (1993) book *Letters to my son: Reflections on becoming a man* and underscores that aging is something that we all share. Many people, especially after they reach mid-life, may find the idea that they are aging to be distressing, yet research shows that older adults experience more happiness than most other age groups (e.g., Blanchflower & Oswald, 2008; Thomas et al., 2016). Moreover, thanks to advances in the health sciences and prevention efforts, life expectancy has been increasing so that young people today can expect that, on average, they are likely to live longer than their parents and grandparents (World Health Organization, 2015). Despite such optimistic predictions, there are health concerns that affect a portion of older persons and these issues are the focus of this chapter. Older adults represent the fastest-growing segment of the US and Canadian populations, with the leading edge of the baby boomers turning 65 in 2011. Over 46 million adults in the United States are 65 years of age and older, and the portion of those over the age of 85 is increasing especially rapidly (Mather, Jacobsen, & Pollard, 2015) (see Figure 14.1). In Canada, the numbers of seniors are expected to increase from 5.7 million to 9.8 million between 2005 and 2036 (Statistics Canada, 2015) (see Figure 14.2).

The prevalence of most types of **disability** (e.g., problems in mobility, agility, hearing, vision, and pain) increases with age, with the highest rates occurring in those aged 75 and older. Pearson, Bhat-Schelbert, and Probst (2012) examined the prevalence of nine chronic illnesses in the United States: angina/coronary heart disease, arthritis, asthma, cancer, diabetes, heart attack, hypertension, obesity, and stroke. All conditions except obesity and asthma increase across the lifespan. By age 70, 7 per cent of the population have hypertension and 55 per cent have arthritis. Similar patterns of chronic illness are seen across the lifespan of Canadian adults (Health Canada, 2003; Public Health Agency of Canada [PHAC], 2009a; 2009b; 2011; 2012). Prevalence rates of asthma

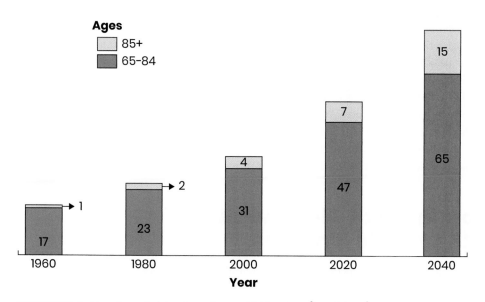

FIGURE 14.1 Number of older Americans, 1960–2040 (in millions).

Source: Urban Institute. Data source: U.S. Census Bureau (2004a, 2004b, 2004c).

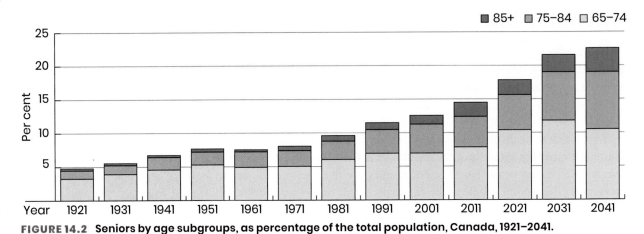

FIGURE 14.2   Seniors by age subgroups, as percentage of the total population, Canada, 1921–2041.

(PHAC, 2012) and obesity decrease as age increases, with obesity rates being the highest in adults 55 to 64 years old (PHAC, 2009b) and asthma being greatest in children 12 and younger (PHAC, 2012). At the age of 75 and older, 23 per cent of Canadians have cardiovascular disease (PHAC, 2009a). **Dementia**, which refers to a variety of conditions that affect the brain (e.g., Alzheimer's disease [AD]) and produce symptoms such as memory loss and impairments in language skills, also represents a significant public health need in older populations. According to a report released by the Alzheimer Society of Canada (2016), 11.6 per cent of females and 10.4 of males 74 to 85 years of age have a diagnosis of dementia with the prevalence rising to 37.1 per cent and 28.1 per cent for females and males over 85 years respectively. The majority of people with dementia suffer from AD. In the United States, 5.4 million Americans are estimated to suffer from AD (Alzheimer's Association, 2016).

Health disparities (see Chapter 15) reduce the ability to achieve the best health outcomes among minority groups, including people of colour, women, those with low education and income, and rural-dwelling individuals (Centers for Disease Control, 2012). Health disparities arise due to poverty, poor access to health care, and educational differences. Notably, lifespan and health are determined by both genetic and environmental or lifestyle influences, with genetics accounting for roughly 35 per cent and health behaviours (e.g., smoking, poor diet, inactivity) accounting for the largest percentage. These health behaviours may be changed through culturally competent educational programs.

Ability to decrease risk factors is important for health geropsychology, but the childhood and adult obesity epidemic threatens longevity and health for people as they grow older. Overweight individuals are at increased risk for heart disease, type 2 diabetes, high blood pressure, stroke, osteoarthritis, respiratory problems, and some cancers. Interventions to increase physical activity and promote self-management of chronic illness are needed for the benefit of public health in North America.

Working with Older Adults with Chronic Illnesses

Approximately 75 million people in the United States have more than one chronic condition (Parekh & Barton, 2010). Poor health outcomes associated with multiple chronic illnesses include increased hospitalizations, complicated medication schedules, duplicated medical tests, conflicting medical advice, increased disability, and death. Research findings are often slow to reach and be applied in clinical practice. This is because research studies usually include only people with one illness, so applying treatments developed in research to people with multiple chronic illnesses in a practice setting may not work. Although research studies with older adults present findings about treatments that work, health professionals tend not to apply these findings because seniors are seen as a more complex age group.

Interdisciplinary and Collaborative Care

Chronic conditions often are accompanied by psychological disorders (Solano, Gomes, & Higginson, 2006) such as depression and anxiety (Scherrer et al., 2003). This has led to the development of integrated health programs that combine mental health screening (Scogin & Shah, 2006) and services into medical care settings treating patients with chronic conditions. This form of health care is called **collaborative care** (Scherrer et al., 2003), an approach in which physicians and mental health–care providers work together in an organized way to manage common mental disorders and chronic disease. These programs are practical and apply principles of chronic disease management, including establishing and sustaining effective communication and teamwork among primary care, mental health–care providers, and care managers (Boyd et al., 2005). This collaboration supports systematic diagnosis and health or mental health outcomes tracking. It also facilitates adjustment of treatments based on these outcomes (Scogin, Hanson, & Welsh, 2003; Thielke, Vannoy, & Unützer, 2007). Collaborative care represents best clinical practice, particularly given the multiple chronic conditions experienced by many older adults (Parekh & Barton, 2010).

Advance Care Planning

The National Hospice and Palliative Care Organization (2017) defines **advance care planning** as, "making decisions about the care you would want to receive if you become unable to speak for yourself." Advance care planning includes: (1) getting information on the types of life-sustaining treatments that are available; (2) deciding what types of treatment you would or would not want should you be diagnosed with a life-limiting illness; (3) sharing your personal values with your loved ones; and (4) completing advance directives to put into writing what types of treatment you would or would not want should you be unable to speak for yourself. Advance directives usually are written documents designed to allow competent patients the opportunity to guide future health-care decisions in the event that they are unable to participate directly in medical decision making. In order to make the process of advance care planning, including advance directives, easier for individuals to complete, multiple methods have emerged. Five Wishes and Making Your Wishes Known are two self-guided, web-based programs that provide individuals with documented end-of-life care goals. Respecting Choices˙ is a program designed and verified to improve advance care planning by training individuals to engage patients in these discussions. People from minority groups are disproportionately less likely to complete advance directives, but with targeted intervention, using these tools, successful engagement and completion of the task of documenting their wishes for end-of-life care has been demonstrated (Huang et al., 2016; Pecanac et al., 2014).

Family Caregiving and Chronic Illness

Family members often provide care to people living with chronic illness in the community (Family Caregiver Alliance, 2006). Despite the many positive aspects of caregiving, providing care to an older family member with a chronic illness can be associated with psychological distress

In Practice
The Need to Understand Cognitive Impairment

Mrs Land, living at her daughter's home, is an 82-year-old widow receiving palliative care for congestive heart failure. She has suffered a series of strokes, leaving her with moderate cognitive impairment. She is morbidly obese and confined to her bed. Her daughter, a substitute middle-school teacher, occasionally leaves Mrs Land at home alone when she substitute teaches. She always leaves the house telephone within her mother's reach and alerts her neighbour to the possibility that her mother will call during the school day if the need arises. The consulting health psychologist has been educating the daughter regarding caregiving issues and the potential need for respite care.

On one occasion, the home health aide arrived to find Mrs Land had become incontinent of bowel and was covered in her own feces. Mrs Land reported that she had called out for her daughter, but that her daughter did not appear to be home. The telephone sat beside Mrs Land on a bed stand.

The home health aide provided continence care and bathed Mrs Land. Upon returning to the home health agency, the aide reported the incident to her supervisor. After consulting with the interdisciplinary team, the medical director of the home health agency reported the incident to Adult Protective Services.[*] The daughter continued her work with the health psychologist but the relationship with the medical director was irreparable and the services of another home health agency were engaged.

---

[*]Legislation and regulations concerning reporting of such incidents vary from jurisdiction to jurisdiction. Individuals are advised to be familiar with the laws and regulations of their jurisdiction. For health professionals, any decision concerning reporting must be in accordance with professional standards and ethics codes adopted by their discipline.

and feelings of caregiver burden (Aneshensel, Pearlin, Mullan, Zarit, & Whitlach, 1995; Family Caregiver Alliance, 2006). For example, family caregivers of individuals approaching the end of life are at risk for stress, depression, and health problems (McMillan, 2005; McMillan et al., 2006), especially when there have not been previous discussions of the dying person's wishes for medical care at the end of life. In ethnic minority groups, inclusion of family in medical decision making is common; for example, among Hispanics and African Americans the use of family to communicate the wishes of the patient is often seen as more relevant than a written directive (Volker, 2005). Chapter 15 provides a detailed discussion of cross-cultural issues.

In the context of caregiving, family behaviours and communication patterns are important in the overall outcomes of patients living with chronic health problems. Critical, overprotective, controlling, and distracting family responses to illness management have been associated with negative patient outcomes (Rosland, Heisler, & Piette, 2012). Therefore, interventions aimed at improving chronic illness outcomes should emphasize increased family use of attentive coping techniques and family support for the patient's autonomous motivation.

The Caregiver Stress–Health Model (Monin & Schulz, 2009) suggests ways in which an older adult's suffering (as displayed through physical and emotional symptoms) may influence family members' emotion regulation and, thus, provision of care. Two possible family member response patterns are proposed: **cognitive empathy** and conditioned emotional responses. Cognitive empathy refers to the shared or complementary emotional experience of the family member in response to the older adult's physical and emotional suffering. Conditioned emotional responses may occur when the family member has paired certain emotions with past experiences of the older person's suffering (i.e., becoming angry when the older relative displays fatigue or pain) and can cause defensive emotions (e.g., denial, fatalism) and withdrawal from the older patient. Health geropsychologists and other health professionals consider the history of the relationship and long-term familial coping patterns when designing family-based interventions for care of chronic illness in the home.

As the In Practice box above illustrates, family members of people with chronic illnesses may be inadequately prepared for caregiving tasks and require intervention and education in order to provide care at home. For example, the adult daughter described in the case study may not have understood the impact of cognitive impairment on an individual's ability to meet his or her needs, such as calling a neighbour for help when in distress. Effectively educating this caregiver about respite care and sitter services may have prevented the episode and subsequent involvement of Adult Protective Services; this type of caregiver education can be facilitated by health geropsychologists.

Chronic Pain

Chronic pain affects at least 50 per cent of older adults who live in the community and as many as 80 per cent of seniors who live in long-term care (LTC) facilities (Charlton, 2005, Patel, Guralnik, Dansie, & Turk, 2013). A detailed discussion of the experience of pain and health psychologists' role in its assessment and management has been included in Chapter 9. In this section, we focus on special issues pertaining to pain in older adults.

Older Adults Who Live Independently in the Community

Although there are many similarities between the way psychologists assess and treat younger and older pain patients, there are also unique challenges to working with older persons. Gauthier and Gagliese (2010) have discussed some of the issues specific to pain assessment and have pointed out that some commonly seen age-related changes (e.g., changes in visual acuity, auditory impairments) may make it more difficult for older adults to complete psychological questionnaires and to participate in clinical interviews. Accommodations, such as use of larger type on written materials, are often needed. Aside from such practical considerations, a complicating factor relates to commonly held false beliefs such as the idea that pain is an inevitable part of aging that must be endured (e.g., Martin, Williams, Hadjistavropoulos, Hadjistavropoulos, & MacLean, 2005). Pain is not the result of aging per se, but the result of pathology that ought to be treated irrespective of a person's age. Beliefs that pain in old age is natural may make older persons less likely to seek assessment and treatment of their pain and contribute to the under-treatment of pain that is often seen in this population (Herr, 2010).

Although a wide variety of tools are available to assess the pain experience and co-morbid psychological concerns, only a portion of these have been validated in older populations. As such, it is critical that psychologists select their assessment tools carefully and that they ensure these have been appropriately researched with older persons (Hadjistavropoulos et al., 2007a).

Cognitive behavioural therapy (CBT) is frequently employed in the psychological management of chronic pain. The CBT methods used with older adults are similar to those employed with younger persons, although the focus may be different. For example, older adults often present with inaccurate beliefs about pain and aging such as the aforementioned idea that pain is inevitable in old age and must be endured. The psychologist will challenge such beliefs with Socratic dialogue.

In other words, the psychologist queries the client regarding the logic underlying inaccurate beliefs about pain experienced by older adults. Moreover, the types of stressors that older adults face (and that consequently are addressed in therapy) often are different from those typically seen among younger persons (e.g., younger persons are concerned about their ability to perform the duties of their occupation whereas retired older persons are more likely to be preoccupied with such issues as widowhood and empty nest).

As discussed in Chapter 9, CBT has been found to be effective in the management of pain (Butler, Chapman, Forman, & Beck, 2006), and several studies have investigated its effectiveness specifically with older persons (e.g., Green, Hadjistavropoulos, Hadjistavropoulos, Martin, & Sharpe, 2009; Lunde, Nordhus, & Pallesen, 2009; Nicholas et al., 2013). Lunde and colleagues (2009) found CBT to be moderately effective, with demonstrated benefit on self-reported pain but not on physical function, depression, or patterns of medication use. Moreover, **acceptance and commitment therapy (ACT)** approaches, incorporating mindfulness, are also gaining popularity in the management of chronic pain in older adults (e.g., Scott, Daily, Yu, & McCracken, 2017). Initial results have demonstrated promising findings with respect to number of days off from work, medical care utilization (Dahl, Wilson, & Nilsson, 2004), illness-focused coping strategies, catastrophic thinking, and global distress levels over time (Cosio, 2016). Psychologists have also developed bibliotherapy interventions (i.e., self-help treatments involving the use of books and manuals) to help older adults deal with chronic pain (Hadjistavropoulos & Hadjistavropoulos, 2019), although the effectiveness of such programs requires further study (Hadjistavropoulos, 2012).

Older Adults with Dementia Who Live in Long-Term Care Facilities

While pain tends to be under-treated in older adults in general (Herr, 2010), this under-treatment is an even more significant concern when focusing specifically on older adults who live in LTC facilities. There is evidence that older persons who live in LTC in both the United States (e.g., Horgas, Nichols, Schapson, & Vietes, 2007; Morrison & Siu, 2000; Robinson, 2007) and Canada (Martin et al., 2005; Hadjistavropoulos et al., 2009) suffer from unnecessary pain. One of the factors contributing to this under-treatment is the communication challenge (Hadjistavropoulos et al., 2011) associated with advanced dementia.

Advanced AD and other dementias are associated with major impairments in judgement and language abilities. As a result, older adults with dementia often do not report their pain. Given subjectivity in the experience of pain and fluctuations in pain intensity, underlying physical problems may be missed when pain is not self-reported. Health psychologists and other professionals have played an active role in trying to solve the problem of pain under-reporting by developing behavioural observation assessment methods, emphasizing non-verbal pain behaviours (e.g., vocalizations, grimaces). Such automatic, reflexive pain behaviours tend to be less affected by advanced dementia compared to self-report. As such, observational procedures focusing on such behaviours have been shown to be helpful in identifying pain and its fluctuations. One of the most effective standardized assessment tools for identifying pain in this population is the Pain Assessment Checklist for Seniors with Limited Ability to Communicate[1] (PACSLAC) (Fuchs-Lacelle, Hadjistavropoulos, & Lix, 2008; Lints-Martindale, Hadjistavropoulos, Lix, & Thorpe, 2012) and the PACSLAC-II (Chan, Hadjistavropoulos, Williams, & Lints-Martindale, 2014), which require health-care personnel to observe the patient and evaluate him or her for pain behaviours (for more detailed assessment protocols, see Hadjistavropoulos, Fitzgerald, & Marchildon, 2010; Hadjistavropoulos et al., 2007a). Increasingly, LTC facilities are employing observational pain assessment procedures such as the PACSLAC, although challenges remain (e.g., nursing staff may be unfamiliar with such procedures).*

Untreated pain in LTC can lead to behavioural disturbances (e.g., aggression, loud vocalizations), which can easily be misattributed to psychiatric conditions and can lead to unnecessary and risky pharmacological therapies (Balfour & O'Rourke, 2003; Ballard et al., 2009). In response to this, psychologists increasingly are involved in the development of appropriate interventions designed to identify and modify the sources of behavioural disturbance (e.g., whether or not the disturbance is due to pain). For example, psychologist Jane Fisher and her colleagues developed the Functional Analytic Model of Intervention (Fisher, Drossel, Ferguson, Cherup, & Sylvester, 2008). This model recognizes that all behaviours are influenced by a person's psychological and physiological history and his or her current social and physical context. Through appropriate assessment (e.g., observing the antecedents and consequences of a behaviour), sources of distress are identified and managed through a variety of integrated approaches, including behavioural interventions (e.g., Cohen-Mansfield, 2001; Opie, Doyle, & O'Connor, 2002), structured activities, and environmental design. More research is needed to determine the extent to which such interventions are effective in the management of pain in seniors who reside in LTC facilities.

Falls represent a frequent cause of injury in older persons.

Falls

Falls represent one of the most frequent sources of painful injury among older adults. Approximately one in three older persons experiences a fall, with roughly half of these individuals falling more than once per year (Hawk, Hyland, Rupert, Colonvega, & Hall, 2006). Such falls are a leading cause of injury and hospitalization, with hospitalization rates doubling in seniors above age 75 (Rubenstein, 2006). In an American study, Stevens, Mack, Paulozzi, & Ballesteros (2008) found that 31 per cent of falls reported over one year resulted in at least one medical visit and at least one day of restricted activity. In a Canadian six-month longitudinal study (i.e., a study in which information is collected from the same people over relatively long periods of time) involving 571 older adults over age 69, Hadjistavropoulos and colleagues (2007b) found that 199 falls occurred, with 50 per cent of these falls leading to significant injury and 22 per cent leading to pain lasting more than a few days. Moreover, 18 per cent of the falls resulted in seeking medical attention.

While a variety of medical factors increase the risk of falling (e.g., visual problems, significant orthopedic diagnosis, use of medications that affect balance), psychological factors also increase the risk of falling. This is consistent with biopsychosocial models of health discussed throughout this volume. For example, depression (e.g., Ivziku, Matarese, & Pedone, 2011) and excessive fear of falling can predict future falls (e.g., Hadjistavropoulos, 2007b). It is often assumed that fear of falling leads to excessive avoidance of activity, which in turn leads to loss of muscle tone and fitness, which

---

* Disclosure of conflict of interest: Thomas Hadjistavropoulos, who is a co-author of this chapter, is also one of the developers of the PACSLAC and the PACSLAC-II.

iStock.com/PeopleImages

Meaningful activity is an important component of quality of life.

then leads to falls (e.g., Brummel-Smith, 1989), but this is not necessarily the case. Specifically, in their longitudinal investigation, Hadjistavropoulos and colleagues (2007b) did not find an association between fear-related avoidance of activity and future falls and speculated that fear of falling may have a direct negative effect on balance. This has now been confirmed (i.e., older people walk in a less stable way when they become anxious) (Delbaere, Sturnieks, Crombez, & Lord, 2009; Feltner, MacRae, & McNitt-Gray, 1994; Hadjistavropoulos et al., 2012). These changes in gait are less likely to appear when people are not anxious.

Educational interventions often focus on preventing falls (e.g., by recommending appropriate footwear and environmental modifications), but given the association between fear of falling—as well as depression—and increased fall risk, it is not surprising that CBT has also been employed in this context. CBT has been found to be effective in reducing fear of falling and recurrent falls, especially when it is combined with an appropriately supervised physical exercise program (Zijlstra et al., 2007; Zijlstra et al., 2009). CBT interventions aim to increase self-efficacy beliefs regarding falls as well as the sense of control over falling. An emphasis is also placed on correcting misconceptions about falls and fall risk, setting realistic goals for safely increasing physical activity, and changing the home environment to reduce risk (Zijlstra et al., 2009). In cases where physical exercise is involved in preventing falls, it is appropriate and usually necessary for psychologists to collaborate with other treating professionals such as physical therapists.

Behavioural Interventions in Long-Term Care

Many options for sheltered housing are available to older individuals, including independent senior housing with services, assisted living facilities, continuing care retirement communities, and skilled nursing facilities (Stone & Reinhard, 2007). Transition to any residential care may result in depression and loneliness (Rossen, 2007). Six to 25 per cent of LTC residents have a diagnosis of major depression, 12 to 25 per cent suffer from mild depressive disorders, and 30 to 50 per cent display significant depressive symptoms (e.g., Parmelee, Katz, & Lawton, 1992; Teresi, Abrams, Holmes, Ramirez, & Eimicke, 2001). Transitions to LTC often are precipitated by increasing physical or cognitive impairments, which are associated with decreased quality of life in multiple domains, such as privacy, individuality, relationship, and mood (Abrahamson, Clark, Perkins, & Arling, 2012). Passage of the Nursing Home Reform Act as part of the Omnibus Budget Reconciliation Act of 1987 in the United States mandated that adequate care in skilled nursing facilities include psychosocial and quality-of-life assessments (Fields, Kramer, & Lubin, 1993) and required certified LTC facilities to employ activities personnel (e.g., activities director, recreation therapist). Engagement in pleasant and meaningful activity is a fundamental component of quality of life (Colombo, Della Buono, Smania, Raviola, & De Leo, 2006; Glass, de Leon, Bassuk, & Berkman, 2006; Moos & Björn, 2006) and has been used as an intervention for improving mood and decreasing symptoms of depression (Glass et al., 2006; Lawton, 1997).

Behavioural Activation in Long-Term Care

The Brief Behavioural Activation Treatment for Depression (BATD) (Lejuez, Hopko, & Hopko, 2001) focuses on unique environmental contingencies that maintain depressed behaviour across settings. The intervention seeks to increase participation in meaningful events through goal setting and activity planning. A modified version of BATD with inpatients in a geropsychiatric facility involving eight sessions over a four-week period improved depression in patients (Snarski et al., 2011).

Animal-assisted therapy in LTC has health benefits. It can improve psychological states and self-worth, and increase morale (Beck & Katcher, 2003). Nursing home residents have demonstrated improvements in physical functioning, self-care, depression and anxiety, cognitive functioning, social functioning, and life satisfaction after taking care of a canary in comparison with caring for a plant or doing nothing. The canary group also demonstrated significant decreases in somatic complaints compared to the control group and significant decreases in anxiety and psychotic symptoms compared to the plant group (Colombo et al., 2006).

The amount of total activity, including group and individual activities, is positively related to interest and pleasure among nursing home residents. Residents vary greatly in terms of the activities that generate positive affect, and for some residents, participation in an activity increased negative affect. Depressed residents are less likely to engage in informal spontaneous activities and may benefit from more structured activities (Meeks, Young, & Looney, 2007). Thus, particularly for depressed residents, individually tailored activity programs are needed to increase their engagement in activities that are meaningful to them. It would be important for health geropsychologists and other mental health professionals to consider LTC settings as a primary practice arena. When mental health consultants have worked with LTC residents and staff to evaluate individualized activity plans and then implemented interventions engaging residents in pleasurable activities, both residents and staff reported satisfaction with this intervention (Meeks & Depp, 2002; Meeks, Looney, Van Haitsma, & Teri, 2008).

End-of-Life Care

End-of-life care is a continuum that spans from the time people receive a diagnosis of life-limiting illness until they take their last breath. Psychology can contribute across the continuum of care in many ways. The American Psychological Association (APA, 2005) defines **end of life** as the period when health-care providers would not be surprised if death occurred within six months. The APA ad-hoc committee on end-of-life issues identified four time periods when psychologists can contribute to end-of-life care: (1) before illness strikes; (2) after illness is diagnosed; (3) during advanced illness and the dying process; and (4) after the death of the patient with bereaved caregivers. Research has since demonstrated an important role for psychologists and trained retired senior volunteers in assisting caregivers throughout the caregiving process as well (Allen, Hilgeman, Ege, Shuster, & Burgio, 2008; Allen et al., 2014; Allen et al., 2016).

Palliative and hospice care are medical specialties related to end-of-life care (Kelley & Morrison, 2015). **Palliative care** is defined by the World Health Organization (2017) as an approach that improves the quality of life of patients and their families facing the problems associated with life-threatening illness, through the prevention and relief of suffering by means of early identification and impeccable assessment and treatment of pain and other physical, psychosocial, and spiritual problems. **Hospice** requires a prognosis of six months or less with focus on physical and emotional comfort, not curing illness. It can be provided in the patient's home, in freestanding hospice centres, hospitals, nursing homes, and other LTC facilities. Patients receiving palliative care can be receiving curative therapy; therefore, all hospice care is palliative care, but not all palliative care is hospice care. In order to meet goals of improved quality of life, the team approach is employed and often includes psychologists as well as social workers, chaplains, complementary and alternative practitioners (massage therapists, music therapists, art therapists, etc) in addition to physicians and nurses.

Another role for hospice is also to recognize and help the patient and family with grief. One of the most familiar models of grief is the work of Elisabeth Kübler-Ross, which describes five stages of grief: denial, anger, bargaining, depression, and acceptance (Kübler-Ross, 1969). More recently, grief has been conceptualized as a life process that varies in intensity (Wessel & Garon, 2005) rather than a single experience or series of stages as described by Kübler-Ross. Bruce (2007) outlined an updated view of "denial" that recognizes the griever's experience of "setting aside reality" while ". . . body, mind, and soul adjust to the distressful situation by closing down to protect and rebuild in small increments." The Fraser Health Hospice Psychosocial Care Guidelines (2006) describe that "the outcome of grief work is not so much about 'acceptance' as it is about exploring and adjusting to life without the person who has died." They recommend that, for the person still living, healing is about taking on the changes the loss has created, developing a new sense of self, and investing in new roles and relationships. They also describe normalizing and validating the grief process as an important part of grief work. Of note, 75 per cent of individuals are resilient and experience emotional recovery following the loss of a loved one, but that does not mean they do not experience sadness and emotional pain (Bonanno et al., 2002). Each grief experience is unique and personal and the length of time required to heal varies with each person. That said, when grieving becomes more complicated, usually adversely affecting daily functioning, a referral for more intense grief counselling should be considered. The following are risk factors for persistent complex bereavement disorder: sudden and unexpected death; loss of a child; death after a lengthy illness; death that the mourner perceives as having been preventable; a relationship with the deceased that was markedly angry, ambivalent, or dependent; multiple losses (past or present) or additional stressors; mental health concerns; and a mourner's perception of lack of support (Fraser Health, 2006). The APA (2005) outlined how psychologists can use their clinical skills on these teams. Evaluation and treatment of clinical depression and other mental health problems is important as research has demonstrated under-diagnosis and under-treatment of psychological distress in this population (Azuero, Allen, Kvale, Azuero, & Parmelee, 2012). Psychologists also help caregivers and family members with facilitating emotional expression and how to effectively be good listeners for people who are dying. They work with issues of mourning and loss, traumatic stress, and serve as advocates for good medical care and advance care planning across the care continuum. Psychologists not working on palliative care teams can also help their suffering patients by educating families about these services and providing them with referrals to palliative care as indicated.

Reminiscence Therapy

Although older adults experience declines in episodic memory with advancing age (Radvansky, 2011), considerable evidence demonstrates that **life review** and **reminiscence** interventions are effective in reducing symptoms of depression in this population (Bohlmeijer, Smit, & Cuijpers,

2003; Haight, Michel, & Hendrix, 2000; Haight & Webster, 1995; Scogin, Welsh, Hanson, Stump, & Coates, 2005); improving social interaction, quality of life, and aspects of well-being (Haber, 2006; Moos & Björn, 2006); and assisting in the integration, maintenance, or development of the self (Haber, 2006; Moos & Björn, 2006). Haber (2006) clearly differentiates reminiscence (the universal, passive recall of memories) from life review. Life review describes a structured, potentially multi-session interview focused around one or more life themes such as family, work, major turning points, the impact of historical events, the arts, aging, dying and death, and socialization issues such as meaning, values, and purpose in life.

Reminiscence interventions are often effective in reducing symptoms of depression in older persons.

We discuss reminiscence therapy in relation to three different populations: older adults in community, LTC residents, and persons in palliative care settings. Notably, across settings, incorporation of volunteer-delivered interventions incorporating schoolchildren, a folklorist/oral historian, or same-aged peer may be effective means of improving accessibility of reminiscence interventions to older adults with chronic illness (Allen et al., 2014; Kazdin & Blaise, 2011).

In Focus

The Legacy Project

The Legacy Project (Allen et al., 2008; Allen et al., 2014), conducted with palliative care patients and their informal family caregivers living in the community, combined reminiscence with creative activity. Both the individual with chronic illness and a member of his or her family were active participants in the intervention.

"You told me, you said, 'If you can't go forward, don't go backward. Stand still.' And that meant a whole lot to me."—Mrs J, caregiver and Legacy Project participant (2014).

This 70-year-old African-American woman, Mrs M, was living with chronic kidney disease in a rural community and receiving dialysis three times per week. Her lifelong friend (Mrs J) had taken up the task of caregiving, providing instrumental and emotional support on a daily basis. Mrs M was struggling with a desire for

primary control over her chronic illness (she wanted her illness to be cured), but her advanced-stage kidney disease left her in a position of vulnerability and in need of help from her friend (her chronic illness could not be cured and she needed to receive care).

Mrs M displayed significant symptoms of depression related to her diminished physical function and need for care. In a despondent tone, she stated, "I'm just not worth nothin.' I'm so sorry I'm putting you through all of this!" Mrs J response, quoted above, was a reminder that Mrs M had been a source of comfort and support in the past when Mrs J was in need. Mr. J emphasized their lifelong connection and stated it was time she repaid the favour. The two of them continued to work together in the Legacy Project to reminisce and to create a cookbook of recipes from Mrs M's family.

Treatments in the Community

Reminiscence has received support as an evidence-based treatment for depression among community-dwelling older adults. Using specific coding criteria developed by the Committee on Science and Practice of the Society for Clinical Psychology (Division 12) of the American Psychological Association, Scogin and colleagues (Scogin et al., 2005) found life review to be one of six treatments that are beneficial in reducing geriatric depression, and it is the only intervention developed specifically for older adults. Advanced-practice psychiatric nurses have been shown to effectively deliver life review and reminiscence therapy in the community with depressed patients and to decrease their anxiety, denial, despair, and isolation (McDougall, Buxen, & Suen, 1997).

Treatments in Long-Term Care

In 28 studies, published between 1990 and 2003, using life review with nursing home patients with mild to moderate dementia, benefits were found in self-esteem and self-integration, quality of life, and modification of problematic behaviour (Moos & Björn, 2006). Specifically, the individuals with mild to moderate dementia appeared to benefit most in the five interventions that targeted self-integration (e.g., Bourgeois, Dijkstra, Burgio, & Allen-Burge, 2001; Burgio et al., 2001) in comparison with the nine interventions targeting general quality-of-life outcomes and 11 targeting specific behaviour change. The features of the interventions associated with an enhanced sense of identity were (1) a thorough and encompassing treatment of the individual's life story; (2) the translation of the life story into care interactions with nursing home staff (e.g., mutual reminiscence); and (3) active encouragement of the residents' meaningful activity. Kitwood (1997) has argued that the emphasis on personhood and subjectivity in dementia care is in the process of being adopted as a best practice within LTC, with a humanistic emphasis on seeing the person with dementia as a person capable of having experiences within physical, social, and cultural contexts. However, Moos and Björn (2006) note several methodological problems within life-review studies, including inadequate information on the staging of dementia, limitations of personalized content as a result of group sessions, and poor documentation of unprompted or spontaneous recall of memories or events.

A relatively new intervention not included in these reviews was conducted by Cohen-Mansfield and colleagues (Cohen-Mansfield, Parpura-Gill, & Golander, 2006) based on their prior work in developing the Self-Identity in Dementia Questionnaire (Cohen-Mansfield, Golander, & Arnheim, 2000). Older persons with dementia most frequently report the following salient identity roles, in order of prevalence: (1) family heritage; (2) success of a relative; (3) academic achievement; (4) occupations; (5) traits; and (6) survival. Notably, better cognitive functioning was shown to be consistently related to a greater saliency of identity role in their sample (Cohen-Mansfield et al., 2000).

Using the Self-Identity in Dementia Questionnaire (Cohen-Mansfield et al., 2000), meaningful activity interventions were individualized for 93 older persons with severe dementia. Individuals with moderate dementia provided more salient input regarding their prior roles; the saliency of caregiver input increased as the severity of dementia within an individual increased. In all cases, interventions were designed to match the demographics and cognitive abilities of the person with dementia while still providing purposeful or meaningful activity (Cohen-Mansfield et al., 2006). A family role intervention, for example, involved the creation of a family tree using family photographs or watching videos from close family members. Self-identity awareness, affect, involvement, agitation, well-being, cognitive functioning, and provision of activities were assessed before and during the intervention. In comparison with usual care, the treatment group showed a significant increase in interest, pleasure, and involvement with activities; fewer agitated behaviours; and increased orientation during the treatment period (Cohen-Mansfield et al., 2006). Notably, feedback was not systematically gathered from family members about their impressions of the effectiveness of this intervention.

A product called CIRCA was developed by Scottish computer designers and psychologists to support reminiscence among individuals with dementia working with family and professional caregivers in adult daycare settings. It is a touch-screen interface to support reminiscence. Opinions of potential users and their caregivers are elicited and a guided system design uses an iterative (i.e., recurrent trial-and-error) approach. The interface was designed to be attractive and as simple as possible, with command prompts at the bottom of the screen to lessen fatigue. The system contains 10 videos, 23 music items, and 80 historic photographs of the local city organized into three themes: (1) recreation; (2) entertainment; and (3) city life. In comparison with traditionally administered reminiscence therapy, CIRCA sessions are more conversational with more varied topics and materials (Alm et al., 2007).

Although longitudinal intervention outcome studies are scarce, Haight and colleagues (2000) examined the potential therapeutic effects of a face-to-face structured life review with a therapeutic listener over three years. Half of the residents in this study received the life-review intervention whereas the other half received a friendly visit. Measures consisted of life satisfaction, well-being, self-esteem, depression, hopelessness, and suicide intent. Results indicated that the life-review intervention was beneficial. Scores on the baseline and post-test measures stayed the same in the intervention group but went down in the friendly visit control group, indicating the life-review intervention helped residents maintain stability in affect and identity over three years.

Treatment for Individuals Approaching the End of Life

Two intervention models using reminiscence and life review with individuals with advanced chronic illness and either health-care professionals or family caregivers have been applied in palliative care settings: (1) Chochinov's Dignity Therapy (Chochinov, 2012; Chochinov et al., 2011); and (2) the Legacy Project (Allen, 2009; Allen et al., 2008; Allen et al., 2014). Chochinov's Dignity Therapy (Chochinov, 2012; Chochinov et al., 2011) is a combination treatment approach that borrows elements from supportive therapy with its emphasis on empathy and connectedness; existential psychotherapy with engagement of issues such as meaning, hope, and mortality; and life review. One component of Chochinov's (2012) dignity-conserving repertoire is "generativity or legacy," an exercise that attempts to provide comfort through the telling of the life story and sense that one's life will transcend death. In the Dignity intervention (Chochinov et al., 2011), treatment was delivered individually over three to four sessions to terminally ill cancer patients in the hospital and those receiving home-based palliative care. A semi-structured interview was administered individually and the interviews were transcribed verbatim and edited by the treatment team to end with the patient's overall life message. After the therapist read the transcript to the patient, who could edit the life narrative, the patient could then share the life-story transcript with his or her family. Results indicated that Dignity Therapy was effective in improving positive affect and was perceived by patients and families as beneficial (Chochinov et al., 2011). Moreover, patients' belief that the Dignity interviews would be helpful to family members was associated with perceptions that life was more meaningful.

As mentioned in the case of Mrs M, the Legacy Project (Allen et al., 2008) has been found to decrease caregiving stress and increase positive affect and family communication as the

Harvey Chochinov of the University of Manitoba developed Dignity Therapy.

patient was approaching the end of life. Specifically, caregivers show reduced caregiving stress and patients report increased religious meaning and decreased difficulty breathing. Caregivers and patients report greater perceived social interaction in the care recipient. And they both report that completing the Legacy Project improved family communication (Allen et al., 2008).

A review of supportive interventions to improve psychological and physical health of informal caregivers and those with terminal illness found 11 randomized controlled trials (Candy, Jones, Drake, Leurent, & King, 2011). These research projects involved 1836 caregivers (and some patients). The review authors concluded that there is weak evidence that supportive interventions with caregivers of individuals with terminal illness may reduce caregiving distress; however, more evidence is needed.

To summarize, reminiscence and life-review interventions have yielded mostly successful outcomes and promoted successful aging among community-dwelling and institutionalized older adults as well as those approaching the end of life. However, very few studies have assessed outcomes of the life-review process on caregivers as well as patients, and greater research attention is needed in this area (Candy et al., 2011).

A new, promising area of psychological treatment for those facing life-limiting illness is **acceptance and commitment therapy** (ACT). ACT is a new wave of therapy within CBT (Hayes, 2004). The ACT treatment model is designed to help people change how they cognitively approach problems using techniques related to mindfulness, acceptance, and values-based living (Hayes & Smith, 2005). Interventions using ACT have been employed with cancer patients and have been found to be as effective as standard CBT for improving quality of life (Feros, Lane, Ciarrochi, & Blackledge, 2013). There is certainly much more to be explored regarding the effectiveness of ACT for improving quality of life and decreasing emotional suffering in those living with life-limiting illness or who are at the end of life, but preliminary findings are promising.

Medically Assisted Death

Although controversial (e.g., Materstvedt et al., 2003), medically assisted death for individuals facing life-limiting illness is becoming a more available option for consideration in some jurisdictions. On October 27, 1997, Oregon enacted the Death with Dignity Act, which allows terminally ill Oregonians to end their lives through the voluntary self-administration of lethal medications expressly prescribed by a physician for that purpose (Oregon Health Authority, 2018). Overall, Oregonians who have chosen to end their lives this way have been 65 years or older with cancer (Oregon Health Authority, Public Health Division, 2018). As of February 2017, California, Colorado, District of Columbia, Oregon, Vermont, and Washington have Death with Dignity statutes. In Montana, physician-assisted dying is legal by State Supreme Court ruling (Death with Dignity National Center, 2018). In their resolution on this issue, the American Psychological Association has not taken a stance, but does outline the complexities involved and the continuous need for evaluation, research, and advocacy from a full range of disciplines (APA, 2017).

In 2016, new Canadian federal legislation created a regulatory framework for medically assisted death (Health Law Institute, Dalhousie University, n.d.). Medically assisted death is now legal in Canada, if strict eligibility criteria are met (e.g., over the age of 18 years, must be eligible for medical services funded by the Government of Canada, incurable illness/disease/disability, natural death is "reasonably foreseeable", suffering is intolerable to the person and cannot be relieved under acceptable conditions). The legislation includes numerous safeguards and requirements to ensure that the criteria are met and that consent is voluntary. Some literature on this topic for psychologists working with terminally ill patients is available but a recent survey of Canadian psychologists demonstrated that participants had limited confidence in their ability to assess the competency of terminally ill patients to consent to medically assisted death (Karesa & McBride, 2016). Moreover, the psychologists who responded to the survey expressed interest in more professional training in this emerging area.

Cognitive Rehabilitation

Cognitive decline frequently is conceptualized as a part of normal aging. Cognitive processing speed slows with age, and is, sometimes, further slowed by cognitive impairment that sometimes occurs (Lezak, Howieson, & Loring, 2004) (see Figure 14.3). Poor decision making is a consequence of cognitive decline among some older persons without dementia (i.e., those widely considered cognitively healthy) (Boyle et al., 2012). Divided attention is the ability to pay attention to multiple streams of information simultaneously, or to ignore competing information or stimulation while concentrating on a task. Divided attention is slightly compromised by age, and more so by cognitive impairments (Lezak et al., 2004). According to the Society for Cognitive Rehabilitation (2013), **cognitive rehabilitation therapy** is "the process of relearning cognitive skills that have been lost or altered as a result of damage to brain cells/ chemistry." Examples of cognitive rehabilitation strategies that can improve encoding (use of context and existing knowledge to understand and store information) are providing instruction about activities at a slower pace, controlling the environment to cut down on distractions, and providing instruction in multiple modalities (i.e., demonstrating the task, then explaining the task in words) (Lezak et al., 2004). Other strategies can facilitate encoding by improving engagement, thereby increasing attention to the activity. Examples of such strategies include providing activities that have high levels of initial success and using adaptive or supportive environments and assistive devices (e.g., provision of electronic reminders) as needed (Camp, Cohen-Mansfield, & Capezuti, 2002). This intermediate strategy is important because Sperling and colleagues (2011) found that older persons who exhibit cognitive decline, but do not yet meet accepted criteria for mild cognitive impairment (MCI) or Alzheimer's disease (AD), may be most likely to benefit from early intervention and offer a unique opportunity to reduce the public health burden posed by AD.

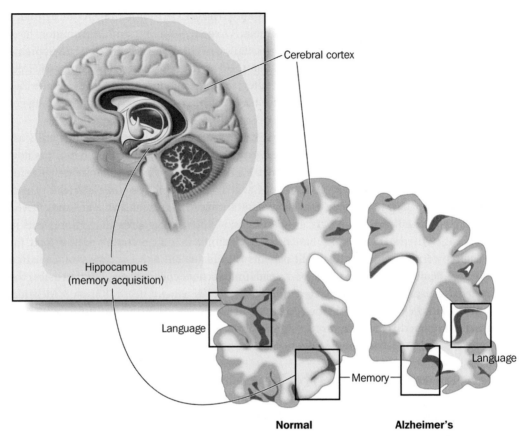

FIGURE 14.3 Neuronal loss associated with Alzheimer's disease results in atrophy of the affected brain regions. A cure for Alzheimer's disease has yet to be found.

Source: © Can Stock Photo Inc. / Blambs

There is growing evidence that cognitive training may be beneficial (Aguirre et al., 2010; Willis et al., 2006). Plassman, Williams, Burke, Holsinger and Benjamin (2009) reviewed factors associated with risk and possible prevention of cognitive decline and found insufficient evidence for most factors but acknowledged some promise for exercise, cognitive training, and certain nutritional patterns (i.e., a Mediterranean diet and fruits and vegetables). Yamaguchi, Maki, and Yamagami (2010) recommend a new approach to maintaining cognitive function called brain-activation rehabilitation. They recommend that activities designed to maintain cognitive function should include five principles: (1) enjoyable and comfortable activities; (2) activities that promote two-way communication; (3) efforts to enhance motivation among patients; (4) engagement in social roles that tap lifelong interests and abilities; and (5) pleasant environmental settings that are patient-centred.

Dementia

The available evidence is limited and there are no significant benefits of cognitive training in individuals with early stage AD or vascular dementia (Clare & Woods, 2003). This is attributed to a lack of randomized control trials in cognitive rehabilitation studies (Clare & Woods, 2003). In 2012, a clinical study examining cognitive rehabilitation also demonstrated no effect on the everyday functioning of participants with early-onset dementia (Kurz et al., 2012). Therefore, at this time, the efficacy of this treatment lacks sufficient scientific support in individuals with early-onset or vascular dementia (i.e., dementia related to problems in the flow of blood to the brain).

Future Directions

In addition to funding more graduate training in gerontology and geriatric medicine, professional organizations must focus continuing education efforts for currently practising professionals on the needs of older adults in North America. Practitioners interested in focusing assessment and intervention efforts on the needs of older adults with

Appropriately supervised physical exercise can have many benefits for older adults.

chronic illness need to be proactive in identifying their competencies and training needs (Karel, Emery, & Molinari, 2010; Knight, Karel, Hinrichsen, Qualls, & Duffy, 2009). Technology-based continuing education opportunities such as "webinars" are becoming increasingly available to meet the training needs of a diverse workforce. Through interdisciplinary collaboration and increased focus on health geropsychology, it is possible that the public health crisis in caring for older adults with chronic illness faced by the United States and Canada can be met in an effective manner.

Although technology use varies around the world, 80 per cent of Americans 50 to 64 years old use the Internet (Pew Research Center, 2017). Assisted technologies and information and communication technologies are showing promise to change the landscape for practice delivery and general connectedness of older adults. Interventions utilizing technology have demonstrated improved quality of life (Eastman & Iyer, 2004) for older adults and caregivers (Blazer, 2003). Although more research is needed to establish efficacy of cyber-based treatments, it is the future of education and service delivery. Nonetheless, there are ethical and practice concerns when utilizing technology clinically. Specifically, concerns such as privacy, access to technology, security, and ensuring the balance between patient autonomy and the beneficent responsibility of health-care providers must be addressed before technological interventions can be used on a larger scale (Bush, Allen, & Molinari, 2017). As Reed, McLaughlin, and Millholland (2000) outline in their guidance for practising ethical mental health care, providers' ethical and professional requirements do not change with the introduction of new technologies; therefore, it is incumbent upon the provider to ensure best practices in risk management and overall application of core ethical principles to each case.

Summary

In this chapter, we considered the prevalence of chronic illness among older people in the United States and Canada, clinical needs in working with these patients (e.g., considerations of multi-morbidity, the need for interdisciplinary teams, and a focus on the family), the impact of pain and falls, and how individuals cope with chronic illness and death and dying. Moreover, we considered specific areas of intervention, including behavioural interventions in LTC, reminiscence therapy, and cognitive rehabilitation. Because the numbers of older adults are growing rapidly, the public health burden of chronic disease and multi-morbidity will impact health-care costs, policy, and employment opportunities for the foreseeable future. A multi-faceted approach, including technology use, is critical to train the numbers of health geropsychologists needed to meet this burgeoning need.

Critical Thought Questions

1. Considering the different health-care systems operating within the United States and Canada, how might health geropsychologists structure their practice to best meet the needs of older clients with chronic illness?
2. What are the barriers and facilitators to collaborative or stepped care in different practice settings (i.e., community, primary care, LTC)?
3. How might the training needs of practising professionals and current health geropsychology students be met within technology-based workshops on working with older adults with chronic illness?

Recommended Reading

Aldwin. C.M., Park, C.L., & Spiro, A. (Eds.). (2007). *Handbook of health psychology and aging.* New York, NY: Guilford Press.

Bush, S.S., Allen, R. S., & Molinari, V. (2017). *Ethical practice in geropsychology.* Washington, DC: American Psychological Association.

Lichtenberg, P.A. (Ed.). (2010). *Handbook of assessment in clinical gerontology* (2nd ed.). Burlington, MA: Elsevier.

Mast, B.T. (2011). *Whole person dementia assessment.* Baltimore, MD: Health Professions Press.

Cross-Cultural Issues in Health Psychology

15

Jaime Williams

Chantelle Richmond

Learning Objectives

In this chapter you will:

- Discover how culture influences health and how people respond to illness and use support or treatment.

- Recognize how culture may function in a biopsychosocial model to explain better the etiology of illness, as well as to improve illness prevention and management strategies.

- Learn to describe key causes of disparities in health outcomes among different cultural groups and the key health disparities that exist in North America.

- Become familiar with the cross-cultural presentation of mental disorders, treatment implications, and the relationship to physical conditions.

Introduction: The Importance of Cross-Cultural Issues in Health Psychology

The award-winning film *God Grew Tired of Us* tells the story of three Sudanese "lost boys" as they are accepted into the refugee program of the United States. Approximately 40,000 children fled their country during the Second Sudanese Civil War from 1983–2005, often following the death of their families—a story of displacement, poverty, hunger, and war. They wandered in the desert of Sudan and other east African countries sometimes for years before reaching a refugee camp. This documentary gives us a unique view of the continued struggle of refugees as they strive to improve their quality of life despite the stresses of a new country and culture.

Our society is becoming increasingly multicultural and globally conscious. In recent years, the cultural composition of North America has shifted. In the United States in 2001, 25 to 30 per cent of people self-reported as being of minority status; this statistic increased to 34 per cent in 2010 and is expected to rise to approximately 50 per cent by the year 2050 (US Census Bureau, 2001; 2011). In Canada, visible minority persons (of non-Indigenous descent) constituted approximately 16 per cent of the population in 2006 and this portion is projected to double by 2031 (Statistics Canada, 2008). Indigenous persons (i.e., First Nations, Métis, Inuit) comprised approximately 3 per cent of the population in 2001 and almost 4 per cent in 2006; the Indigenous population is growing at a pace exceeding that of other Canadian ethnic groups (Statistics Canada, 2003, 2005).

Shifting demographics have a direct impact on the practice of health psychologists (Keefe & Blumenthal, 2004). We work with clients from many different cultural backgrounds and contexts and this is reflected in the current training and practice of psychology. Professional associations, researchers, and training programs recognize the importance of becoming culturally competent by understanding how different groups respond to physical and psychological symptoms and view medical services (Dana, 2002; Yali & Revenson, 2004). This chapter serves as a primer for the study of culture and health in psychology, with a focus on North American people of non-European/Western cultural backgrounds. In this chapter, we draw from a biopsychosocial model to describe and explain health disparities that exist among North Americans of differing cultures. This model is useful as it enables accounting for cultural differences and the ways these differences affect health. Such understanding allows for insight into the psychological impact of illness, responses to illness, challenges, and strengths that affect people of all ethnic and cultural backgrounds.

What Is Diversity? Distinguishing among Race, Ethnicity, and Culture

The terms **race**, **ethnicity**, and **culture**, although related, can also be distinguished from one another. Originally, the term "race" was intended to capture differences in biological substrates through physical characteristics such as skin colour and hair type (APA, 2002; Watt & Norton, 2004). However, the genetic and/or biological basis of race has been debated and the term is contentious given current understanding of genetics (Watt & Norton, 2004). Watt and Norton stress that genetic differences contributing to health and disease among various racial groups should not be dismissed. However, Mountain and Risch (2004) found that genetics only contributes to racial group differences in physical traits, complex diseases, and behaviour to a limited extent. They concluded that "we are far from characterizing the contribution of genes to between-group variation (racial group differences) of any complex trait and are likely to continue struggling in the future"

(p. s52). Nevertheless, the term "race" still reflects how others assign individuals to categories (or how people self-identify) (Cokley, 2007). Some argue that underlying concepts referenced by the term "race" (e.g., belonging, ownership, citizenship, and racism) have important implications for identity among African Americans (Airhihenbuwa & Liburd, 2006).

Some authors do not distinguish between the terms "race" and "ethnicity" or they use them interchangeably (e.g., Kressin, Raymond, & Manze, 2008; Skrentny, 2008). Kaplan and Bennett (2003) note that the term "race," as opposed to "ethnicity," however, is almost always linked to the idea of biological variation between groups. The American Psychological Association (APA) describes ethnicity as "the acceptance of the group mores and practices of one's culture of origin and the concomitant sense of belonging" (APA, 2002, p. 9), thereby recognizing the subjectivity and self-reflective nature of the concept, which is often captured through self-report measures. The APA further states that individuals may hold more than one ethnic identity with varying salience at different times (APA, 2002). Unfortunately, even among researchers, there is no consistency, with some arguing for the term "ethnicity" to encompass both the terms "race" and "culture" (Kaplan & Bennett, 2003).

"Culture" is an open and dynamic daily experience (e.g., language, family structure). People are exposed to multiple cultures of which their individual identities are composed. Culture is learned or transmitted through interaction with members already indoctrinated in the culture, yet changes over time (Lewis-Fernández & Krishan Aggarwal, 2013). These ideas may include implicitly and explicitly learned assumptions about individualism, equality, and health and illness (Yali & Revenson, 2004). Language is also considered a fundamental aspect of culture and its transmission (Marshall et al., 2011). Airhihenbuwa and Liburd (2006) note that culture as "collective consciousness" is reinforced through society. Society may promote health-supporting (protective) or health-hindering values, beliefs, and behaviours. Further, Stephens (2011) notes that representations of illness, appropriate responses to illness, the relationship between the mind and body, and the role of medical knowledge may all be culturally transmitted. Given that culture is primarily learned, it remains dynamic, ever-changing, and responsive to new situations depending on resources that are available vs required, and our roles and responsibilities (Andrews & Boyle, 2015; Watt & Norton, 2004). Of particular note in these definitions is the inclusivity of the term; all persons from all racial and ethnic origins are cultural producers and consumers (APA, 2002).

Hofstede's Value Dimensions of Culture

A highly influential framework for considering how values may vary across cultures was developed by Dutch social psychologist Geert Hofstede, and is referred to as **Hofstede's value dimensions of culture** (Hofstede, 2001; Taras & Kirkman, 2010). Hofstede conducted a pioneering study on how values in the workplace are influenced by culture through survey data from 88,000 IBM employees in 40 countries (20 languages) during the 1960s and 1970s (Hofstede, 2001; Taras & Kirkman, 2010). His framework originally included four dimensions of culture, with a fifth dimension being added later (Figure 15.1) (Hofstede & Bond, 1988). The first, *individualism–collectivism*, refers to the degree to which people within a society act individually rather than as part of a group, depending on how close or loose their interpersonal frameworks are. The second, *power distance*, refers to societal acceptance of the equal or unequal distribution of power within institutions. Third, *uncertainty avoidance* involves the ability of societies to tolerate ambiguity, as indicated by the presence or absence of clear rules. *Masculinity–femininity* is the extent to which a society values assertiveness and monetary acquisition ("ego-oriented" or "masculine") as opposed to co-operation, position security, and a friendly atmosphere ("relationship-oriented"

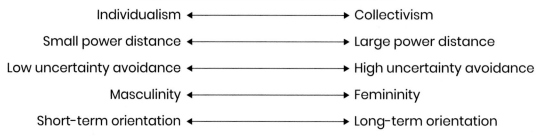

FIGURE 15.1   **Hofstede's value dimensions of culture.**

or "feminine"). The fifth dimension, *Confucian dynamism* (long-term vs short-term orientation), refers to future-oriented values (e.g., persistence) as compared with present/past orientation (e.g., traditions, social engagements). Both in Hofstede's original research (1980) and in more recent cross-cultural re-examinations of those dimensions (Fernandez, Carlson, Stepina, & Nicholson, 1997), inter-country differences have been found. Fernandez et al. (1997) examined differences in Hofstede's dimensions using a sample of respondents from nine countries. Overall, they found several differences, of note being that people from Western countries (e.g., the United States, Germany) score higher on individualism and those from non-Western cultures (e.g., Japan, China, Russia) were found to be more collectivist in orientation.

Studies of Hofstede's theories were compiled and meta-analyzed (i.e., statistically combined) by Taras and Kirkman (2010). In their review of 598 empirical investigations, several hypotheses were tested concerning the predictive power of Hofstede's cultural dimensions for individual traits such as emotional responses and attitudes. They found that the cultural dimensions predict most strongly participants' emotional responses (e.g., depression, anxiety) rather than their attitudes (e.g., religiosity, perceived justice, life satisfaction) or job satisfaction. This cultural trend was especially true for managers and employees, men, and those of higher levels of education. They concluded that cultural values are useful in predicting emotional responses (Taras & Kirkman, 2010). There have also been criticisms of Hofstede's work (Jones, 2007; McSweeney, 2002; Moulettes, 2007; Yeh, 1988). McSweeney (2002) notes the core assumption of Hofstede's view of culture is that it is implicit, causal, territorially unique, and shared. McSweeney further notes that this idea of culture has been debated at length. In other words, Hofstede's work has been criticized for minimizing the possibility of many cultures operating simultaneously within a country and also for assuming that national boundaries demarcate different cultural orientations (Jones, 2007). Moulettes (2007) provides a critique of the cultural value dimensions by asking whether the theory overall engenders Westernized, patriarchial structures. Moulettes and others raise their questions using **postcolonial theory**, which makes an attempt to understand the process and problems stemming from European colonization (Ashcroft, Griffiths, & Tiffin, 2006).

Cultural Factors and a Biopsychosocial Formulation of Health

Although past medical models and traditional views of health have somewhat neglected cultural differences in health and illness, this is changing. Alternatively, within health psychology the biopsychosocial formulation posits that biological, psychological, and social processes interact and contribute reciprocally to health and illness (Suls & Rothman, 2004); people's psychological and social experiences and behaviours are proposed to be interconnected with their biological processes. Culture and ethnicity have increasingly been recognized within a biopsychosocial formulation of health as important for the causation, prevention, and management of illness (Suls & Rothman, 2004). It is important to consider all the influences that culture exerts on health, including coping styles, economic resources, appraisals of and exposure to stress, and illness exposure (Suls & Rothman, 2004). Diversity is accelerating in multiple contexts, including social, religious, educational, and economic spheres (Keefe & Blumenthal, 2004), and these, in turn, have been shown to impact on health and mental health through such factors as language barriers and access to health insurance and health care (Yali & Revenson, 2004).

Susan Mogae (far left), diversity co-ordinator for Public Health, helped co-ordinate a multicultural fair that provided newcomers to Canada and service providers an opportunity to share information and learn about different resources supporting the health of Nova Scotians. To encourage interaction, volunteer interpreters trained by the Immigrant Settlement and Integration Service interpretation program were on hand to provide simultaneous interpretation in several languages.

To illustrate, Marshall and colleagues (2011) demonstrate how culture may be a central consideration within a biopsychosocial model of health for patients diagnosed with cancer and for their families. They emphasize socio-cultural and family-systems models in which culture, family, and social class interconnect and influence the trajectory of cancer illness. Although they recognize the role of biology in cancer, they present evidence suggesting that differences between groups of patients in the rates of cancers and recovery can be accounted for, at least in part, by socio-cultural factors. They describe, for example, findings that link cancer outcome disparities to low economic class, culture, and injustice, concluding that poverty, in particular, has strong explanatory power. Their model considers the "cancer experience" and treatment to involve all members of the family, rather than just the patient to the exclusion of his or her support people. They stress the personal influence of culture on individuals and families and, in turn, the individual's role as a producer of culture. Finally, Marshall and colleagues (2011) describe how cancer education may become more responsive to culture by considering language, transportation, finances, flexible care provision (e.g., time of treatments, setting), family-friendly treatment settings, and appropriate follow-up.

Health Beliefs Expressed Cross-Culturally

Within a biopsychosocial approach, health psychologists often focus on the *health beliefs* of the patient (e.g., Rabia, Knauper, & Miquelon, 2006; Sarafino & Smith, 2014). The health beliefs model of social cognition (also see Chapter 1) explains how beliefs interact to produce behavioural effects (health behaviours) (Rosenstock, 1974; Rosenstock, Strecher, & Becker, 1988). It is based on the assumption that people are motivated to be healthy (value) and that they hold beliefs about the helpfulness of their behaviours (expectancy)—hence, *value expectancy* theory. The likelihood that behaviours will occur depends on how effective a person believes that behaviour will be and his or her perceived level of risk for an illness (Abraham & Sheeran, 2007). Culture may affect people's health beliefs about disease and wellness, feelings about medical treatment and providers, and use of traditional medicines (Vaughn, Jacquez, & Baker, 2009).

Similarly, culture may affect *attributions* about health, which are causal explanations people assign to illness and wellness. For instance, Kottak (2011) describes three different styles of health attributions that may differ cross-culturally. Naturalistic theories (most characteristic of Western medicine) seek to explain illness scientifically, systematically, and impersonally. This approach is contrasted with personalistic theories that attribute illness to sorcerers, spirits, and ghosts, and emotionalistic theories that ascribe illness to extreme states of emotion. Some research has suggested that individuals from developing countries may more likely attribute causes of illness (mental and physical) to spiritual, social, and supernatural beliefs whereas those from more developed countries make attributes based on naturalistic, individual-centred theories of illness (e.g., Mulatu & Berry, 2001; Teferra & Shibre, 2012; Tenkorang, Gyimah, Maticka-Tyndale, & Adiei, 2011), although it is difficult to support generalizations (Kirmayer & Sartorius, 2007). Health beliefs and health attributions have a reciprocal relationship wherein attributions influence the development of health beliefs, which in turn affect how people make attributions (Vaughn et al., 2009). Health beliefs and attributions provide information to the patient about the meaning and seriousness of symptoms and influence health behaviours.

One may begin to gain insight into cross-cultural differences in health beliefs through the examination of values associated with systems of non-Western medicine (Gurung, 2011). Gurung (2011) describes a number of culturally based systems of medicine that are likely to influence health beliefs. For example, in traditional Chinese medicine (TCM), practitioners work *holistically* with the human body and environment. Forces in the body, along with pairings of organs and *qi* (chee; energy circulating in bodies, which is popularly conceptualized as the human-energy complex) are sought to be balanced and harmonized, which is considered central in health and illness (Jahnke, Larkey, Rogers, Etnier, & Lin, 2010). Health is viewed as optimizing balance between states and illness occurs from unbalance (Figure 15.2). Food is principal for balancing the body and optimizing the flow of *qi*.

As a second example, Cohen (2003) notes that among Native Americans, medicine is more akin to healing than to curing and focuses on restoring well-being and harmony to the body; these practices are often referred to as "traditional healing." Gurung (2011) notes that many elements of Native American medicine are similar to TCM, and that the values of both contrast with values in Western medicine. Elements of the natural world are considered alongside the human world wherein everything is connected. Healers co-ordinate medical practices and work with patients to find connections among their life experiences and their illness. Ritual, ceremony, and the spirit world are also often given consideration (Gurung, 2011).

Within Western medicine, many of these traditional systems of healing are being incorporated into complementary and alternative approaches to treating illness, perhaps reflecting the changing health beliefs of our multicultural society. Although many people use the terms "alternative" and "complementary" medicine interchangeably, the National Center for Complementary and Alternative Medicine (NCCAM) in the United States distinguishes between the two. It defines alternative medicine as non-mainstream approaches to health that are used *in place of* conventional medicine whereas complementary approaches refer to the use of non-mainstream approaches *in conjunction with* conventional medicine (NCCAM, 2013). It is further noted that the array of specific approaches can be divided into natural products and mind–body practices. Several mind–body practices are adaptations from non-Western medicine, such as meditation, yoga, Tai Chi, and qigong. Some empirical evidence supports the use of complementary and alternative approaches for the management of some health conditions. Although not perfectly consistent across studies, for example, some investigations have led to the conclusion that yoga has beneficial effects for patients with musculoskeletal pain problems (Cramer, Lauche, Langhorst, & Dobos, 2013; Ward, Stebbings, Cherkin, & Baxter, 2013).

Despite their potential importance, it is not easy to examine etiological (i.e., concerning the origins or causes) and other beliefs about physical and mental disorders cross-culturally (Kirmayer & Sartorius, 2007; Vaughn et al., 2009), and many have cautioned against the categorical measurement of ethnicity or race as proxy for culture (e.g., Ford & Kelly, 2005; Rudell & Diefenbach, 2008). For these reasons, few summative statements can be made concerning differences in health beliefs cross-culturally. For example, Sheikh and Furnham (2000) examined health beliefs among three cultural groups (community sample, total $N = 287$) including British Western, Asian British (Indo-Asian background residing in Britain), and Pakistani (residing in Pakistan) persons, expecting that Asian British and Pakistani people would endorse more non-Western and fewer Western health beliefs compared to British Western individuals. Although they found these

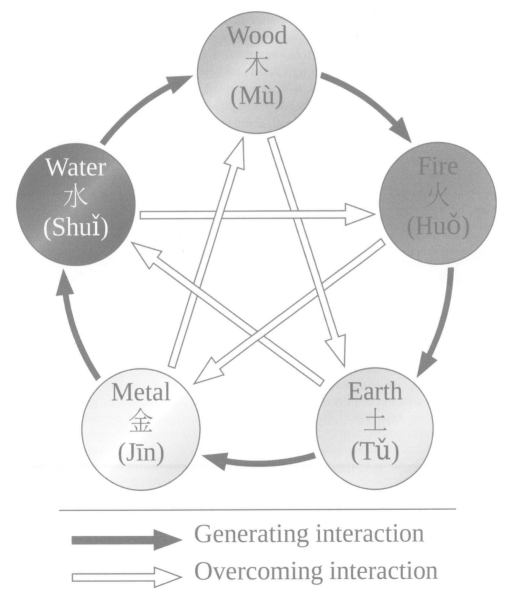

FIGURE 15.2 **The five elements of traditional Chinese medicine.**

Source: Wikipedia/Ju gatsu mikka based on works of Benoît Stella.

expected patterns for Asian British and British Western participants, Pakistani participants scored higher on measures of Western attributions of illness as well as non-Western attributions of illness than British Western participants. The authors admitted this was unexpected and suggested speculatively that plurality within the Pakistani medical system may explain the differences.

Health Disparities among Cultural Groups

Health disparities refer to the gap between the incidence (i.e., number of new cases of an illness in a given time period) and prevalence (i.e., number of total cases of an illness in a given time period) rates of illness and death among different groups of people, for example, socio-economic status groups; cultural groups; older adults; and lesbian, gay, bi, transgendered, and queer (LGBTQ) persons (Carter-Pokras & Baquet, 2002; Centers for Disease Control and Prevention [CDC], 2011). These differences can be evaluated quantitatively and qualitatively in terms of *inequality* (i.e., an unequal condition) and also *inequity* (i.e., an unequal condition deemed to be unfair or unjust) (Carter-Pokras & Baquet, 2002). Although significant health disparities exist among Caucasian people and people representing visible minority populations, Indigenous people, and Hispanic and Latino people, the relationship between health disparities and ethnic status is not straightforward; it generally is considered to be mostly mediated. Mediation occurs when a third variable accounts for the measured relationship between two variables such as socio-economic status and health behaviours (Carter-Pokras & Baquet, 2002; CDC, 2011). To understand health disparities, researchers use multiple health-related outcomes/indicators including health status (e.g., life expectancy), subjective self-rated health, disease presence (e.g., diabetes), health-care access and use, and health behaviours (e.g., smoking) (Frohlich, Ross, & Richmond, 2006).

In Focus

Cultural Loss, Environmental Change, and Contemporary Patterns of Health

Indigenous knowledge (IK) is understood as the knowledge held by local people concerning their everyday realities of living in, and as part of, their environments and greater ecosystems (Cajete, 1999; Ermine, Nilson, Sauchyn, Sauve, & Smith, 2005). Indigenous knowledge refers to the cultural traditions, values, and belief systems that have enabled many generations of Indigenous people to have nourishing relationships with their natural and social environments, thereby allowing them not only to survive, but to flourish (Battiste & Henderson, 2000). Traditionally, IK has been expressed through oral tradition—language and stories—about the ways Indigenous peoples live their lives (Battiste & Henderson, 2000). Over time, processes of environmental dispossession have altered the maintenance and transmission of IK. Environmental dispossession refers to the processes by which Indigenous people's access to their traditional lands and resources is reduced or severed (see Richmond & Ross, 2009; Luginaah, Smith, & Lockridge, 2010). This occurs through direct and indirect forms. Direct forms of environmental dispossession involve physical processes that block use of land, such as contamination events or industrial development, which physically sever ties to traditional foods or resources required for sustaining daily activities. Indirect forms of dispossession occur as a result of policies intended to sever links to the environment, such as the residential school

Significant Health Disparities in North America

Richmond and Cook (2016) review the evidence for health disparities in Canada. They note that although some health disparities have narrowed, Canada still shows clear differences among groups of people regardless of the indicators used (e.g., health status, health behaviours, disease outcomes). Most notably, Canada's Indigenous peoples fare much worse than non-Indigenous Canadians on indicators such as life expectancy and infant mortality, chronic disease outcomes, and health behaviours (Mitrou et al., 2014). For example, Indigenous men living off reserve have a life expectancy of 72.1 years whereas the general Canadian population has a life expectancy of 76 years. For Indigenous women, life expectancy is 77.7 years off reserve compared to 81.5 years for the general population. When Indigenous persons living on reserves are considered, this gap widens to nearly 9 years for men and 8.5 years for women. Smylie, Fell, and Ohlsson (2010) examined infant mortality rates among Indigenous people in Canada, noting that these rates are important indicators of the overall level of health of a population. They found sizable and persistent elevations in infant mortality rates among First Nations people residing both on and off reserve as well as among Inuit people compared to the general population of Canada. Infant mortality is an important indicator of health disparity, reflecting several underlying mechanisms, such as maternal health, quality of health care, socio-economic conditions, and public health practices (Elias, 2014; MacDorman & Mathews, 2011). The Inuit of Quebec have a rate of infant mortality greater than five times that of the general Canadian population (23.1 deaths/1000 vs 4.4 deaths/1000). Similar findings have been reported for life expectancy and infant mortality for Indigenous populations in the United States, Australia, and New Zealand (Smylie et al., 2010).

Regarding specific illness outcomes, diabetes and its complications are particularly problematic for Indigenous persons. Health Canada has reported that rates of diabetes among First

system, which was regulated under Canada's Indian Act, and which forcibly removed 150,000 Indigenous children from their homes. Because of the special links between First Nations people and their physical environments (Richmond, Elliott, Mathews, & Elliott, 2005; Parlee, Berkes, & Gwich'in, 2005; Wilson, 2003), environmental dispossession has had disastrous implications for the health and well-being of affected communities (Adelson, 2005; Gracey & King, 2009; Guimond & Cooke, 2008; Richmond & Ross, 2009).

In contemporary times, these processes manifest in the health of the population as social upheaval, mental illness, violence, crime, suicide, disease (Adelson, 2005), and culture stress, which is often apparent in societies that have undergone massive, imposed, or uncontrollable change. Berry (2005) notes that cultural change may include both indirect change that is "ecological" in nature (e.g., the ethnic constituency of neighbourhoods) and delayed change of internal adjustments (i.e., psychological transformation takes time). In cultures under stress, people tend to lose confidence in what they know to be true, and they also begin to question their own value as human beings (Bartlett, 2003). The effects of culture stress have been particularly prominent among Canada's Indigenous youth population, leading to a disproportionate incidence of accidents, violence, substance/drug abuse, and suicide, as well as lower high school completion rates and reduced workforce participation (Adelson, 2005; Browne, Smye, & Varcoe, 2005; Chandler, Lalonde, Sokol, & Hallet, 2003; Gideon, Gray, Nicholas, & Ha, 2008; Richmond, 2007; Richmond & Ross, 2008; Wilson & Rosenberg, 2002).

Nations persons living on reserve are three to five times higher than among other Canadians (Health Canada, 2011): 19.7 per cent of First Nations people are diagnosed with diabetes, compared to 5.2 per cent in the general population. Although rates of diabetes are somewhat lower among Métis and First Nations persons living off reserve (Reading & Wien, 2009), health disparities are still present and Health Canada (2011) expects these rates to increase due to a significant presence of risk factors, such as obesity and physical inactivity. In the United States, Native Americans and Alaska Natives are more than twice as likely to have a diagnosis of diabetes as their non-Hispanic White counterparts (American Diabetes Association, 2012). The American Diabetes Association (2012) notes that there have been steady increases in diabetes over the past 15 years, especially among youth. For more information about Indigenous knowledge and patterns of health in Canada, see the accompanying In Focus box.

In the United States, health disparities among African-American and other ethnic groups are of particular note (e.g., CDC, 2011; Mensah, Mokdad, Ford, Greenlund, & Croft, 2005). The health disparities between African-American men and other groups in the United States have been described as "staggering" (Xanthos, Treadwell, & Braithwaite Holden, 2010, p. 11). The CDC (2011) reported that in terms of life expectancy, African Americans live six to ten years less than non-Hispanic White Americans and have twice the infant mortality rate (13.35 per 1000 live births compared to 5.58 per 1000). Cardiovascular health and cardiovascular risk factors are other key outcomes that pose a particular problem for African-American men and women (Keenan & Shaw, 2011; Mensah et al., 2005). Cardiovascular disease mortality in general and premature death rates from cardiovascular disease and stroke are highest among African Americans compared to all other ethnic groups, including non-Hispanic White, Hispanic, American Indian/Alaskan Native, and Asian/Pacific Islander (Keenan & Shaw, 2011; Mensah et al., 2005) (see Figure 15.3). Keenan and Shaw (2011) in their literature review also examined health disparities for cardiovascular disease risk factors and found that major disparities exist among younger individuals aged 23 to 25. With regard to these risk factors, obesity (especially among women) and hypertension are particularly problematic for African Americans compared to other ethnic groups (Mensah et al., 2005). However, concerning ethnic group differences in cardiovascular disease and risk, Mensah et al. (2005) note that these relationships are complex. Similar to other conclusions about health disparities, they stress the importance of mediating variables such as education level and poverty.

Among the US Hispanic population, there are several notable health disparities. Vega, Rodriguez, and Gruskin (2009) describe diabetes, certain types of cancer, liver disease, and human immunodeficiency virus (HIV) as being particularly problematic. Regarding diabetes, Hispanic people living in the United States experience greater disparities in risk, greater complications from diabetes, and both men and women experience higher diabetes-related mortality rates (Osborn, de Groot, & Wagner, 2013; Vega et al., 2009). Moreover, these mortality rates are increasing at a greater rate than in the general population (Vega et al., 2009). Specific types of cancers, especially cervical cancer among women and stomach and liver cancers among men, also reflect disparities among US Hispanics, although the overall cancer rates are not elevated within this population (Vega et al., 2009). Moreover, there are disparities in the rates of mortality due to liver disease among the Hispanic population, although the rates of these conditions are not elevated (Vega et al., 2009). It is somewhat unclear why these disparities occur, although several secondary variables (e.g., patterns of alcohol consumption, obesity, socio-economic status) may be responsible (see Determinants of Health Disparities below). Finally, HIV mortality reflects an important health disparity among the US Hispanic population, although this gap has narrowed (Henao-Martinez & Castillo-Mancilla, 2013; Vega et al., 2009). Despite progress in this area, mortality rates from

HIV among Hispanics are almost three times the rate for White people (Vega et al., 2009). Moreover, the number of new cases of HIV is disproportionately large among Hispanic people, and those being infected are on average younger than White non-Hispanics (Vega et al., 2009).

Determinants of Health Disparities

Carter-Pokras and Baquet (2002) note that health disparities are not thought to occur due to ethnicity/race/culture per se but rather because of a complex chain of secondary mediating variables (e.g., health-care access) contributing to disease outcomes (e.g., recovery from illness) (Carter-Pokras & Baquet, 2002; CDC, 2011). These secondary variables can be described as *health-care*

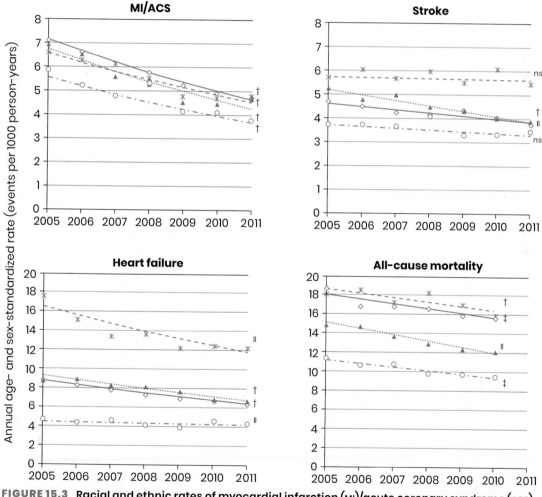

FIGURE 15.3 Racial and ethnic rates of myocardial infarction (MI)/acute coronary syndrome (ACS), stroke, heart failure, and all-cause mortality from 2005 to 2011 among 1.25 million insured persons with diabetes mellitus across 11 health care systems. Cross indicates ✕ = non-Hispanic Black; ▲ = solid triangle, Hispanic; ◇ = open diamond, non-Hispanic White; and ○ = open circle, non-Hispanic Asian. Annual rate of change (Poisson regression): ns, nonsignificant; ‡P<0.05 ; ‖P<0.01 ; †P<0.001.

Source: Desai, J. R., Vazquez-Benitez, G., Xu, Z., Schroeder, E. B., Karter, A. J., Steiner, J. F., ... O'Connor, P. J. (2015). Who must we target now to minimize future cardiovascular events and total mortality? *Circulation: Cardiovascular Quality and Outcomes, 8*, 508–516.

disparities (i.e., differences that exist among people of various cultures regarding access to health-care services, facilities, and providers). Therefore, determining and predicting health status among groups of people requires the examination of multiple factors. These multi-dimensional approaches to understanding health disparities are in accordance with biopsychosocial perspectives of health.

Government agencies responsible for researching population health often identify *determinants* that are given priority within a health-care platform. **Determinants of health** can be defined as the range of factors (i.e., personal, socio-economic, environmental) that account for the health status of groups of people (WHO, 1998). The US Department of Health and Human Services (HealthyPeople.gov, 2012) groups determinants of health into policy making, social factors, health services, individual behaviour, and biology and genetics. Health Canada (2011) considers 12 key determinants of health, 11 of which are socially based and one that recognizes "biology and genetic endowment." The full list includes income and social status, social support networks,

Former Canadian federal Minister of Health Leona Aglukkaq (left), signs an agreement on 13 October 2011 ensuring a new First Nations health governance structure. This structure ensures a major role for the First Nations of British Columbia in the management and planning of health services for First Nations. Also pictured are BC Minister of Health Michael de Jong (sitting, second from left), members of the BC First Nations Health Council and the BC First Nations Health Society, and Assembly of First Nations National Chief, Shawn A-in-chut Atleo (standing, second from right).

education and literacy, employment/working conditions, social environments, physical environments, personal health practices and coping skills, healthy child development, biology and genetic endowment, health services, gender, and culture. Although ethnicity (i.e., "culture") is included, Health Canada emphasizes that the risks to health evident through group membership are due to the socio-economic environment in which dominant cultural values serve to marginalize, devalue, and reduce health-care access. Indeed, when considering why health disparities occur among different ethnic groups, one must account for the entire set of determinants (Reading & Wien, 2009), including processes such as colonialism, racism, and discrimination. As Adelson (2005) notes, Indigenous health disparities are related to economic, political, and social disparities—not to any inherent Indigenous trait—and exist because of the limited autonomy Indigenous peoples have in determining and addressing their health needs. And in fact, in an important new addition to the base of Indigenous health scholarship in Canada *Determinants of Indigenous Peoples' Health in Canada: Beyond the Social* (Greenwood, de Leeuw, Lindsay, & Reading, 2015), a compelling case is made that colonialism must be viewed as the most important determinant of Indigenous people's health.

Socio-Economic Status: A Critical Determinant of Health Disparity

Socio-economic status (SES), which is generally established through a combination of education, income, and work status, is emphasized as a leading cause of health disparities (e.g., APA, 2007; Brawley, 2007). Brawley (2007), the chief medical officer of the American Cancer Society, notes that it is appropriate to define disparities in socio-economic terms rather than racial terms, given the substantial numbers of disadvantaged persons of all ethnicities who are at increased risk for health problems. Nevertheless, there are many complexities when examining the relationships among culture/race/ethnicity, socio-economic status, and health. Socio-economic status does not account for all disparities in health; some ethnic health disparities persist at similar levels of SES (Xanthos et al., 2010).

The APA's Task Force on Socioeconomic Status (APA, 2007) describes three conceptualizations of SES: materialist, gradient, and social-class perspectives. The materialist perspective uses education, income, and occupation to explain varying levels of *access to resources*, which is the primary explanatory mechanism of disparities. A gradient perspective considers the *relative gap* between groups of people as important for health and often focuses on mediating pathways (e.g., coping styles, belief structures) as explanatory mechanisms. The social-class perspective considers aspects of society that promote closed perpetuation of wealth and power. Unequal access to resources is viewed as important for understanding health, but unlike a materialist perspective, the focus is on a broad societal level. The APA (2007) notes that only recently have researchers focused on systemic factors within broader societal systems that reinforce inequality and disparities.

Overall, a well-known positive association exists between health and SES; those of higher status tend to have better health (Matthews & Gallo, 2011; Ram, 2006). People of lower SES are more likely to suffer from diseases, to experience lowered functioning due to illness, to have higher physical and cognitive impairment, and to have higher mortality rates (e.g., Anderson, Bulatao, & Cohen, 2004; Matthews & Gallo, 2011; Zheng, 2009). Visible minorities, Indigenous people, and Hispanic and Latino persons are over-represented among those living in poverty (Statistics Canada, 2008, US Census Bureau, 2011). In the United States and Canada, adults of African descent are over-represented in the lowest income bracket and under-represented in the highest brackets (Attewell, Kasinitz, & Dunn, 2010). Attewell et al. (2010) further note that Black

Eric Fowke / Alamy Stock Photo

The National School Lunch Program, administered by the US Department of Agriculture, promotes nutrition and prevents hunger for approximately 31 million students throughout the United States through federal assistance to schools and child-care centres.

households have significantly lower household income than White households and that these income gaps "are not simply a matter of educational differences or differences in household composition between Blacks and Whites in each country. After controlling for education and the other factors, the racial income gaps remain substantial, and of roughly similar magnitude in Canada and the US" (Attewell et al., 2010, p. 484). In Canada, Indigenous people are among the poorest in the country and the income gap has not substantially closed since 1996 (Wilson & Macdonald, 2010). Morales, Lara, Kington, and Valdez (2002) note that socio-economic status for Hispanic Americans is comparable to African Americans and is much lower than among non-Hispanic Whites, although this finding varies by Hispanic subgroup (e.g., Puerto Rican, Cuban, Mexican).

To illustrate the relationships among race, socio-economic status, and health, consider that African-American men are disadvantaged economically compared to Caucasian men as evidenced through lower earnings, higher unemployment, and greater representation in lower-income jobs; these economic factors contribute to social disadvantages such as poorer neighbourhood conditions and environmental hazards (Xanthos et al., 2010). As previously discussed, African-American men also experience disparities in health in many regards in comparison to men from other ethnic groups, including Caucasians (CDC, 2011; Mensah et al., 2005). Xanthos et al. (2010) note that lower SES has been linked to poorer health in this population through a stress-related mechanism, which may result from reduced opportunities (e.g., educational, occupational, health). However, socio-economic conditions do not account for all the differences between African Americans and other groups, with disparities in health remaining after SES has been controlled for (Hayward, Miles, Crimmins, & Yang, 2000; Xanthos et al., 2010). Xanthos et al. (2010) recommend examination of other social conditions (related to SES) to further understand health disparities, specifically racial discrimination and elevated incarceration rates among Black (young especially) males, and call for these social conditions to be examined in conjunction with their effects on health behaviours in order to begin to close the gap in health outcomes for Black men.

The Effect of Acculturation

When people relocate to another culture, they undergo a socio-cultural process of **acculturation** wherein they adapt to and take on characteristics (i.e., behavioural, lifestyle) of the "new" culture via continual contact (Kazarian & Evans, 2001; Morales et al., 2002; Sam & Berry, 2016). Some argue that characteristics from the first culture are lost during acculturation, whereas others maintain that aspects of both cultures can be held concomitantly (Morales et al., 2002). A useful theory for understanding acculturation is Berry's (1997) two-factor model of acculturation (Figure 15.4), in which levels of identification with the native and host cultures are considered. Four outcomes are possible: (1) *marginalization* occurs when there is low affiliation with either culture; (2) *separation* occurs when an individual has a high affiliation with the culture of origin but a low identification with the new culture; (3) *assimilation* involves a low affiliation with the culture of origin but a high affiliation with the new culture; and (4) *integration* involves high affiliation with both cultures. More recent theories consider a multi-dimensional view in defining and measuring acculturation (Lopez-Class, Castro, & Ramirez, 2011). Acculturation is not necessarily a straightforward process, but rather occurs in stages across several domains such as language and socio-economic status; the characteristics of acculturation and the degree to which changes manifest depend on the differences between the two cultures (Lopez-Class et al., 2011).

Acculturation is important for explaining variation in health behaviours as well as discrepancies in health conditions within cultural groups (e.g., Lara, Gamboa, Kahramanian, Morales, & Hayes Bautista, 2005). Morales et al. (2002) note that acculturation can have positive or negative effects on health behaviours depending on the frequency of the behaviour in the original and new cultures. For example, if reliance on fast food is more common in the new culture, acculturation would have a negative effect evidenced through increased consumption of fast food. Conversely, if rates of obesity were higher in the original culture, acculturation may exert a positive influence.

Consider the effect of acculturation on the Hispanic population living in the United States. It has been observed that indicators of health such as age-adjusted mortality rates and birth outcomes are *more* favourable among Hispanic persons compared to other groups (including Caucasians) and compared to what would be expected given their levels of poverty (Lara et al., 2005); this is sometimes referred to as the *Hispanic paradox* (Cutler, Lleras-Muney, & Vogl, 2008). Acculturation has been examined as a factor in this discrepancy. Morales et al. (2002) found that acculturation had a positive impact on some behaviours and a negative impact on others. Specifically, acculturation to mainstream America resulted in increased alcohol consumption. Concerning diet, acculturation can have both

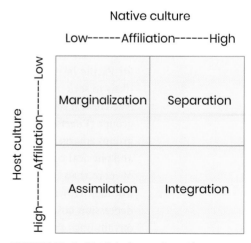

FIGURE 15.4 **Model of acculturation.**

Source: Adapted from Berry (1997).

negative and positive effects, but overall the effects tend to be more negative (i.e., traditional diets are protective and a typical North American diet may lead to health deterioration). Acculturation's *positive* effects for Latinos seem to be in health-system use and perceptions of one's own health (Lara et al., 2005). However, the Hispanic population is heterogeneous (e.g., Cuban, Puerto Rican, Mexican, South and Central American) and health outcomes differ greatly among subgroups (Ortega, Feldman, Canino, Steinman, & Alegria, 2006). For example, infant mortality rates have been found to be higher among Puerto Rican women (8.01) compared to non-Hispanic White women (5.58), but Mexican, South and Central American, and Cuban women have marginally lower infant mortality rates (5.34, 4.52, and 5.08 per 1000, respectively) (MacDorman & Mathews, 2011), underscoring the complexities in understanding health disparities and the importance of considering mediating variables.

Mental Health Issues and Health

The APA (2012) describes clinical health psychologists as working at the intersection between physical and emotional conditions. In order to treat clients, they need to have knowledge of how diseases affect the body physically and psychologically and how psychological states may affect physical well-being. They must also be aware of how culture, race, and ethnicity affect both physical illnesses and mental disorders, which may be co-morbid (Scott, McGee, Schaaf, & Baxter, 2008). Although the relationship between mental disorders and physical conditions has been well established, possible cross-cultural differences have not often been researched despite significant impetus to do so (Scott et al., 2008). Researching cross-cultural differences may provide insight into the mechanisms linking physical and psychological conditions more generally, and health disparities could be narrowed (Scott et al., 2008). At this point, more research into the area is needed.

Scott and colleagues (2008) conducted one of only a few studies examining patients presenting with mental and physical health co-morbidities. They examined a general population survey ($N = 7435$) in New Zealand, focusing on cultural groups (Indigenous Maōri, Pacific Islanders, and those of European descent), physical conditions (chronic pain, cardiovascular disease, diabetes, and respiratory disease), and psychological difficulties. Few differences were found based on cultural/ethnic group. The only noteworthy finding was that the association between respiratory disease and mood disorders was stronger for the Pacific group, but the authors were unable to explain this finding (Scott et al., 2008).

In another study, Scott, Kokaua, and Baxter (2011) found that having a physical condition resulted in *increased* help-seeking behaviour for mental health problems. This finding was strongest for Pacific Islanders. However, Pacific Islanders, in the absence of a physical problem, were *less* likely to seek mental health treatment compared to other ethnic groups. Ortega et al. (2006) analyzed health survey data on concurrent physical and psychological problems from four US Latino groups (Puerto Ricans, Cubans, Mexicans, and other Latinos/Latinas). Differences between the groups emerged, with Puerto Ricans faring the worst: the highest levels of concurrent psychiatric and physical conditions; higher lifetime prevalence for any psychiatric disorders; the highest rate of more than one disorder; and the highest level of having a depressive disorder or an anxiety disorder. However, their findings overall suggested that Latinos/Latinas do not have significant depression co-occurring with cardiovascular disorders or diabetes, which is contrary to previous findings that indicated these associations (Anderson, Freedland, Clouse, & Lustman, 2001; Möller-Leimkühler, 2007; Ortega et al., 2006). Nonetheless, there is limited evidence of different patterns of co-occurrence of physical and mental conditions among different cultural groups.

In the context of the co-occurrence between physical and psychological disorders, it is important to note that immigrants in general across countries have increased rates of psychological disorders compared to native populations (Bhugra & Jones, 2001). In addition, Canadian First Nations people have been found to have higher rates of suicide (some estimates indicate twice the rate), alcoholism, and incidences of violence (e.g., Health Canada, 2008; Kirmayer, 1994; Kirmayer et al., 1993; Royal Commission on Aboriginal Peoples, 1995). For example, Frideres (2011, p. 128) notes that "For the past decade, over one-third of all First Nation deaths have resulted from accidents and violence, compared to 8 per cent for non–First Nations deaths." Moreover, minority populations in North America have fewer psychological services available to them and have difficulty accessing these services; they have a lower likelihood of seeking out, receiving, and retaining services, and there is less probability they will receive high-quality care and obtain benefits of therapy (e.g., Saha, Arbelaez, & Cooper, 2003; Shin et al., 2005; Smedley, Stith, & Nelson, 2002).

Cross-Cultural Presentation of Psychological Symptoms and Disorders

Much of the mental health research conducted in North America and Europe primarily focuses on Caucasian populations. Although this research has relevance to minority groups, there is also evidence that rates of mental disorders, patterns of psychopathology, and presentation of symptoms are influenced by cultural factors (Blumentritt, Angle, & Brown, 2004; Kirmayer, 2001; Thakker & Ward, 1998; Weisz et al., 1993). Also, some physical and psychological conditions are specific to various cultures. These are referred to as **culture-bound syndromes**, which have been described as recurrent patterns of abnormal behaviour and troubling experience that occur specifically to a local culture/community (American Psychiatric Association, 2000; Vaughn et al., 2009). Clinicians should understand both symptom presentation and culture-bound syndromes to improve assessment, diagnosis, and treatment (Vaughn et al., 2009).

Cultural factors have been investigated within many categories and types of mental disorders such as anxiety disorders, mood disorders, schizophrenia, and conduct disorder, as well as general symptoms of distress (Muris, Schmidt, Engelbrecht, & Perold, 2002; Oates et al., 2004; Suhail & Cochrane, 2002). To illustrate, consider a research investigation on postpartum depression (Oates et al., 2004). The researchers describe the universality of feelings of distress and unhappiness following childbirth in women in 11 countries as diverse as France, Uganda, Japan, and the United States. Using a qualitative approach, they found that women from all countries attributed insufficient sleep and fatigue to unhappiness following delivery. Women from all the countries recognized the phenomenon of morbid unhappiness (i.e., postpartum depression). However, the term "postnatal depression" was not consistently used and not all of the cultural groups considered these feelings abnormal or to require professional treatment.

As another example, Lewis-Fernández et al. (2009) reviewed the cross-cultural literature on anxiety disorders, including panic attacks, panic disorder, agoraphobia, specific phobia, social anxiety disorder, obsessive compulsive disorder, and generalized anxiety disorder. They found that research studies supported the importance of cultural factors in the expression of panic disorder, social anxiety disorder, and generalized anxiety disorder especially. With regard to social anxiety disorder, prevalence rates were found to be higher in US populations compared to other countries such as Japan and Mexico. The situation within the United States was more complex. There, higher prevalence of social anxiety disorder was associated with being American Indian and lower prevalence associated with being Asian, Latino/Latina, African American, or Caribbean Black; however, these associations varied depending on other variables such as education, age, and immigration status. In terms of cultural

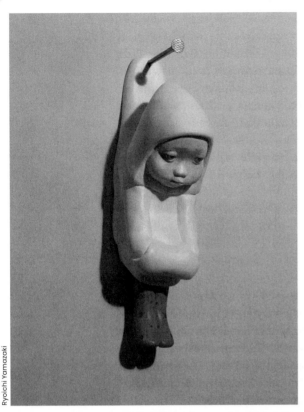

Ryoichi Yamazaki

Japanese artist Ryoichi Yamazaki creates diminutive ceramic sculptures that explore the culture-bound syndrome, *hikikomori*, such as in the above example entitled, "Nobody helps me." *Hikikomori* is described as extreme social isolation and withdrawal of Japanese youth to their bedrooms within their parents' homes and is often associated with extreme apathy.

variation within symptom presentation, Lewis-Fernandéz et al. (2009) describe a cultural variant of social anxiety, *Taijin kyofusho*, a culture-bound syndrome, although the distinct status of *Taijin kyofusho* from social anxiety disorder has been debated (American Psychiatric Association, 2000; Suzuki, Takei, Kawai, Minabe, & Mori, 2003). In Japan and South Korea, a subgroup of patients who have fear of social situations and avoidance express concerns that are not typically found among North American samples. Specifically, these individuals have social fears of doing something that will embarrass *the other person*. These concerns may involve staring at another person's body parts inappropriately, having offensive body odour, or appearing physically offensive.

Empirically Supported Therapies with Cultural Groups

Of particular interest in the cross-cultural clinical psychology literature is the effectiveness of evidence-based therapy for people of various cultural/ethnic groups. It has been noted that the evidence-based therapy literature and the literature on multicultural therapies have developed separately and, unfortunately, minority groups have been under-represented in most psychotherapy studies (Bernal & Scharrón-Del-Río, 2001; Hall, 2001; Morales & Norcross, 2010). Furthermore, these studies give little formal consideration to the external validity (i.e., whether the results of a study can be generalized/extended to other settings, populations, or conditions) of the intervention relevant to people from diverse cultures (i.e., cultural, interpretative, population, ecological, and construct validities) (Bernal & Scharrón-Del-Río, 2001). Nevertheless, newer commentary by Morales and Norcross (2010) notes that the gap between evidence-based practice and multicultural interventions has closed. Beginning in 2002, they describe a proliferation of national conferences, federal initiatives, and discipline-specific guidelines highlighting the need for cultural inclusion in empirically based practice (Morales & Norcross, 2010). They note that the APA has a definition of empirically based practice that is culturally inclusive—that is, empirically based practice is "the integration of the best available research with clinical expertise in the context of patient characteristics, culture, and preferences" (APA Task Force, 2006, p. 273).

Cultural Competence

Cultural competence, as it relates to psychotherapists' ability to provide interventions to clients from diverse ethnic backgrounds, is necessary in our multicultural society (APA, 2002). Both the APA and the Canadian Psychological Association (CPA) have incorporated diversity training into their professional training standards (Trilateral Forum on Professional Psychology, 2000; as cited in Pettifor, 2004). Sue, Zane, Nagayama Hall, and Berger (2009) define competence as having the required training, experience, and qualifications to adequately complete a task. When individuals from different cultures are considered, a therapist's degree of competence may shift, as different client groups often require differing approaches to treatment (Sue et al., 2009). "Competence" and "cultural competence" are related constructs sharing common ingredients, such as empathy and therapeutic alliance, but there is also evidence that cultural competence predicts client satisfaction with therapy beyond competence alone (Fuertes & Brobst, 2002; Fuertes, Costa, Mueller, & Hersh, 2005). Cultural competence then can be described as care that acknowledges the importance of culture at multiple levels, is sensitive to differences in cultural dynamics, and adapts services to meet the client's culturally unique needs (Danish, Forneris, & Wilder Schaaf, 2007). A culturally responsive psychologist must understand both general psychopathology and his or her client's specific cultural background and should be proficient at navigating the specificities of ethnic groups in practice (Sue, 2006).

Cultural competence can be further distinguished from two related terms, "cultural sensitivity" and "patient-centred cultural sensitivity." Cultural sensitivity refers to a general, ongoing awareness of and responsiveness to cultural differences and similarities (Majumdar, Browne, Roberts, & Carpio, 2004). Patient-centred cultural sensitivity is a more specific term applied to health-care workers. It comprises several characteristics, including sensitivity wherein professionals provide care that indicates respect for the patient's culture. It considers the provider and patient as partners in care and is oriented towards empowering the patient (Tucker, Marsiske, Rice, Jones, & Herman, 2011). Cultural competence may be conceptualized as the outcome of the process a professional has undergone in order to be both culturally sensitive and to provide patient-centred culturally sensitive care.

Several prominent scholars have proposed theoretical models of multicultural counselling competencies that stress three components: *cultural awareness and beliefs, cultural knowledge,* and *cultural skills* (Constantine & Ladany, 2000; Kitaoka, 2005; Purnell, 2002; Sue, 2001; Sue et al., 2009). The therapist must be aware of his or her own assumptions, values, and biases associated with racism, sexism, disability, and ageism, and the way this affects his or her practice. He or she must strive to understand that the worldviews of clients are culturally diverse. This may occur through empathetic practice, but, more importantly, through a learning process aimed to uncover the scope and nature of the client's background and daily experiences through cultural encounters (Campinha-Bacote, 1999). Based on this knowledge, the therapist works with the client to develop appropriate interventions. Therapists who assume that their mode of therapy may be applied to everyone, regardless of culture, do not account for the fact that interactions require approaches consistent with the person's life experiences (Purnell, 2002; Ponterotto, Casas, Suzuki, & Alexander, 2009). Some view cultural competence as similar to other skill-based competencies in that the therapist can use specific strategies to improve cultural competence (Whaley & Davis, 2007). However, Sue et al. (2009) note that it is difficult to isolate and operationalize components of cultural competence (i.e., assigning specific indicators) and, thus, these models still require empirical grounding.

Racial/ethnic similarities between client and therapist are important for culturally responsive care, with "race" used as a proxy for "shared cultural experiences" (Maramba & Hall, 2002). Early efforts examined therapists and clients of the same or different racial/ethnic backgrounds and, despite some mixed evidence (Flaskerud, 1990; Shin et al., 2005), found that ethnic matching was related to better client outcomes (Flaskerud, 1990; Gamst, Dana, Der-Karaberian, & Kramer, 2000; Smith & Glass, 1977). However, it has been argued that racial or ethnic match is not necessarily a good indicator of cultural match, which would include, for instance, shared language, understanding of the client's cultural background, and an openness to modify and match treatment approach (Hall, 2001; Jacob & Kuruvilla, 2012). It is important to note, however, that clients' preferences and perceptions about the importance of the ethnicity of their therapist may differ, including both positive and negative appraisals of ethnic match or mismatch (Chang & Yoon, 2011).

In Practice
Adapting Practice to Meet Client Needs

Mr L (82 years of age) has been referred to Dr W for support in caring for his wife, who has moderate dementia. Mrs L (79 years of age) was diagnosed with Alzheimer's disease approximately four years ago and since this time Mr L has cared for her in their home. Mr L reported that his wife's memory difficulties and level of impairment remained fairly minimal for the first three years following diagnosis. However, in the past year, her illness has progressed more quickly and she has deteriorated in her level of independence and ability to communicate. She also started to resist some aspects of personal care. Mr L reported feelings of depression and frustration, stating that he "does not know what to do" any more.

Mr and Mrs L, along with their young son, immigrated to Canada from China in 1956. Although their son had little trouble adjusting to life in Canada, Mr L reported that he and his wife had always felt isolated from those outside their own cultural circle and had little interaction with other cultural groups. Upon assessment, Mr L spoke English somewhat brokenly and reported sometimes having trouble finding the right words to describe his situation. He stated that his wife is still quite limited in speaking and understanding English and that they speak their native language in their home. Mr L describes both himself and his wife as traditional and that their Chinese heritage is of primary importance. Mr L also noted that he specifically asked for a referral to a Chinese therapist.

Dr W (age 36) is fourth-generation Canadian and until recently felt little cultural affiliation with the Chinese community. Dr W recently began learning about his Chinese culture and ancestry to provide culturally responsive psychotherapy. This has resulted in increased referrals of Asian clients. To support his new expertise, Dr W regularly seeks consultation from a more experienced therapist to ensure he is appropriately attending to cultural issues.

Following their initial interview, Dr W offered the services of an experienced translator, but Mr L declined, stating they could communicate in English. In the first treatment session, Dr W clarified his and Mr L's roles and the two discussed some differences and similarities in their worldviews. They jointly established the treatment goals of improved mood, more homecare support, and more behavioural strategies for aiding Mrs L. Throughout the weeks, Dr W tailored the content of the sessions to facilitate Mr L's goals. He further discussed the process of therapy in his consultation sessions, focusing on language barriers, cultural dissimilarities (e.g., views on receiving professional support for adjustment difficulties), and differing social roles. Through these discussions, Mr L reported feeling respected and understood specifically in regard to his culture. This provided a portal for communication and enhanced rapport, which facilitated the success of the psychotherapy. Mr L improved substantially in terms of his mood and noted improved ability to assist his wife. Upon termination of therapy, Dr W referred Mr L to a support group for family caregivers of seniors with dementia. He acknowledged Mr L's ongoing need for support and thus left the door to therapy "ajar," indicating that Mr L could make additional appointments if necessary.

Future Directions

Research that compares ethnic or cultural groups in terms of group averages is ill-suited to capture this process of cultural shaping of illness experience. The majority of epidemiological studies that report on ethnoracial blocs . . . cannot shed much light on the impact of culture on psychopathological processes. Specifying ethnicity more precisely does not get at the real issue, which is the heterogeneity within even well-defined ethnic groups. . . . For research to advance on cultural variations in psychopathology, we need to go beyond conventional group labels to examine the specific biological, psychological, or social mediators of cultural difference. (Kirmayer & Sartorius, 2007, p.832)

Adequate representation of different cultural groups is important in health psychology research and the importance of such representation has been emphasized by research-governing bodies in both Canada and the United States (Government of Canada, 2011; National Institutes of Health, 2012). There are both ethical and scientific reasons for representing minority groups in research. Rudell and Diefenbach (2008) note that accounting for cultural factors in research may enrich theories of health behaviour and aid in the interpretation of research findings. They caution that it is not sufficient to rely solely on proxy variables when defining culture (i.e., nationality, race, ethnicity); rather, the interplay among varying cultures, cultural change, and potentially the degree of immersion in a second culture must be examined. It has been suggested that, in research, race be defined in social-psychological and social-political terms, including factors such as perception of racism, level of acculturation, and socio-economic status (Ford & Kelly, 2005; Kao, Hsu, & Clark, 2004).

It has been widely noted that ethnic minority groups are under-represented in health-care research, although there has been improvement, and it is somewhat unclear why this under-representation occurs (e.g., Corbie-Smith, Thomas, & St George, 2002; Fisher & Kalbaugh, 2011; Wendler et al., 2005; Yancey, Ortega, & Kumanyika, 2006). Historically, researchers thought under-representation likely occurs because members of minority groups may distrust the research community, biases and negative attitudes among the gatekeepers to research participation, decreased access to health-care research, and less willingness to participate, although this may be changing (Corbie-Smith et al., 2002; Fisher & Kalbaugh, 2011; Wendler et al., 2005). Researchers often cite the Tuskegee Syphilis Study (1932–72) as a contributing factor to distrust of research by African Americans (Freimuth et al., 2001). In this study, 399 African-American men who had previously contracted syphilis were enrolled in a research study and were told they would receive medical care for their "bad blood" (CDC, 2011; Freimuth et al., 2001). They were not told they had syphilis and were deliberately denied treatment so the researchers could document the natural progression of the disease. Even after penicillin was found to effectively treat syphilis in the 1940s, these men were not treated.

However, Wendler et al. (2005) noted that it does not appear that people from minority groups are less willing to participate or have negative attitudes towards research; rather, health-care access functions as the primary barrier to recruitment and retention of minority research participants. For example, Fisher and Kalbaugh (2011) examined the distribution of minority participants among phases I, II, and III clinical trials. They note that minority research participants, while under-represented in phase III clinical trials (the treatment phase considered to have the most potential for benefit and a low risk of harmful side effects), are actually over-represented in phase I trials (safety studies that provide monetary compensation, but have a lower probability of providing benefit and greater risk of adverse effects). They note that this finding is not consistent with the literature, which cites distrust, attitudes, and access as reasons for under-representation. Instead, they point to broader (structural) socio-economic and political concerns, such as the greater amount of money paid for participation in a phase I trial. Fisher and Kalbaugh (2011, p. 2221) conclude that "minorities share a disproportionately greater risk and enjoy disproportionately fewer benefits (from a health and disease standpoint) from participating in clinical trials."

Kao and colleagues (2004) describe a number of strategies researchers can employ to integrate better the concept of culture into their study designs. They advocate for mixed-methods research, combining quantitative and qualitative approaches in order to understand cultural aspects from multiple perspectives. They stress that culture needs to be deeply integrated into the research paradigm; when cultural factors are eliminated because they are not expected to exert an effect, the reason for the omission should be thoroughly explored. Kao et al. (2004)

state that instruments and frameworks should be carefully chosen to ensure they are *culturally sensitive* (i.e., valid, reliable, and appropriate) for the research participant. They note the importance of dialogue with communities throughout the stages of research to better understand an "emic" (cultural insider) perspective. It is also of value to consider historical contexts for populations. Finally, they state that interventions need to be replicated across populations to improve their ecological validity and determine their clinical applicability for individuals from different cultural backgrounds.

Immigration to both the United States and Canada has risen, creating culturally complex communities with diverse health concerns, potentially in need of psychological services. For example, Canada is undergoing immigration from a variety of countries, the largest source of which is Asia including the Middle East (Statistics Canada, 2013). When considering the mental health needs of a diverse community, refugee status is one area of critical focus. Since November 2015 (and as of the time of this writing), Canada has accepted over 35,000 Syrian refugees, many of whom suffer mental health concerns due to pre-arrival trauma such as war, torture, and bombings, and post-arrival factors such as stress and unemployment or underemployment (Hadfield, Ostrowski, & Ungar, 2017). Concerning stress specifically, moving to a new country can be associated with new responsibilities in childcare and other domestic duties, because family members who previously took on these roles have died, or other separation has occurred. Further stress is associated with discrimination, which can predict problematic behaviours focused towards the self (e.g., social withdrawal, somatic complaints) and towards others (e.g., bullying, vandalism), as well as lower levels of happiness among young refugees (Hadfield et al., 2017). A great deal of benefit is associated with refugees feeling a sense of belonging in their new communities and this may be aided through activities that bring together refugees and other community members (Hadfield et al., 2017).

Post-traumatic stress disorder (PTSD) is especially problematic for Syrian refugees, especially amongst women and children, and unfortunately many do not receive treatment for this disorder (Ghumman, McCord, & Chang, 2016). Ghumman et al. (2016) report that approximately 30 to 50 per cent of Syrian and other Arab refugees are found to have or be at risk for PTSD, compared to approximately 9 per cent of the US population. This is understandable given the nature and frequency of traumatic events witnessed or experienced by refugees. Although treatment can be beneficial for refugees, it can be further complicated by cultural and language differences, making communication with counsellors difficult and, possibly due to past negative experiences with authority, preventing counsellors from being fully trusted. Trauma-related psychotherapy is highly effective in treating PTSD for refugees, but barriers for those seeking treatment and for clinicians providing treatment must be overcome. Aside from general considerations in providing culturally sensitive mental

Waiting for Syrian refugees to arrive at the Toronto airport.

Steve Russell/Toronto Star via Getty Images

health care, one promising solution proposed by Ghumman et al. (2016) is to utilize telehealth, whereby technology is used for service delivery. This could allow psychotherapy to be delivered at a distance, affording early care to refugees, perhaps before they reach their new country.

Given the increasing multiculturalism associated with the Canadian population, it is unsurprising that there is an increase in Muslim, Hindu, Sikh, and Buddhist religious affiliations (Statistics Canada, 2013). Furthermore, a substantial number of the population, in both Canada and the United States, adheres to Indigenous spirituality beliefs (Fleming & Ledogar, 2008). Cultural and religious diversity create a unique set of challenges for technological advances that have received substantial support in health psychology (Cuijpers, Van Straten & Andersson, 2008; Webb, Joseph, Yardley, Michie, 2010). For example, online tools in the assessment, treatment, and self-management (e.g., self-help websites) of health-related psychological functioning have all received support (e.g., Barak, Klein, & Proudfoot, 2009; Kalichman et al., 2003; Wright & Bell, 2003). However, in turn, each must respond to the culturally responsive wave being mitigated in these advances in the standard health psychology literature. For instance, a significant forum may be provided by asking questions such as how the technology can be responsive to cultural issues and how people's needs may be met from different cultural backgrounds through online discussion groups. Moreover, ways that the specificity of empirically supported online interventions can be ensured for varied cultures would be beneficial. Clearly, future research is needed with regard to these possibilities.

Summary

Shifting demographics in Canada and the United States have resulted in an increased focus on cultural issues in health psychology training, research, and clinical work. It is important that distinctions among the terms "race," "culture," and "ethnicity" be acknowledged. While "race" denotes a biological basis for some obvious difference (e.g., skin colour), "ethnicity" accounts for the subjectivity of self-report in group identification, and "culture" focuses on shared ideologies. Researchers have emphasized the importance of incorporating culture, including health beliefs and attributions, into a biopsychosocial framework to help explain health disparities in the general population. Indigenous and African-American populations are at particular risk for experiencing several negative health outcomes, including lower life expectancy, higher infant mortality rates, diabetes among Indigenous people, and heart disease among African Americans. It must be stressed that health disparities are *not* a consequence of group membership or ethnicity, but rather, they are the result of a chain of events and other determinants of health, such as socio-economic status, racial discrimination, health-care access and treatment quality, and health behaviour, all of which can be influenced by acculturation. When considering the influence of culture on mental disorders that may be co-morbid with physical disorders, differing cross-cultural symptom presentations may be relevant. Consideration of the literature on psychological therapies with different cultural groups and cultural competence in clinical work are also important. We provide relevant considerations for people who may work with minority populations, urging for the appropriate application of terminology (e.g., "race," "ethnicity," "culture") and noting the distinctions among these terms. Finally, we place emphasis on the need for multi-dimensional conceptualizations of culture.

Critical Thought Questions

1. In what ways might it be possible to research health disparities that are present among different cultural groups *without* directly assessing race or ethnicity and how would you justify the decision *not* to assess these constructs?
2. The Tuskegee Syphilis Study is often cited as an example of how a historical occurrence may continue to influence attitudes towards research among African Americans. What other North American historical occurrences continue to exert their influence on health variables within cultural groups and through what mechanisms?

Recommended Reading

Miranda, J., Bernal, G., Lau, A., Kohn, L., Hwang, W.C., & LaFromboise, T. (2005). State of the science on psychosocial interventions for ethnic minorities. *Annual Review of Clinical Psychology, 1,* 113–42.

Morales, E., & Norcross, J.C. (2010). Evidence-based practices with ethnic minorities: Strange bedfellows no more. *Journal of Clinical Psychology, 66,* 821–9.

Richmond, C.A.M., & Cook, C. (2016). Creating conditions for Canadian aboriginal health equity: The promise of healthy public policy. *Public Health Reviews, 37*(2).

US Department of Health and Human Services, Centers for Disease Control and Prevention. (2011). *CDC health disparities and inequalities report—United States 2011* (Morbidity and Mortality Weekly Report, No. 60).

Yali, A.M., & Revenson, T.A. (2004). How changes in population demographics will impact health psychology: Incorporating a broader notion of cultural competence into the field. *Health Psychology, 23,* 147–55.

Glossary

10,000 steps a day: A method for gaining and maintaining good health (this is equal to walking about 8 kilometres).

Acceptance and commitment therapy (ACT): An evidence-based psychological intervention that emphasizes acceptance and mindfulness strategies as well as commitments towards living consistently with one's values.

Acculturation: A socio-cultural process that occurs when people relocate to another culture wherein they adapt to and take on characteristics (i.e., behavioural, belief, and lifestyle) of the "new" second culture via continual contact.

Acquired immunodeficiency syndrome (AIDS): A disease that occurs when an individual infected with HIV can no longer fight the infection. It takes on average more than 10 years to progress from HIV infection to AIDS.

Acute coronary syndrome (ACS): A set of symptoms caused by the restriction of blood flow through circulatory vessels depriving heart muscle tissues of blood supply and hence access to oxygen and nutrients, which may lead to myocardial infarction.

Adherence (*in the context of health care*): Observance of medication or treatment schedules in accordance with the prescription by health-care personnel.

Adrenal glands: Two small glands located near the kidneys that release a number of hormones involved in the stress response.

Advance care planning: A process of planning and documenting one's wishes for future health and personal care. The idea behind advance care planning is to provide instructions for family and health-care workers in the event that an individual becomes ill and unable to communicate his or her wishes.

Advance directives: A legal document prepared by an individual when in a state of competence regarding the specific actions that should be taken medically if the individual loses decision-making capacity or is no longer able to communicate with his or her medical team.

Aerobic exercise: Any physical activity that increases heart rate and breathing. It strengthens the heart and lungs, increases the rate at which one burns calories (metabolism), tones muscles, lowers blood pressure, and can help with weight loss.

Angina: A symptom of ischemic heart disease characterized by chest, shoulder, jaw, or neck pain; occurs when part of the heart muscle does not receive enough oxygen.

Anorexia nervosa: An eating disorder characterized by extreme weight loss due to very low caloric intake stemming from an intense fear of being or becoming overweight.

Appraisal support: Helping someone identify a stressor and potential coping options.

Autonomic nervous system: The portion of the peripheral nervous system involved in control of organs that support muscle activity and behaviour (the heart, lungs, etc.).

Avoidant coping: Ignoring or trying to ignore a problem and its resulting consequences and emotions.

Bacteria: Single-celled microorganisms that can multiply given ideal environments. Antibiotic medications are most commonly used to treat bacterial infections.

Basal metabolic rate: The specific amount of food energy or calories needed to maintain bodily functions while at rest.

Behavioural medicine: "The field concerned with the development of behavioral-science knowledge and techniques relevant to the understanding of physical health and illness and the application of this knowledge and these techniques to diagnosis, prevention, treatment and rehabilitation. Psychosis, neurosis and substance abuse are included only insofar as they contribute to physical disorders as an end point" (Schwartz & Weiss, 1977).

Beveridge systems: Health systems financed through general taxation that involve a government overseeing the co-ordination and integration of a broad range of health services; named after William Beveridge, the civil servant whose recommendations led to the creation of the National Health Service in the United Kingdom.

Binge eating disorder: A condition that is characterized by food binges in which a person eats an excessive amount of food within a discrete period of time with a sense of lack of control during the binging episode. The person experiences distress in response to the binge.

Binge eating: Consuming, usually a large amount of food, with a sense of loss of control during the episodes.

Biofeedback: A procedure that helps clients become more aware of specific physiological functions (e.g., muscle tension) using psychophysiological measuring instruments.

Biopsychosocial model: Model that proposes that health is a function of biological, psychological, and social factors, which interact.

Biopsychosocial models of pain: These models tend to be consistent with the gate control theory of pain. While they recognize the importance of biological/physiological factors (e.g., tissue damage) in the pain experience, they also stress and describe the role of psychological and social (cultural) influences on pain.

Blood alcohol level: The amount of alcohol in the bloodstream.

Breast-conserving surgery: Surgical treatment for breast cancer that removes the cancerous tumour along with a margin of normal tissue. Accompanying radiation therapy over several weeks often is used to eliminate any remaining cancer cells.

Buffering hypothesis: The notion that social support leads to better health outcomes by buffering or protecting the individual from the negative effects of stress.

Bulimia nervosa: An eating disorder that is characterized by binge eating and purging episodes (e.g., vomiting or taking laxatives) to rid the body of the excess calories.

Carcinogen: An environmental factor or substance that increases the risk of developing cancer.

Cardiovascular rehabilitation: A comprehensive secondary prevention program providing cardiovascular risk factor modification through education, counselling (for health behaviours such as pharmacological therapy adherence, nutrition and weight management, smoking cessation, etc.) and individualized exercise training.

Cartesian dualism: The idea that mind and body are separate entities and explanations for illness can be found in the body alone.

Cause (*as related to illness representation*): Beliefs about what caused one's illness.

Chronic disease: A disease of long duration and generally slow progression. Not all chronic diseases are progressive.

Chronic obstructive pulmonary disease: Refers to a family of progressive lung diseases that result in difficulty breathing. Asthma, emphysema, and chronic bronchitis are examples of obstructive pulmonary disease.

Chronic pain: Recurrent and frequent pain (e.g., headaches, stomach aches, backaches). Chronic pain is common in children and adolescents, as well as in older people, and can occur as a result of an associated medical condition or in the absence of any identifiable organic pathology.

Clinical health psychology: Subfield of health psychology focused on applying or translating knowledge from health psychology into practices that promote health, prevent and treat illness or disability, and improve the health system.

Co-action: The increased probability that those who are successful at changing one behaviour can change a second behaviour.

Cognitive behavioural therapy (CBT): A structured psychological intervention of short duration that involves the identification and modification of maladaptive cognitive patterns and behaviours that contribute to a patient's psychological distress.

Cognitive empathy: Shared or complementary emotional experience in response to another person's physical and emotional suffering.

Cognitive rehabilitation therapy: The process of relearning cognitive skills that have been lost or altered as a result of damage to brain cells/chemistry.

Collaborative care: An approach in which physicians and mental health–care providers work together to manage common mental disorders and chronic disease.

Combination antiretroviral therapy (CART): A type of drug therapy in which a combination of multiple antiretroviral drugs is used to treat HIV and other retroviruses. This combination treatment is sometimes also known as Highly Active Antiretroviral Therapy (HAART).

Common-sense model (CSM) of self-regulation/CSM of illness representations: A theoretical framework that describes the way in which people process and cope with health threats.

Community health psychology: Subspecialty of health psychology focused on health status, health needs, and health-care systems to effect change and to promote access and cultural competence within those systems.

Comorbidity: The presence of two or more conditions simultaneously.

Confirmatory bias: When individuals with anxiety tend to focus on information that confirms their fears and ignore information that disconfirms their fears.

Consequences (*as related to illness representation*): Beliefs about how illness impacts one's everyday life (e.g., self-care, household responsibilities, family, work).

Controllability (*as related to illness representation*): Beliefs about whether we have control over our illness and how efficacious treatment will be.

Coping: The ability to manage a chronic medical condition or how a person responds to medical procedures. Coping responses include simple behavioural strategies (e.g., distraction, deep breathing) as well as more complex cognitive strategies (e.g., cognitive restructuring) and vary by the person's age and development. Effective coping skills are related positively with many patient outcomes.

Cortisol: A key adrenal hormone that increases blood glucose and has numerous effects on metabolism and immune function.

Cultural competence: Having the required training, experience, and qualifications to provide care to clients from different cultural backgrounds by acknowledging the importance of culture at multiple levels, being sensitive to differences in cultural dynamics, and adapting services to meet the client's culturally unique needs.

Culture: A set of values, ideals, beliefs, and assumptions about life shared among a particular group of people and transmitted generationally, rarely with implicit instruction.

Culture-bound syndromes: A recurrent pattern of abnormal behaviour and experience, specifically in relation to a local culture/community that may or may not be linked to a recognized Western category of mental disorders (e.g., anxiety disorders).

Decisional balance: Conceptualized by Janis and Mann as a decisional "balance sheet" of comparative potential gains and losses or pros and cons.

Dementia: Cognitive loss beyond what would be expected as a result of normal aging. Among the most common types of dementia are Alzheimer's disease and vascular dementia.

Determinants of health: The range of personal, socio-economic, and environmental factors that determine the health status of people or groups of people. Government agencies often prioritize sets of determinants within a health-care platform.

Diabetes (type 1 and type 2): Diabetes is a disease in which the body's ability to produce or use insulin is impaired. This results in high levels of sugar in the blood. Type 1 diabetes occurs when the immune system attacks and kills the cells that produce, store, and release insulin in the pancreas (beta cells). Type 1 diabetes requires insulin therapy. Type 2 diabetes occurs when the body does not make enough insulin or resists the effects of insulin. Type 2 diabetes may require insulin therapy, but may also be managed through diet and exercise changes.

Dialysis: Dialysis is a treatment procedure used in patients whose kidneys are no longer removing enough wastes and fluids from the blood. In peritoneal dialysis, the lining of the abdomen and a cleaning solution are used to remove wastes and extra fluid from the body.

Disability: A condition that limits an individual's mobility, senses, speech, or activities.

Distraction: A widely used and effective behavioural coping strategy involving directing one's attention away from a painful stimulus (e.g., blowing bubbles, listening to music, talking with others, humour). Distraction is often used to deal with acute pain, such as a medical procedure, and can be self-led or parent/other-led.

Distress: A negative form of stress in which demands outweigh resources, which can lead to negative health outcomes.

e-Health (Electronic Health): The use of digital technologies to deliver health services and information.

Emotional support: Providing encouragement and empathy.

Emotion-focused coping: A type of coping in which one addresses and regulates the negative emotions caused by stressful events.

Encopresis: A problem of toileting that involves the passage of feces in inappropriate places (e.g., clothing) and occurs as the direct result of involuntary overflow incontinence, resulting from constipation.

Endocrine system: Glands that release hormones into the bloodstream to influence different aspects of physiology.

End of life: When life expectancy is not anticipated to exceed six months.

Enuresis: A problem of toileting that involves the involuntary passage of urine, most often during the night (e.g., bedwetting).

Ethnicity: Subjectively identifying with a group by accepting group customs and practices from one's culture of origin in conjunction with a feeling a belonging.

Eustress: A positive form of stress when situations do not overwhelm resources, and so it can lead to mastery and a sense of meaning.

Fetal alcohol spectrum disorder: A condition in which the child potentially experiences mental impairment, stunted growth, and facial abnormalities as a result of exposure to alcohol during the fetal stages of development.

Fibromyalgia: A chronic condition that is characterized by widespread musculoskeletal pain, fatigue, and tenderness to touch in areas of the body.

Gate control theory: Theory that conceptualizes pain as a complex psychological phenomenon and postulates that there is a gating mechanism at the level of the spinal cord that either blocks potentially painful ascending signals or allows them to continue travelling to the brain. Signals travelling via small nerve fibres tend to open the "gate" whereas signals of large-diameter fibres tend to close the "gate." The "gate" can also be opened and closed through descending messages from the brain. This theory provides an explanation for the important role of social and psychological factors in the pain experience.

General Adaptation Syndrome: Selye's term for the general response of the body to all threats; also known as the fight-or-flight response.

Genetic counsellor: A professional (usually with a Master of Science degree) certified to provide information on hereditary conditions, their health and familial implications, preventive options and management, and possible genetic testing to determine mutation carrier status. Genetic counsellors are experts in educating patients and translating complex medical information.

Health anxiety: The experience of anxiety about one's present or future health.

Health belief model: Model postulating that readiness to take action in relation to health problems is a function of people's beliefs and their perception of the benefits of taking action in order to prevent health problems.

Health disparities: Preventable differences in the burden of disease, injury, violence, and opportunities to achieve optimal health experienced by socially disadvantaged populations.

Health psychology: A discipline-specific descriptor within the broad interdisciplinary field of behavioural medicine; discipline of psychology focused on the promotion and maintenance of health, the prevention and treatment of illness, and the identification of etiologic and diagnostic correlates of health, illness, and related dysfunction.

Health system: The complex array of governance, funding, administrative, and service-delivery arrangements established to deliver personal and population-based health services, all in an effort to improve health and health-care outcomes.

Heart failure: The heart's inability to adequately pump enough blood with oxygen and nutrients to meet the needs of the body.

Hemodialysis: A form of renal replacement therapy that uses an artificial dialyzer to filter the blood. It is usually performed under medical supervision in a hospital or clinic setting.

Hofstede's value dimensions of culture: A framework of five cultural dimensions that may vary across cultures: individualism–collectivism; power distance; uncertainty avoidance; masculinity–femininity; and Confucian dynamism (long- vs short-term orientation).

Hospice: Health care focused on providing symptom management for individuals at the end of life.

Human immunodeficiency virus (HIV): A virus that attacks the immune system, resulting in a chronic progressive illness that leaves individuals vulnerable to opportunistic infections and cancers.

Hypnosis: A psychological intervention involving a disassociation from a painful experience through suggestion, which has been shown to be effective in decreasing pain and distress associated with medical procedures.

Hypochondriasis: Extreme health anxiety based on misinterpretation of bodily symptoms that persists despite medical reassurance, and results in significant distress and/or disability for at least six months.

Identity: Beliefs about the distinctive characteristics of one's illness.

Immune system: A system involving organs and circulating blood cells devoted primarily to protecting the body from foreign substances.

Immunosurveillance: The immune system's detection and destruction of cancerous cells.

Inflammation: A co-ordinated reaction of the body especially in response to injury or infection. Specifically, in response to injury, blood vessel dilation and migration of fluid and immune cells occur in order to seal the area and speed healing.

Inflammatory bowel disease: Disease that involves chronic inflammation of all or part of the digestive tract. The two most common types of inflammatory bowel disease are Crohn's disease and ulcerative colitis. Inflammation in Crohn's disease can occur anywhere but is commonly found in the lower part of the small intestine (ileum). Inflammation in ulcerative colitis affects only the colon (large intestine).

Informational support: Providing valuable information relevant to addressing a stressful situation.

Instrumental support: Providing tangible goods and services.

Intoxication: Diminished physical or mental control due to the effects of psychoactive substances.

Irritable bowel syndrome: A condition that affects the large intestine that can cause cramping, abdominal pain, diarrhea, bloating, and constipation. Irritable bowel syndrome is distinct from inflammatory bowel disease in that it typically does not cause changes, such as inflammation and ulcers, in bowel tissues.

Job stress: Generally thought to be not so much a function of a particular position, but instead to having job demands without sufficient authority, autonomy, or rewards.

Knowledge translation: The creation, dissemination, and application of research evidence in a practical and accessible way so that it can be used by relevant stakeholders (e.g., patients, caregivers, health-care providers, policy makers) to strengthen health systems and improve health.

Life review: A structured, potentially multi-session interview focused around one or more life themes such as family, work, major turning points, the impact of historical events, the arts, aging, dying and death, and socialization issues such as meaning, values, and purpose in life.

Lymphedema: Buildup of lymphatic fluid in a limb, often as a result of surgery or radiation treatment; a chronic and progressive problem resulting in swelling, aching, pain, and hardening of tissue.

Main effects model: An approach to stress and health positing that social support is generally beneficial to well-being, whether we are carefree or stress-ridden.

Maladaptive behaviour: Dysfunctional or disruptive behaviours that interfere with successful adjustment and/or successful adaptation to specific situations.

Mastectomy: Surgical treatment for breast cancer that removes the entire breast.

Medical cost offset: The net savings in medical costs resulting from an intervention.

Meta-analysis: A statistical method that considers the results of multiple studies within a single analysis.

Metastasis: The ability of malignant neoplasm cells to spread to distant parts of the body and grow at those sites.

m-Health (Mobile Health): A type of eHealth that uses mobile phones and other wireless technology to deliver health services and information.

Moderate exercise: Any exercise where you're working hard enough to raise your heart rate and break a sweat. One way to tell if you're working hard enough is that you'll be able to talk, but not sing the words to your favourite song.

Multiple sclerosis: A chronic disease of the central nervous system (brain and spinal cord) that involves progressive damage to the myelin sheath (the protective covers) of the nerve fibres.

Myocardial infarction (MI): A complete blockage of an artery causing the death of heart muscle in the surrounding area due to the deprivation of oxygen and nutrients to the tissues.

Neuromatrix model: Model complementary to the gate control theory of pain positing that the multi-dimensional pain experience is associated with a "neurosignature" or pattern of nerve impulses generated by a widely distributed neural network in the brain (the body–self neuromatrix).

Neuroticism: A tendency to experience negative emotions and emotional instability; also referred to as negative affectivity or trait anxiety.

Nociception: The activity of nociceptors (sensory receptors that respond to stimulation) that has the potential to be perceived as painful.

Obesity: Having too much body fat. Obesity develops over time when you eat more calories than you use.

Occupational health psychology: A subspecialty of health psychology focused on the prevention and management of occupational stress, the prevention of injury, and the maintenance of workers' health.

Opportunistic infection: An infection caused by pathogens that usually do not cause disease in a host with a healthy immune system, but can cause disease in an individual with a compromised immune system.

Osteoarthritis: The most common form of arthritis in which the protective cartilage on the ends of the bones wears down over time. It commonly occurs in the weight-bearing joints of the hips, knees, and spine.

Overdiagnosis (*in the context of cancer*): The detection and diagnosis, for example, of a tumour that will not become malignant or is slow growing enough that it is unlikely to be the cause of death.

Pain: According to the International Association for the Study of Pain, an unpleasant sensory and emotional experience associated with actual or potential tissue damage, or described in terms of such damage.

Palliative care: Care provided to those who have been diagnosed with a range of medical conditions where curative treatments have failed or to those who require intensive long-term treatment aimed at maintaining quality of life.

Parasympathetic nervous system: The portion of the autonomic nervous system that usually reduces cardiac and smooth muscle activity.

Patient navigator: Lay person or health-care professional who assists patients at all stages of cancer care. While first conceived as a role to help under-served patients obtain early diagnosis and treatment, navigators now guide patients through coping with diagnosis, treatment, and making the transition to survivorship.

Pediatric psychology: A specialized psychological field that encompasses areas of health, clinical, and developmental psychology and integrates both scientific research and clinical practice to address the psychological aspects of children's medical conditions and the promotion of health behaviours in children and their families.

Peripheral nervous system: Neurons that lie outside the central nervous system (brain and spinal cord) that allow the brain to influence physiology.

Postcolonial theory: Literary and cultural theory that attempts to understand the process and problems stemming from European colonization and its effects. It is often noted that historical texts represent the perspectives of the colonizers with little acknowledgement of the experiences of those who were colonized.

Primary appraisal: A determination of whether a situation presents a threat, and the magnitude of that threat.

Primary care: First level of personal care for common conditions, focused on both prevention and treatment, from which access to specialized care is co-ordinated.

Primary control: An individual's attempts to maintain equilibrium and a sense of efficacy by using active, problem-focused coping strategies to change environmental circumstances.

Private health insurance systems: Health systems in which the majority of payments are made through individual or employment-based private insurance contracts.

Problem-focused coping: A type of coping in which one takes specific actions to address the demands of the stressful situation.

Procedural pain: Pain experienced as a result of a medical treatment or procedure (e.g., venepuncture, immunization, intravenous tube placement, etc.)

Processes of change: Ten experiential and behavioural activities that people use to progress through the stages of change.

Quality of life: An individual's general well-being, including emotional, social, and physical aspects of one's life. Health-related quality of life may be impacted by numerous illnesses and diseases, such as CVD.

Race: A term intended to capture differences in biological substrates based on physical characteristics such as skin colour and hair type; however, the term is contentious, given current understandings of genetics.

Regular physical activity: Either 150 minutes of moderate exercise or 75 minutes of vigorous exercise a week, plus muscle-strengthening activities for all major muscle groups at least two days a week.

Reminiscence: The universal, passive recall of memories.

Revascularization: A medical procedure performed in a hospital to restore blood flow to the heart tissues; includes percutaneous coronary intervention (e.g., stents) and coronary artery bypass graft (CABG) surgery.

Rheumatoid arthritis: A chronic and progressive form of arthritis in which inflammation occurs in the joints, causing swelling and pain around the joints. The most commonly affected joints are those of the hands, feet, wrists, elbows, knees, and ankles.

Rumination: Dwelling on the events that caused acute stress so that the stress becomes chronic.

Safety behaviours: Behaviours that anxious individuals engage in because they believe the behaviours will keep them safe, such as information-seeking, reassurance-seeking, body-checking, and cleaning, but that, in fact, serve to increase anxiety.

Saturated fats: A type of fat in which the fatty acids all have single bonds. Saturated fats are typically solid at room temperature.

Secondary appraisal: A determination of whether one has sufficient resources to cope with the threat. If resources are sufficient, then the situation can be viewed as a challenge rather than a threat, and it will be less damaging to the system.

Secondary care: Specialized health-care services provided by medical specialists and other health professionals who generally do not have first contact with patients.

Self-efficacy: A construct from Bandura that reflects the degree of confidence individuals have in maintaining a desired behaviour change in situations that often trigger relapse.

Self-management (*in the context of health and illness*): A process in which the patient is actively engaged in understanding and implementing the day-to-day tasks involved in managing a chronic health condition.

Sexually transmitted infections (STIs): Infections spread primarily through intimate person-to-person contact.

Social cognitive theory: Theory that emphasizes the importance of self-efficacy beliefs (developed through personal experiences, observing others, and social experiences as well any internal experiences) as a determinant of health behaviour. Personal factors, environmental influences, and behaviour are believed to interact.

Social health insurance systems: Health systems financed largely through compulsory employer–employee insurance contributions regulated by the state.

Social support: A social network in which others care about one's well-being and provide help and assistance.

Somatic nervous system: The portion of the peripheral nervous system involved in control of voluntary, striated muscle activity.

Specificity theory of pain: View based on the idea that there is a one-to-one correspondence between pain and tissue damage.

Stress management: Any method or activity that helps a person manage stress, such as deep breathing, meditation, yoga, visualizing a calming place, exercising, or seeking support from a friend.

Substance use disorder: Patterns of symptoms resulting from use of a substance which the individual continues to take, despite experiencing problems as a result.

Sympathetic nervous system: The portion of the autonomic nervous system that often stimulates cardiac and smooth muscle activity.

Syndemic: Two or more linked afflictions, interacting in synergy as contributors to excess disease burden in the population. This is also known as synergestic epidemic.

Tend-and-befriend: The hypothesis put forth by Taylor and colleagues suggesting that women's stress response is marked by efforts at social bonding and caring for offspring.

Tertiary care: Care provided in a facility that has specialized personnel and facilities for advanced medical investigation and treatment.

Theory of planned behaviour: A view of behaviour as determined by three types of beliefs: behavioural, normative, and control beliefs.

Timeline (*as related to illness representation*): Beliefs about how long an illness will last and whether the illness will fluctuate or persist over time.

Tolerance: Requiring noticeably larger amounts of a substance, over time, to get the desired effect or noticing less of an effect over time after repeated use of the same amount.

Trans fats: A type of unsaturated fat that can be found naturally in some animal-based foods or can be industrially produced.

Type A personality: A personality type characterized by hostility, competitiveness, and impatience.

Venepuncture: Intravenous access for the purpose of blood sampling, performed by a phlebotomist or other health professional. It is one of the most routinely performed invasive medical procedures.

Viruses: Submicroscopic organisms that require a host to survive—they can only reproduce by taking over the host cell's cellular machinery. Vaccines and antiviral medications aid in the treatment and prevention of viral infections.

Yo-yo dieting: Frequently losing and regaining weight or weight cycling.

References

Chapter 1

Ajzen, I. (1991). The theory of planned behavior. *Organizational Behavior and Human Decision Processes, 50*, 179–211.

Ajzen, I. (n.d.). *Constructing a theory of planned behaviour questionnaire.* Retrieved from people.umass.edu/aizen/pdf/tpb.measurement.pdf

Ajzen, I., & Fishbein, M. (1980). *Understanding attitudes and predicting social behavior.* Englewood Cliffs, NJ: Prentice-Hall.

Allen, J.K., Becker, D.M., & Swank, R.T. (1990). Factors related to functional status after coronary artery bypass surgery. *Heart & Lung: The Journal of Critical Care, 19*, 337–43.

American Psychological Association. (2011). *Public description of clinical health psychology.* Retrieved from www.apa.org/ed/graduate/specialize/health.aspx

American Psychological Association. (2016). *2015 survey of psychology health service providers.* Washington, DC: Author.

American Psychological Association Division 38. (2014). *Health psychology.* Retrieved from www.health-psych.org/CompetenciesinResearch.cfm

Antoni, M.H., August, S., LaPerriere, A., Baggett, H.L., Klimas, N., Ironson, G., . . . Fletcher, M.A. (1990). Psychological and neuroendocrine measures related to functional immune changes in anticipation of HIV-1 serostatus notification. *Psychosomatic Medicine, 52*, 496–510.

Armitage, C.J., & Conner, M. (2001). Efficacy of the theory of planned behaviour: A meta-analytic review. *British Journal of Social Psychology, 40*, 471–99.

Arving, C., Brandberg, Y., Feldman, I., Johansson, B., & Glimelius B. (2014). Cost-utility analysis of individual psychosocial support interventions for breast cancer patients in a randomized controlled study. *Psychooncology, 23*(3), 251–8.

Bandura, A. (1986). *Social foundations of thought and action: A social cognitive theory.* Englewood Cliffs, NJ: Prentice-Hall.

Bandura, A. (1991a). Self-efficacy mechanism in physiological activation and health-promoting behavior. In J. Madden IV (Ed.), *Neurobiology of learning, emotion and affect* (pp. 229–70). New York: Raven.

Bandura, A. (1991b). Self-regulation of motivation through anticipatory and self-regulatory mechanisms. In R.A. Dienstbier (Ed.), *Perspectives on motivation: Nebraska symposium on motivation* (Vol. 38, pp. 69–164). Lincoln: University of Nebraska Press.

Bandura, A. (1998). Health promotion from the perspective of social cognitive theory. *Psychology and Health, 13*, 623–49.

Bastone, E.C., & Kerns, R.D. (1995). Effects of self-efficacy and perceived social support on recovery-related behaviours after coronary artery bypass graft surgery. *Annals of Behavioral Medicine, 17*, 324–30.

Beck, A.T., & Dozois, D.J.A. (2011). Cognitive therapy: Current status and future directions. *Annual Review of Medicine, 62*, 397–409.

Beck, A.T. & Haigh, E.A. (2014). Advances in cognitive theory and therapy: The generic cognitive model. *Annual Review of Clinical Psychology, 10*, 1–24. doi: 10.1146/annurev-clinpsy-032813-153734

Beckham, J.C., Burker, E.J., Lytle, B.L., Feldman, M.E., & Costakis, M.J. (1997). Self-efficacy and adjustment in cancer patients: A preliminary report. *Behavioural Medicine, 23*, 138–42.

Belar, C. (1997). Clinical health psychology: A specialty for the 21st century. *Health Psychology, 16*, 411–16.

Belar, C.D., Mendonca McIntyre, T.M., & Matarazzo, J.D. (2003). Health psychology. In D.K. Freedheim (Ed.), *Handbook of psychology* (pp. 451–64). Hoboken, NJ: John Wiley & Sons.

Brus, H., van de Laar, M., Taal, E., Rasker, J., & Wiegman, O. (1999). Determinants of compliance with medication in patients with rheumatoid arthritis: The importance of self-efficacy expectations. *Patient Education and Counseling, 36*, 57–64.

Centers for Disease Control and Prevention. (2012). Occupational health psychology. Retrieved from www.cdc.gov/niosh/topics/ohp

Champion, V.L., & Skinner, C.S. (2008). The health belief model. In K. Glanz, B.K. Rimer, & K. Viswanath (Eds.), *Health behavior and health education* (pp. 45–65). San Francisco: John Wiley & Sons.

Child, N. (2000). The limits of the medical model in child psychiatry. *Clinical Child Psychology and Psychiatry, 5*, 11–21.

Cutrona, C.E., & Troutman, B.R. (1986). Social support, infant temperament, and parenting self-efficacy: A mediational model of postpartum depression. *Child Development, 57*, 1507–18.

De Geest, S., Borgermans, L., Gemoets, H., Abraham, I., Vlaminck, H., Evers, G., & Vanrenterghem, Y. (1995). Incidence, determinants, and consequences of subclinical noncompliance with immunosuppressive therapy in renal transplant recipients. *Transplantation, 59*, 340–7.

De La Cancela, V., Lau Chin, J., & Jenkins, Y.M. (1998). What is community health psychology? Empowerment for diverse communities. In V. De La Cancela, J. Lau Chin, & Y.M. Jenkins (Eds.), *Community health psychology: Empowerment for diverse communities.* New York: Routledge.

Devins, G.M., Binik, Y.M., Borman, P., Dattel, M., McCloskey, B., Oscar, G., & Briggs, J. (1982). Perceived self-efficacy, outcome expectancies, and negative mood states in end-stage renal disease. *Journal of Abnormal Psychology, 91*, 241–4.

Duncan, T.E., & McAuley, E. (1993). Social support and efficacy cognitions in exercise adherence: A latent growth curve analysis. *Journal of Behavioral Medicine, 16*, 199–218.

Ehde, D.M., Dillworth, T.M., & Turner, J.A. (2014). Cognitive-behavioral therapy for individuals with chronic pain: Efficacy, innovations, and directions for research. *American Psychologist, 69*(2), 153–66.

Engel, G.L. (1977). The need for a new medical model: A challenge for biomedicine. *Science, 196*, 129–36.

Fisher, E.B., Thorpe, C.T., Devellis, B.M., & Devellis, R.F. (2007). Healthy coping, negative emotions, and diabetes management: A systematic review and appraisal. *The Diabetes Educator, 33*(6), 1080–1103.

France, C. (2011, spring). The future of APA division 38. *Health Psychologist, 33*. Retrieved from www.health-psych.org/PDF/Spring2011.pdf

Gatchel, R.J., Baum, A., & Krantz, D.S. (1989). *An introduction to health psychology.* New York: Random House.

Glanz, K., & Bishop, D.B. (2010). The role of behavioral science theory in development and implementation of public health interventions. *Annual Review of Public Health, 31*, 399–418.

Grover, N., Kumaraiah, V., Prasadrao, P.S., & D'souza, G. (2002). Cognitive behavioural intervention in bronchial asthma. *Journal of the Association of Physicians of India, 50*, 896–900.

Gruber, B.L., Hall, N.R., Hersh, S.P., & Dubois, P. (1988). Immune system and psychological changes in metastatic cancer patients using relaxation and guided imagery: A pilot study. *Scandinavian Journal of Behaviour Therapy, 17*, 25–46.

Guze, S.B., Matarazzo, J.D., & Saslow, G. (1953). A formulation of principles of comprehensive medicine with special reference to learning theory. *Journal of Clinical Psychology, 9*, 127–36.

Haran, M.L., Kim, K.K., Gendler, P., Froman, R.D., & Patel, M.D. (1998). Development and evaluation of the osteoporosis self-efficacy scale. *Research in Nursing & Health, 21*, 395–403.

Hunsley, J. (2003). Cost effectiveness and medical cost-offset considerations in psychological service provision. *Canadian Psychology, 44*, 61–73.

Janz, N.K., & Becker, M.H. (1984). The health belief model: A decade later. *Health Education Quarterly, 11*, 1–47.

Jensen, S.E., Pereira, D.B., Whitehead, N., Buscher, I., McCalla, J., Andrasik, M., . . . Antoni, M.H. (2013). Cognitive-behavioral stress management and psychological well-being in HIV plus racial/ethnic minority women with human papillomavirus. *Health Psychology, 32*(2), 227–30.

Jones, C.J., Smith, H.E., & Llewellyn, C.D. (2016). A systematic review of the effectiveness of interventions using the Common Sense Self-Regulatory Model to improve adherence behaviours. *Journal of Health Psychology, 21*(11), 2709–24.

Kerns, R.D., Burns, J.W., Shulman, M., Jensen, M.P., Nielson, W.R., Czlapinski, R., . . . Rosenberger, P. (2014). Can we improve cognitive-behavioral therapy for chronic back pain treatment engagement and adherence? A controlled trial of tailored versus standard therapy. *Health Psychology, 33*(9), 938–47.

Kiecolt-Glaser, J., Glaser, R., Strain, E.C., Stout, J.C., Tarr, K.L., Holliday, J.E., & Speicher, C.E. (1986). Modulation of cellular immunity in medical students. *Journal of Behavioral Medicine, 9*, 5–21.

Larson, E.B., Olsen, E., Cole, W., & Shortell, S. (1979). The relationship of health beliefs and a postcard reminder in influenza vaccination. *Journal of Family Practice, 8*, 1207–11.

Leventhal, H., Meyer, D., & Nerenz, D. (1980). The common sense representation of illness danger. In S. Rachman (Ed.), *Contributions to medical psychology* (Vol. II, pp. 7–30). New York: Pergamon Press.

Leventhal, H., Phillips, L.A. & Burns, E. (2016). The common-sense model of self-regulation: A dynamic framework for understanding illness self-management. *Journal of Behavioral Medicine, 39*, 935–46.

Lipsitt, D. (1999). A century of psychosomatic medicine: Successes and failures. In M. Dinis (Ed.), *Reflexões sobre psicossomatica* [Reflections on psychosomatics] (pp. 11–22). Lisbon, Portugal: Sociedade Portuguesa de Psicossomatica [Portuguese Society of Psychosomatics].

Lopez-Olivo, M.A., Landon, G.C., Siff, S.J., Edelstein, D., Pak, C., Kallen, M.A., . . . Suarez-Almazor, M.E. (2011). Psychosocial determinants of outcomes in knee replacement. *Annals of the Rheumatic Diseases, 70*, 1775–81.

Lyons, A.C., & Chamberlain, K. (2006). *Health psychology: A critical introduction.* New York: Cambridge University Press.

McAlister, A.L., Perry, C.L., & Parcel, G.S. (2008). How individuals, environments and health behaviors interact: Social cognitive theory. In K. Glanz, B.K. Rimer, & K. Viswanath (Eds.), *Health behavior and health education* (pp. 45–65). San Francisco: John Wiley & Sons.

McGregor, B.A., Antoni, M.H., Boyers, A., Alferi, S.M., Blomberg, B.B., & Carver, C.S. (2002). Cognitive-behavioral stress management increases benefit finding and immune function among women with early-stage breast cancer. *Journal of Psychosomatic Research, 56*, 1–8.

Major, B., Mueller, P., & Hildebrandt, K. (1985). Attributions, expectations, and coping with abortion. *Journal of Personality and Social Psychology, 48*, 585–99.

Matarazzo, J.D. (1980). Behavioral health and behavioral medicine: Frontiers for a new health psychology. *American Psychologist, 35*, 807–17.

Matarazzo, J.D. (1982). Behavioral health's challenge to academic, scientific, and professional psychology. *American Psychologist, 37*, 1–14.

Miller, G., Chen, E., & Cole, S.W. (2009). Health psychology: Developing biologically plausible models linking the social world and physical health. *Annual Review of Psychology, 60*, 501–24.

Munro, S., Lewin, S., Swart, T., & Volmink, J. (2007). A review of health behaviour theories: How useful are these for developing interventions to promote long-term medication adherence for TB and HIV/AIDS? *BMC Public Health, 7*, 1–16.

Noar, S.M., Benac, C.N., & Harris, M.S. (2007). Does tailoring matter? Meta-analytic review of tailored print health behavior change interventions. *Psychological Bulletin, 133*(4), 673–93.

Payne, H.E., Lister, C., West, J.H., & Bernhardt, J.M. (2015). Behavioral functionality of mobile apps in health interventions: A systematic review of the literature. *JMIR mHealth and uHealth, 3*(1), e20.

Prochaska, J.O., Wright, J.A., & Velicer, W.F. (2008). Evaluating theories of health behavior change: A hierarchy of criteria applied to the transtheoretical model. *Applied Psychology: An International Review, 57*(4), 561–88.

Rosenstock, I.M. (1974). The health belief model and preventive health behavior. *Health Education Monographs, 2*, 354–86.

Rozanski, A., Blumenthal, J.A., & Kaplan, J. (1999). Impact of psychological factors on the pathogenesis of cardiovascular disease and implications for therapy. *Clinical Cardiology: New Frontiers, 99*, 2192–2217.

Salyer, J., Schubert, C.M., & Chiaranai, C. (2012). Supportive relationships, self-care confidence, and heart failure self-care. *Journal of Cardiovascular Nursing, 27*(5), 384–93.

Schneiderman, N., Antoni, M.H., Saab, P.G., & Ironson, G. (2001). Health psychology: Psychosocial and biobehavioral aspects of chronic disease management. *Annual Review of Psychology, 52*, 555–80.

Schwartz, G.E., & Weiss, S.M. (1977). What is behavioral medicine? *Psychosomatic Medicine, 39*, 377–81.

Segerstrom, S.C., & Miller, G.E. (2004). Psychological stress and the human immune system: A meta-analytic study of 30 years of inquiry. *Psychological Bulletin, 130*, 601–30.

Simpson, J.S.A., Carlson, L.E., & Trew, M.E. (2001). Effect of group therapy for breast cancer on healthcare utilization. *Cancer Practice, 9*, 19–26.

Smith, T.W., Orleans, C.T., & Jenkins, C.D. (2004). Prevention and health promotion: Decades of progress, new challenges, and an emerging agenda. *Health Psychology, 23*, 115–18.

Smith, T.W., & Ruiz, J.M. (2002). Psychosocial influences on the development and course of coronary heart disease: Current status and implications for research and practice. *Journal of Consulting and Clinical Psychology, 70*, 548–68.

Smith Fawzi, M.C., Eustache, E., Oswald, C., Louis, E., Surkan, P.J., Scanlan, F., . . . Mukherjee, J.S. (2012). Psychosocial support intervention for HIV-affected families in Haiti: Implications for programs and policies for orphans and vulnerable children. *Social Science & Medicine, 74*, 1494–1503.

Stagl, J.M., Antoni, M.H., Lechner, S.C., Bouchard, L.C., Blomberg, B.B., Gluck, S., . . . Carver, C.S. (2015). Randomized controlled trial of cognitive behavioral stress management in breast cancer: A brief report of effects on 5-year depressive symptoms. *Health Psychology, 34*(2), 176–80.

Straub, R.O. (2007). *Health psychology: A biopsychological approach* (2nd ed.). New York: Worth Publishers.

Suls, J., & Rothman, A. (2004). Evolution of the biopsychosocial model: Prospects and challenges for health psychology. *Health Psychology, 23*, 119–25.

Turner, L.W., Hunt, S.B., Dibrezzo, R., & Jones, C. (2009). Design and implementation of an osteoporosis prevention program using the health belief model. In J.A. Hayden (Ed.), *Introduction to health behavior theory* (pp. 37–42). Wayne, NJ: Jones and Bartlett.

Vallance, J.K., Lavallee, C., Culos-Reed, N.S., & Trudeau, M.G. (2012). Predictors of physical activity among rural and small town breast cancer survivors: An application of the theory of planned behaviour. *Psychology, Health, & Medicine, 17*(6), 685–97.

Welsh, D., Lennie, T.A., Marcinek, R., Biddle, M.J., Abshire, D., Bentley, B., & Moser, D.K. (2013). Low-sodium diet self-management intervention in heart failure: Pilot study results. *European Journal of Cardiovascular Nursing, 12*(1), 87–95.

White, C.A. (2001). Cognitive behaviour therapy for chronic medical problems: A guide to assessment and treatment in practice. Chichester, UK: John Wiley & Sons.

Chapter 2

Abdel-Sater, K.A., Abdel-Daiem, W.M., & Sayyed Bakheet, M. (2012). The gender difference of selective serotonin reuptake inhibitor, fluoxetine in adult rats with stress-induced gastric ulcer. *European Journal of Pharmacology, 688*, 42–8.

Ader, R., & Cohen, N. (1975). Behaviorally conditioned immunosuppression. *Psychosomatic Medicine, 37*, 333–40.

Alexander, F. (1939). Psychoanalytic study of a case of essential hypertension. *Psychosomatic Medicine, 1*, 139–52.

Andersen, B.L., Yang, H.C., Farrar, W.B., Golden-Kreutz, D.M., Emery, C.F., Thornton, L.M., & Carson, W.E. (2008). Psychologic intervention improves survival for breast cancer patients: A randomized clinical trial. *Cancer, 113*, 3450–8.

Aoyama, N., Kinoshita, Y., Fujimoto, S., Himeno, S., Todo, A., Kasuga, M., & Chiba, T. (1998). Peptic ulcers after the Hanshin-Awaji earthquake: Increased incidence of bleeding gastric ulcers. *American Journal of Gastroenterology, 93*, 311–16.

Ax, A.F. (1953). The physiological differentiation between fear and anger in humans. *Psychosomatic Medicine, 15*, 433–42.

Benschop, R.J., Jacobs, R., Sommer, B., Schurmeyer, T.H., Raab, J.R., Schmidt, R.E., & Schedlowski, M. (1996). Modulation of the immunologic response to acute stress in humans by beta-blockade or benzodiazepines. *FASEB Journal, 10*, 517–24.

Bernatova, I., Puzserova, A., & Dubovicky, M. (2010). Sex differences in social stress-induced pressor and behavioral responses in normotensive and prehypertensive rats. *General Physiology and Biophysics, 29*, 346–54.

Bonga, S.E.W. (1997). The stress response in fish. *Physiological Reviews, 77*, 591–625.

Bracha, H.S. (2004). Freeze, flight, fight, fright, faint: Adaptationist perspectives on the acute stress response spectrum. *CNS Spectrums, 9*, 679–85.

Brady, J.V., Porter, R.W., Conrad, D.G., & Mason, J.W. (1958). Avoidance behavior and the development of gastroduodenal ulcers. *Journal of the Experimental Analysis of Behavior, 1*, 69–72.

Cannon, W.B. (1929). *Bodily changes in pain, hunger, fear, and rage.* Oxford, UK: Appleton.

Cannon, W.B. (1942). "Voodoo" death. *American Anthropologist, 44*, 169–81.

Cao-Lei, L., Veru, F., Elgbelli, G., Szy, M., Laplante, D.P., & King, S. (2016). DNA methylation mediates the effect of exposure to prenatal maternal stress on cytokine production in children at age 13 ½ years: Project Ice Storm. *Clinical Epigenetics, 8*, 1–15.

Chen, E., Miller, G.E., Walker, H.A., Arevalo, J.M., Sung, C.Y., & Cole, S.W. (2009). Genome-wide transcriptional profiling linked to social class in asthma. *Thorax, 64*, 38–43.

Choy, D.S.J., & Ellis, R. (1998). Multiple hearts in animals other than Barosaurus. *Lancet, 352*, 744.

Cohen, S. (2005). Keynote presentation at the Eight International Congress of Behavioral Medicine: The Pittsburgh common cold studies: Psychosocial predictors of susceptibility to respiratory infectious illness. *International Journal of Behavioral Medicine, 12*, 123–31.

Cohen, S., Janicki-Deverts, D., Doyle, W.J., Miller, G.E., Frank, E., Rabin, B.S., & Turner, R.B. (2012). Chronic stress, glucocorticoid receptor resistance, inflammation, and disease risk. *Proceedings of the National Academy of Sciences of the United States of America, 109*, 5995–99.

Cole, S.W., Hawkley, L.C., Arevalo, J.M., Sung, C.Y., Rose, R.M., & Cacioppo, J.T. (2007). Social regulation of gene expression in human leukocytes. *Genome Biology, 8(9)*, R189.

Darwin, C.R. (1872). *The expression of emotions in man and animals*. London: John Murray.

Davies, S.A., Overend, G., Sebastian, S., Cundall, M., Cabrero, P., Dow, J.A., & Terhzaz, S. (2012). Immune and stress response "cross-talk" in the Drosophila Malpighian tubule. *Journal of Insect Physiology, 58*, 488–97.

Diehl, R.R. (2005). Vasovagal syncope and Darwinian fitness. *Clinical Autonomic Research, 15*, 126–9.

Ditto, B., Gilchrist, P.T., & Holly, C.D. (2012). Fear-related predictors of vasovagal symptoms during blood donation: It's in the blood. *Journal of Behavioral Medicine, 35*, 393–9.

Dutour, A., Boiteau, V., Dadoun, F., Feissel, A., Atlan, C., & Oliver, C. (1996). Hormonal response to stress in brittle diabetes. *Psychoneuroendocrinology, 21*, 525–43.

Epel, E.S., McEwen, B., Seeman, T., Matthews, K., Castellazzo, G., Brownell, K.D., Ickovics, J.R. (2000). Stress and body shape: Stress-induced cortisol secretion is consistently greater among women with central fat. *Psychosomatic Medicine, 62*, 623–32.

Fink, G. (2011). Stress controversies: Post-traumatic stress disorder, hippocampal volume, gastroduodenal ulceration. *Journal of Neuroendocrinology, 23*, 107–17.

Fitch, D.R., & Rippert, E.T. (1992). Syncope in military formations: A persistent problem. *Military Medicine, 157*, 577–8.

Folino, A.F. (2006). Cerebral autoregulation in neurally mediated syncope: Victim or executioner? *Heart, 92*, 724–6.

Giese-Davis, J., Collie, K., Rancourt, K.M., Neri, E., Kraemer, H.C., & Spiegel, D. (2011). Decrease in depression symptoms is associated with longer survival in patients with metastatic breast cancer: A secondary analysis. *Journal of Clinical Oncology, 29*, 413–20.

Glaser, R. (2005). Stress-associated immune dysregulation and its importance for human health: A personal history of psychoneuroimmunology. *Brain, Behavior, and Immunity, 19*, 3–11.

Graham, D.T., Kabler, J.D., & Lunsford, L., Jr. (1961). Vasovagal fainting: A diphasic response. *Psychosomatic Medicine, 23*, 493–507.

Grenon, S.M., Owens, C.D., Alley, H., Perez, S., Whooley, M.A., Neylan, T.C., . . . Cohen, B.E. (2016). Posttraumatic stress disorder is associated with worse endothelial function among veterans. *Journal of the American Heart Association, 5*, 1–7.

Harkness, E.F., Abbot, N.C., & Ernst, E. (2000). A randomized trial of distant healing for skin warts. *American Journal of Medicine, 108*, 448–52.

Ishigami, T. (1919). The influence of psychic acts on the progress of pulmonary tuberculosis. *American Review of Tuberculosis, 2*, 470–84.

Kiecolt-Glaser, J.K., Garner, W., Speicher, C., Penn, G.M., Holliday, J., & Glaser, R. (1984). Psychosocial modifiers of immunocompetence in medical students. *Psychosomatic Medicine, 46*, 7–14.

Kin, N.W., & Sanders, V.M. (2006). It takes nerve to tell T and B cells what to do. *Journal of Leukocyte Biology, 79*, 1093–1104.

Leserman, J., Petitto, J.M., Gu, H., Gaynes, B.N., Barroso, J., Golden, R.N., & Evans, D.L. (2002). Progression to AIDS, a clinical AIDS condition and mortality: Psychosocial and physiological predictors. *Psychological Medicine, 32*, 1059–73.

Levenson, R.W., & Ditto, W.B. (1981). Individual differences in ability to control heart rate: Personality, strategy, physiological and other variables. *Psychophysiology, 18(2)*, 91–100.

Levenstein, S. (2000). The very model of a modern etiology: A biopsychosocial view of peptic ulcer. *Psychosomatic Medicine, 62*, 176–85.

Miller, G.E., Cohen, S., & Ritchey, A.K. (2002). Chronic psychological stress and the regulation of pro-inflammatory cytokines: A glucocorticoid-resistance model. *Health Psychology, 21*, 531–41.

Ost, L.G. (1992). Blood and injection phobia: Background and cognitive, physiological, and behavioral variables. *Journal of Abnormal Psychology, 101*, 68–74.

Pereira, D.B., Antoni, M.H., Danielson, A., Simon, T., Efantis-Potter, J., Carver, C.S., O'Sullivan, M.J. (2003). Life stress and cervical squamous intraepithelial lesions in women with human papillomavirus and human immunodeficiency virus. *Psychosomatic Medicine, 65*, 427–34.

Regecova, V., & Kellerova, E. (1995). Effects of urban noise pollution on blood pressure and heart rate in preschool children. *Journal of Hypertension, 13(4)*, 405–12.

Sapolsky, R.M. (2000). Glucocorticoids and hippocampal atrophy in neuropsychiatric disorders. *Archives of General Psychiatry, 57*, 925–35.

Sapolsky, R.M. (2004). *Why zebras don't get ulcers* (3rd ed.). New York, NY: Holt.

Schneider, R.H., Alexander, C.N., Staggers, F., Orme-Johnson, D.W., Rainforth, M., Salerno, J.W., & Nidich, S.I. (2005). A randomized controlled trial of stress reduction in African Americans treated for hypertension for over one year. *American Journal of Hypertension, 18*, 88–98.

Schuster, J.P., Limosin, F., Levenstein, S., & Le Strat, Y. (2010). Association between peptic ulcer and personality disorders in a nationally representative US sample. *Psychosomatic Medicine, 72*, 941–6.

Segerstrom, S.C., & Miller, G.E. (2004). Psychological stress and the human immune system: A meta-analytic study of 30 years of inquiry. *Psychological Bulletin, 130*, 601–30.

Selye, H. (1956). *The stress of life*. New York, NY: McGraw-Hill.

Sherwin, E., Rea, K., Dinan, T.G., & Cryan, J.F. (2016). A gut (microbiome) feeling about the brain. *Current Opinion in Gastroenterology, 32*, 96–102.

Sinha, R., Lovallo, W.R., & Parsons, O.A. (1992). Cardiovascular differentiation of emotions. *Psychosomatic Medicine, 54*, 422–35.

Sontag, S. (1978). *Illness as metaphor*. New York, NY: Farrar, Straus, & Giroux.

Spanos, N.P., Williams, V., & Gwynn, M.I. (1990). Effects of hypnotic, placebo, and salicylic acid treatments on wart regression. *Psychosomatic Medicine, 52*, 109–14.

Sternberg, E. M. (2002). Walter B. Cannon and "Voodoo Death": A perspective from 60 years on. *American Journal of Public Health, 92*, 1564–6.

Taylor, S.E., Gonzaga, G.C., Klein, L.C., Hu, P., Greendale, G.A., & Seeman, T.E. (2006). Relation of oxytocin to psychological stress responses and hypothalamic-pituitary-adrenocortical axis activity in older women. *Psychosomatic Medicine, 68*, 238–45.

Tomfohr, L., Cooper, D.C., Mills, P.J., Nelesen, R.A., & Dimsdale, J.E. (2010). Everyday discrimination and nocturnal blood pressure dipping in Black and White Americans. *Psychosomatic Medicine, 72*, 266–272.

van Kempen, E., & Babisch, W. (2012). The quantitative relationship between road traffic noise and hypertension: A meta-analysis. *Journal of Hypertension, 30*, 1075–86.

Weiss, J.M., Pohorecky, L.A., Salman, S., & Gruenthal, M. (1976). Attenuation of gastric lesions by psychological aspects of aggression in rats. *Journal of Comparative and Physiological Psychology, 90*, 252–9.

Chapter 3

Åkerstedt, T., Kecklund, G., & Axelsson, J. (2007). Impaired sleep after bedtime stress and worries. *Biological Psychology, 76*(3), 170–3.

Åkerstedt, T., Knutsson, A., Westerholm, P., Theorell, T., Alfredsson, L., & Kecklund, G. (2002). Sleep disturbances, work stress and work hours: A cross-sectional study. *Journal of Psychosomatic Research, 53*(3), 741–8.

Alexander, F. (1939). Emotional factors in essential hypertension. *Psychosomatic Medicine, 1*, 173–9.

Almqvist, K., & Brandell-Forsberg, M. (1997). Refugee children in Sweden: Post-traumatic stress disorder in Iranian preschool children exposed to organized violence. *Child Abuse & Neglect, 21*(4), 351–66.

American Psychiatric Association (2013). *Diagnostic and statistical manual of mental disorders* (5th ed.). Arlington, Va.: American Psychiatric Publishing.

Arora, N., Rutten, L., Gustafson, D., Moser, R., & Hawkins, R. (2007). Perceived helpfulness and impact of social support provided by family, friends, and health care providers to women newly diagnosed with breast cancer. *Psycho-Oncology, 16*, 474–86.

Banerjee, B., Vadiraj, H.S., Ram, A., Rao, R., Jayapal, M., Gopinath, K.S., & Prakash Hande, M. (2007). Effects of an integrated yoga program in modulating psychological stress and radiation-induced genotoxic stress in breast cancer patients undergoing radiotherapy. *Integrated Cancer Therapy, 6*, 242–50.

Barak, A., Boniel-Nissim, M., & Suler, J. (2008). Fostering empowerment in online support groups. *Computers in Human Behavior, 24*(5), 1867–83.

Barefoot, J.C., Dodge, K.A., Peterson, B.L., Dahlstrom, W.G., & Williams, R.B. (1989). The Cook-Medley Hostility Scale: Item content and ability to predict survival. *Psychosomatic Medicine, 51*, 46–57.

Benham, G. (2010). Sleep: An important factor in stress–health models. *Stress and Health, 26*(3), 204–14.

Berset, M., Elfering, A., Lüthy, S., Lüthi, S., & Semmer, N. K. (2011). Work stressors and impaired sleep: Rumination as a mediator. *Stress and Health, 27*(2), e71–e82.

Bevan, J.L., Gomez, R., & Sparks, L. (2014). Disclosures about important life events on Facebook: Relationships with stress and quality of life. *Computers in Human Behavior, 39*, 246–53.

Bombay, A., Matheson, K., & Anisman, H. (2011). The impact of stressors on second generation Indian residential school survivors. *Transcultural Psychiatry, 48*(4), 367–91.

Brady, J.V. (1958). Ulcers in executive monkeys. *Scientific American, 199*, 95–100.

Brady, J.V., Porter, R.W., Conrad, D.G., & Mason, J.W. (1958). Avoidance behavior and the development of duodenal ulcers. *Journal of the Experimental Analysis of Behavior, 1*, 69–72.

Brondolo, E., Grantham, K.I., Karlin, W., Taravella, J., Mencía-Ripley, A., Schwartz, J.E., . . . Contrada, R.J. (2009). Trait hostility and ambulatory blood pressure among traffic enforcement agents: The effects of stressful social interactions. *Journal of Occupational Health Psychology, 14*, 110–21.

Brown, G.W, & Harris, T.O. (1978). Social origins of depression: A study of psychiatric disorder in women. New York: Free Press.

Brummett, B.H., Maynard, K.E., Haney, T.L., Siegler, I.C., & Barefoot, J.C. (2000). Reliability of interview-assessed hostility ratings across mode of assessment and time. *Journal of Personality Assessment, 75*, 225–36.

Bryant, R.A., Harvey, A.G., Dang, S.T., Sackville, T., & Basten, C. (1998). Treatment of acute stress disorder: A comparison of cognitive-behavioral therapy and supportive counseling. *Journal of Consulting and Clinical Psychology, 66*, 862–6.

Buss, A.H., & Perry, M. (1992). The aggression questionnaire. *Journal of Personality and Social Psychology, 63*, 452–9.

Butler, A.C., Chapman, J.E., Forman, E.M., & Beck, A.T. (2006). The empirical status of cognitive-behavioral therapy: A review of meta-analyses. *Clinical Psychology Review, 26*, 17–31.

Campisi, J., Bynog, P., McGehee, H., Oakland, J. C., Quirk, S., Taga, C., & Taylor, M. (2012). Facebook, stress, and incidence of upper respiratory infection in undergraduate college students. *Cyberpsychology, Behavior, and Social Networking, 15*(12), 675–81.

Cannon, W.C (1929). *Bodily changes in pain, hunger, fear, and rage*. New York: Appleton-Century-Crofts.

Carver, C.S., Scheier, M.F., & Weintraub, J.K. (1989). Assessing coping strategies: A theoretically based approach. *Journal of Personality and Social Psychology, 56*, 267–83.

Chafin, S., Christenfeld, N., & Gerin, W. (2008). Improving cardiovascular recovery from stress with brief poststress exercise. *Health Psychology, 27*(1 Suppl), S64–72.

Chandra, V., Szklo, M., Goldberg, R., & Tonascia, J. (1983). The impact of marital status on survival after an acute myocardial infarction: A population-based study. *American Journal of Epidemiology, 117*, 320–5.

Chen, W., & Lee, K. H. (2013). Sharing, liking, commenting, and distressed? The pathway between Facebook interaction and psychological distress. *Cyberpsychology, Behavior, and Social Networking, 16*(10), 728–34.

Chesney, M.A., Chambers, D.B., Taylor, J.M., Johnson, L.M., & Folkman, S. (2003). Coping effectiveness training for men living with HIV: Results from a randomized clinical trial testing a group-based intervention. *Psychosomatic Medicine, 65*(6), 1038–46.

Christenfeld, N., Glynn, L.M., Phillips, D.P., & Shrira, I. (1999). New York City as a risk factor for heart attack mortality. *Psychosomatic Medicine, 61*, 740–3.

CIA World Factbook. (2017). Retrieved from www.cia.gov/library/publications/the-world-factbook.

Clarke, H.F., Dalley, J.W., Crofts, H.S., Robbins, T.W., & Roberts, A.C. (2004). Cognitive inflexibility after prefrontal serotonin depletion. *Science, 304*, 878–80.

Cohen, S., Doyle, W.J., Skoner, D.P., Rabin, B.S., & Gwaltney, J.M., Jr. (1997). Social ties and susceptibility to the common cold. *Journal of the American Medical Association, 277*, 1940–4.

Cohen, S., & Wills, T.A. (1985). Stress, social support, and the buffering hypothesis. *Psychological Bulletin, 98*, 310–57.

Cook, W.W., & Medley, D.M. (1954). Proposed hostility and pharisaic virtue scales for the MMPI. *Journal of Applied Psychology, 38*, 414–18.

Coulson, N.S., & Knibb, R.C. (2007). Coping with food allergy: Exploring the role of the online support group. *Cyberpsychology & Behavior, 10*(1), 145–8.

Coverman, S. (1989). Role overload, role conflict, and stress: Addressing consequences of multiple role demands. *Social Forces, 67*, 965–82.

Colhoun, H.M., Hemingway, H., & Poulter, N.R. (1998). Socio-economic status and blood pressure: An overview analysis. *Journal of Human Hypertension, 12*(2), 91–110.

Coyne, J.C., Rohrbaugh, M.J., Shoham, V., Sonnega, J.S., Nicklas, J.M., & Cranford, J.A. (2001). Prognostic importance of marital quality for survival of congestive heart failure. *American Journal of Cardiology, 88*, 526–9.

Cutler, D. M., & Lleras-Muney, A. (2012). *Education and health: Insights from international comparisons* (No. w17738). National Bureau of Economic Research.

Cutrona, C.E., Russell, D.W., Brown, P.A., Clark, L.A., Hessling, R.M., & Gardner, K.A. (2005). Neighborhood context, personality, and stressful life events as predictors of depression among African American women. *Journal of Abnormal Psychology, 114*, 3–15.

D'Atri, D.A., Fitzgerald, E.F., Kasl, S.K., & Ostfeld, A.M. (1981). Crowding in prison: The relationship between changes in housing mode and blood pressure. *Psychosomatic Medicine, 43*, 95–105.

Dressier, W.W. (1990). Lifestyle, stress, and blood pressure in a southern Black community. *Psychosomatic Medicine, 52*, 182–98.

Dressier, W.W. (1991). Social support, lifestyle incongruity, and arterial blood pressure in a southern Black community. *Psychosomatic Medicine, 53*, 608–20.

Edwards, K.M., Burns, V.E., Reynolds, T., Carroll, D., Drayson, M., & Ring, C. (2006). Acute stress exposure prior to influenza vaccination enhances antibody response in women. *Brain, Behavior, and Immunity, 20*, 159–68.

Eibner, C., & Evans, W.N. (2005). Relative deprivation, poor health habits, and mortality. *Journal of Human Resources, 40*, 592–620.

Ellis, A. (1962). *Reason and emotion in psychotherapy*. New York: L. Stuart.

Ellis, B. H., MacDonald, H. Z., Lincoln, A. K., & Cabral, H. J. (2008). Mental health of Somali adolescent refugees: The role of trauma, stress, and perceived discrimination. *Journal of Consulting and Clinical Psychology, 76*(2), 184–93.

Epel, E.S., Blackburn, E.H., Lin, J., Dhabhar, F.S., Adler, N.E., Morrow, J.D., & Cawthon, R.M. (2004). Accelerated telomere shortening in response to life stress. *Proceedings of the National Academies of Science, 101*, 17312–5.

Eysenbach, G., Powell, J., Englesakis, M., Rizo, C., & Stern, A. (2004). Health related virtual communities and electronic support groups: Systematic review of the effects of online peer to peer interactions. *BMJ, 328*(7449), 1166.

Eysenck, H.J. (1991). Type A behaviour and coronary heart disease: The third stage. In M.J. Strube (Ed.) *Type A behavior*. Newbury Park, Calif.: Sage.

Folkman, S., & Lazarus, R.S. (1980). An analysis of coping in a middle-aged community sample. *Journal of Health and Social Behavior, 21*, 219–39.

Folkman, S., Lazarus, R.S., Dunkel-Schetter, C., DeLongis, A., & Gruen, R.J. (1986). Dynamics of a stressful encounter: Cognitive appraisal, coping, and encounter outcomes. *Journal of Personality and Social Psychology, 50*, 992–1003.

Folkow, B. (1978). Cardiovascular structural adaptation: Its role in the initiation and maintenance of primary hypertension. *Clinical Science and Molecular Medicine, 55* (Suppl. 4), IV-3–IV-22.

Francis, M.E., & Pennebaker, J.W. (1992). Putting stress into words: The impact of writing on physiological, absentee, and self-reported emotional well-being measures. *American Journal of Health Promotion, 6*, 280–7.

Frankenhaeuser, M. (1983). The sympathetic-adrenal and pituitary-adrenal response to challenge: Comparison between the sexes. In T.M. Dembroski, T.H. Schmidt, & G. Blomchen (Eds.), *Biobehavioral bases of coronary heart disease* (pp. 91–105). Basel, Switzerland: Karger.

French, J.R., Caplan, R.D., & Harrison, R.V. (1982). *The mechanisms of job stress and strain*. Chichester, UK: Wiley.

Friedman, M., & Rosenman, R. (1959). Association of specific overt behaviour pattern with blood and cardiovascular findings. *Journal of the American Medical Association, 169*, 1286–96.

Geary, D.C., & Flinn, M.V. (2002). Sex differences in behavioral and hormonal response to social threat: Commentary on Taylor et al. (2000). *Psychological Review, 109*, 745–50.

George, D. R., Dellasega, C., Whitehead, M. M., & Bordon, A. (2013). Facebook-based stress management resources for first-year medical students: A multi-method evaluation. *Computers in Human Behavior, 29*(3), 559–62.

Gerber, M., Hartmann, T., Brand, S., Holsboer-Trachsler, E., & Puhse, U. (2010). The relationship between shift work, perceived stress, sleep and health in Swiss police officers. *Journal of Criminal Justice, 38*(6), 1167–75.

Gerin, W., Zawadzki, M., Brosschot, J., Thayer, J., Christenfeld, N., Campbell, T.S., & Smyth, J.M. (2012). Rumination as a mediator of chronic stress effects on hypertension: A causal model. *International Journal of Hypertension.*

Gerstel, N., Riessman, C.K., & Rosenfield, S. (1985). Explaining the symptomatology of separated and divorced women and men: The role of material conditions and social networks. *Social Forces, 64*, 84–101.

Galdas, P.M., Cheater, F., & Marshall, P. (2005). Men and health help-seeking behaviour: Literature review. *Journal of Advanced Nursing, 49*(6), 616–23.

Glynn, L.M., Christenfeld, N., & Gerin, W. (1999). Gender, social support, and cardiovascular responses to stress. *Psychosomatic Medicine, 61*, 234–42.

Glynn, L.M., Christenfeld, N., & Gerin, W. (2002). The role of rumination in recovery from reactivity: Cardiovascular consequences of emotional states. *Psychosomatic Medicine, 64*, 714–26.

Goodwin, P.J., Leszcz, M., Ennis, M., Koopmans, J., Vincent, L., Guther, H., . . . Speca, M. (2001). The effect of group psychosocial support on survival in metastatic breast cancer. *New England Journal of Medicine, 345*(24), 1719–26.

Goodwin, J.S., Hunt, W.C., Key, C.R., & Samet, J.M. (1987). The effect of marital status on stage, treatment, and survival of cancer patients. *Journal of the American Medical Association, 258*, 3125–30.

Graham, A.L., Papandonatos, G.D., Erar, B., & Stanton, C.A. (2015). Use of an online smoking cessation community promotes abstinence: Results of propensity score weighting. *Health Psychology, 34*(S), 1286.

Helgeson, V.S., Cohen, S., Schulz, R., & Yasko, J. (2000). Group support interventions for women with breast cancer: Who benefits from what? *Health Psychology, 19*, 107–14.

Hemingway, H., & Marmot, M. (1999). Clinical evidence: Psychosocial factors in the etiology and prognosis of coronary heart disease: Systematic review of prospective cohort studies. *Western Journal of Medicine, 171*, 342–50.

Hofmann, S.G., Sawyer, A.T., Witt, A.A., & Oh, D. (2010). The effect of mindfulness-based therapy on anxiety and depression: A meta-analytic review. *Journal of Consulting and Clinical Psychology, 78*(2), 169.

Holahan, C.J., & Moos, R.H. (1986). Personality, coping, and family resources in stress resistance: A longitudinal analysis. *Journal of Personality and Social Psychology, 51*, 389–95.

Holmes, D.S., & Houston, B.K. (1974). Effect of avoidant thinking and reappraisal for coping with threat involving temporal uncertainty. *Journal of Personality and Social Psychology, 30*, 382–8.

Holmes, T.H., & Rahe, R.H. (1967). The Social Readjustment Rating Scale. *Journal of Psychosomatic Research, 11*, 213–18.

Irvine, J., Garner, D.M., Craig, H.M., & Logan, A.G. (1991). Prevalence of Type A behavior in untreated hypertensive individuals. *Hypertension, 18*, 72–8.

Jacobs, G.D. (2001). Clinical applications of the relaxation response and mind–body interventions. *Journal of Alternative and Complementary Medicine, 7* (Suppl 1), S93–101.

Jain, S., Shapiro, S.L., Swanick, S., Roesch, S.C., Mills, P.J., Bell, I., & Schwartz, G.E. (2007). A randomised controlled trial of mindfulness meditation versus relaxation training: Effects on distress, positive states of mind, rumination, and distraction. *Annals of Behavioral Medicine, 33*, 11–21.

Jones, S. (1996). The association between objective and subjective caregiver burden. *Archives of Psychiatric Nursing, 10*, 77–84.

Kabat-Zinn, J., Massion, A.O., Kristeller, J., Peterson, L.G., Fletcher, K., Pbert, L., . . . Santorelli, S.F. (1992). Effectiveness of a meditation-based stress reduction program in the treatment of anxiety disorders. *American Journal of Psychiatry, 149*, 936–43.

Kanner, A.D., Coyne, J.C., Schaefer, C., & Lazarus, R.S. (1981). Comparison of two modes of stress measurement: Daily hassles and uplifts versus major life events. *Journal of Behavioral Medicine, 4*, 1–39.

Karasek, R.A., Theorell, T., Schwartz, J.E., Schnall, P.L., Pieper, C.F., & Michela, J.L. (1988). Job characteristics in relation to the prevalence of myocardial infarction in the U.S. Health Examination Survey (HES) and the Health and Nutrition Examination Survey (HANES). *American Journal of Public Health, 78*, 910–18.

Kenny, D.T. (2006). A systematic review for treatments of music performance anxiety. *Anxiety, Stress, & Coping, 18*, 183–208.

Kiecolt-Glaser, J.K., & Newton, T.L. (2001). Marriage and health: His and hers. *Psychological Bulletin, 127*, 472–503.

Kivimaki, M., Leino-Arjas, P., Luukkonen, R., Riihimäi, H., Vahtera, J., & Kirjonen, J. (2002). Work stress and risk of cardiovascular mortality: Prospective cohort study of industrial employees. *British Medical Journal, 325*, 857–60.

Knight, W.E., & Rickard, N.S. (2001). Relaxing music prevents stress-induced increases in subjective anxiety, systolic blood pressure, and heart rate in healthy males and females. *Journal of Music Therapy, 38*(4), 254–72.

Knudsen, H. K., Ducharme, L. J., & Roman, P. M. (2007). Job stress and poor sleep quality: Data from an American sample of full-time workers. *Social Science & Medicine, 64*(10), 1997–2007.

Kross, E., Verduyn, P., Demiralp, E., Park, J., Lee, D. S., Lin, N., . . . Ybarra, O. (2013). Facebook use predicts declines in subjective well-being in young adults. *PLOS ONE, 8*(8), e69841.

Kulik, J.A., & Mahler, H.I. (1987). Effects of preoperative roommate assignment on preoperative anxiety and recovery from coronary-bypass surgery. *Health Psychology, 6*, 525–43.

Kulik, J.A., & Mahler, H.I. (1989). Social support and recovery from surgery. *Health Psychology, 8*, 221–38.

Lanska, D.J., & Kuller, L.H. (1995). The geography of stroke mortality in the United States and the concept of a Stroke Belt. *Stroke, 26*, 1145–9.

Larsen, B.A., & Christenfeld, N.J.S. (2009). Cardiovascular disease and psychiatric comorbidity: The potential role of perseverative cognition. *Cardiovascular Psychiatry and Neurology*.

Lawton, M.P., Moss, M., Kleban, M.H., Glicksman, A., & Rovine, M. (1991). A two-factor model of caregiving appraisal and psychological well-being. *Journal of Gerontology, 46*, 181–9.

Lazarus, R.S. (1966). *Psychological stress and the coping process*. New York: McGraw-Hill.

Lazarus, R.S., & Folkman, S. (1984). *Stress, appraisal and coping*. New York: Springer.

Le Fevre, M., Matheny, J., & Kilt, G. (2003). Eustress, distress, and interpretation in occupational stress. *Journal of Managerial Psychology, 18*, 726–44.

Li, X., Chen, W., & Popiel, P. (2015). What happens on Facebook stays on Facebook? The implications of Facebook interaction for perceived, receiving, and giving social support. *Computers in Human Behavior, 51*, 106–13.

Luxton, D.D., Hansen, R.N., & Stanfill, K. (2014). Mobile app self-care versus in-office care for stress reduction: A cost minimization analysis. *Journal of Telemedicine and Telecare, 20*(8), 431–5.

Mani, M., Kavanagh, D.J., Hides, L., & Stoyanov, S.R. (2015). Review and evaluation of mindfulness-based iPhone apps. *JMIR mHealth and uHealth, 3*(3), e82.

McCloskey, W., Iwanicki, S., Lauterbach, D., Giammittorio, D.M., & Maxwell, K. (2015). Are Facebook "friends" helpful? Development of a Facebook-based measure of social support and examination of relationships among depression, quality of life, and social support. *Cyberpsychology, Behavior, and Social Networking, 18*(9), 499–505.

McCrae, R.R. (1990). Controlling neuroticism in the measurement of stress. *Stress Medicine, 6*, 237–41.

McEwen, B.S. (1998). Protective and damaging effects of stress mediators. *New England Journal of Medicine, 338*, 1771–9.

McNutt, L., Strogatz, D.S., Coles, F.B., & Fehrs, L.J. (1994). Is the high ischemic heart disease rate in New York State just an urban effect? *Public Health Reports, 109*, 567–77.

Matschinger, H., Siegrist, J., Siegrist, K., & Dittmann, K.H. (1986). Type A as a coping career: Towards a conceptual and methodological redefinition. In T.H. Schmidt, T.M. Dembroski, & G. Blümchen (Eds.), *Biological and psychological factors in cardiovascular disease* (pp. 104–26). Berlin: Springer.

Maurin, J., & Boyd, C. (1990). Burden of mental illness on the family: A critical review. *Archives of Psychiatric Nursing, 4*, 99–107.

Minkel, J.D., Banks, S., Htaik, O., Moreta, M.C., Jones, C.W., McGlinchey, E.L., . . . Dinges, D.F. (2012). Sleep deprivation and stressors: Evidence for elevated negative affect in response to mild stressors when sleep deprived. *Emotion, 12*(5), 1015–20.

Mioshi, E., Bristow, M., Cook, R., & Hodges, J.R. (2009). Factors underlying caregiver stress in frontotemporal dementia and Alzheimer's disease. *Dementia and Geriatric Cognitive Disorders, 27*(1), 76–81.

Nabi, R.L., Prestin, A., & So, J. (2013). Facebook friends with (health) benefits? Exploring social network site use and perceptions of social support, stress, and well-being. *Cyberpsychology, Behavior, and Social Networking, 16*(10), 721–7.

Nandi, A., Glymour, M.M., & Subramanian, S.V. (2014). Association among socioeconomic status, health behaviors, and all-cause mortality in the United States. *Epidemiology, 25*(2), 170–7.

Nijboer, C., Triemstra, M., Tempelaar, R., Sanderman, R., & Van den Bos, G. (1999). Determinants of caregiving experiences and mental health of partners of cancer patients. *Cancer, 86*, 577–88.

Nolan, M., Grant, G., & Ellis, N. (1990). Stress is in the eye of the beholder: Reconceptualizing the measurement of career burden. *Journal of Advanced Nursing, 15*, 544–55.

Nolen-Hoeksema, S. (2000). The role of rumination in depressive disorders and mixed anxiety/depressive symptoms. *Journal of Abnormal Psychology, 109*, 504–11.

Norris, R., Carroll, D., & Cochrane, R. (1992). The effects of physical activity and exercise training on psychological stress and well-being in an adolescent population. *Journal of Psychosomatic Research, 36*, 55–65.

Obrist, P. (1981). Cardiovascular psychophysiology: A perspective. New York: Plenum Press.

Oparil, S. (1995). Hypertension in postmenopausal women: Pathophysiology and management. *Current Opinion in Nephrology and Hypertension, 4*, 438–42.

Orzech, K.M., Grandner, M.A., Roane, B.M., & Carskadon, M.A. (2016). Digital media use in the 2 h before bedtime is associated with sleep variables in university students. *Computers in Human Behavior, 55*, 43–50.

O'Sullivan, G. (2010). The relationship between hope, eustress, self-efficacy, and life satisfaction among undergraduates. *Social Indicators Research, 101*, 155–72.

Padesky, C.A., & Hammen, C.L. (1981). Sex differences in depressive symptom expression and help-seeking among college students. *Sex Roles, 7*, 309–20.

Palanza, P., Gioiosa, L., & Parmigiani, S. (2001). Social stress in mice: Gender differences and effects of estrous cycle and social dominance. *Physiology & Behavior, 73*(3), 411–20.

Pascoe, E. A., & Smart Richman, L. (2009). Perceived discrimination and health: A meta-analytic review. *Psychological Bulletin, 135*(4), 531–54.

Penedo, F.J., & Dahn, J.R. (2005). Exercise and well-being: A review of mental and physical health benefits associated with physical activity. *Current Opinion in Psychiatry, 18*, 189–93.

Pennebaker, J. W. (1997). Writing about emotional experiences as a therapeutic process. *Psychological Science, 8*(3), 162–6.

Pennebaker, J.W., Colder, M., & Sharp, L.K. (1990). Accelerating the coping process. *Journal of Personality and Social Psychology, 58*, 528–37.

Pennebaker, J.W., & Seagal, J.D. (1999). Forming a story: The health benefits of narrative. *Journal of Clinical Psychology, 55*, 1243–54.

Pérez-Stable, E.J., Marín, G., & Marín, B.V. (1994). Behavioral risk factors: A comparison of Latinos and non-Latino Whites in San Francisco. *American Journal of Public Health, 84*, 971–6.

Petrie, K.J., Booth, R.J., Pennebaker, J.W., Davison, K.P., & Thomas, M.G. (1995). Disclosure of trauma and immune response to a hepatitis B vaccination program. *Journal of Consulting and Clinical Psychology, 63*, 787–92.

Pinquart, M., & Sörensen, S. (2006). Gender differences in caregiver stressors, social resources, and health: An updated meta-analysis. *The Journals of Gerontology Series B: Psychological Sciences and Social Sciences, 61*(1), P33–P45.

Puttonen, S., Harma, M., & Hublin, C. (2010). Shift work and cardiovascular disease—pathways from circadian stress to morbidity. *Scandinavian Journal of Work, Environment & Health, 36*, 96–108.

Rabkin, J.G., & Struening, E.L. (1976). Life events, stress, and illness. *Science, 194*, 1013–20.

Repetti, R.L., & Wood, J. (1997). Effects of daily stress at work on mothers' interaction with preschool children. *Journal of Family Psychology, 11*, 90–108.

Rosengren, A., Orth-Gomer, K., Wedel, H., & Wilhelmsen, L. (1993). Stressful life events, social support, and mortality in men born in 1933. *British Medical Journal, 307*, 1102–5.

Sandlund, E.S., & Norlander, T. (2000). The effects of Tai Chi Chuan relaxation and exercise on stress responses and well-being: An overview of research. *International Journal of Stress Management, 7*, 139–49.

Sapolsky, R.M. (2004). Why zebras don't get ulcers: The acclaimed guide to stress, stress related diseases, and coping (3rd rev. ed.). New York: W.H. Freeman.

Saunders, T., Driskell, J.E., Johnston, J.H., & Salas, E. (1996). The effect of stress inoculation training on anxiety and performance. *Journal of Occupational Health Psychology, 1*, 170–86.

Schell, F.J., Allolio, B., & Schonecke, O.W. (1994). Physiological and psychological effects of Hatha-Yoga exercise in healthy women. *International Journal of Psychosomatics, 41*, 46–52.

Schulz, R., & Beach, S.R. (1999). Caregiving as a risk factor for mortality. *Journal of the American Medical Association, 282*, 2215–19.

Seligman, M.E.P., & Maier, S.F. (1967). Failure to escape traumatic shock. *Journal of Experimental Psychology, 74*, 1–9.

Selye, H. (1976). *The stress of life* (rev. ed.). New York: McGraw-Hill.

Shakespeare, W. (2003). *Hamlet* (The New Folger Library Shakespeare). New York: Simon & Schuster, New Folger Edition.

Siegrist, J. (1996). Adverse health effects of high-effort/low reward conditions. *Journal of Occupational Health Psychology, 1*, 27–41.

Smyth, J.M., Stone, A.A., Hurewitz, A., & Kaell, A. (1999). Effects of writing about stressful experiences on symptom reduction in patients with asthma or rheumatoid arthritis: A randomized trial. *Journal of the American Medical Association, 281*, 1304–9.

Son, J., Erno, A., Shea, D.G., Femia, E.E., Zarit, S.H., & Parris Stephens, M.A. (2007). The caregiver stress process and health outcomes. *Journal of Aging and Health, 19*, 871–87.

Spielberger, C.D., Johnson, E.H., Russell, S.F., Crane, R.J., Jacobs, G.A., & Worden, T.I. (1985). The experience and expression of anger: Construction and validation of an anger expression scale. In M.A. Chesney & R.H. Rosenman (Eds.), *Anger and hostility in cardiovascular and behavioral disorders*. New York: Hemisphere/McGraw-Hill.

Stone, A.A., & Neale, J.M. (1984). New measure of daily coping. Development and preliminary results. *Journal of Personality and Social Psychology, 46*, 892–906.

Szanton, S.L., Rifkind, J.M., Mohanty, J.G., Miller, E.R., Thorpe, R.J., Nagababu, E., . . . Evans, M.K. (2011). Racial discrimination is associated with a measure of red blood cell oxidative stress: A potential pathway for racial health disparities. *International Journal of Behavioral Medicine*, September.

Taylor, S.E. (2006). Tend and befriend biobehavioral bases of affiliation under stress. *Current Directions in Psychological Science, 15*(6), 273–7.

Taylor, S.E., Klein, L.C., Gruenewald, T.L., Gurung, R.A., & Taylor, S.F. (2003). Affiliation, social support, and biobehavioral responses to stress. In J.M. Suls & K.A. Wallston (Eds.), *Social psychological foundations of health and illness* (pp. 314–32). Boston: Blackwell.

Taylor, S.E., Klein, L.C., Lewis, B.P., Gruenewald, T.L., Gurung, R.A., & Updegraff, J.A. (2000). Biobehavioral responses to stress in females: Tend-and-befriend, not fight-or-flight. *Psychological Review, 107*, 411–29.

Tennant, C. (2001). Work-related stress and depressive disorders. *Journal of Psychosomatic Research, 51*, 697–704.

Theorell, T., DeFaire, U., Johnson, J., Hall, E., Perski, A., & Stewart, W. (1991). Job strain and ambulatory blood pressure profiles. *Scandinavian Journal of Work Environment and Health, 17*, 380–5.

Timio, M., Verdecchia, P., Venanzi, S., Gentili, S., Ronconi, M., Francucci, B., . . . Bichisao, E. (1988). Age and blood pressure changes: A 20-year follow-up study in nuns in a secluded order. *Hypertension, 12*, 457–61.

Tomaka, J., Blascovich, J., Kelsey, R.M., & Leitten, C.L. (1993). Subjective, physiological, and behavioral effects of threat and challenge appraisal. *Journal of Personality and Social Psychology, 65*, 248–60.

Uchino, B.N., Cacioppo, J.T, & Kiecolt-Glaser, J.K. (1996). The relationship between social support and physiological processes: A review with emphasis on underlying mechanisms and implications for health. *Psychological Bulletin, 119*, 488–531.

Umberson, D. (1987). Family status and health behaviors: Social control as a dimension of social integration. *Journal of Health and Social Behavior, 28*, 306–19.

Verhaeghe, S., Defloor, T., & Grypdonck, M. (2005). Stress and coping among families of patients with traumatic brain injury: A review of the literature. *Journal of Clinical Nursing, 14*, 1004–12.

Verlander, L. A., Benedict, J. O., & Hanson, D. P. (1999). Stress and sleep patterns of college students. *Perceptual and Motor Skills, 88*(3), 893–8.

Wareham, S., Fowler, K., & Pike, A. (2007). Determinants of depression severity and duration in Canadian adults: The moderating effects of gender and social support. *Journal of Applied Social Psychology, 37*, 2951–79.

Weiss, J.M. (1968). Effects of coping responses on stress. *Journal of Comparative and Physiological Psychology, 65,* 251–60.

White, M., & Dorman, S. M. (2001). Receiving social support online: implications for health education. *Health Education Research, 16*(6), 693–707.

Williams, R.B., & Barefoot, J.C. (1988). Coronary-prone behavior: The emerging role of the hostility complex. In B.K. Houston & C.R. Snyder (Eds.), *Type A behavior Pattern—Research, theory, and intervention* (pp. 189–211). New York: Wiley.

Wills, T.A. (1990). Social support and interpersonal relationships. In M.S. Clark (Ed.), *Prosocial Behavior* (pp. 265–89). Thousand Oaks, Calif.: Sage.

Yadav, R. K., Magan, D., Mehta, N., Sharma, R., & Mahapatra, S. C. (2012). Efficacy of a short-term yoga-based lifestyle intervention in reducing stress and inflammation: Preliminary results. *The Journal of Alternative and Complementary Medicine, 18*(7), 662–7.

Chapter 4

Abramson, J.S., Oshea, T.M., Ratledge, D.L., Lawless, M.R., & Givner, L.B. (1995). Development of a vaccine tracking system to improve the rate of age-appropriate primary immunization in children of lower socioeconomic-status. *Journal of Pediatrics, 126,* 583–6.

Alemayehu, B., & Warner, K.E. (2004). The lifetime distribution of health care costs. *Health Services Research, 39,* 627–42.

American College Health Association. (2017). American College Health Association–National College Health Assessment: Fall 2017 Reference Group Executive Summary. Retrieved from http://www.acha-ncha.org/docs/NCHA-II_FALL_2017_REFERENCE_GROUP_EXECUTIVE_SUMMARY.pdf

American Psychiatric Association. (2013). *Diagnostic and statistical manual of mental disorders* (5th ed.). Washington, DC: Author.

Andrade, L.H., Alonso, J., Mneimneh, Z., Wells, J.E., Al-Hamzawi, A., Borges, G., . . . Kessler, R.C. (2014). Barriers to mental health treatment: Results from the WHO World Mental Health surveys. *Psychological Medicine, 44*(6), 1303–17.

Barsky, A.J., Peekna, H.M., & Borus, J.F. (2001). Somatic symptom reporting in women and men. *Journal of General Internal Medicine, 16,* 266–75.

Béland, D., Rocco, P., & Waddan, A. (2016). *Obamacare wars: Federalism, state politics, and the Affordable Care Act.* Lawrence, KS: University Press of Kansas.

Belar, C.D. (1997). Clinical health psychology: A specialty for the 21st century. *Health Psychology, 16,* 411–16.

Blackwell, D.L., Martinez, M.E., Gentleman, J.F., Sanmartin, C., & Berthelot, J.M. (2009). Socioeconomic status and utilization of health care services in Canada and the United States: Findings from a binational health survey. *Medical Care, 47,* 1136–46.

Bobevski, I., Clarke, D. M., & Meadows, G. (2016). Health anxiety and its relationship to disability and service use: Findings from a large epidemiological survey. *Psychosomatic Medicine, 78*(1), 13–25.

Burau, V., & Blank, R.H. (2006). Comparing health policy: An assessment of typologies of health systems. *Journal of Comparative Policy Analysis, 8,* 63–76.

Burgess, D.J., Ding, Y., Hargreaves, M., van Ryn, M., & Phelan, S. (2008). The association between perceived discrimination and underutilization of needed medical and mental health care in a multi-ethnic community sample. *Journal of Health Care for the Poor and Underserved, 19,* 894–911.

Centers for Disease Control and Prevention. (2016). *Early release of selected estimates based on data from the 2015 National Health Interview Survey.* Washington, DC: U.S. Department of Health and Human Services, Centers for Disease Control and Prevention, National Center for Health Statistics. Retrieved from https://www.cdc.gov/nchs/data/nhis/earlyrelease/earlyrelease201605.pdf

Chiles, J.A., Lambert, M.J., & Hatch, A.L. (1999). The impact of psychological interventions on medical cost offset: A meta-analytic review. *Clinical Psychology Science and Practice, 6,* 204–20.

Davidson, K.W., Gidron, Y., Mostofsky, E., & Trudeau, K.J. (2007). Hospitalization cost offset of a hostility intervention for coronary heart disease patients. *Journal of Consulting and Clinical Psychology 75,* 657–62.

Deacon, B., Lickel, J., & Abramowitz, J.S. (2008). Medical utilization across the anxiety disorders. *Journal of Anxiety Disorders, 22,* 344–50.

DiMatteo, M.R. (2004). Social support and patient adherence to medical treatment: A meta-analysis. *Health Psychology, 23,* 207–18.

DiMatteo, M.R., Giordani, P.J., Lepper, H.S., & Croghan, T.W. (2002). Patient adherence and medical treatment outcomes—A meta-analysis. *Medical Care, 40,* 794–811.

DiMatteo, M.R., Haskard-Zolnierek, K.B., & Martin, L.R. (2012). Improving patient adherence: A three-factor model to guide practice. *Health Psychology Review, 6,* 74–91.

Figueras, J., McKee, M., Lessof, S., Duran, A., & Menabde, N. (2008). *Health systems, health and wealth: Assessing the case for investing in health systems.* Copenhagen: WHO on behalf on the European Observatory on Health Systems and Policies.

Flood, C.M., & Archibald, T. (2001). The illegality of private health care in Canada. *Canadian Medical Association Journal, 164,* 825–30.

Frank, G., McDaniel, S.H., Bray, J.H., & Heldring, M. (2004). *Primary care psychology.* Washington, DC: American Psychological Association.

Freeman, R., & Frisina, L. (2010). Health care systems and the problem of classification. *Journal of Comparative Health Policy Analysis, 12,* 163–78.

Glozier, N., Christensen, H., Naismith, S., Cockayne, N., Donkin, L., Neal, B., . . . Hickie, I. (2013). Internet-delivered cognitive behavioural therapy for adults with mild to moderate depression and high cardiovascular disease risks: A randomised attention-controlled trial. *PLOS ONE, 8*(3), e59139.

Gray, B.H. (2006). The rise and decline of the HMO: A chapter in U.S. health-policy history. In R. Stevens, C.E. Rosenberg, & L.R. Burns (Eds.), *History and health policy in the United*

States: Putting the past back in (pp. 309–440). Piscataway, NJ: Rutgers University Press.

Gray, V., Lowery, D., & Godwin, E.K. (2007). The political management of managed care: Explaining variations in state health maintenance organization regulations. *Journal of Health Politics, Policy and Law, 32*, 457–95.

Hacke, W., Donnan, G., Fieschi, C., Kaste, M., von Kummer, R., Broderick, J. P., . . . Hamilton, S. (2004). Association of outcome with early stroke treatment: Pooled analysis of ATLANTIS, ECASS, and NINDS RT-PA stroke trials. *Lancet, 363*, 768–74.

Hacker, J. S. (2002). *The divided welfare state: The battle over public and private social benefits in the United States*. New York, NY: Cambridge University Press.

Hagger, M.S., & Orbell, S. (2003). A meta-analytic review of the common-sense model of illness representations. *Psychology & Health, 18*, 141–84.

Hagger, M.S., Wood, C., Stiff, C., & Chatzisarantis, N.L.D. (2009). The strength model of self-regulation failure and health-related behaviour. *Health Psychology Review, 3*, 208–38.

Hand, M., Brown, C., Horan, M., & Simons-Morton, D. (1998). The National Heart Attack Alert Program: Progress at 5 years in educating providers, patients, and the public and future directions. *Journal of Thrombosis and Thrombolysis, 6*, 9–17.

Hedman, E., Andersson, E., Lindefors, N., Andersson, G., Ruck, C., & Ljotsson, B. (2013). Cost-effectiveness and long-term effectiveness of Internet-based cognitive behaviour therapy for severe health anxiety. *Psychological Medicine, 43*(2), 363–74.

Hunsley, J. (2003). Cost-effectiveness and medical cost-offset considerations in psychological service provision. *Canadian Psychology, 44*, 61–73.

Ingersoll, K.S., & Cohen, J. (2008). The impact of medication regimen factors on adherence to chronic treatment: A review of literature. *Journal of Behavioral Medicine, 31*, 213–24.

Kainth, A., Hewitt, A., Sowden, A., Duffy, S., Pattenden, J., Lewin, R., . . . Thompson, D. (2004). Systematic review of interventions to reduce delay in patients with suspected heart attack. *Emergency Medicine Journal, 21*, 506–8.

Kimerling, R., Ouimette, P.C., Cronkite, R.C., & Moos, R.H. (1999). Depression and outpatient medical utilization: A naturalistic 10-year follow-up. *Annals of Behavioral Medicine, 21*, 317–21.

Kraft, S., Puschner, B., Lambert, M.J., & Kordy, H. (2006). Medical utilization and treatment outcome in mid- and long-term outpatient psychotherapy. *Psychotherapy Research, 16*, 241–9.

LaVeist, T.A., Isaac, L.A., & Williams, K.P. (2009). Mistrust of health care organizations is associated with underutilization of health services. *Health Services Research, 44*, 2093–105.

Luepker, R.V., Raczynski, J.M., Osganian, S., Goldberg, R.J., Finnegan, J.R., Hedges, J.R., . . . Grp, R.S. (2000). Effect of a community intervention on patient delay and emergency medical service use in acute coronary heart disease—The Rapid Early Action for Coronary Treatment (REACT) trial. *Journal of the American Medical Association, 284*, 60–7.

McDonald, H.P., Garg, A.X., & Haynes, R.B. (2002). Interventions to enhance patient adherence to medication prescriptions—Scientific review. *Journal of the American Medical Association, 288*, 2868–79.

Marchildon, G.P. (2013). *Health systems in transition: Canada* (2nd ed.). Toronto, ON: University of Toronto Press.

Marchildon, G.P., & Lockhart, W. (2012). Common trends in public stewardship in health care. In B. Rosen, A. Israeli, & S. Shortell (Eds.), *Accountability and responsibility in health care: Issues in addressing an emerging global challenge* (pp. 255–76). Hackensack, NJ: World Scientific.

Mechanic, D., & Olfson M. (2016). The relevance of the Affordable Care Act for improving mental health care. *Annual Review of Clinical Psychology, 11*, 515–42.

Moser, D.K., Kimble, L.P., Alberts, M.J., Alonzo, A., Croft, J.B., Dracup, K., . . . Zerwic, J.J. (2007). Reducing delay in seeking treatment by patients with acute coronary syndrome and stroke: A scientific statement from the American Heart Association Council on Cardiovascular Nursing and Stroke Council. *Journal of Cardiovascular Nursing, 22*, 326–43.

Nicassio, P.M., Meyerowitz, B.E., & Kerns, R.D. (2004). The future of health psychology interventions. *Health Psychology, 23*, 132–7.

Organisation for Economic Co-operation and Development (OECD). (2011). *Health at a glance: OECD indicators*. Paris: OECD.

Organisation for Economic Co-operation and Development (OECD). (2013). *OECD health status statistics*. Paris: OECD. Retrieved from http://stats.oecd.org

Prins, M.A., Verhaak, P.F.M., Smit, D., & Verheij, R.A. (2014). Healthcare utilization in general practice before and after psychological treatment: A follow-up data linkage study in primary care. *Scandinavian Journal of Primary Health Care, 32*(3), 117–23.

Quan, H., Fong, A., De Coster, C., Wang, J.L., Musto, R., Noseworthy, T.W., & Ghali, W.A. (2006). Variation in health services utilization among ethnic populations. *Canadian Medical Association Journal, 174*, 787–91.

Romanow, R.J., & Marchildon, G.P. (2003). Psychological services and the future of health care in Canada. *Canadian Psychology, 44*, 283–95.

Roter, D.L., Hall, J.A., & Aoki, Y. (2002). Physician gender effects in medical communication: A meta-analytic review. *Journal of the American Medical Association, 288*, 756–64.

Saltman, R.B., & Dubois, H.F.W. (2004). The historical and social base of social health insurance systems. In R.B. Saltman, R. Busse, & A. Figueras (Eds.), *Social health insurance systems in Europe* (pp. 33–80). Maidenhead, UK: Open University Press for European Observatory on Health Systems and Policies.

Saltman, R.B., & Ferroussier-Davis, O. (2000). The concept of stewardship in health policy. *Bulletin of the World Health Organization, 78*, 732–9.

Scheppers, E., van Dongen, E., Dekker, J., Geertzen, J., & Dekker, J. (2006). Potential barriers to the use of health services among ethnic minorities: A review. *Family Practice, 23*, 325–48.

Schoen, C. (2011). New 2011 survey of patients with complex care needs in 11 countries finds that care is often poorly coordinated. *Health Affairs 30*, 2437–48.

Schoen, C., Osborn, R., Doty, M.M., Squires, D., Peugh, J., & Applebaum, S. (2009). A survey of primary care physicians in eleven countries, 2009: Perspectives on care costs, and experiences. *Health Affairs Web Exclusive, 28,* w1171–w1183.

Sheeran, P., Maki, A., Montanaro, E., Avishai-Yitshak, A., Bryan, A., Klein, W.M.P., . . . Rothman, A.J. (2016). The impact of changing attitudes, norms, and self-efficacy on health-related intentions and behavior: A meta-analysis. *Health Psychology, 35*(11), 1178–88.

Sitzia, J., & Wood, N. (1997). Patient satisfaction: A review of issues and concepts. *Social Science & Medicine, 45,* 1829–43.

Smith, T.W., Orleans, C.T., & Jenkins, C.D. (2004). Prevention and health promotion: Decades of progress, new challenges, and an emerging agenda. *Health Psychology, 23,* 126–31.

Starr, P. (2011). *Remedy and reaction: The peculiar American struggle over health care reform.* New Haven, CT: Yale University Press.

Suls, J., & Rothman, A. (2004). Evolution of the biopsychosocial model: Prospects and challenges for health psychology. *Health Psychology, 23,* 119–25.

Tak, H., Ruhnke, G. W., & Shih, Y. C. T. (2015). The association between patient-centered attributes of care and patient satisfaction. *Patient-Patient Centered Outcomes Research, 8*(2), 187–97.

Taylor, C. J., La Greca, A., Valenzuela, J. M., Hsin, O., & Delamater, A. M. (2016). Satisfaction with the health care provider and regimen adherence in minority youth with Type 1 diabetes. *Journal of Clinical Psychology in Medical Settings, 23*(3), 257–68.

Tomenson, B., McBeth, J., Chew-Graham, C.A., Macfarlane, G., Davies, I., Jackson, J., . . . Creed, F.H. (2012). Somatization and health anxiety as predictors of health care use. *Psychosomatic Medicine, 74,* 656–64.

Tovian, S.M. (2004). Health services and health care economics: The health psychology marketplace. *Health Psychology, 23,* 138–41.

Turner, J.C., Keller, A., Wu, H., Zimmerman, M., Zhang, J., & Barnes, L.E. (2018). Utilization of primary care among college students with mental health disorders. *Health Psychology, 37,* 385–93. http://dx.doi.org/10.1037/hea0000580

United States Census Bureau (2016). *Health Insurance Coverage in the United States: 2015.* Retrieved from https://www.census.gov/content/dam/Census/library/publications/2016/demo/p60-257.pdf

Weise, C., Kleinstauber, M., & Andersson, G. (2016). Internet-delivered cognitive-behavior therapy for tinnitus: A randomized controlled trial. *Psychosomatic Medicine, 78*(4), 501–10.

Wood, W., & Runger, D. (2016). Psychology of habit. *Annual Review of Psychology, 67,* 289–314.

World Health Organization (WHO). (2000). *The World Health Report 2000: Health systems: improving performance.* Geneva: WHO.

Worthington, C. (2005). Patient satisfaction with health care: Recent theoretical developments and implications for evaluation practice. *Canadian Journal of Program Evaluation, 20,* 41–63.

Xiao, H., & Barber, J.P. (2008). The effect of perceived health status on patient satisfaction. *Value in Health, 11,* 719–25.

Zolnierek, K.B., & DiMatteo, M.R. (2009). Physician communication and patient adherence to treatment: A meta-analysis. *Medical Care, 47,* 826–34.

Chapter 5

Abrams, D.B., Herzog, T.A., Emmons, K.M., & Linnan, L. (2000). Stages of change versus addiction: A replication and extension. *Nicotine & Tobacco Research, 2,* 223–29.

Aveyard, P., Cheng, K.K., Almond, J., Sherratt, E., Lancashire, R., Lawrence, T., . . . Evans, O. (1999). Cluster randomized controlled trial of expert system based on the transtheoretical ("stages of change") model for smoking prevention and cessation in schools. *British Medical Journal, 319,* 948–53.

Azjen, I., and Madden, T. (1986). Prediction of goal-directed behavior: Attitudes, intentions, and perceived behavioral control. *Journal of Experimental Social Psychology, 22,* 453–74.

Bandura, A. (1982). Self-efficacy mechanism in human agency. *American Psychologist, 37,* 122–47.

Blissmer, B., Prochaska, J.O., Velicer, W.F., Redding, C.A., Rossi, J.S., Greene, G.W., . . . Robbins, M.L. (2010). Common factors predicting long-term changes in multiple health behaviours. *Journal of Health Psychology, 15,* 201–14.

Broderick, L., Johnson, S.S., Cummins, C.O., & Castle, P. (2015, November). Effectiveness of liveWell: An online program to promote student well-being. Paper presented at the annual conference of the American Public Health Association, Chicago, IL.

CDC AIDS Community Demonstration Projects Research Group. (1999). Community-level HIV intervention in 5 cities: Final outcome data from the CDC AIDS community demonstration projects. *American Journal of Public Health, 89,* 336–45.

DiClemente, C.C., & Prochaska, J.O. (1982). Self-change and therapy change of smoking behaviour: A comparison of processes of change in cessation and maintenance. *Addictive Behaviour, 7,* 133–42.

DiClemente, C.C., Prochaska, J.O., Fairhurst, S.K., Velicer, W.F., Valesquez, M.M., & Rossi, J.S. (1991). The processes of smoking cessation: An analysis of precontemplation, contemplation, and preparation stages of change. *Journal of Consulting and Clinical Psychology, 59,* 295–304.

Dijkstra, A., Conijm, B., & De Vries, H. (2006). A match-mismatch test of a stage model of behaviour change in tobacco smoking. *Addiction, 101,* 1035–43.

Edington, D.W. (2001). Emerging research: A view from one research center. *American Journal of Health Promotion, 15,* 341–9.

Etter, J.F., Perneger, T.V., & Ronchi, A. (1997). Distributions of smokers by stage: International comparison and association with smoking prevalence. *Preventive Medicine, 26*(4), 580–5.

Evers, K.E., Prochaska, J.O., Van Marter, D.F., Johnson, J.L., & Prochaska, J.M. (2007). Transtheoretical-based bullying prevention effectiveness trials in middle schools and high schools. *Education Research, 49,* 397–414.

Farkas, A.J., Pierce, J.P., Zhu, S.H., Rosbrook, B., Gilpin, E.A., Berry, C., & Kaplan, R.M. (1996). Addiction versus stages of change models in predicting smoking cessation. *Addiction, 91*, 1271–80.

Goldstein, M.G., Pinto, B.M., Marcus, B.H., Lynn, H., Jette, A.M., Rakowski, W., . . . Tennstedt, S. (1999). Physician-based physical activity counseling for middle-aged and older adults: A randomized trial. *Annals of Behavioural Medicine, 21*, 40–7.

Hall, J.S., & Rossi, J.S. (2008). Meta-analytic examination of the strong and weak principles across 48 health behaviours. *Preventive Medicine, 46*, 266–74.

Herzog, T.A., Abrams, D.B., Emmons, K. A., & Linnan, L. (2000). Predicting increases in readiness to quit smoking: A prospective analysis using the contemplation ladder. *Psychology & Health, 15*, 369–81.

Herzog, T.A., Abrams, D.B., Emmons, K.A., Linnan, L., & Shadel, W.G. (1999). Do processes of change predict stage movements? A prospective analysis of the transtheoretical model. *Health Psychology, 18*, 369–75.

Hoffman A., Redding, C.A., Goldberg, D.N., Añel, D., Prochaska, J.O., Meyer, P.M., & Pandey, D. (2006). Computer expert systems for African American smokers in physicians' offices: A feasibility study. *Preventive Medicine, 43*, 204–11.

Hollis, J.F., Polen, M.R., Whitlock, E.P., Lichtenstein, E., Mullooly, J., Velicer, W.F., & Redding, C.A. (2005). Teen REACH: Outcomes from a randomized controlled trial of a tobacco reduction program for teens seen in primary medical care. *Pediatrics, 115*, 981–9.

Janis, I.L., & Mann, L. (1977). Decision making: A psychological analysis of conflict, chance and commitment. London: Cassil & Collier Macmillan.

Johnson, J.L., Regan, R., Maddock, J.E., Fava, J.L., Velicer, W.F., Rossi, J.S., & Prochaska, J.O. (2000). What predicts stage of change for smoking cessation? *Annals of Behavioural Medicine, 22*, S173. (Abstract).

Johnson, S.S., Paiva, A.L., Cummins, C.O., Johnson, J.L., Dyment, S.J., Wright, J.A., . . . Sherman, K. (2008). Transtheoretical model-based multiple behaviour intervention for weight management: Effectiveness on a population basis. *Preventive Medicine, 46*, 238–46.

Johnson, S.S., Paiva, A, Mauriello,L. Prochaska, J.O., Redding, C.A., & Velier, W.F. (2014). Coaction in multiple behavior change interventions: Consistency across multiple studies on weight management & obesity prevention. *Health Psychology, 33*(5), 475–80.

Jordan P.J., Evers, K.E., Spira, J.L., King, L.A., & Lid, V. (2013). *Computerized tailored interventions improve outcomes and reduce barriers to care.* Poster presented at the 17th Annual International meeting and Exposition of the American Telemedicine Association, Austin, TX.

Levesque, D.A., Johnson, J.L., Welch, C.A., Prochaska, J.M., & Paiva, A.L. (2016). Teen dating violence prevention: Cluster-randomized trial of teen choices, an online, stage-based program for healthy, nonviolent relationships. *Psychology of Violence, 6*(3), 421–32.

Khaw, K.T., Wareham, N., Bingham, S., Welch, A., Luben, R., & Day, N. (2008). Combined impact of health behaviours and mortality in men and women: The EPIC-Norfolk Prospective Population Study. *PLOS Medicine 5*, e12.

Kreuter, M.W., Strecher, V.J., & Glassman, B. (1999). One size does not fit all: The case for tailoring print materials. *Annals of Behavioural Medicine, 21*, 276–83.

Mauriello, L.M., Ciavatta, M.M.H., Paiva, A.L., Sherman, K.J., Castle, P.H., Johnson, J.L., and Prochaska, J.M. (2010). Results of a multi-media multiple behaviour obesity prevention program for adolescents. *Preventive Medicine, 51*, 451–6.

Mauriello, L.M., Sherman, K.J., Driskell, M.M., & Prochaska, J.M. (2007). Using interactive behaviour change technology to intervene on physical activity and nutrition with adolescents. *Adolescent Medicine, 8*, 383–99. PMID: 18605653.

Mauriello, L.M., Van Marter, D.F., Umanzor, C.D., Castle, P.H., & de Aquiar, E.L. (2016). Using mHealth to deliver behavior change interventions within prenatal care at community health centers. *American Journal of Health Promotion, 30*(7), 554–62.

Noar, S.M., Benac, C., & Harris, M. (2007). Does tailoring matter? Meta-analytic review of tailored print health behaviour change interventions. *Psychological Bulletin, 133*, 673–93.

Norman, G.J., Adams, M.A., Calfas, K.J., Covin, J., Sallis, J.F., Rossi, J.S., . . . Patrick, K. (2007). A randomized controlled trial of a multicomponent intervention for adolescent sun protection behaviours. *Archives of Pediatric & Adolescent Medicine, 161*, 146–52.

Paiva, A.L., Prochaska, J.O., Hui-Qing Yin, H., Redding, C.R., Rossi, J.S., Blissmer, B., . . . Horiuchi, S. (2012). Treated individuals who progress to action or maintenance for one behavior are more likely to make similar progress on another behavior: Coaction results of a pooled data analysis of three trials. *Preventive Medicine, 54*, 331–4.

Peterson, A.V., Kealey, K.A., Mann, S.L., Marek, P.M., & Sarason, I.G. (2000). Hutchinson Smoking Prevention Project: Long-term randomized trial in school-based tobacco use prevention—results on smoking. *Journal of the National Cancer Institute, 92*, 1979–91.

Prochaska, J.J., Velicer, W.F., Prochaska, J.O., Delucchi, K., & Hall, S.M. (2006). Comparing intervention outcomes in smokers treated for single versus multiple behavioural risks. *Health Psychology, 25*, 380–8.

Prochaska, J.M., Prochaska, J.O., Cohen, F.C., Gomes, S.O., Laforge, R.G., & Eastwood, A. (2004). The transtheoretical model of change for multi-level interventions for alcohol abuse on campus. *Journal of Alcohol and Drug Education, 47*, 34–50.

Prochaska, J.O. (1979). *Systems of psychotherapy: A transtheoretical analysis.* Pacific Grove, CA.: Brooks-Cole. (8th ed., 2014).

Prochaska, J.O., Butterworth, S., Redding, C.A., Burden, V., Perrin, N., Leo, M., . . . Prochaska, J.M. (2008). Initial efficacy of MI, TTM tailoring and HRI's with multiple behaviours for employee health promotion. *Preventive Medicine, 45*, 226–31.

Prochaska, J.O., & DiClemente, C.C. (1983). Stages and processes of self-change of smoking: Toward an integrative model of change. *Journal of Consulting and Clinical Psychology, 51*, 390–5.

Prochaska, J.O., DiClemente, C.C., Velicer, W.F., Ginpil, S., & Norcross, J.C. (1985). Predicting change in smoking status for self-changers. *Addictive Behaviours, 10*, 407–12. PMID: 4091072.

Prochaska, J.O., Evers, K.E., Castle, P.H., Johnson, J.L., Prochaska, J.M., Rula, E.Y., . . . Pope, J.E. (2012). Enhancing multiple domains of well-being by decreasing multiple health risk behaviours: A randomized clinical trial. *Population Health Management, 15*, 276–86.

Prochaska, J.O., & Prochaska, J.M. (2016). Changing to thrive: Using the stages of change to overcome the top threats to your health and happiness. Center City, MN.: Hazelden Publishing.

Prochaska, J.O., & Velicer, W.F. (1996). On models, methods and premature conclusions. *Addictions, 91*, 1281–3.

Prochaska, J.O., & Velicer, W.F. (1997). The transtheoretical model of health behaviour change. *American Journal of Health Promotion, 12*, 38–48.

Prochaska, J.O., Velicer, W.F., Fava, J.L., Ruggiero, L., Laforge, R.G., Rossi, J.S., . . . Lee, P.A. (2001). Counselor and stimulus control enhancements of a stage-matched expert system intervention for smokers in a managed care setting. *Preventive Medicine, 32*, 23–32.

Prochaska, J.O., Velicer, W.F., Guadagnoli, E., Rossi, J.S., & DiClemente, C.C. (1991). Patterns of change: Dynamic typology applied to smoking cessation. *Multivariate Behavioural Research, 26*, 83–107.

Prochaska, J.O., Velicer, W.F., Redding, C.A., Rossi, J.S., Goldstein, M., DePue, J., . . . Plummer, B.A. (2005). Stage-based expert systems to guide a population of primary care patients to quit smoking, eat healthier, prevent skin cancer, and receive regular mammograms. *Preventive Medicine, 41*, 406–16.

Prochaska, J.O., Velicer, W.F., Rossi, J.S., Goldstein, M.G., Marcus, B.H., Rakowski, W., . . . Rossi, S.R. (1994). Stages of change and decisional balance for twelve problem behaviours. *Health Psychology, 13*, 39–46.

Prochaska, J.O., Velicer, W.F, Rossi, J.S., Redding, C.A., Greene, G.W., Rossi, S.R., . . . Plummer, B.A. (2004). Impact of simultaneous stage-matched expert system interventions for smoking, high fat diet, and sun exposure in a population of parents. *Health Psychology, 23*, 503–16.

Prochaska, J.O., Wright, J.A., & Velicer, W.F. (2008). Evaluating theories of health behaviour change: A hierarchy of criteria applied to the transtheoretical model. *Applied Psychology: An International Review, 57*, 561–88.

Pronk, N.P., Lowry, M., Kottke, T.E., Austin, E., Gallagher, J., & Katz, A. (2010). The association between optimal lifestyle adherence and short-term incidence of chronic conditions among employees. *Population Health Management, 13*, 289–95.

Rakowski, W.R., Ehrich, B., Goldstein, M.G., Rimer, B.K., Pearlman, D.N., Clark, M.A., . . . Woolverton, H. (1998). Increasing mammography among women aged 40–74 by use of a stage-matched, tailored intervention. *Preventive Medicine, 27*, 748–56.

Redding, C.A., Maddock, J.E., & Rossi, J.S. (2006). The sequential approach to measurement of health behaviour constructs: Issues in selecting and developing measures. *Californian Journal of Health Promotion, 4*, 83–101.

Reeves, M.J., & Rafferty, A.P. (2005). Healthy lifestyle characteristics among adults in the United States, 2000. *Archives of Internal Medicine, 165*, 854–7.

Rosen, C.S. (2000). Is the sequencing of change processes by stage consistent across health problems? A meta-analysis. *Health Psychology, 19*, 593–604.

Rosenstock, I.M. (1960). What research in motivation suggests for public health. *American Journal of Public Health, 50*, 295–302.

Rossi, J.S. (1992a). Stages of change for 15 health risk behaviours in an HMO population. Paper presented at 13th meeting of the Society for Behavioural Medicine, New York, NY.

Rossi, J.S. (1992b). Common processes of change across nine problem behaviours. Paper presented at 100th meeting of American Psychological Association, Washington, D.C.

Ruggiero, L., Glasgow, R., Dryfoos, J.M., Rossi, J.S., Prochaska, J.O., Orleans, C.T., . . . Johnson, S. (1997). Diabetes self-management: Self-reported recommendations and patterns in a large population. *Diabetes Care, 20*, 568–76.

Skinner, C.S., Campbell, M.D., Rimer, B.K., Curry, S., & Prochaska, J.O. (1999). How effective is tailored print communication? *Annals of Behavioural Medicine, 21*, 290–8.

Snow, M.G., Prochaska, J.O., & Rossi, J.S. (1992). Stages of change for smoking cessation among former problem drinkers: A cross-sectional analysis. *Journal of Substance Abuse, 4*, 107–16.

Sun, X., Prochaska, J.O., Velicer, W.F., & Laforge, R.G. (2007). Transtheoretical principles and processes for quitting smoking: A 24-month comparison of a representative sample of quitters, relapsers and non-quitters. *Addictive Behaviours, 32*, 2707–26.

US Department of Health and Human Services (USDHHS). (1990). *The health benefits of smoking cessation: A report of the Surgeon General* (DHHS Publication No. CDC 90-8416). Washington, D.C.: U.S. Government Printing Office.

van den Brandt, P.A. (2011). The impact of a Mediterranean diet and healthy lifestyle on premature mortality in men and women. *American Journal of Clinical Nutrition, 94*, 913–20.

Velicer, W.F., Fava, J.L., Prochaska, J.O., Abrams, D.B., Emmons, K.M., & Pierce, J. (1995). Distribution of smokers by stage in three representative samples. *Preventive Medicine, 24*, 401–11.

Velicer, W.F., Prochaska, J.O., Bellis, J.M., DiClemente, C.C., Rossi, J.S., Fava, J.L., & Steiger, J.H. (1993). An expert system intervention for smoking cessation. *Addictive Behaviours, 18*, 269–90.

Velicer, W.F., Redding, C.A., Paiva, A.L., Mauriello, L.M., Blissmer, B., Oatley, K., . . . & Fernandez, A.C. (2013). Multiple behavior interventions to prevent substance abuse and increase energy balance behaviors in middle school students. *Translational Behavioral Medicine: Practice, Policy and Research, 3*(1), 82–93.

Velicer, W.F., Redding, C.A., Sun, X., & Prochaska, J.O. (2007). Demographic variables, smoking variables, and outcome across five studies. *Health Psychology, 26*, 278–87.

Voorhees, C.C., Stillman, F.A., Swank, R.T., Heagerty, P.J., Levine, D.M., & Becker, D.M. (1996). Heart, body, and soul: Impact of church-based smoking cessation interventions on readiness to quit. *Preventive Medicine, 25*, 277–85.

Wewers, M.E., Stillman, F.A., Hartman, A.M., & Shopland, D.R. (2003). Distribution of daily smokers by stage of change: Current population survey results. *Preventive Medicine, 36*, 710–20.

World Health Organization. (1998). Health promotion glossary. Geneva: Author.

Yang, G., Ma, J., Chen, A., Zhang, Y., Samet, J.M., Taylor, C.E., & Becker, K. (2001). Smoking cessation in China: Findings from the 1996 national prevalence survey. *Tobacco Control, 10*, 170–4.

Chapter 6

Advertising Standards Canada. (1998). *The 1998 ad complaints report*. Toronto, ON: Author.

Alhassan, S., Kim, S., Bersamin, A., King, A. C., & Gardner, C.D. (2008). Dietary adherence and weight loss success among overweight women: Results from the A TO Z weight loss study. *International Journal of Obesity, 32*, 985–91.

American Psychiatric Association. (2013). *Diagnostic and statistical manual of mental disorders* (5th ed.). Arlington, VA: American Psychiatric Publishing.

Andreyeva, T., Long, M.W., Henderson, K.E., & Grode, G.M. (2010). Trying to lose weight: Diet strategies among Americans with overweight or obesity in 1996 and 2003. *Journal of the American Dietetic Association, 110*(4), 535–42.

Arria, A.M., Garnier-Dykstra, L.M., Caldeira, K.M., Vincent, K.B., Winick, E.R., & O'Grady, K.E. (2013). Drug use patterns and continuous enrollment in college: Results from a longitudinal study. *Journal of Studies on Alcohol and Drugs, 74*, 71–83.

Ashare, R.L., Falcone, M., & Lerman, C. (2014). Cognitive function during nicotine withdrawal: Implications for nicotine dependence treatment. *Neuropharmacology, 76*, 581–91.

Atluri, S., Sudarshan, G., & Manchikanti, L. (2014). Assessment of the trends in medical use and misuse of opioid analgesics from 2004 to 2011. *Pain Physician, 17*, E119–E128.

Bandura, A. (1977). *Social learning theory*. Englewood Cliffs, NJ: Prentice Hall.

Bardone-Cone, A.M., Wonderlich, S.A., Frost, R.O., Bulik, C.M., Mitchell, J.E., Uppala, S., & Simonich, H. (2007). Perfectionism and eating disorders: Current status and future directions. *Clinical Psychology Review, 27*(3), 384–405.

Berglund, M. (2005). A better widget? Three lessons for improving addiction treatment from a meta-analytical study. *Addiction, 100*, 742–50.

Berman, A.H., Bergman, H., Palmstierna, T., & Schlyter, F. (2005). Evaluation of the Drug Use Disorders Identification Test (DUDIT) in criminal justice and detoxification settings and in a Swedish population sample. *European Addiction Research, 11*(1), 22–31.

Beydoun, M.A. (2014). The interplay of gender, mood, and stress hormones in the association between emotional eating and dietary behaviour. *The Journal of Nutrition, 144*(8), 1139–41.

Bickel, W.K., Christensen, D.R., & Marsch, L.A. (2011). A review of computer-based interventions used in the assessment, treatment, and research of drug addiction. *Substance Use & Misuse, 46*, 4–9.

Boden, J.M., & Fergusson, D.M. (2011). Alcohol and depression. *Addiction, 106*(5), 906–14.

Bohn, K., & Fairburn, C.G. (2008). The clinical impairment assessment questionnaire (CIA 3.0). In C.G. Fairburn (Ed.), *Cognitive behavior therapy and eating disorders* [Appendix III]. New York: Guildford Press.

Bolton, J.M., Robinson, J., & Sareen, J. (2009). Self-medication of mood disorders with alcohol and drugs in the National Epidemiologic Survey on Alcohol and Related Conditions. *Journal of Affective Disorders, 115*(3), 367–75.

Boone, L., Claes, L., & Luyten, P. (2014). Too strict or too loose? Perfectionism and impulsivity: The relation with eating disorder symptoms using a person-centered approach. *Eating Behaviours, 15*(1), 17–23.

Boumparis, N., Karyotaki, E., Schaub, M.P., Cuijpers, P., & Riper, H. (2017). Internet interventions for adult illicit substance users: A meta-analysis. *Addiction, 112*, 1521–32.

Boyce, W. (2004). *Young people in Canada: Their health and well-being*. Ottawa, ON: Health Canada. Retrieved from https://www.jcsh-cces.ca/upload/hbsc_report_2004_e.pdf.

Brown, R.L., & Rounds, L.A. (1995). Conjoint screening questionnaires for alcohol and other drug abuse: Criterion validity in a primary care practice. *Wisconsin Medical Journal, 94*(3) 135–40.

Bruce, S.G., Riediger, N.D., Zacharias, J.M., & Young, T.K. (2010). Obesity and obesity-related comorbidities in a Canadian First Nation population. *Chronic Diseases and Injuries in Canada, 31*(1), 27–32.

Butt, P., Beirness, D., Gliksman, L., Paradis, C., & Stockwell, T. (2011). *Alcohol and health in Canada: A summary of evidence and guidelines for low-risk drinking*. Ottawa, ON: Canadian Centre on Substance Abuse.

Carod-Artel, F.J. (2015). Hallucinogenic drugs in pre-Columbian Mesoamerican cultures. *Nerologia, 30*(1), 42–9.

Cassin, S.E., & von Ranson, K.M. (2005). Personality and eating disorders: A decade in review. *Clinical Psychology Review, 25*(7), 895–916.

Caulkins, J.P., & Bond, B.M. (2012). Marijuana price gradients: Implications for exports and export-generated tax revenue for California after legalization. *Journal of Drug Issues, 42*(1), 28–45.

Centers for Disease Control and Prevention (CDC). (2017). *Smoking & tobacco use*. Retrieved from https://www.cdc.gov/tobacco/data_statistics/fact_sheets/economics/econ_facts/index.htm

Center on Alcohol Marketing and Youth. (2012). *Youth exposure to alcohol advertising on television, 2001–2009*. Retrieved from http://www.camy.org/research/Youth_Exposure_to_Alcohol_Ads_on_TV_Growing_Faster_Than_Adults.

Chassin, L., Pitts, S.C., & Prost, J. (2002). Binge drinking trajectories from adolescence to emerging adulthood in a high-risk sample: Predictors and substance abuse outcomes. *Journal of Consulting and Clinical Psychology, 70*(1), 67–78.

Chassin, L., Sher, K.J., Hussong, A., & Curran, P. (2013). The developmental psychopathology of alcohol use and alcohol disorders: Research achievements and future directions. *Development and Psychopathology, 25*(4 Pt 2), 1567–84.

Chiesa, A., & Serretti, A. (2014). Are mindfulness-based interventions effective for substance use disorders? A systematic review of the evidence. *Substance Use & Misuse, 49*(5), 492–512.

Combs, J.L., Smith, G.T., Flory, K., Simmons, J.R., & Hill, K.K. (2010). The acquired preparedness model of risk for bulimic symptom development. *Psychology of Addictive Behaviours, 24*, 475–86.

Cooper, K., Chatters, R., Kaltenthaler, E., & Wong, R. (2015). Psychological and psychosocial interventions for cannabis cessation in adults: A systematic review short report. *Health Technology Assessment, 19*(56).

Cotton, M.A., Ball, C., & Robinson, P. (2003). Four simple questions can help screen for eating disorders. *Journal of General Internal Medicine, 18*(1), 53–6.

Creswell, J.D. (2017). Mindfulness interventions. *Annual Review of Psychology, 68*, 18.1–18.26.

Crocq, M. A. (2007). Historical and cultural aspects of man's relationship with addictive drugs. *Dialogues in Clinical Neuroscience, 9*(4), 355–61.

Culbert, K.M., Racine, S.E., & Klump, K.L. (2015). Research review: What we have learned about the causes of eating disorders – A synthesis of sociocultural, psychological, and biological research. *Journal of Child Psychology and Psychiatry, 56*(11), 1141–64.

Curtis, T., Kvernmo, S., & Bjerregaard, P. (2005). Changing living conditions, life style and health. *International Journal of Circumpolar Health, 64*(5), 442–50.

Darmon, N., & Drewnowski, A. (2008). Does social class predict diet quality? *The American Journal of Clinical Nutrition, 87*(5), 1107–17.

Darvishi, N., Farhadi, M., Haghtalab, T., & Poorolajal, J. (2015). Alcohol-related risk of suicidal ideation, suicide attempt, and completed suicide: A meta-analysis. *PLOS ONE, 10*(5), e0126870.

Davis, D.R., Kurti, A.N., Skelly, J.M., Redner, R., White, T.J., & Higgins, S.T. (2016). A review of the literature on contingency management in the treatment of substance use disorders, 2009–2014. *Preventative Medicine, 92*, 36–46.

De Ridder, D., De Vet, E., Stok, F.M., Adriaanse, M.A., & De Wit, J.B.F. (2013). Obesity, overconsumption and self-regulation failure: The unsung role of eating appropriateness standards. *Health Psychology Review, 7*, 148–65.

De Ridder, D., Kroese, F., Evers, C., Adriaanse, M., & Gillebaart, M. (2017). Healthy diet: Health impact, prevalence, correlates, and interventions. *Psychology & Health, 32*, 907–41.

De Jong R., & Bijleveld C. (2015). Child sexual abuse and family outcomes. *Crime Science, 4*(34).

Dick, D.M., Smith, G., Olausson, P., Mitchell, S.H., Leeman, R.F., O'Malley, S.S., & Sher, K. (2010). Understanding the construct of impulsivity and its relationship to alcohol use disorders. *Addiction Biology, 15*(2), 217–26.

Dietz, W.H., & Gortmaker, S.L. (2001). Preventing obesity in children and adolescents. *Annual Review of Public Health, 22*(1), 337–53.

Doughty, K.N., Njike, V.Y., & Katz, D.L. (2015). Effects of a cognitive-behavioral therapy-based immersion obesity treatment program for adolescents on weight, fitness, and cardiovascular risk factors: A pilot study. *Childhood Obesity, 11*(2), 215–18.

Duffey, K.J., & Popkin, B.M. (2011). Energy density, portion size, and eating occasions: Contributions to increased energy intake in the United States, 1977–2006. *PLOS Medicine, 8*(6), e1001050.

Earnshaw, V.A., Elliott, M.N., Reisner, S.L., Mrug, S., Windle, M., Emery, S.T., . . . Schuster, M.A. (2017). Peer victimization, depressive symptoms, and substance use: a longitudinal analysis. *Pediatrics, 139*, e20163426.

Elkins, I.J., King, S.M., McGue, M., & Iacono, W.G. (2006). Personality traits and the development of nicotine, alcohol, and illicit drug disorders: Prospective links from adolescence to young adulthood. *Journal of Abnormal Psychology, 115*(1), 26–39.

Elwyn, G., Dehlendorf, C., Epstein, R.M., Marrin, K., White, J., & Frosch, D.L. (2014). Shared decision making and motivational interviewing: Achieving patient-centered care across the spectrum of health care problems. *The Annals of Family Medicine, 12*(3), 270–5.

Emslie, C., Hunt, K., & Lyons, A. (2015). Transformation and time-out: The role of alcohol in identity construction among Scottish women in early midlife. *International Journal on Drug Policy, 26*(5), 437–45.

Enoch, M.A. (2012). The influence of gene-environment interactions on the development of alcoholism and drug dependence. *Current Psychiatry Reports, 14*(2), 150–8.

Ervin, R.B., Kit, B.K., Carroll, M.D., & Ogden, C.L. (2012). Consumption of added sugar among U.S. children and adolescents, 2005–2008. *NCHS Data Brief, 87*, 1–8.

Evans, D.E., & Drobes, D.J. (2009). Nicotine self-medication of cognitive-attentional processing. *Addiction Biology, 14*(1), 32–42.

Ewing, J.A. (1984). Detecting alcoholism: The CAGE questionnaire. *JAMA, 252*(14), 1905–7.

Fairburn, C.G., & Beglin, S.J. (2008). Eating disorder examination questionnaire (6.0). In C. G. Fairburn (Ed.). *Cognitive behavior therapy and eating disorders*. New York: Guilford Press.

Fairburn, C.G., & Cooper, Z. (2014). Eating disorders: A transdiagnostic protocol. In D.H. Barlow (Ed.). *Clinical handbook of psychological disorders: A step-by-step treatment manual*. New York: Guilford Press.

Fairburn, C.G., & Harrison, P.J. (2003). Eating disorders. *The Lancet, 361*(9355), 407–16.

Fairburn, C.G., Bailey-Straebler, S., Basden, S., Doll, H.A., Jones, R., Murphy, R., . . . Cooper, Z. (2015). A transdiagnostic comparison of enhanced cognitive behaviour therapy (CBT-E) and interpersonal psychotherapy in the treatment of eating disorders. *Behaviour Research and Therapy, 70*, 64–71.

Fischer, B., Ialomiteanu, A., Boak, A., Adlaf, E., Rehm, J., & Mann, R.E. (2013). Prevalence and key covariates of non-medical prescription opioid use among the general secondary student and adult populations in Ontario, Canada. *Drug and Alcohol Review, 32*(3), 276–87.

Flett, G., Kocovski, N., Blankstein, K.R., Davison, G.C., & Neale, J.M. (2017). *Abnormal psychology* (6th Canadian ed.). Toronto, ON: Wiley.

Frone, M.R. (2016). Work stress and alcohol use: Developing and testing a biphasic self-medication model. *Work & Stress, 30*(4), 374–94.

Gade, H., Hjlmesaeth, J., Rosenvinge, J.H., & Friborg, O. (2014). Effectiveness of a cognitive behavioral therapy for dysfunctional eating among patients admitted for bariatric surgery: A randomized controlled trial. *Journal of Obesity, 2014,* 127936.

Garriguet, D. (2007). Canadians' eating habits. *Health Reports, 18*(2), 17–32.

Ghosh, S., & Bouchard, C. (2017). Convergence between biological, behavioural and genetic determinants of obesity. *Nature Reviews Genetics, 18*(12), 731–748.

Goldschmidt, A.B., Wall, M.M., Choo, T.H.J., Bruening, M., Eisenberg, M.E., & Neumark-Sztainer, D. (2014). Examining associations between adolescent binge eating and binge eating in parents and friends. *International Journal of Eating Disorders, 47*(3), 325–8.

Government of Canada. (2017). *Canadian tobacco, alcohol and drug survey (CTADS): 2015 summary.* Available online: https://www.canada.ca/en/health-canada/services/canadian-tobacco-alcohol-drugs-survey/2015-summary.html

Grazioli, V.S., Bagge, C.L., Studer, J., Bertholet, N., Rougemont-Bücking, A., Mohler-Kuo, M., . . . Gmel, G. (2018). Depressive symptoms, alcohol use and coping drinking motives: Examining various pathways to suicide attempts among young men. *Journal of Affective Disorders.* Advance online publication. https://doi.org/10.1016/j.jad.2018.02.028

Guh, D.P., Zhang, W., Bansback, N., Amarsi, Z., Birmingham, C.L., & Anis, A.H. (2009). The incidence of co-morbidities related to obesity and overweight: A systematic review and meta-analysis. *BMC Public Health, 9*(1), 88.

Hajek, P., Etter, J.F., Benowitz, N., Eissenberg, T., & McRobbie, H. (2014). Electronic cigarettes: Review of use, content, safety, effects on smokers and potential for harm and benefit. *Addiction, 109*(11), 1801–10.

Hall, W. (2015). What has research over the past two decades revealed about the adverse health effects of recreational cannabis use? *Addiction, 110*(1), 19–35.

Harden, K.P., & Tucker-Drob, E.M. (2011). Individual differences in the development of sensation seeking and impulsivity during adolescence: Further evidence for a dual systems model. *Developmental Psychology, 47*(3), 739–46.

Hart, A.B., & Kranzler, H.R. (2015). Alcohol dependence genetics: Lessons learned from genome-wide association studies (GWAS) and post-GWAS analyses. *Alcoholism, Clinical and Experimental Research, 39*(8), 1312–27.

Hartmann-Boyce, J., Stead, L.F., Cahill, K., & Lancaster, T. (2014). Efficacy of interventions to combat tobacco addiction: Cochrane update of 2013 reviews. *Addiction, 109*(9), 1414–25.

Heishman, S.J., Kleykamp, B.A., & Singleton, E.G. (2010). Meta-analysis of the acute effects of nicotine and smoking on human performance. *Psychopharmacology, 210*(4), 453–69.

Herrera, B.M., & Lindgren, C.M. (2010). The genetics of obesity. *Current Diabetes Reports, 10*(6), 498–505.

Hittner, J.B., & Swickert, R. (2006). Sensation seeking and alcohol use: A meta-analytic review. *Addictive Behaviours, 31*(8), 1383–1401.

Hogue, A., Henderson, C.E., Ozechowski, T.J., & Robbins, M.S. (2014). Evidence base on outpatient behavioural treatments for adolescent substance use: Updates and recommendations 2007–2013. *Journal of Clinical Child & Adolescent Psychology, 43*(5), 695–720.

Holzel, B.K., Lazar, S.W., Gard, T., Schuman-Olivier, Z., Vago, D.R., & Ott, U. (2011). How does mindfulness meditation work? Proposing mechanisms of action from a conceptual and neural perspective. *Perspectives on Psychological Science, 6*(6), 537–59.

Jamal, A., King, B.A., Neff, L.J., Whitmill, J., Babb, S.D., & Graffunder, C.M. (2016). Current cigarette smoking among adults – United States, 2005–2015. *Morbidity and Mortality Weekly Report, 65*(44), 1205–11.

Jungquist, C.R., Flannery, M., Perlis, M.L., & Grace, J.T. (2012). Relationship of chronic pain and opioid use with respiratory disturbance during sleep. *Pain Management Nursing, 13*(2), 70–9.

Kaplan, M.S., Huguet, N., Caetano, R., Giesbrecht, N., Kerr, W.C., & McFarland, B.H. (2016). Heavy alcohol use among suicide decedents relative to a nonsuicide comparison group: Gender-specific effects of economic contraction. *Alcoholism, Clinical and Experimental Research, 40*(7), 1501–6.

Keesman, M., Aarts, H., Häfner, M., & Papies, E.K. (2017). Mindfulness reduces reactivity to food cues: Underlying mechanisms and applications in daily life. *Current Addiction Reports, 4*(2), 151–7.

Keith, S.W., Redden, D.T., Katzmarzyk, P.T., Boggiano, M.M., Hanlon, E.C., Benca, R.M., . . . Allison, D.B. (2006). Putative contributors to the secular increase in obesity: Exploring the roads less traveled. *International Journal of Obesity, 30*(11), 1585–94.

Kelly, S.M., Gryczynski, J., Mitchell, S.G., Kirk, A., O'Grady, K.E., & Schwartz, R.P. (2014). Validity of brief screening instrument for adolescent tobacco, alcohol, and drug use. *Pediatrics, 133*(5), 819–26.

Kelly, J.F., Magill, M., & Stout, R.L. (2009). How do people recover from alcohol dependence? A systematic review of the research on mechanisms of behavior change in Alcoholics Anonymous. *Addiction Research and Theory, 17*(3), 236–59.

Kerr, W.C., Kaplan, M. S., Huguet, N., Caetano, R., Giesbrecht, N., & McFarland, B.H. (2017). Economic recession, alcohol, and suicide rates: Comparative effects of poverty, foreclosure, and job loss. *American Journal of Preventive Medicine, 52*(4), 469–75.

Khawandanah, J., & Tewfik, I. (2016). Fad diets: Lifestyle promises and health challenges. *Journal of Food Research, 5*(6), 80–94.

Kilmer, B. (2014). Policy designs for cannabis legalization: Starting with the eight Ps. *The American Journal of Drug and Alcohol Abuse, 40*(4), 259–61.

Kolahdooz, F., Sadeghirad, B., Corriveau, A., & Sharma, S. (2017). Prevalence of overweight and obesity among Indigenous populations in Canada: A systematic review and meta-analysis. *Critical Reviews in Food Science and Nutrition, 57*(7), 1316–27.

Kozo, J., Sallis, J.F., Conway, T.L., Kerr, J., Cain, K., Saelens, B.E., & Owen, N. (2012). Sedentary behaviours of adults in relation to neighborhood walkability and income. *Health Psychology, 31*, 704–13.

Larimer, M.E., & Palmer, R.S. (1999). Relapse prevention: An overview of Marlatt's cognitive-behavioural model. *Alcohol Research and Health, 23*(2), 151–60.

Legroux-Gerot, I., Vignau, J., Collier, F., & Cortet, B. (2005). Bone loss associated with anorexia nervosa. *Joint, Bone, Spine, 72*(6), 489–95.

Leonardi-Bee, J., Jere, M.L., & Britton, J. (2011). Exposure to parental and sibling smoking and the risk of smoking uptake in childhood and adolescence: A systematic review and meta-analysis. *Thorax, 66*(10), 847–55.

Lev-Ran, S., Le Strat, Y., Imtiaz, S., Rehm, J., & Le Foll, B. (2013). Gender differences in prevalence of substance use disorders among individuals with lifetime exposure to substances: Results from a large representative sample. *The American Journal on Addictions, 22*(1), 7–13.

Luppino, F.S., de Wit, L.M., Bouvy, P.F., Stijnen, T., Cuijpers, P., Penninx, B.W., & Zitman, F.G. (2010). Overweight, obesity, and depression: A systematic review and meta-analysis of longitudinal studies. *Archives of General Psychiatry, 67*(3), 220–9.

Lupoli, R., Lembo, E., Saldalamacchia, G., Avola, C.K., Angrisani, L., & Capaldo, B. (2017). Bariatric surgery and long-term nutritional issues. *World Journal of Diabetes, 8*(11), 464–74.

MacArthur, J., Sean, H., Deborah, M., Matthew, H., & Rona, C. (2016). Peer-led interventions to prevent tobacco, alcohol and/ or drug use among young people aged 11–21 years: A systematic review and meta-analysis. *Addiction, 111*(3), 391–407.

Maisto, S.A., Galizio, M., & Connors, G.J. (2011). *Drug use and abuse.* Belmont, CA: Wadsworth Publishing.

Management of Substance Use Disorders Work Group. (2015). *VA/DoD clinical practice guidelines.* Retrieved from https:// www.healthquality.va.gov/guidelines/mh/sud

Marlatt, G.A., & Gordan J.R. (Eds.). (1985). Relapse prevention: Maintenance strategies in the treatment of addictive behaviors. New York: The Guilford Press.

Marlatt, G.A., & Witkiewitz, K. (2002). Harm reduction approaches to alcohol use: Health promotion, prevention and treatment. *Addictive Behaviors, 27*, 867–86.

Marlatt, G.A., & Witkiewitz, K. (2010). Update on harm-reduction policy and intervention research. *Annual Review of Clinical Psychology, 6*, 591–606.

Marsch, L.A., & Dallery, J. (2012). Advances in the psychosocial treatment of addiction: The role of technology in the delivery of evidence-based psychosocial treatment. *The Psychiatric Clinics of North America, 35*(2), 481–93.

Mason, M.J., Mennis, J., Linker, J., Bares, C., & Zaharakis, N. (2014). Peer attitudes effects on adolescent substance use: The moderating role of race and gender. *Prevention Science, 15*(1), 56–64.

Mayer, B. (2014). How much nicotine kills a human? Tracing back the generally accepted lethal dose to dubious self-experiments in the nineteenth century. *Archives of Toxicology, 88*(1), 5–7.

McCambridge, J., & Cunningham, J.A. (2014). The early history of ideas on brief interventions for alcohol. *Addiction, 109*(4), 538–46.

McCann, E., & Temenos, C. (2015). Mobilizing drug consumption rooms: Inter-place networks and harm reduction drug policy. *Health & Place, 31*, 216–23.

McGrew, K.S., & Bruininks, R.H. (1990). Defining adaptive and maladaptive behaviour within a model of personal competence. *School Psychology Review, 19*(1), 53–73.

McHugh, R.K., Hearon, B.A., & Otto, M.W. (2010). Cognitive behavioural therapy for substance use disorders. *Psychiatric Clinics of North America, 33*(3), 511–25.

McKenzie, D. (2000). *Under the influence? The impact of alcohol advertising on youth.* North York, ON: Association to Reduce Alcohol Promotion in Ontario.

McTavish, F.M., Chih, M.Y., Shah, D., & Gustafson, D.H. (2012). How patients recovering from alcoholism use a smartphone intervention. *Journal of Dual Diagnosis, 8*, 294–304.

Mehler, P.S., & Brown, C. (2015). Anorexia nervosa—medical complications. *Journal of Eating Disorders, 3*(11).

Melioli, T., Bauer, S., Franko, D.L., Moessner, M., Ozer, F., Chabrol, H., & Rodgers, R.F. (2016). Reducing eating disorder symptoms and risk factors using the internet: A meta-analytic review. *International Journal of Eating Disorders, 49*(1), 19–31.

Menary, K.R., Corbin, W.R., Leeman, R.F., Fucito, L.M., Toll, B.A., DeMartini, K., & O'Malley, S.S. (2015). Interactive and indirect effects of anxiety and negative urgency on alcohol-related problems. *Alcoholism, Clinical and Experimental Research, 39*(7), 1267–74.

Middlekauff, H.R. (2015). Rebuttal from Dr Middlekauff. *Chest Journal, 148*(3), 585–6.

Milara, J., & Cortijo, J. (2012). Tobacco, inflammation, and respiratory tract cancer. *Current Pharmaceutical Design, 18*(26), 3901–38.

Miller, W.R., & Rollnick, S. (1991). Motivational interviewing, preparing people to change addictive behavior. New York: The Guildford Press.

Montani, J.P., Schutz, Y., & Dulloo, A.G. (2015). Dieting and weight cycling as risk factors for cardiometabolic diseases: Who is really at risk? *Obesity Reviews, 16*(S1), 7–18.

Morgan, J.F., Reid, F., & Lacey, H. (1999). The SCOFF questionnaire: Assessment of a new screening tool for eating disorders. *BMJ, 319*, 1467–8.

National Institute on Alcohol Abuse and Alcoholism. (2015). *Alcohol facts and statistics.* Retrieved from https:// www.niaaa.nih.gov/alcohol-health/overview-alcohol-consumption/alcohol-facts-and-statistics

National Institute on Drug Abuse. (2016). *Nationwide drug trends.* Retrieved from https://www.drugabuse.gov/ publications/drugfacts/nationwide-trends

Nederkoorn, C., Houben, K., Hofmann, W., Roefs, A., & Jansen, A. (2010). Control yourself or just eat what you like? Weight gain over a year is predicted by an interactive effect of response inhibition and implicit preference for snack foods. *Health Psychology, 29*(4), 389–93.

Norström, T., & Rossow, I. (2016). Alcohol consumption as a risk factor for suicidal behavior: A systematic review of associations at the individual and at the population level. *Archives of Suicide Research, 20*(4), 489–506.

O'Leary-Barrett, M., Topper, L., Al-Khudhairy, N., Pihl, R.O., Castellanos-Ryan, N., Mackie, C.J., & Conrod, P.J. (2013). Two-year impact of personality-targeted, teacher-delivered interventions on youth internalizing and externalizing problems: A cluster-randomized trial. *Journal of the American Academy of Child and Adolescent Psychiatry, 52*, 911–20.

O'Reilly, G.A., Cook, L., Spruijt-Metz, D., & Black, D.S. (2014). Mindfulness-based interventions for obesity-related eating behaviours: A literature review. *Obesity Reviews, 15*(6), 453–61.

Onrust, S.A., Otten, R., Lammers, J., & Smit, F. (2016). School-based programmes to reduce and prevent substance use in different age groups: What works for whom? Systematic review and meta-regression analysis. *Clinical Psychology Review, 44*, 45–59.

Ouzir, M., & Errami, M. (2016). Etiological theories of addiction: A comprehensive update on neurobiological, genetic and behavioural vulnerability. *Pharmacology Biochemistry and Behaviour, 148*, 59–68.

Pacula, R.L., & Smart, R. (2017). Medical marijuana and marijuana legalization. *Annual Review of Clinical Psychology, 13*, 397–419.

Palazzolo, D.L., Crow, A.P., Nelson, J.M., & Johnson, R.A. (2017). Trace metals derived from Electronic Cigarette (ECIG) generated Aerosol: Potential problem of ECIG devices that contain nickel. *Frontiers in Physiology, 7*(663).

Pan-Canadian Public Health Network. (2017). *Towards a healthier Canada—Health inequalities data table*. Retrieved from http://www.phn-rsp.ca/thcpr-vcpsre-2017/pdf/table2-eng.pdf.

Pechey, R., & Monsivais, P. (2016). Socioeconomic inequalities in the healthiness of food choices: Exploring the contributions of food expenditures. *Preventive Medicine, 88*, 203–9.

Potier, C., Laprévote, V., Dubois-Arber, F., Cottencin, O., & Rolland, B. (2014). Supervised injection services: What has been demonstrated? A systematic literature review. *Drug & Alcohol Dependence, 145*, 48–68.

Prochaska, J.J., & Benowitz, N.L. (2016). The past, present, and future of nicotine addiction therapy. *Annual Review of Medicine, 67*, 467–86.

Puccio, F., Fuller-Tyszkiewicz, M., Youssef, G., Mitchell, S., Byrne, M., Allen, N., & Krug, I. (2017). Longitudinal bi-directional effects of disordered eating, depression and anxiety. *European Eating Disorders Review, 25*(5), 351–8.

Rahman, M.A., Hann, N., Wilson, A., Mnatzaganian, G., & Worrall-Carter, L. (2015). E-cigarettes and smoking cessation: Evidence from a systematic review and meta-analysis. *PLOS ONE, 10*(3), e0122544.

Riper, H., Andersson, G., Hunter, S.B., Wit, J., Berking, M., & Cuijpers, P. (2014). Treatment of comorbid alcohol use disorders and depression with cognitive-behavioural therapy and motivational interviewing: A meta-analysis. *Addiction, 109*(3), 394–406.

Rotgers, F., Fromme, K., & Larimer, M. (2012). In memoriam: G. Alan Marlatt. *Addiction Research & Theory, 20*(3), 183–5.

Rutledge, P. C., & Sher, K. J. (2001). Heavy drinking from the freshman year into early young adulthood: The roles of stress, tension-reduction drinking motives, gender and personality. *Journal of Studies on Alcohol, 62*(4), 457–66.

Ruwaard, J., Lange, A., Broeksteeg, J., Renteria-Agirre, A., Schrieken, B., Dolan, C.V., & Emmelkamp, P. (2013). Online cognitive–behavioural treatment of bulimic symptoms: A randomized controlled trial. *Clinical Psychology & Psychotherapy, 20*(4), 308–18.

Sabourin, B.C., & Stewart, S. (2007). Alcohol use and anxiety disorders. In M J. Zvolensky & J.A. Smits (Eds.), *Anxiety in health behaviors and physical illness* (pp. 29–54). New York, NY: Springer.

Salvy, S.J., De La Haye, K., Bowker, J.C., & Hermans, R.C. (2012). Influence of peers and friends on children's and adolescents' eating and activity behaviors. *Physiology & Behavior, 106*(3), 369–78.

Saunders, J.B., Aasland, O.G., Babor, T.F., De la Fuente, J.R., & Grant, M. (1993). Development of the alcohol use disorders identification test (AUDIT): WHO collaborative project on early detection of persons with harmful alcohol consumption-II. *Addiction, 88*(6), 791–804.

Schauer, G.L., King, B.A., Bunnell, R.E., Promoff, G., & McAfee, T.A. (2016). Toking, vaping, and eating for health or fun: Marijuana use patterns in adults, U.S., 2014. *American Journal of Preventive Medicine, 50*(1), 1–8.

Schiltenwolf, M., Akbar, M., Hug, A., Pfuller, U., Gantz, S., Neubauer, E., & Wang, H. (2014). Evidence of specific cognitive deficits in patients with chronic low back pain under long-term substitution treatment of opioids. *Pain Physician, 17*(1), 9–20.

Scull, T.M., Kupersmidt, J.B., & Erausquin, J.T. (2014). The impact of media-related cognitions on children's substance use outcomes in the context of parental and peer substance use. *Journal of Youth and Adolescence, 43*(5), 717–28.

Selzer, M.L., Vanosdall, F.E., & Chapman, M. (1971). Alcoholism in a problem driver group: A field trial of the Michigan Alcoholism Screening Test (MAST). *Journal of Safety Research, 3*(4), 176–81.

Sharma, S. (2010). Assessing diet and lifestyle in the Canadian Arctic Inuit and Inuvialuit to inform a nutrition and physical activity intervention programme. *Journal of Human Nutrition and Dietetics, 23*(Suppl 1), 5–17.

Sinha, R., & Jastreboff, A.M. (2013). Stress as a common risk factor for obesity and addiction. *Biological Psychiatry, 73*(9), 827–35.

Skinner, H.A. (1982). The drug abuse screening test. *Addictive Behaviors, 7*(4), 363–71.

Sobell, M.B., & Sobell, L.C. (1995). Controlled drinking after 25 years: How important was the great debate? *Addiction, 90*(9), 1149–53.

Spronk, I., Kullen, C., Burdon, C., & O'Connor, H. (2014). Relationship between nutrition knowledge and dietary intake. *British Journal of Nutrition, 111*(10), 1713–26.

Strandheim, A., Coombes, L., Bentzen, N., & Holmen, T.L. (2009). Alcohol intoxication and mental health among adolescents–a population review of 8983 young people, 13–19 years in North-Trøndelag, Norway: The Young-HUNT Study. *Child and Adolescent Psychiatry and Mental Health, 3*(18).

Statistics Canada. (2012). *Prevalence and correlates of marijuana use in Canada, 2012.* Retrieved from http://www.statcan.gc.ca/pub/82-003-x/2015004/article/14158-eng.htm

Statistics Canada. (2016) *Canadian Community Health Survey, 2016.* Retrieved from http://www.statcan.gc.ca/daily-quotidien/170927/dq170927a-eng.htm

Stead, L.F., Koilpillai, P., Fanshawe, T.R., & Lancaster, T. (2016). Combined pharmacotherapy and behavioural interventions for smoking cessation. *Cochrane Database of Systematic Reviews,* (3), CD008286.

Strike, C., Watson, T.M., Lavigne, P., Hopkins, S., Shore, R., Young, D., . . . Millson, P. (2011). Guidelines for better harm reduction: Evaluating implementation of best practice recommendations for needle and syringe programs (NSPs). *International Journal of Drug Policy, 22*(1), 34–40.

Suisman, J.L., Thompson, J.K., Keel, P.K., Burt, S.A., Neale, M., Boker, S., & Klump, K.L. (2014). Genetic and environmental influences on thin-ideal internalization across puberty and preadolescent, adolescent, and young adult development. *International Journal of Eating Disorders, 47*(7), 773–83.

Sweet, L.H., Mulligan, R.C., Finnerty, C.E., Jerskey, B.A., David, S.P., Cohen, R.A., & Niaura, R.S. (2010). Effects of nicotine withdrawal on verbal working memory and associated brain response. *Psychiatry Research: Neuroimaging, 183,* 69–74.

Swift, R.M., & Aston, E.R. (2015). Pharmacotherapy for alcohol use disorder: Current and emerging therapies. *Harvard Review of Psychiatry, 23*(2), 122–33.

Taber, D.R., Chriqui, J.F., Perna, F.M., Powell, L.M., & Chaloupka, F.J. (2012). Weight status among adolescents in states that govern competitive food nutrition content. *Pediatrics, 130*(3), 437–44.

Tan, W.C., Lo, C., Jong, A., Xing, L., FitzGerald, M.J., Vollmer, W.M., . . . Sin, D.D. (2009). Marijuana and chronic obstructive lung disease: A population-based study. *Canadian Medical Association Journal, 180*(8), 814–20.

Taylor, G., Aveyard, P., Van der Meer, R., Toze, D., Stuijfzand, B., Kessler, D., & Munafò, M. (2017). Impact of variation in functions and delivery on the effectiveness of behavioural and mood management interventions for smoking cessation in people with depression: Protocol for a systematic review and meta-analysis. *BMJ Open, 7*(11), e018617.

Trace, S.E., Baker, J.H., Peñas-Lledó, E., & Bulik, C.M. (2013). The genetics of eating disorders. *Annual Review of Clinical Psychology, 9,* 589–620.

Twells, L.K., Gregory, D.M., Reddigan, J., & Midodzi, W.K. (2014). Current and predicted prevalence of obesity in Canada: A trend analysis. *CMAJ Open, 2*(1), E18.

Vartanian, L.R., Herman, C.P., & Wansink, B. (2008). Are we aware of the external factors that influence our food intake? *Health Psychology, 27*(5), 533–8.

Wagner, B., Nagl, M., Dölemeyer, R., Klinitzke, G., Steinig, J., Hilbert, A., & Kersting, A. (2016). Randomized controlled trial of an Internet-based cognitive-behavioural treatment program for binge-eating disorder. *Behaviour Therapy, 47*(4), 500–14.

Ward, V. B. (2008). Eating disorders in pregnancy. *BMJ, 336*(7635), 93–6.

Watson, T.M., Strike, C., Challacombe, L., Demel, G., Heywood, D., & Zurba, N. (2017). Developing national best practice recommendations for harm reduction programmes: Lessons learned from a community-based project. *International Journal of Drug Policy, 41,* 14–18.

Westmoreland, P., Krantz, M.J., & Mehler, P.S. (2016). Medical complications of anorexia nervosa and bulimia. *The American Journal of Medicine, 129,* 30–7.

Wettlaufer, A., Florica, R.O., Asbridge, M., Beirness, D., Brubacher, J., Callaghan, R., & McKiernan, A. (2017). Estimating the harms and costs of cannabis-attributable collisions in the Canadian provinces. *Drug and Alcohol Dependence, 173,* 185–90.

White, H.R., Larimer, M.E., Sher, K.J., & Witkiewitz, K. (2011). In memoriam: G. Alan Marlatt 1941–2011. *Journal of Studies on Alcohol and Drugs, 72,* 357–60.

Whitesell, M., Bachand, A., Peel, J., & Brown, M. (2013). Familial, social, and individual factors contributing to risk for adolescent substance use. *Journal of Addiction, 2013,* 579310.

Wilfley, D.E., Tibbs, T.L., Van Buren, D., Reach, K.P., Walker, M.S., & Epstein, L.H. (2007). Lifestyle interventions in the treatment of childhood overweight: A meta-analytic review of randomized controlled trials. *Health Psychology, 26*(5), 521–32.

Wirt, A., & Collins, C.E. (2009). Diet quality–What is it and does it matter? *Public Health Nutrition, 12*(12), 2473–92.

Witkiewitz, K., & Marlatt, G.A. (2006). Overview of harm reduction treatments for alcohol problems. *International Journal of Drug Policy, 17*(4), 285–94.

WHO ASSIST Working Group (2002). The alcohol, smoking and substance involvement screening test (ASSIST): Development, reliability and feasibility. *Addiction, 97*(9), 1183–94.

World Health Organization. (2000). *Obesity: Preventing and managing the global epidemic: Report of a WHO consultation* (WHO Technical Report Series No. 894). Geneva, Switzerland: Author.

World Health Organization. (2017a). *Obesity and overweight.* Retrieved from http://www.who.int/mediacentre/factsheets/fs311/en

World Health Organization. (2017b). *Psychoactive substances.* Retrieved from http://www.who.int/substance_abuse/terminology/psychoactive_substances/en/

Xiao, L., Bechara, A., Gong, Q., Huang, X., Li, X., Xue, G., & Jia, Y. (2013). Abnormal affective decision making revealed in adolescent binge drinkers using a functional magnetic resonance imaging study. *Psychology of Addictive Behaviours, 27*(2), 443–54.

Chapter 7

Abramowitz, J.S., & Braddock, A.E. (2008). *Psychological treatment of health anxiety and hypochondriasis: A biopsychosocial approach.* Ashland, Ohio: Hogrefe & Huber.

Abramowitz, J.S., & Moore, E.L. (2007). An experimental analysis of hypochondriasis. *Behaviour Research and Therapy, 45*, 413–24.

Alberts, N.M., & Hadjistavropoulos, H.D. (2014). Parental illness, attachment dimensions, and health beliefs: Testing the cognitive-behavioural and interpersonal models of health anxiety. *Anxiety, Stress, & Coping, 27*(2), 216–28.

American Psychiatric Association. (2013). *Diagnostic and statistical manual of mental disorders* (5th ed.). Washington: Author.

Arntz, A., Rauner, M., & Vandenhout, M. (1995). If I feel anxious, there must be danger—Ex-consequentia reasoning in inferring danger in anxiety disorders. *Behaviour Research and Therapy, 33*, 917–25.

Asmundson, G.J., Taylor, S., & Cox, B.J. (Eds.). (2001). *Health anxiety: Clinical and research perspectives on hypochondriasis and related conditions.* New York: Wiley.

Avia, M.D., Ruiz, M., Olivares, M., Crespo, M., Guisado, A.B., Sánchez, A., & Varela, A. (1996). The meaning of psychological symptoms: Effectiveness of a group intervention with hypochondriacal patients. *Behaviour Research and Therapy, 34*, 23–31.

Barsky, A.J., & Ahern, D.K. (2004). Cognitive behavior therapy for hypochondriasis: A randomized controlled trial. *Journal of the American Medical Association, 291*, 1464–70.

Barsky, A.J., Frank, C.B., Cleary, P.D., Wyshak, G., & Klerman, G. (1991). The relation between hypochondriasis and age. *American Journal of Psychiatry, 148*, 923–8.

Barsky, A.J., Wyshak, G., Klerman, G., & Latham, K. (1990). The prevalence of hypochondriasis in medical outpatients. *Social Psychiatry and Psychiatric Epidemiology, 25*, 89–94.

Bijsterbosch, J., Scharloo, M., Visser, A.W., Watt, I., Mieulenbelt, I., Huizinga, T.W.J., . . . Kloppenburg, M. (2009). Illness perceptions in patients with osteoarthritis: Change over time and association with disability. *Arthritis & Rheumatism— Arthritis Care & Research, 61*, 1054–61.

Birley, A.J., Gillespie, N.A., Heath, A.C., Sullivan, P.F., Boomsma, D.I., & Martin, N.G. (2006). Heritability and nineteen-year stability of long and short EPQ-R neuroticism scales. *Personality and Individual Differences, 40*, 737–47.

Bobevski, I., Clarke, D. M., & Meadows, G. (2016). Health anxiety and its relationship to disability and service use: Findings from a large epidemiological survey. *Psychosomatic Medicine, 78*(1), 13–25.

Bourgault-Fagnou, M.D., & Hadjistavropoulos, H.D. (2009). Understanding health anxiety among community dwelling seniors with varying degrees of frailty. *Aging & Mental Health, 13*, 226–37.

Bourgault-Fagnou, M.D., & Hadjistavropoulos, H.D. (2013). A randomized trial of two forms of cognitive behaviour therapy for an older adult population with subclinical health anxiety. *Cognitive Behaviour Therapy, 42*(1), 31–44.

Buwalda, F.M., Bouman, T., & van Duijn, M.A. (2007). Psychoeducation for hypochondriasis: A comparison of a cognitive-behavioural approach and a problem-solving approach. *Behaviour Research and Therapy, 45*, 887–99.

Cameron, L.D., & Jago, L. (2008). Emotion regulation interventions: A common-sense model approach. *British Journal of Health Psychology, 13*, 215–21.

Cannon, N. (Producer). (2012a, April 2). *NCredible health hustle: Episode 1.* [Video file] Retrieved from www.youtube.com/watch?v=jSTyfZUX2ps

Cannon, N. (Producer). (2012b, May 10). *Ncredible health hustle: Episode 6.* [Video file] Retrieved from www.essence.com/2012/05/10/must-see-nick-cannons-ncredible-health-hustle-episode-6/

Cannon, N. (Producer). (2012c, May 15). *NCredible health hustle: Episode 7.* [Video file] Retrieved from www.youtube.com/watch?v=RAEVrcPHIMc

Charles, S.T., Gatz, M., Kato, K., & Pedersen, N.L. (2008). Physical health 25 years later: The predictive ability of neuroticism. *Health Psychology, 27*, 369–78.

Clark, D.M., Salkovskis, P. M., Hackmann, A., Wells, A., Fennell, M., Ludgate, J., . . . Gelder, M. (1998). Two psychological treatments for hypochondriasis: A randomised controlled trial. *British Journal of Psychiatry, 173*, 218–25.

Costa, P.T., & McCrae, R.R. (1985). Hypochondriasis, neuroticism, and aging—When are somatic complaints unfounded. *American Psychologist, 40*, 19–28.

Cousins, N. (1976). Anatomy of an illness as perceived by the patient. *New England Journal of Medicine, 295*, 1458–63.

Craig, K.D., & Weiss, S.M. (1971). Vicarious influences on pain-threshold determinations. *Journal of Personality and Social Psychology, 19*, 53–7.

Croyle, R.T., & Uretsky, M.B. (1987). Effects of mood on self-appraisal of health status. *Health Psychology, 6*, 239–53.

Dahlquist, L.M., Gil, K.M., Armstrong, F.D., Delawyer, D.D., Greene, P., & Wuori, D. (1986). Preparing children for medical examinations—The importance of previous medical experience. *Health Psychology, 5*, 249–59.

de Zubiria Salgado, A., & Herrera-Diaz, C. (2012). Lupus nephritis: An overview of recent findings. *Autoimmune Diseases, 2012*, 849684.

Diefenbach, M.A., & Leventhal, H. (1996). The common-sense model of illness representation: Theoretical and practical considerations. *Journal of Social Distress and the Homeless, 5*, 11–38.

Faravelli, C., Salvatori, S., Galassi, F., Aiazzi, L., Drei, C., & Cabras, P. (1997). Epidemiology of somatoform disorders: A community survey in Florence. *Social Psychiatry and Psychiatric Epidemiology, 32*, 24–9.

Fergus, T. A. (2014). Health-related dysfunctional beliefs and health anxiety: Further evidence of cognitive specificity. *Journal of Clinical Psychology, 70*(3), 248–59.

Ferguson, E. (2009). A taxometric analysis of health anxiety. *Psychological Medicine, 39*, 277–85.

Fischer, M., Scharloo, M., Abbink, J., van't Hul, A., van Ranst, D., Rudolphus, A., . . . Kaptein, A.A. (2010). The dynamics of illness perceptions: Testing assumptions of Leventhal's common-sense model in a pulmonary rehabilitation setting. *British Journal of Health Psychology, 15*, 887–903.

Ford, D., Zapka, J., Gebregziabher, M., Yang, C.W., & Sterba, K. (2010). Factors associated with illness perception among critically ill patients and surrogates. *Chest, 138*, 59–67.

Fulton, J.J., Marcus, D.K., & Merkey, T. (2011). Irrational health beliefs and health anxiety. *Journal of Clinical Psychology, 67*, 527–38.

Furer, P., Walker, J.R., & Stein, M.B. (2007). *Treating health anxiety and fear of death: A practitioner's guide*. New York: Springer Science + Business Media.

Giannousi, Z., Karademas, E.C., & Dimitraki, G. (2016). Illness representations and psychological adjustment of Greek couples dealing with a recently-diagnosed cancer: dyadic, interaction and perception-dissimilarity effects. *Journal of Behavioral Medicine, 39*(1), 85–93.

Gil, K.M., Carson, J.W., Porter, L.S., Scipio, C., Bediako, S.M., & Orringer, E. (2004). Daily mood and stress predict pain, health care use, and work activity in African American adults with sickle-cell disease. *Health Psychology, 23*, 267–74.

Gillespie, N.A., Zhu, G., Heath, A., Hickie, I., & Martin, N. (2000). The genetic aetiology of somatic distress. *Psychological Medicine: A Journal of Research in Psychiatry and the Allied Sciences, 30*, 1051–61.

Gorgen, S.M., Hiller, W., & Witthoft, M. (2014). Health anxiety, cognitive coping, and emotion regulation: A latent variable approach. *International Journal of Behavioral Medicine, 21*(2), 364–74.

Greeven, A., van Balkom, A.J., Visser, S., Merkelbach, J.W., van Rood, Y.R., van Dyck, R., . . . Spinhoven, P. (2007). Cognitive behavior therapy and paroxetine in the treatment of hypochondriasis: A randomized controlled trial. *American Journal of Psychiatry, 164*, 91–9.

Grewal, K., Stewart, D.E., & Grace, S.L. (2010). Differences in social support and illness perceptions among South Asian and Caucasian patients with coronary artery disease. *Heart & Lung, 39*, 180–7.

Griva, K., Jayasena, D., Davenport, A., Harrison, M., & Newman, S.P. (2009). Illness and treatment cognitions and health related quality of life in end stage renal disease. *British Journal of Health Psychology, 14*, 17–34.

Hadjistavropoulos, H.D., Alberts, N.M., Nugent, M., & Marchildon, G. (2014). Improving access to psychological services through therapist-assisted, Internet-delivered cognitive behaviour therapy. *Canadian Psychology-Psychologie Canadienne, 55*(4), 303–11.

Hadjistavropoulos, H.D., Janzen, J.A., Kehler, M.D., Leclerc, J.A., Sharpe, D., & Bourgault-Fagnou, M.D. (2012). Core cognitions related to health anxiety in self-reported medical and non-medical samples. *Journal of Behavioural Medicine, 35*, 167–78.

Hagger, M.S., & Orbell, S. (2003). A meta-analytic review of the common-sense model of illness representations. *Psychology & Health, 18*, 141–84.

Hedman, E., Andersson, G., Andersson, E., Ljotsson, B., Ruck, C., Asmundson, G.J., & Lindefors, N. (2011). Internet-based cognitive-behavioural therapy for severe health anxiety: Randomised controlled trial. *British Journal of Psychiatry, 198*, 230–236.

Hedman, E., Axelsson, E., Gorling, A., Ritzman, C., Ronnheden, M., El Alaoui, S., . . . Ljotsson, B. (2014). Internet-delivered exposure-based cognitive-behavioural therapy and behavioural stress management for severe health anxiety: randomised controlled trial. *British Journal of Psychiatry, 205*(4), 307–14.

Hedman, E., Lekander, M., Karshikoff, B., Ljotsson, B., Axelsson, E., & Axelsson, J. (2016). Health anxiety in a disease-avoidance framework: Investigation of anxiety, disgust and disease perception in response to sickness cues. *Journal of Abnormal Psychology, 125*(7), 868–78.

Hedman, E., Lindefors, N., Andersson, G., Andersson, E., Lekander, M., Ruck, C., & Ljotsson, B. (2013). Predictors of outcome in Internet-based cognitive behavior therapy for severe health anxiety. *Behavior Research and Therapy, 51*, 711–17.

Hedman, E., Ljotsson, B., Andersson, E., Ruck, C., Andersson, G., & Lindefors, N. (2010). Effectiveness and cost offset analysis of group CBT for hypochondriasis delivered in a psychiatric setting: An open trial. *Cognitive Behaviour Therapy, 39*, 239–50.

Henselmans, I., Sanderman, R., Helgeson, V.S., de Vries, J., Smink, A., & Ranchor, A.V. (2010). Personal control over the cure of breast cancer: Adaptiveness, underlying beliefs and correlates. *Psycho-Oncology, 19*, 525–34.

Jessop, D.C., & Rutter, D.R. (2003). Adherence to asthma medication: The role of illness representations. *Psychology & Health, 18*, 595–612.

Jimenez, S., Cervera, R., Font, J., & Ingelmo, M. (2003). The epidemiology of systemic lupus erythematosus. *Clinical Reviews in Allergy and Immunology, 25*, 3–12.

Jones, C.J., Smith, H.E., & Llewellyn, C.D. (2016). A systematic review of the effectiveness of interventions using the Common Sense Self-Regulatory Model to improve adherence behaviours. *Journal of Health Psychology, 21*(11), 2709–24.

Jones, S.L., Hadjistavropoulos, H.D., & Gullickson, K. (2014). Understanding health anxiety following breast cancer diagnosis. *Psychology, Health & Medicine, 19*(5), 525–35.

Krautwurst, S., Gerlach, A.L., & Witthoft, M. (2016). Interoception in pathological health anxiety. *Journal of Abnormal Psychology, 125*(8), 1179–84.

Landrine, H., & Klonoff, E.A. (1992). Culture and health-related schemas—A review and proposal for interdisciplinary integration. *Health Psychology, 11*, 267–76.

Lawson, V.L., Bundy, C., Lyne, P.A., & Harvey, J.N. (2004). Using the IPQ and PMDI to predict regular diabetes care-seeking among patients with type 1 diabetes. *British Journal of Health Psychology, 9*, 241–52.

Leventhal, H., Meyer, D., & Nerenz, D. (1980). The common sense representation of illness danger. In S. Rachman (Ed.), *Contributions to medical psychology* (Vol. II, pp. 7–30). New York: Pergamon Press.

Leventhal, H., Phillips, L. A. & Burns, E. (2016). The common-sense model of self-regulation: a dynamic framework for understanding illness self-management. *Journal of Behavioral Medicine, 39*, 935–46.

McGrady, M.E., Peugh, J.L., & Hood, K.K. (2014). Illness representations predict adherence in adolescents and young adults with type 1 diabetes. *Psychology & Health, 29*(9), 985–98.

McManus, F., Surawy, C., Muse, K., Vazquez-Montes, M., & Williams, J. M. (2012). A randomized clinical trial of mindfulness-based cognitive therapy versus unrestricted services for health anxiety (hypochondriasis). *Journal of Consulting and Clinical Psychology, 80*(5), 817–28.

McSharry, J., Moss-Morris, R., & Kendrick, T. (2011). Illness perceptions and glycaemic control in diabetes: A systematic review with meta-analysis. *Diabetic Medicine, 28*, 1300–10.

Moss-Morris, R., Weinman, J., Petrie, K.J., Horne, R., Cameron, L.D., & Buick, D. (2002). The revised Illness Perception Questionnaire (IPQ-R). *Psychology & Health, 17*, 1–16.

Norton, S., Hughes, L.D., Chilcot, J., Sacker, A., van Os, S., Young, A., . . . Done, I. (2014). Negative and positive illness representations of rheumatoid arthritis: a latent profile analysis. *Journal of Behavioral Medicine, 37*(3), 524–32.

Noyes, R., Happel, R.L., & Yagla, S.J. (1999). Correlates of hypochondriasis in a nonclinical population. *Psychosomatics, 40*, 461–9.

Olatunji, B.O., Etzel, E.N., Tomarken, A.J., Ciesielski, B.G., & Deacon, B. (2011). The effects of safety behaviors on health anxiety: An experimental investigation. *Behaviour Research and Therapy, 49*, 719–28.

Owens, K.M.B., & Antony, M. (2011). *Overcoming health anxiety: Letting go of your fear of illness*. Oakland, Calif.: New Harbinger.

Pennebaker, J.W. (1982). *The psychology of physical symptoms*. New York: Springer-Verlag.

Petrie, K.J., Cameron, L.D., Ellis, C.J., Buick, D., & Weinman, J. (2002). Changing illness perceptions after myocardial infarction: An early intervention randomized controlled trial. *Psychosomatic Medicine, 64*, 580–6.

Pollard, T.M., & Schwartz, J.E. (2003). Are changes in blood pressure and total cholesterol related to changes in mood? An 18-month study of men and women. *Health Psychology, 22*, 47–53.

Rachman, S. (2012). Health anxiety disorders: A cognitive construal. *Behaviour Research and Therapy, 50*, 502–12.

Radomsky, A.S., Shafran, R., Coughtrey, A.E., & Rachman, S. (2010). Cognitive-behavior therapy for compulsive checking in OCD. *Cognitive and Behavioral Practice, 17*, 119–31.

Rask, C.U., Munkholm, A., Clemmensen, L., Rimvall, M. K., Ornbol, E., Jeppesen, P., . . . Skovgaard, A.M. (2016). Health anxiety in preadolescence—Associated health problems, healthcare expenditure, and continuity in childhood. *Journal of Abnormal Child Psychology 44*(4), 823–32.

Salkovskis, P.M., & Warwick, H.M.C. (1986). Morbid preoccupations, health anxiety and reassurance—A cognitive behavioral approach to hypochondriasis. *Behaviour Research and Therapy, 24*, 597–602.

Seivewright, H., Green, J., Salkovskis, P., Barrett, B., Nur, U., & Tyrer, P. (2008). Cognitive-behavioural therapy for health anxiety in a genitourinary medicine clinic: Randomised controlled trial. *British Journal of Psychiatry, 193*, 332–7.

Shafran, R., & Rachman, S. (2004). Thought-action fusion: A review. *Journal of Behavior Therapy and Experimental Psychiatry, 35*, 87–107.

Shapiro, M.F., Ware, J.E., Jr., & Sherbourne, C.D. (1986). Effects of cost sharing on seeking care for serious and minor symptoms: Results of a randomized controlled trial. *Annals of Internal Medicine, 104*, 246–51.

Singh, K., & Brown, R.J. (2014). Health-related internet habits and health anxiety in university students. *Anxiety, Stress, & Coping, 27*(5), 542–54.

Sorensen, P., Birket-Smith, M., Wattar, U., Buemann, I., & Salkovskis, P. (2011). A randomized clinical trial of cognitive behavioural therapy versus short-term psychodynamic psychotherapy versus no intervention for patients with hypochondriasis. *Psychological Medicine: A Journal of Research in Psychiatry and the Allied Sciences, 41*, 431–41.

Stein, M.B., Jang, K.L., & Livesley, W. (1999). Heritability of anxiety sensitivity: A twin study. *American Journal of Psychiatry, 156*, 246–51.

Taylor, S., & Asmundson, G.J.G. (2004). *Treating health anxiety: A cognitive-behavioral approach*. New York: Guilford Press.

Taylor, S., Asmundson, G.J., & Coons, M.J. (2005). Current directions in the treatment of hypochondriasis. *Journal of Cognitive Psychotherapy, 19*, 285–304.

Torgerson, S. (1986). Genetics of somatoform disorders. *Archives of General Psychiatry, 43*, 502–5.

Tyrer, P., Cooper, S., Crawford, M., Dupont, S., Green, J., Murphy, D., . . . Tyrer, H. (2011). Prevalence of health anxiety problems in medical clinics. *Journal of Psychosomatic Research, 71*, 392–94.

Vilchinsky, N., Dekel, R., Leibowitz, M., Reges, O., Khaskia, A., & Mosseri, M. (2011). Dynamics of support perceptions among couples coping with cardiac illness: The effect on recovery outcomes. *Health Psychology, 30*, 411–19.

Warwick, H.M., Clark, D.M., Cobb, A.M., & Salkovskis, P.M. (1996). A controlled trial of cognitive-behavioural treatment of hypochondriasis. *British Journal of Psychiatry, 169*, 189–95.

Warwick, H.M., & Salkovskis, P.M. (1990). Hypochondriasis. *Behaviour Research and Therapy, 28*, 105–17.

Wattar, U., Sorensen, P., Buemann, I., Birket-Smith, M., Salkovskis, P.M., Albertsen, M., & Strange, S. (2005). Outcome of cognitive-behavioural treatment for health anxiety (hypochondriasis) in a routine clinical setting. *Behavioural and Cognitive Psychotherapy, 33*, 165–75.

Weck, F., Neng, J.M., Richtberg, S., Jakob, M., & Stangier, U. (2015). Cognitive therapy versus exposure therapy for hypochondriasis (health anxiety): A randomized controlled trial. *Journal of Consulting and Clinical Psychology, 83*(4), 665–76.

Weinman, J., Petrie, K.J., Moss Morris, R., & Horne, R. (1996). The illness perception questionnaire: A new method for assessing the cognitive representation of illness. *Psychology & Health, 11*, 431–45.

Yohannes, A.M., Yalfani, A., Doherty, P., & Bundy, C. (2007). Predictors of drop-out from an outpatient cardiac rehabilitation programme. *Clinical Rehabilitation, 21,* 222–29.

Zolnierek, K.B., & DiMatteo, M.R. (2009). Physician communication and patient adherence to treatment: A meta-analysis. *Medical Care, 47,* 826–34.

Chapter 8

Abbott, C.A., Malik, R.A., van Ross, E.R.E., Kulkarni, J., & Boulton, A.J.M. (2011). Prevalence and characteristics of painful diabetic neuropathy in a large community-based diabetic population in the U.K. *Diabetes Care, 34*(10), 2220–4.

Ahn, S., Basu, R., Smith, M.L., Jiang, L., Lorig, K., Whitelaw, N., & Ory, M.G. (2013). The impact of chronic disease self-management programs: Healthcare savings through a community-based intervention. *BMC Public Health, 13*(1), 1141.

Alberts, N.M., Hadjistavropoulos, H.D., Dear, B.F., & Titov, N. (2017). Internet-delivered cognitive-behaviour therapy for recent cancer survivors: A feasibility trial. *Psycho-Oncology, 26*(1), 137–9.

American Academy of Allergy Asthma & Immunology. (2017). *Asthma statistics.* Retrieved from http://www.aaaai.org/about-aaaai/newsroom/asthma-statistics

Amercian Academy of Pediatrics. (2016). *American Academy of Pediatrics supports childhood sleep guidelines.* Retrieved from https://www.aap.org/en-us/about-the-aap/aap-press-room/pages/American-Academy-of-Pediatrics-Supports-Childhood-Sleep-Guidelines.aspx

American Psychological Association. (2017). *Clinical health psychology.* Retrieved from http://www.apa.org/ed/graduate/specialize/health.aspx

Anand, S.S., Yusuf, S., Jacobs, R., Davis, A.D., Yi, Q., Gerstein, H., . . . Lonn, E. (2001). Risk factors, atherosclerosis, and cardiovascular disease among Aboriginal people in Canada: The Study of health assessment and risk evaluation in Aboriginal peoples (SHARE-AP). *Lancet, 358*(9288), 1147–53.

Anderson, R.J., Freedland, K.E., Clouse, R.E., & Lustman, P.J. (2001). The prevalence of comorbid depression in adults with diabetes: A meta-analysis. *Diabetes Care, 24*(6), 1069–78.

Artese, A., Ehley, D., Sutin, A.R., & Terracciano, A. (2017). Personality and actigraphy-measured physical activity in older adults. *Psychology and Aging, 32*(2), 131–8. http://doi.org/10.1037/pag0000158

Asthma Society of Canada. (2014). *Severe asthma: The Canadian patient journey.* Retrieved from http://www.asthma.ca/pdfs/SAstudyES.pdf

Astin, J.A., Berman, B.M., Bausell, B., Lee, W.-L., Hochberg, M., & Forys, K.L. (2003). The efficacy of mindfulness meditation plus Qigong movement therapy in the treatment of fibromyalgia: A randomized controlled trial. *The Journal of Rheumatology, 30*(10), 2257–62.

Axelsson, M., Brink, E., Lundgren, J., & Lötvall, J. (2011). The influence of personality traits on reported adherence to medication in individuals with chronic disease: An epidemiological study in West Sweden. *PLOS ONE, 6*(3), e18241. http://doi.org/10.1371/journal.pone.0018241

Ayas, N.T., White, D.P., Manson, J.E., Stampfer, M.J., Speizer, F.E., Malhotra, A., & Hu, F.B. (2003). A prospective study of sleep during and coronary heart disease in women. *Archives of Internal Medicine, 163*(2), 203–9. http://doi.org/10.1001/archinte.163.2.205

Bailey, S.J., LaChapelle, D.L., LeFort, S.M., Gordon, A., & Hadjistavropoulos, T. (2013). Evaluation of chronic pain-related information available to consumers on the internet. *Pain Medicine, 14*(6), 855–64. http://doi.org/10.1111/pme.12087

Barlow, J., Wright, C., Sheasby, J., Turner, A., & Hainsworth, J. (2002). Self-management approaches for people with chronic conditions: a review. *Patient Education and Counseling, 48*(2), 177–87.

Barnes, J.D., Cameron, C., Carson, V., Chaput, J.-P., Faulkner, G.E.J., Janson, K., . . . Tremblay, M. S. (2016). Results from Canada's 2016 ParticipACTION report card on physical activity for children and youth. *Journal of Physical Activity and Health, 13*(11 Suppl 2), S110–S116. http://doi.org/10.1123/jpah.2016-0300

Beatty, L., Koczwara, B., & Wade, T. (2011). "Cancer coping online": A pilot trial of a self-guided CBT internet intervention for cancer-related distress. *E-Journal of Applied Psychology, 7*(2). http://doi.org/10.7790/ejap.v7i2.256

Bello, A.K., Peters, J., Rigby, J., Rahman, A.A., & El Nahas, M. (2008). Socioeconomic status and chronic kidney disease at presentation to a renal service in the United Kingdom. *Clinical Journal of the American Society of Nephrology, 3*(5), 1316–23. http://doi.org/10.2215/CJN.00680208

Benchimol, E.I., Bernstein, C.N., Bitton, A., Carroll, M.W., Singh, H., Otley, A.R., . . . Kaplan, G.G. (2017). Trends in epidemiology of pediatric inflammatory bowel disease in Canada: Distributed network analysis of multiple population-based provincial health administrative databases. *The American Journal of Gastroenterology.* Advance online publication. http://doi.org/10.1038/ajg.2017.97

Bhat, M., Nguyen, G.C., Pare, P., Lahaie, R., Deslandres, C., Bernard, E.-J., . . . Bitton, A. (2009). Phenotypic and genotypic characteristics of inflammatory bowel disease in French Canadians: Comparison with a large North American repository. *The American Journal of Gastroenterology, 104*(9), 2233–40. http://doi.org/10.1038/ajg.2009.267

Blackwell, D.L., & Villarroel, M.A. (2016). *Tables of summary health statistics for U.S. adults: 2015 National Health Interview Survey.* Atlanta, GA: National Center for Health Statistics. Retrieved from https://www.cdc.gov/nchs/nhis/shs/tables.htm

Blankespoor, R.J., Schellekens, M.P.J., Vos, S.H., Speckens, A.E.M., & de Jong, B.A. (2017). The effectiveness of mindfulness-based stress reduction on psychological distress and cognitive functioning in patients with multiple sclerosis: A pilot study. *Mindfulness.* Advance online publication. http://doi.org/10.1007/s12671-017-0701-6

Bloch, G., Rozmovits, L., & Giambrone, B. (2011). Barriers to primary care responsiveness to poverty as a risk factor for health. *BMC Family Practice, 12*(1), 62. http://doi.org/10.1186/1471-2296-12-62

Bohlmeijer, E., Prenger, R., Taal, E., & Cuijpers, P. (2010). The effects of mindfulness-based stress reduction therapy on mental health of adults with a chronic medical disease: A meta-analysis. *Journal of Psychosomatic Research, 68*(6), 539–44. http://doi.org/10.1016/j.jpsychores.2009.10.005

Borson, S., McDonald, G.J., Gayle, T., Deffebach, M., Lakshminarayan, S., & VanTuinen, C. (1992). Improvement in mood, physical symptoms, and function with nortriptyline for depression in patients with chronic obstructive pulmonary disease. *Psychosomatics, 33*(2), 190–201. http://doi.org/10.1016/S0033-3182(92)71995-1

Braverman, P.A., Cubbin, C., Egerter, S., Williams, D.R., & Pamuk, E. (2010). Socioeconomic disparities in health in the United States: What the patterns tell us. *American Journal of Public Health, 10*(S1), S186–S196. http://doi.org/10.2105/AJPH.2009.166082

Breslau, N., & Peterson, E.L. (1996). Smoking cessation in young adults: Age at initiation of cigarette smoking and other suspected influences. *American Journal of Public Health, 86*(2), 214–20.

Brown, M.T., & Bussell, J.K. (2011). Medication adherence: WHO cares? *Mayo Clinic Proceedings, 86*(4), 304–14. http://doi.org/10.4065/mcp.2010.0575

Bruce, J.M., Hancock, L.M., Arnett, P., & Lynch, S. (2010). Treatment adherence in multiple sclerosis: Association with emotional status, personality, and cognition. *Journal of Behavioral Medicine, 33*(3), 219–27. http://doi.org/10.1007/s10865-010-9247-y

Bruce, S.G., Riediger, N.D., Zacharias, J.M., & Young, T.K. (2010). Obesity and obesity-related comorbidities in a Canadian First Nation population. *Chronic Diseases in Canada, 31*(1), 27–32.

Bucholz, E.M., Butala, N.M., Rathore, S.S., Dreyer, R.P., Lansky, A.J., & Krumholz, H.M. (2014). Sex differences in long-term mortality after myocardial infarction: A systematic review. *Circulation, 130*(9), 757–67. http://doi.org/10.1161/CIRCULATIONAHA.114.009480

Burns, M.N., Nawacki, E., Kwasny, M.J., Pelletier, D., & Mohr, D.C. (2014). Do positive or negative stressful events predict the development of new brain lesions in people with multiple sclerosis? *Psychological Medicine, 44*(2), 349–59. http://doi.org/10.1017/S0033291713000755

Butler, A., Chapman, J., Forman, E., & Beck, A. (2006). The empirical status of cognitive-behavioral therapy: A review of meta-analyses. *Clinical Psychology Review, 26*(1), 17–31. http://doi.org/10.1016/j.cpr.2005.07.003

Butt, Z., Rosenbloom, S.K., Abernethy, A.P., Beaumont, J.L., Paul, D., Hampton, D., . . . Cella, D. (2008). Fatigue is the most important symptom for advanced cancer patients who have had chemotherapy. *Journal of the National Comprehensive Cancer Network, 6*(5), 448–55. http://doi.org/10.6004/jnccn.2008.0036

Cappuccio, F.P., D'Elia, L., Strazzullo, P., & Miller, M.A. (2010). Sleep duration and all-cause mortality: A systemic review and meta-analysis of prospective studies. *Sleep, 33*(5), 585–92.

Carver, C.S., Scheier, M.F., & Segerstrom, S.C. (2010). Optimism. *Clinical Psychology Review, 30*(7), 879–89. http://doi.org/10.1016/j.cpr.2010.01.006

Centers for Disease Control and Prevention. (2015). *Excessive alcohol use.* Retrieved from https://www.cdc.gov/chronicdisease/resources/publications/aag/alcohol.htm

Centers for Disease Control and Prevention. (2016). *Current cigarette smoking among adults in the United States.* Retrieved from https://www.cdc.gov/tobacco/data_statistics/fact_sheets/adult_data/cig_smoking/

Ch'Ng, A.M., French, D., & Mclean, N. (2008). Coping with the challenges of recovery from stroke. *Journal of Health Psychology, 13*(8), 1136–46. http://doi.org/10.1177/1359105308095967

Chan, R., Dear, B.F., Titov, N., Chow, J., & Suranyi, M. (2016). Examining internet-delivered cognitive behaviour therapy for patients with chronic kidney disease on haemodialysis: A feasibility open trial. *Journal of Psychosomatic Research, 89,* 78–84. http://doi.org/10.1016/j.jpsychores.2016.08.012

Chapman, B.P., van Wijngaarden, E., Seplaki, C.L., Talbot, N., Duberstein, P., & Moynihan, J. (2011). Openness and conscientiousness predict 34-SSweek patterns of Interleukin-6 in older persons. *Brain, Behavior, and Immunity, 25*(4), 667–73. http://doi.org/10.1016/j.bbi.2011.01.003

Chapman, D.P., Perry, G.S., & Strine, T.W. (2005). The vital link between chronic disease and depressive disorders. *Preventing Chronic Disease, 2*(1), A14.

Christensen, A.J., Ehlers, S.L., Wiebe, J.S., Moran, P.J., Raichle, K., Ferneyhough, K., & Lawton, W.J. (2002). Patient personality and mortality: A 4-year prospective examination of chronic renal insufficiency. *Health Psychology, 21*, 315–20. doi: 10.1037/0278-6133.21.4.315

Ciechanowski, P.S., Katon, W.J., & Russo, J.E. (2000). Depression and diabetes: Impact of depressive symptoms on adherence, function, and costs. *Archives of Internal Medicine, 160*(21), 3278–85.

Ciechanowski, P.S., Katon, W.J., Russo, J.E., & Hirsch, I.B. (2003). The relationship of depressive symptoms to symptom reporting, self-care and glucose control in diabetes. *General Hospital Psychiatry, 25*(4), 246–52. https://doi.org/10.1016/S0163-8343(03)00055-0

Ciesla, J.A., & Roberts, J.E. (2001). Meta-analysis of the relationship between HIV infection and risk for depressive disorders. *The American Journal of Psychiatry, 158*(5), 725–30. http://doi.org/10.1176/appi.ajp.158.5.725

Cohen, S., Kessler, R.C., & Gordon, U.L. (1995). Strategies for measuring stress in studies or psychiatric and physical disorders. In S. Cohen, R.C. Kessler, & U.L. Gordon (Eds.), *Measuring stress: A guide for health and social scientists* (pp. 3–26). New York, NY: Oxford University Press.

Collins Jr., F., Sorocco, K., Haala, K., Miller, B., & Lovallo, W. (2003). Stress and health. In L. Cohen, D. McCHargue, & F. Collins Jr. (Eds.), *The health psychology handbook: Practical issues for the behavioral medicine specialist* (pp. 169–86). London, UK: Sage Publications.

Con, D., & De Cruz, P. (2016). Mobile phone apps for inflammatory bowel disease self-management: A systematic assessment of content and tools. *JMIR mHealth and uHealth, 4*(1), e13. http://doi.org/10.2196/mhealth.4874

Cook, J.A., Grey, D., Burke, J., Cohen, M.H., Gurtman, A.C., Richardson, J.L., . . . Hessol, N. A. (2004). Depressive symptoms and AIDS-related mortality among a multisite cohort of HIV-positive women. *American Journal of Public Health, 94*(7), 1133–40.

Corrao, G. (2004). A meta-analysis of alcohol consumption and the risk of 15 diseases. *Preventive Medicine, 38*(5), 613–19. http://doi.org/10.1016/j.ypmed.2003.11.027

Cramer, H., Haller, H., Lauche, R., & Dobos, G. (2012). Mindfulness-based stress reduction for low back pain. A systematic review. *BMC Complementary and Alternative Medicine, 12*(1), 1162. http://doi.org/10.1186/1472-6882-12-162

Crohn's & Colitis Foundation of America. (2009). *Managing flares and other IBD symptoms.* New York, NY. Retrieved from http://www.crohnscolitisfoundation.org/assets/pdfs/flares_brochure_final.pdf

Cunningham, W.E., Hays, R.D., Duan, N., Andersen, R., Nakazono, T.T., Bozzette, S.A., & Shapiro, M.F. (2005). The effect of socioeconomic status on the survival of people receiving care for HIV infection in the United States. *Journal of Health Care for the Poor and Underserved, 16*(4), 655–76. http://doi.org/10.1353/hpu.2005.0093

Cushman, W.C. (2001). Alcohol consumption and hypertension. *Journal of Clinical Hypertension, 3*, 166–70. doi: 10.1111/j.1524-6175.2001.00443.x

Dew, M.A., Simmons, R.G., Roth, L.H., Schulberg, H.C., Thompson, M.E., Armitage, J.M., & Griffith, B.P. (1994). Psychosocial predictors of vulnerability to distress in the year following heart transplantation. *Psychological Medicine, 24*(4), 929–45.

DiMatteo, M.R., Lepper, H.S., & Croghan, T.W. (2000). Depression is a risk factor for noncompliance with medical treatment. *Archives of Internal Medicine, 160*(14), 2101. http://doi.org/10.1001/archinte.160.14.2101

Drulovic, J., Basic-Kes, V., Grgic, S., Vojinovic, S., Dincic, E., Toncev, G., . . . Pekmezovic, T. (2015). The prevalence of pain in adults with multiple sclerosis: A multicenter cross-sectional survey. *Pain Medicine, 16*(8), 1597–1602. http://doi.org/10.1111/pme.12731

Duggan, K.A., Friedman, H.S., McDevitt, E.A., & Mednick, S.C. (2014). Personality and healthy sleep: The importance of conscientiousness and neuroticism. *PLOS ONE, 9*(3), e90628. http://doi.org/10.1371/journal.pone.0090628

Dyck, R., Osgood, N., Lin, T.H., Gao, A., & Stang, M.R. (2010). Epidemiology of diabetes mellitus among First Nations and non-First Nations adults. *Canadian Medical Association Journal, 182*(3), 249–56. http://doi.org/10.1503/cmaj.090846

Ediger, J.P., Walker, J.R., Graff, L., Lix, L., Clara, I., Rawsthorne, P., . . . Bernstein, C.N. (2007). Predictors of medication adherence in inflammatory bowel disease. *The American Journal of Gastroenterology, 102*(7), 1417–26. http://doi.org/10.1111/j.1572-0241.2007.01212.x

Eisner, M.D., Blanc, P.D., Omachi, T.A., Yelin, E.H., Sidney, S., Katz, P.P., . . . Iribarren, C. (2011). Socioeconomic status, race and COPD health outcomes. *Journal of Epidemiology and Community Health, 65*(1), 26–34. http://doi.org/10.1136/jech.2009.089722

Feros, D.L., Lane, L., Ciarrochi, J., & Blackledge, J.T. (2011). Acceptance and commitment therapy (ACT) for improving the lives of cancer patients: A preliminary study. *Psycho-Oncology, 22*(2), 459–64. http://doi.org/10.1002/pon.2083

Finkelstein, E.A., Tangka, F.K., Trogdon, J.G., Sabatino, S.A., & Richardson, L.C. (2009). The personal financial burden of cancer for the working-aged population. *The American Journal of Managed Care, 15*(11), 801–6.

Forman, E.M., Herbert, J.D., Moitra, E., Yeomans, P.D., & Geller, P.A. (2007). A randomized controlled effectiveness trial of acceptance and commitment therapy and cognitive therapy for anxiety and depression. *Behavior Modification, 31*(6), 772–99. http://doi.org/10.1177/0145445507302202

Fredriksen, K., Rhodes, J., Reddy, R., & Way, N. (2004). Sleepless in Chicago: Tracking the effects of adolescent sleep loss during the middle school years. *Child Development. 75*(1), 84–95. http://doi.org/10.1111/j.1467-8624.2004.00655.x

Fredriksen-Goldsen, K., Kim, H., Barkan, S.E., Muraco, A., & Hoy-Ellis, C.P. (2013). Health disparities among lesbian, gay, and bisexual older adults: Results from a population-based study. *American Journal of Public Health, 103*(10), 1802–09. http://doi.org/10.2105/AJPH.2012.301110

Friedman, M., & Rosenman, R.H. (1959). Association of specific overt behavior pattern with blood and cardiovascular findings. *Journal of the American Medical Association, 169*(12), 1286. http://doi.org/10.1001/jama.1959.03000290012005

Friesen, L.N., Hadjistavropoulos, H.D., Schneider, L.H., Alberts, N.M., Titov, N., & Dear, B.F. (2017). Examination of an internet-delivered cognitive behavioural pain management course for adults with fibromyalgia. *PAIN, 158*(4), 593–604. http://doi.org/10.1097/j.pain.0000000000000802

Frolkis, A., Dieleman, L.A., Barkema, H.W., Panaccione, R., Ghosh, S., Fedorak, R.N., . . . Alberta IBD Consortium. (2013). Environment and the inflammatory bowel diseases. *Canadian Journal of Gastroenterology/Journal Canadien de Gastroenterologie, 27*(3), e18–24.

Gamble, J., Stevenson, M., McClean, E., & Heaney, L.G. (2009). The prevalence of nonadherence in difficult asthma. *American Journal of Respiratory and Critical Care Medicine, 180*(9), 817–22. http://doi.org/10.1164/rccm.200902-0166OC

Garriguet, D. (2009). Diet quality in Canada. *Health Reports, 20*(3), 41–52.

Gatchel, R.J., Peng, Y.B., Peters, M.L., Fuchs, P.N., & Turk, D.C. (2007). The biopsychosocial approach to chronic pain: Scientific advances and future directions. *Psychological Bulletin, 133*(4), 581–624. http://doi.org/10.1037/0033-2909.133.4.581

Gayner, B., Esplen, M.J., DeRoche, P., Wong, J., Bishop, S., Kavanagh, L., & Butler, K. (2012). A randomized controlled trial of mindfulness-based stress reduction to manage affective symptoms and improve quality of life in gay men living with HIV. *Journal of Behavioral Medicine, 35*(3), 272–285. http://doi.org/10.1007/s10865-011-9350-8

Gerteis, J., Izrael, D., Deitz, D., LeRoy, L., Ricciardi, R., Miller, T., & Basu, J. (2014). *Multiple chronic conditions chartbook.*

Rockville, MD. Retrieved from https://www.ahrq.gov/sites/default/files/wysiwyg/professionals/prevention-chronic-care/decision/mcc/mccchartbook.pdf

Gibson, P.G., Powell, H., Coughlan, J., Wilson, A.J., Abramson, M., Haywood, P., . . . Walters, E.H. (2003). Self-management education and regular practitioner review for adults with asthma. *The Cochrane Database of Systematic Reviews*, (1), CD001117. http://doi.org/10.1002/14651858.CD001117

Gifford, A.L., Laurent, D.D., Gonzales, V.M., Chesney, M.A., & Lorig, K.R. (1998). Pilot randomized trial of education to improve self-management skills of men with symptomatic HIV/AIDS. *Journal of Acquired Immune Deficiency Syndromes and Human Retrovirologyn*, *18*(2), 136–44.

Gillisen, A. (2007). *Patient's adherence in asthma. Journal of Physiology and Pharmacology 58 Suppl 5(Pt 1)*, 205–22.

Gonzalez, J.S., McCarl, L., Wexler, D.D., Cagliero, E., Delahanty, L., Soper, T.D., . . . Safren, S.A. (2010). Cognitive Behavioral Therapy for Adherence and Depression (CBT-AD) in Type 2 Diabetes. *Journal of Cognitive Psychotherapy, 24*(4), 329–343. doi:10.1891/0889-8391.24.4.329

Goodwin, C.L., Forman, E.M., Herbert, J.D., Butryn, M.L., & Ledley, G.S. (2012). A pilot study examining the initial effectiveness of a brief acceptance-based behavior therapy for modifying diet and physical activity among cardiac patients. *Behavior Modification*, *36*(2), 199–217. http://doi.org/10.1177/0145445511427770

Graff, L.A., Walker, J.R., & Bernstein, C.N. (2009). Depression and anxiety in inflammatory bowel disease: A review of comorbidity and management. *Inflammatory Bowel Diseases*, *15*(7), 1105–18. http://doi.org/10.1002/ibd.20873

Green, C.R., Hart-Johnson, T., & Loeffler, D.R. (2011). Cancer-related chronic pain. *Cancer, 117*(9), 1994–2003. http://doi.org/10.1002/cncr.25761

Gregg, J.A., Callaghan, G.M., Hayes, S.C., & Glenn-Lawson, J.L. (2007). Improving diabetes self-management through acceptance, mindfulness, and values: A randomized controlled trial. *Journal of Consulting and Clinical Psychology*, *75*(2), 336–43. http://doi.org/10.1037/0022-006X.75.2.336

Grossman, P., Tiefenthaler-Gilmer, U., Raysz, A., & Kesper, U. (2007). Mindfulness training as an intervention for fibromyalgia: Evidence of postintervention and 3-year follow-up benefits in well-being. *Psychotherapy and Psychosomatics*, *76*(4), 226–33. http://doi.org/10.1159/000101501

Gu, F., Han, J., Laden, F., Pan, A., Caporaso, N.E., Stampfer, M.J., . . . Schernhammer, E.S. (2015). Total and cause-specific mortality of U.S. nurses working rotating night shifts. *American Journal of Preventive Medicine*, *48*(3), 241–52. https://doi.org/10.1016/j.amepre.2014.10.018

Hack, T.F., & Degner, L.F. (2004). Coping responses following breast cancer diagnosis predict psychological adjustment three years later. *Psycho-Oncology*, *13*(4), 235–47. http://doi.org/10.1002/pon.739

Hadjistavropoulos, T., & Hadjistavropoulos, H. (2019). *Pain management for older adults : A self-help guide* (2nd ed.). Philadelphia, PA: Wolters Kluwer.

Hagedoorn, M., Sanderman, R., Bolks, H.N., Tuinstra, J., & Coyne, J.C. (2008). Distress in couples coping with cancer: A meta-analysis and critical review of role and gender

effects. *Psychological Bulletin*, *134*(1), 1–30. http://doi.org/10.1037/0033-2909.134.1.1

Hanauer, D.A., Wentzell, K., Laffel, N., & Laffel, L.M. (2009). Computerized automated reminder diabetes system (CARDS): E-Mail and SMS cell phone text messaging reminders to support diabetes management. *Diabetes Technology & Therapeutics*, *11*(2), 99–106. http://doi.org/10.1089/dia.2008.0022

Harper, F.W.K., Nevedal, A., Eggly, S., Francis, C., Schwartz, K., & Albrecht, T.L. (2013). "It's up to you and God": Understanding health behavior change in older African American survivors of colorectal cancer. *Translational Behavioral Medicine*, *3*(1), 94–103. http://doi.org/10.1007/s13142-012-0188-6

Harris, M.D. (2003). Psychosocial aspects of diabetes with an emphasis on depression. *Current Diabetes Reports*, *3*, 49–55. doi: 10.1007/s11892-003-0053-6

Hart, J.T. (1971). The inverse care law. *Lancet, 1*(7696), 405–12. https://doi.org/10.1016/S0140-6736(71)92410-X

Hart, S.L., Vella, L., & Mohr, D.C. (2008). Relationships among depressive symptoms, benefit-finding, optimism, and positive affect in multiple sclerosis patients after psychotherapy for depression. *Health Psychology*, *27*(2), 230–238. http://doi.org/10.1037/0278-6133.27.2.230

Hayes, S.C., Strosahl, K.D., & Wilson, K.G. (2012). *Acceptance and commitment therapy: The process and practice of mindful change* (2nd ed.). New York: NY: Guilford.

Health Canada. (2011a). *Canada's food guide*. Ottawa, ON. Retrieved from http://www.hc-sc.gc.ca/fn-an/alt_formats/hpfb-dgpsa/pdf/food-guide-aliment/view_eatwell_vue_bienmang-eng.pdf

Health Canada. (2011b). *Smoking and your body*. Retrieved from http://www.hc-sc.gc.ca/hc-ps/tobac-tabac/body-corps/index-eng.php

Helgeson, V.S. (2012). Gender and health: A social psychological perspective. In A. Baum, T. Revenson, & J. Singer (Eds.), *Handbook of health psychology* (pp. 519–37). New York, NY: Psychology Press.

Helgeson, V.S., Snyder, P., & Seltman, H. (2004). Psychological and physical adjustment to breast cancer over 4 years: Identifying distinct trajectories of change. *Health Psychology*, *23*(1), 3–15. http://doi.org/10.1037/0278-6133.23.1.3

Helgeson, V.S., & Zajdel, M. (2017). Adjusting to chronic health conditions. *Annual Review of Psychology*, *68*(1), 545–71. http://doi.org/10.1146/annurev-psych-010416-044014

Heron, M. (2016). Deaths: Leading causes for 2014. *National Vital Statistics Reports*, *65*(5).

Hewitt, M., Rowland, J.H., & Yancik, R. (2003). Cancer survivors in the United States: Age, health, and disability. *The Journals of Gerontology Series A: Biological Sciences and Medical Sciences*, *58*(1), M82–M91. http://doi.org/10.1093/gerona/58.1.M82

Honda, K., & Goodwin, R.D. (2004). Cancer and mental disorders in a national community sample: Findings from the National Comorbidity Survey. *Psychotherapy and Psychosomatics*, *73*(4), 235–42. http://doi.org/10.1159/000077742

Hunt-Shanks, T., Blanchard, C., & Reid, R.D. (2009). Gender differences in cardiac patients: A longitudinal investigation of exercise, autonomic anxiety, negative affect and depression. *Psychology, Health & Medicine, 14*(3), 375–85. http://doi.org/10.1080/13548500902866939

Hunt, M.G., Moshier, S., & Milonova, M. (2009). Brief cognitive-behavioral internet therapy for irritable bowel syndrome. *Behaviour Research and Therapy, 47*(9), 797–802. http://doi.org/10.1016/j.brat.2009.05.002

Ickovics, J.R., Hamburger, M.E., Vlahov, D., Schoenbaum, E.E., Schuman, P., Boland, R.J., . . . for the HIV Epidemiology Research Study Group. (2001). Mortality, CD_4 cell count decline, and depressive symptoms among HIV-seropositive women. *JAMA, 285*(11), 1466. http://doi.org/10.1001/jama.285.11.1466

Iida, M., Parris Stephens, M.A., Rook, K.S., Franks, M.M., & Salem, J.K. (2010). When the going gets tough, does support get going? Determinants of spousal support provision to type 2 diabetic patients. *Personality & Social Psychology Bulletin, 36*(6), 780–91. http://doi.org/10.1177/0146167210369897

Islam, T., Dahlui, M., Majid, H.A., Nahar, A.M., Mohd Taib, N.A., Su, T.T., & MyBCC study group. (2014). Factors associated with return to work of breast cancer survivors: a systematic review. *BMC Public Health, 14*(Suppl 3), S8. http://doi.org/10.1186/1471-2458-14-S3-S8

Jacklin, K.M., Henderson, R.I., Green, M.E., Walker, L.M., Calam, B., & Crowshoe, L.J. (2017). Health care experiences of Indigenous people living with type 2 diabetes in Canada. *Canadian Medical Association Journal, 189*(3), E106–E112. http://doi.org/10.1503/cmaj.161098

Janz, T. (2015). *Current smoking trends.* Ottawa, ON. Retrieved from http://www.statcan.gc.ca/pub/82-624-x/2012001/article/11676-eng.htm#n13

Jha, P., Ramasundarahettige, C., Landsman, V., Rostron, B., Thun, M., Anderson, R.N., . . . Peto, R. (2013). 21st-century hazards of smoking and benefits of cessation in the United States. *New England Journal of Medicine, 368*(4), 341–50. http://doi.org/10.1056/NEJMsa1211128

Jim, H.S., Richardson, S.A., Golden-Kreutz, D.M., & Andersen, B.L. (2006). Strategies used in coping with a cancer diagnosis predict meaning in life for survivors. *Health Psychology 25*(6), 753–61. http://doi.org/10.1037/0278-6133.25.6.753

Kabat-Zinn, J. (1990). *Full Catastrophe Living: Using the Wisdom of Your Body and Mind to Face Stress, Pain and Illness.* New York, NY: Hyperion Books.

Kabat-Zinn, J. (1994). *Wherever you go, there you are: Mindfulness meditation in everyday life.* New York, NY: Hyperion.

Karlsen, B., & Bru, E. (2002). Coping styles among adults with type 1 and type 2 diabetes. *Psychology, Health & Medicine, 7*(3), 245–59. http://doi.org/10.1080/13548500220139403

Katon, W., Lin, E.H.B., & Kroenke, K. (2007). The association of depression and anxiety with medical symptom burden in patients with chronic medical illness. *General Hospital Psychiatry, 29*(2), 147–55. http://doi.org/10.1016/j.genhosppsych.2006.11.005

Katz, P.P., & Yelin, E.H. (2001). Activity loss and the onset of depressive symptoms: Do some activities matter more than others? *Arthritis & Rheumatism, 44*(5), 1194–1202. http://doi.org/10.1002/1529-0131(200105)44:5<1194::AID-ANR203>3.0.CO;2-6

Kennard, B.D., Brown, L.T., Hawkins, L., Risi, A., Radcliffe, J., Emslie, G.J., . . . Thornton, S. (2014). Development and implementation of health and wellness CBT for individuals with depression and HIV. *Cognitive and Behavioral Practice, 21*(2), 237–46. http://doi.org/10.1016/j.cbpra.2013.07.003

Kennedy, A.P. (2004). A randomised controlled trial to assess the effectiveness and cost of a patient orientated self management approach to chronic inflammatory bowel disease. *Gut, 53*(11), 1639–45. http://doi.org/10.1136/gut.2003.034256

Kiebles, J.L., Doerfler, B., & Keefer, L. (2010). Preliminary evidence supporting a framework of psychological adjustment to inflammatory bowel disease. *Inflammatory Bowel Diseases, 16*(10), 1685–95. http://doi.org/10.1002/ibd.21215

Kim, H.-S. (2007). A randomized controlled trial of a nurse short-message service by cellular phone for people with diabetes. *International Journal of Nursing Studies, 44*(5), 687–92. http://doi.org/10.1016/j.ijnurstu.2006.01.011

Kivimäki, M., Virtanen, M., Elovainio, M., Kouvonen, A., Väänänen, A., & Vahtera, J. (2006). Work stress in the etiology of coronary heart disease—A meta-analysis. *Scandinavian Journal of Work, Environment & Health, 32*(6), 431–42.

Kochanek, K.D., Murphy, S.L., Xu, J., & Tejada-Vera, B. (2016). Deaths: Final data for 2014. *National Vital Statistics Reports, 65*(4).

Krantz, D.S., & McCeney, M.K. (2002). Effects of psychological and social factors on organic disease: A critical assessment of research on coronary heart disease. *Annual Review of Psychology, 53*, 341–69. http://doi.org/10.1146/annurev.psych.53.100901.135208

Kübler-Ross, E. (1973). *On death and dying.* New York, NY: McMillan.

Kwan, K.S.H., Roberts, L.J., & Swalm, D.M. (2005). Sexual dysfunction and chronic pain: The role of psychological variables and impact on quality of life. *European Journal of Pain, 9*(6), 643–643. http://doi.org/10.1016/j.ejpain.2004.12.008

Lee, M.M., Lin, S.S., Wrensch, M.R., Adler, S.R., & Eisenberg, D. (2000). Alternative therapies used by women with breast cancer in four ethnic populations. *Journal of the National Cancer Institute, 92*(1), 42–7. https://doi.org/10.1093/jnci/92.1.42

LeFort, S.M., Gray-Donald, K., Rowat, K.M., & Jeans, M.E. (1998). Randomized controlled trial of a community-based psychoeducation program for the self-management of chronic pain. *Pain, 74*(2), 297–306. http://doi.org/10.1016/S0304-3959(97)00190-5

Li, Q.P., Mak, Y.W., & Loke, A.Y. (2013). Spouses' experience of caregiving for cancer patients: A literature review. *International Nursing Review, 60*(2), 178–87. http://doi.org/10.1111/inr.12000

Lilly, C.L., Bryant, L.L., Leary, J.M., Vu, M.B., Hill-Briggs, F., Samuel-Hodge, C.D., . . . Keyserling, T.C. (2014). Evaluation of the effectiveness of a problem-solving intervention addressing barriers to cardiovascular disease prevention behaviors in 3 underserved populations: Colorado, North Carolina, West Virginia, 2009. *Preventing Chronic Disease*, *11*, 130249. http://doi.org/10.5888/pcd11.130249

Lin, E.H.B., Katon, W., Von Korff, M., Tang, L., Williams, Jr, J.W., Kroenke, K., . . . for the IMPACT Investigators. (2003). Effect of improving depression care on pain and functional outcomes among older adults with arthritis. *JAMA*, *290*(18), 2428. http://doi.org/10.1001/jama.290.18.2428

Ljótsson, B., Falk, L., Vesterlund, A.W., Hedman, E., Lindfors, P., Rück, C., . . . Andersson, G. (2010). Internet-delivered exposure and mindfulness based therapy for irritable bowel syndrome – A randomized controlled trial. *Behaviour Research and Therapy*, *48*(6), 531–9. http://doi.org/10.1016/j.brat.2010.03.003

Longo, C.J., Fitch, M., Deber, R.B., & Williams, A.P. (2006). Financial and family burden associated with cancer treatment in Ontario, Canada. *Supportive Care in Cancer*, *14*(11), 1077–85. http://doi.org/10.1007/s00520-006-0088-8

Lorig, K.R., Mazonson, P.D., & Holman, H.R. (1993). Evidence suggesting that health education for self-management in patients with chronic arthritis has sustained health benefits while reducing health care costs. *Arthritis and Rheumatism*, *36*, 439–46. doi: 10.1002/art.1780360403

Lorig, K., Ritter, P.L., Laurent, D.D., & Plant, K. (2008). The internet-based arthritis self-management program: A one-year randomized trial for patients with arthritis or fibromyalgia. *Arthritis & Rheumatism*, *59*(7), 1009–17. http://doi.org/10.1002/art.23817

Lorig, K., Ritter, P.L., Villa, F.J., & Armas, J. (2009). Community-based peer-led diabetes self-management. *The Diabetes Educator*, *35*(4), 641–51. http://doi.org/10.1177/0145721709335006

Lorig, K., Ritter, P., Stewart, A.L., Sobel, D.S., Brown, B.W., Bandura, A., . . . Holman, H.R. (2001). Chronic disease self-management program: 2-year health status and health care utilization outcomes. *Medical Care*, *39*(11), 1217–23.

Lovasi, G.S., Hutson, M.A., Guerra, M., & Neckerman, K.M. (2009). Built environments and obesity in disadvantaged populations. *Epidemiologic Reviews*, *31*, 7–20. http://doi.org/10.1093/epirev/mxp005

Ludman, E.J., Katon, W., Russo, J., Von Korff, M., Simon, G., Ciechanowski, P., . . . Young, B. (2004). Depression and diabetes symptom burden. *General Hospital Psychiatry*, *26*(6), 430–6. http://doi.org/10.1016/j.genhosppsych.2004.08.010

Mahler, H.I.M., & Kulik, J.A. (2000). Optimism, pessimism and recovery from coronary bypass surgery: Prediction of affect, pain and functional status. *Psychology, Health & Medicine*, *5*(4), 347–58. http://doi.org/10.1080/713690216

Marrie, R.A., Patten, S.B., Greenfield, J., Svenson, L.W., Jette, N., Tremlett, H., . . . Fisk, J.D. (2016). Physical comorbidities increase the risk of psychiatric comorbidity in multiple sclerosis. *Brain and Behavior*, *6*(9), e00493. http://doi.org/10.1002/brb3.493

Martins, R.K., & McNeil, D.W. (2009). Review of motivational interviewing in promoting health behaviors. *Clinical Psychology Review*, *29*(4), 283–93. http://doi.org/10.1016/j.cpr.2009.02.001

Masoli, M., Fabian, D., Holt, S., & Beasley, R. (2004). The global burden of asthma: Executive summary of the GINA Dissemination Committee Report. *Allergy*, *59*(5), 469–78. http://doi.org/10.1111/j.1398-9995.2004.00526.x

Matthews, K.A. (2004). Hostile behaviors predict cardiovascular mortality among men enrolled in the multiple risk factor intervention trial. *Circulation*, *109*(1), 66–70. http://doi.org/10.1161/01.CIR.0000105766.33142.13

Matthews, K.A., & Gallo, L.C. (2011). Psychological perspectives on pathways linking socioeconomic status and physical health. *Annual Review of Psychology*, *62*(1), 501–30. http://doi.org/10.1146/annurev.psych.031809.130711

McEwen, B.S. (2006a). Protective and damaging effects of stress mediators: Central role of the brain. *Dialogues in Clinical Neuroscience*, *8*(4), 367–81.

McEwen, B.S. (2006b). Sleep deprivation as a neurobiologic and physiologic stressor: Allostasis and allostatic load. *Metabolism*, *55*, S20–S23. http://doi.org/10.1016/j.metabol.2006.07.008

Meng, Y., Babey, S., & Wolstein, J. (2012). Asthma-related school absenteeism and school concentration of low-income students in California. *Preventing Chronic Disease*, *9*, E98. http://doi.org/10.5888/pcd9.110312

Merkes, M. (2010). Mindfulness-based stress reduction for people with chronic diseases. *Australian Journal of Primary Health*, *16*(3), 200. http://doi.org/10.1071/PY09063

Milgrom, H., Bender, B., Ackerson, L., Bowry, P., Smith, B., & Rand, C. (1996). Noncompliance and treatment failure in children with asthma. *The Journal of Allergy and Clinical Immunology*, *98*, 1051–7. doi: 10.1016/S0091-6749(96)80190-4

Miller, T., & DiMatteo, R. (2013). Importance of family/social support and impact on adherence to diabetic therapy. *Diabetes, Metabolic Syndrome and Obesity: Targets and Therapy*, *6*, 421–6. http://doi.org/10.2147/DMSO.S36368

Mohr, D.C., Goodkin, D.E., Bacchetti, P., Boudewyn, A.C., Huang, L., Marrietta, P., . . . Dee, B. (2000). Psychological stress and the subsequent appearance of new brain MRI lesions in MS. *Neurology*, *55*(1), 55–61. http://doi.org/10.1212/WNL.55.1.55

Morone, N.E., Greco, C.M., & Weiner, D.K. (2008). Mindfulness meditation for the treatment of chronic low back pain in older adults: A randomized controlled pilot study. *Pain*, *134*(3), 310–19. http://doi.org/10.1016/j.pain.2007.04.038

Musselman, D.L., Evans, D.L., & Nemeroff, C.B. (1998). The relationship of depression to cardiovascular disease. *Archives of General Psychiatry*, *55*(7), 580. http://doi.org/10.1001/archpsyc.55.7.580

National Sleep Foundation. (2006). *Teens and sleep: Sleep in America polls*. Washington, DC. Retrieved from https://sleepfoundation.org/sites/default/files/2006_summary_of_findings.pdf

Nicassio, P.M., Moxham, E.G., Schuman, C.E., & Gevirtz, R.N. (2002). The contribution of pain, reported sleep quality, and depressive symptoms to fatigue in fibromyalgia. *Pain*, *100*(3), 271–9. http://doi.org/10.1016/S0304-3959(02)00300-7

Nicholas, S.B., Kalantar-Zadeh, K., & Norris, K.C. (2015). Socioeconomic disparities in chronic kidney disease. *Advances in Chronic Kidney Disease, 22*(1), 6–15. http://doi.org/10.1053/j.ackd.2014.07.002

Office of Disease Prevention and Health Promotion. (2017). *A closer look at current intakes and recommended shifts.* Retrieved from https://health.gov/dietaryguidelines/2015/guidelines/acknowledgments

Pan, A., Schernhammer, S., Sun, Q., & Hu, F.B. (2011). Rotating night shift work and risk of type 2 diabetes: Two prospective cohort studies in women. *PLOS Medicine, 8*(12), e1991141. https://doi.org/10.1371/journal.pmed.1001141

Parker, R., Stein, D.J., & Jelsma, J. (2014). Pain in people living with HIV/AIDS: A systematic review. *Journal of the International AIDS Society, 17*, 18719. doi: 10.7448/IAS.17.1.18719

Peek, M.E., Odoms-Young, A., Quinn, M.T., Gorawara-Bhat, R., Wilson, S.C., & Chin, M.H. (2010). Race and shared decision-making: perspectives of African-Americans with diabetes. *Social Science & Medicine (1982), 71*(1), 1–9. http://doi.org/10.1016/j.socscimed.2010.03.014

Peyrot, M., Rubin, R.R., Lauritzen, T., Snoek, F.J., Matthews, D.R., & Skovlund, S.E. (2005). Psychosocial problems and barriers to improved diabetes management: Results of the Cross-National Diabetes Attitudes, Wishes and Needs (DAWN) Study. *Diabetic Medicine, 22*(10), 1379–85. http://doi.org/10.1111/j.1464-5491.2005.01644.x

Physical & Health Education Canada. (2016). *Global comparisons with ParticipACTION report card.* Retrieved from http://www.phecanada.ca/resources/news/global-comparisons-participaction-report-card

Plantinga, L.C., Fink, N.E., Harrington-Levey, R., Finkelstein, F.O., Hebah, N., Powe, N.R., & Jaar, B.G. (2010). Association of social support with outcomes in incident dialysis patients. *Clinical Journal of the American Society of Nephrology, 5*(8), 1480–8. http://doi.org/10.2215/CJN.01240210

Pong, R.W., DesMeules, M., Heng, D., Lagacé, C., Guernsey, J.R., Kazanjian, A., . . . Luo, W. (2011). Chronic diseases and injuries in Canada, *31*(supplement 1), 1–30. Retrieved from http://www.phac-aspc.gc.ca/publicat/hpcdp-pspmc/31-1-supp/ar_01-eng.php

Pong, R.W., DesMeules, M., & Lagacé, C. (2009). Rural-urban disparities in health: How does Canada fare and how does Canada compare with Australia. *The Australian Journal of Rural Health, 17*(1), 58–64. http://doi.org/10.1111/j.1440-1584.2008.01039.x

Pradhan, E.K., Baumgarten, M., Langenberg, P., Handwerger, B., Gilpin, A.K., Magyari, T., . . . Berman, B.M. (2007). Effect of mindfulness-based stress reduction in rheumatoid arthritis patients. *Arthritis & Rheumatism, 57*(7), 1134–42. http://doi.org/10.1002/art.23010

Public Health Agency of Canada. (2014). *Economic burden of illness in Canada 2005–2008.* Ottawa, ON. Retrieved from http://www.phac-aspc.gc.ca/publicat/ebic-femc/2005-2008/assets/pdf/ebic-femc-2005-2008-eng.pdf

Public Health Agency of Canada. (2015). *Centre for Chronic Disease Prevention strategic plan 2016–2019: Improving health outcomes a paradigm shift.* Ottawa, ON. Retrieved from http://www.phac-aspc.gc.ca/cd-mc/assets/pdf/ccdp-strategic-plan-2016-2019-plan-strategique-cpmc-eng.pdf

Public Health Agency of Canada. (2016). *How healthy are Canadians? A trend analysis of the health of Canadians from a healthy living and chronic disease perspective.* Ottawa, ON. Retrieved from https://www.canada.ca/en/public-health/services/publications/healthy-living/how-healthy-canadians.html

Quintana-Hernández, D.J., Miró-Barrachina, M.T., Ibáñez-Fernández, I.J., Pino, A.S., Quintana-Montesdeoca, M.P., Rodríguez-de Vera, B., . . . Bravo-Caraduje, N. (2015). Mindfulness in the maintenance of cognitive capacities in Alzheimer's disease: A randomized clinical trial. *Journal of Alzheimer's Disease, 50*(1), 217–32. http://doi.org/10.3233/JAD-143009

Quittner, A.L., Espelage, D.L., Opipari, L.C., Carter, B., Eid, N., & Eigen, H. (1998). Role strain in couples with and without a child with a chronic illness: Associations with marital satisfaction, intimacy, and daily mood. *Health Psychology, 17*(2), 112–24. http://doi.org/10.1037/0278-6133.17.2.112

Qureshi, A.I., Giles, W.H., Croft, J.B., & Bliwise, D.L. (1997). Habitual sleep patterns and risk for stroke and coronary heart disease: A 10-year follow-up from NHANES I. *Neurology, 48*(4), 904–11.

Rasmussen, H.N., Wrosch, C., Scheier, M.F., & Carver, C.S. (2006). Self-regulation processes and health: The importance of optimism and goal adjustment. *Journal of Personality, 74*(6), 1721–48. http://doi.org/10.1111/j.1467-6494.2006.00426.x

Rehm, J., Room, R., Graham, K., Monteiro, M., Gmel, G., & Sempos, C.T. (2003). The relationship of average volume of alcohol consumption and patterns of drinking to burden of disease: An overview. *Addiction, 98*(9), 1209–28. http://doi.org/10.1046/j.1360-0443.2003.00467.x

Reid, D., Abramson, M., Raven, J., & Walters, H.E. (2000). Management and treatment perceptions among young adults with asthma in Melbourne: The Australian experience from the European Community Respiratory Health Survey. *Respirology, 5*, 281–7. doi: 10.1046/j.1440-1843.2000.00265.x

Revenson, T. (2003). Scenes from a marriage: Examining support, coping, and gender within the context of chronic illness. In J. Suls and K.A. Wallston (Eds.), *Social psychological foundations of health and illness* (pp. 530–59). Malden, MA: Wiley.

Reynolds, K., Lewis, B., Nolen, J.D.L., Kinney, G.L., Sathya, B., & He, J. (2003). Alcohol Consumption and Risk of Stroke. *JAMA, 289*(5), 579. http://doi.org/10.1001/jama.289.5.579

Richard, A.A., & Shea, K. (2011). Delineation of self-care and associated concepts. *Journal of Nursing Scholarship, 43*(3), 255–64. http://doi.org/10.1111/j.1547-5069.2011.01404.x

Riediger, N.D., Bruce, S.G., & Young, T.K. (2010). Cardiovascular risk according to plasma apolipoprotein and lipid profiles in a Canadian First Nation. *Chronic Diseases in Canada, 31*(1), 33–8.

Ritz, T., & Janssens, T. (2014). Asthmas and chronic obstructive pulmonary disease. In T. Hadjistavropoulos & H.

Hadjistavropoulos (Eds.), *Fundamentals of health psychology* (pp. 223–36). Toronto, ON: Oxford University Press.

Rodríguez-Artalejo, F., Guallar-Castillón, P., Herrera, M.C., Otero, C.M., Chiva, M.O., Ochoa, C.C., . . . Pascual, C.R. (2006). Social network as a predictor of hospital readmission and mortality among older patients with heart failure. *Journal of Cardiac Failure, 12*(8), 621–7. http://doi.org/10.1016/j.cardfail.2006.06.471

Rohrbaugh, M.J., Cranford, J.A., Shoham, V., Nicklas, J.M., Sonnega, J.S., & Coyne, J.C. (2002). Couples coping with congestive heart failure: Role and gender differences in psychological distress. *Journal of Family Psychology, 16*(1), 3–13. http://dx.doi.org/10.1037/0893-3200.16.1.3

Rozanski, A., Blumenthal, J.A., & Kaplan, J. (1999). Impact of psychological factors on the pathogenesis of cardiovascular disease and implications for therapy. *Circulation, 99*(16), 2192–217. https://doi.org/10.1161/01.CIR.99.16.2192

Safren, S.A., Gonzalez, J.S., Wexler, D.J., Psaros, C., Delahanty, L.M., Blashill, A.J., . . . Cagliero, E. (2014). A randomized controlled trial of cognitive behavioral therapy for adherence and depression (CBT-AD) in patients with uncontrolled type 2 diabetes. *Diabetes Care, 37*(3), 625–33. http://doi.org/10.2337/dc13-0816

Sanmartin, C., & Healthy Analysis Division. (2015). *Research highlights on health and aging.* Ottawa, ON. Retrieved from http://www.statcan.gc.ca/pub/11-631-x/11-631-x2016001-eng.htm

Saydah, S., & Lochner, K. (2010). Socioeconomic status and risk of diabetes-related mortality in the U.S. *Public Health Reports, 125*(3), 377–88. http://doi.org/10.1177/003335491012500306

Scheier, M.F., Matthews, K.A., Owens, J.F., Magovern, G.J., Lefebvre, R.C., Abbott, R.A., & Carver, C.S. (1989). Dispositional optimism and recovery from coronary artery bypass surgery: The beneficial effects on physical and psychological well-being. *Journal of Personality and Social Psychology, 57*(6), 1024–40. http://dx.doi.org/10.1037/0022-3514.57.6.1024

Schmidt, E.Z., Hofmann, P., Niederwieser, G., Kapfhammer, H.-P., & Bonelli, R.M. (2005). Sexuality in multiple sclerosis. *Journal of Neural Transmission, 112*(9), 1201–11. http://doi.org/10.1007/s00702-005-0275-7

Schouffoer, A.A., Schoones, J.W., Terwee, C.B., & Vliet Vlieland, T.P.M. (2012). Work status and its determinants among patients with systemic sclerosis: A systematic review. *Rheumatology, 51*(7), 1304–14. http://doi.org/10.1093/rheumatology/ker523

Schulman-Green, D., Jaser, S., Martin, F., Alonzo, A., Grey, M., McCorkle, R., . . Whittemore, R. (2012). Processes of self-management in chronic illness. *Journal of Nursing Scholarship, 44*(2), 136–44. http://doi.org/10.1111/j.1547-5069.2012.01444.x

Sember, V., Starc, G., Jurak, G., Golobič, M., Kovač, M., Samardžija, P.P., & Morrison, S.A. (2016). Results from the Republic of Slovenia's 2016 report card on physical activity for children and youth. *Journal of Physical Activity and Health, 13*(11 Suppl 2), S256–S264. http://doi.org/10.1123/jpah.2016-0294

Shayeghian, Z., Hassanabadi, H., Aguilar-Vafaie, M.E., Amiri, P., & Besharat, M.A. (2016). A randomized controlled trial of acceptance and commitment therapy for type 2 diabetes management: The moderating role of coping styles. *PLOS ONE, 11*(12), e0166599. http://doi.org/10.1371/journal.pone.0166599

Shigaki, C.L., Smarr, K.L., Gong, Y., Donovan-Hanson, K., Siva, C., Johnson, R.A., . . . Musser, D.R. (2008). Social interactions in an online self-management program for rheumatoid arthritis. *Chronic Illness, 4*(4), 239–46. http://doi.org/10.1177/1742395308097862

Smart, C.M., Segalowitz, S.J., Mulligan, B.P., Koudys, J., & Gawryluk, J.R. (2016). Mindfulness training for older adults with subjective cognitive decline: Results from a pilot randomized controlled trial. *Journal of Alzheimer's Disease, 52*(2), 757–74. http://doi.org/10.3233/JAD-150992

Smeja, C., & Brassard, P. (2000). Tuberculosis infection in an Aboriginal (First Nations) population of Canada. *The International Journal of Tuberculosis and Lung Disease, 4*(10), 925–30.

Smith, J.E., Richardson, J., Hoffman, C., & Pilkington, K. (2005). Mindfulness-based stress reduction as supportive therapy in cancer care: systematic review. *Journal of Advanced Nursing, 52*(3), 315–27. http://doi.org/10.1111/j.1365-2648.2005.03592.x

Speca, M., Carlson, L.E., Goodey, E., & Angen, M. (2000). A randomized, wait-list controlled clinical trial: The effect of a mindfulness meditation-based stress reduction program on mood and symptoms of stress in cancer outpatients. *Psychosomatic Medicine, 62*(5), 613–22.

Srinath, A.I., Walter, C., Newara, M.C., & Szigethy, E.M. (2012). Pain management in patients with inflammatory bowel disease: Insights for the clinician. *Therapeutic Advances in Gastroenterology, 5*(5), 339–57. http://doi.org/10.1177/1756283X12446158

Stanford School of Medicine. (2017a). *Positive self-management program for HIV (PSMP).* Retrieved from http://patienteducation.stanford.edu/programs/psmp.html

Stanford School of Medicine. (2017b). S*tanford small-group self-management programs in English.* Retrieved from http://patienteducation.stanford.edu/programs/

Stanton, A.L., & Revenson, T.A. (2007). Adjustment to chronic disease: Progress and promise in research. In H.S. Friedman & R. Cohen Silver (Eds.), *Foundations of health psychology* (pp. 203–33). New York, NY: Oxford University Press.

Stanton, A.L., & Revenson, T.A. (2011). Adjustment to chronic disease: Progress and promise in research. In H.S. Friedman (Ed.), *The Oxford handbook of health psychology* (pp. 241–68). New York, NY: Oxford University Press.

Stanton, A.L., Revenson, T.A., & Tennen, H. (2007). Health psychology: Psychological adjustment to chronic disease. *Annual Review of Psychology, 58*(1), 565–92. http://doi.org/10.1146/annurev.psych.58.110405.085615

Statistics Canada. (2015a). *Asthma, 2014.* Retrieved from http://www.statcan.gc.ca/pub/82-625-x/2015001/article/14179-eng.htm

Statistics Canada. (2015b). *The 10 leading causes of death, 2011*. Retrieved from http://www.statcan.gc.ca/pub/82-625-x/2014001/article/11896-eng.htm

Statistics Canada. (2017). *Health fact sheets: Smoking, 2015*. Retrieved from http://www.statcan.gc.ca/pub/82-625-x/2017001/article/14770-eng.htm

Stone, A.A., Broderick, J.E., Porter, L.S., & Kaell, A.T. (1997). The experience of rheumatoid arthritis pain and fatigue: Examining momentary reports and correlates over one week. *Arthritis Care and Research, 10*(3), 185–93.

Straif, K., Baan, R., Grosse, Y., Secretan, B., El Ghissassi, F., Bouvard, V., . . . Cogliano, V. (2007). Carcinogenicity of shift-work, painting, and fire-fighting. *Lancet Oncology, 8*(12), 1065–6. http://dx.doi.org/10.1016/S1470-2045(07)70373-X

Strik, J.J.M. ., Lousberg, R., Cheriex, E.C., & Honig, A. (2004). One year cumulative incidence of depression following myocardial infarction and impact on cardiac outcome. *Journal of Psychosomatic Research, 56*(1), 59–66. http://doi.org/10.1016/S0022-3999(03)00380-5

Strine, T.W., & Chapman, D.P. (2005). Association of frequent sleep insufficiency with health-related quality of life and health behaviours. *Sleep Medicine, 6*(1), 23–7. https://doi.org/10.1016/j.sleep.2004.06.003

Suls, J., & Fletcher, B. (1985). The relative efficacy of avoidant and nonavoidant coping strategies: A meta-analysis. *Health Psychology, 4*, 249–88. doi: 10.1037//0278-6133.4.3.249

Sutin, A.R., Ferrucci, L., Zonderman, A.B., & Terracciano, A. (2011). Personality and obesity across the adult life span. *Journal of Personality and Social Psychology, 101*(3), 579–92. http://doi.org/10.1037/a0024286

Sutin, A.R., Zonderman, A.B., Ferrucci, L., & Terracciano, A. (2013). Personality traits and chronic disease: Implications for adult personality development. *The Journals of Gerontology Series B: Psychological Sciences and Social Sciences, 68*(6), 912–20. http://doi.org/10.1093/geronb/gbt036

Symister, P., & Friend, R. (2003). The influence of social support and problematic support on optimism and depression in chronic illness: A prospective study evaluating self-esteem as a mediator. *Health Psychology, 22*(2), 123–9. http://dx.doi.org/10.1037/0278-6133.22.2.123

Symplur. (2017). *Healthcare hashtag project*. Retrieved from https://www.symplur.com/healthcare-hashtags/

Targownik, L.E., Sexton, K.A., Bernstein, M.T., Beatie, B., Sargent, M., Walker, J.R., & Graff, L.A. (2015). The relationship among perceived stress, symptoms, and inflammation in persons with inflammatory bowel disease. *The American Journal of Gastroenterology, 110*(7), 1001–12. http://doi.org/10.1038/ajg.2015.147

Taylor, D.J., Mallory, L.J., Lichstein, K.L., Durrence, H.H., Riedel, B.W., & Bush, A.J. (2007). Comorbidity of chronic insomnia with medical problems. *Sleep, 30*(2), 213–8.

Terracciano, A., Löckenhoff, C.E., Crum, R.M., Bienvenu, O.J., & Costa, P.T. (2008). Five-factor model personality profiles of drug users. *BMC Psychiatry, 8*(1), 22. http://doi.org/10.1186/1471-244X-8-22

The Comfort Ability. (2016). *Online health chats*. Retrieved from https://www.thecomfortability.com/pages/online-health-chats

Timms, C., Forton, D., & Poullis, A. (2014). Social media use in patients with inflammatory bowel disease and chronic viral hepatitis. *Clinical Medicine, 14*(2), 215. http://doi.org/10.7861/clinmedicine.14-2-215

Tjepkema, M., Wilkins, R., Senécal, S., Guimond, E., & Penney, C. (2010). Mortality of urban Aboriginal adults in Canada, 1991–2001. *Chronic Diseases in Canada, 31*(1), 4–21.

Tremblay, M.S., Warburton, D.E.R., Janssen, I., Paterson, D.H., Latimer, A.E., Rhodes, R.E., . . . Duggan, M. (2011). New Canadian physical activity guidelines. *Applied Physiology, Nutrition, and Metabolism, 36*(1), 36–46. http://doi.org/10.1139/H11-009

Uchino, B.N. (2006). Social support and health: A review of physiological processes potentially underlying links to disease outcomes. *Journal of Behavioral Medicine, 29*(4), 377–87. http://doi.org/10.1007/s10865-006-9056-5

Van Dongen, H.P.A., Maislin, G., Mullington, J.M., & Dinges, D.F. (2003). The cumulative cost of additional wakefulness: Dose-response effects on neurobehavioral functions and sleep physiology from chronic sleep restriction and total sleep deprivation. *Sleep, 26*(2), 117–26.

Veehof, M.M., Oskam, M.-J., Schreurs, K.M.G., & Bohlmeijer, E.T. (2011). Acceptance-based interventions for the treatment of chronic pain: A systematic review and meta-analysis. *Pain, 152*(3), 533–42. http://doi.org/10.1016/j.pain.2010.11.002

Wagner, C.D., Bigatti, S.M., & Storniolo, A.M. (2006). Quality of life of husbands of women with breast cancer. *Psycho-Oncology, 15*(2), 109–20. http://doi.org/10.1002/pon.928

Wang, X., Ouyang, Y., Liu, J., Zhu, M., Zhao, G., Bao, W., & Hu, F.B. (2014). Fruit and vegetable consumption and mortality from all causes, cardiovascular disease, and cancer: Systematic review and dose-response meta-analysis of prospective cohort studies. *BMJ, 349*, g4490. http://doi.org/10.1136/bmj.g4490

Ward, B.W., Schiller, J.S., & Goodman, R.A. (2014). Multiple chronic conditions among US adults: A 2012 Update. *Preventing Chronic Disease, 11*, 130389. http://doi.org/10.5888/pcd11.130389

Webel, A.R., Lorig, K., Laurent, D., Gonzalez, V., Gifford, A.L., Sobel, D., & Minor, M. (2016). *Living a healthy life with HIV* (4th ed.). Boulder, CO: Bull Publishing.

Wehner, M.R., Chren, M.-M., Shive, M.L., Resneck, J.S., Pagoto, S., Seidenberg, A.B., & Linos, E. (2014). Twitter: An opportunity for public health campaigns. *The Lancet, 384*(9938), 131–2. http://doi.org/10.1016/S0140-6736(14)61161-2

Wetherell, J.L., Afari, N., Rutledge, T., Sorrell, J.T., Stoddard, J.A., Petkus, A.J., . . . Atkinson, H.J. (2011). A randomized, controlled trial of acceptance and commitment therapy and cognitive-behavioral therapy for chronic pain. *Pain, 152*(9), 2098–2107. http://doi.org/10.1016/j.pain.2011.05.016

Willems, S., De Maesschalck, S., Deveugele, M., Derese, A., & De Maeseneer, J. (2005). Socio-economic status of the patient and doctor-patient communication: Does it make a difference? *Patient Education and Counseling, 56*(2), 139–46. http://doi.org/10.1016/j.pec.2004.02.011

Willett, W.C., Koplan, J.P., Nugent, R., Dusenbury, C., Puska, P., & Gaziano, T.A. (2006). Prevention of chronic disease by means of diet and lifestyle changes. In D.T. Jamison, J.G. Breman, A.R. Measham, G. Alleyne, M. Claeson, D.B. Evans, . . . P. Musgrove (Eds.), *Disease control priorities in developing countries* (2nd ed.). Washington, DC: The World Bank.

Williams, D.R. (2002). Racial/ethnic variations in women's health: The social embeddedness of health. *American Journal of Public Health, 92*(4), 588–97.

Williamson, D.L., Stewart, M.J., Hayward, K., Letourneau, N., Makwarimba, E., Masuda, J., . . . Wilson, D. (2006). Low-income Canadians' experiences with health-related services: Implications for health care reform. *Health Policy, 76*(1), 106–21. http://doi.org/10.1016/j.healthpol.2005.05.005

Wilson, K.E., & Dishman, R.K. (2015). Personality and physical activity: A systematic review and meta-analysis. *Personality and Individual Differences, 72*, 230–42. http://doi.org/10.1016/j.paid.2014.08.023

Wilson, S.R., Scamagas, P., German, D.F., Hughes, G.W., Lulla, S., Coss, S., . . . Stancavage, F.B. (1993). A controlled trial of two forms of self-management education for adults with asthma. *The American Journal of Medicine, 94*(6), 564–76. https://doi.org/10.1016/0002-9343(93)90206-5

World Health Organization (WHO). (2003). *Adherence to long-term therapies: Evidence for Action*. Geneva. Retrieved from http://www.who.int/chp/knowledge/publications/adherence_full_report.pdf

World Health Organization (WHO). (2013). *WHO report on the global tobacco epidemic, 2013*. Geneva. Retrieved from http://doi.org/http://apps.who.int/iris/bitstream/10665/85380/1/9789241505871_eng.pdf

World Health Organization (WHO). (2017a). *Fact sheet about health benefits of smoking cessation*. Retrieved from http://www.who.int/tobacco/quitting/benefits/en/

World Health Organization (WHO). (2017b). *Health promotion*. Retrieved from http://www.who.int/topics/health_promotion/en/

World Health Organization (WHO). (2017c). *Noncommunicable diseases*. Retrieved from http://www.who.int/topics/noncommunicable_diseases/en/

Wortman, C.B., & Silver, R.C. (2001). The myths of coping with loss revisited. In M. S. Stroebe, R. . Hansson, W. Stroeve, & H. Schut (Eds.), *Handbook of Bereavement Research: Consequences, Coping, and Care* (pp. 402–29). Washington, DC: American Psychological Association.

Yamout, B., Itani, S., Hourany, R., Sibaii, A.M., & Yaghi, S. (2010). The effect of war stress on multiple sclerosis exacerbations and radiological disease activity. *Journal of the Neurological Sciences, 288*(1–2), 42–4. http://doi.org/10.1016/j.jns.2009.10.012

Yeom, J.H., Sim, C.S., Lee, J., Yun, S.H., Park, S.J., Yoo, C.I., & Sung, J.H. (2017). Effect of shift work on hypertension: Cross-sectional study. *Annals of Occupational and Environmental Medicine, 29*(11), http://doi.org/10.1186/s40557-017-0166-z

Younger, J., Aron, A., Parke, S., Chatterjee, N., & Mackey, S. (2010). Viewing pictures of a romantic partner reduces experimental pain: Involvement of neural reward systems. *PLOS ONE, 5*(10), e13309. http://doi.org/10.1371/journal.pone.0013309

Ziegelstein, R.C., Fauerbach, J.A., Stevens, S.S., Romanelli, J., Richter, D.P., & Bush, D.E. (2000). Patients with depression are less likely to follow recommendations to reduce cardiac risk during recovery from a myocardial infarction. *Archives of Internal Medicine, 160*, 1818–23.doi: 10.1001/archinte.160.12.1818

Chapter 9

Bailey, S.J., LaChapelle, D.L., LeFort, S.M., Gordon, A., & Hadjistavropoulos, T. (2013). Evaluation of chronic pain-related information available to consumers on the Internet. *Pain Medicine, 14*(6), 855–64.

Bair, M.J., Robinson, R.L., Katon, W., & Kroenke, K. (2003). Depression and pain comorbidity. *Archives of Internal Medicine, 163*, 2433–2445.

Bates, D. (2011, November 10). I thought, "I can't exist like this": George Clooney reveals how he contemplated suicide after agonizing spinal injury. *The Daily Mail*. Retrieved from http://www.dailymail.co.uk/tvshowbiz/article-2059563/George-Clooney-I-considered-suicide-agonising-spinal-injury.html

Bishop, S.R., Lau, M., Shapiro, S., Carlson, L., Anderson, N.D., Carmody, J., . . . Devins, G. (2004). Mindfulness: A proposed operational definition. *Clinical Psychology: Science and Practice, 11*, 230–41.

Boothby, J.L., Thorn, B.E., Overduin, L.Y., & Ward, L.C. (2004). Catastrophizing and perceived partner responses to pain. *Pain, 109*, 500–506.

Breau, L.M., Finley, G.A., McGrath, P.J. & Camfield, C.S. (2002). Validation of the non-communicating children's pain checklist—post operative version. *Anesthesiology, 96*, 528–35.

Breivik, H., Collett, B., Ventafridda, V., Cohen, R., & Gallacher, D. (2006). Survey of chronic pain in Europe: Prevalence, impact on daily life, and treatment. *European Journal of Pain 10*, 287–333.

Bruehl, S., & Chung, O.Y. (2004). Interactions between the cardiovascular systems: An updated review of mechanisms and possible alterations in chronic pain. *Neuroscience and Biobehavioral Reviews, 28*, 395–414.

Budell, L., Kunz, M., Jackson, P.L., & Rainville, P. (2015). Mirroring pain in the brain: Emotional expression versus motor imitation. *PLOS ONE, 10*(2), e0107526.

Canadian Pain Society (2011). *Call to action: The need for a national pain strategy for Canada*. Toronto: Author.

Cascella, M., & Muzio, M.R. (2017). Pain insensitivity in a child with a de novo interstitial deletion of the long arm of the chromosome 4: Case report. *Revista Chilena de Pediatria, 88*(3), 411–16.

Chambers, C.T., Craig, K.D., & Bennett, S.M. (2002). The impact of maternal behavior on children's pain experiences: An experimental analysis. *Journal of Pediatric Psychology, 27*, 293–301.

Cimmino, M.A., Ferrone, C., & Cutolo, M. (2011). Epidemiology of chronic musculoskeletal pain. *Best Practice and Research Clinical Rheumatology, 25*, 173–83.

Covic, T., Adamson, B., & Hough, M. (2000). The impact of passive coping on rheumatoid arthritis pain. *Rheumatology, 39*, 1027–30.

Craig, K.D. (1986). Social modeling influences: Pain in context. In R.A. Sternbach (Ed.), *The psychology of pain* (2nd ed., pp. 67–96). New York: Raven Press.

Craig, K.D., & Weiss, S.M. (1972). Verbal reports of pain without noxious stimulation. *Perceptual and Motor Skills, 34*, 943–8.

Day, M.A., Thorn, B.E., & Burns, J.W. (2012). The continuing evolution of biopsychosocial interventions for chronic. *Journal of Cognitive Psychotherapy, 26*, 114–29.

Dear, B. F., Titov, N., Perry, K. N., Johnston, L., Wootton, B. M., Terides, M. D., Hudson, J. L. (2013). The pain course: A randomised controlled trial of a clinician-guided Internet-delivered cognitive behaviour therapy program for managing chronic pain and emotional well-being. *Pain, 154*(6), 942–50.

Dube, A.A., Duquette, M., Roy, M., Lepore, F., Duncan, G., & Rainville, P. (2009). Brain activity associated with the electrodermal reactivity to acute heat pain. *NeuroImage, 45*, 169–180.

Dubuisson, D., & Melzack, R. (1976). Classification of clinical pain descriptions by multiple group discriminant analysis. *Experimental Neurology, 51*, 480–487.

Eccleston, C., Williams, A.C.D.C., & Morley S. (2009). Psychological therapies for the management of chronic pain (excluding headache) in adults. *Cochrane Database of Systematic Reviews*, UK: John Wiley & Sons.

Ehde, D.M., Dillworth, T.M. & Turner, J.A. (2014). Cognitive-behavioral therapy for individuals with chronic pain: Efficacy, innovations, and directions for research. *American Psychologist, 69*, 153–66.

Facco, E., Casiglia, E., Masiero, S., Tikhonoff, V., Giacomello, M., & Zanette, G. (2011). Effects of hypnotic focused analgesia on dental pain threshold. *International Journal of Clinical and Experimental Hypnosis, 59*, 454–68.

Faucett, J.A., & Levine, J.D. (1991). The contributions of interpersonal conflict to chronic pain in the presence or absence of organic pathology. *Pain, 44*, 35–43.

Flor, H., Knost, B., & Birbaumer, N. (2002). The role of operant conditioning in chronic pain: An experimental investigation. *Pain, 95*, 111–18.

Fordyce, W.E. (1976). *Behavioral methods for chronic pain and illness*. St Louis: Mosby.

Fordyce, W.E., Shelton, J.L., & Dundore, D.E. (1982). The modification of avoidance learning pain behaviors. *Journal of Behavioral Medicine, 5*, 405–14.

Fritz, J.M., George, S.Z., & Delitto, A. (2001). The role of fear-avoidance beliefs in acute low back pain: Relationships with current and future disability and work status. *Pain, 94*, 7–15.

Gallagher, R., & Beattie, B.L. (2019). The role of medications. In T. Hadjistavropoulos & H. Hadjistavropoulos (Eds.), *Pain management in older adults: A self-help guide* (2nd ed.), pp. 147–161. Philadelphia: Wolters Kluwer.

Gerrig, R.J., Zimbardo, P.G., Desmarais, S., & Ivanco, T. (2010). *Psychology and life*. Toronto: Pearson.

Guerriere, D.N., Choiniere, M., Dion, D., Peng, P., Stafford-Coyte, E., Zagorski, B., . . . Ware, M. (2010). The Canadian STOP-PAIN project—Part 2: What is the cost of pain for patients on waitlists of multidisciplinary pain treatment facilities? *Canadian Journal of Anesthesia, 57*, 549–58.

Gureje, O., Von Korff, M., Simon, G.E., & Gater, R. (1998). Persistent pain and well-being. *Journal of the American Medical Association, 280*, 147–51.

Hadjistavropoulos, H.D., Thompson, M., Ivanov, M., Drost, C., Butz, C.J., Klein, B., & Austin, D.W. (2011). Considerations in the development of a therapist-assisted Internet cognitive behavior therapy service. *Professional Psychology: Research and Practice, 42*, 463–71.

Hadjistavropoulos, T. (1999). Chronic pain on trial: The influence of compensation and litigation on chronic pain syndromes. In A.R. Block, E.F. Kremer, & E. Fernandez (Eds.), *Handbook of pain syndromes: Biopsychosocial perspectives* (pp. 59–76). Mahwah, NJ: Lawrence Erlbaum.

Hadjistavropoulos, T., Breau, L.M., & Craig, K.D. (2011). Assessment of pain in adults and children with limited ability to communicate. In D.C. Turk and R. Melzack (Eds.), *Handbook of pain assessment* (3rd ed., pp. 260–80). New York: Guilford.

Hadjistavropoulos, T., & Craig, K.D. (2002). A theoretical framework for understanding self-report and observational measures of pain: A communications model. *Behaviour Research and Therapy, 40*, 551–70.

Hadjistavropoulos, T., & Craig, K.D. (Eds.). (2004). *Pain: Psychological perspectives*. Mahwah, NJ: Lawrence Erlbaum.

Hadjistavropoulos, T., Craig, K.D., Duck, S., Cano, A., Goubert, L., Jackson, P., . . . Dever Fitzgerald, T. (2011). A biopsychosocial formulation of pain communication. *Psychological Bulletin, 137*, 910–939.

Hadjistavropoulos, T., Herr, K., Prkachin, K., Craig, K., Gibson, S., Lukas, L., & Smith, J. (2014). Pain assessment in elderly adults with dementia. *The Lancet Neurology, 13*, 1216–27.

Hadjistavropoulos, T., LaChapelle, D., MacLeod, F., Hale, C., O'Rourke, N., & Craig, K.D. (1998). Cognitive functioning and pain reactions in hospitalized elders. *Pain Research and Management, 3*, 145–51.

Hadjistavropoulos, T., von Baeyer, C., & Craig, K.D. (2001). Pain assessment in persons with limited ability to communicate. In D.C. Turk and R. Melzack (Eds.), *Handbook of pain assessment* (2nd ed., pp. 134–49). New York: Guilford.

Hale, C., & Hadjistavropoulos, T. (1997). Emotional components of pain. *Pain Research and Management, 2*, 217–25.

Hanley, M.A., Jensen, M.P., Ehde, D.M., Hoffman, A.J., Patterson, D.R., & Robinson, L.R. (2004). Psychosocial predictors of long-term adjustment to lower-limb amputation and phantom limb pain. *Disability and Rehabilitation, 26*, 882–93.

Hayes, S.C., Strosahl, K.D. & Wilson, K.G. (2012). *Acceptance and commitment therapy: The process and practice of mindful change* (2nd ed.). New York: Guilford Press.

Haythornthwaite, J.A., Clark, M.R., Pappagallo, M., & Raja, S.N. (2003). Pain coping strategies play a role in the persistence of pain in post-herpetic neuralgia. *Pain, 106*, 453–60.

Henschke, N., Ostello, R.W.J.G., val Tulder, M.W., Vlaeyen, J.W.S., Morley, S., Assendelft, W.J.J., & Main, C.J. (2010). Behavioural treatment for chronic low-back pain. *Cochrane Database of Systematic Reviews*, UK: John Wiley & Sons.

Institute of Medicine, Committee on Advancing Pain Research, Care, and Education. (2011). *Relieving pain in America: Blue for transforming prevention, care, education, and research*. Washington: National Academies Press.

Jensen, M.P., Moore, M.R., Bockow, T.B., Ehde, D.M., & Engel, J.M. (2011). Psychosocial factors and adjustment to chronic pain in persons with physical disabilities: A systematic review. *Archives of Physical Medicine and Rehabilitation, 92*(1), 146–60.

Jolliffe, C.D., & Nicholas, M.K. (2004). Verbally reinforcing pain reports: An experimental test of the operant model of chronic pain. *Pain, 107*, 167–75.

Kerns, R. D., Rosenberg, R., & Otis, J. D. (2002). Self-appraised problem solving and pain-relevant social support as predictors of the experience of chronic pain. *Annals of Behavioral Medicine, 24*(2), 100–5.

Koranyi, S., Barth, J., Trelle, S., Strauss, B.M., & Rosendahl, J. (2014). Psychological interventions for acute pain after open heart surgery. *Cochrane Database of Systematic Reviews*, UK: John Wiley & Sons.

LaChapelle, D.L., Lavoie, S., Higgins, N.C., & Hadjistavropoulos, T. (2014). Attractiveness, diagnostic ambiguity, and disability cues impact perceptions of women with pain. *Rehabilitation Psychology, 59*(2), 162–70.

Lamm, C., Decety, J., & Singer, T. (2011). Meta-analytic evidence for common and distinct neural networks associated with directly experienced pain and empathy for pain. *NeuroImage, 54*(3), 2492–2502.

Li, A., Montaño, Z., Chen, V.J., & Gold, J.I. (2011). Virtual reality and pain management: Current trends and future directions. *Pain Management, 1*, 147–57.

Linton, S.J. (2005). Do psychological factors increase the risk for back pain in the general population in both a cross-sectional and prospective analysis? *European Journal of Pain, 9*, 355–61.

Loeser, J.D., & Melzack, R. (1999). Pain: an overview. *Lancet, 353*, 1607–1609.

Loeser, J. D., & Treede, R. D. (2008). The Kyoto protocol of IASP basic pain terminology. *Pain, 137*(3), 473–7.

Macea, D.D., Gajos, K., Daglia Calil, Y.A., & Fregni, F. (2010). The efficacy of web-based cognitive behavioral interventions for chronic pain: A systematic review and meta-analysis. *Journal of Pain, 11*, 917–29.

MacLeod, F., LaChapelle, D., Hadjistavropoulos, T., & Pfeifer, J. (2001). The effect of disability claimants' coping styles on judgments of pain, disability and compensation. *Rehabilitation Psychology, 46*, 417–35.

McCracken, L.M. (2005). Social context and acceptance of chronic pain: The role of solicitous and punishing responses. *Pain, 113*, 155–9.

McGrath, P. (1998). We all failed the Latimers. *Journal of Paediatrics and Child Health, 2*, 153–4.

Melzack, R. (1975). The McGill Pain Questionnaire: Major properties and scoring methods. *Pain, 1*, 277–99.

Melzack, R. (2001). Pain and the neuromatrix in the brain. *Journal of Dental Education, 65*, 1378–82.

Melzack, R. (2005). Evolution of the neuromatrix theory of pain. The Prithvi Raj lecture: Presented at the Third World Congress of World Institute of Pain, Barcelona 2004. *Pain Practice, 5*, 85–94.

Melzack, R., & Katz, J. (2004). The gate control theory: Reaching for the brain. In T. Hadjistavropoulos & K.D. Craig (Eds.), *Pain: psychological perspectives* (pp. 13–34). Mahwah, NJ: Lawrence Erlbaum.

Melzack, R., Terrence, C., Fromm, G., & Amsel, R. (1986). Trigeminal neuralgia and atypical facial pain: Use of the McGill Pain Questionnaire for discrimination and diagnosis. *Pain, 27*, 297–302.

Melzack, R., & Wall, P.D. (1965). Pain mechanisms: A new theory. *Science, 150*, 971–9.

Melzack, R., & Wall, P.D. (2004). *The challenge of pain*. London: Penguin Global.

Merskey, H., & Bogduk, N. (Eds.). (1994). *Classification of chronic pain: Descriptions of chronic pain syndromes and definitions of pain terms*. Seattle: IASP Press.

Meulders, A., Vansteenwegen, D., & Vlaeyen, J.W.S. (2011). The acquisition of fear of movement-related pain and associative learning: A novel pain-relevant human fear conditioning paradigm. *Pain, 152*, 2460–9.

Miller, L.R., & Cano, A. (2009). Comorbid chronic pain and depression: Who is at risk? *Journal of Pain, 10*, 619–27.

Morasco, B.J., Corson, K., Turk, D.C., & Dobscha, S.K. (2011). Association between substance use disorder status related function following 12 months of treatment in primary care patients with musculoskeletal pain. *Journal of Pain, 12*, 352–9.

Moseley, G.L. (2011). A new direction for the fear avoidance model? *Pain, 152*, 2447–28.

National Center for Health Statistics (2006). *Health, United States, 2006. With chartbook on trends in the health of Americans*. Hyattsville, MD: Author.

Nayak, S., Shiflett, S.C., Eshun, S., & Levine, F.M. (2000). Culture and gender effects in pain beliefs and the prediction of pain tolerance. *Cross-Cultural Research, 34*, 135–151.

Phillips, C.J., & Schopflocher, D. (2008). The economics of chronic pain. In S. Rashiq, D. Schopflocher, P. Taenzer, & E. Jonsson (Eds.), *Chronic pain: A health policy perspective* (pp. 41–50). Weinheim, Germany: Wiley.

Picavet, H.S., Vlaeyen, J.W., & Schouten, J.S. (2002). Pain catastrophizing and kinesiophobia: Predictors of chronic low back pain. *American Journal of Epidemiology, 156*, 1028–34.

Piva, S.R., Fitzgerald, G.K., Wisniewski, S. & Delitto, A. (2009). Predictors of pain and function outcome in patients with patellofemoral pain syndrome. *Journal of Rehabilitation Medicine, 8*, 604–12.

Price, D.D. (2000). Psychological and neural mechanisms of the affective dimension of pain. *Science, 288*, 1769–72.

Prkachin, K.M., & Craig, K.D. (1994). Expressing pain: The communication and interpretation of facial pain signals. *Journal of Nonverbal Behavior, 19*, 191–205.

Rainville, P. (2002). Brain mechanisms of pain affect and pain modulation. *Current Opinion in Neurobiology, 12*, 195–204.

Rosenthal, R. (1982). Conducting judgement studies. In K. Scherer & P. Ekman (Eds.), *Handbook of methods in nonverbal behavior research* (pp. 287–361). New York: Cambridge University Press.

Ruskin, D.A., Amaria, K.A., Warnock, F.F., & McGrath, P.A. (2001). Assessment of pain in infants, children, and adolescents. In D.C. Turk & R. Melzack (Eds.), *Handbook of pain assessment* (3rd ed., pp. 213–41). New York: Guilford Press.

Schopflocher, D., Taenzer, P., & Jovey, R. (2011). The prevalence of chronic pain in Canada. *Pain Research and Management, 16*, 445–50.

Schwartz, L., Jensen, M. P., & Romano, J. M. (2005). The development and psychometric evaluation of an instrument to assess spouse responses to pain and well behavior in patients with chronic pain: The spouse response inventory. *The Journal of Pain, 6*(4), 243–52.

Sessle, B. (2011). Unrelieved pain: A crisis. *Pain Research and Management, 16*, 16–20.

Sharp, T.J. (2001). Chronic pain: A reformulation of the cognitive-behavioural model. *Behaviour Research and Therapy, 39*, 787–800.

Skinner, M., Wilson, H.D., & Turk, D.C. (2012). Cognitive-behavioral perspective and cognitive-behavioral therapy for people with chronic pain—Distinctions, outcomes, & innovations. *Journal of Cognitive Psychotherapy, 26*, 93–113.

Stanford, E.A., Chambers, C.T., Biesanz, J.C., & Chen, E. (2008). The frequency, trajectories and predictors of adolescent recurrent pain: A population-based approach. *Pain, 138*, 11–21.

Staud, R., Craggs, J.G., Robinson, M.E., Perlstein, W.M., & Price, D.D. (2007). Brain activity related to temporal summation of c-fibre evoked pain. *Pain, 129*, 130–142.

Sullivan, M.J.L., Bishop, S.R., & Pivik, J. (1995). The pain catastrophizing scale: Development and validation. *Psychological Assessment, 7*, 524–32.

Sullivan, M.J.L., Feuerstein, M., Gatchel, R., Linton, S.J., & Pransky, G. (2005). Integrating psychosocial and behavioral interventions to achieve optimal rehabilitation outcomes. *Journal of Occupational Rehabilitation, 15*, 475–89.

Tsang, A., Von Korff, M., Lee, S., Alonso, J., Karam, E., Angermeyer, M.C., . . . Watanabe, M. (2008). Common chronic pain conditions in developed and developing countries: Gender and age differences and comorbidity with depression-anxiety disorders. *Journal of Pain, 9*, 883–91.

Turk, D.C., Meichenbaum, D., & Genest, M. (1987). *Pain and behavioral medicine: A cognitive-behavioral perspective.* New York: Guilford Press.

Turk, D.C., & Melzack, R. (2011). The measurement of pain and the assessment of people experiencing pain. In D.C. Turk & R. Melzack (Eds.), *Handbook of pain assessment* (3rd ed., pp. 242–59). New York: Guilford Press.

Turk, D.C., Wilson, H.D., & Cahana, A. (2011). Treatment of chronic non-cancer pain. *Lancet, 377*, 2226–35.

Veehof, M.M., Oskam, M.J., Schreurs, K.M., & Bohlmeijer, E.T. (2011). Acceptance-based interventions for the treatment of chronic pain: A systematic review and meta-analysis. *Pain, 152*, 533–42.

Vlaeyen, J.W.S., & Linton, S.J. (2000). Fear-avoidance and its consequences in chronic musculoskeletal pain: A state of the art. *Pain, 85*, 317–32.

Waddell, G. (1987). A new clinical model for the treatment of low-back pain. *Spine, 12*, 632–44.

Waddell, G. (1991). Low back disability. A syndrome of Western civilization. *Neurosurgery Clinics of North America, 2*, 719–38.

Waddell, G. (1992). Biopsychosocial analysis of low back pain. *Clinical Rheumatology, 6*, 523–57.

Waddell, G., Newton, M., Henderson, I., Somerville, D., & Main, C.J. (1993). A fear-avoidance beliefs questionnaire (FABQ) and the role of fear-avoidance in chronic low back pain and disability. *Pain, 52*, 157–68.

Wenn. (2012, April 17). George Clooney reveals extent of back pain, and tortuous medical sessions that made him want to die. *The Huffington Post UK.* Retrieved from http://www.huffingtonpost.co.uk/2012/02/17/george-clooney-back-surgery-syriana_n_1283856.html

Chapter 10

Aboa-Éboulé, C., Brisson, C., Blanchette, C., Maunsell, E., Bourbonnais, R., Abdous, B., . . . Dagenais, G.R. (2011). Effort-reward imbalance at work and psychological distress: A validation study of post-myocardial infarction patients. *Psychosomatic Medicine, 73*, 448–55.

Aboa-Éboulé, C., Brisson, C., & Maunsell, E. (2011). Effort-reward imbalance at work and recurrent coronary heart disease events: A 4-year prospective study of post-myocardial infarction patients. *Psychosomatic Medicine, 73*, 436–47.

Aboa-Éboulé, C., Brisson, C., Maunsell, E., Mâsse, B., Bourbonnais, R., Vézina, M., . . . Dagenais, G.R. (2007). Job strain and risk of acute recurrent coronary heart disease events. *Journal of American Medical Association, 298*, 1652–60.

Ahmadi, N., Hajsadeghi, F., Mirshkarlo, H.B., Budoff, M., Yehuda, R., & Ebrahimi, R. (2011). Post-traumatic stress disorder, coronary atherosclerosis, and mortality. *American Journal of Cardiology, 108*, 29–33.

Akashi, Y.J., Nef, H.M., & Lyon, A.R. (2015). Epidemiology and pathophysiology of takotsubo syndrome. *Nature Reviews Cardiology, 12*, 387–97.

Albert, C.M., Chae, C.V., Rexrode, K.M., Manson, J.E., & Kawachi, I. (2005). Phobic anxiety and risk of coronary heart disease and sudden cardiac death among women. *Circulation, 111*, 480–7.

Aldwin, C.M. (1994). *Stress, coping, and development: An integrative perspective.* New York: Guilford Press.

Allgulander C. (2016). Anxiety as a risk factor in cardiovascular disease. *Current Opinion in Psychiatry, 29*, 13–17.

Allegra, J.R., Mostashari, F., Rothman, J., Milano, P., & Cochrane, D.G. (2005). Cardiac events in New Jersey after the

September 11, 2001, terrorist attack. *Journal of Urban Health: Bulletin of the New York Academy of Medicine, 82*, 358–63.

Alter, D.A., Ko, D.T., Tu, J.V., Stukel, T.A., Lee, D.S., Laupacis, A., . . . Austin, P.C. (2012). The average lifespan of patients discharged from hospital with heart failure. *Journal of General Internal Medicine, 27*, 1171–79.

American Heart Association. (2014). *Warning signs of heart attack, stroke & cardiac arrest.* Retrieved from www.heart.org/HEARTORG/Conditions/Conditions_UCM_305346_SubHomePage.jsp

American Heart Association. (2016). *Is broken heart syndrome real?* Retrieved from http://www.heart.org/HEARTORG/Conditions/More/Cardiomyopathy/Is-Broken-Heart-Syndrome-Real_UCM_448547_Article.jsp#.Who378aZO8U

American Psychiatric Association. (2013). *Diagnostic and statistical manual of mental disorders* (5th ed.). Arlington, VA: American Psychiatric Publishing.

Anand, S.S., Islam, S., Rosengren, A., Franzosi, M.G., Steyn, K., Yusufali, A.H., . . . Yusuf, S. (2008). Risk factors for myocardial infarction in women and men: Insights from the INTERHEART study. *European Heart Journal, 29*, 932–40.

Andersson, G., Hesser, H., Veilord, A., Svedling, L., Andersson, F., Sleman, O., . . . Lamminen, M. (2013). Randomised controlled non-inferiority trial with 3-year follow-up of internet-delivered versus face-to-face group cognitive behavioural therapy for depression. *Journal of Affective Disorders, 151*, 986–94.

Anderson, L., & Taylor, R.S. (2014). Cardiac rehabilitation for people with heart disease: An overview of Cochrane systematic reviews. *The Cochrane Database of Systematic Reviews, 12*, CD011273.

Andrews, G., Cuijpers, P., Craske, M. G., McEvoy, P., & Titov, N. (2010). Computer therapy for the anxiety and depressive disorders is effective, acceptable and practical health care: A meta-analysis. *PLOS ONE, 5*, e13196.

Antman, E.M., Anbe, D.T., Armstrong, P.W., Bates, E.R., Green, L.A., Hand, M., . . . Jacobs, A.K. (2004). ACC/AHA guidelines for the management of patients with ST-elevation myocardial infarction-executive summary: A report of the American College of Cardiology/American Heart Association Task Force on Practice Guidelines (Writing Committee to Revise the 1999 Guidelines for the Management of Patients With Acute Myocardial Infarction). *Circulation, 110*, 588–636.

Azar, K.M., Lesser, L.I., Laing, B.Y., Stephens, J., Aurora, M.S., Burke, L.E., & Palaniappan, L.P. (2013). Mobile applications for weight management: Theory-based content analysis. *American Journal of Preventive Medicine, 45*, 583–9.

Barefoot, J.C., Peterson, B.L., & Harrell, F.E. (1989). Type A behaviour and survival: A follow-up study of 1,467 patients with coronary artery disease. *American Journal of Cardiology, 64*, 427–32.

Barth, J., Schumacher, M., & Herrmann-Lingen, C. (2004). Depression as a risk factor for mortality in patients with coronary heart disease: A meta-analysis. *Psychosomatic Medicine, 66*, 802–13.

Berkman, L.F., Blumental, J., Burg, M., Carney, R.M., Catellier, D., Cowan, M.J., . . . Schneiderman, N.

(2003). Effects of treating depression and low perceived social support on clinical events after myocardial infarction: The Enhancing Recovery in Coronary Heart Disease Patients (ENRICHD) Randomized Trial. *Journal of the American Medical Association, 289*, 3106–16.

Blumenthal, J.A., Sherwood, A., Babyak, M.A., Watkins, L.L., Waugh, R., Georgiades, A., . . . Hinderliter, A. (2005). Effects of exercise and stress management training on markers of cardiovascular risk in patients with ischemic heart disease: A randomized controlled trial. *Journal of the American Medical Association, 293*, 1626–34.

Blumenthal, J.A., Sherwood, A., Smith, P.J., Watkins, L., Mabe, S., Kraus, W.E., . . . Hinderliter, A. (2016). Enhancing cardiac rehabilitation with stress management training: A randomized, clinical efficacy trial. *Circulation, 133*, 1341–50.

Blumenthal, J.A., Wang, J.T., Babyak, M., Watkins, L., Kraus, W., Miller, P., . . . Sherwood, A. (2010). Enhancing standard cardiac rehabilitation with stress management training: Background, methods, and design for the enhanced study. *Journal of Cardiopulmonary Rehabilitation and Prevention, 30*, 77–84.

Boehm, J.K., & Kubzansky, L.D. (2012). The heart's content: The association between positive psychological well-being and cardiovascular health. *Psychological Bulletin, 138*, 655–91.

Bradley, S.M., & Rumsfeld, J.S. (2015). Depression and cardiovascular disease. *Trends in Cardiovascular Medicine, 25*, 614–22.

Burg, M.M., Barefoot, J., Berkman, L., Catellier, D.J., Czajkowski, S., Saab, P., . . . Taylor, C.B. (2005). Low perceived social support and post-myocardial infarction prognosis in the enhancing recovery in coronary heart disease clinical trial: The effects of treatment. *Psychosomatic Medicine, 67*, 879–88.

Burke, L.E., Ma, J., Azar, K.M., Bennett, G.G., Peterson, E.D., Zheng, Y., . . . Quinn, C.C. (2015). Current science on consumer use of mobile health for cardiovascular disease prevention: A scientific statement from the American Heart Association. *Circulation, 132*, 1157–1213.

Cahill, M.C., Bilanovic, A., Kelly, S., Bacon, S., & Grace, S.L. (2015). Screening for depression in cardiac rehabilitation: A review. *Journal of Cardiopulmonary Rehabilitation and Prevention, 35*, 225–30.

Carey, I.M., Shah, S.M., DeWilde, S., Harris, T., Victor, C.R., & Cook, D.G. (2014). Increased risk of acute cardiovascular events after partner bereavement: A matched cohort study. *JAMA Internal Medicine, 174*, 598–605.

Carney, R.M., Blumenthal, J.A., Freedland, K.E., Youngblood, M., Veith, R.C., Burg, M.M., . . . Jaffe, A.S. (2004). Depression and later mortality after myocardial infarction in the Enhancing Recovery in Coronary Heart Disease (ENRICHD) study. *Psychosomatic Medicine, 66*, 466–474.

Carney, R.M., & Freedland, K.E. (2017). Depression and coronary heart disease. *Nature Reviews Cardiology, 14*, 145–55.

Caro, M.A., Rosenthal, J.L., Kendall, K., Pozuelo, L., & Funk, M.C. (2016). What the psychiatrist needs to know about ventricular assist devices: A comprehensive review. *Psychosomatics, 57*, 229–37.

Chan, I.W.S., Lai, J.C.L., & Wong, K.W.N. (2006). Resilience is associated with better recovery in Chinese people diagnosed with coronary artery disease. *Psychology & Health, 21*, 335–349.

Chida, Y., & Steptoe, A. (2009). The association of anger and hostility with future coronary heart disease: A meta-analytic review of prospective evidence. *Journal of the American College of Cardiology, 53*, 936–946.

Cossette, S., Frasure-Smith, N., & Lespérance, F. (2001). Clinical implications of a reduction in psychological distress on cardiac prognosis in patients participating in a psychosocial intervention program. *Psychosomatic Medicine, 63*, 257–66.

Cowan, M.J., Freedland, K.E., Burg, M.M., Saab, P.G., Youngblood, M.E., Cornell, C.E., & Czajkowski, S.M. (2008). Predictors of treatment response for depression and inadequate social support—The ENRICHD randomized clinical trial. *Psychotherapy and Psychosomatics, 77*, 27–37.

Cuijpers, P., Donker, T., van Straten, A., Li, J., & Andersson, G. (2010). Is guided self-help as effective as face-to-face psychotherapy for depression and anxiety disorders? A systematic review and meta-analysis of comparative outcome studies. *Psychological Medicine, 40*, 1943–57.

Czarny, M.J., Arthurs, E., Coffie, D.F., Smith, C., Steele, R.J., Ziegelstein, R.C., & Thombs, B.D. (2011). Prevalence of antidepressant prescription or use in patients with acute coronary syndrome: A systematic review. *PLOS ONE, 6*, e27671.

Davidson, K.W., Bigger, J.T., Burg, M.M., Carney, R.M., Chaplin, W.F., Czajkowski, S., . . . Ye, S. (2013). Centralized, stepped, patient preference-based treatment for patients with post-acute coronary syndrome depression: CODIACS vanguard randomized controlled trial. *JAMA Internal Medicine, 173*, 997–1004.

Davies, E., Moxham, T.I., Rees, K., Singh, S., Coats, A.S., Ebrahim, S., . . . Taylor, R.S. (2010). Exercise training for systolic heart failure: Cochrane systematic review and meta-analysis. *European Journal of Heart Failure, 12*, 706–15.

Deforche, B., Van Dyck, D., Deliens, T., & De Bourdeaudhuij, I. (2015). Changes in weight, physical activity, sedentary behaviour and dietary intake during the transition to higher education: A prospective study. *International Journal of Behavioral Nutrition and Physical Activity, 12*, 1–10.

de Jonge, P., Ormel, J., van den Brink, R.H., van Melle, J.P., Spikerman, T.A., Kuijper, A., . . . Schene, A.H. (2006). Symptom dimensions of depression following myocardial infarction and their relationship with somatic health status and cardiovascular prognosis. *American Journal of Psychiatry, 163*, 138–44.

Denollet, J. (2005). DS14: Standard assessment of negative affectivity, social inhibition, and Type D personality. *Psychosomatic Medicine, 67*, 89–97.

Denollet, J., & Brutsaert, D.L. (1998). Personality, disease severity, and the risk of long-term cardiac events in patients with a decreased ejection fraction after myocardial infarction. *Circulation, 97*, 167–73.

de Voogd, J.N., Sanderman, R., & Coyne, J.C. (2012). A meta-analysis of spurious associations between type D personality and cardiovascular disease endpoints. *Annals of Behavioral Medicine, 44*, 136–7.

Dickens, C.M., McGowan, L., Percival, C., Douglas, J., Tomenson, B., Cotter, L., . . . Creed, F.H. (2004). Lack of a close confidant, but not depression, predicts further cardiac events after myocardial infarction. *Heart, 90*, 518–22.

Donker, T., Bennett, K., Bennett, A., Mackinnon, A., van Straten, A., Cuijpers, P., . . . Griffiths, K.M. (2013). Internet-delivered interpersonal psychotherapy versus internet-delivered cognitive behavioral therapy for adults with depressive symptoms: Randomized controlled noninferiority trial. *Journal of Medical Internet Research, 15*, e82.

DuBois, C.M., Beach, S.R., Kashdan, T.B., Nyer, M.B., Park, E.R., Celano, C.M., & Huffman, J.C. (2012). Positive psychological attributes and cardiac outcomes: Associations, mechanisms, and interventions. *Psychosomatics, 53*, 303–18.

DuBois, C.M., Lopez, O.V., Beale, E.E., Healy, B.C., Boehm, J.K., & Huffman, J.C. (2015). Relationships between positive psychological constructs and health outcomes in patients with cardiovascular disease: A systematic review. *International Journal of Cardiology, 195*, 265–80.

Douglas, G., & Channon, K.M. (2014). The pathogenesis of atherosclerosis. *Medicine, 42*, 480–4.

Eaker, E.D., Sullivan, L.M., Kelley-Hayes, M., D'Agostino, R.B., & Benjamin, E.J. (2007). Marital status, marital strain, and risk of coronary heart disease of total mortality: The Framingham Offspring Study. *Psychosomatic Medicine, 69*, 509–13.

Feinstein, M., Ning, H., Kang, J., Bertoni, A., Carnethon, M., & Lloyd-Jones, D.M. (2012). Racial differences in risks for first cardiovascular events and noncardiovascular death: The atherosclerosis risk in communities study, the cardiovascular health study, and the multi-ethnic study of atherosclerosis. *Circulation, 126*, 50–9.

Ferris, P.A, Kline, T.J., & Bourdage, J.S. (2012). He said, she said: Work, biopsychosocial, and lifestyle contributions to coronary heart disease risk. *Health Psychology, 31*, 503–11.

Fiedorowicz, J.G., He, J., & Merikangas, K.R. (2011). The association between mood and anxiety disorders with vascular diseases and risk factors in a nationally representative sample. *Journal of Psychosomatic Research, 70*, 145–54.

Fleet, R., Lavoie, K., & Beitman, B.D. (2000). Is panic disorder associated with coronary artery disease? A critical review of the literature. *Journal of Psychosomatic Research, 48*, 347–56.

Frasure-Smith, N., & Lespérance, F. (2008). Depression and anxiety as predictors of 2-year cardiac events in patients with stable coronary artery disease. *Archives of General Psychiatry, 65*, 62–71.

Frasure-Smith, N., Lespérance, F., & Talajic, M. (1995). The impact of negative emotions on prognosis following myocardial infarction: Is it more than depression? *Health Psychology, 14*, 388–98.

Freedland, K.E., Hesseler, M.J., Carney, R.M., Steinmeyer, B.C., Skala, J.A., Dávila-Román, V.G., & Rich, M.W. (2016). Major depression and long-term survival of patients with heart failure. *Psychosomatic Medicine, 78*, 896–903.

Freedland, K.E., Skala, J.A., Carney, R.M., Raczynski, J.M., Taylor, C.B., Mendes de Leon, C.F., . . . Veith, R.C. (2002). The Depression Interview and Structured Hamilton (DISH):

Rationale, development, characteristics, and clinical validity. *Psychosomatic Medicine, 64*, 897–905.

Friedman, M., & Rosenman, R.H. (1959). Association of specific overt behaviour pattern with blood and cardiovascular findings: Blood cholesterol level, blood clotting time, incidence of arcus senilis, and clinical coronary artery disease. *Journal of the American Medical Association, 169*, 1286–96.

Friedmann, E., & Thomas, A. (1995). Pet ownership, social support, and one-year survival after acute myocardial infarction in the cardiac arrhythmia suppression trial (CAST). *American Journal of Cardiology, 76*, 1213–17.

Garcia-Retamero, R., Petrova, D., Arrebola-Moreno, A., Catena, A., & Ramírez-Hernández, J.A. (2016). Type D personality is related to severity of acute coronary syndrome in patients with recurrent cardiovascular disease. *British Journal of Health Psychology, 21*, 694–711.

Gerin, W., Chaplin, W., Schwartz, J.E., Holland, J., Alter, R., Wheeler, D., . . . Pickering, T.G. (2005). Sustained blood pressure increase after an acute stressor: The effects of the 11 September 2001 attack on the New York City World Trade Center. *Journal of Hypertension, 23*, 279–84.

Ghisi, G.L., Abdallah, F., Grace, S.L., Thomas, S., & Oh, P. (2014). A systematic review of patient education in cardiac patients: Do they increase knowledge and promote health behavior change? *Patient Education and Counseling, 95*, 160–74.

Ghisi, G.L., Polyzotis, P., Oh, P., Pakosh, M., & Grace, S.L. (2013). Physician factors affecting cardiac rehabilitation referral and patient enrollment: A systematic review. *Clinical Cardiology, 36*, 323–35.

Gilbody, S., House, A., & Sheldon, T. (2005). Screening and case finding instruments for depression. *Cochrane Database of Systematic Reviews, 4*, CD002792.

Gilbody, S., Sheldon, T., & House, A. (2008). Screening and case-finding instruments for depression: A meta-analysis. *Canadian Medical Association Journal, 178*, 997–1003.

Glassman, A.H., Bigger, J.T., & Gaffney, M. (2009). Psychiatric characteristics associated with long-term mortality among 361 patients having an acute coronary syndrome and major depression: Seven-year follow-up of SADHART participants. *Archives of General Psychiatry, 66*, 1022–9.

Glassman, A.H., O'Connor, C.M., Califf, R.M., Swedberg, K., Schwartz, P., Bigger, J.T., . . . McIvor, M. (2002). Sertraline treatment of major depression in patients with acute MI or unstable angina. *Journal of the American Medical Association, 288*, 701–9.

Glozier, N., Christensen, H., Naismith, S., Cockayne, N., Donkin, L., Neal, B., . . . Hickie, I. (2013). Internet-delivered cognitive behavioural therapy for adults with mild to moderate depression and high cardiovascular disease risks: A randomised attention-controlled trial. *PLOS ONE, 8*, e59139.

Grace, S.L., Abbey, S.E., Pinto, R., Shnek, Z.M., Irvine, J., & Stewart, D.E. (2005). Longitudinal course of depressive symptomology after a cardiac event: Effects of gender and cardiac rehabilitation. *Psychosomatic Medicine, 67*, 52–8.

Grace, S.L., Turk-Adawi, K.I., Contractor, A., Atrey, A., Campbell, N., Derman, W., . . . Sarrafzadegan, N. (2016). Cardiac rehabilitation delivery model for low-resource settings. *Heart, 102*, 1449–55.

Grace, S.L., Turk-Adawi, K., Santiago Pio, C., & Alter, D.A. (2016). Ensuring cardiac rehabilitation access for the majority of those in need: A call to action for Canada. *Canadian Journal of Cardiology, 32*, S358–S364.

Grande, G., Romppel, M., Vesper, J.M., Schubmann, R., Glaesmer, H., & Herrmann-Lingen, C. (2011). Type D personality and all-cause mortality in cardiac patients—Data from a German cohort study. *Psychosomatic Medicine, 73*, 548–56.

Griggs, R.A. (2017). *Psychology: A concise introduction.* New York, NY: Macmillan.

Gulliksson, M., Burell, G., Vessby, B., Lundin, L., Toss, H., & Svärdsudd, K. (2011). Randomized controlled trial of cognitive behavioural therapy vs. standard treatment to prevent recurrent cardiovascular events in patients with coronary artery disease: Secondary Prevention in Uppsala Primary Health Care project (SUPRIM). *Archives of Internal Medicine, 171*, 134–40.

Haley, W.E., Roth, D.L., Howard, G., & Safford, M.M. (2010). Caregiving strain and estimated risk for stroke and coronary heart disease among spouse caregivers: Differential effects by race and sex. *Stroke, 41*, 331–6.

Hare, D.L., Toukhsati, S.R., Johansson, P., & Jaarsma, T. (2014). Depression and cardiovascular disease: A clinical review. *European Heart Journal, 35*, 1365–72.

Haupt, C.M., Alte, D., Dorr, M. Robinson, D.M., Felix, S.B., John, U., & Völzke, H. (2008). The relation of exposure to shift work with atherosclerosis and myocardial infarction in a general population. *Atherosclerosis, 201*, 205–11.

Hedman, E., Ljótsson, B., & Lindefors, N. (2012). Cognitive behavior therapy via the Internet: A systematic review of applications, clinical efficacy and cost–effectiveness. *Expert Review of Pharmacoeconomics & Outcomes Research, 12*, 745–64.

Helsel, D.L., Jakicic, J.M., & Otto, A.D. (2007). Comparison of techniques for self-monitoring eating and exercise behaviors on weight loss in a correspondence-based intervention. *Journal of the American Dietetic Association, 107*, 1807–10.

Hemingway, H., & Marmot, M. (1999). Evidence-based cardiology: Psychosocial factors in the aetiology and prognosis of coronary artery disease: Systematic review of prospective cohort studies. *British Medical Journal, 318*, 1460–7.

Heron, M. (2016). Deaths: Final data for 2013. *National Vital Statistics Reports, 65, 1–95.*

Herrmann, C., Brand-Driehorst, S., Buss, U., & Ruger, U. (2000). Effects of anxiety and depression on 5-year mortality in 5,057 patients referred for exercise testing. *Journal of Psychosomatic Research, 48*, 455–62.

Honig, A., Kuyper, A.M., Schene, A.H., van Melle, J.P., de Jonge, P., Tulner, D.M., . . . Ormel, J. (2007). Treatment of post-myocardial infarction depressive disorder: A randomized, placebo-controlled trial with mirtazapine. *Psychosomatic Medicine, 69*, 606–13.

Huang, K., Liu, W., He, D., Huang, B., Xiao, D., Peng, Y., . . . Huang, D. (2015). Telehealth interventions versus center-based cardiac rehabilitation of coronary artery disease: A systematic review and meta-analysis. *European Journal of Preventive Cardiology, 22*, 959–71.

Huffman, J. C., Mastromauro, C. A., Boehm, J. K., Seabrook, R., Fricchione, G. L., Denninger, J. W., & Lyubomirsky, S. (2011). Development of a positive psychology intervention for patients with acute cardiovascular disease. *Heart International, 6*, e14.

Hunt, S.A., Abraham, W.T., Chin, M.H., Feldman, A.M., Francis, G.S., Ganiats, T.G., . . . Heart Rhythm Society. (2005). ACC/AHA 2005 guideline update for the adult: A report of the American College of Cardiology/American Heart Association task force on practice guidelines (writing committee to update the 2001 guidelines for the evaluation and management of heart failure): Developed in collaboration with the American College of Chest Physicians and the International Society for Heart and Lung Transplantation: endorsed by the Heart Rhythm Society. *Circulation, 112*, e154–e235.

Hunt-Shanks, T., Blanchard, C., Reid, R., Fortier, M., & Cappelli, M. (2010). A psychometric evaluation of the Hospital Anxiety and Depression Scale in cardiac patients: Addressing factor structure and gender invariance. *British Journal Health Psychology, 15*, 97–114.

Hurley, M.C., Arthur, H.M., Chessex, C., Oh, P., Turk-Adawi, K., & Grace, S.L. (2017). Burden, screening, and treatment of depressive and anxious symptoms among women referred to cardiac rehabilitation: A prospective study. *BMC Women's Health, 17*, 1–11.

Johnson-Lawrence, V., Kaplan, G., & Galea, S. (2013). Socioeconomic mobility in adulthood and cardiovascular disease mortality. *Annals of Epidemiology, 4*, 167–71.

Karasek, R., & Theorell, T. (1990). *Healthy work: Stress, productivity, and the reconstruction of working life.* New York, NY: Basic Books.

Kario, K., McEwen, B.S., & Pickering, T.G. (2003). Disasters and the heart: A review of the effects of earthquake-induced stress on cardiovascular disease. *Hypertension Research, 26*, 355–67.

Kawachi, I., Colditz, G.A., Ascherio, A., Rimm, E.B., Giovonnucci, E., Stampfer, M.J., & Willett, W.C. (1994). Prospective study of phobic anxiety and risk of coronary heart disease in men. *Circulation, 89*, 1992–7.

Kawachi, I., Colditz, G.A., Stampfer, M.J., Willett, W.C., Manson, J.E., Speizer, F.E., & Hennekens, C.H. (1995). Prospective study of shift work and risk of coronary heart disease in women. *Circulation, 92*, 3178–82.

Kessler, R.C., Chiu, W.T., Demler, O., & Walters, E.E. (2005). Prevalence, severity, and comorbidity of twelve-month DSM-IV disorders in the National Comorbidity Survey Replication (NCS-R). *Archives of General Psychiatry, 62*, 617–27.

Kim, Y., Hogan, K., D'Onofrio, G., Chekijian, S. & Safdar, B. (2017). Patient ethnicity predicts poor health access and gaps in perception of personal cardiovascular risk factors. *Critical Pathways in Cardiology, 16*, 147–57.

Kroenke, K., Spitzer, R.L., & Williams, J.B. (2003). The Patient Health Questionnaire-2: Validity of a two-item depression screener. *Medical Care, 32*, 1284–92.

Kronish, I.M., Rieckmann, N., Burg, M.M., Edmondson, D., Schwartz, J.E., & Davidson, K.W. (2012). The effect of enhanced depression care on adherence to risk reducing behaviors after acute coronary syndromes: Findings from the COPES trial. *American Heart Journal, 164*, 524–9.

Kuper, H., Singh-Manoux, A., Siegrist, J., & Marmot, M. (2002). When reciprocity fails: Effort-reward imbalance in relation to coronary heart disease and health functioning within the Whitehall II study. *Occupational Environmental Medicine, 59*, 777–84.

Lane, D., Caroll, D., Ring, C., Beevers, D.G., & Lip, G.Y. (2000). Mortality and quality of life 12 months after myocardial infarction: Effects of depression and anxiety. *Psychosomatic Medicine, 63*, 221–30.

Leifheit-Limson, E.C., Reid, K.J., Kasl, S.V., Lin, H., Jones, P.G., Buchanan, D.M., . . . Lichtman, J.H. (2010). The role of social support in health status and depressive symptoms after acute myocardial infarction: Evidence for a stronger relationship among women. *Circulation: Cardiovascular Quality and Outcomes, 3*, 143–50.

Lespérance, F., Frasure-Smith, N., Koszycki, D., Laliberte, M.A., van Zyl, L.T., Baker, B., . . . Guertin, M.C. (2007). Effects of citralopram and interpersonal psychotherapy on depression in patients with coronary artery disease: The Canadian Cardiac Randomized Evaluation of Antidepressant and Psychotherapy Efficacy (CREATE) trial. *Journal of the American Medical Association, 297*, 367–79.

Lichtman, J.H., Froelicher, E.S., Blumenthal, J.A., Carney, R.M., Doering, L.V., Frasure-Smith, N., . . . Wulsin, L. (2014). Depression as a risk factor for poor prognosis among patients with acute coronary syndrome: Systematic review and recommendations: A scientific statement from the American Heart Association. *Circulation, 129*, 1350–69.

Low, C.A., Thurston, R.C., & Matthews, K.A. (2010). Psychosocial factors in the development of heart disease in women: Current research and future directions. *Psychosomatic Medicine, 72*, 842–54.

Lund, L.H., Edwards, L.B., Dipchand, A.I., Goldfarb, S., Kucheryavaya, A.Y., Levvey, B.J., . . . Stehlik, J. (2016). The registry of the international society for heart and lung transplantation: Thirty-third adult heart transplantation report—2016; Focus theme: Primary diagnostic indications for transplant. *The Journal of Heart and Lung Transplantation, 35*, 1158–69.

Martikainen, P., & Valkonen, T. (1996). Mortality after the death of a spouse: Rates and causes of death in a large Finnish cohort. *American Journal of Public Health, 86*, 1087–93.

Martins, R.K., & McNeil, D.W. (2009). Review of motivational interviewing in promoting health behaviors. *Clinical Psychology Review, 29*, 283–93.

Mavrides, N., & Nemeroff, C. (2013). Treatment of depression in cardiovascular disease. *Depression and Anxiety, 30*, 328–41.

Meijer, A., Conradi, H.J., Bos, E.H., Anselmino, M., Carney, R.M. Denollet, J., . . . de Jonge, P. (2013). Adjusted prognostic association of depression following myocardial infarction with mortality and cardiovascular events: Individual patient data meta-analysis. *British Journal of Psychiatry, 203*, 90–102.

Mensah, G.A., Mokdad, A.H., Ford, E.S., Greenlund, K.J., & Croft, J.B. (2005). State of disparities in cardiovascular health in the United States. *Circulation, 111*, 1233–41.

Milani, R.V., & Lavie, C.J. (2009). Reducing psychosocial stress: A novel mechanism of improving survival from exercise training. *American Journal of Medicine, 122*, 931–8.

Miller, W.R. (1996). Motivational interviewing: Research, practice, and puzzles. *Addictive Behaviors, 21*, 835–42.

Mitchell, P.H., Powell, L., Blumenthal, J., Norten, J., Ironson, G., Pitula, C.R., . . . Berkman, L.F. (2003). A short social support measure for patients recovering from myocardial infarction: The ENRICHD Social Support Inventory. *Journal of Cardiopulmonary Rehabilitation, 23*, 398–403.

Moser, D.K., & Dracup, K. (1996). Is anxiety early after myocardial infarction associated with subsequent ischemic and arrhythmic events? *Psychosomatic Medicine, 58*, 395–401.

Mozaffarian, D., Benjamin, E.J., Go, A.S., Arnett, D.K., Blaha, M.J., Cushman, M., . . . Turner, M.B. (2016). Heart disease and stroke statistics—2016 update: A report from the American Heart Association. *Circulation, 133*, e38–360.

National Institute of Health. (2004). *NHLBI working group assessment and treatment of depression in patients with cardiovascular disease*. Retrieved from www.nhlbi.nih.gov/meetings/workshops/depression/index.htm

Oosenbrug, E., Marinho, R.P., Zhang, J., Marzolini, S., Colella, T.J., Pakosh, M., & Grace, S.L. (2016). Sex differences in cardiac rehabilitation adherence: A meta-analysis. *Canadian Journal of Cardiology, 32*, 1316–24.

Ormel, J., Von Korff, M., Burger, H., Scott, K., Demyttenaere, K., Huang, Y.Q., . . . Kessler, R. (2007). Mental disorders among persons with heart disease—Results from World Mental Health surveys. *General Hospital Psychiatry, 29*, 325–34.

Orth-Gomer, K., Rosengren, A., & Wilhelmsen, L. (1993). Lack of social support and incidence of coronary heart disease in middle-aged Swedish men. *Psychosomatic Medicine, 55*, 37–43.

Orth-Gomer, K., Wamala, S.P., Horsten, M., Schenck-Gustafsson, K.C., Schneiderman, N., & Mittleman, M.A. (2000). Marital stress worsens prognosis in women with coronary heart disease: The Stockholm female coronary risk study. *Journal of the American Medical Association, 284*, 3008–14.

O'Shea, J.C., Wilcox, R.G., Skene, A.M., Stebbins, A.L., Granger, C.B., Armstrong, P.W., . . . Ohman, E.M. (2002). Comparison of outcomes of patients with myocardial infarction when living alone versus those not living alone. *American Journal of Cardiology, 90*, 1374–7.

Parker, G.B., Owen, C.A., Brotchie, H.L., & Hyett, M.P. (2010). The impact of differing anxiety disorders on outcome following an acute coronary syndrome: Time to start worrying? *Depression and Anxiety, 27*, 302–9.

Pratt, L.A., & Brody, D.J. (2014). *Depression in the U.S. household population, 2009–2012*. Retrieved from https://www.cdc.gov/nchs/data/databriefs/db172.pdf

Prior, P.L., Francis, J., Reitav, J., & Stone, J.A. (2009). Behavioural, psychological and functional issues in cardiovascular disease and cardiac rehabilitation. In J.A. Stone, H.M. Arthur, & N.G. Suskin (Eds.), *Canadian guidelines for cardiac rehabilitation and cardiovascular disease prevention: Translating knowledge into action*. Winnipeg, MB: Canadian Association for Cardiac Rehabilitation.

Public Health Agency of Canada. (2009). *2009 Tracking heart disease and stroke in Canada*. Retrieved from www.phac--aspc.gc.ca/publicat/2009/cvd-avc/report-rapport-eng.php

Public Health Agency of Canada. (2014). *Economic burden of illness in Canada, 2005-2008*. Retrieved from http://www.phac-aspc.gc.ca/publicat/ebic-femc/2005-2008/index-eng.php

Rawstorn, J.C., Gant, N., Direito, A., Beckmann, C., & Maddison, R. (2016). Telehealth exercise-based cardiac rehabilitation: A systematic review and meta-analysis. *Heart, 102*, 1183–92.

Reid, R., Blanchard, C.M., Wooding, E., Harris, J., Krahn, M., Pipe, A., . . . Grace, S.L. (2016). Ecologically optimizing exercise maintenance in men and women in post-cardiac rehabilitation: Protocol for a randomized controlled trial of efficacy with economics (ECO-PCR). *Contemporary Clinical Trials, 50*, 116–23.

Rodriguez, C.J., Elkind, M.S., Clemow, L., Jin, Z., Di Tullio, M., Sacco, R.L., . . . Boden-Albala, B. (2011). Association between social isolation and left ventricular mass. *American Journal of Medicine, 124*, 164–70.

Roest, A.M., Martens, E.J., Denollet, J., & de Jonge, P. (2010). Prognostic association of anxiety post myocardial infarction with mortality and new cardiac events: A meta-analysis. *Psychosomatic Medicine, 72*, 563–9.

Rosengren, A., Hawken, S, Ounpuu, S., Sliwa, K., Zubaid, M., Almahmeed, W.A., . . Yusuf, S. (2004). Association of psychosocial risk factors with risk of myocardial infarction in 11119 cases and 13648 controls from 52 countries (the INTERHEART study: Case control study). *Lancet, 364*, 953–62.

Roth, D.L., Fredman, L., & Haley, W.E. (2015). Informal caregiving and its impact on health: A reappraisal from population-based studies. *The Gerontologist, 55*, 309–19.

Roth, D.L., Perkins, M., Wadley, V.G., Temple, E., & Haley, W.E. (2009). Family caregiving and emotional strain: Associations with psychological health in a national sample of community-dwelling middle-aged and older adults. *Quality of Life Research, 18*, 679–88.

Rozanski, A., Bairey, C.N., Krantz, D.S., Friedman, J., Resser, K.J., Morell, M., . . . Berman, D.S. (1988). Mental stress and the induction of silent myocardial ischemia in patients with coronary artery disease. *New England Journal of Medicine, 318*, 1005–12.

Rozanski, A., Blumenthal, J.A., & Davidson, K.W. (2005) The epidemiology, pathophysiology, and management of psychosocial risk factors in cardiac practice: The emerging field of behavioural cardiology. *Journal of the American College of Cardiology, 45*, 637–51.

Rugulies, R. (2002). Depression as a predictor for coronary heart disease: A review and meta-analysis. *American Journal of Preventive Medicine, 23*, 51–61.

Rutledge, T., Redwine, L.S., Linke, S.E., & Mills, P.J. (2013). A meta-analysis of mental health treatments and cardiac rehabilitation for improving clinical outcomes and depression among patients with coronary heart disease. *Psychosomatic Medicine, 75*, 335–49.

Santo, K., Richtering, S.S., Chalmers, J., Thiagalingam, A., Chow, C.K., & Redfern, J. (2016). Mobile phone apps to improve medication adherence: A systematic stepwise process to identify high-quality apps. *JMIR mHealth and uHealth, 4*, e132.

Schmaltz, H.N., Southern, D., Ghali, W.A., Jelinski, S.E., Parsons, G.A., King, K.M., & Maxwell, C.J. (2007). Living alone, patient sex and mortality after acute myocardial infarction. *Society of General Internal Medicine, 22*, 572–8.

Shakespeare, W. (2008). *Romeo and Juliet* (J. L. Levenson, Ed.). Oxford: Oxford University Press.

Shankar, A., McMunn, A., Banks, J., & Steptoe, A. (2011). Loneliness, social isolation, and behavioural and biological health indicators in older adults. *Health Psychology, 30*, 377–85.

Sidney, S. (2013). Post-traumatic stress disorder and coronary heart disease. *Journal of the American College of Cardiology, 62*, 979–80.

Siegrist, J. (2010). Effort-reward imbalance at work and cardiovascular disease. *International Journal of Occupational Medicine and Environmental Health, 23*, 279–85.

Siegrist, J., Starke, D., Chandola, T., Gordon, I., Marmot, M., Niedhammer, I., & Peter, R. (2004). The measurement of effort-reward imbalance at work: European comparisons. *Social Science & Medicine, 58*, 1483–99.

Simon, G.E., & Von Korff, M. (2006). Medical co-morbidity and validity of DSM-IV depression criteria. *Psychological Medicine, 36*, 27–36.

Smith, T., & Ruiz, J. (2002). Psychosocial influences on the development and course of coronary heart disease: Current status and implications for research and practice. *Journal of Consulting and Clinical Psychology, 70*, 548–68.

Smith, T.W., Uchino, B.N., Berg, C.A., Florsheim, P., Pearce, G., Hawkins, M., . . . Olsen-Cerny, C. (2009). Conflict and collaboration in middle-aged and older couples: II. Cardiovascular reactivity during marital interaction. *Psychological Aging, 24*, 274–86.

Sorabella, R. A., Yerebakan, H., Walters, R., Takeda, K., Colombo, P., Yuzefpolskaya, M., . . . Naka, Y. (2015). Comparison of outcomes after heart replacement therapy in patients over 65 years old. *The Annals of Thoracic Surgery, 99*, 582–8.

Spek, V., Cuijpers, P., Nyklícek, I., Riper, H., Keyzer, J., & Pop, V. (2007). Internet-based cognitive behaviour therapy for symptoms of depression and anxiety: A meta-analysis. *Psychological Medicine, 37*, 319–28.

Statistics Canada. (2011). Mortality, summary list of causes (2008 numbers: CVD).

Statistics Canada. (2015). Deaths, by cause, chapter IX: Diseases of the circulatory system (I00-I99), age group and sex, Canada, annual (number). CANSIM (database). Retrieved from http://www5.statcan.gc.ca/cansim/a26

Stone, J.A., & Mancini, G.M.J. (2009). The pathophysiology of atherosclerosis and cardiovascular disease. In J.A. Stone, H.M. Arthur, & N.G. Suskin (Eds.), *Canadian guidelines for cardiac rehabilitation and cardiovascular disease prevention: Translating knowledge into action.* Winnipeg, MB: Canadian Association for Cardiac Rehabilitation.

Strik, J.J., Denollet, J., Lousberg, R., & Honig, A. (2003). Comparing symptoms of depression and anxiety as predictors of cardiac events and increased health care consumption after myocardial infarction. *Journal of the American College of Cardiology, 42*, 1801–7.

Tedeschi, R.G., Park, C.L., & Calhoun, L.G. (1998). *Posttraumatic growth: Positive change in the aftermath of crisis.* Mahwah, NJ: Lawrence Erlbaum.

Thakkar, J., Redfern, J., Thiagalingam, A., & Chow, C.K. (2016). Patterns, predictors and effects of texting intervention on physical activity in CHD —Insights from the TEXT ME randomized clinical trial. *European Journal of Preventive Cardiology, 23*, 1894–1902.

Thombs, B.D., Bass, E.B., Ford, D.E., Stewart, K.J., Tsilidis, K.K., Patel, U., . . . Ziegelstein, R.C. (2006). Prevalence of depression in survivors of acute myocardial infarction. *Journal General Internal Medicine, 21*, 30–8.

Thombs, B.D., de Jonge, P., Coyne, J.C., Whooley, M.A., Frasure-Smith, N., Mitchell, A.J., . . . Ziegelstein, R.C. (2008). Depression screening and patient outcomes in cardiovascular care: A systematic review. *Journal of the American Heart Association, 300*, 2161–71.

Thombs, B.D., Roseman, M., Coyne, J.C., de Jonge, P., Delisle, V.C., Arthurs, E., . . . Ziegelstein, R.C. (2013). Does evidence support the American Heart Association's recommendations to screen patients for depression in cardiovascular care? An updated systematic review. *PLOS ONE, 8*, e52654.

Todaro, J.F., Shen, B.J., Raffia, S.D., Tilkemeir, P.L., & Niaura, R. (2007). Prevalence of anxiety disorders in men and women with established coronary artery disease. *Journal of Cardiopulmonary Rehabilitation and Prevention, 27*, 86–91.

Turk-Adawi, K., & Grace, S.L. (2014). Smartphone-based cardiac rehabilitation. *Heart, 100*, 1737–8.

Vaccarino, V., Goldberg, J., Rooks, C., Shah, A.J., Veledar, E., Faber, T.L., & Bremner, J.D. (2013). Post-traumatic stress disorder and incidence of coronary heart disease: A twin study. *Journal of the American College of Cardiology, 62*, 970–8.

Vaglio, J., Conard, M., Poston, W., O'Keefe, J., Haddock, K., House, J., & Spertus, J.A. (2004). Testing the performance of the ENRICHD Social Support Instrument in cardiac patients. *Health & Quality of Life Outcomes, 2*, 24–9.

Van der Kooy, K., van Hout, H., Marwijk, H., Marten, H., Stewouwer, C., & Beekman, A. (2007). Depression and the risk for cardiovascular diseases: A systematic review and meta-analysis. *International Journal of Geriatric Psychiatry, 22*, 613–26.

Vasamreddy, C.R., Ahmed, D., Gluckman, T.J., & Blumenthal, R.S. (2004). Cardiovascular disease in athletes. *Clinics in Sports Medicine, 23*, 455-71.

Wagner, B., Horn, A.B., & Maercker, A. (2014). Internet-based versus face-to-face cognitive-behavioral intervention for depression: A randomized controlled non-inferiority trial. *Journal of Affective Disorders, 152*, 113–21.

Watkins, L.L., Blumenthal, J.A., Davidson, J.R., Babyak, M.A., McCants, C.B., & Sketch, M.H. (2006). Phobic anxiety, depression, and risk of ventricular arrhythmias in patients with coronary heart disease. *Psychosomatic Medicine, 68*, 651–6.

Whittaker, R., McRobbie, H., Bullen, C., Rodgers, A., & Yulong, G. (2016). Mobile phone-based interventions for smoking cessation. *Cochrane Database of Systematic Reviews, 4*, CD006611.

Wulsin, L., & Singal, B. (2003). Do depressive symptoms increase the risk for the onset of coronary disease? A systematic quantitative review. *Psychosomatic Medicine, 65*, 201–10.

Yohannes, A.M., Doherty, P., Bundy, C., & Yalfani, A. (2010). The long-term benefits of cardiac rehabilitation on depression, anxiety, physical activity and quality of life. *Journal of Clinical Nursing, 19*, 2806–13.

Zen, A.L., Whooley, M.A., Zhao, S., & Cohen, B.E. (2012). Post-traumatic stress disorder is associated with poor health behaviors: Findings from the heart and soul study. *Health Psychology, 31*, 194–201.

Ziegelstein, R.C., Thombs, B.D., Coyne, J.C., & de Jonge, P. (2009). Routine screening for depression in patients with coronary heart disease never mind. *Journal of the American College of Cardiology, 54*, 886–90.

Zigmond, A.S., & Snaith, R.P. (1983). The hospital anxiety and depression scale. Acta Psychiatrica Scandinavica, *67*, 361–70.

Chapter 11

Ajzen, I. (1991). The theory of planned behavior. *Organizational Behavior and Human Decision Processes, 50*, 179–211.

Ajzen, I., & Fishbein, M. (1980). *Understanding attitudes and predicting social behavior.* Englewood Cliffs, NJ: Prentice-Hall.

Al-Dakkak, I., Patel, S., McCann, E., Gadkari, A., Prajapati, G., & Maiese, E. M. (2013). The impact of specific HIV treatment-related adverse events on adherence to antiretroviral therapy: A systematic review and meta-analysis. *AIDS Care, 25*(4), 400–14.

Alghazo, R., Upton, T.D., & Cioe, N. (2011). Duty to warn versus duty to protect confidentiality: Ethical and legal considerations relative to individuals with AIDS/HIV. *Journal of Applied Rehabilitation Counseling, 42*, 1, 43–9.

Al-Tayyib, A.A., McFarlane, M., Kachur, R., & Rietmeijer, C.A. (2009). Finding sex partners on the Internet: What is the risk for sexually transmitted infections? *Sexually Transmitted Infections, 85*, 216–20.

American Civil Liberties Union. (2008). *Lesbian & Gay Rights Project AIDS Project: State criminal statutes on HIV transmission—2008*. Retrieved from www.aclu.org/files/images/asset_upload_file292_35655.pdf

Ammassari, A., Trotta, M.P., Murri, R., Castelli, F., Narciso, P., Noto, P., . . . Antinori, A. (2002). Correlates and predictors of adherence to highly active antiretroviral therapy: Overview of published literature. *Journal of Acquired Immune Deficiency Syndromes, 31*, S123–S127.

Anderson, S.E.H. (1995). Personality, appraisal, and adaptational outcomes in HIV seropositive men and women. *Research in Nursing and Health, 18*, 303–12.

Antinori, A., Arendt, G., Becker, J.T., Brew, B.J., Byrd, D.A., Cherner, M., . . . Wojna, V.E. (2007). Updated research nosology for HIV-associated neurocognitive disorders. *Neurology, 69*(18), 1789–99.

Antoni, M.H. (2003). Stress management effects on psychological, endocrinological and immune functioning in men with HIV infection: Empirical support for a psychoneuroimmunological model. *Stress, 6*, 173–88.

Aral, S.O., Adimora, A.A., & Fenton, K.A. (2008). Understanding and responding to disparities in HIV and other sexually transmitted infections in African Americans. *Lancet, 372*(9635), 337–40.

Arts, E.J., & Hazuda, D.J. (2012). HIV-1 antiretroviral drug therapy. *Cold Spring Harbor Perspectives in Medicine, 2*(4).

Ashton, E., Vosvick, M., Chesney, M., Gore-Felton, C., Koopman, C., O'Shea, K., . . . Spiegel, S. (2005). Social support and maladaptive coping as predictors of the change in physical health symptoms among persons living with HIV/AIDS. *AIDS Patient Care and STDs, 19*, 587–98.

AVERT. (2016). *The Science of HIV and AIDS—overview*. Retrieved from www.avert.org/hiv-virus.htm

Balfe, M., Brugha, R., O'Connell, E., McGee, H., O'Donovan, D., & Vaughan, D. (2010). Why don't young women go for chlamydia testing? A qualitative study employing Goffman's stigma framework. *Health, Risk & Society, 12*, 131–48.

Bandura, A. (1998). Health promotion from the perspective of social cognitive theory. *Personality and Social Psychology, 13*, 623–49.

Bartholomew, L.K, Parcel, G.S., Kok, G., Gottlieb, N.H., & Fernández, M.E. (2011). *Planning health promotion programs: An intervention mapping approach.* San Francisco, CA: Jossey-Bass.

Bayoumi, A.M., & Zaric, G.S. (2008). The cost-effectiveness of Vancouver's supervised injection facility. *Canadian Medical Journal Association, 179*, 1143–51.

BC Centre for Disease Control (BCCDC). (2016a). *Sexually transmitted infections (STIs)*. Retrieved from http://www.bccdc.ca/health-info/diseases-conditions/sexually-transmitted-infections-(stis)

BC Centre for Disease Control (BCCDC). (2016b). *Human papillomavirus (HPV)/genital warts*. Retrieved from http://www.bccdc.ca/health-info/diseases-conditions/human-papillomavirus-(hpv)-genital-warts

BC Centre for Disease Control (BCCDC). (2016c). *Genital herpes/herpes simplex virus*. Retrieved from http://www.bccdc.ca/health-info/diseases-conditions/genital-herpes-herpes-simplex-virus

BC Centre for Disease Control (BCCDC). (2016d). *Hepatitis A.* Retrieved from http://www.bccdc.ca/health-info/diseases-conditions/hepatitis-a

BC Centre for Disease Control (BCCDC). (2016e). *Hepatitis B.* Retrieved from http://www.bccdc.ca/health-info/diseases-conditions/hepatitis-b

BC Centre for Disease Control (BCCDC). (2016f). *Hepatitis C.* Retrieved from http://www.bccdc.ca/health-info/diseases-conditions/hepatitis-c

BC Centre for Disease Control (BCCDC). (2016g). *Chlamydia.* Retrieved from http://www.bccdc.ca/health-info/diseases-conditions/chlamydia

BC Centre for Disease Control (BCCDC). (2016h). *Gonorrhea.* Retrieved from http://www.bccdc.ca/health-info/diseases-conditions/gonorrhea

BC Centre for Disease Control (BCCDC). (2016i). *Syphilis.* Retrieved from http://www.bccdc.ca/health-info/diseases-conditions/syphilis

BC Centre for Disease Control (BCCDC). (2016j). *Trichomoniasis.* Retrieved from http://www.bccdc.ca/health-info/diseases-conditions/trichomoniasis

BC Centre for Disease Control (BCCDC). (2016k). *Pubic lice.* Retrieved from http://www.bccdc.ca/health-info/diseases-conditions/pubic-lice

BC Centre for Disease Control (BCCDC). (2016l). *Scabies.* Retrieved from http://www.bccdc.ca/health-info/diseases-conditions/scabies

Becker, M., Cox, J., Evans, G.A., Haider, S., & Shafran, S.D. (2016). AMMI Canada position statement: The use of early antiretroviral therapy in HIV-infected persons. *Official Journal of the Association of Medical Microbiology and Infectious Disease Canada, 1*(2).

Beekmann, S. E., & Henderson, D. K. (2014). Prevention of HIV/AIDS: Post-exposure prophylaxis (including healthcare workers). *Infectious Disease Clinics of North America, 28*(4), 601–13.

Begley, K., McLaws, M.-L., Ross, M.W., & Gold, J. (2008). Cognitive and behavioural correlates of non-adherence to HIV anti-retroviral therapy: Theoretical and practical insight for clinical psychology and health psychology. *Clinical Psychologist, 12*, 9–17.

Bennett, D.S., Hersh, J., Herres, J., & Foster, J. (2016). HIV-related stigma, shame, and avoidant coping: Risk factors for internalizing symptoms among youth living with HIV? *Child Psychiatry and Human Development, 47*(4), 657–64.

Boarts, J.M., Sledjeski, E.M., Bogart, L.M., & Delahanty, D.L. (2006). The differential impact of PTSD and depression on HIV disease markers and adherence to HAART in people living with HIV. *AIDS and Behavior, 10*, 253–61.

Bolding, G., Davis, M., Hart, G., Sherr, L., & Elford, J. (2005). Gay men who look for sex on the Internet: Is there more HIV/STI risk with online partners? *AIDS, 19*, 961-968.

Bradley, H., Hall, R., Wolitski, R.J., Van Handel, M.M., Stone, A.E., LaFlam, M., . . . Valleroy L.A. (2014). Vital signs: HIV diagnosis, care, and treatment among persons living with HIV—United States, 2011. *Morbidity and Mortality Weekly Report, 63*(47), 1113–17.

Brandt, C.P., Sheppard, D.P., Zvolensky, M.J., Morgan, E.E., Atkinson, J.H., & Woods, S.P. (2016). Does age influence the frequency of anxiety symptoms and disorders in HIV disease? *Journal of HIV/AIDS & Social Services, 15*(4), 380–403.

Brew, B.J., & Gonzalez-Scarano, F. (2007). HIV-associated dementia: An inconvenient truth. *Neurology, 68*, 324–5.

Brown, J.L., & Vanable, P.A. (2007). Alcohol use, partner type, and risky sexual behaviour among college students: Findings from an event-level study. *Addictive Behaviors, 32*, 2940–52.

Brown, L., Macintyre, K., & Trujillo, L. (2003). Interventions to reduce HIV/AIDS stigma: What have we learned? *AIDS Education and Prevention, 15*, 49–69.

Budhiraja, R., Roth, T., Hudgel, D.W., Budhiraja, P., & Drake, C.L. (2011). Prevalence and polysomnographic correlates of insomnia comorbid with medical disorders. *Sleep, 34*(7), 859–67.

Calin, T., Green, J., Hetherton, J., & Brook, G. (2007). Disclosure of HIV among Black African men and women attending a London HIV clinic. *AIDS Care, 19*, 385–91.

Campos, L.N., Guimarães, M.D.C., & Remien, R.H. (2010). Anxiety and depression symptoms as risk factors for non-adherence to antiretroviral therapy in brazil. *AIDS and Behavior, 14*(2), 289–99.

Canadian Broadcasting Corporation (CBC). (2011). *Vancouver's Insite drug injection clinic will stay open: Top court rules on clinic's exemption from federal drug laws.* Retrieved from www.cbc.ca/news/canada/british-columbia/-story/2011/09/29/bc-insite-supreme-court-ruling-advancer.html

Canadian Broadcasting Corporation (CBC). (2016). *It's about to get easier to set up supervised drug injection sites in Canada.* Retrieved from www.cbc.ca/news/politics/it-s-about-to-get-easier-to-set-up-supervised-drug-injection-sites-in-canada-1.3890401

Canadian HIV/AIDS Legal Network. (2011). *Criminalization of HIV non-disclosure: Current Canadian law.* Retrieved from www.aidslaw.ca/publications/interfaces/downloadFile.php?ref=1887

Canadian HIV/AIDS Legal Network. (2014). *Criminal law and HIV non-disclosure in Canada.* Retrieved from http://www.aidslaw.ca/site/criminal-law-and-hiv/?lang=en

Capaldi, D.M., Stoolmiller, M., Clark, S., & Owen, L.D. (2002). Heterosexual risk behaviors in at-risk young men from early adolescence to young adulthood: Prevalence, prediction, and association with STD contraction. *Developmental Psychology, 38*, 394–406.

Catz, S.L., Kelly, J.A., Bogart, L.M., Benotsch, E.G., & McAuliffe, T.L. (2000). Patterns, correlates, and barriers to medication adherence among persons prescribed new treatments for HIV disease. *Health Psychology, 19*, 124–133.

Centers for Disease Control and Prevention (CDC). (2003). Incorporating HIV prevention into the medical care of persons living with HIV. *Morbidity and Mortality Weekly Report, 52*, 1–24.

Centers for Disease Control and Prevention (CDC). (2010). *Parasites: Scabies.* Retrieved from www.cdc.gov/parasites/scabies/gen_info/faqs.html

Centers for Disease Control and Prevention (CDC). (2011). *10 ways STDs impact women differently from men.* Retrieved from www.cdc.gov/nchhstp/newsroom/docs/STDs-Women-042011.pdf

Centers for Disease Control and Prevention (CDC). (2012). *African Americans and sexually transmitted diseases.*

Retrieved from www.cdc.gov/nchhstp/newsroom/docs/AAs-and-STD-Fact-Sheet.pdf

Centers for Disease Control and Prevention (CDC). (2013a). *Parasites—Lice – Pubic "crab" lice.* Retrieved from https://www.cdc.gov/parasites/lice/pubic/gen_info/faqs.html

Centers for Disease Control and Prevention (CDC). (2013b). *Condoms and STDs: Fact sheet for public health personnel.* Retrieved from www.cdc.gov/condomeffectiveness/latex.htm.

Centers for Disease Control and Prevention (CDC). (2015a). *Viral hepatitis—Hepatitis A information.* Retrieved from https://www.cdc.gov/hepatitis/hav/

Centers for Disease Control and Prevention (CDC). (2015b). *Viral hepatitis—Hepatitis B information.* Retrieved from https://www.cdc.gov/hepatitis/hbv/index.htm

Centers for Disease Control and Prevention (CDC). (2015c). *Viral hepatitis—Hepatitis C information.* Retrieved from https://www.cdc.gov/hepatitis/hcv/index.htm

Centers for Disease Control and Prevention (CDC). (2015d). *Trichomoniasis—the facts.* Retrieved from https://www.cdc.gov/std/trichomonas/the-facts/default.htm

Centers for Disease Control and Prevention (CDC). (2016a). *Sexually Transmitted Disease Surveillance 2015.* Retrieved from https://www.cdc.gov/std/stats15/std-surveillance-2015-print.pdf

Centers for Disease Control and Prevention (CDC). (2016b). *CDC fact sheet: HIV among African Americans.* Retrieved from https://www.cdc.gov/nchhstp/newsroom/docs/factsheets/cdc-hiv-aa-508.pdf

Centers for Disease Control and Prevention (CDC). (2016c). *CDC fact sheets.* Retrieved from https://www.cdc.gov/std/healthcomm/fact_sheets.htm

Centers for Disease Control and Prevention (CDC). (2016d). *Diagnoses of HIV infection in the United States and dependent areas, 2015.* Retrieved from https://www.cdc.gov/hiv/pdf/library/reports/surveillance/cdc-hiv-surveillance-report-2015-vol-27.pdf

Centers for Disease Control and Prevention (CDC). (2016e). *Genital HPV infection—fact sheet.* Retrieved from https://www.cdc.gov/std/hpv/stdfact-hpv.htm

Centers for Disease Control and Prevention (CDC). (2016f). *Genital herpes—CDC fact sheet.* Retrieved from https://www.cdc.gov/std/herpes/stdfact-herpes.htm

Centers for Disease Control and Prevention (CDC). (2016g). *Chlamydia—CDC fact sheet.* Retrieved from https://www.cdc.gov/std/chlamydia/stdfact-chlamydia.htm

Centers for Disease Control and Prevention (CDC). (2016h). *Gonorrhea—CDC fact sheet.* Retrieved from https://www.cdc.gov/std/gonorrhea/stdfact-gonorrhea.htm

Centers for Disease Control and Prevention (CDC). (2016i). *Syphilis—CDC fact sheet.* Retrieved from https://www.cdc.gov/std/syphilis/STDFact-Syphilis.htm

Centers for Disease Control and Prevention (CDC). (2016j). Updated guidelines for antiretroviral postexposure prophylaxis after sexual, injection drug use, or other nonoccupational exposure to HIV—United States. Retrieved from www.cdc.gov/hiv/pdf/programresources/cdc-hiv-npep-guidelines.pdf

Chang, L.W., Serwadda, D., Quinn, T.C., Wawer, M.J., Gray, R.H., & Reynolds, S.J. (2013). Combination implementation for HIV prevention: Moving from clinical trial evidence to population-level effects. *The Lancet Infectious Diseases, 13*(1), 65–76.

Chesney, M.A., Ickovics, J.R., Chambers, D.B., Gifford, A.L., Neidig, J., Zwickl, B., & Wu, A.W. (2000). Self-reported adherence to antiretroviral medications among participants in HIV clinical trials: The AACTG adherence instruments. *AIDS Care, 12*, 255–66.

Chesney, M.A., & Smith, A.W. (1999). Critical delays in HIV testing and care: The potential role of stigma. *American Behavioral Scientist, 42*, 1162–74.

Chiu, C.J., Menacho, L., Fisher, C., & Young, S.D. (2015). Ethics issues in social media-based HIV prevention in low- and middle-income countries. *The International Journal of Healthcare Ethics Committees, 24*(3), 303–10.

Chung, K., Yeung, W., Ho, F.Y., Yung, K., Yu, Y., & Kwok, C. (2015). Cross-cultural and comparative epidemiology of insomnia: The Diagnostic and Statistical Manual (DSM), International Classification of Diseases (ICD) and International Classification of Sleep Disorders (ICSD). *Sleep Medicine, 16*(4), 477–82.

Ciesla, J.A., & Roberts, J.E. (2001). Meta-analysis of the relationship between HIV infection and risk for depressive disorder. *American Journal of Psychiatry, 158*, 725–30.

Clifford, D.B., & Ances, B.M. (2013). HIV-associated neurocognitive disorder. *The Lancet Infectious Diseases, 13*(11), 976–86.

Crosby, R.A., DiClemente, R.J., Wingood, G.M., Cobb, B.K., Harrington, K., Davies, S.L., . . . Oh, M.K. (2002). Condom use and correlates of African American adolescent females' infrequent communication with sex partners about preventing sexually transmitted diseases and pregnancy. *Health Education & Behavior, 29*, 219–31.

Dayer, L., Heldenbrand, S., Anderson, P., Gubbins, P.O., & Martin, B.C. (2013). Smartphone medication adherence apps: Potential benefits to patients and providers. *Journal of the American Pharmaceutical Association, 53*(2), 172–81.

DeLonga, K., Torres, H.L., Kamen, C., Evans, S.N., Lee, S., Koopman, C., & Gore-Felton, C. (2011). Loneliness, internalized homophobia, and compulsive Internet use: Factors associated with sexual risk behaviour among a sample of adolescent males seeking services at a community LGBT center. *Sexual Addiction & Compulsivity, 18*, 61–74.

Dew, B.J., & Chaney, M.P. (2005). The relationship among sexual compulsivity, internalized homophobia, and HIV at-risk sexual behaviour in gay and bisexual male users of Internet chat rooms. *Sexual Addiction & Compulsivity, 12*, 259–73.

DiIorio, C., Dudley, W.N., Kelly, M., Soet, J.E., Mbwara, J., & Potter, J.S. (2001). Social cognitive correlates of sexual experience and condom use among 13- through 15-year-old adolescents. *Journal of Adolescent Health, 29*, 208–16.

Dooling, K., & Rachlis, M. (2010). Vancouver's supervised injection facility challenges Canada's drug laws. *Canadian Medical Association Journal, 182*, 1440–44.

Drumright, L.N., Patterson, T.L., & Strathdee, S.A. (2006). Club drugs as causal risk factors for HIV acquisition among men who have sex with men: A review. *Substance Use & Misuse, 41*, 1551–1601.

Enns, E.A., Zaric, G.S., Strike, C.J., Jairam, J.A., Kolla, G., & Bayoumi, A.M. (2016). Potential cost-effectiveness of supervised injection facilities in Toronto and Ottawa, Canada. *Addiction, 111*(3), 475–89.

Evans, D.L., Ten Have, T.R., Douglas, S.D., Gettes, D.R., Morrison, M., Chiappini, M.S., . . . Pettito, J.M. (2002). Association of depression with viral load, CD8 T lymphocytes, and natural killer cells in women with HIV infection. *American Journal of Psychiatry, 159*, 1752–9.

Farmer, M.A., & Meston, C.M. (2006). Predictors of condom use self-efficacy in an ethnically diverse university sample. *Archives of Sexual Behavior, 35*, 313–26.

Feldman, B.J., Fredericksen, R.J., Crane, P.K., Safren, S.A., Mugavero, M.J., Willig, J.H., . . . Crane, H.M. (2013). Evaluation of the single-item self-rating adherence scale for use in routine clinical care of people living with HIV. *AIDS and Behavior, 17*(1), 307–18.

Fisher, J.D., & Fisher, W.A. (1992). Changing AIDS-risk behavior. *Psychological Bulletin, 111*, 455–74.

Ford, N., Shubber, Z., Calmy, A., Irvine, C., Rapparini, C., Ajose, O., . . . Mayer, K. H. (2015). Choice of antiretroviral drugs for postexposure prophylaxis for adults and adolescents: A systematic review. *Clinical Infectious Diseases, 60*(Suppl 3), S170–6.

Fortenberry, J.D., McFarlane, M., Bleakley, A., Bull, S., Fishbein, M., Grimley, D.M., . . . Stoner, B.P. (2002). Relationships of stigma and shame to gonorrhea and HIV screening. *American Journal of Public Health, 92*, 378–81.

French, S. E., & Holland, K. J. (2013). Condom negotiation strategies as a mediator of the relationship between self-efficacy and condom use. *Journal of Sex Research, 50*(1), 48–59.

Garett, R., Smith, J., & Young, S.D. (2016). A review of social media technologies across the global HIV care continuum. *Current Opinion in Psychology, 9*, 56–66.

Gaynes, B.N., O'Donnell, J., Nelson, E., Heine, A., Zinski, A., Edwards, M., . . . Pence, B.W. (2015). Psychiatric comorbidity in depressed HIV-infected individuals: Common and clinically consequential. *General Hospital Psychiatry, 37*(4), 277–82.

Gaynes, B.N., Pence, B.W., Eron, J.J. Jr., & Miller, W.C. (2008). Prevalence and comorbidity of psychiatric diagnoses based on reference standard in an HIV+ patient population. *Psychosomatic Medicine, 70*(4), 505–11.

Geraci, A.P., & Simpson, D.M. (2001). Neurological manifestations of HIV-1 infection in the HAART era. *Comprehensive Therapy, 27*, 232–41.

Gilliam, P.P., & Straub, D.M. (2009). Prevention with positives: A review of published research, 1998–2008. *Journal of the Association of Nurses in AIDS Care, 20*, 92–109.

Glanz, K., & Bishop, D. B. (2010). The role of behavioral science theory in development and implementation of public health interventions. *Annual Review of Public Health, 31*, 399–418.

Goffman, E. (1963). *Stigma: Notes on the management of spoiled identity.* Englewood Cliffs, NJ: Prentice-Hall.

Goforth, H.W., Cohen, M.A., & Murrough, J. (2008). Mood disorders. In M.A. Cohen & J.M. Gorman (Eds.), *Comprehensive textbook of AIDS psychiatry.* New York, NY: Oxford University Press.

Golin, C., Isasi, F., Bontempi, J.B., & Eng, E. (2002). Secret pills: HIV-positive patients' experiences taking antiretroviral therapy in North Carolina. *AIDS Education and Prevention, 14*, 318–29.

Granich, R., Crowley, S., Vitoria, M., Smyth, C., Kahn, J.G., Bennett, R., . . . Williams, B. (2010). Highly active antiretroviral treatment as prevention of HIV transmission: Review of scientific evidence and update. *Current Opinion in HIV and AIDS, 5*, 298–304.

Grimley, D.M., Annang, L., Houser, S., & Chen, H. (2005). Prevalence of condom use errors among STD clinic patients. *American Journal of Health Behavior, 29*, 324–30.

Guse, K., Levine, D., Martins, S., Lira, A., Gaarde, J., Westmorland, W., & Gilliam, M. (2012). Interventions using new digital media to improve adolescent sexual health: A systematic review. *The Journal of Adolescent Health, 51*(6), 535–43.

Hagan, H., & Des Jarlais, D.C. (2000). HIV and HCV infection among injecting drug users. *Mount Sinai Journal of Medicine, 67*, 423–8.

Hardy, D. J., & Vance, D. E. (2009). The neuropsychology of HIV/AIDS in older adults. *Neuropsychology Review, 19*(2), 263–72.

Harling, G., Subramanian, S., Barnighausen, T., & Kawachi, I. (2013). Socioeconomic disparities in sexually transmitted infections among young adults in the United States: Examining the interaction between income and race/ethnicity. *Sexually Transmitted Diseases, 40*(7), 575–81.

Hart, T.A., & Hart, S.L. (2010). The future of cognitive behavioral interventions within behavioral medicine. *Journal of Cognitive Psychotherapy, 24*, 344–53.

Hart, T.A., & Heimberg, R.G. (2005). Social anxiety as a risk factor for unprotected intercourse among gay and bisexual male youth. *AIDS and Behavior, 9*, 505–12.

Hart, T.A., James, C.A., Purcell, D.W., & Farber, E. (2008). Social anxiety and HIV transmission risk among HIV-seropositive male patients. *AIDS Patient Care and STDs, 22*, 879–86.

Hart, T.A., Noor, S.W., Adam, B.D., Vernon, J.R., Brennan, D.J., Gardner, S., . . . Myers, T. (2017). Number of psychosocial strengths predicts reduced HIV sexual risk behaviors above and beyond syndemic problems among gay and bisexual men. *AIDS and Behavior.* doi: 10.1007/s10461-016-1669-2.

Hedrich, D., Kerr, T., & Dubois-Arber, F. (2010). In T. Rhodes & D. Hedrich (Eds.), *Drug consumption facilities in Europe and beyond* (10th ed.). Luxembourg: European Monitoring Centre for Drugs and Drug Addiction. Retrieved from www.emcdda.europa.eu/publications/monographs/harm-reduction

Heldenbrand, S., Martin, B.C., Gubbins, P.O., Hadden, K., Renna, C., Shilling, R., & Dayer, L. (2016). Assessment of medication adherence app features, functionality, and health literacy level and the creation of a searchable Web-based adherence app resource for health care professionals and patients. *Journal of the American Pharmaceutical Association, 56*(3), 293–302.

Herek, G.M. (1999). AIDS and stigma. *American Behavioral Scientist, 42*, 1102–12.

Herek, G.M., Capitanio, J.P., & Widaman, K.F. (2002). HIV-related stigma and knowledge in the United States: Prevalence and trends, 1991–1999. *American Journal of Public Health, 92*, 371–7.

Hofman, P., & Nelson, A.M. (2006). The pathology induced by highly active antiretroviral therapy against human immunodeficiency virus: An update. *Current Medicinal Chemistry, 13*, 3121–32.

Holzemer, W.L., Human, S., Arudo, J., Rosa, M., Hamilton, M.J., Corless, I., . . . Maryland, M. (2009). Exploring HIV stigma and quality of life for persons living with HIV infection. *Journal of the Association of Nurses in AIDS Care, 20*, 161–8.

Horvath, K.J., Rosser, B.S., & Remafedi, G. (2008). Sexual risk taking among young Internet-using men who have sex with men. *American Journal of Public Health, 98*, 1059–67.

Houston, E., Mikrut, C., Guy, A., Fominaya, A.W., Tatum, A.K., Kim, J.H., & Brown, A. (2016). Another look at depressive symptoms and antiretroviral therapy adherence: The role of treatment self-efficacy. *Journal of Health Psychology, 21*(10), 2138–47.

Hurt, C.B., Matthews, D.D., Calabria, M.S., Green, K.A., Adimora, A.A., Golin, C.E., & Hightow-Weidman, L. (2010). Sex with older partners is associated with primary HIV infection among men who have sex with men in North Carolina. *Journal of Acquired Immune Deficiency Syndromes, 54*, 185–90.

Ickovics, J.R., Beren, S.E., Grigorenko, E.L., Morrill, A.C., Druley, J.A., & Rodin, J. (2002). Pathways of risk: Race, social class, stress, and coping as factors predicting heterosexual risk behaviors for HIV among women. *AIDS and Behavior, 6*, 339–50.

Ickovics, J.R., Hamburger, M.E., Vlahov, D., Schoenbaum, E.E., Schuman, P., Boland, R.J., & Moore, J. (2001). Mortality, CD4 count decline, and depressive symptoms among HIV-seropositive women: Longitudinal analysis from the HIV epidemiology research study. *Journal of the American Medical Association, 285*, 1466–74.

Ivanova, E.L., Hart, T.A., Wagner, A.C., Aljassem, K., & Loutfy, M.R. (2012). Correlates of anxiety in women living with HIV of reproductive age. *AIDS and Behavior, 16*, 2181–91.

James, C.A., Hart, T.A., Roberts, K.E., Ghai, A., Petrovic, B., & Lima, M.D. (2011). Religion versus ethnicity as predictors of unprotected vaginal intercourse among young adults. *Sexual Health, 8*, 363–71.

Jemmott, J.B. (2012). The reasoned action approach in HIV risk-reduction strategies for adolescents. *The Annals of the American Academy of Political and Social Science, 640*(1), 150–72.

Johnson, B.T., Scott-Sheldon, L.A., Huedo-Medina, T.B., & Carey, M.P. (2011). Interventions to reduce sexual risk for human immunodeficiency virus in adolescents. *Archives of Pediatrics & Adolescent Medicine, 165*, 77–84.

Jozaghi, E., & Jackson, A. (2015). Examining the potential role of a supervised injection facility in Saskatoon, Saskatchewan, to avert HIV among people who inject drugs. *International Journal of Health Policy and Management, 4*, 373–9.

Jozaghi, E., Reid, A.A., & Andresen, M.A. (2013). A cost-benefit/cost-effectiveness analysis of proposed supervised injection facilities in Montreal, Canada. *Substance Abuse Treatment, Prevention, and Policy, 8*(25).

Jozaghi, E., Reid, A.A., Andresen, M.A., & Juneau, A. (2014). A cost-benefit/cost-effectiveness analysis of proposed supervised injection facilities in Ottawa, Canada. *Substance Abuse Treatment, Prevention, and Policy, 9*(31).

Kahn, J.A., Kaplowitz, R.A., Goodman, E., & Emans, S.J. (2002). The association between impulsiveness and sexual risk behaviors in adolescent and young adult women. *Journal of Adolescent Health, 30*, 229–32.

Kalichman, S.C., & Cain, D. (2004). A prospective study of sensation seeking and alcohol use as predictors of sexual risk behaviors among men and women receiving sexual transmitted infection clinic services. *Psychology of Addictive Behaviors, 18*, 367–73.

Kalichman, S.C., Rompa, D., Cage, M., DiFonzo, K., Simpson, D., Austin, J., . . . Graham, J. (2001). Effectiveness of an intervention to reduce HIV transmission risks in HIV-positive people. *American Journal of Preventive Medicine, 21*, 84–92.

Kann, L., McManus, T., Harris, W.A., Shanklin, S.L., Flint, K.H., Hawkins, J., . . . Zaza, S. (2016). Youth Risk Behavior Surveillance – United States, 2015. *MMWR Surveillance Summaries, 65*(6), 1–174.

Kashubeck-West, S., & Szymanski, D.M. (2008). Risky sexual behaviour in gay and bisexual men: Internalized heterosexism, sensation seeking, and substance use. *Counseling Psychologist, 36*, 595–614.

Kaufman, M.R., Cornish, F., Zimmerman, R.S., & Johnson, B.T. (2015). Health behavior change models for HIV prevention and AIDS care: Practical recommendations for a multi-level approach. *Journal of Acquired Immune Deficiency Syndromes, 66*, S250–S258.

Kegeles, S.M., Rebchook, G., Pollack, L., Huebner, D., Tebbetts, S., Hamiga, J., . . . Zovod, B. (2012). An intervention to help community-based organizations implement an evidence-based HIV prevention intervention: The Mpowerment project technology exchange system. *American Journal of Community Psychology, 49*(1–2), 182–98.

Kerr, T., Stoltz, J., Tyndall, M., Li, K., Zhang, R., Montaner, J., & Wood, E. (2006). Impact of a medically supervised safer injection facility on community drug use patterns: A before and after study. *British Medical Journal, 332*, 220–2.

Kerr, T., Tyndall, M., Li, K., Montaner, J.S., & Wood, E. (2005). Safer injecting facility use and syringe sharing in injection drug users. *Lancet, 366*, 316–18.

Kessler, R.C., Berglund, P., Demler, O., Jin, R., & Walters, E.E. (2005). Lifetime prevalence and age-of-onset distributions of DSM-IV disorders in the national comorbidity survey replication. *Archives of General Psychiatry, 62*, 593–602.

Kinsler, J.J., Wong, M.D., Sayles, J.N., Davis, C., & Cunningham, W.E. (2007). The effect of perceived stigma from a health care provider on access to care among a low-income HIV-positive population. *AIDS Patient Care and STDs, 21*, 584–92.

Kitahata, M.M., Reed, S.D., Dillingham, P.W., Van Rompaey, S.E., Young, A.A., Harrington, R.D., & Holmes, K.K. (2004). Pharmacy-based assessment of adherence to HAART predicts virologic and immunologic treatment response and clinical progression to AIDS and death. *International Journal of STD & AIDS, 15*, 803–10.

Klinkenberg, W.D., & Sacks, S. (2004). Mental disorders and drug abuse in persons living with HIV/AIDS. *AIDS Care, 16*, S22–S42.

Kobin, A.B., & Sheth, N.U. (2011). Levels of adherence required for virologic suppression among newer antiretroviral medications. *Annals of Pharmacotherapy, 45*(3), 372–9.

Koblin, B.A., Chesney, M.A., Husnik, M.J., Bozeman, S., Celum, C.L., Buchbinder, S., . . . Coates, T.J. (2003). High-risk behaviors among men who have sex with men in 6 US cities: Baseline data from the EXPLORE study. *American Journal of Public Health, 93*, 926–32.

Kohler, P.K., Manhart, L.E., & Lafferty, W.E. (2008). Abstinence-only and comprehensive sex education and the initiation of sexual activity and teen pregnancy. *Journal of Adolescent Health, 42*, 344–51.

Kulig, J. (2003). Condoms: The basics and beyond. *Adolescent Medicine Clinics, 14*, 633–45.

Kurtz, S.P., Buttram, M.E., Surratt, H.L., & Stall, R.D. (2012). Resilience, syndemic factors, and serosorting behaviors among HIV-positive and HIV-negative substance-using MSM. *AIDS Education and Prevention, 24*(3), 193–205.

Latka, M.H., Hagan, H., Kapadia, F., Golub, E.T., Bonner, S., Campbell, J.V., . . . Strathdee, S.A. (2008). A randomized intervention trial to reduce the lending of used injection equipment among injection drug users infected with hepatitis C. *American Journal of Public Health, 98*, 853–61.

Lazarus, R.S., & Folkman, S. (1984). *Stress, appraisal, and coping.* New York, NY: Springer.

Lee, R.S., Kochman, A., & Sikkema, K.J. (2002). Internalized stigma among people living with HIV–AIDS. *AIDS and Behavior, 6*, 309–19.

Lehman, J.S., Carr, M.H., Nichol, A.J., Ruisanchez, A., Knight, D.W., Langford, A.E., . . . Mermin, J.H. (2014). Prevalence and public health implications of state laws that criminalize potential HIV exposure in the United States. *AIDS and Behavior, 18*(6), 997–1006.

Liu, Y., Canada, K., Shi, K., & Corrigan, P. (2012). AIDS care: Psychological and socio-medical aspects of AIDS/HIV. *AIDS Care, 24*, 129–35.

Logan, T.K., Cole, J., & Leukefeld, C. (2002). Women, sex, and HIV: Social and contextual factors, meta-analysis of published interventions, and implications for practice and research. *Psychological Bulletin, 128*, 851–85.

Lu, M., Safren, S.A., Skolnik, P.R., Rogers, W.H., Coady, W., Hardy, H., & Wilson, I.B. (2008). Optimal recall period and response task for self-reported HIV medication adherence. *AIDS and Behavior, 12*(1), 86–94.

Lyles, C.M., Crepaz, N., Herbst, J.H., & Kay, L.S. (2006). Evidence-based HIV behavioral prevention from the perspective of the CDC's HIV/AIDS Prevention Research Synthesis team. *AIDS Education & Prevention, 18*, 21–31.

Lyles, C.M., Kay, L.S., Crepaz, N., Herbst, J.H., Passin, W.F., Kim, A.S., . . . Mullins, M.M. (2007). Best-evidence interventions: Findings from a systematic review of HIV behavioral interventions for US populations at high risk, 2000–2004. *American Journal of Public Health, 97*(1), 133–43.

Ma, W., Detels, R., Feng, Y., Wu, Z., Shen, L., Li, Y., . . . Liu, T. (2007). Acceptance of and barriers to voluntary HIV counselling and testing among adults in Guizhou Province, China. *AIDS, 21*, S129–S135.

Mahajan, A.P., Sayles, J.N., Patel, V.A., Remien, R.H., Sawires, S.R., Ortiz, D.J., . . . Coates, T.J. (2008). Stigma in the HIV/AIDS epidemic: A review of the literature and recommendations for the way forward. *AIDS, 22*, S67–S79.

Marhefka, S.L., Buhi, E.R., Baldwin, J., Chen, H., Johnson, A., Lynn, V., & Glueckauf, R. (2014). Effectiveness of healthy relationships video-group — A videoconferencing group intervention for women living with HIV: Preliminary findings from a randomized controlled trial. *Telemedicine Journal and e-Health, 20*(2), 128–34.

Marino, P., Simoni, J.M., & Bordeaux Silverstein, L. (2007). Peer support to promote medication adherence among people living with HIV /AIDS: The benefits to peers. *Social Work in Health Care, 45*, 67–80.

Martin, L., & Kagee, A. (2011). Lifetime and HIV-related PTSD among persons recently diagnosed with HIV. *AIDS and Behavior, 15*(1), 125–31.

Mayberry, L.S., & Osborn, C.Y. (2014). Empirical validation of the information-motivation-behavioral skills model of diabetes medication adherence: A framework for intervention. *Diabetes Care, 37*(5), 1246–53.

Mayne, T.J., Vittinghoff, E., Chesney, M.A., Barrett, D.C., & Coates, T.J. (1996). Depressive affect and survival among gay and bisexual men infected with HIV. *Archives of Internal Medicine, 156*, 2233–8.

McCoul, M.D., & Haslam, N. (2001). Predicting high risk sexual behaviour in heterosexual and homosexual men: The roles of impulsivity and sensation seeking. *Personality and Individual Differences, 31*, 1303–10.

McFarlane, M., Kachur, R., Bull, S., & Rietmeijer, C. (2004). Women, the Internet, and sexually transmitted infections. *Journal of Women's Health, 13*, 689–94.

Medley, A., Kennedy, C., O'Reilly, K., & Sweat, M. (2009). Effectiveness of peer education interventions for HIV prevention in developing countries: A systematic review and meta-analysis. *AIDS Education and Prevention, 21*, 181–206.

Meyer, I.H. (1995). Minority stress and mental health in gay men. *Journal of Health and Social Behavior, 36*, 38–56.

Meyer, I.H. (2003). Prejudice, social stress, and mental health in lesbian, gay, and bisexual populations: Conceptual issues and research evidence. *Psychological Bulletin, 129*, 674–97.

Miguez-Burbano, M.J., Espinoza, L., & Lewis, J.E. (2008). HIV treatment adherence and sexual functioning. *AIDS and Behavior, 12*, 78–85.

Milloy, M.J.S., Kerr, T., Tyndall, M., Montaner, J., & Wood, E. (2008). Estimated drug overdose deaths averted by North America's first medically-supervised safer injection facility. *PLOS ONE, 3*, e3351.

Molina, J., Capitant, C., Spire, B., Pialoux, G., Cotte, L., Charreau, I., . . . Delfraissy, J. (2015). On-demand preexposure prophylaxis in men at high risk for HIV-1 infection. *New England Journal of Medicine, 373*(23), 2237–46.

Montaño, D.E., & Kasprzyk, D. (2015). Theory of reasoned action, theory of planned behavior, and the integrated behavioral model. In K. Glanz, B.K. Rimer, & K. Viswanath (Eds.), *Health behavior: Theory, research and practice* (pp. 95–124). San Francisco, CA: Jossey-Bass.

Mustanski, B.S. (2007). Are sexual partners met online associated with HIV/STI risk behaviours? Retrospective and daily diary data in conflict. *AIDS Care, 19*, 822–7.

National Institutes of Health. (2016a). *HIV overview: The HIV life cycle*. Retrieved from https://aidsinfo.nih.gov/education-materials/fact-sheets/19/73/the-hiv-life-cycle

National Institutes of Health. (2016b). *HIV overview: The stages of HIV infection*. Retrieved from https://aidsinfo.nih.gov/education-materials/fact-sheets/19/46/the-stages-of-hiv-infection

Navaline, H.A., Snider, E.C., Petro, C.J., Tobin, D., Metzger, D., Alterman, A.I., & Woody, G.E. (1994). Preparations for AIDS vaccine trials. An automated version of the Risk Assessment Battery (RAB): Enhancing the assessment of risk behaviors. *AIDS Research and Human Retroviruses, 10*, S281–S283.

Newcomb, M.E., & Mustanski, B. (2011). Moderators of the relationship between internalized homophobia and risky sexual behaviour in men who have sex with men: A meta-analysis. *Archives of Sexual Behavior, 40*, 189–99.

Newman, P.A., & Poindexter, C.C. (2010). HIV prevention innovations and challenges. In P.A. Newman & C.C. Poindexter (Eds.), *Handbook of HIV and social work: Principles, practice, and populations* (pp. 183–96). Hoboken, NJ: John Wiley & Sons.

Noar, S.M., Carlyle, K., & Cole, C. (2006). Why communication is crucial: Meta-analysis of the relationship between safer sexual communication and condom use. *Journal of Health Communication, 11*(4), 365–90.

Noar, S.M., Morokoff, P.J., & Harlow, L.L. (2002). Condom negotiation in heterosexually active men and women: Development and validation of a condom influence strategy questionnaire. *Psychology & Health, 17*(6), 711–35.

Obermeyer, C.M., & Osborn, M. (2007). The utilization of testing and counseling for HIV: A review of the social and behavioral evidence. *American Journal of Public Health, 97*, 1762–74.

Ogilvie, G.S., Taylor, D.L., Trussler, T., Marchand, R., Gilbert, M., Moniruzzaman, A., & Rekart, M.L. (2008). Seeking sexual partners on the Internet: A marker for risky sexual behaviour in men who have sex with men. *Canadian Journal of Public Health, 99*, 185–8.

Owe-Larsson, B., Säll, L., Salamon, E., & Allgulander, C. (2009). HIV infection and psychiatric illness. *African Journal of Psychiatry, 12*, 115–28.

Pakenham, K.I., & Rinaldis, M. (2001). The role of illness, resources, appraisal, and coping strategies in adjustment to HIV/AIDS: The direct and buffering effects. *Journal of Behavioral Medicine, 24*, 259–79.

Peterson, J.L., Folkman, S., & Bakeman, R. (1996). Stress, coping, HIV status, psychosocial resources, and depressive mood in African gay, bisexual, and heterosexual men. *American Journal of Community Psychology, 24*, 461–87.

Pinkerton, S.D. (2011). How many HIV infections are prevented by Vancouver Canada's supervised injection facility? *International Journal of Drug Policy, 22*(3), 179–83.

Pitpitan, E.V., Kalichman, S.C., Eaton, L.A., Cain, D., Sikkema, K.J., Skinner, D., . . . Pieterse, D. (2012). AIDS-related stigma, HIV testing, and transmission risk among patrons of informal drinking places in Cape Town, South Africa. *Annals of Behavioral Medicine, 43*(3), 362–71.

Poulin, C., & Graham, L. (2001). The association between substance use, unplanned sexual intercourse and other sexual behaviours among adolescent students. *Addiction, 96*, 607–21.

Prochaska, J.O., & Velicer, W.F. (1997). The transtheoretical model of health behavior change. *American Journal of Health Promotion, 12*, 38–48.

Public Health Agency of Canada (PHAC). (2008). *Canadian guidelines for sexual health education*. Ottawa, ON: Sexual Health & Sexually Transmitted Infections Section, Community Acquired Infections Division, Public Health Agency of Canada.

Public Health Agency of Canada (PHAC). (2009). *Acquired Immunodeficiency Syndrome*. Retrieved from http://www.phac-aspc.gc.ca/publicat/ccdr-rmtc/09vol35/35s2/AIDS_SIDA-eng.php

Public Health Agency of Canada (PHAC). (2013). The Chief Public Health Officer's Report on the State of Public Health in Canada, 2013: Infectious Disease – The never-ending threat. Retrieved from http://www.phac-aspc.gc.ca/cphorsphc-respcacsp/2013/assets/pdf/2013-eng.pdf

Public Health Agency of Canada (PHAC). (2015a). *Sexual health and sexually transmitted infections*. Retrieved from http://www.phac-aspc.gc.ca/std-mts/

Public Health Agency of Canada (PHAC). (2015b). Report on sexually transmitted infections in Canada: 2012 – Appendix B: Reported cases and rates of chlamydia, gonorrhea, and infectious syphilis. Retrieved from http://www.phac-aspc.gc.ca/sti-its-surv-epi/rep-rap-2012/app-ann-b-eng.php

Public Health Agency of Canada (PHAC). (2016a). *HIV in Canada: Surveillance summary tables, 2014–2015*. Retrieved from http://healthycanadians.gc.ca/publications/diseases-conditions-maladies-affections/hiv-aids-surveillance-2015-vih-sida/index-eng.php

Public Health Agency of Canada (PHAC). (2016b). *Summary: Measuring Canada's progress on the 90-90-90 HIV targets*. Retrieved from http://healthycanadians.gc.ca/publications/diseases-conditions-maladies-affections/hiv-90-90-90-vih/index-eng.php

Rabkin, J.G. (1996). Prevalence of psychiatric disorders in HIV illness. *International Review of Psychiatry, 8*, 157–66.

Radcliffe, J., Landau Fleisher, C., Hawkins, L.A., Tanney, M., Kassam-Adams, N., Ambrose, C., & Rudy, B.J. (2007). Posttraumatic stress and trauma history in adolescents and young adults with HIV. *AIDS Patient Care and STDs, 21*, 501–8.

Rathus, S.A., Nevid, J.S., Fichner-Rathus, L., Herold, E.S., & McKenzie, S.W. (2007). Sexually transmitted infections. In S.A. Rathus, J.S. Nevid, & L. Fichner-Rathus (Eds.), *Human sexuality in a world of diversity* (2nd Canadian ed., pp. 406–439). Toronto, ON: Pearson.

Ray, M., Logan, R., Sterne, J.A., Hernández-Díaz , S., Robins, J.M., Sabin, C., . . . HIV-CAUSAL Collaboration. (2010). The effect of combined antiretroviral therapy on the overall mortality of HIV-infected individuals. *AIDS, 24*(1), 123–37.

Rietmeijer, C.A., Bull, S.S., McFarlane, M., Patnaik, J.L., & Douglas, J.M. (2003). Risks and benefits of the Internet for populations at risk for sexually transmitted infections (STIs): Results of an STI clinic survey. *Sexually Transmitted Diseases, 30*, 15–19.

Rintamaki, L.S., Davis, T.C., Skripkauskas, S., Bennett, C.L., & Wolf, M.S. (2006). Social stigma concerns and HIV medication adherence. *AIDS Patient Care and STDs, 20*, 359–68.

Rosenstock, I.M. (1974). The health belief model and preventive health behavior. *Health Education Monographs, 2*, 354–86.

Rosser, B.S., Miner, M.H., Bockting, W.O., Ross, M.W., Konstan, J., Gurak, L., . . . Mazin, R. (2009a). HIV risk and the Internet: Results of the Men's INTernet Sex (MINTS) Study. *AIDS and Behavior, 13*, 746–56.

Rosser, B.S., Oakes, J.M., Horvath, K.J., Konstan, J.A., Danilenko, G.P., & Peterson, J.L. (2009b). HIV sexual risk behavior by men who use the Internet to seek sex with men: Results of the Men's INTernet Sex Study-II (MINTS-II). *AIDS and Behavior, 13*, 488–98.

Rotermann, M. (2012). Sexual behavior and condom use of 15- to 24-year-olds in 2003 and 2009/2012. *Statistics Canada: Health Reports, 23*, 1–5.

Rubinstein, M.L., & Selwyn, P.A. (1998). High prevalence of insomnia in an outpatient population with HIV infection. *Journal of Acquired Immune Deficiency Syndromes and Human Retrovirology, 19*, 260–5.

Saberi, P., Neilands, T.B., Vittinghoff, E., Johnson, M.O., Chesney, M., & Cohn, S.E. (2015). Barriers to antiretroviral therapy adherence and plasma HIV RNA suppression among AIDS Clinical Trials Group study participants. *AIDS Patient Care & STDs, 29*(3), 111–16.

Safren, S.A., Gershuny, B.S., & Hendriksen, E. (2003). Symptoms of posttraumatic stress and death anxiety in persons with HIV and medication adherence difficulties. *AIDS Patient Care and STDs, 17*, 657–64.

Safren, S.A., O'Cleirigh, C., Tan, J.Y., Raminani, S.R., Reilly, L.C., Otto, M.W., & Mayer, K.H. (2009). A randomized controlled trial of cognitive behavioral therapy for adherence and depression (CBT-AD) in HIV-infected individuals. *Health Psychology, 28*, 1–10.

Safren, S.A., Otto, M.W., & Worth, J.L. (1999). Life-steps: Applying cognitive-behavioral therapy to HIV medication adherence. *Cognitive and Behavioral Practice, 6*, 332–41.

Santelli, J., Ott, M.A., Lyon, M., Rogers, J., Summers, D., & Schleifer, R. (2006). Abstinence and abstinence-only education: A review of U.S. policies and programs. *Journal of Adolescent Health, 38*, 72–81.

Sarkar, N. N. (2008). Barriers to condom use. The European Journal of Contraception & Reproductive Health Care, 13(2), 114–22.

Seeley, J., Watts, C.H., Kippax, S., Russell, S., Heise, L., & Whiteside, A. (2012). Addressing the structural drivers of HIV: A luxury or necessity for programmes? *Journal of the International AIDS Society, 15*(Suppl 1), 1–4.

Selik, R.M., Mokotoff, E.D., Branson, B., Owen, S.M., Whitmore, S., & Hall, H.I. (2014). Revised surveillance case definition for HIV infection—United States, 2014. *MMWR Recommendations and Reports, 63*(3), 1–10.

Shiely, F., Horgan, M., & Hayes, K. (2009). Increased sexually transmitted infection incidence in a low risk population: Identifying the risk factors. *European Journal of Public Health, 20*, 207–12.

Siegel, K., & Schrimshaw, E.W. (2000). Coping with negative emotions: The cognitive strategies of HIV-infected gay/ bisexual men. *Journal of Health Psychology, 5*, 517–30.

Sikkema, K.J., Hansen, N.B., Kochman, A., Santos, J., Watt, M.H., Wilson, P.A., . . . Mayer, G. (2011). The development and feasibility of a brief risk reduction intervention for newly HIV-diagnosed men who have sex with men. *Journal of Community Psychology, 39*, 717–32.

Simbayi, L.C., Kalichman, S., Strebel, A., Cloete, A., Henda, N., & Mqeketo, A. (2007). Internalized stigma, discrimination, and depression among men and women living with HIV/AIDS in Cape Town, South Africa. *Social Science & Medicine, 64*, 1823–31.

Simoni, J.M., Nelson, K.M., Franks, J.C., Yard, S.S., & Lehavot, K. (2011). Are peer interventions for HIV efficacious? A systematic review. *AIDS and Behavior, 15*(8), 1589–95.

Singer, M. (2009). Introduction to syndemics: A critical systems approach to public and community health. San Francisco, CA: Wiley.

Small, E., Weinman, M.L., Buzi, R.S., & Smith, P.G. (2009). Risk factors, knowledge, and attitudes as predictors of intent to use condoms among minority female adolescents attending family planning clinics. *Journal of HIV/AIDS & Social Services, 8*, 251–68.

Smith, M.T., Huang, M I., & Manber, R. (2005). Cognitive behavior therapy for chronic insomnia occurring within the context of medical and psychiatric disorders. *Clinical Psychology Review, 25*, 559–92.

Sperber, K., & Shao, L. (2003). Neurologic consequences of HIV infection in the era of HAART. *AIDS Patient Care and STDs, 17*, 509–18.

Stanger-Hall, K., & Hall, D.W. (2011). Abstinence-only education and teen pregnancy rates: Why we need comprehensive sex education in the U.S. *PLOS ONE, 6*, e24658.

Taibi, D. M. (2013). Sleep disturbances in persons living with HIV. *Journal of the Association of Nurses in AIDS Care, 24*(1), S72–S85.

Tapert, S.F., Aarons, G.A., Sedlar, G.R., & Brown, S.A. (2001). Adolescent substance use and sexual risk-taking behaviour. *Journal of Adolescent Health, 28*, 181–9.

Taylor, S.E., Kemeny, M.E., Aspinwall, L.G., Schneider, S.G., Rodriguez, R., & Herbert, M. (1992). Optimism, coping, psychological distress, and high-risk sexual behaviour among men at risk for acquired immunodeficiency syndrome (AIDS). *Journal of Personality and Social Psychology, 63*, 460–73.

Teitelman, A.M., Tennille, J., Bohinski, J.M., Jemmott, L.S., & Jemmott, J.B. (2011). Unwanted unprotected sex: Condom coercion by male partners and self-silencing of condom negotiation among adolescent girls. *Advances in Nursing Science, 34*, 243–59.

Teva, I., Bermudez, M.P., & Buela-Casal, G. (2010). Sexual sensation seeking, social stress, and coping styles as predictors of HIV/STD risk behaviors in adolescents. *Youth & Society, 42*, 255–77.

Theuninck, A.C., Lake, N., & Gibson, S. (2010). HIV-related posttraumatic stress disorder: Investigating the traumatic events. *AIDS Patient Care and STDs, 24*, 458–91.

Toronto Star. (2016). *Feds ease rules on supervised drug injection sites, mail inspections at border.* Retrieved from www.thestar.com/news/canada/2016/12/12/more-supervised-drug-injection-sites-expected-to-open-in-canada.html

Treisman, G., & Angelino, A. (2007). Interralation between psychiatric disorders and the prevention and treatment of HIV infection. *Clinical Infectious Diseases, 45*, S313–S317.

Tulloch, T.G., Rotondi, N.K., Ing, S., Myers, T., Calzavara, L.M., Loutfy, M.R., & Hart, T.A. (2015). Retrospective reports of developmental stressors, syndemics, and their association with sexual risk outcomes among gay men. *Archives of Sexual Behavior, 44*(7), 1879–89.

UNAIDS. (2008). *Criminalization of HIV transmission: Policy brief.* Retrieved from data.unaids.org/pub/basedocument/2008/20080731_jc1513_policy_criminalization_en.pdf

UNAIDS. (2014). *90-90-90: An ambition treatment target to help end the AIDS epidemic.* Retrieved from http://www.unaids.org/sites/default/files/media_asset/90-90-90_en_0.pdf

UNAIDS. (2016). *AIDS by the numbers.* Retrieved from http://www.unaids.org/sites/default/files/media_asset/AIDS-by-the-numbers-2016_en.pdf

US Public Health Service. (2014). *Preexposure prophylaxis for the prevention of HIV infections in the United States.* Retrieved from https://www.cdc.gov/hiv/pdf/prepguidelines2014.pdf

Vanable, P.A., Carey, M.P., Blair, D.C., & Littlewood, R.A. (2006). Impact of HIV-related stigma on health behaviors and psychological adjustment among HIV-positive men and women. *AIDS and Behavior, 10*, 473–82.

van de Vijver, D.A., Nichols, B.E., Abbas, U.L., Boucher, C.A.B., Cambiano, V., Eaton, J.W., . . . Hallett, T.B. (2013). Preexposure prophylaxis will have a limited impact on HIV-1 drug resistance in sub-Saharan Africa: A comparison of mathematical models. *AIDS, 27*(18), 2943-2951.

van Servellen, G., Chang, B., Garcia, L., & Lombardi, E. (2002). Individual and system-level factors associated with treatment nonadherence in human immunodeficiency virus-infected men and women. *AIDS Patient Care and STDs, 16*, 269–281.

Wagner, A.C., Hart, T.A., Mohammed, S., Ivanova, E., Wong, J., & Loutfy, M.R. (2010). Correlates of HIV stigma in HIV-positive women. *Archives of Women's Mental Health, 13*, 207–214.

Wagner, G.J., Goggin, K., Remien, R.H., Rosen, M.I., Simoni, J., Bangsberg, D.R., & Liu, H. (2011). A closer look at depression and its relationship to HIV antiretroviral adherence. *Annals of Behavioral Medicine, 42*(3), 352–60.

Whetten, K., Reif, S., Whetten, R., & Murphy-MacMillan, L.K. (2008). Trauma, mental health, distrust, and stigma among HIV-positive persons: Implications for effective care. *Psychosomatic Medicine, 70*, 531–8.

Williams, B., Wood, R., Dukay, V., Delva, W., Ginsburg, D., Hargrove, J., . . . Welte, A. (2011). Treatment as prevention: Preparing the way. *Journal of the International AIDS Society, 14*, S6.

Wilson, P.A., Nanin, J., Amesty, S., Wallace, S., Cherenack, E.M., & Fullilove, R. (2014). Using syndemic theory to understand vulnerability to HIV infection among Black and Latino men in New York City. *Journal of Urban Health, 91*(5), 983–98.

Winters, K.C., Botzet, A.M., Fahnhorst, T., Baumel, L., & Lee, S. (2009). Impulsivity and its relationship to risky sexual behaviors and drug abuse. *Journal of Child & Adolescent Substance Abuse, 18*, 43–56.

Wolitski, R.J., & Fenton, K.A. (2011). Sexual health, HIV, and sexually transmitted infections among gay, bisexual, and other men who have sex with men in the United States. *AIDS and Behavior, 15*(1), 9–17.

Wood, E., Tyndall, M.W., Montaner, J.S., & Kerr, T. (2006a). Summary of findings from the evaluation of a pilot medically supervised safer injecting facility. *Canadian Medical Association Journal, 175*, 1399–1404.

Wood, E., Tyndall, M.W., Zhang, R., Montaner, J.S.G., & Kerr, T. (2007). Rate of detoxification service use and its impact among a cohort of supervised injection facility users. *Addiction, 102*, 916–19.

Wood, E., Tyndall, M.W., Zhenguo, Q., Zhang, R., Montaner, J.S.G., & Kerr, T. (2006b) Service uptake and characteristics of injection drug users utilizing North America's first medically supervised safer injecting facility. *American Journal of Public Health, 96*, 770–3.

World Health Organization (WHO). (2008). Essential prevention and care interventions for adults and adolescents living with HIV in resource-limited settings. Retrieved from www.who.int/hiv/pub/prev_care/OMS_EPP_AFF_en.pdf

World Health Organization (WHO). (2016a). *Global health sector strategy on Sexually Transmitted Infections, 2016-2021: Towards ending STIs.* Retrieved from http://apps.who.int/iris/bitstream/10665/246296/1/WHO-RHR-16.09-eng.pdf?ua=1

World Health Organization (WHO). (2016b). *Global health sector strategy on HIV 2016-2021: Towards ending AIDS.* Retrieved from http://apps.who.int/iris/bitstream/10665/246178/1/WHO-HIV-2016.05-eng.pdf?ua=1

World Health Organization (WHO). (2016c). *HIV/AIDS*. Retrieved from http://www.who.int/features/qa/71/en/

Zarani, F., Besharat, M. A., Sadeghian, S., & Sarami, G. (2010). The effectiveness of the information-motivation-behavioral skills model in promoting adherence in CABG patients. *Journal of Health Psychology, 15*(6), 828–37.

Zuckerman, M. (2009). Sensation seeking. In M.R. Leary & R.H., Hoyle (Eds.), *Handbook of individual differences in social behavior* (pp. 455–65). New York, NY: Guilford.

Chapter 12

Adler, N.E., & Page, A.E.K. (Eds.), Institute of Medicine Committee on Psychosocial Services to Cancer Patients/ Families in a Community Setting. (2008). *Cancer care for the whole patient: Meeting psychosocial and health needs.* Washington: National Academies Press.

Ahmed, R.L., Thomas, W., Yee, D., & Schmitz, K.H. (2006). Randomized controlled trial of weight training and lymphedema in breast cancer survivors. *Journal of Clinical Oncology, 24*, 2765–72.

American Cancer Society (ACS). (2015a). *Breast cancer facts & figures 2015–2016.* Atlanta, GA: American Cancer Society.

American Cancer Society (ACS). (2015b). *Cancer prevention & early detection facts & figures 2015–2016.* Atlanta, GA: American Cancer Society.

American Cancer Society (ACS). (2016). *Cancer facts & figures 2016.* Atlanta, GA: American Cancer Society.

Andersen, B.L., Farrar, W.B., Golden-Kreutz, D., Kutz, L.A., MacCallum, R., Courtney, M.E., & Glaser, R. (1998). Stress and immune responses after surgical treatment for regional breast cancer. *Journal of the National Cancer Institute, 90*, 30–6.

Ando, M., Morita, T., Akechi, T., & Okamoto, T. (2010). Efficacy of short-term life-review interviews on the spiritual well-being of terminally ill cancer patients. *Journal of Pain and Symptom Management, 39*, 993–1002.

Antoni, M.H., Lutgendorf, S.K., Cole, S.W., Dhabhar, F.S., Sephton, S.E., McDonald, P.G., . . . Sood, A.K. (2006). The influence of bio-behavioural factors on tumour biology: Pathways and mechanisms. *Nature Reviews Cancer, 6*, 240–8.

Benson, J.R., & Liau, S.-S. (2010). The nature and development of cancer. In D.A. Warrell, T.M. Cox, & J.D. Firth (Eds.), *Oxford textbook of medicine* (5th ed., Vol. 1. pp. 333–357). New York: Oxford.

Bleiker, E.M.A., Hendriks, J.H.C.L., Otten, J.D.M., Verbeek, A.L.M., & van der Ploeg, H.M. (2008). Personality factors and breast cancer risk: A 13-year follow-up. *Journal of the National Cancer Institute, 100*, 213–18.

Booth, C.M., Li, G., Zhang-Salomons, J., & Mackillop, W.J. (2010). The impact of socioeconomic status on stage of cancer at diagnosis and survival. *Cancer, 116*, 4160–7.

Brett, J., Bankhead, C., Henderson, B., Watson, E., & Austoker, J. (2005). The psychological impact of mammographic screening: A systematic review. *Psycho-Oncology, 14*, 917–38.

Brewer, N.T., Salz, T., & Lillie, S.E. (2007). Systematic review: The long-term effects of false-positive mammograms. *Annals of Internal Medicine, 146*, 502–10.

Brown, J.C., Huedo-Medina, T.B., Pescatello, L.S., Pescatello, S.M., Ferrer, R.A., & Johnson, B.T. (2011). Efficacy of exercise interventions in modulating cancer-related fatigue among adult cancer survivors: A meta-analysis. *Cancer Epidemiology, Biomarkers & Prevention, 20*, 123–33.

Buck, C.B., & Ratner, L. (2014). Oncogenic viruses. In V.T. Devita, Jr., T.S. Lawrence, & S.T. Rosenberg. (Eds.) *DeVita, Hellman, and Rosenberg's cancer: Principles & practice of oncology* (10th ed., pp. 70–83). Philadelphia: Wolters Kluwer.

Canadian Cancer Society's (CCS) Advisory Committee on Cancer Statistics. (2016). *Canadian cancer statistics 2016.* Toronto, ON: Canadian Cancer Society.

Canadian Cancer Society (CCS). (2018). *Types of hormone therapy.* Retrieved from: http://www.cancer.ca/en/cancer-information/diagnosis-and-treatment/chemotherapy-and-other-drug-therapies/hormonal-therapy/types-of-hormonal-therapy/?region=on

Canadian Partnership Against Cancer. (January 2015). Cancer screening in Canada: An overview of screening participation for breast, cervical and colorectal cancer. Toronto, ON: Canadian Partnership Against Cancer.

Canadian Task Force on Preventive Health Care. (2011). Recommendations on screening for breast cancer in average-risk women aged 40–74 years. *Canadian Medical Association Journal, 183*, 1991–2001.

Canadian Task Force on Preventive Health Care. (2014). Recommendations on screening for prostate cancer with the prostate-specific antigen test. *Canadian Medical Association Journal, 186*, 1225–34.

Centers for Disease Control and Prevention (CDC). (2016, July 20). *What are the risk factors for lung cancer?* Retrieved from cdc.gov/cancer/lung/basic_info/risk_factors.htm.

Champion, V.L., & Skinner, C.S. (2003). Differences in perceptions of risk, benefits, and barriers by stage of mammography adoption. *Journal of Women's Health, 12*, 277–86.

Chida, Y., Hamer, M., Wardle, J., & Steptoe, A. (2008). Do stress-related psychosocial factors contribute to cancer incidence and survival? *Nature Clinical Practice Oncology, 5*, 466–75.

Classen, C.C., Kraemer, H.C., Blasey, C., Giese-Davis, J., Koopman, C., Palesh, O.G., . . . Spiegel, D. (2008). Supportive-expressive group therapy for primary breast cancer patients: A randomized prospective multicenter trial. *Psycho-Oncology, 17*, 438–47.

Clegg, L.X., Reichman, M.E., Miller, B.A., Hankey, B.F., Singh, G.K., Dan Lin, Y., . . . Edwards, B.K. (2009). Impact of socioeconomic status on cancer incidence and stage at diagnosis: Selected findings from the surveillance, epidemiology, and end results: National Longitudinal Mortality Study. *Cancer Causes and Control, 20*, 417–35.

Cole, S.W., Nagaraja, A.S., Lutgendorf, S.K., Green, P.A., & Sood, A.K. (2015). Sympathetic nervous system regulation of the tumour microenvironment. *Nature Reviews Cancer, 15*, 563–72.

Costa, D.S.J., Mercieca-Bebber, R., Rutherford, C., Gabb, L., & King, M.T. (2016). The impact of cancer on psychological and social outcomes. *Australian Psychologist, 51*, 89–99.

Costanzo, E.S., Lutgendorf, S.K., Sood, A.K., Andersen, B., Sorosky, J., & Lubaroff, D.M. (2005). Psychosocial factors and interleukin-6 among women with advanced ovarian cancer. *Cancer, 104*, 305–13.

Costanzo, E.S., Sood, A.K., & Lutgendorf, S.K. (2011). Biobehavioral influences on cancer progression. *Immunology and Allergy Clinics of North America, 31*, 109–32.

Curtis, E., Quale, C., Haggstrom, D., & Smith-Bindman, R. (2008). Racial and ethnic differences in breast cancer survival: How much is explained by screening, tumor severity, biology, treatment, comorbidities, and demographics? *Cancer, 112*, 171–80.

De Faye, B.J., Wilson, K.G., Chater, S., Viola, R.A., & Hall, P. (2006). Stress and coping with advanced cancer. *Palliative and Supportive Care, 4*, 239–49.

Dunn, G.P., Koebel, C.M., & Schreiber, R.D. (2006). Interferons, immunity and cancer immunoediting. *Nature Reviews Immunology, 6*, 836–48.

Edelman, S., & Kidman, A.D. (1999). Description of a group cognitive behaviour therapy programme with cancer patients. *Psycho-Oncology, 8*, 306–14.

Engel, G.L. (1977). The need for a new medical model: A challenge for biomedicine. *Science, 196*, 129–36.

Ferlay, J., Soerjomataram, I., Ervik, M., Dikshit, R., Eser, S., Mathers, C., . . . Bray, F. (November 2015). *GLOBOCAN 2012 v1.2, Cancer Incidence and Mortality Worldwide: IARC CancerBase No. 11* [Internet]. Lyon, France: International Agency for Research on Cancer. Retrieved from: http://globocan.iarc.fr

Fortner, B., Baldwin, S., Schwartzberg, L., & Houts, A.C. (2006). Validation of the cancer care monitor items for physical symptoms and treatment side effects using expert oncology nurse evaluation. *Journal of Pain and Symptom Management, 31*, 207–14.

Franks, H.M., & Roesche, S.C. (2006). Appraisals and coping in people with cancer: A meta-analysis. *Psycho-Oncology, 15*, 1027–37.

Glaser, R., & Kiecolt-Glaser, J.K. (2005). Stress-induced immune dysfunction: Implications for health. *Nature Reviews Immunology, 5*, 243–51.

Hart, S.L., Hoyt, M.A., Diefenbach, M., Anderson, D.R., Kilbourn, K.M., Craft, L.L., . . . Stanton, A.L. (2012). Meta-analysis of efficacy of interventions for elevated depressive symptoms in adults diagnosed with cancer. *Journal of the National Cancer Institute, 104*, 990–1004.

Hastert, T.A., Beresford, S.A.A., Sheppard, L., & White, E. (2015). Disparities in cancer incidence and mortality by area-level socioeconomic status: A multilevel analysis. *Journal of Epidemiology & Community Health, 69*, 168–76.

Helgeson, V.S., & Cohen, S. (1996). Social support and adjustment to cancer: Reconciling descriptive, correlational, and intervention research. *Health Psychology, 15*, 135–48.

Holland, J.C., & Weiss, T.R. (2010). Principles of psycho-oncology. In W.K. Hong, R.C. Bast, Jr., W.N. Hait, D. W. Kufe, R. E. Pollock, R. R. Weichselbaum, . . . E. Frei III. (Eds.), *Holland-Frei cancer medicine* (8th ed., pp. 793–809). Shelton, Connecticut: People's Medical Publication House.

Howlader, N., Noone, A.M., Krapcho, M., Miller, D., Bishop, K., Altekruse, S.F., . . . Cronin K.A. (Eds). (April 2016). *SEER Cancer Statistics Review, 1975–2013*. Bethesda, MD: National Cancer Institute. Retrieved from http://seer.cancer.gov/csr/1975_2013/

Iqbal J., Ginsburg O., Rochon P.A., Sun P., & Narod S.A. (2015). Differences in breast cancer stage at diagnosis and cancer-specific survival by race and ethnicity in the United States. *Journal of the American Medical Association, 313*, 165–73.

Jolie Pitt, A. (2015, March 24). Diary of a surgery. *New York Times*. Retrieved from https://www.nytimes.com/2015/03/24/opinion/angelina-jolie-pitt-diary-of-a-surgery.html?_r=0

Kawachi, I., & Kroenke, C. (2006). Socioeconomic disparities in cancer incidence and mortality. In D. Schottenfeld & J.F. Fraumeni, Jr. (Eds.), *Cancer epidemiology and prevention* (3rd ed., pp. 174–188). New York: Oxford University Press.

Keegan, T.H.M., Gomez, S.L., Clarke, C.A., Chan, J.K., & Glaser, S.L. (2007). Recent trends in breast cancer incidence among 6 Asian groups in the Greater Bay Area of Northern California. *International Journal of Cancer, 120*, 1324–9.

Kolonel, L.N., & Wilkens, L.R. (2006). Migrant studies. In D. Schottenfeld & J.F. Fraumeni, Jr. (Eds.), *Cancer epidemiology and prevention* (3rd ed., pp. 189–201). New York: Oxford University Press.

Krebber, A.M.H., Buffart, L.M., Kleijn, G., Riepma, I.C., de Bree, R., Leemans, C.R., . . . Verdonck-de Leeuw, I.M. (2014). Prevalence of depression in cancer patients: A meta-analysis of diagnostic interviews and self-report instruments. *Psycho-Oncology, 23*, 121–30.

Kroenke, C.H., Kubzansky, L.D., Schernhammer, E.S., Holmes, M.D., & Kawachi, I. (2006). Social networks, social support, and survival after breast cancer diagnosis. *Journal of Clinical Oncology, 24*, 1105–11.

Lerner, B.H. (2001). *The breast cancer wars*. New York: Oxford University Press.

Levav, I., Kohn, R., Iscovich, J., Abramson, J.H., Tsai, W.Y., & Vigdorovich, D. (2000). Cancer incidence and survival following bereavement. *American Journal of Public Health, 90*, 1601–7.

Levin, B., & Prorock, P.C. (2006). Principles of screening. In D. Schottenfeld & J.F. Fraumeni, Jr. (Eds.), *Cancer epidemiology and prevention*, (3rd ed., pp. 1310–17). New York: Oxford University Press.

Levy, S.M., Heberman, R.B., Whiteside, T., Sanzo, K., Lee, J., & Kirkwood, J. (1990). Perceived social support and tumor estrogen/progesterone receptor status as predictors of natural killer cell activity in breast cancer patients. *Psychosomatic Medicine, 52*, 73–85. Retrieved from www.psychosomaticmedicine.org/content/52/1/73.long

Lillberg, K., Verkasalo, P.K., Kaprio, J., Teppo, L., Helenius, H., & Koskenvuo, M. (2003). Stressful life events and risk of breast cancer in 10,808 women: A cohort study. *American Journal of Epidemiology, 157*, 415–23.

Ljungman, M. (2014). Physical factors. In V.T. Devita, Jr., T.S. Lawrence, & S.T. Rosenberg. (Eds). *DeVita, Hellman, and Rosenberg's cancer: Principles & practice of oncology* (10th ed., pp. 95–102). Philadelphia: Wolters Kluwer.

Løberg, M., Lousdal, M.L., Bretthauer, M., & Kalager, M. (2015). Benefits and harms of mammography screening. *Breast Cancer Research, 17*, 1–12.

Lutgendorf, S.K., & Andersen, B.L. (2015). Biobehavioral approaches to cancer progression and survival: Mechanisms and interventions. *American Psychologist, 70*, 186–97.

Lutgendorf, S.K., Johnsen, E.L., Cooper, B., Anderson, B., Sorosky, J.I., Buller, R.E., & Sood, A.K. (2002). Vascular endothelial growth factor and social support in patients with ovarian carcinoma. *Cancer, 95*, 808–15.

Lutgendorf, S.K., & Sood, A.K. (2011). Biobehavioral factors and cancer progression physiological pathways and mechanisms. *Psychosomatic Medicine, 73*, 724–30.

Lynch, J., Venne, V., & Berse, B. (2015). Genetic tests to identify risk for breast cancer. *Seminars in Oncology Nursing, 31*, 100–7.

Manne, S., Rini, C., Rubin, S., Rosenblum, N., Bergman, C., Edelson, M., . . . Rocereto, T. (2008). Long-term trajectories of psychological adaptation among women diagnosed with gynecological cancers. *Psychosomatic Medicine, 70*, 677–87.

Massie, M.J. (2004). Prevalence of depression in patients with cancer. *Journal of the National Cancer Institute Monographs, 32*, 57–71.

Matloff, E., & Caplan, A. (2008). Direct to confusion: Lessons learned from marketing BRCA testing. *American Journal of Bioethics, 8*, 5–8.

Miller, S.J., O'Hea, E.L., Block Lerner, J., Moon, S., & Foran-Tuller, K.A. (2011). The relationship between breast cancer anxiety and mammography: Experiential avoidance as a moderator. *Behavioral Medicine, 37*, 113–18.

Moyer, A., Goldenberg, M., Hall, M.A., Knapp-Oliver, S.K., Sohl, S.J., Sarma, E.A., & Schneider, S. (2012). Mediators of change in psychosocial interventions for cancer patients: A systematic review. *Behavioral Medicine, 38*, 90–114.

Moyer, A., Sohl, S.J., Knapp-Oliver, S.K., & Schneider, S. (2009). Characteristics and methodological quality of 25 years of research investigating psychosocial interventions for cancer patients. *Cancer Treatment Reviews, 35*, 475–84.

Moyer, V.A. on behalf of the U.S. Preventive Services Task Force. (2012). Screening for prostate cancer: U.S. Preventive Services Task Force recommendation statement. *Annals of Internal Medicine, 157*, 120–34.

National Cancer Institute (NCI). (2015a). *What is cancer?* Retrieved from cancer.gov/cancertopics/cancerlibrary/what-is-cancer.

National Cancer Institute (NCI). (2015b). *BRCA1 and BRCA 2: Cancer risk and genetic testing.* Retrieved from cancer.gov/cancertopics/factsheet/Risk/BRCA

National Cancer Institute (NCI). (2016, August 8). *Cancer Prevention Overview (PDQ˚) Health Professional Version.* Bethesda, MD: National Cancer Institute. Retrieved from cancer.gov/about-cancer/causes-prevention/hp-prevention-overview-pdq. [PMID: 26389451]

National Cancer Institute (NCI). (2017). *A to Z list of cancer drugs.* Retrieved from https://www.cancer.gov/about-cancer/treatment/drugs

National Cancer Institute (NCI). (2018). *Cisplatin.* Retrieved from: https://www.cancer.gov/about-cancer/treatment/drugs/cisplatin

National Center for Health Statistics (NCHS). (2016). *Health, United States, 2015, with special feature on racial and ethnic health disparities.* Hyattsville, MD.

Nelson, H.D., Fu, R., Cantor, A., Pappas, M., Daeges, M., & Humphrey, L. (2016a). Effectiveness of breast cancer screening: Systematic review and meta-analysis to update the 2009 U.S. Preventive Services Task Force recommendation. *Annals of Internal Medicine, 164*, 244–55.

Nelson, H.D., Pappas, M., Cantor, A., Griffin, J., Daeges, M., & Humphrey, L. (2016b). Harms of breast cancer screening: Systematic review to update the 2009 U.S. Preventive Services Task Force recommendation. *Annals of Internal Medicine, 164*, 256–67.

Nicholas, D.R., & Veach, T.A. (2000). The psychosocial assessment of the adult cancer patient. *Professional Psychology: Research and Practice, 31*, 206–15.

Ogedegbe, G., Cassells, A.N., Robinson, C.M., DuHamel, K., Tobin, J.N., Sox, C.H., & Dietrich, A.J. (2005). Perceptions of barriers and facilitators of cancer early detection among low-income minority women in community health centers. *Journal of the National Medical Association, 97*, 162–70. Retrieved from www.ncbi.nlm.nih.gov/pmc/articles/PMC2568778/

Palesh, O., Butler, L.D., Koopman, C., Giese-Davis, J., Carlson, R., & Spiegel, D. (2007). Stress history and breast cancer recurrence. *Journal of Psychosomatic Research, 63*, 233–9.

Parkin, D.M., & Bray, F.I. (2006). International patterns of cancer incidence and mortality. In D. Schottenfeld & J.F. Fraumeni, Jr. (Eds), *Cancer epidemiology and prevention* (3rd ed., pp. 101–38). New York: Oxford University Press.

PDQ˚ Screening and Prevention Editorial Board. (2016). *PDQ Cancer Screening Overview.* Bethesda, MD: National Cancer Institute. Retrieved from http://www.cancer.gov/about-cancer/screening/hp-screening-overview-pdq. [PMID: 26389235]

Penninx, B.W.J.H., Guralnik, J.M., & Havlik, R.J. (1998). Chronically depressed mood and cancer risk in older persons. *Journal of the National Cancer Institute, 90*, 1888–93.

Petticrew, M., Bell, R., & Hunter, D. (2002). Influence of psychological coping on survival and recurrence in people with cancer: A systematic review. *British Medical Journal, 325*, 1–10.

Pinquart, M., & Duberstein, P.R. (2010). Associations of social networks with cancer mortality: A meta-analysis. *Critical Reviews in Oncology/Hematology, 75*, 122–37.

Pinquart, M., Fröhlich, C., & Silbereisen, R.K. (2007). Optimism, pessimism, and change of psychological well-being in cancer patients. *Psychology, Health, & Medicine, 12*, 421–32.

Plummer, M., de Martel, C., Vignat, J., Ferlay, J., Bray, F., & Franceschi, S. (2016). Global burden of cancer attributable to infection in 2012: A synthetic analysis. *The Lancet Global Health, 4*, e609–e616.

Price, M.A., Butow, P.N., Bell, M.L., deFazio, A., Friedlander, M., Fardell, J.E., . . . AOCS. (2016). Helplessness/hopelessness, minimization and optimism predict survival in women with invasive ovarian cancer: A role for targeted support during initial treatment decision-making? *Support Care Cancer, 24,* 2627–34.

Puetz, T.W., & Herring, M.P. (2012). Differential effects of exercise on cancer-related fatigue during and following treatment: A meta-analysis. *American Journal of Preventive Medicine, 43,* e1–e24.

Rawl, S.M., Champion, V.L., Menon, U., & Foster, J.L. (2000). The impact of age and race on mammography practices. *Health Care for Women International, 21,* 583–97.

Reiche, E.M.V., Nunes, S.O.V., & Morimoto, H.K. (2004). Stress, depression, immune system, and cancer. *Lancet Oncology, 5,* 617–25.

Reynolds, P., Hurley, S., Torres, M., Jackson, J., Boyd, P., & Chen, V.W. (2000). Use of coping strategies and breast cancer survival: Results from the Black/White Cancer Survival Study. *American Journal of Epidemiology, 152,* 940–9.

Reynolds, P., & Kaplan, G.A. (1990). Social connections and risk for cancer: Prospective evidence from the Alameda County study. *Behavioral Medicine, 16,* 101–10.

Rosenbaum, E.H., & Rosenbaum, I.R. (2005). Genetics and cancer. In E.H. Rosenbaum & I. Rosenbaum (Eds.), *Everyone's guide to cancer supportive care: A comprehensive handbook for patients and their families* (pp. 9–15). Kansas City: Andrews McMeel.

Rosenbaum, E.H., Rosenbaum, I.R., Margolis, L., Meyler, T.S., Haas-Kogan, D., Benz, C., & Hawn, M. (2005). Cancer therapy. In E.H. Rosenbaum & I. Rosenbaum (Eds.), *Everyone's guide to cancer supportive care: A comprehensive handbook for patients and their families* (pp. 9–15). Kansas City: Andrews McMeel.

Rosenstock, I.M., Strecher, V.J., & Becker, M.H. (1988). Social learning theory and the Health Belief Model. *Health Education and Behavior, 15*(2), 175–83.

Salz, T., Richman, A.R., & Brewer, N.T. (2010). Meta-analysis of the effect of false-positive mammograms on generic and specific psychosocial outcomes. *Psycho-Oncology, 19,* 1026–34.

Sanchez, M.A., Rabin, B.A., Gaglio, B., Henton, M., Elzarrad, M.K., Purcell, P., & Glasgow, R.E. (2013). A systematic review of eHealth cancer prevention and control interventions: New technology, same methods and designs? *Translational Behavioral Medicine, 3,* 392–401.

Sarma, E.A. (2015). Barriers to screening mammography. *Health Psychology Review, 9,* 42–62.

Satin, J.R., Linden, W., & Phillips, M.J. (2009). Depression as a predictor of disease progression and mortality in cancer patients: A meta-analysis. *Cancer, 115,* 5349–61.

Schneider, S., Moyer, A., Knapp-Oliver, S., Sohl, S., Cannella, D., & Targhetta, V. (2010). Pre-intervention distress moderates the efficacy of psychosocial treatment for cancer patients: A meta-analysis. *Journal of Behavioral Medicine, 33,* 1–14.

Segerstrom, S.C., & Miller, G.E. (2004). Psychological stress and the human immune system: A meta-analytic study of 30 years of inquiry. *Psychological Bulletin, 130,* 601–30.

Siu, A.L. on behalf of the U.S. Preventive Services Task Force. (2016). Screening for breast cancer: U.S. Preventive Services Task Force recommendation statement. *Annals of Internal Medicine, 164,* 279–96.

Sklar, L.S., & Anisman, H. (1981). Stress and cancer. *Psychological Bulletin, 89,* 369–406.

Spiegel, D., & Giese-Davis, J. (2003). Depression and cancer: Mechanisms and disease progression. *Society of Biological Psychiatry, 54,* 269–82.

Sprehn, G.C., Chambers, J.E., Saykin, A.J., Konski, A., & Johnstone, P.A. (2009). Decreased cancer survival in individuals separated at time of diagnosis: Critical period for cancer pathophysiology? *Cancer, 115,* 5108–16.

Stanton, A.L., Danoff-Burg, S., Cameron, C.L., Bishop, M., Collins, C.A., Kirk, S.B., . . . Twillman, R. (2000). Emotionally expressive coping predicts psychological and physical adjustment to breast cancer. *Journal of Consulting and Clinical Psychology, 68,* 875–82.

Stanton, A.L., Luecken, L.J., Mackinnon, D.P., & Thompson, E.H. (2012). Mechanisms in psychosocial interventions for adults living with cancer: Opportunity for integration of theory, research, and practice. *Journal of Consulting and Clinical Psychology, 81,* 318–25.

Statistics Canada. (2015, December 10). *Leading causes of death, 2012.* Retrieved from http://www.statcan.gc.ca/pub/82-625-x/2015001/article/14296-eng.htm

Swerdlow, A.J., Peto, R., & Doll, R.S. (2010). Epidemiology of cancer. In D.A. Warrell, T.M. Cox, & J.D. Firth (Eds.), *Oxford textbook of medicine* (5th ed., Vol. 1, pp. 299–332). New York: Oxford University Press.

Tamagawa, R., Garland, S., Vaska, M., & Carlson, L.E. (2012). Who benefits from psychosocial interventions in oncology? A systematic review of psychological moderators of treatment outcome. *Journal of Behavioral Medicine.* Advance online publication.

Taylor, S.E., & Lobel, M. (1989). Social comparison activity under threat: Downward evaluation and upward contacts. *Psychological Review, 96,* 569–75.

U.S. Department of Health and Human Services (USDHHS). (2014). *The Health Consequences of Smoking: 50 Years of Progress. A Report of the Surgeon General.* Atlanta, GA: USDHHS, CDC, National Center for Chronic Disease Prevention and Health Promotion, Office on Smoking and Health.

van der Spek, N., van Uden-Kraan, C.F., Vos, J., Breitbart, W., Tollenaar, R.M., van Asperen, C.J., . . . Verdonck-de Leeuw, I.M. (2014). Meaning-centered group psychotherapy in cancer survivors: A feasibility study. *Psycho-Oncology, 23,* 827–31.

van't Spijker, A., Trijsburg, R.W., & Duivenvoorden, H.J. (1997). Psychological sequelae of cancer diagnosis: A meta-analytical review of 58 studies after 1980. *Psychosomatic Medicine, 59,* 280–93.

Watson, M., Haviland, J.S., Greer, S., Davidson, J., & Bliss, J.M. (1999). Influence of psychological response on survival in breast cancer a population-based cohort study. *Lancet, 354,* 1331–6.

Watson, M., & Kissane, D. (Eds.). (2011). *Handbook of psychotherapy in cancer care*. Hoboken, NJ: John Wiley & Sons.

Wilt, T.J., Brawer, M.K., Jones. K.M., Barry, M.J., Aronson, W.J., Fox, S., . . . Wheeler, T. (Prostate Cancer Intervention versus Observation Trial (PIVOT) Study Group). (2012). Radical prostatectomy versus observation for localized prostate cancer. *New England Journal of Medicine, 367*, 203–13.

Wood, J.V., Taylor, S.E., & Lichtman, R.R. (1985). Social comparison in adjustment to breast cancer. *Journal of Personality and Social Psychology, 49*, 1169–83.

Woods, L.M., Rachet, B., & Coleman, M.P. (2006). Origins of socio-economic inequalities in cancer survival: A review. *Annals of Oncology, 17*, 5–19.

World Health Organization (WHO). (2009). Global health risks: Mortality and burden of disease attributable to selected major risks. Geneva, Switzerland: WHO.

Wortman, C.B., & Dunkel-Schetter, C. (1979). Interpersonal relationships and cancer: A theoretical analysis. *Journal of Social Issues, 35*, 120–55.

Yaffe, M.J., & Mainprize, J.G. (2011). Risk of radiation-induced breast cancer from mammographic screening. *Radiology, 258*, 98–105.

Ziegler, R.G., Hoover, R.N., Pike, M.C., Hildesheim, A., Nomura, A.M.Y., West, D.W., . . . Hyer, M.B. (1993). Migration patterns and breast cancer risk in Asian-American women. *Journal of the National Cancer Institute, 85*, 1819–27.

Chapter 13

Akard, T.F., Wray, S., & Gilmer, M.J. (2015). Facebook advertisements recruit parents of children with cancer for an online survey of web-based research preferences. *Cancer Nursing, 38*, 155–61.

Allen, S.L., Howlett, M.D., Coulombe, J.A., & Corkum, P.V. (2016). ABCs of SLEEPING: A review of the evidence behind pediatric sleep practice recommendations. *Sleep Medicine Reviews, 29*, 1–14.

Barlow, J.H., & Ellard, D.R. (2004). Psycho-educational interventions for children with chronic disease, parents and siblings: An overview of the research evidence base. *Child: Care, Health & Development, 30*, 637–45.

Beale, I.L. (2006). Scholarly literature review: Efficacy of psychological interventions for pediatric chronic illnesses. *Journal of Pediatric Psychology, 31*, 437–51.

Beck, M.H., Cataldo, M., Slifer, K.J., Pulbrook, V., & Ghuman, J.K. (2005). Teaching children with attention deficit hyperactivity disorder (ADHD) and autistic disorder (AD) how to swallow pills. *Clinical Pediatrics, 44*, 515–526.

Beran, T.N., Ramirez-Serrano, A., Vanderkooi, O.G., & Kuhn, S. (2013). Reducing children's pain and distress towards flu vaccinations: A novel and effective application of humanoid robotics. *Vaccine, 31*, 2772–7.

Bergstraesser, E. (2013). Pediatric palliative care—When quality of life becomes the main focus of treatment. *European Journal of Pediatrics, 172*(2), 139–50.

Bethell, C.D., Kogan, M.D., Strickland, B.B., Schor, E.L., Robertson, J., & Newacheck, P.W. (2011). A national and state profile of leading health problems and health care quality for US children: Key insurance disparities and across-state variations. *Academic Pediatrics, 11*, S22–S33.

Birch, L.L., & Fisher, J.A. (1995). Appetite and eating behavior in children. *Pediatric Nutrition, 42*, 931–53.

Birch, L.L., & Fisher, J.A. (1998). Development of eating behaviors among children and adolescents. *Pediatrics, 101*, 539–49.

Birnie, K.A., Boerner, K.E., & Chambers, C.T. (2013). Families and pain. In P.J. McGrath, B. Stevens, S. Walker, & W. Zempsky (Eds.), *Oxford text of paediatric pain* (pp. 111–18). Oxford: Oxford University Press.

Birnie, K.A., Chambers, C.T., Taddio, A., McMurtry, C.M., Noel, M., Pillai Riddell, R., . . . HELPinKids&Adults Team. (2015). Psychological interventions for vaccine injections in children and adolescents: Systematic review of randomized and quasi-randomized controlled trials. *The Clinical Journal of Pain, 31*(10 Suppl), S72–S89.

Birnie, K.A., Noel, M., Parker, J.A., Chambers, C.T., Uman, L.S., Kisely, S.R., & McGrath, P.J. (2014). Systematic review and meta-analysis of distraction and hypnosis for needle-related pain and distress in children and adolescents. *Journal of Pediatric Psychology, 39*, 783–808.

Birnie, K.A., Uman, L.S., & Chambers, C.T. (2013). Impact of familial factors on children's chronic pain. In R.F. Schmidt & G.F. Gebhart (Eds.), *Encyclopedia of pain* (2nd ed., pp. 1577–84). New York: Springer-Verlag.

Blount, R.L., Cohen, L.L., Frank, N.C., Bachanas, P.J., Smith, A.J., Manimala, M.R., & Pate, J.T. (1997). The child–adult medical procedure interaction scale-revised: An assessment of validity. *Journal of Pediatric Psychology, 22*, 73–88.

Blount, R.L., Corbin, S.M., Sturges, J.W., Wolfe, V.V., Prater, J.M., & James, L.D. (1989). The relationship between adult's behavior and child coping and distress during BMA LP procedures: A sequential analysis. *Behavior Therapy, 20*, 585–601.

Blount, R.L., Dahlquist, L.M., Baer, R.A., & Wuori, D. (1984). A brief effective method for teaching children to swallow pills. *Behavior Therapy, 15*, 381–7.

Blount, R.L., Simons, L.E., Devine, K.A., Jaaniste, T., Cohen, L.L., Chambers, C.T., & Hayutin, L.G. (2008). Evidence-based assessment of coping and stress in pediatric psychology. *Journal of Pediatric Psychology, 33*, 1021–45.

Boerner, K.E., Gillespie, J.M., McLaughlin, E.N., Kuttner, L., & Chambers, C.T. (2014). Implementation of evidence-based psychological interventions for pediatric needle pain. *Clinical Practice in Pediatric Psychology, 2*, 224–35.

Borowitz, S.M., Cox, D.J., Sutphen, J.L., & Kovatchev, B. (2002). Treatment of childhood encopresis: A randomized trial comparing three treatment protocols. *Journal of Pediatric Gastroenterology and Nutrition, 34*(4), 378–84.

Broome, M.E., Bates, T.A., Lillis, P.P., & McGahee, T.W. (1990). Children's medical fears, coping behaviors, and pain perceptions during a lumbar puncture. *Oncology Nursing Society, 17*, 361–7.

Brown, M.L., Pope, A.W., & Brown, E.J. (2010). Treatment of primary noctural enuresis in children: A review. *Child: Care, Health and Development, 37*, 153–60.

Brummelte, S., Grunau, R.E., Chau, V., Poskitt, K.J., Brant, R., Vinall, J., . . . Miller, S.P. (2012). Procedural pain and brain development in premature newborns. *Annals of Neurology, 71*, 385–96.

Bull, S.S., Breslin, L.T., Wright, E.E., Black, S.R., Levine, D., & Santelli, J.S. (2011). Case study: An ethics case study of HIV prevention research on Facebook: The Just/Us study. *Journal of Pediatric Psychology, 36*(10), 1082–92.

Butler-Jones, D. (2009). The chief public health officer's report on the state of public health in Canada 2009: Growing up well — Priorities for a healthy future. Ottawa, ON.: Public Health Agency of Canada. Retrieved from http://publichealth.gc.ca/CPHOreport

Canadian Institutes of Health Research. (2016, June 20). *It doesn't have to hurt*. Retrieved from http://www.cihr-irsc.gc.ca/e/49821.html

Chambers, C.T. (2003). The role of family factors in pediatric pain. In P.J. McGrath & G.A. Finley (Eds.), *Pediatric pain: Biological and social context* (pp. 99–130). Seattle: IASP Press.

Chambers, C.T. (2012). Pill swallowing and children. *Progress Notes: Newsletter of the Society for Pediatric Psychology, 36*(2), 4–5.

Chambers, C.T., & Craig, K.D. (1998). An intrusive impact of anchors in children's faces pain scales. *Pain, 78*, 27–37.

Chambers, C.T., Craig, K.D., & Bennett, S.M. (2002). The impact of maternal behavior on children's pain experiences: An experimental analysis. *Journal of Pediatric Psychology, 27*, 293–301.

Chambers, C.T., Giesbrecht, K., Craig, K.D., Bennett, S.M., & Huntsman, E. (1999). A comparison of faces scales for the measurement of pediatric pain: Children's and parents' ratings. *Pain, 83*, 25–35.

Chambers, C.T., Hardial, J., Craig, K.D., Court, C., & Montgomery, C. (2005). Faces scales for the measurement of postoperative pain intensity in children following minor surgery. *Clinical Journal of Pain, 21*, 277–85.

Chambers, C.T., Reid, G.J., Craig, K.D., McGrath, P.J., & Finley, G.A. (1998). Agreement between child and parent reports of pain. *Clinical Journal of Pain, 14*, 336–42.

Cheung, Y.T., & Krull, K.R. (2015). Neurocognitive outcomes in long-term survivors of childhood acute lymphoblastic leukemia treated on contemporary treatment protocols: A systematic review. *Neuroscience and Biobehavioral Reviews, 53*, 108–20.

Christopherson, E. (2010). *Elimination disorders in children and adolescents*. New York: Hogrefe & Huber.

Cohen, L.L., & MacLaren, J.E. (2007). Breaking down the barriers to pediatric procedural preparation. *Clinical Psychology: Science and Practice, 14*, 144.

Compas, B.E., Jaser, S.S., Dunn, M.J., & Rodriguez, E.M. (2012). Coping with chronic illness in childhood and adolescence. *Annual Review of Clinical Psychology, 8*, 455–80.

Coulombe, J.A., Reid, G.J., Boyle, M.H., & Racine, Y. (2010). Concurrent associations among sleep problems, indicators of inadequate sleep, psychopathology, and shared risk factors in a population-based sample of healthy Ontario children. *Journal of Pediatric Psychology, 35*, 790–9.

Craig, K.D., Lilley, C.M., & Gilbert, C.A. (1996). Social barriers to optimal pain management in infants and children. *Clinical Journal of Pain, 12*, 232–42.

Craig, K.D., Whitfield, M.F., Grunau, R.V.E., Linton, J., & Hadjistavropoulos, H.D. (1993). Pain in the preterm neonate: Behavioral and physiological indices. *Pain, 52*, 287–99.

Crist, W., & Napier-Phillips, A. (2001). Mealtime behaviors of young children: A comparison of normative and clinical data. *Journal of Developmental and Behavioral Pediatrics, 22*, 279–86.

Cruz-Arrieta, E. (2008). Pill-swallowing training: A brief pediatric oncology report. *Primary Psychiatry, 15*, 49–53.

Curran, E. (2007) *Guided imagery for healing children and teens*. New York: Atria Books.

Dean, A.J., Walters, J., & Hall, A. (2010). A systematic review of interventions to enhance medication adherence in children and adolescents with chronic illness. *Archives of Disease in Childhood, 95*, 717–23.

Drotar, D., & Bonner, M.S. (2009). Influences on adherence to pediatric asthma treatment: A review of correlates and predictors. *Journal of Developmental and Behavioral Pediatrics, 30*, 574–82.

Duggan, M., Lenhart, A., Lampe, C., & Ellison, N. (2015). *Parents and social media*. Washington, DC: Pew Research Center. Retrieved from http://www.pewinternet.org/2015/07/16/parents-and-social-media

Eccleston, C., Fisher, E., Law, E., Bartlett, J., & Palermo, T.M. (2015). Psychological interventions for parents of children and adolescents with chronic illness. *The Cochrane Database of Systematic Reviews, 4*, CD009660.

Eccleston, C., Palermo, T. M., Williams, A. C.., Lewandowski Holley, A., Morley, S., Fisher, E., & Law, E. (2014). Psychological therapies for the management of chronic and recurrent pain in children and adolescents. *The Cochrane Database of Systematic Reviews, 5*(5), CD003968.

Feeney, J.A., (2000). Implications of attachment style for patterns of health and illness. *Child: Care, Health and Development, 26*, 277–88.

Fisher, E., Law, E., Palermo, T. M., & Eccleston, C. (2015). Psychological therapies (remotely delivered) for the management of chronic and recurrent pain in children and adolescents. *The Cochrane Database of Systematic Reviews*, (3), CD011118.

Funk, M.J., Mullins, L.L., & Olson, R.A. (1984). Teaching children to swallow pills: A case study. *Children's Health Care, 3*, 20–3.

Garvie, P.A., Lensing, S., & Rai, S.N. (2007). Efficacy of a pill-swallowing training intervention to improve antiretroviral medication adherence in pediatric patients with HIV/AIDS. *Pediatrics, 119*, e893–e899.

Gerrard, A. (2016, June 22). Improving knowledge of kids' cancer pain through social media. *Dalhousie University Faculty of Medicine News*. Retrieved from https://medicine.dal.ca/news/news/2016/06/22/improving_knowledge_of_kids____cancer_pain_through_social_media.html

Ghuman, J.K., Cataldo, M.D., Beck, M.H., & Slifer, K.J. (2004). Behavioral training for pill-swallowing difficulties in young children with autistic disorder. *Journal of Child and Adolescent Psychopharmacology, 14*, 601–11.

Gorman, J.R., Roberts, S.C., Dominick, S.A., Malcarne, V.L., Dietz, A.C., & Su, H.I. (2014). A diversified recruitment approach incorporating social media leads to research participation among young adult-aged female cancer survivors. *Journal of Adolescent and Young Adult Oncology, 3*, 59–65.

Grunau, R.V.E., Whitfield, M.F., Petrie, J.H., & Fryer, E.L. (1994). Early pain experience, child and family factors, as precursors of somatization: A prospective study of extremely premature and fullterm children. *Pain, 56*, 353–9.

Hamm, M.P., Shulhan, J., Williams, G., Milne, A., Scott, S.D., & Hartling, L. (2014). A systematic review of the use and effectiveness of social media in child health. *BMC Pediatrics, 14*(138).

Hechler, T., Kanstrup, M., Holley, A.L., Simons, L.E., Wicksell, R., Hirschfeld, G., & Zernikow, B. (2015). Systematic review on intensive interdisciplinary pain treatment of children with chronic pain. *Pediatrics, 136*, 115–27.

Henderson, E.M., Rosser, B.A., Keogh, E., & Eccleston, C. (2012). Internet sites offering adolescents help with headache, abdominal pain, and dysmenorrhoea: A description of content, quality, and peer interactions. *Journal of Pediatric Psychology, 37*, 262–71.

Hicks, C.L., von Baeyer, C.L., Spafford, P.A., van Korlaar, I., & Goodenough, B. (2001). The faces pain scale—revised: Toward a common metric in pediatric pain measurement. *Pain, 93*, 173–83.

Hogendorf, A.M., Fendler, W., Sieroslawski, J., Bobeff, K., Wegrewicz, K., Malewska, K. I., . . . Mlynarski, W.M. (2017). Alcohol and cigarette use among adolescents with type 1 diabetes. *European Journal of Pediatrics, 176*(6), 713–22.

Honaker, S.M., & Meltzer, L.J. (2016). Sleep in pediatric primary care: A review of the literature. *Sleep Medicine Reviews, 25*, 31–9.

Huguet, A., & Miro, J. (2008). The severity of chronic pediatric pain: An epidemiological study. *Journal of Pain, 9*, 226–36.

Incledon, E., Williams, L., Hazell, T., Heard, T. R., Flowers, A., & Hiscock, H. (2015). A review of factors associated with mental health in siblings of children with chronic illness. *Journal of Child Health Care: For Professionals Working with Children in the Hospital and Community, 19*, 182–94.

Jaaniste, T., Hayes, B., & von Baeyer, C.L. (2007). Providing children with information about forthcoming medical procedures: A review and synthesis. *Clinical Psychology: Science and Practice, 14*, 124–43.

Kahana, S., Drotar, D., & Frazier, T. (2008). Meta-analysis of psychological interventions to promote adherence to treatment in pediatric chronic health conditions. *Journal of Pediatric Psychology, 33*, 590–611.

King, S., Chambers, C.T., Huguet, A., MacNevin, R.C., McGrath, P.J., Parker, L., & MacDonald, A.J. (2011). The epidemiology of chronic pain in children and adolescents revisited: A systematic review. *Pain, 152*, 2729–38.

La Greca, A.M., & Race Mackey, E. (2009). Adherence to pediatric treatment regimens. In M.C. Roberts & R.G. Steele (Eds.), *Handbook of pediatric psychology* (4th ed., pp. 130–152). New York: Guilford Press.

Lalloo, C., Jibb, L.A., Rivera, J., Agarwal, A., & Stinson, J.N. (2015). "There's a pain app for that": Review of patient-targeted Smartphone applications for pain management. *The Clinical Journal of Pain, 31*, 557–63.

Lenhart, A. (2015). *Teens, Social Media & Technology Overview 2015*. Washington, DC: Pew Research Center. Retrieved from http://www.pewinternet.org/2015/04/09/teens-social-media-technology-2015/

Lescano, C.M., Koinis-Mitchell, D., & McQuaid, E.L. (2016). Introduction to the special issue on diversity and health disparities: Where have we been and where are we going? *Journal of Pediatric Psychology, 41*(4), 385–90.

Lewandowski, A.S., Ward, T.M., & Palermo, T.M. (2011). Sleep problems in children and adolescents with common medical conditions. *Pediatric Clinics of North America, 58*, 699–713.

Luersen, K., Davis, S.A., Kaplan, S.G., Abel, T.D., Winchester, W.W., & Feldman, S.R. (2012). Sticker charts: A method for improving adherence to treatment of chronic diseases in children. *Pediatric Dermatology, 29*, 403–8.

McCulloch, R., Comac, M., & Craig, F. (2008). Paediatric palliative care: Coming of age in oncology? *European Journal of Cancer, 44*, 1139–45.

McGrath, P.J., Walco, G.A., Turk, D.C., Dworkin, R.H., Brown, M.T., Davidson, K., . . . Zeltzer, L. (2008). Core outcome domains and measures for pediatric acute and chronic/recurrent pain clinical trials: PedIMMPACT recommendations. *Journal of Pain, 9*, 771–83.

McMurtry, C.M., Chambers, C.T., McGrath, P.J., & Asp, E. (2010). When "don't worry" communicates fear: Children's perceptions of parental reassurance and distraction during a painful medical procedure. *Pain, 150*, 52–8.

McMurtry, C.M., McGrath, P.J., Asp, E., & Chambers, C.T. (2007). Parental reassurance and pediatric procedural pain: A linguistic description. *Journal of Pain, 8*, 95–101.

McMurtry, C.M., McGrath, P.J., & Chambers, C.T. (2006). Reassurance can hurt: Parental behavior and painful medical procedures. *Journal of Pediatrics, 148*, 560–1.

Meltzer, L.J., & Montgomery-Downs, H.E. (2011). Sleep in the family. *Pediatric Clinics of North America, 58*, 765–74.

Meltzer, E.O., Welch, M.J., & Ostrom, N.K. (2006). Pill swallowing ability and training in children 6 to 11 years of age. *Clinical Pediatrics, 45*, 725–33.

Modi, A.C., Pai, A.L., Hommel, K.A., Hood, K.K., Cortina, S., Hilliard, M.E., . . . Drotar, D. (2012). Pediatric self-management: A framework for research, practice, and policy. *Pediatrics, 129*, e473–e485.

Moody, K., Siegel, L., Scharbach, K., Cunningham, L., & Cantor, R.M. (2011). Pediatric palliative care. *Primary Care: Clinics in Office Practice, 38*, 327–61.

Moon, E.C., Chambers, C.T., & McGrath, P.J. (2011). "He says, she says": A comparison of fathers' and mothers' verbal behavior during child cold pressor pain. *Journal of Pain, 12*, 1174–81.

Moreno, M.A., Goniu, N., Moreno, P.S., & Diekema, D. (2013). Ethics of social media research: Common concerns and practical considerations. *Cyberpsychology, Behavior, and Social Networking, 16,* 708–13.

Nguyen, E., Bugno, L., Kandah, C., Plevinsky, J., Poulopoulos, N., Wojtowicz, A., . . . Greenley, R.N. (2016). Is there a good app for that? Evaluating m-Health apps for strategies that promote pediatric medication adherence. *Telemedicine and E-Health, 22,* 929–37.

Noel, M., Petter, M., Parker, J.A., & Chambers, C.T. (2012). Cognitive behavioural therapy for pediatric chronic pain: The problem, research, and practice. *Journal of Cognitive Psychotherapy, 26,* 143–56.

Olson, A.L., Johansen, S.G., Powers, L.E., Pope, J.B., & Klein, R.B. (1993). Cognitive coping strategies of children with chronic illness. *Journal of Developmental and Behavioral Pediatrics, 14,* 217–23.

Padovani, L., André, N., Constine, L.S., & Muracciole, X. (2012). Neurocognitive function after radiotherapy for paediatric brain tumours. *Nature Reviews Neurology, 8,* 578–88.

Palermo, T.M. (2000). Impact of recurrent and chronic pain on child and family daily functioning: A critical review of the literature. *Journal of Developmental & Behavioral Pediatrics, 21,* 58–69.

Palermo, T.M., Janicke, D.M., McQuaid, E.L., Mullins, L.L., Robins, P.M., & Wu, Y.P. (2014). Recommendations for training in pediatric psychology: Defining core competencies across training levels. *Journal of Pediatric Psychology, 39,* 965–84.

Pearson, C., Janz, T., & Ali, J. (2013). *Mental and substance use disorders in Canada.* Retrieved from http://www.statcan.gc.ca/pub/82-624-x/2013001/article/11855-eng.pdf.

Peters, D.H., Adam, T., Alonge, O., Agyepong, I.A., & Tran, N. (2013). Implementation research: What it is and how to do it. *BMJ, 347,* f6753.

Pillai Riddell, R., Taddio, A., McMurtry, C.M., Chambers, C., Shah, V., Noel, M., & HELPinKIDS Team. (2015a). Psychological interventions for vaccine injections in young children 0 to 3 years: Systematic review of randomized controlled trials and quasi-randomized controlled trials. *The Clinical Journal of Pain, 31*(10 Suppl), S64–S71.

Pillai Riddell, R., Taddio, A., McMurtry, C.M., Shah, V., Noel, M., Chambers, C.T., & HELPinKIDS&Adults Team. (2015b). Process interventions for vaccine injections: Systematic review of randomized controlled trials and quasi-randomized controlled trials. *The Clinical Journal of Pain, 31*(10 Suppl), S99–S108.

Pless, I.B., Power, C., & Peckham, C.S. (1993). Long-term psychosocial sequelae of chronic physical disorders in childhood. *Pediatrics, 91,* 1131–6.

Porter, F.L., Grunau, R.E., & Anand, K.J.S. (1999). Long-term effects of pain in infants. *Journal of Developmental and Behavioral Pediatrics, 20,* 253–61.

Powers, K.S., & Rubenstein, J.S. (1999). Family presence during invasive procedures in the pediatric intensive care unit. *Archives of Pediatric and Adolescent Medicine, 153,* 955–8.

Reid, G.J., Gilbert, C.A., & McGrath, P.J. (1998). The pain coping questionnaire: Preliminary validation. *Pain, 76,* 83–96.

Reid, G.J., Hong, R.Y., & Wade, T.J. (2009). The relation between common sleep problems and emotional and behavioral problems among 2- and 3-year-olds in the context of known risk factors for psychopathology. *Journal of Sleep Research, 18,* 49–59.

Reid, K., Simmonds, M., Verrier, M., & Dick, B. (2016). Supporting teens with chronic pain to obtain high school credits: Chronic Pain 35 in Alberta. *Children, 3*(4), E31.

Reitman, D., & Passeri, C. (2008). Use of stimulus fading and functional assessment to treat pill refusal with an 8-year-old boy diagnosed with ADHD. *Clinical Case Studies, 7,* 224–37.

Repetti, R.L., Taylor, S.E., Seeman, T.E. (2002). Risky families: Family social environments and the mental and physical health of offspring. *Psychological Bulletin, 128,* 330–6.

Rodriguez, E.M., Dunn, M.J., Zuckerman, T., Vannatta, K., Gerhardt, C.A., & Compas, B.E. (2012). Cancer-related sources of stress for children with cancer and their parents. *Journal of Pediatric Psychology, 37,* 185–97.

Rudolph, K.D., Dennig, M.D., & Weisz, J.R. (1995). Determinants and consequences of children's coping in the medical setting: Conceptualization, review and critique. *Psychological Bulletin, 118,* 328–57.

Schmidt, S., Peterson, C., & Bullinger, M. (2003). Coping with chronic disease from the perspective of children and adolescents: A conceptual framework and its implications for participation. *Child: Care, Health and Development, 29,* 63–75.

Schwartz, L.A., Tuchman, L.K., Hobbie, W.L., & Ginsberg, J.P. (2011). A social-ecological model of readiness for transition to adult-oriented care for adolescents and young adults with chronic health conditions. *Child: Care, Health & Development, 37,* 883–95.

Shah, V., Taddio, A., McMurtry, C.M., Halperin, S.A., Noel, M., Pillai Riddell, R., . . . HELPinKIDS Team. (2015). Pharmacological and combined interventions to reduce vaccine injection pain in children and adults: Systematic review and meta-analysis. *The Clinical Journal of Pain, 31*(10 Suppl), S38–S63.

Shepard, J.A., Poler, J.E., Jr., & Grabman, J.H. (2017). Evidence-based psychosocial treatments for pediatric elimination disorders. *Journal of Clinical Child & Adolescent Psychology,* https://www.ncbi.nlm.nih.gov/pubmed/27911597.

Siegel, R.L., Miller, K.D., & Jemal, A. (2016). Cancer statistics, 2016. *CA: A Cancer Journal for Clinicians, 66,* 7–30.

Silverman, A.H. (2015). Behavioral management of feeding disorders of childhood. *Annals of Nutrition and Metabolism, 66,* 33–42.

Simons, L.E., & Basch, M.C. (2016). State of the art in biobehavioral approaches to the management of chronic pain in childhood. *Pain Management, 6,* 49–61.

Spirito, A., Stark, L.J., & Williams, C. (1988). Development of a brief coping checklist for use with pediatric populations. *Journal of Pediatric Psychology, 13,* 555–74.

Stanford, E.A., Chambers, C.T., Biesanz, J.C., & Chen, E. (2007). The frequency, trajectories and predictors of adolescent recurrent pain: A population-based approach. *Pain, 138,* 11–21.

Stevens, B., Johnston, C., Petryshen, P., & Taddio, A. (1996). Premature infant pain profile: Development and initial validation. *Clinical Journal of Pain, 12,* 13–22.

Stevens, B.J., Abbott, L.K., Yamada, J., Harrison, D., Stinson, J., Taddio, A., . . . Finley, G.A. (2011). Epidemiology and management of painful procedures in children in Canadian hospitals. *Canadian Medical Association Journal, 183,* E403–E410.

Stinson, J., Wilson, R., Gill, N., Yamada, J., & Holt, J. (2009). A systematic review of Internet-based self-management interventions for youth with health conditions. *Journal of Pediatric Psychology, 34,* 495–510.

Taddio, A., Chambers, C.T., Halperin, S.A., Ipp, M., Lockett, D., Rieder, M.J., & Shah, V. (2009). Inadequate pain management during routine childhood immunizations: The nerve of it. *Clinical Therapeutics, 31*(Suppl. B), S152–S167.

Taddio, A., Goldbach, M., Ipp, M., Stevens, B., & Koren, G. (1995). Effect of neonatal circumcision on pain responses during vaccinations in boys. *Lancet, 345,* 291–2.

Taddio, A., Katz, J., Ilersich, A.L., & Koren, G. (1997). Effect of neonatal circumcision on pain response during subsequent routine vaccination. *Lancet, 349,* 599–603.

Taddio, A., McMurtry, C.M., Shah, V., Riddell, R.P., Chambers, C.T., Noel, M., . . . HELPinKIDS&Adults. (2015a). Reducing pain during vaccine injections: Clinical practice guideline. *CMAJ: Canadian Medical Association Journal = Journal de l'Association Medicale Canadienne, 187,* 975–82.

Taddio, A., Shah, V., McMurtry, C.M., MacDonald, N.E., Ipp, M., Riddell, R.P., . . . HELPinKIDS&Adults Team. (2015b). Procedural and physical interventions for vaccine injections: Systematic review of randomized controlled trials and quasi-randomized controlled trials. *The Clinical Journal of Pain, 31*(10 Suppl), S20–S37.

Thompson, R.J., & Gustafson, K.E. (1996). *Adaptation to chronic childhood illness.* Washington, DC: APA.

Thompson Jr, R.J., Gustafson, K.E., Hamlett, K.W., & Spock, A. (1992). Stress, coping, and family functioning in the psychological adjustment of mothers of children and adolescents with cystic fibrosis. *Journal of Pediatric Psychology, 17,* 573–85.

Uman, L.S., Birnie, K.A., Noel, M., Parker, J.A., Chambers, C.T., McGrath, P.J., & Kisely, S.R. (2013). Psychological interventions for needle-related procedural pain and distress in children and adolescents. *The Cochrane Database of Systematic Reviews,* (10), CD005179.

Uman, L.S., Chambers, C.T., McGrath, P.J., & Kisely, S. (2008). A systematic review of randomized controlled trials examining psychological interventions for needle-related procedural pain and distress in children and adolescents: An abbreviated Cochrane review. *Journal of Pediatric Psychology, 33,* 842–54.

Vermaes, I.P., van Susante, A.M., & van Bakel, H.J. (2012). Psychological functioning of siblings in families of children with chronic health conditions: A meta-analysis. *Journal of Pediatric Psychology, 37,* 166–84.

von Gontard, A. (2003). Elimination disorders in childhood. How to make children dry and clean. [Ausscheidungsstorungen differenziert behandeln. Wie Sie Kinder trocken und sauber bekommen]. *MMW Fortschritte Der Medizin, 145,* 26–30.

von Gontard, A., Baeyens, D., Van Hoecke, E., Warzak, W.J., & Bachmann, C. (2011). Psychological and psychiatric issues in urinary and fecal incontinence. *Journal of Urology, 185,* 1432–6.

Vriend, J., Davidson, F., Rusak, B., & Corkum, P. (2015). Emotional and cognitive impact of sleep restriction in children. *Sleep Medicine Clinics, 10,* 107–15.

Walco, G.A. (1986). A behavioral treatment for difficulty in swallowing pills. *Journal of Behavior Therapy and Experimental Psychiatry, 17,* 127–8.

Walker, L.S., Sherman, A.L., Bruehl, S., Garber, J., & Smith, C.A. (2012). Functional abdominal pain patient subtypes in childhood predict functional gastrointestinal disorders with chronic pain and psychiatric comorbidities in adolescence and adulthood. *Pain, 153,* 1798–1806.

Wallander, J.L., & Varni, J.W. (1992). Adjustment in children with chronic physical disorders: Programmatic research on a disability-stress-coping model. In A.M. LaGreca, L. Siegal, J.L. Wallander, & C.E. Walker (Eds.), *Stress and coping in child health* (pp. 279–98). New York: Guilford Press.

Wittmeier, K., Holland, C., Hobbs-Murison, K., Crawford, E., Beauchamp, C., Milne, B., . . Keijzer, R. (2014). Analysis of a parent-initiated social media campaign for Hirschsprung's disease. *Journal of Medical Internet Research, 16,* e288.

Woody, S.R., Weisz, J., & McLean, C. (2005). Empirically supported treatments: 10 years later. *The Clinical Psychologist, 58,* 5–11.

World Health Organization. (2015). Reducing pain at the time of vaccination: WHO position paper. *Weekly Epidemiological Record, 90,* 505–516.

Wright, L. (1967). The pediatric psychologist: A role model. *American Psychologist, 22*(4), 323–5.

Yamada, J., Squires, J.E., Estabrooks, C.A., Victor, C., Stevens, B., & CIHR Team in Children's Pain. (2017). The role of organizational context in moderating the effect of research use on pain outcomes in hospitalized children: A cross sectional study. *BMC Health Services Research, 17*(68).

Zhou, H., Roberts, P., & Horgan, L. (2008). Association between self-report pain ratings of child and parent, child and nurse and parent and nurse dyads: Meta-analysis. *Journal of Advanced Nursing, 63,* 334–42.

Chapter 14

Abrahamson, K., Clark, D., Perkins, A., & Arling, G. (2012). Does cognitive impairment influence quality of life among nursing home residents? *Gerontologist, 52,* 632–40.

Aguirre, E., Spector, A., Hoe, J., Russell, I.T., Knapp, M., Woods, R.T., & Orrell, M. (2010). Maintenance Cognitive Stimulation Therapy (CST) for dementia: A single-blind, multi-centre, randomized controlled trial of maintenance CST versus CST for dementia. *Trials, 11,* 1–10.

Allen, R.S. (2009). The Legacy Project intervention to enhance meaningful family interactions: Case examples. *Clinical Gerontologist, 32,* 164–76.

Allen, R. S., Azuero, C. B., Csikai, E. L., Parmelee, P. A., Shin, H. J., Kvale, E., . . . Burgio, L.D. (2016). "It was very rewarding for me . . .": Senior volunteers' experiences with implementing a reminiscence and creative activity intervention. *The Gerontologist, 56*(2), 357–67.

Allen, R.S., Harris, G.M., Burgio, L.D., Azuero, C.B., Miller, L.A., Shin, H., . . . Parmelee, P. (2014). Can senior volunteers deliver reminiscence and creative activity interventions? Results of the Legacy Intervention Family Enactment (LIFE) randomized controlled trial. *Journal of Pain and Symptom Management, 48*(4), 590–601.

Allen, R.S., Hilgeman, M.M., Ege, M.A., Shuster, J.L., Jr, & Burgio, L.D. (2008). Legacy activities as interventions approaching the end of life. *Journal of Palliative Medicine, 11*, 1029–38.

Alm, N., Dye, R., Gowans, G., Campbell, J., Astell, A., & Ellis, M. (2007). A communication support system for older people with dementia. *Computer, 40*, 35–41.

Alzheimer's Association. (2016). Alzheimer's Disease facts and figures. *Alzheimer's & Dementia, 12*, 459–509.

Alzheimer Society of Canada. (2016). *Prevalence and monetary costs of dementia in Canada.* Toronto, ON: Alzheimer Society of Canada.

American Psychological Association. (2005). *The role of psychology in end-of-life decisions and quality of care.* Retrieved from http://www.apa.org/research/action/end.aspx

American Psychological Association. (2017). *Resolution on assisted dying.* Retrieved from http://www.apa.org/about/policy/assisted-dying-resolution.aspx

Aneshensel, C.S., Pearlin, L.I., Mullan, J.T., Zarit, S.H., & Whitlatch, C.J. (1995). *Profiles in caregiving: The unexpected career.* San Diego, CA: Academic Press.

Azuero, C., Allen, R.S., Kvale, E., Azuero, A., & Parmelee, P. (2014). Determinants of psychology service utilization in a palliative care outpatient population. *Psycho-oncology, 23*(6), 650–7.

Balfour, J.E., & O'Rourke, N. (2003). Older adults with Alzheimer disease, comorbid arthritis and prescription of psychotropic medications. *Pain Research and Management, 8*, 198–204.

Ballard, C., Hanney, M.L., Theodoulou, M., Douglas, S., McShane, R., Kossakowski, K., . . . Jacoby, R. (2009). The dementia antipsychotic withdrawal trial (DART-AD): Long-term follow-up of a randomised placebo-controlled trial. *Lancet Neurology, 8*, 151–7.

Beck, A.M., & Katcher, A.H. (2003). Future directions in human–animal bond research. *American Behavioral Scientist, 47*, 79–93.

Blanchflower, D.G., & Oswald, A.J. (2008). Is well-being U-shaped over the life cycle? *Social Science & Medicine, 66*(8), 1733–49.

Blazer, D.G. (2003). Depression in late life: Review and commentary. *Journals of Gerontology – Series A Biological Sciences and Medical Sciences, 58*(3), 249–65.

Bohlmeijer, E., Smit, F. & Cuijpers, P. (2003). Effects of reminiscence and life review on late-life depression. *International Journal of Geriatric Psychiatry, 18*, 1088–94.

Bonanno, G.A., Wortman, C.B., Lehman, D.R., Tweed, R.G., Haring, M., Sonnega, J., . . . Nesse, P.M. (2002). Resilience to loss and chronic grief: A prospective study from preloss to 18-months postloss. *Journal of Personality and Social Psychology, 83*(5), 1150–64.

Bourgeois, M.S., Dijkstra, K., Burgio, L., & Allen-Burge, R. (2001). Memory aids as an augmentative and alternative communication strategy for nursing home residents with dementia. *Augmentative and Alternative Communication, 17*, 196–210.

Boyd, C.M., Darer, J., Boult, C., Fried, L.P., Boult, L., & Wu, A.W. (2005). Clinical practice guidelines and quality of care for older patients with multiple comorbid diseases: Implications for pay for performance. *Journal of the American Medical Association, 294*, 716–24.

Boyle, P.A., Yu, L., Wilson, R.S., Gamble, K., Buchman, A.S., & Bennett, D.A. (2012). Poor decision making is a consequence of cognitive decline among older persons without Alzheimer's disease or mild cognitive impairment. *PLOS ONE, 7*(8), e43647.

Bruce, C. (2007). Helping patients, families, caregivers and physicians in the grieving process. *Journal of the American Osteopathic Association, 107*(7), 33–40.

Brummel-Smith, K. (1989). Falls in the aged. *Primary Care, 16*(2), 377–393.

Burgio, L.D., Allen-Burge, R., Roth, D.L., Bourgeois, M.S., Dijkstra, K., Gerstle, J., . . . Bankester, L. (2001). Come talk with me: Improving communication between nursing assistants and nursing home residents during care routines. *Gerontologist, 41*, 449–60.

Bush, S.S., Allen, R.S., & Molinari, V. (2017). *Ethical practice in geropsychology.* Washington, DC: American Psychological Association.

Butler, A.C., Chapman, J.E., Forman, E.M., & Beck, A.T. (2006). The empirical status of cognitive-behavioural therapy: A review of meta-analyses. *Clinical Psychology Review, 26*, 17–31.

Camp, C.J., Cohen-Mansfield, J., & Capezuti, E.A. (2002). Use of nonpharmacologic interventions among nursing home residents with dementia. *Psychiatric Services, 53*, 1397–1401.

Candy, B., Jones, L., Drake, R., Leurent, B., & King, M. (2011). Interventions for supporting informal caregivers of patients in the terminal phase of a disease. *Cochrane Database of Systematic Reviews, 7*, 1–77.

Centers for Disease Control (2012). *Health disparities.* Retrieved from www.cdc.gov/healthyyouth/disparities/index.html

Chan, S., Hadjistavropoulos, T., Williams, J., & Lints-Martindale, A. (2014). Evidence-based development and initial validation of the Pain Assessment Checklist for Seniors with Limited Ability to Communicate-II (PACSLAC-II). *Clinical Journal of Pain, 30*(9), 816–24.

Charlton, J.E. (2005). *Core curriculum for professional education in pain* (3rd ed.). Seattle, WA: IASP Press.

Chochinov, H.M. (2012). *Dignity therapy: Final words for final days.* New York, NY: Oxford University Press.

Chochinov, H.M., Kristjanson, L.J., Breitbart, W., McClement, S., Hack, T.F., Hassard, T., & Harlos, M. (2011). Effect of dignity therapy on distress and end-of-life experience in terminally ill patients: A randomised controlled trial. *Lancet Oncology, 12*(8), 753–62.

Clare, L., & Woods, B. (2003). Cognitive rehabilitation and cognitive training for early-stage Alzheimer's disease and vascular dementia. *Cochrane Database of Systematic Reviews, 4,* CD003260.

Cohen-Mansfield, J. (2001). Nonpharmacologic interventions for inappropriate behaviours in dementia: A review, summary, and critique. *American Journal of Geriatric Psychiatry, 9,* 361–81.

Cohen-Mansfield, J., Golander, H., & Arnheim, G. (2000). Self-identity in older persons suffering from dementia: Preliminary results. *Social Science & Medicine, 51,* 381–94.

Cohen-Mansfield, J., Parpura-Gill, A., & Golander, H. (2006) Utilization of self-identity roles for designing interventions for persons with dementia. *Journals of Gerontology, Series B: Psychological Sciences and Social Sciences, 61,* 202–12.

Colombo, G., Dello Buono, M., Smania, K., Raviola, R., & De Leo, D. (2006). Pet therapy and institutionalized elderly: A study on 144 cognitively unimpaired subjects. *Archives of Gerontology and Geriatrics, 42,* 207–16.

Cosio, D. (2016). Practice-based evidence for outpatient, acceptance & commitment therapy for veterans with chronic, non-cancer pain. *Journal of Contextual Behavioral Science, 5,* 23–32.

Dahl, J., Wilson, K. G., & Nilsson, A. (2004). Acceptance and commitment therapy and the treatment of persons at risk for long-term disability resulting from stress and pain symptoms: A preliminary randomized trial. *Behavior Therapy, 35,* 785–802.

Death with Dignity National Center. (2018). *How to access and use death with dignity laws.* Retrieved from https://www.deathwithdignity.org/learn/access

Delbaere, K., Sturnieks, D.L., Crombez, G., & Lord, S.R. (2009). Concern about falls elicits changes in gait parameters in conditions of postural threat in older people. *Journals of Gerontology, Series A: Biological Sciences and Medical Sciences, 64,* 237–42.

Eastman, J.K., & Iyer, R. (2004). The elderly's uses and attitudes towards the internet. *Journal of Consumer Marketing, 21*(3), 208–20.

Family Caregiver Alliance. (2006). *Caregiver assessment: Voices and views from the field.* Report form a National Consensus Development Conference (Vol. II). San Francisco, CA: Family Caregiver Alliance.

Feltner, M.E., MacRae, P.G., & McNitt-Gray, J.L. (1994). Quantitative gait assessment as a predictor of prospective and retrospective falls in community-dwelling older women. *Archives of Physical Medicine and Rehabilitation, 75,* 447–53.

Feros, D.L., Lane, L., Ciarrochi, J., & Blackledge, J.T. (2013). Acceptance and commitment therapy (ACT) for improving the lives of cancer patients: A preliminary study. *Psycho-Oncology, 22*(2), 459–64.

Fields, J.A., Kramer, J.A., & Lubin, W. (1993). Challenges and opportunities in the provision of long-term care. *Benefits Quarterly, 9,* 6–11.

Fisher, J.E., Drossel, C., Ferguson, K., Cherup, S., & Sylvester, M. (2008). Treating persons with dementia in context. In D. Gallagher-Thompson, A.M. Steffen, & L.W. Thompson (Eds.), *Handbook of behavioral and cognitive therapies with older adults* (pp. 200–18). New York, NY: Springer Science + Business Media, LLC.

Fraser Health. (2006). *Hospice palliative care program symptom guidelines: Psychosocial care.* Retrieved from http://www.fraserhealth.ca/media/psychosocial%20care.pdf

Fuchs-Lacelle, S., Hadjistavropoulos, T., & Lix, L. (2008). Pain assessment as intervention: A study of older adults with severe dementia. *Clinical Journal of Pain, 24,* 697–707.

Gauthier, L.R., & Gagliese, L. (2010). Assessment of pain in older persons. In D.C. Turk & R. Melzack (Eds.), *Handbook of pain assessment* (3rd ed., pp. 242–59). New York, NY: Guilford Press.

Glass, T.A., de Leon, C.F., Bassuk, S.S., & Berkman, L.F. (2006). Social engagement and depressive symptoms in late life: Longitudinal findings. *Journal of Aging and Health, 18,* 604–28.

Green, S.M., Hadjistavropoulos, T., Hadjistavropoulos, H., Martin, R., & Sharpe, D. (2009). A controlled investigation of a cognitive behavioural pain management program for older adults. *Behavioural and Cognitive Psychotherapy, 37,* 221–6.

Haber, D. (2006). Life review: Implementation, theory, research, and therapy. *International Journal on Aging and Human Development, 63,* 153–71.

Hadjistavropoulos, T. (2012). Self-management of pain in older persons: Helping people help themselves. *Pain Medicine, 13,* S67–S71.

Hadjistavropoulos, T., Carleton, R.N., Delbaere, K., Barden, J., Zwakhalen, S., Fitzgerald, B., . . . Hadjistavropoulos, H. (2012). The relationship of fear of falling and balance confidence with balance and dual tasking performance. *Psychology and Aging, 27,* 1–13.

Hadjistavropoulos, T., Craig, K.D., Duck, S., Cano, A., Goubert, L., Jackson, P., . . . Fitzgerald, T.D. (2011). A biopsychosocial formulation of pain communication. *Psychological Bulletin, 137,* 910–39.

Hadjistavropoulos, T., Fitzgerald, T.D., & Marchildon, G. (2010). Practice guidelines for assessing pain in older persons who reside in long-term care facilities. *Physiotherapy Canada, 62,* 104–13.

Hadjistavropoulos, T., & Hadjistavropoulos, H.D. (Eds.). (2019). *Pain management for older adults: A self help guide* (2nd ed.). Philadelphia, PA: Wolters Kluwer.

Hadjistavropoulos, T., Herr, K., Turk, D.C., Fine, P.G., Dworkin, R.H., Helme, R., . . . Williams, J. (2007a). An interdisciplinary expert consensus statement on assessment of pain in older persons. *Clinical Journal of Pain, 23,* S1–S43.

Hadjistavropoulos, T., Marchildon, G., Fine, P., Herr, K., Palley, H., Kaasalainen, S., & Beland, F. (2009). Transforming long-term care pain management in North America: The policy clinical interface. *Pain Medicine, 10,* 506–20.

Hadjistavropoulos, T., Martin, R., Sharpe, D., Lints-Martindale, A.C., McCreary, D., & Asmundson, G.J.G. (2007b). A longitudinal investigation of fear of falling, fear of pain, and activity avoidance in community dwelling older adults. *Journal of Aging and Health, 19,* 965–84.

Haight, B., Michel, Y., & Hendrix, S. (2000). The extended effects of the life review in nursing home residents. *International Journal on Aging and Human Development, 50,* 151–68.

Haight, B., & Webster, J.D. (1995). The art and science of reminiscing: Theory, research, methods and applications. Washington, DC: Taylor and Francis.

Hawk, C., Hyland, J.K., Rupert, R., Colonvega, M., & Hall, S. (2006). Assessment of balance and risk for falls in a sample of community-dwelling adults aged 65 and older. *Chiropractic & Osteopathy, 14*(3).

Hayes, S.C. (2004). Acceptance and commitment therapy, relational frame theory, and the third wave of behavior therapy. *Behavior Therapy, 35,* 639–65.

Hayes, S.C., & Smith, S. (2005). Get out of your mind and into your life: The new acceptance and commitment therapy. Oakland, CA: New Harbinger Publications.

Health Canada (2003). *Arthritis in Canada—An ongoing challenge.* Ottawa: Health Canada. Retrieved from www.phac-aspc.gc.ca/publicat/ac/pdf/ac_e.pdf

Health Law Institute, Dalhousie University. (n.d.). End-of-life law & policy in Canada. Retrieved from http://eol.law.dal.ca

Herr, K. (2010). Pain in the older adult: An imperative across all health care settings. *Pain Management Nursing, 11,* S1–S10.

Horgas, A.L., Nichols, A.L., Schapson, C.A., & Vietes, K. (2007). Assessing pain in persons with dementia: Relationships among the non-communicative patient's pain assessment instrument, self-report, and behavioral observations. *Pain Management Nursing, 8,* 77–85.

Huang, C. H., Crowther, M., Allen, R. S., DeCoster, J., Kim, G., Azuero, C., . . . Kvale, E. (2016). A pilot feasibility intervention to increase advance care planning among African Americans in the deep south. *Journal of Palliative Medicine, 19*(2), 164–73.

Ivziku, D., Matarese, M., & Pedone, C. (2011). Predictive validity of the Hendrich fall risk model II in an acute geriatric unit. *International Journal of Nursing Studies, 48*(4), 468–74.

Karel, M., Emery, E., & Molinari, V. (2010). Development of a tool to evaluate geropsychology knowledge and skill competencies. *International Psychogeriatrics, 22,* 886–95.

Karesa, S., & McBride, D. (2016). A sign of the changing times? Perceptions of Canadian psychologists on assisted death. *Canadian Psychology/Psychologie canadienne, 57*(3), 188–92.

Kazdin, A.E., & Blase, S.L. (2011). Rebooting psychotherapy research and practice to reduce the burden of mental illness. *Perspectives on Psychological Science, 6,* 21–37.

Kelley, A.S., & Morrison, R.S. (2015). Palliative care for the seriously ill. *New England Journal of Medicine, 373*(8), 747–55.

Kitwood, T. (1997). *Dementia reconsidered: The person comes first.* Buckingham, UK: Open University Press.

Knight, B.G., Karel, M.J., Hinrichsen, G.A., Qualls, S.H., & Duffy, M. (2009). Pikes Peak model for training in professional gerospychology. *American Psychologist, 64,* 205–14.

Kübler-Ross, E. (1969). On death and dying: What the dying have to teach doctors, nurses, clergy and their own families. New York, NY: Macmillan.

Kurz, A., Thone-Otto, A., Cramer, B., Egert, S., Frolich, L., Gertz, H., . . . Werheid, K. (2012). CORDIAL: Cognitive rehabilitation and Cognitive-behavioral Treatment for Early

Dementia in Alzheimer Disease: A multicenter, randomized, controlled trial. *Alzheimer Disease & Associated Disorders, 26,* 246–53.

Lawton, M.P. (1997). Positive and negative affective states among older people in long-term care. In R.L. Rubenstein & M.P. Lawton (Eds.), *Depression in long term and residential care: Advances in research and treatment* (pp. 29–54). New York, NY: Springer.

Lejuez, C.W., Hopko, D.R., & Hopko, S.D. (2001). A brief behavioral activation treatment for depression: Treatment manual. *Behavior Modification, 25,* 255–86.

Lezak, M.D., Howieson, D.B., & Loring, D.W. (2004). *Neuropsychological assessment.* Oxford, UK: Oxford University Press.

Lints-Martindale, A.C., Hadjistavropoulos, T., Lix, L.M., & Thorpe, L. (2012). A comparative investigation of observational pain assessment tools for older adults with dementia. *Clinical Journal of Pain, 28,* 226–37.

Lunde, L., Nordhus, I.H., & Pallesen, S. (2009). The effectiveness of cognitive and behavioural treatment of chronic pain in the elderly: A quantitative review. *Journal of Clinical Psychology in Medical Settings, 16,* 254–62.

Martin, R., Williams, J., Hadjistavropoulos, T., Hadjistavropoulos, H.D., & MacLean, M. (2005). A qualitative investigation of seniors' and caregivers' views on pain assessment and management. *Canadian Journal of Nursing Research, 37,* 142–64.

Materstvedt, L.J., Clark, D., Ellershaw, J., Forde, R., Gravgaard, A.M., Muller-Busch, H.C., . . . EAPC Ethics Task Force. (2003). Euthanasia and physician-assisted suicide: A view from an EAPC ethics task force. *Palliative Medicine, 17,* 97–101.

Mather, M., Jacobsen, L.A., & Pollard, K.M. (2015). Aging in the United States. *Population Bulletin, 70*(2). Washington, DC: Population Reference Bureau.

McDougall, G.J., Buxen, C.E., & Suen, L.J. (1997). The process and outcome of life review psychotherapy with depressed homebound older adults. *Nursing Research, 46,* 277–83.

McMillan, S.C. (2005). Interventions to facilitate family caregiving at the end of life. *Journal of Palliative Medicine, 8*(S1), S132–S139.

McMillan, S.C., Small, B.J., Weitzer, M., Schonwetter, R., Tittle, M., Moody, L., & Haley, W. (2006). Impact of a coping skills intervention with family caregivers of hospice patients with cancer: A randomized clinical trial. *Cancer, 106,* 214–22.

Meeks, S., & Depp, C.A. (2002). Pleasant events-based behavioral intervention for depression in nursing home residents: A conceptual and empirical foundation. *Clinical Gerontologist, 25,* 125–48.

Meeks, S., Looney, S.W., Van Haitsma, K., & Teri, L. (2008). BE-ACTIV: A staff-assisted behavioral intervention for depression in nursing homes. *Gerontologist, 48,* 105–14.

Meeks, S., Young, C.M., & Looney, S.W. (2007). Activity participation and affect among nursing home residents: Support for a behavioural model of depression. *Aging and Mental Health, 11,* 751–60.

Monin, J.K., & Schulz, R. (2009). Interpersonal effects of suffering in older adult caregiving relationships. *Psychology and Aging, 24*, 681–95.

Moos, I., & Björn, A. (2006). Use of the life story in the institutional care of people with dementia: A review of intervention studies. *Ageing and Society, 26*, 431–54.

Morrison, R.S., & Siu, A.L. (2000). A comparison of pain and its treatment in advanced dementia and cognitively impaired patients with hip fracture. *Journal of Pain and Symptom Management, 19*, 240–8.

Nerburn, K. (1993). *Letters to my son: Reflections on becoming a man*. San Rafael, CA: New World Library.

Nicholas, M.K., Asghari, A., Blyth, F.M., Wood, B.M., Murray, R., McCabe, R., . . . Overton, S. (2013). Self-management intervention for chronic pain in older adults: A randomised controlled trial. *Pain, 154*(6), 824–35.

Opie, J., Doyle, C., & O'Connor, D.W. (2002). Challenging behaviours in nursing home residents with dementia: A randomised controlled trial of multi-disciplinary interventions. *International Journal of Geriatric Psychiatry, 17*, 6–13.

Oregon Health Authority. (2018). *Oregon death with dignity act: 2017 data summary*. Retrieved from www.oregon.gov/oha/PH/PROVIDERPARTNERRESOURCES/EVALUATIONRESEARCH/DEATHWITHDIGNITYACT/Documents/year20.pdf

Oregon Health Authority, Public Health Division. (2018). Physician assisted suicide. Retrieved from: www.oregon.gov/oha/ph/ProviderPartnerResources/EvaluationResearch/DeathwithDignityAct/Pages/index.aspx

Parekh, A.K., & Barton, M.B. (2010). The challenge of multiple comorbidity for the US healthcare system. *Journal of the American Medical Association, 202*, 1303–4.

Parmelee, P.A., Katz, I.R., & Lawton, M.P. (1992). Incidence of depression in long-term care settings. *Journals of Gerontology: Series A, Biological and Medical Sciences, 47*, M189–M196.

Patel, K.V., Guralnik, J.M., Dansie, E.J., & Turk, D.C. (2013). Prevalence and impact of pain among older adults in the United States: Findings from the 2011 National Health and Aging Trends Study. *Pain, 154*(12), 2649–57.

Pearson, W.S., Bhat-Schelbert, K., & Probst, J.C. (2012). Multiple chronic conditions and the aging of America. *Journal of Primary Care & Community Health, 3*, 51–6.

Pecanac, K.E., Repenshek, M.F., Tennenbaum, D., & Hammes, B. (2014). Respecting Choices® and advance directives in a diverse community. *Journal of Palliative Medicine, 17*(3), 282–7.

Pew Research Center. (2017). *Internet/broadband fact sheet*. Retrieved from http://www.pewinternet.org/fact-sheet/internet-broadband/#

Plassman, B.L., Williams, J.W., Burke, J.R., Holsinger, T., & Benjamin, S. (2009). NIH conference and systematic review: Factors associated with risk for and possible prevention of cognitive decline in later life. *Annals of Internal Medicine, 153*, 182–93.

Public Health Agency of Canada (PHAC). (2009a). *Tracking heart disease and stroke in Canada*. Retrieved from www.phac-aspc.gc.ca/publicat/2009/cvd-avc/pdf/cvd-avs-2009-eng.pdf

Public Health Agency of Canada (PHAC). (2009b). *Obesity in Canada—snapshot*. Retrieved from www.phac-aspc.gc.ca/publicat/2009/oc/pdf/oc-eng.pdf

Public Health Agency of Canada (PHAC). (2011). *Diabetes in Canada: Facts and figures from a public health perspective*. Retrieved from www.phac-aspc.gc.ca/cd-mc/publications/diabetes-diabete/facts-figures-faits-chiffres-2011/pdf/facts-figures-faits-chiffres-eng.pdf

Public Health Agency of Canada (PHAC). (2012). *Asthma facts and figures*. Retrieved from www.phac-aspc.gc.ca/cd-mc/crd-mrc/asthma_figures-asthme_figures-eng.php

Radvansky, G.A. (2011). *Human memory* (2nd ed.). New York, NY: Pearson.

Reed, G.M, McLaughlin, C.J, & Millholland, K. (2000). Ten interdisciplinary principles for professional practice in telehealth. *Professional Psychology Research and Practice, 31*, 170–8.

Robinson, C.L. (2007). Relieving pain in the elderly. *Health Progress, 88*, 48–53, 70.

Rosland, A.M., Heisler, M., & Piette, J.D. (2012). The impact of family behaviors and communication patterns on chronic illness outcomes: A systematic review. *Journal of Behavioral Medicine, 35*, 221–39.

Rossen, E.K. (2007). Assessing older persons' readiness to move to independent congregate living. *Clinical Nurse Specialist, 21*, 292–6.

Rubenstein, L.Z. (2006). Falls in older people: Epidemiology, risk factors and strategies for prevention. *Age and Ageing, 35*, 37–41.

Scherrer, J.F., Bucholz, K.K., Eisen, S.A., Lyons, M.J., Goldberg, J., Tsuang, M., & True, W.R. (2003). A twin study of depression symptoms, hypertension, and heart disease in middle-aged men. *Psychosomatic Medicine, 65*, 548–57.

Scogin, F., Hanson, A., & Welsh, D. (2003). Self-administered treatment in stepped-care models of depression treatment. *Journal of Clinical Psychology, 59*, 341–9.

Scogin, F., & Shah, A. (2006). Screening older adults for depression in primary care settings. *Health Psychology, 25*, 675–7.

Scogin, F., Welsh, D., Hanson, A., Stump, J., & Coates, A. (2005). Evidence-based psychotherapies for depression in older adults. *Clinical Psychology: Science and Practice, 12*, 222–37.

Scott, W., Aisling, D., Yu, L. & McCraken, L.M. (2017). Treatment of chronic pain for adults 65 and over: Analyses of outcomes and changes in psychological flexibility following Acceptance and Commitment Therapy. *Pain Medicine, 18*, 252–264.

Snarski, M., Scogin, F., DiNapoli, E., Presnell, A., McAlpine, J., & Marcinak, J. (2011). The effects of behavioral activation therapy with inpatient geriatric psychiatry patients. *Behavior Therapy, 42*, 100–8.

Society for Cognitive Rehabilitation. (2013). *What is cognitive rehabilitation therapy?* Retrieved from www.societyforcognitiverehab.org/patient-family-resources/what-is-cognitive-rehab.php

Solano, J.P., Gomes, B., & Higginson, I.J. (2006). A comparison of symptom prevalence in far advanced cancer, AIDS, heart disease, chronic obstructive pulmonary disease and renal disease. *Journal of Pain and Symptom Management, 31*, 58–69.

Sperling, R.A., Aisen, P.S., Beckett, L.A., Bennett, D.A., Craft, S., Fagan, A.M., . . . Phelps, C.H. (2011). Toward defining the preclinical stages of Alzheimer's disease: Recommendations from the National Institute on Aging-Alzheimer's Association workgroups on diagnostic guidelines for Alzheimer's disease. *Alzheimer's Dementia, 7*, 280–92.

Statistics Canada. (2015). *Canada's population estimates: Age and sex, July 1, 2015.* Retrieved from http://www.statcan.gc.ca/daily-quotidien/150929/dq150929b-eng.pdf

Stevens, J.A., Mack, K.A., Paulozzi, L.J., & Ballesteros, M.F. (2008). Self-reported falls and fall-related injuries among persons aged greater than or equal to 65 years—United States, 2006. *Journal of Safety Research, 39*, 345–9.

Stone, R.I., & Reinhard, S.C. (2007). The place of assisted living in long-term care and related service systems. *Gerontologist, 47*, 23–32.

Teresi, J., Abrams, R., Holmes, D., Ramirez, M., & Eimicke, J. (2001). Prevalence of depression and depression recognition in nursing homes. *Social Psychiatry and Psychiatric Epidemiology, 36*, 613–20.

The National Hospice and Palliative Care Organization. (2017). *Advance care planning.* Retrieved from https://www.nhpco.org/advance-care-planning.

Thielke, S., Vannoy, S., & Unützer, J. (2007). Integrating mental health and primary care. *Primary Care: Clinics in Office Practice, 34*(3), 571–92.

Thomas, M.L., Kaufmann, C.N., Palmer, B.W., Depp, C.A., Martin, A.S., Glorioso, D.K., . . . Jeste, D.V. (2016). Paradoxical trend for improvement in mental health with aging: A community-based study of 1,546 adults aged 21–100 years. *Journal of Clinical Psychiatry, 77*(8), 1019–25.

Volker, D.L. (2005). Control and end-of-life care: Does ethnicity matter? *American Journal of Hospice and Palliative Medicine, 22*, 442–6.

Wessel, E., & Garon, M. (2005). Introducing reflective narratives into palliative home care education. *Home Healthcare Nurse, 23*(8), 516–22.

Willis, S.L., Tennstedt, S.L., Marsiske, M., Ball, K., Elias, J., Koepke, J.M., . . . Wright, E. (2006). Long-term effects of cognitive training on everyday functional outcomes in older adults. *Journal of the American Medical Association, 296*, 2805–14.

World Health Organization. (2015). *World report on ageing and health.* Geneva, Swizerland: Author.

World Health Organization. (2017). *WHO definition of palliative care.* Retrieved from www.who.int/cancer/palliative/definition/en/

Yamaguchi, H., Maki, Y., & Yamagami, T. (2010). Overview of non-pharmacological intervention for dementia and principles of brain-activating rehabilitation. *Psychogeratrics: Official Journal of the Japanese Psychogeriatric Society, 10*, 206–13.

Zijlstra, G.A.R., Van Haastregt, J.C.M., Ambergen, T., Van Rossum, E., Van Eijk, J.T.M., Tennstedt, S.L., & Kempen, G. (2009). Effects of a multicomponent cognitive behavioral group intervention on fear of falling and activity avoidance in community-dwelling older adults: Results of a randomized controlled trial. *Journal of the American Geriatrics Society, 57*, 2020–8.

Zijlstra, G.A.R., Van Haastregt, J.C.M., Van Rossum, E., Van Eijk, J.T.M., Yardley, L., & Kempen, G. (2007). Interventions to reduce fear of falling in community-living older people: A systematic review. *Journal of the American Geriatrics Society, 55*, 603–15.

Chapter 15

Abraham, C. & Sheeran, P. (2007). The health belief model. In S. Ayers, A. Baum, C. McManus, S. Newman, K. Wallston, J. Weinman, & R. West, (Eds.). *Cambridge handbook of psychology health and medicine* (2nd ed., pp. 97–101). Cambridge: Cambridge University Press.

Adelson, N. (2005). The embodiment of inequality: Health disparities in Aboriginal Canada. *Canadian Journal of Public Health, 96*, S45–S61.

Airhihenbuwa, C.O., & Liburd, L. (2006). Eliminating health disparities in the African American population: The interface of culture, gender, and power. *Health Education & Behavior, 33*, 488–501.

American Diabetes Association. (2012). *Living with diabetes: Native American complications.* Retrieved from www.diabetes.org/living-with-diabetes/complications/native-americans.html

American Psychiatric Association. (2000). *Diagnostic and statistical manual of mental disorders*, (4th ed. text revision.).Washington: American Psychiatric Association.

American Psychological Association (APA). (2002). *Guidelines on multicultural education, training, research, practice, and organizational change for psychologists.* Retrieved from www.apa.org/pi/oema/resources/policy/multicultural-guideline.pdf

American Psychological Association (APA). (2007). *Report of the APA Task Force on Socioeconomic Status.* Retrieved from www.apa.org/pi/ses/resources/publications/task-force-2006.pdf

American Psychological Association (APA). (2012). *Public description of clinical health psychology.* Retrieved from www.apa.org/ed/graduate/specialize/health.aspx

American Psychological Association Presidential Task Force on Evidence-Based Practice. (2006). Evidence-based practice in psychology. *American Psychologist, 61*, 271–285.

Anderson, N.B., Bulatao, R.A., & Cohen, B. (Eds.). (2004). *Critical perspectives on racial and ethnic differences in health and late life.* Washington: National Academies Press.

Anderson, R.J., Freedland, K.E., Clouse, R.E., & Lustman, P.J. (2001). The prevalence of comorbid depression in adults with diabetes: A meta-analysis. *Diabetes Care, 24*, 1069–78.

Andrews, M.M., & Boyle, J.S. (2015). *Transcultural concepts in nursing care* (6th ed.). Philadelphia, PA: Wolters Kluwer.

Ashcroft, B., Griffiths, G., & Tiffin, H. (2006). *The post-colonial studies reader* (2nd ed.). New York: Taylor & Francis.

Attewell, P., Kasinitz, P., & Dunn. K. (2010). Black Canadians and Black Americans: Racial income inequality in comparative perspective. *Ethnic and Racial Studies, 33*, 473–95.

Barak, A., Klein, B., & Proudfoot, J.G. (2009). Defining internet-supported therapeutic interventions. *Annals of Behavioral Medicine, 38*, 4–17.

Bartlett, J.G. (2003). Involuntary cultural change, stress phenomenon and Aboriginal health status. *Canadian Journal of Public Health, 94*, 165–167.

Battiste, M., & Henderson, J. (2000). *Protecting indigenous knowledge and heritage: A global challenge.* Saskatoon: Purich Publishing.

Bernal, G., & Scharrón-Del-Río, M. (2001). Are empirically supported treatments valid for ethnic minorities? Toward an alternative approach for treatment research. *Journal of Cultural Diversity and Ethnic Minority Psychology, 7*, 328–42.

Berry, J.W. (2005). Acculturation: Living successfully in two cultures. *International Journal of Intercultural Relations, 29*, 697–712.

Berry, J.W. (1997). Immigration, acculturation, and adaptation. *Applied Psychology, 46*, 5–34.

Bhugra, D., & Jones, P. (2001). *Advances in Psychiatric Treatment, 7*, 216–222.

Blumentritt, T.L., Angle, R.L., & Brown, J.M. (2004). MACI personality patterns and DSM-IV symptomology in a sample of troubled Mexican-American adolescents. *Journal of Child & Family Studies, 13*, 163–78.

Brawley, O.W. (2007). Health-care disparites, civil rights, and human rights. *Oncology, 21*, 499–503.

Browne, A.J., Smye, V.L., & Varcoe, C. (2005). The relevance of postcolonial theoretical perspectives to research in Aboriginal health. *Canadian Journal of Nursing Research, 37*, 16–37.

Cajete, G. (1999). *Native science: Natural laws of interdependence.* Sante Fe, NM: Clear Light Publishers.

Campinha-Bacote, J. (1999). A model and instrument for addressing cultural competence in health care. *Journal of Nursing Education, 38*, 203–7.

Carter-Pokras, O., & Baquet, C. (2002). What is a "health disparity"? *Public Health Reports, 117*, 426–34.

Centers for Disease Control and Prevention (CDC), US Department of Health and Human Services. (2011). CDC *HEALTH DISPARITIES AND INEQUALITIES REPORT—UNITED STATES 2011* (Morbidity and Mortality Weekly Report, No. 60). Retrieved from www.cdc.gov/mmwr/pdf/other/su6001.pdf

Chandler, M.J., Lalonde, C.E., Sokol, B.W., & Hallet, D. (2003). Personal persistence, identity, development, and suicide: A study of Native and non-Native North American adolescents. *Monographs for the Society for Research in Child Development, 68*(2), 1–130.

Chang, D.F., & Yoon, P. (2011). Ethnic minority clients' perceptions of the significance of race in cross-racial therapy relationships. *PsychotherapyResearch, 21*, 567–82.

Cohen, K. (2003). Honoring the medicine: The essential guide to Native American healing. *Alternative Therapies in Health and Medicine, 9*, 68–73.

Cokley, K. (2007). Critical issues in the measurement of ethnic and racial identity: A referendum on the state of the field. *Journal of Counseling Psychology, 54*, 224 –34.

Constantine, M.G., & Ladany, N. (2000). Self-report multicultural counseling competence scales: Their relation to social desirability attitudes and multicultural case conceptualization ability. *Journal of Counseling Psychology, 47*, 155–64.

Corbie-Smith, G., Thomas, S.B., & St George, D.M.M. (2002). Distrust, race, and research. *Archives of Internal Medicine, 162*, 2458–63.

Cramer, H., Lauche, R., Langhorst, J., & Dobos, G. (2013). Yoga for rheumatic diseases: A systematic review. *Rheumatology, 52*(11), 2025–30.

Cuijpers, P., Van Straten, A., & Andersson, G. (2008). Internet-administered cognitive behavior therapy for health problems: a systematic review. *Journal of Behavioral Medicine, 31*, 169–77.

Cutler, D.M., Lleras-Muney, A., & Vogl, T. (2008). *Socioeconomic status and health: Dimensions and mechanisms.* NBER Working Paper No. 1433.

Dana, R.H. (2002). Mental health services for African Americans: A cultural/racial perspective. *Cultural Diversity and Ethnic Minority Psychology, 8*, 3–18.

Danish, S.J., Forneris, T., & Wilder Schaaf, K. (2007). Counseling psychology and culturally competent health care: Limitations and challenges. *Counseling Psychologist, 35*, 716–25.

Elias, B. (2014). Moving beyond the historical quagmire of measuring infant mortality for the First Nations population in Canada. *Social Science Medicine, 123*, 125–32.

Ermine, W., Nilson, R., Sauchyn, D., Sauve, E., & Smith, R.Y. (2005). Isi Askiwan—The state of the land: Summary of the Prince Albert grand council Elders' forum on climate change. *Journal of Aboriginal Health, 2*, 62–72.

Fernandez, D.R., Carlson, D.S., Stepina, L.P., & Nicholson, J.D. (1997). Hofstede's country classification 25 years later. *Journal of Social Psychology, 137*, 43–54.

Fisher, J.A., & Kalbaugh, C.A. (2011). Challenging assumptions about minority participation in US clinical research. *American Journal of Public Health, 101*(12), 2217.

Flaskerud, J.H. (1990). Matching client and therapist ethnicity, language, and gender: A review of research. *Issues in Mental Health Nursing, 11*, 321–36.

Fleming, J., & Ledogar, R.J. (2008). Resilience and Indigenous spirituality: A literature review. *Pimatisiwin, 6*, 47–64.

Ford, M.E., & Kelly, P.A. (2005). Conceptualizing and categorizing race and ethnicity in health services research. *Health Research and Educational Trust, 40*, 1659–75.

Freimuth, V.S., Quinn, S.C., Thomas, S.B., Cole, G., Zook, E., & Duncan, T. (2001). African Americans' views on research and the Tuskegee Syphilis Study. *Social Science & Medicine, 52*, 797–808.

Frideres, J.S. (2011). *First nations in the twenty-first century.* Toronto: Oxford University Press.

Frohlich, K.L., Ross, N., & Richmond, C. (2006). Health disparities in Canada today: Some evidence and a theoretical framework. *Health Policy, 79*, 132–43.

Fuertes, J.N., & Brobst, K. (2002). Clients' ratings of counselor multicultural competency. *Cultural Diversity and Ethnic Minority Psychology, 8*, 214–23.

Fuertes, J.N., Costa, C.I., Mueller, L.N., & Hersh, M. (2005). Psychotherapy process and outcome from a racial-ethnic perspective. In R.T. Carter (Ed.), *Handbook of racial-cultural psychology and counseling, Volume One, Theory and Research* (pp. 256–77). Hoboken, NJ: Wiley.

Gamst, G., Dana, R.H., Der-Karaberian, A., & Kramer, T. (2000). Ethnic match and client ethnicity effects on global assessment and visitation. *Journal of Community Psychology, 28*, 547–64.

Ghumman, U., McCord, C.E., & Chang, J.E. (2016). Posttraumatic stress disorder in Syrian refugees: A review. *Canadian Psychology/Psychologie Canadienne, 57*(4), 246–53.

Gideon, V., Gray, J., Nicholas, W., & Ha, P. (2008). First Nations youth health: Recognizing the challenges, recognizing the potential. *Horizons: Policy Research Initiative, 10*, 83–7.

Government of Canada. (2011). TCPS 2—2nd edition of Tri-Council Policy Statement: Ethical conduct for research involving humans. Panel on Research Ethics. Retrieved from www.pre.ethics.gc.ca/eng/policy-politique/initiatives/tcps2-eptc2/Default

Gracey, M., & King, M. (2009). Indigenous health part 1: Determinants and disease patterns. *Lancet, 374*, 65–75.

Greenwood, M., de Leeuw, S., Lindsay, N.M., & Reading, C. (2015). *Determinants of Indigenous Peoples' health in Canada: Beyond the social*. Toronto, On: Canadian Scholars' Press.

Guimond, E., & Cooke, M.J. (2008). The current well-being of registered Indian youth: Concerns for the future? *Horizons: Policy Research Initiative, 10*, 26–30.

Gurung, R.A.R. (2011). Cultural influences on health. In K.D. Keith (Ed.), *Cross-cultural psychology: Contemporary themes and perspectives* (pp. 259–73). West Sussex, UK: Wiley-Blackwell.

Hadfield, K., Ostrowski, A., & Ungar, M. (2017). What can we expect of the mental health and well-being of Syrian refugee children and adolescents in Canada? *Canadian Psychology/ Psychologie Canadienne, 58*(2), 194–201.

Hall, G.C.N. (2001). Psychotherapy research with ethnic minorities: Empirical, ethical, and conceptual issues. *Journal of Consulting and Clinical Psychology, 69*, 502–10.

Hayward, M.D., Miles, T.P., Crimmins, E.M., & Yang, Y. (2000). The significance of socioeconomic status in explaining the racial gap in chronic health conditions. *American Sociological Review, 65*, 910–30.

Health Canada. (2008). *A statistical profile on the health of First Nations in Canada: Self-rated health and selected conditions, 2002 to 2005* (Government of Canada Publication, No. 3556). Retrieved from www.hc-sc.gc.ca/fniah-spnia/pubs/aborig-autoch/index-eng.php

Health Canada. (2011). *Diabetes in Canada: Facts and figures from a public health perspective*. Ottawa. Retrieved from www.phac-aspc.gc.ca/cd-mc/diabetes-diabete/index-eng.php

HealthyPeople.gov. (2012). *Healthy People 2020: Improving the health of Americans*. Washington: US Department of Health and Human Services. Retrieved from www.healthypeople.gov/2020/default.aspx

Henao-Martinez, A.F., & Castillo-Mancilla, J.R. (2013). The Hispanic HIV epidemic. *Current Infectious Disease Reports, 15*, 46–51.

Hofstede, G.H. (1980). Culture's consequences: International differences in work-related values. Newbury Park, CA: Sage Publications.

Hofstede, G. (2001). *Culture's consequences: Comparing values, behaviors, institutions, and organizations across nations* (2nd ed.). Thousand Oaks, Calif.: Sage.

Hofstede, G., & Bond, M.H. (1988). The Confucius connection: From cultural roots to economic growth. *Organizational Dynamics, 16*, 5–21.

Jacob, K.S., & Kuruvilla, A. (2012). Psychotherapy across cultures: The form-content dichotomy. *Clinical Psychology and Psychotherapy, 19*, 91–5.

Jahnke, R., Larkey, L., Rogers, C., Etnier, J., & Lin, F. (2010). A comprehensive review of health benefits of qigong and tai chi. *American Journal of Health Promotion, 24*, e1–e25.

Jones, M.L. (2007). *Hofstede—Culturally questionable?* (Published for Research Online [University of Wollongong]). Retrieved from ro.uow.edu.au/cgi/viewcontent.cgi?article=1389&context=commpapers

Kao, H.F.S., Hsu, M.T., & Clark, L. (2004). Conceptualizing and critiquing culture in health research. *Journal of Transcultural Nursing, 15*, 269–77.

Kaplan, J.B., & Bennett, T. (2003). Use of race and ethnicity in biomedical publication. *Journal of the American Medical Association, 289*, 2709–16.

Kalichman, S.C., Benotsch, E.G., Weinhardt, L., Austin, J., Luke, W., & Cherry, C. (2003). Health-related Internet use, coping, social support, and health indicators in people living with HIV/AIDS: Preliminary results from a community survey. *Health Psychology, 22*, 111–16.

Kazarian, S.S., & Evans, D.R. (Eds.). (2001). *Handbook of cultural health psychology*. San Diego: Academic Press.

Keefe, F.J., & Blumenthal, J.A. (2004). Health psychology: What will the future bring? *Health Psychology, 23*, 156–7.

Keenan, M.L., & Shaw, K.M. (2011). Coronary heart disease and stroke deaths—United States, 2006. In Centers for Disease Control and Prevention, US Department of Health and Human Services, *CDC health disparities and inequalities report—United States 2011* (pp. 62–66) (Morbidity and Mortality Weekly Report, No. 60). Retrieved from www.cdc.gov/mmwr/pdf/other/su6001.pdf

Kirmayer, L.J. (1994). Suicide among Canadian Aboriginal people. *Transcultural Psychiatric Research Review, 31*, 3–58.

Kirmayer, L.J. (2001). Cultural variations in the presentation of depression and anxiety: Implications for diagnosis and treatment. *Journal of Clinical Psychiatry, 63*(suppl. 13), 22–8.

Kirmayer, L.J., Gill, K., Fletcher, C., Ternar, Y., Boothroyd, L., Quesney, C., . . . Hayton, B. (1993). *Emerging trends in research on mental health among Canadian Aboriginal people*.

Montreal: Sir Mortimer B. Davis—Jewish General Hospital and Department of Psychiatry, McGill University.

Kirmayer, L.J., & Sartorius, N. (2007). Cultural models and somatic syndromes. *Psychosomatic Medicine, 69*, 832–840.

Kitaoka, S.K. (2005). Multicultural counseling competencies: Lessons from assessment. *Journal of Multicultural Counseling and Development, 33*, 37–47.

Kottak, C.P. (2011). *Cultural anthropology: Appreciating cultural diversity.* New York: McGraw-Hill.

Kressin, N.R., Raymond, K.L., & Manze, M. (2008). Perceptions of race/ethnicity-based discrimination: A review of measures of evaluation of their usefulness for the health care setting. *Journal of Health Care for the Poor and Underserved, 19*, 697–730.

Lara, M., Gamboa, C., Kahramanian, M.I., Morales, L.S., & Hayes Bautista, D.E. (2005). Acculturation and Latino health in the United States: A review of the literature and its socio-political context. *Annual Review of Public Health, 26*, 367–97.

Lewis-Fernández, R., Hinton, D.E., Laria, A.J., Patterson, E.H., Hofmann, S.G., Craske, M., . . . Liao, B. (2009). Culture and the anxiety disorders: Recommendations for DSM-V. *Depression and Anxiety, 27*, 212–29.

Lewis-Fernández, R., & Krishan Aggarwal, N. (2013). Culture and psychiatric diagnosis. *Advances in Psychosomatic Medicine, 33*, 15–30.

Lopez-Class, M., Castro, F.G., & Ramirez, A.G. (2011). Conceptions of acculturation: A review and statement of critical issues. *Social Science & Medicine, 72*, 1555–62.

Luginaah, I., Smith, K., & Lockridge, A. (2010). Surrounded by chemical valley and "living in a bubble": Health impacts and coping strategies of the Aamjiwnaang First Nation, Ontario. *Journal of Environmental Planning and Management, 53*, 353–70.

MacDorman, M.F., & Mathews, T.J. (2011). Infant Deaths—United States, 2000–2007. In Centers for Disease Control and Prevention, US Department of Health and Human Services, *CDC health disparities and inequalities report—United States 2011* (pp. 59–61) (Morbidity and Mortality Weekly Report, No. 60). Retrieved from www.cdc.gov/mmwr/pdf/other/su6001.pdf

McSweeney, B. (2002). Hofstede's model of national cultural differences and their consequences: A triumph of faith—a failure of analysis. *Human Relations, 55*, 89–118.

Majumdar, B., Browne, G., Roberts, J., & Carpio, B. (2004). Effects of cultural sensitivity training on health care provider attitudes and patient outcomes. *Journal of Nursing Scholarship, 36*, 161–6.

Maramba, C.G., & Hall, G.C.N. (2002). Meta-analyses of ethnic match as a predictor of dropout, utilization, and level of functioning. *Cultural Diversity and Ethnic Minority Psychology, 8*, 290–7.

Marshall, C.A., Larkey, L.K., Curran, M.A., Weihs, K.L., Badger, T.A., Armin, J., & Garcia, F. (2011). Considerations of culture and social class for families facing cancer: The need for a new model for health promotion and psychosocial intervention. *Families, Systems, & Health, 29*, 81–94.

Matthews, K.A., & Gallo, L.C. (2011). Psychological perspectives on pathways linking socioeconomic status and physical health. *Annual Review of Psychology, 62*, 501–30.

Mensah, G.A., Mokdad, A.H., Ford, E.S., Greenlund, K.J., & Croft, J.B. (2005). State of disparities in cardiovascular health in the United States. *Epidemiology, 111*, 1233–41.

Mitrou, F., Cooke, M., Lawrence, D., Povah, D., Mobilia, E., Guimond, E., & Zubrick, S.R. (2014). Gaps in Indigenous disadvantage not closing: A census cohort study of social determinants of health in Australia, Canada, and New Zealand from 1981–2006. *BMC Public Health, 14*, 1–9.

Möller-Leimkühler, A.M. (2007). Gender differences in cardiovascular disease and comorbid depression. *Dialogues in Clinical Neuroscience, 9*, 71–83.

Morales, E., & Norcross, J.C. (2010). Evidence-based practices with ethnic minorities: Strange bedfellows no more. *Journal of Clinical Psychology, 66*, 821–9.

Morales, L.S., Lara, M., Kington, R.S., & Valdez, R.O. (2002). Socioeconomic, cultural, behavioral factors affecting Hispanic health outcomes. *Journal of Health Care for the Poor and Underserved, 13*, 477–503.

Moulettes, A. (2007). The absence of women's voices in Hofstede's *Cultural consequences:* A postcolonial reading. *Women in Management Review, 22*, 443–55.

Mountain, J.L., & Risch, N. (2004). Assessing genetic contributions to phenotypic differences among "racial" and "ethnic" groups. *Natural Genetics, 36*, S48–S53.

Mulatu, M.S., & Berry, J.W. (2001). Health care practice in a multicultural context: Western and non-western assumptions. In S.S. Kazarian & J.W. Berry (Eds.), *Handbook of cultural health psychology* (pp. 46–63). New York: Academic Press.

Muris, P., Schmidt, H., Engelbrecht, P., & Perold, M. (2002). DSM-IV-defined anxiety disorder symptoms in South African children. *Journal of the American Academy of Child & Adolescent Psychiatry, 41*, 1360–8.

National Center for Complementary and Alternative Medicine (NCCAM). (2013). *Complementary, alternative, or integrative health: What's in a name.* Retrieved from nccam.nih.gov/health/whatiscam

National Institutes of Health. (2012). *National Institute on minority health and health disparities.* Retrieved from www.nih.gov/about/almanac/organization/NIMHD.htm

Oates, M.R., Cox, J.L., Neema, S., Asten, P., Glangeaud-Freudenthal, N., Figueiredo, B., . . . Yoshida, K. (2004). Postnatal depression across countries and cultures: A qualitative study. *British Journal of Psychiatry, 184*, s10–s16.

Ortega, A.N., Feldman, J.M., Canino, G., Steinman, K., & Alegria, M. (2006). Co-occurrence of mental and physical illness in U.S. Latinos. *Social Psychiatry and Psychiatric Epidemiology, 41*, 927–34.

Osborn, C.Y., de Groot, M., & Wagner, J.A. (2013). Racial and ethnic disparities in diabetes complications in the northeastern United States: The role of socioeconomic status. *Journal of the National Medical Association, 105*, 51–8.

Parlee, B., Berkes, F., Gwich'in, T. (2005). Health of the land, health of the people: A case study on Gwich'in berry harvesting in northern Canada. *Ecohealth, 2,* 127–37.

Pettifor, J. L. (2004). Professional ethics across national boundaries. *European Psychologist, 9*(4), 264–72.

Ponterotto, J.G., Casas, J.M., Suzuki, L.A., & Alexander, C.M. (Eds.). (2009). *Handbook of multicultural counseling* (3rd ed.). Thousand Oaks, CA: Sage publications.

Purnell, L. (2002). The Purnell Model for cultural competence. *Journal of Transcultural Nursing, 13,* 193–6.

Rabia, M., Knauper, B., & Miquelon, P. (2006). The eternal quest for optimal balance between maximizing pleasure and minimizing harm: The compensatory health beliefs model. *British Journal of Health Psychology, 11,* 139–53.

Ram, R. (2006). Further examination of the cross-country association between income inequality and population health. *Social Science & Medicine, 62,* 779–91.

Reading, C.L., & Wien, F. (2009). *Health inequalities and social determinants of Aboriginal peoples' health.* Retrieved from www.nccah.ca/docs/social%20determinates/NCCAH-Loppie-Wien_Report.pdf

Richmond, C.A.M. (2007). Social support, material circumstance and health: Understanding the links in Canada's Aboriginal population. Doctoral dissertation, McGill University.

Richmond, C., Elliott, S.J., Mathews, R., and Elliott, B. (2005). The political ecology of health: Perceptions of environment, economy, health and well-being among "Namgis First Nation." *Health & Place, 11,* 349–65.

Richmond, C.A.M., & Ross, N.A. (2008). Social support, material circumstance and health behaviour: Influences on health in First Nation and Inuit communities in Canada. *Social Science & Medicine, 67,* 1423–33.

Richmond, C.A.M., & Ross, N.A. (2009). The determinants of First Nation and Inuit health: A critical population health approach. *Health and Place, 15,* 403–11.

Rosenstock, I. (1974). Historical origins of the health belief model. *Health Education Monographs, 2*(4).

Rosenstock, I.M., Strecher, V.J., & Becker, M.H. (1988). Social learning theory and the Health Belief Model. *Health Education & Behavior, 15,* 175–83.

Royal Commission on Aboriginal Peoples. (1995). *Choosing life: Special report on suicide among Aboriginal people.* Ottawa: Supply and Services.

Rudell, K., & Deifenbach, M.A. (2008). Current issues and new directions in psychology and health: Culture and health psychology. Why health psychologists should care about culture. *Psychology and Health, 23,* 387–90.

Saha, S., Arbelaez, J.J., & Cooper, L.A. (2003). Patient–physician relationships and racial disparities in the quality of health care. *American Journal of Public Health, 93,* 1713–19.

Sam, D.L., & Berry, J.W. (Eds.). (2016). *The Cambridge handbook of acculturation psychology* (2nd ed.). Cambridge, UK: Cambridge University Press.

Sarafino, E.P., & Smith, T.W. (2014). *Health psychology: Biopsychosocial interactions.* Hoboken, NJ: John Wiley & Sons.

Scott, K.M., Kokaua, J., & Baxter, J. (2011). Does having a chronic physical condition affect the likelihood of treatment seeking for a mental health problem and does this vary by ethnicity? *International Journal of Psychiatry in Medicine, 42,* 421–436.

Scott, K., McGee, M.A., Schaaf, D., & Baxter, J. (2008). Mental–physical comorbidity in an ethnically diverse population. *Social Science & Medicine, 66,* 1165–73.

Sheikh, S., & Furnham, A. (2000). A cross-cultural study of mental health beliefs and attitudes towards seeking profession help. *Social Psychiatry and Psychiatric Epidemiology, 35,* 326–34.

Shin, S.M., Chow, C., Camacho-Gonsalves, T., Levy, R., Allen, I.E., & Leff, H.S. (2005). A meta-analytic review of racial-ethnic matching for African American and Caucasian American clients and clinicians. *Journal of Counseling Psychology, 52,* 45–56.

Skrentny, J.D. (2008). Culture and race/ethnicity: Bolder, deeper, and broader. *Annals of the American Academy of Political and Social Science, 619,* 59–77.

Smedley, B.D., Stith, A.Y., & Nelson, A.R. (2002). *Unequal treatment: Confronting racial and ethnic disparities in health care.* Institute of Medicine Report. Washington: National Academy Press.

Smith, M.L., & Glass, G.V. (1977). Meta-analysis of psychotherapy outcome studies. *American Psychologist, 32,* 752–60.

Smylie, J., Fell, D., & Ohlsson, A. (2010). A review of Aboriginal infant mortality rates in Canada: Striking and persistent Aboriginal/non-Aboriginal inequities. *Canadian Journal of Public Health, 101,* 143–8.

Statistics Canada, Ministry of Finance. (2003). *Census 2001 highlights.*

Statistics Canada. (2005). *Projections of the Aboriginal populations, Canada, provinces and territories 2001 to 2017.* Ottawa.

Statistics Canada. (2008). *Canada's ethnocultural mosaic, 2006 census.* Ottawa: Minister of Industry. Retrieved from www12.statcan.ca/census-recensement/2006/as-sa/97-562/pdf/97-562-XIE2006001.pdf

Statistics Canada. (2013). *Immigration and Ethnocultural Diversity in Canada. National Household Survey, 2011.* Ottawa. Retrieved from www12.statcan.gc.ca/nhs-enm/2011/as-sa/99-010-x/99-010-x2011001-eng.pdf

Stephens, C. (2011). Narrative analysis in health psychology research: Personal, dialogical and social stories of health. *Health Psychology Review, 5,* 62–78.

Sue, D.W. (2001). Multidimensional facets of cultural competence. *Counseling Psychologist, 29,* 790–821.

Sue, S. (2006). Cultural competency: From philosophy to research and practice. *Journal of Community Psychology, 34,* 237–45.

Sue, S., Zane, N., Nagayama Hall, G.C., & Berger, L.K. (2009). The case for cultural competency in psychotherapeutic interventions. *Annual Review of Psychology, 60,* 525–48.

Suhail, K., & Cochrane, R. (2002). Effect of culture and environment on the phenomenology of delusions and hallucinations. *International Journal of Social Psychiatry, 48*, 126–38.

Suls, J., & Rothman, A. (2004). Evolution of the biopsychosocial model: Prospects and challenges for health psychology. *Health Psychology, 23*, 119–25.

Suzuki, K., Takei, N., Kawai, M., Minabe, Y., & Mori, N. (2003). Is Taijin Kyofusho a culture-bound syndrome? *American Journal of Psychiatry, 160*, 1358.

Taras, V., & Kirkman, B.L. (2010). Examining the impact of *Culture's consequences*: A three-decade, multilevel, meta-analytic review of Hofstede's cultural value dimensions. *Journal of Applied Psychology, 95*, 405–39.

Teferra, S., & Shibre, T. (2012). Perceived causes of severe mental disturbance and preferred interventions by the Borana semi-nomadic population in southern Ethiopia: A qualitative study. *BMC Psychiatry, 12*, 1–9.

Tenkorang, E.Y., Gyimah, S.O., Maticka-Tyndale, E., & Adjei, J. (2011). Superstition, witchcraft and HIV prevention in sub-Saharan Africa: The case of Ghana. *Culture, Health, and Sexuality, 13*, 1001–14.

Thakker, J., & Ward, T. (1998). Culture and classification: An international follow-up study. *Clinical Psychology Review, 18*, 501–29.

Tucker, C.M., Marsiske, M., Rice, K.G., Jones, J.D., & Herman, K.C. (2011). Patient-centered culturally sensitive health care: Model testing and refinement. *Health Psychology, 30*, 342–50.

US Census Bureau. (2001, January 13). *Projections of the total resident population by 5-year age groups, race, and Hispanic origin with special age categories: Middle series, 2050 to 2070.* Retrieved from www.census.gov/population/projections/nation/summary/np-t4-g.txt

US Census Bureau. (2011, March). *Overview of race and Hispanic origin: 2010. 2010* Census Briefs. Retrieved from www.census.gov/prod/cen2010/briefs/c2010br-02.pdf

Vaughn, L.M., Jacquez, F., & Baker, R.C. (2009). Cultural health attributions, beliefs, and practices: Effects on healthcare and medical education. *Open Medical Education Journal, 2*, 64–74.

Vega, W.A., Rodriguez, M.A., & Gruskin, E. (2009). Health disparities in the Latino population. *Epidemiological Review, 31*, 99–112.

Ward, L., Stebbings, S., Cherkin, D., & Baxter, G.D. (2013). Yoga for functional ability, pain and psychosocial outcomes in musculoskeletal conditions: A systematic review and meta-analysis. *Musculoskeletal Care*. doi: 10.1002/msc.1042

Watt, S., & Norton, D. (2004). Culture, ethnicity, race: What's the difference? *Paediatric Nursing, 16*, 37–42.

Webb, T., Joseph, J., Yardley, L., & Michie, S. (2010). Using the internet to promote health behavior change: A systematic review and meta-analysis of the impact of theoretical basis, use of behavior change techniques, and mode of delivery on efficacy. *Journal of Medical Internet Research, 12*, e4.

Weisz, J.R., Suwanlert, S., Chaiyasit, W., Weiss, B., Achenbach, T.M., & Eastman, K.L. (1993). Behavioral and emotional problems among Thai and American adolescents: Parent reports for ages 12–16. *Journal of Abnormal Psychology, 102*, 395–403.

Wendler, D., Kington, R., Madans, J., Wye, G.V., Christ-Schmidt, H., Pratt, L.A., . . . Emanuel, E. (2005). Are racial and ethnic minorities less willing to participate in health research? *PLOS Medicine, 3*, 201–10.

Whaley, A.L., & Davis, K.E. (2007). Cultural competence and evidence-based practice in mental health services: A complementary perspective. *American Psychologist, 62*, 563–74.

Wilson, D., & Macdonald, D. (2010, April). *The income gap between Aboriginal peoples and the rest of Canada.* Retrieved from v4.policyalternatives.ca/sites/default/files/uploads/publications/reports/docs/Aboriginal%20Income%20Gap.pdf

Wilson, K. (2003). Therapeutic landscapes and First Nations peoples: An exploration of culture, health and place. *Health & Place, 9*, 83–93.

Wilson, K., & Rosenberg, M.W. (2002). Exploring the determinants of health for First Nations peoples in Canada: Can existing frameworks accommodate traditional activities? *Social Science & Medicine, 55*, 2017–31.

Wright, K.B., Bell, S.B. (2003). Health-related support groups on the Internet: Linking empirical findings to social support and computer-mediated communication theory. *Journal of Health Psychology, 8*, 39–54.

World Health Organization (WHO). (1998). *Health promotion glossary*. Geneva. Retrieved from www.who.int/healthpromotion/about/HPR%20Glossary%201998.pdf

Xanthos, C., Treadwell, H.M., & Braithwaite Holden, K. (2010). Social determinants of health among African-American men. *Journal of Men's Health, 7*, 11–19.

Yali, A.M., & Revenson, T.A. (2004). How changes in population demographics will impact health psychology: Incorporating a broader notion of cultural competence into the field. *Health Psychology, 23*, 147–55.

Yancey, A.K., Ortega, A.N., & Kumanyika, S.K. (2006). Effective recruitment and retention of minority research participants. *Annual Review of Public Health, 27*, 1–28.

Yeh, R.S. (1988). On Hofstede's treatment of Chinese and Japanese values. *Asia Pacific Journal of Management, 6*, 149–60.

Zheng, H. (2009). Rising U.S. income inequality, gender and individual self-rated health, 1972–2004. *Social Science & Medicine, 69*, 1333–42.

Name Index

Subject Index